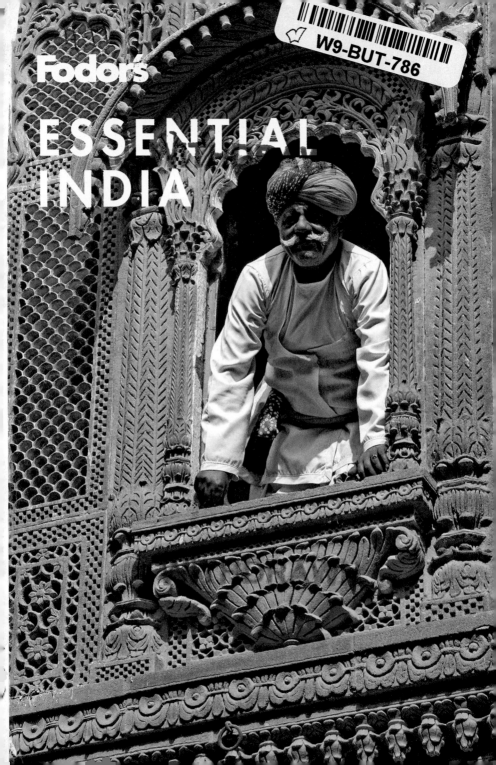

Fodor's

ESSENTIAL
INDIA

Welcome to India

India is a soulful, soul-stirring country, overflowing with cultural treasures, spiritual wonder, and natural beauty. A wondrous land of crowded megacities, Himalayan monasteries, and ancient fishing villages, India sweeps you up in a confounding and beautiful tide of humanity. Float along Kerala's famous backwaters, take a camel ride through Rajasthan, or find peace at the holy Ganges. And whether you drink chai (tea) from the source in Munnar, or savor Marwari cuisine in Jaipur, the land of spices and its remarkable people will linger long in your memory.

TOP REASONS TO GO

★ **Sacred Spaces:** Temples, shrines and holy *ghats* evoke ancient spiritual traditions.

★ **Food:** Rich curries, creamy *daals*, spicy street snacks: India's variety delights.

★ **Architecture:** Delhi's Jama Masjid, the iconic Taj Mahal, Udaipur's Lake Palace.

★ **Beaches:** Palm-fringed golden coastline beckons in Goa, Kerala, and even Mumbai.

★ **Markets:** Jewelry, leather, vibrant fabrics, pungent spices—bargains are plentiful.

★ **Music and Dance:** Bollywood, Bhangra, and festivals like Diwali make a joyful noise.

Contents

Fodor's Features

MAPS

Chapter 1

EXPERIENCE INDIA

22 ULTIMATE EXPERIENCES

India offers terrific experiences that should be on every traveler's list. Here are Fodor's top picks for a memorable trip.

1 Wander the Sprawling City Palace in Udaipur

Set on the banks of gorgeous Lake Pichola, this beautiful whitewashed royal palace-turned-museum is popular for its stunning architecture and regal artifacts. *(Ch. 6)*

2 Enter through the World's Largest Door at Fatehpur Sikri

One of the star attractions of the UNESCO World Heritage Site of Fatehpur Sikri is the Buland Darwaza—or "Victory Gate," which was built by Emperor Akbar in the late 16th century to commemorate his victory over Gujarat. *(Ch. 5)*

3 Search for Elusive Tigers in Ranthambore National Park

One of the best places to spot tigers in the wild, Ranthambore National Park is a popular place for wildlife safaris, particularly for those who dream of witnessing a tiger in its natural habitat. *(Ch. 6)*

4 Catch a Train in Mumbai

The gorgeous Chhatrapati Shivaji Terminus Station is one of the world's finest examples of Indo-Saracenic architecture. *(Ch. 7)*

5 Celebrate Ganesha in Mumbai

This annual festival dedicated to the elephant-headed god Ganesh is celebrated with fervor in Mumbai, with 10 days of religious worship and celebration. *(Ch. 7)*

6 Shop to Your Heart's Content

Delhi is home to numerous bazaars and boutiques selling seemingly everything under the sun, including beautiful jewelry, statues, and accessories. *(Ch. 4)*

7 Learn About Royal Life at the Jaipur City Palace

An active palace to this day (the titular royal family still lives in one wing), Jaipur City Palace offers a glorious glimpse into how Rajasthani royalty live. *(Ch. 6)*

8 Experience an Ayurvedic Detox in Kerala

Kerala is the birthplace of Ayurveda, a traditional Indian system of medicine that often involves some combination of dietary plans, massages using essential oils, and herbal supplements. *(Ch. 9)*

9 Explore Ancient Hindu Cave Temples

The two sets of cave temples at Ajanta and Ellora are celebrated for their intricate interiors and sculptures dating back as early as the 2nd Century BC. *(Ch. 7)*

10 Sample Delhi's Street Food

Known locally as chaat, these vegetarian small bites run the gamut from deep-fried potato patties (aloo tikki) to colorful concoctions made of yoghurt, sweet and spicy chutney, and fried grains. *(Ch. 4)*

11 Join Sufis at Nizamuddin Shrine

Every Thursday, musicians come together at the shrine of beloved Sufi saint Hazrat Nizamuddin to sing qawwalis—traditional Urdu devotional songs performed to a backdrop of harmonium and drums. *(Ch. 4)*

12 Attend the Pushkar Camel Fair

Every year during the full moon of the Hindu month of Kartik, camel and horse traders come from across Rajasthan to Pushkar to sell camels and livestock. *(Ch. 6)*

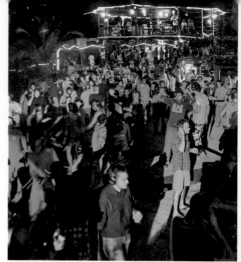

13 Party the Night Away in Goa

India's party capital and home of its own brand of electronic music (the aptly named Goa trance), this beachside state offers tons of clubs and festivals for underground music enthusiasts. *(Ch. 8)*

14 Take a Sunrise Boat Ride on the Ganges

Varanasi is an important pilgrimage city for Hindus who consider it the holiest city on earth. Don't miss taking a sunrise boat ride on the Ganges River to see pilgrims saying their early-morning prayers. *(Ch. 5)*

15 Visit Mother Teresa's Mission in Kolkata

Mother Teresa spent much of her life helping the needy in Kolkata. Although she passed on 20 years ago, her organization is still going strong. *(Ch. 10)*

16 See the Taj Mahal by Moonlight

While India's most famous monument is a sight to behold any time of day, it's particularly magical under the light of the moon. *(Ch. 5)*

17 Tour a Bollywood Studio in Mumbai

Mumbai is ground zero for Hindi cinema, and there are plenty of tours for those who want to visit a studio and see a movie filming in action. *(Ch. 7)*

18 Admire Erotic Art at the Temples of Khajuraho

Often referred to as the "Kama Sutra temples," this UNESCO World Heritage site features stunning, gorgeously preserved temples. *(Ch. 3)*

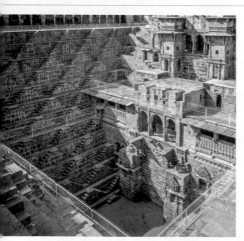

19 Admire the Stunning Chand Baori Stepwell

One of the most beautiful and best-preserved stepwells in the country, this ancient Escher-esque stepwell is celebrated for its beautiful symmetry. *(Ch. 6)*

20 Take a Houseboat Cruise in Kerala

This South Indian state is filled with quiet brackish water lagoons, best explored on your own slow-moving houseboat, either on a day tour or on a multi-night cruise. *(Ch. 9)*

21 Take a Desert Camelback Safari in Jaisalmer

Known for its golden-hued fort and stunning desert landscapes, Jaisalmer—in one of the most remote parts of Rajasthan—is a popular starting point for camel safaris. *(Ch. 6)*

22 Sleep in a Real Palace in Rajasthan

Rajasthan is full of old royal palaces that have been converted into "heritage hotels," some of which date back to the 15th century. *(Ch. 6)*

WHAT'S WHERE

1 Delhi. The capital of India is really two cities: the architecturally planned Central (New) Delhi (including South Delhi), is characterized by broad tree-lined avenues. Old Delhi, by contrast, features labyrinthine alleys and narrow lanes.

2 Delhi Side Trips. Uttar Pradesh, the state neighboring Delhi, has several worthwhile attractions, most notably the Taj Mahal, in Agra. Just west of Agra is the former Mughal capital of Fatehpur Sikri, noted for its urban planning and architecture. In eastern Uttar Pradesh the holy city of Varanasi draws a constant stream of pilgrims to bathe in the river's holy water. The famous Hindu temples at Khajuraho are west of here in Madhya Pradesh.

3 Rajasthan. The "Land of Kings," once 18 princely kingdoms, is probably India's most-visited state. Historic palaces and forts are the prominent attractions here, along with the Pink City of Jaipur, the Jain temples in Ranakpur and Mount Abu, the enchanting lake-city of Udaipur, and Jaisalmer Fort.

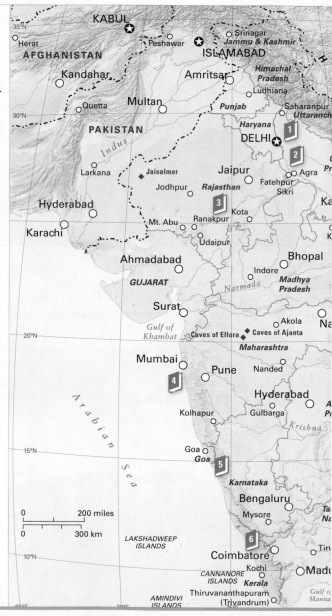

4 Mumbai. This spirited city by the sea sets the tone for the rest of the country with its masala of markets, cafés, art galleries, shops, food carts, and street hawkers. Aurangabad, the base for exploring the caves of Ajanta and Ellora, is about 250 km (150 miles) east of Mumbai.

5 Goa. This former Portuguese colony is blessed with a bright blue coastline stretching down to sparkling, palm-lined beaches along the Arabian Sea. It's as popular for its laid-back values as its legendary seafood and beautiful views.

6 Kerala. On the southwest Malabar coast, Kerala is known for beaches, lush greenery, and ayurvedic massages. Scenic coconut groves and palm trees offer a rustic paradise, while Trivandrum and Kochi preserve a rich culture and vestiges of a colonial past.

7 Kolkata (Calcutta). The former capital of British India, Kolkata has long been at the center of East India's cultural and intellectual life. This city characterized by grandiose architecture and lively markets is also known as the place where Mother Teresa did her charitable work.

What to Eat in India

IDLI SAMBAR
Found at hotel breakfast buffets across India and in homes throughout the southern regions of the country, idli sambar is a dish consisting of idlis (fluffy, sponge-like cakes made of a fermented rice-and-lentil flour and steamed) and sambar (a lentil and vegetable stew cooked with tamarind). It's often served with coconut chutneys.

DAL
The staple source of protein across India, dal is a broad term referring to lentil stews, usually served on rice or with flatbread. Popular varieties include dal tadka (yellow lentils tempered with cumin-infused oil) and dal makhani (black lentils cooked with lots of butter and cream).

VINDALOO
Fans of ultra-spicy food can test their limits by ordering vindaloo, a fiery curry that consists of meat (traditionally pork, but chicken is also common) soaked in vinegar overnight and then cooked with potatoes in a rich, spiced gravy. The dish is popular in the state of Goa, where it originated.

MANGOES
India's national fruit, the mighty mango is beloved across the country, and you can find mango-flavored everything, from candies to chutneys to fruit juice. While there are hundreds of varieties, the most lauded (and priciest) is the Alphonso mango, which grows primarily in the state of Maharashtra.

PANI PURI
Also known as gol gappe and gup chup, this popular street food consists of hollow, crisp, bite-size balls made from flour and deep fried. They are then stuffed with mashed potatoes, onions, coriander, and chickpeas and dipped in a sweet and spicy water and eaten immediately. Just don't try to nibble on them or you'll get messy; the idea is to stuff a whole pani puri into your mouth.

BIRIYANI

Biriyani is a spiced rice dish originating in India's Muslim communities that generally consists of fine basmati rice simmered with aromatic spices along with meat or vegetables. The dish is generally cooked with goat, although vegetarian versions are always available.

JALEBI

This popular snack is commonly served in North Indian roadside sweet shops, particularly in the winter. It's made from a flour batter flavored with a sweet syrup that's squeezed into swirly forms through a pastry bag directly into a vat of hot oil. Jalebis can be eaten cold, but they are best served fresh, when they are still hot and gooey.

MASALA DOSA

A southern Indian breakfast dish, masala dosas are crepes made of fermented black lentil and rice batter stuffed with spiced cooked potatoes. Dosas are generally served with sambar (lentil and veggie stew) and coconut chutney; try the Mysore masala dosa, which comes with a garlic chutney.

PARATHAS

Served at breakfast tables across northern India, parathas are a type of unleavened flaky and layered flatbread that are often stuffed with spiced potatoes, cauliflower, radishes, paneer (tofu-like Indian cheese), and even fenugreek leaves. They are then lightly fried and served hot with pickled vegetables and plain yogurt. The unstuffed variety are often served alongside curries.

CHOLE BHATURE

A popular breakfast item in North India (also commonly eaten as a snack food), chole bhature consists of spicy cooked garbanzo beans paired with gargantuan, deep-fried puff pastries similar to elephant ears. Fresh red onions are often served as an accompaniment to add a little zest.

What to Drink in India

variety is a great alternative to sports drinks if you're feeling dehydrated.

KINGFISHER BEER

Though it's not the only kind of beer available in India, Kingfisher is surely the country's most iconic. While the company makes all sorts of varieties, Kingfisher Premium is the most popular, with a light flavor that pairs well with spicy curries. Beware of the "strong" type, it's designed to get people drunk and known to wreak havoc on the bellies of even the most experienced of drinkers.

DARJEELING TEA

Though most Indian households favor simple, strong teas for making the country's beloved masala chai, those with a taste for lighter, subtler flavor that can be consumed without milk should make sure to sample India's most famous tea: Darjeeling. Dubbed the "Champagne of teas," this tea is grown only in the hilly Darjeeling area of West Bengal, where green, white, and oolong varietals are also beginning to gain popularity.

FRESH LIME SODA

A great alternative to soft drinks, fresh lime soda consists of club soda or sparkling water (just called "soda" in India) mixed with lemon juice (Indian lemons are tiny and kind of look like limes, perhaps explaining the slight misnomer). It's usually served "sweet" (with sugar), "salty" (with salt), or "mixed" (with both sugar

LASSI

If you've been to an Indian restaurant, you've probably had a mango lassi—a frothy mango and yogurt smoothie. In India, lassis take on all sorts of fruit flavors and are made with sugar, yogurt, and water. Some drink them salted, often with a dash of cumin.

MASALA CHAI

India's most popular drink, masala chai (literally translated as spiced tea), can be found everywhere from rural roadside stalls to upscale urban cafes. It's usually made by boiling ample amounts of tea leaves and sugar along with milk, cinnamon, cardamom, cloves, ginger, and sometimes a touch of black pepper. This sweet, spicy concoction is often served in tiny glasses and sometimes accompanied with cookies or biscotti-like biscuit.

OLD MONK

The Russians have their vodka, the Irish have their whiskey, and the Indians have their Old Monk. This ubiquitous brand of saccharine red rum is served throughout the country, often with Coca-Cola and a few ice cubes, though its strong vanilla aroma and overall sweetness may make it a little intense for overseas palates.

NIMBU PANI

India's spin on lemonade, nimbu pani (literally "lemon water") is a refreshing summer drink served in homes and restaurants across India. It can be made sweet (with sugar), salty (with salt), or mixed (with both), and is sometimes spiced up with a little cumin. The mixed and salt), though most restaurants and street vendors are happy to sell it without either if you ask for it plain.

SHERBET
Popular across South Asia and the Middle East, sherbet is a sweet beverage usually made by mixing cold water with concentrated sugary syrup, often flavored with some combination of herbs, fruits, or rose petals. The most popular type is Rooh Afza, made from herbs, roots, and rose petals, while rhododendron syrup is a popular souvenir often sold in resort towns in the foothills of the Himalayas.

SUGARCANE JUICE
Popular in hot countries across the world, sugarcane juice is a refreshing beverage created by grinding sugarcane to a pulp to extract its juice, often using gigantic hand-operated machines. Sugarcane juice often mixed with sulfurous-tasting black salt (*kala namak*), which cuts some of the sweetness and makes for a refreshing alternative to sports beverages. Just be careful where you get it, as drinking sugarcane juice from roadside stalls can be a quick way to end up with a case of Delhi belly.

THANDAI
Sort of like a thin, spiced milkshake, *thandai* is a cooling beverage made with milk, sugar, and a mix of subtle spices, notably cardamom, saffron, rose petals, and almonds. It's often flavored with almonds or almond syrup and is particularly popular during the annual Holi festival, when it's mixed with cannabis paste (known as bhang) and consumed with fervor.

INDIAN SOFT DRINKS
India has a whole slew of homegrown soda pops, the most notable of which are Thums Up and Limca. Thums Up is a fizzy, earthy cola that was created in the late 1970s after Coca-Cola stopped distributing their products in India (due to a refusal to share their secret formula with local partners, though ironically Coca-Cola actually owns the product today). Limca was created around the same time and has a lemon-lime flavor, though it's much more like a French lemonade than Sprite or 7-Up.

KAHWAH
While North Indians tend to drink milky black tea, or chai, the tea of choice in the mountainous Kashmir region is kahwah, a concoction prepared by boiling green tea with cinnamon, cardamom, and sugar or honey (and sometimes strands of saffron). It's generally consumed without the addition of milk, but slivered almonds are usually added to the top.

Masala Chai

SOUTH INDIAN FILTER COFFEE
While most people consider India a nation of tea drinkers, the country has a strong coffee tradition, particularly in the South. While European-style coffee shops abound, the traditional way of enjoying the drink is as "filter coffee," which refers to coffee prepared in a traditional metal filter and then mixed with milk and sugar by pouring it back and forth between a metal tumbler and a high-walled dish that doubles as a coaster. It has a sweet, milky flavor that's more reminiscent of coffee ice cream than bitter espresso, making it an excellent post-meal treat.

POMEGRANATE JUICE
Pomegranates gained popularity during the Mughal Empire, and the trees bearing the red fruit were a feature in many a royal Mughal garden during the Empire's reign. Today, freshly prepared pomegranate (*anar*) juice is readily available at juice stands across the country for a fraction what you'd pay back home for the scarlet superfood.

What to Buy in India

BLOCK-PRINTED TEXTILES

Woodblock printing, creating prints on textiles using inked stamps carved from wood, has been used in India for thousands of years. The method is still popular, particularly in Rajasthan, where woodblock printing is used to create everything from sundresses to tablecloths. The Jaipur-based boutique chain Anokhi is one of the most popular places to pick up woodblock apparel and accessories.

SPICES AND TEA

Many of the world's most celebrated teas come from India, particularly the Assam and Darjeeling regions. If you're looking for edible gifts, pair some Indian tea with a package of premixed "chai masala" (tea spices), or pick up a selection of local spices like mustard seed, saffron, or turmeric.

BOOKS

With the world's largest English-language readership, the publishing industry in India is enormous. You can find everything from coffee table books to inexpensive popular international books. Many of the books in India are hard to find overseas, particularly novels by local authors.

POTTERY

It's not uncommon to see roadside vendors with huge stacks of terracotta pots, sculptures, lanterns, and even disposable tea cups for sale. If you're looking for something to bring home, a piece of traditional blue pottery—everything from doorknobs to vases—from Jaipur might be your best bet.

THANGKAS

India is home to a large Tibetan population. As such, traditional Tibetan crafts and religious items are widely available. The most noteworthy are *thangkas*, intricate paintings of deities or mandalas. They are usually painted on fabric and then sewn into a larger piece of fabric with wooden bars at the top and bottom so that it can be rolled up like a scroll for easy transport.

SHAWLS

Elegant pashminas are a shawl produced in the Kashmir region of India and Pakistan. These draperies come in all sorts of color combinations and often have intricate paisley designs. While true pashminas are made of soft cashmere wool from the Himalayas, synthetic imitations abound.

MUSICAL INSTRUMENTS

Music lovers can find locally produced instruments—popular options include twinned drums known as *tablas* as well as plucked string instruments such as *sitars*, *sarods*, and *veenas*. Most musical instrument vendors in bigger cities can help you figure out the best way of getting instruments home.

JEWELRY

From glass bangles to gold and diamonds, India offers tons of jewelry options. If your budget is modest, you can find all sorts of beautiful silver items, from earrings set with semiprecious stones to enamel-inlaid bangles and pendants, known as *meenakari*, all for a fraction of what you'd pay at home.

SHOES

Popular choices for footwear include *joottis* and *mojaris*, traditional leather slip-on shoes, often covered with some combination of embroidery and sequin work. Sandals and flip-flops, known as *chappals*, are another great choice, and often come with similar embellishments. *Kohal-puris*, hand-made flip-flop-style sandals with extra loops for the big toe are another great find.

INCENSE

Most of the world's incense is made in India, and it's a great place to pick up all sorts of scents, from the ubiquitous sandalwood, known locally as *chandan*, to globally favored aromas such as nag champa. *Dhoop*, a resinous, slightly gooey, stick-free incense often burned outside to keep insects away makes a good gift, as it's not as frequently found outside of India.

India's Best Temples and Shrines

KHAJURAHO TEMPLES, MADHYA PRADESH
Also known as the "Kama Sutra temples" due to the erotic art that adorns them, these beautiful temples dating from the early 10th century are some of the best-preserved structures of their era in all of India. The Kandariya Mahadeva Temple is noteworthy for its medieval temple architecture.

AJANTA AND ELLORA CAVES, MAHARASHTRA
Although miles apart, the approximately 30 caves of Ajanta and Ellora are visited on one trip. These ornately carved cave temples dating from the 2nd through 7th centuries are known for their beautiful rock-hewn interiors and sculptures.

LOTUS TEMPLE, DELHI
The stunning Baha'i House of Worship, more commonly known as the "Lotus temple," is an iconic white-marble building designed to resemble an unfolding lotus. While it's worth visiting just to check out the architecture, those willing to wait in line can visit the interior prayer hall.

TAJ MAHAL, AGRA
India's most iconic attraction, the Taj Mahal has long been celebrated as one of the world's most breathtaking architectural odes to love. Built by Mughal emperor Shah Jahan for his late wife, this striking white-domed mausoleum is picturesque any time of day or night, but is particularly stunning at sunrise or under the light of the full moon.

HAJI ALI SHRINE, MUMBAI
Situated on an islet that juts out into the Mumbai Harbour, the shrine of Sufi saint Haji Ali is one of the holiest sites in Mumbai, particularly for the local Muslim population. It's only accessible via a causeway when the tides are low enough to make walking a possibility. Friday is the best day to visit, as there are often live Qawaali (Sufi devotional music) performances staged here.

ELEPHANTA CAVES, MUMBAI
Situated on an island off the coast of Mumbai, and only accessible by an hour-long ferry ride, the UNESCO World Heritage Elephanta Caves are a series of basalt-hewn Hindu and Buddhist cave temples dating from the 6th-8th centuries AD. Highlights include an 18-foot-tall bas relief of the Hindu Lord Shiva in his three-headed manifestation.

KALIGHAT KALI TEMPLE, KOLKATA
This temple, one of the most famous in Kolkata, is dedicated to the Hindu

Taj Mahal

goddess Kali. It's one of the 51 Shakti Peeths found across India, a collection of important goddess temples and shrines particularly significant to followers of Shakitsim, a strain of Hinduism focused on goddess worship that dominates in West Bengal. The ambience is often lively here, and crowded, and it's a great place to deepen one's understanding of Indian religious traditions.

JAGATPITA SHRI BRAHMA TEMPLE, PUSHKAR

Believed to be the world's only temple dedicated to the Hindu god, Brahma, this14th-century temple is one of the few in the desert town of Pushkar that's open to non-Hindu visitors.

Inside is an idol of Brahma believed to have been blessed by Adi Shankra, the founder of Advaita Vedanta (nondualism) and one of India's most important ancient sages. The temple's saffron-hued spire and blue pillars look particularly stunning against the backdrop of the postcard-perfect Pushkar Lake.

GHATS ON THE GANGES, VARANASI

Varanasi (AKA Kashi and Benares), believed to be one of the oldest continuously inhabited cities on earth, is easily the most sacred city in India for Hindus. It sits on the banks of the Ganges River, which can be safely accessed via the city's 88 ghats, sets of stairs that go down into the water, making it easy to bathe without being swept away by currents. Some ghats have specific purposes, which range from performing cremations to evening prayer ceremonies.

HUMAYAN'S TOMB, DELHI

This UNESCO World Heritage Site, the final resting place of Humayan, son of Barbur (who founded the Mughal Empire), is one of the earliest examples of Mughal architecture. Dating back to the 16th century, it features a large double-domed tomb surrounded by gardens.

India's Best Palaces and Forts

AMER FORT, JAIPUR
Jaipur's 16th-century Amer Fort is a gargantuan, beautifully preserved fortress. This four-story complex features a maze of halls, palaces, and rooms constructed with a mix of red sandstone and white marble, many of which are adorned with intricate mirrorwork and frescoes.

JAISALMER FORT, JAISALMER
Towering over the desert city of Jaisalmer, the UNESCO World Heritage Jaisalmer Fort was built in the 13th century from honey-hued sandstone that blends in gorgeously with its desert surroundings. Unusual for an ancient fort, many people still live within its ramparts—there are even a few hotels, restaurants, guesthouses, and other businesses inside the fort walls.

HAWA MAHAL, JAIPUR
Jaipur's most iconic structure, the pink Hawa Mahal, or "Palace of the Winds" is a five-story structure built in the 18th century as a safe haven for royal women to observe the goings-on of the city. Its prominent feature is its 953 latticed windows that make the palace look like a honeycomb.

AGRA FORT, AGRA
A short jaunt from the Taj Mahal, the UNESCO World Heritage Agra Fort is a 16th-century complex occupying nearly 100 acres. This red sandstone garrison was under the Lodhi Dynasty and remained an imperial stronghold for centuries. Shah Jahan—creator of the Taj Mahal—spent his later life held prisoner here by his son, who interred his father in order to take over the empire.

FATEHPUR SIKRI, UTTAR PRADESH

Just outside of Agra, this UNESCO World Heritage Site is one of the world's best-preserved ghost towns. It's made almost entirely of red sandstone and served as the capital of the Mughal Empire. It's also home to the world's largest door, the Buland Darwaza, which stands a whopping 54 meters (177 feet) high.

CITY PALACE, UDAIPUR

In the heart of the romantic lake city of Udaipur, the City Palace is worth a visit for its stunning palatial architecture dominated by columns, archways, and onion domes. The treasures inside include a wide selection of artifacts, including the world's largest collection of fine crystal.

MEHRANGARH FORT, JODHPUR

On a hill overlooking the "blue city" of Jodhpur, this 15th-century fort is among the largest in India. Along with cannons, ramparts, and beautiful city views, the fort also boasts a number of galleries with artifacts and art, including paintings, palanquins, and a large collection of turbans.

Chittorgarh

CHITTORGARH, RAJASTHAN

Chittorgarh is a gargantuan fortress complex spanning nearly 700 acres. It originated in the 7th century as the capital of the kingdom of Mewar, and fell under siege repeatedly over the years, until a treaty in 1616. Highlights include a reservoir, a number of intricate Jain temples, ancient palaces, plus a 122-foot-high, nine-story "Victory Tower" built in the Middle Ages.

CHAND BAORI ABHANERI, RAJASTHAN

Resembling something out of an M. C. Escher print, this beautiful stepwell dates back to the 9th or 10th century and features a beautiful succession of steep staircases on the interior of a huge well, designed to help people carry water up by hand.

KUMBALGARH, RAJASTHAN

Tucked away in the western Aravalli Mountains, the 15th-century fort of Kumbhalgarh is the second-largest fort in the state (after Chittorgarh) and home to one of the world's longest walls, measuring some 22 miles in length.

What to Read and Watch Before Your Trip

A FINE BALANCE BY ROHINTON MISTRY

A Fine Balance is a 1995 novel that's set during "the Emergency," a period from 1975–77 when then PM Indira Gandhi declared a state of emergency following a war that led to Bangladesh's independence from Pakistan and ensuing civil unrest. The story brings together two tailors fleeing caste violence, a young student, and a young widow, all living together due to situations brought on by the Emergency. It follows them throughout the period, later taking a dip back into their lives in 1984, after Indira Gandhi was assassinated by her Sikh bodyguards and subsequent violent riots targeting Sikh people took place. It provides an exceptional look at life in India under Indira Gandhi and touches on how communitarian ideology can be used to push political agendas, an issue that India still faces to this day.

MIDNIGHT'S CHILDREN BY SALMAN RUSHDIE

One of the world's best-known novels based in India, and a fine example of magic realism in modern literature, *Midnight's Children* tells the story of Indian Independence and Partition from the perspective of a young man, Saleem, who was born at the very moment that India officially gained its independence. Because of his unusual birth time, he (and all children born at the same time) is bestowed with telepathic powers. The 1981 novel won the Booker Prize and was later adapted into a film directed by the renowned Indian-Canadian director, Deepa Mehta.

THE GOD OF SMALL THINGS BY ARUNDHATI ROY

This Booker Prize-winning novel is set in Kerala, in South India, telling the story of two twins, a boy and a girl, who are raised in their maternal grandparents' home with their mother and a host of relatives after their mother flees from her alcoholic husband. The novel chronicles life in Malayali homes, touching on themes of inter-caste romance and its implications, post-colonial identity, and is full of political undertones and the author's insights on Indian society since Independence.

A SUITABLE BOY BY VIKRAM SETH

Set in newly independent India, *A Suitable Boy* tells the story of four different families, though it centers on the tale of a young woman whose mother is trying desperately, and pushily, to arrange her marriage. It devotes well over a thousand pages to the four families, weaving in issues like Indian politics and the role of caste in social relations, as well as the role of women in Indian society.

BEHIND THE BEAUTIFUL FOREVERS BY KATHERINE BOO

Written in 2012, this non-fiction book looks into life in the Annawasi slum next to the Mumbai Airport. The slum was created on a marsh near the airport in the early 1990s by workers hired to construct the airport who needed temporary housing. After the project was complete, many of them stayed on. It's an engaging, elegantly written socio-anthropological study of the slum, and it earned the National Book Award in nonfiction.

TRAIN TO PAKISTAN BY KHUSHWANT SINGH

Arguably one of the finest novels about the Partition to ever be published, Khushwant Singh's *Train to Pakistan* tells the tale of a fictional village on the Pakistan/India border. Most of the people there are Sikh and Muslims, where communitarian ideology and related violence has started to crop up after many years of the two communities living in peace. Rather than delve into the politics behind the division, this book looks at how everyday people contributed to and were impacted by the situation.

MALGUDI DAYS BY R. K. NARAYAN

Malgudi Days is a collection of 32 short stories that's adored by generations of Indians. All of the tales talk about life in a fictional South Indian town by the name of Malgudi, chronicling the lives of locals. Many of the stories were later adapted for television in a 1980s series by the same name.

GANDHI

Directed by Richard Attenborough, this 1982 drama portrays the life of Mohandas Gandhi, the father of Modern India, from his early days in South Africa to his eventual assassination. It provides a fascinating look at India's struggle for independence, highlighting key moments in the decades-long campaign.

DILWALE DULHANIA LE JAYENGE

Known locally as DDLJ, this romantic Bollywood film is one of the most popular films to have ever come out of the subcontinent and it's rare that you'll meet someone in India who hasn't seen it at least once. It follows the story of two young travelers who fall in love on a trip in Europe. The only problem is that the young woman in question is already betrothed to another man, through a family arrangement. It was released in 1995 and is still showing on some screens, making it the longest-running Bollywood film of all time.

THE BEST EXOTIC MARIGOLD HOTEL

While The Best Exotic Marigold Hotel is a fun film to watch both for its great acting and unusual storyline in which a group of seniors move to India to live in a special hotel for the elderly, it's the visual elements that make this film so enthralling. Much of it was filmed in Jaipur and the film is full of beautiful street scenes and lovely shots of the city's elegant architecture. Beyond the eye candy, there's also plenty to glean from the interactions between the British and Indian characters, particularly in terms of cross-cultural understanding.

LAGAAN

One of the highest-grossing Indian films to date, Lagaan is set in the Victorian era, when the British Raj still ruled over India. A British officer has decided to impose taxes on locals and strikes a deal with the community, saying if they can beat the English in a cricket match, he'll waive their tax obligations for three years. Should they lose, they'll have to pay three times the rate.

SLUMDOG MILLIONAIRE

One of the most popular films set in India of the last decade, Slumdog Millionaire tells the story of a young man who was raised in the slums of Mumbai and finds himself a contestant on Kaun Banega Crorepati, India's version of Who Wants to Be a Millionaire. He gets every question right, and is thus accused of cheating, so the film goes into flashback mode, showing how he learned the answers to each question, in many cases demonstrating the atrocities that India's urban poor are faced with in the process. It received mixed reactions due to how it portrayed poverty in the country, though many of the issues it deals with are hard realities.

MONSOON WEDDING

Few things on this earth can match the extravagance of an Indian wedding, and Monsoon Wedding does a fabulous job of not only showing what weddings in India are like (and what they mean), but also shows some of the stresses families go through to organize and pay for them. The award-winning film tells the story of an Indian family whose daughter is betrothed to a young Texan of Indian origin. The film deals with a host of issues faced by families around the world, including infidelity, child abuse, and the insecurities and conflicts that arise when there's great financial disparity among family members, while also illuminating viewers into how big fat Indian weddings are planned and executed.

INDIA BEST BETS

Fodor's writers and editors have chosen our favorites to help you plan. Search individual chapters for more recommendations.

 RESTAURANTS

BEST STREET FOOD
Evergreen Sweet House
Bikanerwala
Lassiwalla

BEST FOR ROMANCE
Indian Accent
Thalassa
The Malabar House

BEST DINING WITH A VIEW
Bellevue
Thalassa
Blue Sky Restaurant
Bristow's Bistro

BEST SEAFOOD
Terrace at Clafouti Beach Resort
6 Ballygunge Place
A Reverie

BEST ITALIAN FOOD
Diva Italian
San Gimignano
Bar Palladio

BEST HOTEL RESTAURANTS
Indian Accent
Suvarana Mahal
Ziya

BEST PUNJABI CUISINE
Punjabi by Nature
Moti Mahal Deluxe
Sher-e-Punjab

BEST SOUTH INDIAN CUISINE
Naivedyam
Sagar Ratna
Tamarind Tree

BEST WINE LIST
Malabar Junction
Risala
Pali Village Café

BEST CAFES
Kashi Art Café
Anokhi Cafe
Latitude 28

BEST INDO-CHINESE FOOD
Chinoiserie
Mainland China
Bar-B-Q

☖ BARS

BEST COCKTAIL BARS
Aqua
Blue Bar
Monkey Bar

BEST HOTEL BARS
Agni
1911
Someplace Else

⌘ HOTELS

BEST FOR HONEYMOONERS
The Oberoi Rajvilas
Alila Diwa Goa
niraamaya - Surya Samudra

BEST DESIGN
Sunbeam
Hyatt Regency Kolkatta
St. Regis

BEST PALACE HOTELS
Umaid Bhawan Palace
Taj Lake Palace
Neemrana Fort Palace

BEST HISTORIC HOTELS
Alsisar Haveli
The Imperial
The Oberoi Grand Kolkata

BEST SPA
ITC Mughal
Taj green Cove Resort & Spa
Park Hyatt Goa Resort and Spa

BEST LUXURY
The Oberoi Udaivilas
Taj Lake Palace
Taj Mahal Palace Hotel

BEST MID-RANGE
Ahuja Residency
Hotel Pushkar Palace
The Malabar House

BEST BUDGET
Singhvi Haveli
Pousada Panjim
Abode

Chapter 2

TRAVEL SMART INDIA

2

Updated by
Margot Bigg

★ CAPITAL
New Delhi

👥 POPULATION
1.34 Billion

💬 LANGUAGE
Hindi, English

€ CURRENCY
Indian rupee (₹) (INR)

☎ COUNTRY CODE
+91

⚠ EMERGENCIES
112

🚗 DRIVING
On the left

⚡ ELECTRICITY
230-250 v/50 cycles;
most plugs have two round
prongs, though heavier
appliances use thick, three-
pronged plugs

🕐 TIME
Nine hours ahead of
New York

🌐 WEB RESOURCES
www.incredibleindia.org
www.cntraveller.in
www.natgeotraveller.in
www.travelandleisureindia.in
www.tripoto.com

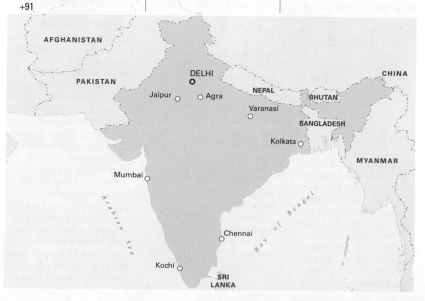

What You Need to Know Before You Visit India

PACK LIGHT (ESPECIALLY WHEN YOU'RE SIGHTSEEING)
India has many climates, but it's mostly hot and sometimes humid. Pack breezy, loose-fitting clothing in light colors that covers your arms and legs, especially for days you plan to visit temples or other religious sites. Bring a scarf or bandana to cover your head if you plan to visit a Sikh temple or a mosque. If you are even remotely interested in shopping, leave half of your suitcase empty. One visit to a market will likely have you wishing you'd brought another suitcase just to take home spices, textiles, clothing, and home décor items. When you're out sightseeing, dress respectfully, wear sunscreen and a wide-brimmed hat, and pack only your camera, phone, wallet, passport, sunscreen, and a bottle of water. If you're visiting the Taj Mahal, it's best to leave as much as you can back at your hotel, as everyday items such as pens, cigarettes, and even cough drops are prohibited.

GETTING AROUND CAN BE TRICKY

Most visitors to India will want to see more than just the city they fly into. Yes, Mumbai and Delhi both make great introductions to the country, but there's so much more to see than just the big cities. Train travel can be romantic, but be prepared for a chaotic scene at the train station. Traffic within cities can be extreme during rush hour, and it can sometimes take hours to get from one end of big cities to the other. Domestic flights within India are easy and inexpensive and the best way to travel if you want to pack as many destinations as possible into your trip. Just like in the United States, airport security can be hectic, especially at larger airports. There are different security lines for men and women, as after passing through metal detectors, women are taken into curtained booths for pat downs by female police officers while men have the experience in the open. Just make sure to arrive early and go with the flow. It's not a bad idea to arrange airport transfers in advance through your hotel, especially on your first night in India.

Insider Tip: If the idea of getting around India is daunting, don't try to do it all on your own. Luxury travel companies such as Abercrombie and Kent offer group trips with set itineraries or custom itineraries for more creative travel. They'll take care of all airport transfers and boarding passes, so you can focus on exploring a new country.

YES, THE POLLUTION, TRAFFIC, AND CROWDS ARE BAD

But it's not any worse than New York or L.A. Try to avoid Delhi between November and February when smog levels are dangerously high, particularly for those with respiratory issues, and air-filtering face masks are necessary if you step outside. However, once you're off the beaten tourist track in places like the Himalayas, you'll find a calm, clean, and peaceful side of India.

THE FOOD IS SO GOOD YOU'LL NEVER BE ABLE TO ENJOY YOUR LOCAL INDIAN RESTAURANT AGAIN

Discovering the flavors of India is a bit like bringing your taste buds into the fourth dimension. You think you've had curry before, but you've never had curry like this. Each of India's 29 states has multiple cuisines and complex flavors with ingredients that don't even exist in America. In the north, you'll find rich meaty stews, and in the south, you'll find spicy vegetarian curries. While there are some ingredients and flavors that are common in dishes across the country, the spices and cooking methods vary from region to region. Dishes you think you've had before (and many you've never even heard of) will be totally unrecognizable (in a good way) from their bland American counterparts. After a week or two of spicy Kerala fish stew and rich saag paneer, you won't be able to enjoy Indian food back home. Many Indians eat with their hands (even rice, in some homes and even in restaurants in some parts of the country), but if this is uncomfortable for you it's fine to ask for cutlery. However, do remember to only use your right hand to pick up food; the left hand is traditionally reserved for toilet duties.

In India, food and food-related hospitality is very important. Indians believe in showing their warmth by feeding a guest endless cups of tea, snacks, and meals. If you refuse entirely to eat a meal or have a cup of tea you may offend your host. Indians also believe in offering food over and over again, to make sure the guest has had enough, in case he or she is too polite or reserved to ask for more. So if you don't want more of something, be firm but polite in your refusals.

SPEAKING OF FOOD, YOU MIGHT GET SICK
But it's avoidable. Most Western travelers to India experience some kind of digestion discomfort (colloquially known as "Delhi Belly") ranging from mild diarrhea or heartburn to severe gastrointestinal issues that require medical attention. Before your trip, head to your local health food store to stock up on Grapefruit Seed Extract (GSE) and other immune-boosting vitamins. Once you're in India, hold fast to the "peel it, cook it, or leave it" rule when it comes to

fresh fruit and vegetables (except in 5-star hotels), though coffee or tea at local shops are usually fine, as both are prepared by boiling ingredients. All meals should be eaten at restaurants and hotels, and street food is best avoided. It's a good idea to pack charcoal, Immodium, and possibly even a Cipro prescription just in case things get really serious, though antibiotics and anti-diarrhea medicines are readily available in pharmacies in even the most remote locations.

Insider Tip: Contrary to popular belief, sit-down toilets are easy to find. Yes, the squat-over-a-hole-in-the-ground toilets are prevalent, but most public restrooms in airports, rest stops, restaurants, and tourist attractions will have both options.

INDIA IS SAFER THAN YOU MAY REALIZE
Making sure you stick to hygienic food and water will be your biggest safety concern in India, and contrary to popular belief, crime against tourists here is relatively low. While you may have someone try to swindle you out of some extra cash, you're unlikely to be robbed. Women do need to take extra precautions when traveling alone, especially at night; your best bet is to sit with families or other women when on public transportation or look for special "ladies' carriages" (found in the Mumbai trains and the Delhi metro) that are reserved for women and children.

LUXURY HERE IS WORTH EVERY PENNY
If you can afford it, India offers some of the world's best luxury travel experiences. However, you don't have to be royalty to travel well. A basic (but luxurious) room in a 5-star hotel in a big city can cost under $200 in some cases. Iconic palace resorts like the Oberoi Rajvilas and Taj Lake Palace are a bit more expensive, but the setting, service, and food are unparalleled anywhere else on earth. If you're mixing high-end hotels with low- to mid-range hotels, make sure to save the luxe places for the end of your stay (and splurge for a spa treatment too).

BUT YOU WILL BE FACED WITH ABJECT POVERTY
Visiting India can be heartbreaking. In cities and tourist sites, you'll see people (even young children) asking for money. If you do decide to give, be discreet about it. If not, be polite but firm, otherwise you may feel harassed. If you'd like to help, seek out an established charity to donate to or consider helping out with service-oriented travel for part of your trip.

DON'T BE INTIMIDATED
If it's your first time, don't try to see everything; you'll surely want an excuse to come back later, anyway. India is like nowhere else on earth and with a little bit of planning and flexibility, you'll be able to plan a fantastic trip.

Getting Here and Around

The major international tourist hubs are Delhi, in the north, and Mumbai, 1,407 km (874 miles) to the south. Major cities are connected by a national highway system, air service, and trains.

Road travel is an easy way to take in local color in a leisurely way. Unfortunately, most roads still have just two lanes and are in poor condition, and progress can be painstaking.

An onslaught of domestic airlines competing for business has made air travel throughout the subcontinent relatively hassle-free and convenient. It's the best option for those who are on a tight schedule, although flight delays and cancellations—due to congestion and weather (usually fog or monsoon rains)—are common.

The Indian train system is an intricate network shuttling millions of people every day. It's reliable, if run-down, and practically every point of interest in the non-mountainous areas of India has a train station nearby.

✈ Air Travel

Flying to and within India has become easier in recent years with new international routes and the emergence of several new low-cost Indian domestic airlines. Domestic tickets can generally be purchased through traditional travel agents, airline websites, travel websites, and even at Indian airports.

Check-in and security in Indian airports, however, often requires considerable time, and it's a good idea to check in at least two hours before a flight within India.

AIRPORTS

India's two major international gateways are Indira Gandhi International Airport (DEL) in New Delhi and Chhatrapati Shivaji International Airport (BOM) in Mumbai. Delhi is best for all the major tourist spots in the north, including Rajasthan. Mumbai is more convenient for Goa and Kerala.

GROUND TRANSPORTATION

The best way to get to and from India's major international airports is by taxi, though taking the Airport Express Line of the Delhi Metro, which connects the airport to the New Delhi Railway Station in about 20 minutes, is also an option for those arriving in Delhi.

Basic non-air-conditioned taxis are available at prepaid government-run stands beyond immigration and customs in most cities. You'll state your destination, pay in advance, and be given a voucher to give to your driver. If you want air-conditioning, book through one of the private taxi companies (their desks resemble those of car-rental companies). They will either charge you a preset or a metered fare, depending on your destination. Room for baggage is ample in taxis in Delhi, but many of the cars used in Mumbai are older and smaller, with less room. Taxi drivers might try to charge you an extra fee (around Rs. 20–Rs. 30) per bag, but again, this varies from city to city.

FLIGHTS
TO INDIA

North America-based travelers can get to India, usually with a stop in Europe, Asia, or the Middle East, on many international carriers. Those offering daily direct flights include United Airlines (Newark to Delhi or to Mumbai) and Air India (New York JFK to Mumbai and Delhi, and Chicago and San Francisco to Delhi).

From Delhi to	Distance	
CITY	DISTANCE IN KILOMETERS	DISTANCE IN MILES
Agra	203	126
Jaipur	258	160
Mumbai	1,407	874
Goa	1,912	1,188

WITHIN INDIA

India's domestic airline scene is booming. In addition to the so-called legacy carriers, Jet Airways and Air India, which both also fly internationally, there is a newer crop of carriers, each with its own quirks.

Jet Airways is often the most expensive carrier, but provides excellent service. Air India, the government carrier, can be a little stodgy and prices a bit high. Vistara is one of the newest (and most comfortable) domestic airlines, and offers old-school perks such as free meals for all passengers. Popular low-cost, no frills carriers include Air India Express, SpiceJet, IndiGo, and GoAir.

🚌 Bus Travel

Bus travel isn't the safest or most comfortable way to travel in India, especially at night. If you decide on bus travel between cities, try to take the most luxurious privately run air-conditioned coaches, and have a local travel agent make the arrangements. Buses rarely if ever have toilets on board, but they usually stop every 2–4 hours at roadside restaurants for bathroom breaks. It's a good idea to bring earplugs or earphones, as many play Bollywood movies or music at high volumes.

Car Travel

Travel by car in India isn't for the faint of heart, but if you can get over India's different road philosophy, it can be an enjoyable, entertaining way to see the country and get from one city to the next.

ROAD CONDITIONS

Roads in India may be wide and smooth in big cities, but they're usually narrow and terribly maintained in the countryside. Traffic in major cities is so erratic and abundant that it is hard to pin down local rush hours. Always be ready for heavy traffic if traveling by car.

HIRING A CAR AND DRIVER

Hiring a car and driver is affordable by Western standards, and even Indians use this option for weekend getaways. However, the price can add up for long trips, so be sure to establish terms, rates, and surcharges in advance. Rates generally include gasoline and tolls.

Shorter trips are usually priced by kilometer, at upwards of Rs. 15 per km, with percentage increase at night (usually after 10). Day rates are usually established for 8 hours and up to 80 km, with additional charges for extra hours.

Be sure to discuss your itinerary up front—what seems like a reasonable day's drive on a map can often take much longer in reality.

🚗 Taxi & Rickshaw Travel

Probably the best way to get around an Indian city is by taxi or motorized auto-rickshaw. Auto-rickshaws, especially, are fast and cheap, although not as comfortable as air-conditioned taxis.

Auto-rickshaws are practically everywhere and are easy to flag down. Taxis are also easy to hail on the street in Mumbai, but harder to find in Delhi, and drivers may speak limited English, so carry a copy of your hotel's business card to show them. Ridesharing apps such as Uber and Ola are also frequently used by taxi companies.

Most importantly, find out in advance the approximate fare for the distance you will be going—someone at your hotel can give you a ballpark figure.

Drivers in areas popular with tourists supplement their incomes by offering to find you a hotel or to take you shopping at the "best" stores, which means they'll get a commission if you get a room or buy anything. The stores are usually very expensive, so if you don't want this kind of detour, you must be very firm.

🚆 Train Travel

Traveling by train in India can be a fine experience if you plan it well. Trains connect the tiniest places across the subcontinent, and train journeys are a terrific way to see off-the-beaten-track India.

Train ticket prices vary greatly depending on where and how you're traveling. The *Shatabdi* and *Rajdhani* express trains are fast and have air-conditioned cars and either reclining seats (in *Shatabdis*) or berths (in *Rajdhanis*), but only offer services between major cities. The next-fastest trains are called "mail" trains. "Passenger" trains, which usually offer only second-class accommodations, make numerous stops, and are crowded.

For long train rides, buy a meter-long chain and a padlock to secure your luggage. Long-distance trains provide meals as part of the tariff, but it's a good idea to bring snacks.

Trains have numerous classes, the nicest of which is first-class air-conditioned (also known as 1AC; lockable compartments with two or four sleeping berths). Second-class air-conditioned (also known as 2AC; two or four berths that convert to sleepers, but no lockable compartments), and third-class air-conditioned (also known as 3AC; just like 2AC but with six berths in each seating bay). The a/c chair car (AC chair class) is a comfortable for day trips, with rows of two or three seats on each side. Sleeper class is laid out just like the 3AC car without the air-conditioning. Finally there's second seating, the cheapest, but it's uncomfortable and not recommended.

If your plans are flexible, you can make reservations once you arrive in India, either through a travel agent, online, or at the station itself. Large urban stations have a special office for foreigners, where you can buy "tourist quota" tickets. (Many trains reserve a few seats for tourists who haven't made reservations.)When it's time to travel, arrive at the station at least half an hour before departure. Seat numbers are displayed on the platform and on each car, along with a list of passengers' names and seat assignments.

E-tickets, which must be printed out and presented with a photo ID, can be purchased at ⊕ *www.irctc.co.in* or on ⊕ *www.cleartrip.com*. A good resource for train schedules is ⊕ *www.indianrail. gov.in*.

Before You Go

🌐 Passport

Unless you hold an Indian passport or are a citizen of Nepal or Bhutan, you need a visa to enter India. This applies to children and infants as well.

🆅 Visa

India offers electronic visas for citizens of a number of countries, including the United States, Canada, and all E.U. member states. Under the new system, applicants are able to apply for permission to visit India online and receive approval within a few days, without having to submit their passports for processing. Once approved, applicants are eligible for a visa on arrival at any of India's major ports, valid for 60 days from the date of entry. Note that travelers are limited to two electronic visas per year; those needing to visit more than twice or wanting to stay longer than 60 days must apply for a different visa with Cox & Kings Global Services.

If you need to extend your visa, go to the Foreigners' Regional Registration Office (FRRO) in one of the major cities. But beware—the Indian government makes it extremely difficult to extend a visa for any reason, and if you overstay your visa, you may be required to get clearance from India's Ministry of Home Affairs to leave the country. Punishment can range from heavy fines to actually being jailed.

✏️ Immunizations

Ultimately you must decide what vaccinations are right for you before you travel to India; it's wise to consult your doctor at least three months before departure.

The Centers for Disease Control and Prevention (CDC) maintain a list of recommended vaccinations for the Indian subcontinent on their website; these include hepatitis A and typhoid fever. No vaccination certificate or inoculations are required to enter India, unless you're coming via certain parts of sub-Saharan Africa, in which case you'll need proof of vaccination against yellow fever. Without such proof, you could be quarantined on arrival in dismal government facilities.

US Embassy/Consulate

The U.S. Embassy is locted in Delhi and is open on weekdays from 8:30–5. Consulates are located in Mumbai, Chennai, Kolkata, and Hyderabad.

📅 When to Go

HIGH SEASON $$$$
India's high season starts in October and runs through March. It winds down around the annual Holi (festival of color) celebrations that traditionally mark the end of winter.

LOW SEASON $
Low season in India is directly correlated to the weather, starting in May, when temperatures peak well over 100°F (especially in North India) and continuning through the monsoon season that runs through August and into September.

VALUE SEASON $$
Travelers wanting to avoid crowds and potentially save money on hotel room rates should consider visiting during either April, when temperatures start to rise but are still bearable, or in September, at the tail-end of the monsoon season.

Essentials

🛏 Lodging

Staying in India can be a pleasure, regardless of whether you've paid top price at a world-class luxury hotel or gone the no-frills route at a local guest house. For average accommodations somewhere in the middle, you often can expect to pay significantly less than what you'd pay at a comparable hotel in North America or Europe, and rooms across price ranges tend to be clean and neat.

Try to secure all room reservations before arrival, especially during peak season and in the major cities and popular tourist destinations such as Mumbai, Delhi, Agra, and Goa. But give yourself a little leeway to make plans on arrival, especially if you have more than two weeks.

Room rates can be extremely expensive in business-oriented cities like Mumbai and Delhi. Urban hotels rarely have off-season discounts, though some international chains have incentive programs for frequent guests. In other areas, hotels may be seeking guests, so you may be able to negotiate your price. Do not agree to an airport pickup or breakfast before checking if these services cost extra. Airport pickups organized by luxury hotels are generally overpriced.

As with restaurants, practically every hotel in India will gladly put up with children running around, and most allow children under a certain age to stay in their parents' room for free.

Category	Cost
$$$$	over Rs. 10,000
$$$	Rs. 6,000–Rs. 10,000
$$	Rs. 4,000–Rs. 5,999
$	under Rs. 4,000

All prices are in rupees for a standard double room in high season, with no meals, excluding tax and service charges, which vary by region.

HERITAGE HOTELS

The Indian government has an excellent incentive program that encourages owners of traditional *havelis* (mansions), forts, and palaces to convert their properties into hotels. Many of these official heritage hotels—noted in reviews throughout this guide—are well outside large cities. Their architecture and style are authentically Indian, not Western. There are more than 60 such establishments in Rajasthan and a smattering elsewhere in India.

HOTELS AND GUESTHOUSES

Hotels and guesthouses are easy to find in most cities. Hotels include chains, company-run, and privately-owned properties—anything from bare-bones budget hotels to luxurious beach resorts. Overall, they tend to be larger, more formal, and more expensive than guesthouses. The term guesthouse refers to small, independent budget digs that usually lack some of the standard hotel amenities (TVs and in-room telephones, for example). Especially popular with foreign backpackers, they often have fewer rooms than hotels and the owners or managers often live on-site. Room service is available at most guesthouses, although meals are not generally included in the rates.

If you opt for room service outside a luxury hotel, here are a few things to keep in mind: tea or coffee usually comes premixed—ask to have a pot of tea or coffee with the milk, sugar, and tea bags or instant coffee brought separately. You can usually get food cooked according to your preferences (non-spicey, etc.), but you have to make the request. Make sure any bottled water you plan to consume is sealed, and do not use water from pitchers in the room unless you are certain it's safe.

🍴 Dining

Indian culture definitely revolves around food, and there are plenty of restaurants, cafés and food stalls serving international cuisine, fast food, and regional specialties, especially in big cities. If you choose to try out street food, be wary of hygiene issues—look for stalls popular with families and avoid shaved ice or anything containing cold water. India is also a haven for vegetarians, with plenty of pure-veg restaurants that don't serve any meat, fish, poultry, or eggs.

For information on food-related health issues, see Health below.

Almost all restaurants in India are family-friendly, even many of the fancier ones in top hotels. If your child doesn't like Indian food, it's usually possible to order sandwiches and pizzas. American fast food is widely available in larger cities.

Category	Cost
$$$$	over Rs. 1,400
$$$	Rs. 1,001–Rs. 1,400
$$	Rs. 500–Rs. 1,000
$	under Rs. 500

Prices are the lowest cost of a standard double room in high season.

MEALS AND MEALTIMES
A typical Indian meal consists of some rice or bread, served with spiced vegetables, meat, and lentils.

Although lots of start the day with toast or cereal, traditional Indian breakfasts are often much heavier South Indian foods such as *idlis* (steamed rice and lentil cakes) with chutney; *dosas* (a crisp crepe, made with a fermented ground-rice-and-lentil batter); *upma* (light semolina, also known as farina, with vegetables); and *aloo poha* (spicy potatoes mixed with rice flakes) feature heavily, though the most popular item in many homes is the *aloo parantha*, flatbread stuffed with potatoes and typically served with yoghurt

A good portion of the Indian population is vegetarian for religious reasons, and while milk is part of the typical vegetarian diet in India, eggs are not. Most people who eat meat don't do so every day (and certainly not at every meal). Hindus consider the cow sacred and do not eat beef. Muslims (and many Hindus) do not touch pork. Some Hindus eat only chicken and seafood and stay away from red meat, while others observe veg-only days on select days of the week (in honor of different gods).

Although South Indian restaurants often start serving lunch early, in North India people tend to eat lunch later in the afternoon than in the United States, sometimes around 3 pm. Restaurants in cities normally stay open until 11 pm , as Indians are known for starting dinner as late as 10 pm. Many five-star hotels have 24-hour restaurants referred to as "coffee shops," but which serve full meals day and night.

Snacking is also popular, and common treats include samosas and other streetside snacks. *Masala chai* (spiced milk tea) is extremely popular and often consumed four to five times a day. But as you go south, coffee becomes increasingly popular and is served with lots of milk and sugar.

Unless otherwise noted, the restaurants listed in this guide are open daily for lunch and dinner.

WINES, BEER, AND SPIRITS

India produces many kinds of liquor, and exorbitant duties make imported spirits unaffordable to all but the wealthiest of citizens and alcohol in luxury hotels is considerably marked up. Its locally produced versions of international brands of rum, vodka, and gin are (called IMFL: Indian-made foreign liquor) are adequate but generally unmemorable. The sweet local red rum, Old Monk, is worth a try. Kingfisher beer is ubiquitous, refreshing, and bland. With every year more and more Indian wine is produced; Sula is the most popular brand.

Dry days—when alcohol isn't available anywhere in the country—are observed on January 26, August 15, October 2, and on certain festival dates. Some states observe additional dry days, which are usually on or around election days.

⊕ Health

No vaccination certificates are required to visit India, unless you are visiting from an area where yellow fever is prevalent (such as sub-Saharan Africa). However, it's a good idea to talk to your doctor about innoculations at least three months before your trip. The Centers for Disease Control and Prevention (CDC) maintain a list of recommended vaccinations for the Indian subcontinent on their website; these include hepatitis A and typhoid fever.

In areas where malaria and dengue fever are prevalent, use mosquito nets, wear long sleeves, apply repellent containing DEET, and use repellents that plug into the wall and release a mosquito-repelling scent or burn anti mosquito coils. You may want to consider taking malaria prophylactics, as the disease exists in many regions of India. There's no vaccine against malaria or dengue, and mosquitoes can pass on other infections, such as the Chikungunya virus, so preventing bites should always be your first line of defense.

The precautions you take for yourself in India are the same ones you should take for your child. Make sure they have all their vaccinations, and consult a pediatrician about antimalaria medication.

The most common types of illnesses are caused by contaminated food and water. If you have problems, mild cases of traveler's diarrhea may respond to Imodium (known generically as loperamide) or Pepto-Bismol. Be sure to drink plenty of water; if you can't keep fluids down, seek medical help. Infectious diseases can be airborne or passed via mosquitoes and ticks and through contact with animals or people. Speak with your physician and/or check the CDC or World Health Organization websites for health alerts, particularly if you're pregnant, traveling with children, or have a compromised immune system.

SPECIFIC ISSUES IN INDIA

The major health risk in India is traveler's diarrhea, caused by ingesting contaminated food or water, so it's important to watch what you eat. Avoid ice, uncooked food, and unpasteurized milk and milk products, and **drink only bottled water.** Avoid tap water, ice, and fresh juice if water may have been added. **You may want to turn down offers of "filtered" water**; it may have been filtered to take out particles but not purified to kill parasites. Water purified through an Aquaguard filter system, however, is generally safe (as long as the filter has been maintained correctly). You'll be fine at most places catering to foreign tourists. **When buying bottled water, make sure that the cap hasn't been tampered with.** Soft drinks and packaged fruit juices are safe, readily available options. And always **keep at least one bottle of water in your hotel room** for brushing your teeth as well as for drinking.

If your stomach does get upset, try to drink plenty of purified water. In severe cases, rehydrate yourself with a salt-sugar solution—½ teaspoon salt and 4 tablespoons sugar per quart of water.

Avoid raw vegetables and fruit outside of fancy restaurants, even those that have been peeled, unless it was you who did the cutting and peeling. Make sure that all meats are thoroughly cooked. Wash your hands before you eat anything, and use hand sanitizer. Many digestion problems often are due more to the heavy amounts of spice and oil that goes into Indian cuisine than to contamination, and it's fine to request your food be made with minimal oil and less spice.

All Indian cities are heavily polluted, and Delhi air quality can get severe in the late autumn and winter. People with breathing problems, especially asthma, should **carry the appropriate respiratory remedies or consider wearing a mask.** India's heat can dehydrate you, and dust can irritate your throat, so **drink plenty of liquids.** Seek air-conditioned areas when possible, and visit tourist sites in the early morning or late afternoon, when the sun is less strong. To avoid sunburn, **use sunscreen** with an SPF of at least 30. While a basic medical kit with band-aids and antiseptic is good for treating wounds immediately, you don't necessarily need to lug a medicine cabinet with you to India—**practically every over-the-counter medication and medical supply under the sun is available** in big cities and small towns alike, should you need them.

CHILDREN'S HEALTH

Bringing your kids to India may seem daunting, but most children love it. Just remember that many diseases are prevalent in India that no longer exist elsewhere, so **check with your pediatrician first** and make sure your child's immunizations are current. It's easiest to bring an infant (who cannot yet crawl, and who is still dependent on breast-feeding or formula) or children who are a bit older and can walk independently.

EMERGENCIES

Delhi's 24-hour East West Rescue has a referral list of doctors, dentists, pharmacists, and lawyers throughout India. Meera Rescue is a professional evacuation service recognized by international insurance companies; the company evacuates from anywhere in the country to hospitals in major cities and overseas if necessary; it's open 24 hours. Both companies can help arrange international evacuation if necessary, but be prepared to pay first and then be reimbursed by your insurance company.

$ Money

A trip to India can be as luxurious and expensive—or as bare-bones and cheap—as you want it to be. There's also a shortage of five-star hotels in the country, and while hotels are generally better value than in more developed countries, room rates in the chicest urban hotels are comparable to those in New York, London, or Paris. You'll pay substantially more for everything in popular tourist spots and big cities compared with the rest of the country, although certain goods (including bottled water and prepackaged snack foods have a maximum retail price (MRP) printed on their packaging. It's illegal to sell such products for more than the printed amount, although sometimes vendors try to charge foreigners more, assuming they are unaware of this price regulation. Many merchants, even in big cities, still only accept payment in cash, although this is changing. It's a good idea to carry small bills when possible, as small change is viewed as a scarce commodity.

Item	Average Cost
Cup of Coffee	Rs. 30–Rs. 50, fancy Rs. 120
Glass of Wine	Rs. 250–Rs. 600
Glass of Beer	Rs. 250–Rs. 400 in a bar or hotel
Sandwich	Rs. 50–Rs. 200
Museum Admission	Rs. 200–Rs. 300 (foreigner rates)

Prices throughout this guide are given for adults. Discounts are available for children, students, and senior citizens at most tourist attractions.

CREDIT CARDS, ATMS, AND BANKS

Master Card and Visa are widely accepted in large Indian cities, especially at retail chains and the upscale restaurants. Smaller merchants and street stalls, however, are likely to take only cash. In rural India, don't ever count on being able to pay with a credit card, and always have enough cash to see you through. It's a good idea to inform your credit-card company and bank that you'll be going abroad, especially if you don't travel internationally very often. Otherwise, the issuing company might put a hold on your card due to unusual activity. Record all your credit-card numbers—as well as the phone numbers to call if your cards are lost or stolen—in a safe place, so you're prepared should something go wrong and sign up for on-line banking so you can check your statement as you go.

Your home bank will probably charge a fee for using ATMs abroad; the foreign bank you use may also charge a fee. Nevertheless, you'll usually get a better rate of exchange at an ATM than you will at a currency-exchange office or even when changing money in a bank. And extracting funds as you need them is a safer option than carrying around a large amount of cash.

CURRENCY AND EXCHANGE

The units of Indian currency are the rupee and the (rare) paisa—100 paise equal one rupee. Paper money comes in denominations of 1 (extremely rare), 5, 10, 20, 50, 100, 200, 500, and 2,000 rupees. Coins come in denominations of 50 paise (rare), 1 rupee, 2 rupees, 5 rupees, and 10 rupees. At this writing, the rate of exchange is approximately US$1 to Rs. 67, so a 500-rupee note is worth around $7.40. The price of big-ticket items, such as real estate or cars, is usually given in units of lakh or crore. A lakh is equal to 100,000, and a crore is equal to 100 lakh. Therefore, 1 lakh rupees is equal to roughly $1,500, and 1 crore is $150,000.

India has strict rules against importing or exporting its currency, so you won't be able to get cash ahead of time. The currency-exchange booths at the international airports are always open for arriving and departing overseas flights. When you change money, remember to get a certain amount in small denominations (in 10s is best) to pay taxi drivers and such. Reject torn, frayed, taped, or soiled bills, as many merchants, hotels, and restaurants won't accept them, and it's a hassle to find a bank to get them exchanged.

Always change money from an authorized moneychanger and ask for a receipt, which you might need if you want to reconvert rupees into your own currency on departure from India.

For the most favorable rates, change money at banks or use ATMs. While ATM transaction fees may be higher abroad than at home, rates are excellent because they're based on wholesale rates offered only by major banks.

💲 Tipping

Tipping is common in India, especially in instances where people help you carry luggage or provide small tasks. Always trust your instincts and reward good service accordingly wherever you are. Rounding up or leaving 10% is common in restaurants and bars and tips are usually given in cash. Keep Rs. 20–50 handy for bellhops at hotels and consider giving your driver and tour guide a couple hundred rupees extra per day. If staying in an Indian home, it's a nice gesture to discreetly slip a token of appreciaton for the house staff if they've been helpful (Rs. 100/day is a good estimate). Tipping taxi drivers is not expected for short trips, but Rs. 100–200 extra per day is a nice gesture for multi-day trips.

💼 Packing

India is full of beautiful, colorful fashions, but your visit here probably shouldn't include lots of fancy things from your own closet. Keep it simple: breathable shirts made of plain cotton or cotton-synthetic blends and a couple of pairs of comfortable pants—all of which can be washed easily and worn again throughout your trip.

Don't worry about looking too casual— India is not a super-dressy society. If

an upscale function or fancy dinner at a big-city restaurant is on the itinerary, men can get away with just a formal shirt and pants. Women can wear simple dresses with sandals.

Bring sunglasses, a bottle of high-SPF sunblock, and two good pairs of footwear—flip-flops and lightweight walking shoes are smart options. Skip anything that's difficult to remove, such as hiking boots—unless you'll be trekking—since you'll often be required to remove your shoes to enter religious sites.

Remember to dress modestly, particularly at sacred sites. In such places, long pants are appropriate for men; women are advised to stick to at- or below-the-knee skirts, dresses, or neat pants. Women may want to avoid tight tank tops or tops that are sheer or have plunging necklines, except in nightclubs and upscale restaurants. Shorts are uncommon and are best worn long or avoided. One-piece bathing suits are the norm for women at public pools frequented by Indians, but bikinis are common at beach resorts and high-end hotels that cater to a foreign clientele.

Keep toilet paper and hand sanitizer handy, especially on long train trips. Good sanitary napkins are sold in India, but tampons with applicators are hard to find. Travelers with children should bring diapers and consider taking a portable car seat along.

If you visit in monsoon season, bring a small umbrella and flip-flops or lightweight water-resistant shoes. In winter, bring a sweater or a light jacket for cool evenings; if you're visiting northern mountainous areas, or plan to ride on any of India's intensely air-conditioned trains, a proper coat is a good idea.

Great Itineraries

India is huge, and it would take months, or even years, to do a full-fledged tour of the country. We've narrowed this book down to what we consider the *essential* India, but even still, unless you have a *really* long vacation, you won't have time to see all the highlights. Keep in mind, too, that the best way to appreciate India is not to rush—in fact, the country tends to run in such a fashion that it's next to impossible to rush while you're here.

To further help you make the most of your time, India's Golden Triangle, spanning roughly 240 km (150 miles) on each of its three sides, links Mughal and Rajput sites in Delhi, Jaipur, and Agra. It's the most well-traveled route in India, and for good reason: for many tourists, the sites here *are* India. What you see—the Taj Mahal, the impressive palace-fort and Islamic monuments in Old Delhi, and the timeless Pink City fairy tale that is Jaipur—are some of the most splendid edifices that India has to offer. Although you could visit most of these sights in a week, or even less, try not to make it a hurried affair if you can. Between the heat and the sometimes tricky dealings of getting around, traveling in India is often more exhausting than elsewhere, and an overpacked day rarely makes for a satisfying visit. We've outlined the basics of the Golden Triangle *below*, with some options and add-ons.

The Golden Triangle, 11 days

DELHI
3–4 days

Fly into Delhi to explore the old and new capitals. Hit the ground running with some light touring on the first day, perhaps doing some shopping or taking in the lovely, pre-Mughal Lodi Gardens. Over the next two days, visit Old Delhi's major Mughal sites, including the Red Fort, Jama Masjid, and Chandni Chowk, now a hodgepodge market. Also highly worth a visit: the Mughal Humayun's tomb and the imperial buildings of the Raj-era. Pay a visit to the excellent collections at the National Museum as well, but make sure to also save time for just getting acquainted with Delhi weather, crowds, and food—the higher-end restaurants and shops in South Delhi are worth the trip. ⇨ *Delhi, Chapter 3.*

Option: If you prefer, head right out to Agra on your second day, leaving time to explore Delhi a little more afterward.

JAIPUR
2–4 days

Set out early for Jaipur (it's about six hours by train or car; the flight is an hour, but factor in airport time). Alternatively, take an extra day and make an overnight stop at the Neemrama Fort Palace, built in the 15th century and now a luxury hotel about midway between Delhi and Jaipur. Once in Jaipur, head out to explore the city's unforgettable bazaars and monuments to see why it's called the Pink City. Set aside a half day to explore the Amber (Amer) Fort and Palace, just north of the city limits. ⇨ *Rajasthan, Chapter 5.* Then head back to Delhi.

Side Trips: If you drive to Jaipur and have the time and desire, add in a few days for a side trip or two. About 160 km (100 miles) south of Jaipur is Ranthambhore National Park, the most likely place in India to see a tiger or other large cat outside of captivity. If you're inclined to explore more of Rajasthan, the "Land of Princes," head farther afield to either

Udaipur, where the sprawling City Palace and Lake Palace seem taken from a fairy-tale book, or the "Blue City" of Jodhpur, the site of the magnificent eight-gated Mehrangarh Fort, built in the 15th century.

Option: Skip Jaipur and go straight to Udaipur: there is more than enough in this magical city to keep you occupied for several days, and there are several spectacular side trips to places like the Jain Temple at Ranakpur.

THE TAJ MAHAL (AGRA) AND FATEHPUR SIKRI
2–3 days

From Delhi, travel by road or take the train to Agra. If you're driving, make a stop during the two- to three-hour trip to visit the splendid royal remnants of the ancient Mughal capital Fatehpur Sikri (if you take the train to Agra, rent a car and driver and backtrack to Fatehpur Sikri). The fast train takes about three hours, but isn't at the most convenient times. Plan to stay overnight in Agra so you can fully appreciate the Taj Mahal and Agra's other sites, the impressive Agra Fort and the tomb of Etmad-ud-Daulah (the so-called "Baby Taj"). Then make your way back to Delhi. ⇨ *Chapter 4, Side Trips from Delhi.*

■TIP➔ **If this is your first time in India, it may seem like a good idea to rent a car and drive it yourself, but it isn't.** India's traffic is fierce and should only be tackled by seasoned drivers familiar with Indian roads and traffic conditions. Hire a car and driver, which costs only a little more than renting a car by itself.

Delhi is one of the most expensive places to stay in India. In the high season, Agra and Jaipur are a close second. These destinations are among the most popular tourist spots in India, so hotels book up quickly. If you have

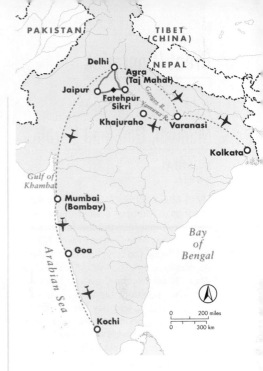

your heart set on a specific hotel, book early. Northern India is also a popular circuit for guided tours. If you like the comfort of a knowledgeable guide and the structure of a set plan, consider a package tour. ⇨ *See the Travel Smart chapter in the back of this book for recommendations.*

Transportation: If getting there is half the fun in your mind, take a train. Although you give up some flexibility with a train, the countryside views are at least partial compensation, as is being able to avoid the loud, manic Indian driving style. If time is limited and you want to have as much freedom as possible with your route, then a car and driver is the better option.

Great Itineraries

Add-Ons from Delhi: Mumbai, Goa, and Kerala

MUMBAI
3–4 days

Fly to Mumbai from Delhi. To get your bearings in Mumbai, start with a visit to the city's most recognizable landmark, the Gateway of India (the nearby Taj Mahal Palace and Tower hotel is a close second in fame). Then visit the Prince of Wales Museum, the Crawford Market, and other signature sights of Raj-era Bombay, ending your day with a visit to Chowpatty Beach, where food stalls and amusement rides line a stretch of sand that comes most alive on Saturday. Another thing that should not to be missed is some time for serious shopping in markets and for experiencing Mumbai's restaurants—two areas in which this often flashy city excels. On one morning, head to Elephanta Island, reached by boat from the Gateway of India; the Hindu and Buddhist cave sculptures there are masterful and mysterious. ⇨ *Mumbai, Chapter 6*.

SIDE TRIP: AJANTA AND ELLORA CAVES, 3 DAYS
The Ajanta and Ellora Caves were built over a period of 700 years starting in the 2nd century BC. To get here, you first must go 400 km (250 miles) east of Mumbai to the city of Aurangabad. Plan on spending the good part of a day at each site (for a total of two days) to avoid getting sculpture fatigue. Aurangabad's impressive Daulatabad Fort, nearly a millennium old, is also worth a visit. ⇨ *Mumbai, Chapter 6*.

Transportation Tips: The number of trains making the seven-hour train ride from Mumbai to Aurangabad is limited, so it probably makes the most sense to fly there and back—it's a 45-minute trip each way. The Ajanta Caves can take up to three hours to reach from Aurangabad, and Ellora is about 30 minutes away. To use your time most efficiently, you will probably want to hire a car and driver to take you to the caves, rather than relying on tour buses.

GOA
4 days

If you're craving some beach time and a look at a totally different part of India, head south to the former Portuguese colony of Goa on the Arabian Sea. You can fly from Mumbai, or take the Konkan Railway, a gorgeous 12-hour trip that tracks the coastline and passes over nearly 150 major bridges on its complete route (book ahead for this popular train). In Goa you'll want to spend time eating seafood and sipping Kingfishers at a beach shack, but make sure to set aside time for a day trip to visit Old Goa's monumental 17-century cathedrals as well as the atmospheric Portuguese-influenced streets of Panjim. When you've had your fill of Goa's many charms, either fly or take the train back to Mumbai. ⇨ *Goa, Chapter 7*.

KERALA
4 days

Remote and serene, Kerala is on the southern coast of the Arabian Sea; you can get there by train or fly into Kochi, Trivandrum, or Calicut. Either way, you'll undoubtedly want to experience nature here. Rent a quaint houseboat for three days to just meander through the majestic backwaters that curve through green hills and the rice paddies of small villages—easily accessible via Kollam. A bit farther inland, the Western Ghats contain vast tea and spice plantations as well as beautiful wildlife. If you want to experience Kerala civilization, the old port city of Kochi is an enchanting mix of traditional South Indian culture and influences from the Portuguese, Jews, Syrian Christians, and Muslims who came this way in the past. ⇨ *Kerala, Chapter 8.*

Add-Ons from Delhi: Kolkata, Khajuraho and Varanasi

KOLKATA
2–3 days

While there are direct overnight trains linking Delhi to Kolkata, the fastest one takes at least 17 hours, and it makes more sense for most people just to fly. When in Kolkata, be sure to take a stroll along Park Street, a colonial era street with excellent restaurants, hotels, and bookshops, and set aside some time to explore the excellent museum housed inside the white marble Victoria Memorial. Other popular attractions include the Mother House, the headquarters of the Missionaries of Charity, which houses a museum and Mother Teresa's tomb, and the Kalighat Kali Temple.

KHAJURAHO
2 days

Fly to Khajuraho on your way to Varanasi and spend two days absorbing the exuberant, often erotic bas-reliefs that adorn the town's 10th- and 11th-century Hindu temples. The temples at Khajuraho are fascinating, but not easy to get to. If you plan to go, visit on the way to Varanasi; at the time of writing, there are no direct air links between Delhi or Kolkata and Khajuraho. While there are direct flights from Khajuraho to Varanasi, stopovers are required when traveling the opposite direction. ⇨ *Chapter 4, Side Trips from Delhi.*

VARANASI
2–3 days

Varanasi, on the holy Ganges River, is the most sacred city for Hindus—and it may also be the oldest continuously populated city in the world. You can visit as a side trip from Delhi if you don't have enough time to do a thorough exploration of Uttar Pradesh. If you can, fly to Varanasi—traveling by train or car eats up a lot of time, and the roads in Uttar Pradesh are not the greatest. Spend your first day getting acquainted with the manic pace of the city's Old Town. Then make it an early night so that you can get up before dawn to take an early morning boat ride on the Ganges and witness morning ablutions along the river. After setting aside some time to wander and take in the Old Town's sights, sounds, and (yes) smells, take an auto-rickshaw south to the Bharat Kala Bhavan Museum, a college institution with some superb examples of local sculpture. ⇨ *Chapter 4, Side Trips from Delhi.*

SIDE TRIP: SARNATH, 1 DAY
After an early breakfast, head to Sarnath, just 11 km (7 miles) north of Varanasi, where the Buddha preached his first sermon. Take an auto-rickshaw or a taxi—you may want to hire the same driver to take you back at the end of the day. Sarnath's Deer Park contains a Buddhist temple, several 5th- and 6th-century monuments, and an outstanding archaeological museum. Have lunch at one of the nearby cafés, then return to Varanasi to see any last-minute sights and get ready for your return to Delhi.

Contacts

✈ Air Travel

AIRLINE SECURITY ISSUES
Transportation Security Administration. ⊕ www.tsa.gov.

AIRPORT INFORMATION
Chhatrapati Shivaji International Airport (Mumbai). ☎ 22/6685–1010 ⊕ www.csia.in. **Indira Gandhi International Airport (Delhi).** ☎ 124/337–6000 ⊕ www.newdelhiairport.in.

AIRLINES
Air India. ☎ 800/223–7776 in U.S.., 800/180–1407 in India ⊕ www.airindia.com. **American Airlines.** ☎ 800/433–7300 in U.S., 124/256–7222 in India ⊕ www.aa.com. **British Airways.** ☎ 800/247–9297 in U.S., 1860/180–3592 in India ⊕ www.britishairways.com. **Delta Airlines.** ☎ 800/241–4141 in U.S., 800/180–0099 in India ⊕ www.delta.com. **Luftansa.** ☎ 800/645–3880 in U.S., 124/488–8888 in India ⊕ www.lufthansa.com. **United Airlines.** ☎ 800/864–8331 in U.S., 124/431–5500 in India ⊕ www.united.com.

WITHIN INDIA
Air India. ☎ 800/160–1407 in India, 800/223–7776 in U.S. ⊕ www.airindia.com. **IndiGo.** ☎ 99/1038–3838, 124/661–3838 ⊕ www.goindigo.in. **Jet Airways.** P800/225–522 in India, 877/835–9538 in U.S. ⊕ www.jetairways.com. **SpiceJet.** ☎ 800/98718–03333 ⊕ www.spicejet.com. **Vistara.** ☎ 92892–28888, 99589–62222 ⊕ www.airvistara.com.

🚆 Train Travel

LUXURY TRAINS
Deccan Odyssey. ☎ 800/111–363 in India wwww.maharashtratourism.gov.in/deccan-odyssey/about. **Heritage Palace on Wheels.** ☎ 11/2338–6069, 800/103–3500 wrtdc.tourism.rajasthan.gov.in/Client/TrainHome.aspx. **Maharajas' Express.** ☎ 97176–35915 in India ⊕ www.the-maharajas.com. **Palace on Wheels.** ☎ 800/103–3500 toll-free in India ⊕ http://rtdc.tourism.rajasthan.gov.in/Client/PalaceOnWheel.aspx.

TRAIN INFORMATION
Indian Railways. ⊕ www.indianrail.gov.in. **Indian Railways International Tourist Bureau.** ⊠ New Delhi Railway Station, Paharganj side, 2nd fl. ☎ 11/4262–5156.

➕ Health/Safety

HEALTH WARNINGS
National Centers for Disease Control & Prevention (CDC). ☎ 800/232–4636 ⊕ www.cdc.gov/travel. **World Health Organization (WHO).** ⊕ www.who.int.

GENERAL EMERGENCY CONTACTS
East West Rescue. ⊠ 38 Golf Links, New Delhi ☎ 11/2464–1494 ⊕ www.eastwestrescue.com. **Meera Rescue.** ⊠ 112 Jor Bagh, New Delhi ☎ 11/2465–3170, 11/2465–3175 ⊕ www.meera-rescue.com.

🏛 Embassies

CONSULATES AND EMBASSIES
U.S. Consulate (Kolkata). ⊠ 38A, J.L.Nehru Rd., Kolkata ☎ 33/3984–6300 win.usembassy.gov/embassy-consulates/kolkata. **U.S. Consulate (Mumbai).** ⊠ Bandra Kurla Complex, C–49, G-Block, Bandra East ☎ 22/2672–4000 ⊕ in.usembassy.gov/embassy-consulates/mumbai. **U.S. Embassy.** ⊠ Shantipath, Chanakyapuri ☎ 11/2419–8000 win.usembassy.gov.

$ Money

REPORTING LOST CARDS
American Express. ☎ 800/528–4800 in U.S., 124/280–1800 in India ⊕ www.americanexpress.com. **Diners Club.** ☎ 800/234–6377 ⊕ www.dinersclub.com. **MasterCard.** ☎ 800/627–8372 in U.S., 636/722–7111 collect from abroad ⊕ www.mastercard.com. **Visa.** ☎ 800/847–2911 in U.S., 800/100–1219 in India ⊕ www.visa.com.

🛂 Passports and Visas

INFORMATION
Cox & Kings Global Services. ⊕ www.in.ckgs.us. **Government of India Electronic Visa Application Page.** ⊕ indianvisaonline.gov.in/evisa/tvoa.html.

Chapter 3

PORTRAIT OF INDIA

3

Updated by
Margot Bigg

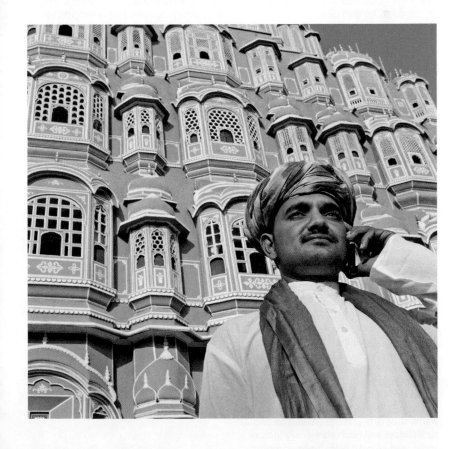

A rich and diverse country, India is difficult to describe in exact terms. We can't completely prepare you for what you'll find, so instead, we will attempt to give a sense of the country through its different elements. From there, it's yours to experience.

From the golden desert of Rajasthan to the palm-fringed beaches of Goa, India is a study in contrasts. So how does the casual visitor get beyond the extremes of the sparkle of tourism's "Incredible India" and the squalor of the country's in-your-face poverty? A good place to start is with the subcontinent's lively **History,** marked by periods of unification and fragmentation, and sparked by associations with foreign traders and invaders—from the Portuguese and the English to Turkic and Mongol tribes. Indeed, the six decades or so of India as a modern nation is short compared to the region's past. An understanding of history will also give context to the intricacies of **Modern Indian Society.**

Diversity and contrast are central themes throughout India. From the austerity of some types of vegetarianism to the excesses of spice-infused meats found in Indian **Cuisine,** and from the ascetic philosophies to extravagant rituals in its **Religions,** India is probably defined better by its deviations than by its norms. This makes for a densely populated portrait: from the panoply of **Hindu Gods and Goddesses** to the vibrant forms of Indian **Dance, Music, and the Performing Arts** and the packed calendar of **Holidays and Festivals**—every inch of India is alive with kaleidoscopic sight, sound, and color. Even in matters of economic consumption, contradiction is king, and **Shopping** options range from crafts and kitschy cultural artifacts found in traditional bazaars and roadside stalls to exquisite designer ware found at megamalls and high-end boutiques.

We've tried to distill India's head-spinning inconsistencies and rich traditions into the thematic pages that follow, starting points for an understanding of India, with an emphasis on the regions covered in this book. This background will help explain the nuances of even the most packaged of tours and—because the unexpected is inevitable in India—help you navigate situations that were not part of your itinerary.

Did You Know?

One form of Kuchipudi classical dance has the dancer keep a pot of water on his or her head while the feet are balanced on a brass plate. The dancer manipulates the plate around the stage without spilling any water.

MODERN INDIAN SOCIETY

At once a stable society, comfortably couched in time-worn traditions, and a chaotic crucible of new ideas, modern India is distinguished by diversity and united by patriotism.

(top left) An information technology center outside of Delhi; (top right) A traditional Indian wedding; (bottom right) Dhobi ghat in Mumbai, where thousands of workers wash clothes by hand

There are countless factors that contribute to India's diversity, including socioeconomic differences and access to basic needs and education; dozens of official languages and various different cuisines; religious differences and the deep gender inequality that transcends even the division between urban and rural populations. And yet many factors unite India. Even in terms of language, English and Hindi are common to most of urbanized North and Central India, though there is some resistance to Hindi in South India, where Dravidian languages and English prevail. And although major urban areas have been joined by roads, the democratizing power of the Indian rail system is not to be underestimated. A shared history of colonialism, active media, a sprawling government bureaucracy, and an engaged political body help create a relatively cohesive Indian society. And, of course, there is the fact that Indian people are, by and large, incredibly warm and welcoming.

ASTROLOGY

Modern India may be known for technology, but this doesn't negate the prevalence of tradition. Many Indians won't make decisions about business, love, or family without consulting the stars. Marriages, if not made in heaven, should at least be consecrated on an auspicious date—on days deemed extra-auspicious for weddings, huge numbers of concurrent ceremonies occur.

URBAN VERSUS RURAL SOCIETY

Possibly the biggest difference in India is one that tourists rarely experience: the division between rural and urban life. India's cities are fueled by labor and resources from India's villages—the majority of the country's population still subsists on an agrarian lifestyle and economy—yet city and small-town life is worlds apart from the fields and dirt roads of the rest of India. While in the cities, access to electricity is frustrated by unannounced power outages, many rural Indian households lack access to any reliable power at all. Education and potable water are often elusive commodities outside of India's cities and towns. Idyllic glimpses of rural life are visible from the road or train—yellow-blossomed mustard fields in north India, coconut plantations along the southern coasts, tractors loaded impossibly high with bales of cotton or other goods—but the realities of rural life are something many travelers never get the chance to see.

RICH, MIDDLE CLASS, POOR

India's cities are microcosms and melting pots. A small, privileged elite drives (or is chauffeured) between the air-conditioned high-rises of south Mumbai, the guarded colonies of south Delhi, and the exclusive resorts of Goa. The denizens of this privileged group frequent five-star restaurants, luxury boutiques, and private clubs. But this is just a tiny segment of society.

A large and rapidly growing middle class fuels the urban economy, powering the country's information-technology hubs. More professionalized and better educated than their parents, members of the urban middle class also feed a mushrooming consumer-goods-and-services sector. Spending money is proof of success, and lavish weddings replete with yards of brocade, miles of fairy lights, kilos of gold jewelry, and bushels of fresh-cut flowers are not uncommon. Coffee shops and fast-food outlets cater to and are staffed by members of the upwardly mobile society.

In stark contrast to the rich and the middle class, India's populated areas are also home to millions of urban poor—from migrants who set up house in tarpaulin shelters while employed in construction and infrastructure projects to low-income families living in slum colonies with open sewers. Many urban migrants live a double life—catering to the wealthy and middle class so they can send money to their families back in their home villages. Besides domestic help, low-income jobs include a wide range of workers—including porters, cycle-rickshaw drivers, and salesmen of cheap goods.

Lunch-wallahs transporting tiffin boxes

GENDER ROLES

Across all walks of life, women and men lead very different, often divergent, lives. While women work the fields and provide manual labor on construction sites right alongside men, these are roles born out of economic necessity. Middle-class and even elite women have less occasion to work outside of the home; although wealthier families may educate daughters as much as sons, the focus for women is squarely on marriage and raising children. Cutting across economic distinctions is a preference for boys—in some states female infanticide is still a serious problem, and it is illegal for doctors to disclose the sex of fetuses. Some villages have such a shortage of marriageable women that they have had to bring in brides from other regions of India—a practice that rubs against the older tradition of marrying within one's caste and culture.

MARRIAGE

Arranged marriages take place all across Indian society. Although the government prohibits child marriage, betrothals and weddings at a very young age still do take place in remote areas. These days, however, the culture of dating also thrives in India's big cities, particularly with the advent of online and app-based dating. Couples can be seen everywhere in Delhi and Mumbai, flirting on the dance floors of nightclubs, sharing coffee and moony looks across a café table, or surreptitiously canoodling under a tree in a public park—often the most convenient meeting ground for poorer youngsters from more conservative families.

CASTE

Marriage classifieds (listings of eligible men and women, living in India or abroad, searchable by caste, religion, profession, and education, etc.) are only one of the many societal phenomena in which caste figures prominently. Caste in India can be as innocuous as a shared community history, signified by a particular last name, or as insidious as a derogatory slur. Although technically abolished, in practical terms caste identity still plays an important role in modern Indian society, particularly in politics. There is still raging debate—akin to but far more polarizing than the American debate over affirmative action—over quotas for historically disadvantaged castes and tribes in government jobs and school admissions.

POLITICS

India's parliamentary democracy is rife with corruption and strange liaisons, and the average Indian is either actively cynical or openly engaged with politics—and sometimes both. A multiparty system means that there are significant blocs of special-interest parties besides the two dominant parties: Congress and the BJP (Bharatiya Janata Party). Unfortunately, some parties attempt to leverage religious differences to garner support, which can turn whole communities against each other.

RELIGION

Religion plays a large part in modern Indian society, and worship is an important component: people often pray regularly in temples, mosques, gurdwaras, and churches, but may also have family shrines at home, composed of icons, portraits, and statues. Ritual fasting is a regular occurrence in many religions, whether weekly for Hindus or yearly during Ramadan for devout Muslims. Religious conventions can often bleed into cultural ones, influencing diet, neighborhood, occupation, and clothing choice.

CLOTHING

Clothing in modern Indian society is a signifier of many things—gender, region, wealth, profession, and, often, religion. In general, men usually wear trousers or jeans with collared shirts or T-shirts. In south India and in rural areas, native forms of dress—long pieces of cloth called *lungis* or *dhotis*—are wrapped around the waist and legs, but loose-fitting pajama-type outfits are more common. These are topped with an undershirt, called a *banyan,* and perhaps a tunic or kurta. Headgear can also be an indicator of religion or region. Rajasthani men are known for their bright, coiled turbans (and grandiose mustaches), Sikh men sweep their long hair into streamlined turbans, and Muslim men usually wear skull caps when praying. Poorer or rural women of all religions tend to cover their heads with thin scarves, particularly in Rajasthan, and urban Muslim women may keep their heads covered and wear body-covering robes as well. Traditional wear for women includes the more typically north Indian tunic or shirt, called a kurta or *kameez.* This is paired with loose pants, or *salwar,* gathered at the ankle or tighter *churidar,* long leggings bunched up at the ankle. Skirts (*lehengas*) with blouses (*cholis*) are also popular, particularly as wedding wear. Saris, yards of cloth that can be tied many different ways around a petticoat and blouse, are worn all over India and come in many regionally and seasonally specific textiles and patterns. Urban women are quite comfortable in jeans and other Western wear, though exposing too much leg or cleavage in public is frowned on (Mumbai and Goa and, increasingly, Delhi are slightly more relaxed in this regard).

A traditional family in a small village in Rajasthan

HISTORY YOU CAN SEE

India's history is marked by periods of cultural and economic exchange and lively empire building. Among the obvious results are the ruins of ancient planned cities and the chaos of modern India's skyrocketing growth.

(top left) Rashtrapati Bhavan, in Delhi, where the president lives; (top right) A carving at Khajuraho; (bottom right) Stone chariot shrine at Hampi

Blessed with an abundance of natural resources, geographical diversity, and many access points along its coasts, India has historically been an attractive place for settlers and conquerors. Part of the reason for the sub-continent's continued diversity of culture and people is that residents have always been influenced by different forces at each of the area's different boundaries, which themselves have been rather fluid over the centuries. At various points, Indian empires have been some of the richest and most cultured in the world. Though its history is marked by cycles of destruction and con-struction, and despite a tendency to neglect all things old, India's past is very much alive in fabulous myths, recorded documents, and phenomenal physical artifacts and archaeological sites.

AGES OF ARCHITECTURE

Mughal architecture is a mélange of influ-ences—vaulted spaces recalling Central Asian campaign tents, Per-sian domes topped with Hindu lotus finials, and Rajput-style pavilions with umbrella-like overhangs. The British adopted what they saw, adding Gothic and art deco touches to create the Indo-Saracenic style of the Victoria Terminus and the Rash-trapati Bhavan.

PREHISTORY

The subcontinent's oldest significant archaeological finds are from the planned cities of the Indus Valley Civilization, which peaked in western India, Pakistan, and points north in the period around 2600–1800 BC. Delhi's **National Museum** has a large collection of artifacts (pottery, toys, copper tools) from this era. Around 1500 BC, Indo-Europeans from Central Asia began to migrate to the region; their Indo-Aryan language was likely influenced by the subcontinent's indigenous Dravidian dialects to form Sanskrit. This gave rise to the Vedic Iron Age, characterized by the oral composition of Sanskrit texts— the underpinnings of Hinduism. Urban centers such as Kashi (modern-day **Varanasi,** the oldest continuously inhabited city in the world) emerged, and India began to split off into various monarchies and republics.

ANCIENT EMPIRES

Succeeding a handful of ancient kingdoms and forays by Macedonian conqueror Alexander the Great, the Hindu Maurya Empire (India's first) was founded in 321 BC. At its peak, under the Buddhist convert Emperor Ashoka, the kingdom encompassed most of the subcontinent. Ashoka built Buddhist shrines and temples at **Sarnath** (where the Buddha preached his first sermon) and at Sanchi. He also furthered the religion through edicts, often inscribed

on pillars. The **Ashokan pillar at Sarnath,** with four lions at the top, later provided the inspiration for modern India's state emblem.

Farther south lay the Dravidian kingdoms of the Cholas, Cheras, and Pandyas. These eventually gave way to other dynasties, while the decline of the Maurya Empire in the north led to smaller kingdoms with ever-shifting boundaries and incursions from the northwest. Most of the north was again united by the Gupta Empire during India's "Golden Age" from the 4th to 6th centuries. Under the tolerant administration of the Guptas, the arts and sciences flourished: the concept of zero, the heliocentric model, and the game of chess are all said to have been invented during this period. Meanwhile, the grandeur of the Vijayanagar Empire in the south, which was strong until the 17th century, is evident in the ruins at Hampi. The rest of India was ruled by other "Middle Kingdoms," like the Vakatakas in central India, who created the Buddhist cave paintings at Ajanta. By the 8th century, martial Rajput clans were a dominant ruling force in north India. Rajput factions built Gwalior's clifftop fort and **Khajuraho**'s erotically embellished temples; their descendents would go on to build forts and palaces in **Jaipur, Udaipur, Jaisalmer,** and other centers of power in **Rajasthan.**

Humayun's tomb, Delhi.

MUSLIM RULERS

India's early Islamic states were several Turkic and Afghan territories, collectively called the Delhi Sultanate. The first, the Mamluk (Slave) Dynasty, was founded by Qutb-ud-din Aibak in the early 13th century. A slave-soldier whose leader had made incursions into north India, Aibak and his successors built Delhi's **Qutub Minar.** Next, the Turkic-Afghan Khilji rulers took over, expanding their territory west from the Ganges River and building Delhi's **Siri Fort.** Around the same time, the breakaway Bahmani Sultanate, which eventually fragmented into smaller kingdoms, carved out parts of the south's Vijayanagara Empire. In 1321, the Tughlaqs sultans came to power, ruling from Tughlaqabad (now in Delhi). Their rule was weakened in 1398, when Timur (Timurlane), a descendent of Genghis Khan, sacked the city. The Sayyid Dynasty ruled briefly, followed by the Afghan Lodhi sultans, some of whom are buried in the tombs in Delhi's **Lodhi Gardens.**

Relative stability came to north India with the first Mughal Emperor, Babur, who hailed from Central Asia and had

Persian, Turkic, and Mongol ancestry. He established his rule in 1526, having defeated the Lodis and neighboring Rajputs. Babur's son was **Humayun,** whose **tomb** in Delhi is an example of the mixing of Islamic and Hindu cultures under the Mughals; it's considered a precursor to the Taj Mahal. Humayun's son, Akbar, reigned for half a century, starting in 1556. Based in **Agra** and nearby **Fatehpur Sikri,** Akbar expanded and consolidated Mughal power through marriage, conquest, and feudal ties. Greatly influenced by Sufi saints, Akbar was curious about and tolerant of other religions. The syncretic Mughal arts and architecture blossomed under his grandson, Shah Jahan, who built his city, **Shahjahanabad (Old Delhi),** including the **Lal Qila (Red Fort)** and the **Jama Masjid,** as well as **Agra Fort** and, of course, the **Taj Mahal.**

COLONIALISM

Following the expansionist policies of the puritanical Emperor Aurangzeb (1658–1707), Mughal power was compromised by war, especially against the strong Maratha Empire, which had its center in Raigad, south of Mumbai.

Meanwhile, Queen Elizabeth I chartered the British East India Company, arguably the world's first corporation, in 1600. Competing with the Dutch, Portuguese, and French for mercantile control, the British East India Company opened trading posts and spread out, building India's **railroads,** from its **forts** in Madras, Calcutta, and Bombay (now Chennai, Kolkata, and Mumbai). The company steadily gained control over the subcontinent by pitting princely states against each other, leveraging economic power, installing governing and educational institutions, and through outright battle. In 1857, the company's Indian troops revolted. Variously called the Sepoy Mutiny or the First War of Independence, the rebellion's ripple effect gave the British government an excuse to clamp down. Raj-era architecture persists in **Delhi,** especially in the **India Gate** area. South Mumbai, too, is littered with Raj reminders; must-sees are the **Prince of Wales Museum** and **Crawford Market.**

INDEPENDENCE AND STATEHOOD

In 1947, after nearly a century of British Raj, India gained independence in the aftermath of World War II. Leading the push for independence through nonviolent resistance was Mohandas K. Gandhi, known as Mahatma (Great Soul). Gandhi and other leaders are honored at museums and memorials across the country, including Delhi's **National Gandhi Museum,** the **Gandhi Smriti** (where he was assassinated), and the **Nehru Memorial Museum.**

Independence came at a price, however. Before their soldiers sailed out from Mumbai's **Gateway of India,** the British partitioned the country, carving out West and East Pakistan (the latter now Bangladesh) as Muslim nations. The violence of Partition (the largest human migration in history, with a population exchange of millions), an early India-Pakistan war, and the problem of incorporating hundreds of princely states were huge challenges. The first prime minister, Jawaharlal Nehru, set about building a socialist nation—creating infrastructure, universities, and nationalized industries, and taking an active part in the fledgling Non-aligned Movement. In its first few decades, India also saw an agricultural revolution, war with China over disputed territory, and more conflicts with Pakistan. When Nehru's daughter, Indira Gandhi, became prime minister, she reacted to the threat of secessionist groups and economic problems by declaring a state of emergency in 1971. The backlash against her and her sons' leadership led to a more dynamic but less predictable coalition-driven Parliament and increased politicization of religion and caste. In the 1990s, economic reforms and the privatization of government-run corporations led to a booming economy and increased participation in global trade. Although its economy is still largely agrarian, India has become an offshore provider of skilled services with a large middle class, evident in the proliferation of call centers and glittering malls.

Photo of Jawaharlal Nehru, on the left, with Mahatma Gandhi, on the right

RELIGIONS OF INDIA

India may be a secular country constitutionally, but religion has a central and vital place in the daily lives of most of its citizens.

(top left) An illustration from the Ramayana; (top right) At a Hindu ceremony; (bottom right) Muslim woman praying at Jama Masjid

To just say that India is 79.8% Hindu oversimplifies the country's complex web of histories, identities, and institutions, many of which were codified in modern terms as "religions" only in the last few centuries. Leaving aside the fact that the population is more than 14.2% Muslim, with significant Christian, Sikh, and other minorities, even the majority Hindu community is extremely diverse. Regional identities often cut deeper than religion (thus some Punjabi Hindus eat meat while many Hindus in South India will not). On top of that, each of India's religions encompass age-old traditions that have survived modernity, new-age movements that focus on spirituality, and politically driven ideologies that justify themselves through mythology. But despite the fact that there are, occasionally, the kind of ugly conflicts that flare up in any pluralistic society, for the most part India is a place where you will find an amazing, often touching, degree of compassion—tolerance that extends to curiosity, and secularism that is expressed as humanity.

JUDAISM

The Jews have a long history in India, starting with the Cochin Jews arriving in Kerala around 500 BC. The Bene Israel came a few centuries later, followed by Middle Eastern and Central Asian Jews. More recently, the Bnei Menashe claimed to be a lost tribe of Israel and were recognized by Israeli rabbis. Some Ben Ephraim Jews, who were converted to Christianity in the 1800s, decided to re-embrace Judaism in the 1980s.

HINDUISM

Just under 80% of India's population identifies as Hindu. The world's third-largest religion, Hinduism is also often regarded as the oldest, with roots that stretch back 5,000 years. It may also be the most varied, as this millennia-old tradition is actually an amalgam of texts, schools, civilizations, and beliefs with a host of leaders and no single founder. Though Hindus generally believe in reincarnation, divinity itself may be multiple or monistic, and practice may involve *dharma* (moral duty), ascetic rigor (as in yoga), devotion through prayer, and many other forms of expression. Modern Hinduism draws from four major Vedic "texts"—Sanskrit ritual verses that were recorded orally beginning with the Iron Age Indus Valley civilization and later written down—as well as corollary philosophical and mystical discourses, treatises on the arts, and the epic poems the *Mahabharata* and the *Ramayana.*

Hinduism today is just as multifaceted as its history. Visitors to India may witness or participate in many aspects of observance including ritual ceremonies, some with fire, ghee, milk, and offerings of flowers and sweets; temple worship, with offerings to deities represented by *murthis* (statues); or physical practices: ascetics who deny material comfort as an expression of devotion, yogis who push their bodies to the physical limit

in order to approach the divine, and ayurvedic doctors who prescribe herbal remedies and offer nutritional advice.

ISLAM

The country's largest minority, India's Muslim population is second only to Indonesia's in numbers. As with Hinduism, Islam in India also encompasses many different schools and practices. Although India's earliest encounter with Islam was through Arab traders along the southwest coast, the religion's first real movement was through the north and west of the subcontinent in the 8th century, and it expanded from the 12th century onward, first under the Delhi Sultanate and then the Mughal Empire. Besides the strength of the Mughal seat of power around Delhi, Muslim communities grew around Islamic rulers around the country.

Like Muslims everywhere, Indian Muslims follow the Koran as the word of Allah revealed to Mohammad in the 7th century. Most Muslims in India belong to the majority Sunni sect, but there are significant portions of Shi'a Muslims as well, who believe in the importance of the Imams and of Mohammad's nephew, Ali. The spread of Islam in India also owes a great deal to mystical Sufi sects, whose founders created centers of learning, music, and charity.

Se (Cathedral), in Old Goa

CHRISTIANITY

India's third-largest religion (about 2.3% of the population), Christianity is most visible in south and southwest India and in the northeastern states. The earliest whispers of Christianity in India are accounts of the arrival of ("Doubting") Thomas the Apostle in Kerala in the 1st century and the establishment of Syrian Christian churches, which likely grew out of extant Indian Jewish communities and populations of Syrian immigrants. Later, European missionaries (like St. Francis Xavier, a Portuguese Jesuit) arrived to proselytize. Most Indian Christians follow Catholic or Orthodox practices, but some Protestant churches were also established. As in other postcolonial countries, Indian Christianity has its own distinct flavors, from the colorful roadside shrines of Kerala to the excesses of Goan Carnival to the pronounced influence of gospel music in the northeast.

SIKHISM

Sikhism grew from the teachings of its founder, Guru Nanak Dev, in the early 1500s. Nanak, a Hindu, broke from that religion's rituals and began to preach a monotheistic faith based on meditation and charity. Nine more *gurus,* or teachers, followed in his footsteps, consolidating and spreading the religion over the next few centuries. Partially as a response to persecution under the later Mughals, Sikhism also acquired a martial flavor, and followers combined elements of both the soldier and the saint. The 11th guru and the spiritual authority for modern Sikhs is the *Guru Granth Sahib Ji,* a sacred text composed of the teachings of previous gurus and other Hindu and Muslim saints. With a majority of its population in Delhi and the northwestern state of Punjab (the Golden Temple in Amritsar is the most important holy site), the Sikh community was directly affected by the violence of India's Partition, as well as suffering later injustices under the Indira Gandhi administration in 1984.

Often identifiable by their uncut hair (which the men tie up under turbans), practicing Sikhs also engage in the singing and chanting of passages of scripture (this can continue over days) and the serving of free daily meals at *gurdwaras* (temples).

BUDDHISM

Although Siddhartha Gautama attained Buddhahood through meditation and became the Buddha in 500 BC in what is now the Indian state of Bihar, India is home to a surprisingly low percentage of the world's Buddhists. In spite of a relatively low number of adherents, Buddhism has had a profound impact on Indian society. With its focus on moderation and individual duty over divisions of caste or divinity, Buddhism peaked in India with the conversion of the Maurya emperor Ashoka around 260 BC. The following centuries saw Buddhist rituals and institutions taking root outside of India, but within the country it was largely subsumed by other systems of faith. Today Buddhists in India include monks (mostly living along India's border with Tibet), low-caste Hindus who converted in large numbers over the last century to improve their social situation, and Tibetan refugees—including the Dalai Lama and the Tibetan government-in-exile in Dharamshala.

JAINISM

While Jainism appears in practice to be a more stringently ascetic, fiercely non-violent cousin of Buddhism, the religion has most likely existed as a complement to and influence on Hinduism for thousands of years. Jains believe in reincarnation and do not believe in an all-powerful creator. However, Jains do follow 24 *tirthankaras* (teachers), the last of whom, Mahavir, was a contemporary of the Buddha. Jain temples house idols of these *tirthankaras*; these temples are also where you might see devout Jain monks or nuns who wear white and cover their mouths to avoid inadvertently swallowing and killing insects and microbes. Jain sects vary in degrees of asceticism (some even eschew clothing), but strict Jains do not eat meat, garlic, or onions. Jain practices have been important to

India's cultural identity, and while they represent just a small portion of the population, Jains are highly influential in political and economic spheres.

BAHÁ'Í FAITH

With the world's largest number of followers living in India, and the landmark House of Worship (Lotus Temple) in Delhi, the syncretic Bahá'í Faith is a significant part of India's spiritual landscape. Founded in Persia in 1863, this faith seeks to unite the world's major religions and claims that Krishna, the Buddha, Abraham, Jesus, Mohammad, the Báb (a 19th-century holy man), and the religion's founder Bahá'u'llah were all divine messengers.

ZOROASTRIANISM

Though Zoroastrianism was once a major monotheistic world religion (founded in Persia by the prophet Zarathustra around 1200 BC), India now has the world's largest contingent of its followers, known as Parsis, a small but well-educated and influential group of Persians who settled in medieval western India. Though many have moved on, Mumbai has a sizeable group, including some prominent industrialists. Mumbai is also home to the Irani community—19th- and 20th-century immigrants who fled persecution in Iran.

Devotees inside Sis Ganj Gurdwara, a Sikh temple

HOLIDAYS AND FESTIVALS OF INDIA

With silk-garbed deities paraded through the streets, and special foods, dancing, and the ritual gifting of everything from saucepans to Swarovski, festivals and holidays bring together the most excessive and ascetic aspects of Indian culture.

(top left) At a Holi festival; (top right) An elaborate tableau for Durga Puja; (bottom right) Republic Day Parade

Holidays in India range from religious days of reflection to patriotic celebrations of nationalism, and festivals can mark time-honored trade fairs or harvest celebrations. Because this is a country of so many regions and religions—with different harvest seasons and different calendars based on the sun, the moon, or both—there are numerous new year's celebrations (sometimes overlapping), different commemorative days for religious or local founders, and any number of minor holidays. There's almost always something going on, and it's worth timing your visit to coincide with a festival. Seeing the elaborate tableaux and dancing; witnessing the masses of people at temples, mosques, and churches; and joining the crowds eating at specially built food stalls is a highlight of many visitors' trips to India.

MAHA NAVRATI

Literally translated as "nine nights," this celebration, which takes place in October and November, marks the beginning of winter. It generally includes worshipping Shakti, the divine Hindu mother goddess. Bengalis honor Shakti in Durga Puja by creating thematic pandals or installations—three-dimensional representations that include a statue of Durga—which are then submerged in the river.

MAKAR SANKRANTI

This January 14 festival marks the end of winter and the beginning of the harvest season, depending on the region. In many places it's celebrated by flying brightly colored paper kites (often "fighting kites," on glass-encrusted string used to strike down other kites).

REPUBLIC DAY

January 26 marks the day that the Constitution came into being in 1950; celebrations include a parade in Delhi, with kitschy floats from every region.

HOLI

The Hindu and Sikh equivalent of Carnival, the northern spring festival of Holi is India's most colorful celebration. All social and religious groups get involved on the last and wildest day (in February or March) by throwing colored powder on each other.

INDEPENDENCE DAY

The celebration of India's independence on August 15 is a dignified affair, with flag-hoisting and public speeches.

EID-UL-FITR

The end of the fasting month of Ramadan consists of three days of feasting on special desserts, buying new clothes, visiting family, and distributing alms.

GANESH CHATHURTHI

Mumbai is the epicenter of this August/September celebration of the

elephant-headed god, Ganesh, which involves submerging Ganesh idols of all sizes and types in the sea.

DIWALI

Diwali is the Hindu New Year and the end of the harvest season. Often called the "festival of lights" because people line their homes with twinkling clay lamps, Diwali is celebrated over five days with firecrackers and gift-giving. On the third day people invite Lakshmi, the goddess of wealth, into their homes. The date varies each year, but is usually between September and November.

EID-UL-ADHA

Also called "Bakr-Id," Eid-ul-Adha marks the end of the Hajj (the Muslim pilgrimage to Mecca). It's celebrated by sacrificing a goat, echoing Abraham's willingness to sacrifice his son, and by distributing food to the poor. The date, based on the Islamic calendar, changes every year.

GURU NANAK JAYANTI

The most important Sikh holiday, also known as Gurpurab, marks the birth of Guru Nanak, the founder of the Sikh religion. It's celebrated with all-night chanting, singing hymns, and cooking meals for the poor. Based on the lunar calendar, it falls either in October or November.

HINDU GODS AND GODDESSES

The vast pantheon of Hindu gods and goddesses originates in ancient Hindu mythology but plays an important role in modern life.

(top left) Durga Puja; (top right) Statue of Krishna; (bottom right) Statue of Vishnu

Most of the Hindu deities are represented in the two great Indian epics, the *Ramayana* and the *Mahabharata,* and in the ancient books of Hindu philosophy known as the Vedas. The stories surrounding the various gods and goddesses are steeped with lore of demons vanquished in the ongoing battle of good versus evil. The deities are richly portrayed, and each of their physical features is deeply symbolic. Many gods and goddesses are also characterized by their *vahana,* or vehicle, the traditional animal mount they ride.

A central concept is that of the Trimurti, which encapsulates the three basic cosmic actions: creation, preservation, and destruction. These are, in turn, personified by Brahma the creator, Vishnu the maintainer or preserver, and Shiva the destroyer or transformer.

One of the key things to look for when you visit a Hindu temple is the intricate carvings and sculptures, which illustrate the gods and goddesses and provide interpretations of Hindu mythology.

PUJA

The tradition of daily *puja,* or prayer, is a central part of Hindu life. Paintings and sculptures of various deities are found in temples and home shrines, where lamps are lit and offerings of food are made to invoke the blessings of the gods. Specific gods or goddesses are often worshipped to deal with specific situations—anything from healing an ailment to doing well on a test or having success in a business venture.

BRAHMA

The God of Creation, Brahma is the first god in the Hindu triumvirate, or Trimurti, and is associated with the daily coming and going of light and dark. He is said to have grown out of the navel of the sleeping Vishnu. Brahma is traditionally depicted with four heads (representing the four Vedas, the four holy books of the Hindu religion), sitting on a lotus. The legends tell that he once had a fifth head but it was lost after he lied to Vishnu and made Shiva angry. In his four arms he holds the Vedas, a *kamandalam* (water pot), a *suruva* (sacrificial spoon), and an *akshamala* (string of beads), which he uses to count time. Brahma has a swan as his *vahana*. Although Brahma is one of the three major gods in Hinduism, there are few temples dedicated to him, the most famous being the Brahma temple at Pushkar in Rajasthan.

VISHNU

Vishnu is the god of preservation, and the second entity in the Trimurti. He is commonly recognized by the blue color of his skin (the color of water) and with four arms that hold the *chakra* (a sharp spinning-discus-like weapon), a conch that produces the mantric Om representing the sound of creation, a lotus representing spiritual liberation, and a *gadha,* or mace. Vishnu is often shown reclining on the ocean, atop Adisesha (a serpent with 1,000 heads) and

alongside his consort Lakshmi, the goddess of wealth. As the divine protector, he is believed to have assumed avatars and descended to Earth to rescue populations from evil rulers and forces, or to restore the balance between good and evil in the world. He is believed to have come to Earth in nine different avatars so far, including one as Krishna, and Hindus believe that he will be reincarnated one last time, right before the end of this world. Mohini is the female form of Vishnu, and usually described as a supremely enchanting maiden.

KRISHNA

Krishna is an avatar, or incarnation, of Vishnu and is often depicted as a young boy or prince, usually with blue skin. He is said to be the embodiment of love and divine joy that destroys all pain and sin. He takes on many different personas, including prankster, lover, divine hero, and Supreme Being. Common representations show him lying back in a relaxed pose, playing the flute, though he is also represented as the divine herdsman, accompanied by cows or *gopis* (milkmaids). Some paintings show him with Radha, his *gopi* consort.

SHIVA

Shiva, the third of the Trimurti, is the god of destruction, and is oftentimes worshipped in the form of the phallus (lingam) fixed on a pedestal. He is vested with the power to destroy the

A Ganesh idol at the Ganesh Chaturthi festival.

universe in order to re-create it—that is, he can destroy the imperfections that can transform the universe. His abilities to both create and destroy give an intimidating aura to his austere, meditative demeanor. He is usually portrayed residing in the Himalayas with an ash-smeared forehead, his body clothed in animal skin, and a king cobra draped around his neck. He has a third eye, believed to be his source of knowledge and wisdom and also the source of his untamed energy, when it is unleashed. He is also often depicted as Nataraj, the Lord of Dance, a metaphor for his ability to masterfully maintain the balance in the universe.

LAKSHMI

The goddess of wealth and prosperity and the consort of Vishnu, Lakshmi is commonly depicted as a beautiful woman standing or sitting on a lotus. She has four arms representing the four ends of human life: *dharma* or righteousness, *kama* or desires, *artha* or wealth, and *moksha* or liberation from the cycle of birth and death. Her portrayal as the goddess of wealth is evident from the cascades of gold

coins flowing from her hands. A representation of her can be found in nearly every business because of her power to bestow prosperity, and she is celebrated with much veneration during the festival of Diwali.

GANESH

Perhaps the most easily recognized of the Hindu gods, and certainly among the most endearing, Ganesh has an elephant head, large belly, and four arms, one of which holds a *laddu,* a ball-shape popular Indian sweet. He is worshipped at the start of any new venture, and before exams, because he is considered to be the god who removes obstacles (*vignam*). He is variously depicted in seated, standing, and dancing postures, and is most often worshipped in people's homes for removing day-to-day challenges. His *vahana* is a tiny mouse, and he has several other names, including Ganapati, Gajanana, Vigneshwara, Pilliar, and Vinayagar.

MURUGAN

Also known as Subramanya or Kartikeya, Murugan is the second son of Shiva and Parvati. He is widely worshipped in South India, especially in the state of Tamil Nadu. He is the God of War. Legend has it that he was so upset with his father, Lord Shiva, whom he believed showed preferential treatment to Ganesh, Shiva's other son, that Murugan left the Himalayas for a hill in Tamil Nadu. It's there that the six most important shrines devoted to him are found; collectively they are known as Arupadai Veedu (literally "six battle camps"), and each is connected to one of the six stages of his life.

HANUMAN

The monkey god, Hanuman, is an ardent devotee of Lord Rama (one of the avatars of Vishnu) and he is among the key characters in the beloved Hindu epic, the *Ramayana*. The story goes that Lord Rama was banished from his father's kingdom for 14 years, during which time his wife Sita is abducted by the evil king Ravana and taken across the seas to Lanka. Hanuman, who belongs to the varanas, an ape-like race of forest dwellers, joins Lord Rama in his mission to rescue Sita. Hanuman is revered and worshipped for his courage and valor in inspiring and leading Rama's army and for being steadfast in his devotion and loyalty to Rama. He is often depicted in temples with a mace in his right hand or kneeling before Lord Rama and Sita.

SARASWATI

As the goddess of knowledge, literature, music, and the arts, Saraswati is said to be the mother of the Vedas, the four holy books of Hinduism. She is also associated with intelligence, creativity, education, and enlightenment. Saraswati is usually pictured dressed in white, sometimes holding a palm-leaf scroll. Her *vahana* is a swan or a peacock. She is the consort of Brahma.

SHAKTI

Shakti is the divine, formless Hindu mother goddess, a creative feminine force. The goddess Durga is the embodiment of her warrior side. Durga is often shown as the mother of Ganesha, Kartikeya, Lakshmi, and Saraswati. The female equivalent of the Trimurti concept is Tridevi (*devi* means goddess in Sanskrit), and can be represented as the conjoined forms of Lakshmi, Parvati, and Saraswati—essentially, the Shaktis of the Trimurti—Vishnu, Shiva, and Brahma, respectively.

KALI

Kali is the goddess of time and change, which come together as death. She has a dual nature of fierceness and motherliness. Although she represents death, she is also seen as a positive force because she is a destroyer of ego and therefore a granter of liberation and freedom of the soul. Kali is often depicted wearing a garland of severed heads while sticking her tongue out. She wields a scimitar and holds a severed head. She is the fierce form of Durga, the consort of Shiva, whose body she is often seen standing upon. Her *vahana* is a jackal.

An enormous Shiva statue

INDIAN CUISINE

Eating in India is an adventure, from the East-meets-West artistry of tandoori-style foie gras to the tangy jumble of flavors in a street snack.

(top left) An assortment of curries and rice dishes; (top right) A dosa with some aloo masala; (bottom right) A bowl of kheer with pistachios

This is a country united by its obsession with food, even as it is divided into countless variations by region, religion, and economics.

Visitors expecting a rigid, prohibitive food culture are often more surprised by the inclusive, evolving nature of Indian cuisines, which absorb and adapt ingredients and cooking techniques from all over the world. Despite many traditional taboos surrounding eating, there's a healthy amount of curiosity and sharing as well. In most cities you'll find diverse fare, from South India's famed breakfast dishes (*dosas, uttapams, idlis*) to North India's rich, meat-heavy curries.

A growing respect for regional cuisines means that visitors are no longer subject to the sanitized menus of yore. Pay a little attention to the changing flavors around you and you'll never again think of Indian food as limited to kebab and curry.

STREET FOOD

In the busy by-lanes of India's urban centers as much as in its truck-stop towns, stalls, and carts are a constant feature and the fuel of street life. For the faint of stomach, watching locals eat at these venues can be a vicarious pleasure—but in the big cities some vendors are sensitive to hygiene (look for signs indicating the use of bottled water), and some sit-down restaurants offer their own clean versions of street dishes.

UBIQUITOUS INDIAN DISHES

Daal, which in India refers to split pulses (lentils, beans, or split peas), is the country's most basic dish, generally boiled, spiced, and tempered with fried cumin seeds, bay leaves, garlic, and onion. Variations in thickness and hue range from pale yellow (*moong daal*) to smoky black (*urad daal*).

Thanks to the inexorable force of Punjabi culture, **chicken tikka** is a widespread dish. Chicken pieces—usually boneless—are marinated in yogurt, lemon, ginger, garlic and spices, then skewered and baked in a clay oven (tandoor) or grilled over coals. Chicken tikkas are found in this simplest form or covered in various spiced gravies.

Though it consists of rice and sweetened, thickened milk, rice pudding is far too prosaic a translation of **kheer.** Ranging from Kashmir's fruit-flavored *phirnis* to coconut milk-based *payasams* in the south, kheer can also be made of broken wheat or vermicelli noodles. Often served in a shallow clay bowl, it can be garnished with nuts or topped with silver leaf.

Definitely a candidate for most ubiquitous dish, the "**Manchurian**" purports to be a Chinese specialty but is as Indian as *saag paneer.* Supposedly invented by Kolkata Chinese chef Nelson Wang in Mumbai in 1975, it consists of strips of battered and deep-fried poultry, doused

in a thickened soy-based sauce. Both chicken and veggie Manchurians are now found on every Indian Chinese menu in the country.

For many North Indians, South Indian food begins and ends with the **dosa.** Popular as a breakfast food, these crisp crepes are made of fermented ground-rice-and-lentil batter. They can be as big as small boats and are served with a thin lentil soup called *sambar.*

Only a small percentage of desserts in any place are regional—the vast majority of Indian confectioners sell the brightly colored **Bengali sweets,** available in an astonishing variety of flavors and pretty, molded shapes. The catalyst for the invention of these candies—by one Nobin Chandra Das in 1860 Bengal—was the Portuguese introduction of intentionally curdling milk to make cheese; the sweets, too, are based on curdled milk.

Whether it's called *puchka, gol-guppa,* **panipuri,** or *gup-chup,* this delightful snack or "chaat" is found all over eastern, northern, and western India. Street vendors crack open hollow puffed crisps, stuff them with bits of boiled vegetable (usually potato and chickpea), dunk them in tamarind sauce and lethally spiced mint-coriander water, and deliver them to salivating customers. Pop each panipuri into your mouth whole and wait for the fireworks.

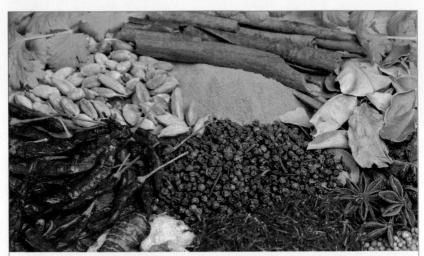

A variety of spices, including coriander, cardamom pods, turmeric, cinnamon, bay leaves, black pepper, cloves, saffron, and red pepper.

EATING PHILOSOPHIES

Indian cuisines have evolved in anything but a vacuum. As part of a subcontinent with landlocked borders along the silk route, India has always been at the crossroads of commerce between East and West, and its culinary traditions have benefited from centuries of cross-pollination.

When it comes to **eating meat,** scholars believe that even during Vedic times, meat was a regular fixture of the Indian diet. This included cattle, which are now considered strictly off-limits to most observant Hindus. In fact, nearly all items that are labeled "beef," "steak," or "burger" in India are actually buffalo meat, and even the sale of buffalo meat is banned in some regions. Only rarely is cow meat encountered in the country. Although the Hindu Vedas discuss meat-eating and animal sacrifice quite openly, these texts also mention the benefits of vegetarianism and allude to the later prohibition against killing cows.

The system of **ayurveda,** which focuses on six flavors (sweet, sour, salty, spicy, bitter, and astringent) and catalogs the benefits and ill effects of various spices, vegetables, fruits, and grains, is also rooted in these texts. Indians are hyperconscious of the consequences of eating certain foods and are quite fond of imparting advice on the subject—this is perhaps best exemplified in the obsessive attention paid to diet in Gandhi's autobiography.

Many historians believe that the protected status of cattle arose first as an economically practical phenomenon and later became codified as religious practice. In general, **vegetarianism** is considered to have spread from North to South India, starting in the 4th century, propelled largely by the rise of Buddhism and Jainism. Contrary to popular belief, about a third of India's population is lacto-vegetarian. Add in vegetarians who eat eggs (who sometimes refer to themselves as "eggetarians") and the number is still less than half. Still, a third of a population as big as India's is substantial, and the country's vegetarian options are arguably the most diverse, creative, and accessible in the world. Regions with high numbers of Jains (whose dietary restrictions surpass kosher laws in their complexity) have rich vegetarian traditions, and orthodox Jains avoid onions, garlic, and other tubers that are pulled from the ground, as their harvest disturbs subterranean life.

INTERNATIONAL INFLUENCES

While everyday spices such as black pepper, cardamom, turmeric, and bay and curry leaf originated in India, many others that are just as commonly used were originally brought from the Mediterranean, Middle East, and Central Asia.

The Spice Traders. Fennel, coriander, cumin, fenugreek, saffron, and asafetida all came to India either over land, following Alexander the Great's route, or by sea, with Arab pepper merchants who plied the eastern coast. Syrian Christians also made their mark, particularly enriching the nonvegetarian traditions of the Malabar region. Later, the Portuguese likely brought chillies and other New World plants to India. Also along eastern and western maritime trade routes, India absorbed tamarind from East Africa, cinnamon from Sri Lanka, and cloves from Southeast Asia.

The Mughal Empire. The Central Asian influence of the Mughals is the best-documented exchange in Indian culinary history. The early Mughal kings often left detailed descriptions of both native food and their own dietary habits. In his autobiography, Babur, the first Mughal king, pines for the grapes and melons of his Central Asian homeland and describes experimenting with planting these fruits in his new kingdom. Muslim rulers—both the Mughals in the north and the Nawabs of Lucknow and Bengal in the east and Hyderabad in the south—introduced elaborate courtly eating rituals to India, as well as the use of raisins, nuts, dried fruit, fragrant essences, and rich, ghee-soaked gravies. They brought their own technique of animal slaughter (halal) and introduced new ways to

cook meat, including fine-ground mince dishes like *haleem*.

Colonizers. Indian cuisine adopted many imported plants introduced by the Portuguese, Dutch, and British traders and colonizers. Such integral ingredients as chillies, potatoes, tomatoes, maize, peanuts, and peanut oil are all New World additions; tea and soybeans are China's major contributions. Besides their role as traders, the British also brought their own culinary traditions to India. Anglo-Indian cuisine, which takes its cues from the chops, bakes, and puddings of Britain, has endured in the country-club culture of urban elites but has also influenced street snacks that are a twist on, for example, teatime sandwiches. The Portuguese introduced soft white cheese to east India, giving rise to the now omnipresent world of Bengali sweets.

Settler Groups. Smaller populations with their own distinct traditions (some of them nearly extinct in modern India) include various Jewish groups and Zoroastrians—both the Parsis who settled in Gujarat around the 10th century and the Iranis, who arrived later. Finally, the influence of India's Chinese population—descendants of settlers from the 19th century onward, and later Tibetan refugees—is formidable. Just as chicken tikka masala has become a

Tandoor prawns

A thali combination plate with a side of rice.

national dish in Britain, dishes such as chilli chicken, "Manchurian," and chow mein are an undeniable part of India's culinary landscape.

THE INDIAN MEAL

Eating out in India could generally be divided into three categories: proper restaurants, holes-in-the-wall or open-air *dhabas* (cheap cafeteria-style eateries), and street food sold out of small stalls or carts. In someone's home or in a sit-down restaurant, a traditional, full meal follows certain general rules. Food is served in a *thali*—a stainless steel plate (silver on special occasions) with raised edges—and in small bowls. The thali contains condiments (a wedge of lime, salt, raw onions, pickles, or chutneys), possibly some fried items, and either rice or bread. The bowls contain servings of vegetable or meat dishes. There's a great deal of regional variation, but a sweet might be included with the savory food. In South India, a banana leaf might substitute for tableware, and in North India, street food or religious offerings are often served on plates made of stitched-together Banyan leaves. It's traditional to scoop up food with the tips of your fingers: curries are generally mixed with rice while torn-off bits of bread are used to pinch food between the fingers. Most places do offer Western cutlery as well. Traditionally, a group of diners shares several dishes, and in *dhabas* you'd usually order a few things for the table. However, some upscale Indian restaurants have started experimenting with single-portion plating; their nouvelle-inspired dishes are well worth a taste.

COMMON SPICES

The word "masala," which loosely translates to "mixture of spices," has become a default adjective for all things Indian—and it's no wonder, given the infinite permutations of seasonings available to the Indian cook. Some of the most commonly used include cumin (*jeera*), turmeric (*haldi*), asafetida (*hing*), powdered and fresh coriander (*dhania*), cloves (*laung*), black pepper (*kalimirch*), dried or powdered red chillies (*lalmirch*), fennel seed (*saunf*), mustard seeds (*rai*), ginger (*adhrak*), garlic (*lasson*), cardamom (*elaichi*), cinnamon (*dalchini*), and bay (*tej patta*). A popular premixed powder called garam (hot) masala includes cumin, coriander, cinnamon, cardamom, and cloves.

COOKING METHODS

In general, special dishes tend toward lower heat and slower processes, while street food is generally quickly fried. But India's vast array of cooking processes includes sun-drying, parboiling, braising, steaming, dry-roasting, grilling, baking, and shallow and deep frying.

The use of the **tandoor,** a clay cylindrical oven, lit from the inside to bake flatbreads and meats, is widespread in North India. In this process, skewers of marinated meat are basted with ghee and suspended in the oven. The tandoor has been made famous by Punjabi restaurants, but it is used right across Central Asia and is an important component in both Mughal and Kashmiri cooking.

Frying is an essential part of street food, which includes a wide variety of fried snacks, from harder, storable munchies like plantain chips to savories and sweets that are meant to be eaten on the spot. The latter include *pakoras* (tempura-like vegetables dipped in gram flour batter), *samosas* (crispy pyramids stuffed with potatoes and peas), and much more. Several kinds of deep-fried wafers or hollow puffs also get incorporated into other snacks, like *paapdi chaat* or *golguppa*.

Most main dishes involve a combination of spices, either powdered or in a paste, fried and added to meat, vegetables, or lentils. **Slow-cooked** dishes are a special treat, and traditional methods include *dhum* cooking, which involves sealing the cooking pots with dough and burying them to cook their contents.

CONDIMENTS

Then there's the wonderful, colorful, and unending array of condiments that spice up every Indian meal. These might be freshly ground, spiced ingredients like mint, coconut, or peanuts. Or they might be sweet, vinegary, or acetic preserve-like chutneys with slivers of mango or dates, or the syrupy, candied *murrabbas* made of fruit and vegetables like carrots or the medicinal Indian gooseberry (*amla*). Then there are *achhars,* spicy, oily pickles composed of everything from dried prawns to fiddlehead ferns, whose name describes their shape.

BREADS

Indian "bread" encompasses an assortment of flat or puffed, pale or golden, griddle-toasted, deep-fried or baked disks, triangles, and ellipses. Unleavened bread is generically called *roti,* and can be of varying thickness and made from refined, unrefined, and other types of flour. *Chapati* or *phulka* is a tortilla-like version made of wheat, cooked on a griddle, and finished on the flame. *Parathas,* rolled with oil to make layers, can be stuffed with all sorts of fillings and are almost a meal in themselves. Leavened breads, like *naan,* can be cooked in a tandoor, while the perfectly round *puri* and its giant cousin, the *bhatura,* are deep-fried so they puff up like crispy-soft balloons. Certain regions consume more rice than others, but every community will have its own recipes for rice and bread, and many meals involve eating both, usually one after the other.

Frying up some street food delicacies

3

Portrait of India **INDIAN CUISINE**

TEXTILES AND SHOPPING

Vibrantly colored shawls, necklaces strung together on the spot, copper pitchers and serving bowls ... these are a few of our favorite Indian things.

(top left) Dolls for sale at the flea market at Anjuna Beach in Goa; (top right) An embroidered pashmina; (bottom right) Painted pottery

With centuries-old crafts and textile traditions preserved from province to province, it's no wonder that shopping factors heavily in many travelers' itineraries on the Indian subcontinent. And these days, knowing where to shop is as important as knowing what to buy. In many cities you'll encounter bazaars and markets lined with street hawkers; in heavily touristed areas you'll mostly find trinkets such as miniature Taj Mahal replicas and carved-wood coasters.

As an alternative, government-run emporiums source good-quality handicrafts from various regions and sell them at fair but nonnegotiable prices. These emporiums (there's at least one in most big cities) carry a wide variety of goods, and are great for one-stop shopping, though tend to be a touch more expensive than local markets.

Bargaining is customary at most markets and bazaars. Keeping a poker face while browsing will help so the seller won't see whether you're really attached to a particular item. If you don't intend to buy, it's best to just voice a firm no to any coaxing and move along.

PASHMINA SHAWLS

Pashmina refers to the cashmere-like wool from the goats that are indigenous to the Himalayas; these days, however, not all shawls labeled pashmina are made from this special wool. Many are silk-wool blends, or man-made viscose, making it important to really understand the fabric before buying. When possible, buy pashminas from government-run emporiums or reputable stores where you can ask questions about the fabric. Many shawls or wraps will also have some embroidery along the borders—look for neatly done threadwork, which gives a good clue about the shawl's quality.

SILVER AND STONE JEWELRY

From eye-catching stones to shimmering silver and gold, from traditional ethnic and tribal designs to chic contemporary pieces, jewelry shopping in India runs the gamut. Jaipur, India's gem-cutting capital, sees thousands of semiprecious stones passing through its gates to markets in Europe and North America. It does pay to carefully examine stones like amazonite, smoky topaz, and chalcedony, as glass beads are sometimes passed off as more precious baubles. If you find a wholesaler who will sell retail to individuals who walk in, these merchants are generally more legitimate because they're not looking to take advantage of retail customers. If you're shopping for silver

pieces, look on the back for a stamp that says 92.5% sterling silver to be assured it's the genuine article.

STONEWARE AND POTTERY

From coasters to jewelry boxes, stoneware, usually featuring floral inlay, is a popular souvenir. Merchants might try to convince you that the stone is marble, but it's more likely soapstone. Also look for terra-cotta and blue pottery, the making of which are traditions dating back hundreds of years. Many blue pottery showrooms in Jaipur sell colorful, antique-style doorknobs, tiles, and platters.

COPPER AND BRASSWARE

Copper-bottom pots and pans might be all the rage at the moment, but copper kitchenware has been a long-standing tradition in India. Ask for *handi*-style pots (similar to a wok) and serving bowls. As for brassware, you'll find stunning Ganesh statues, incense-stick holders, and household items. Many of these can be quite hefty, so be sure to keep your airline's suitcase weight limits in mind. With locations in many big cities, the popular Fabindia brand and the slightly more upscale Good Earth carry quality household products ranging from pottery and brass to linens and beauty products.

Colorful fabrics

TEXTILES

Whether you're shopping for yourself or for convenient presents to take home, Indian textiles are a good way to go: perhaps block-printed tunics in bold hues, embroidered pillow covers, or quilted bedspreads. Established stores like Fabindia, Anokhi, and Cottons, which have locations in many cities, specialize in these types of textiles, as well as hand-woven table linens, rugs, and more, but you'll also find similar goods at markets all over the country. Look for a type of highly durable cotton called *khadi* (popularized by Gandhi himself during the Independence Movement); it's coarse but softens with each wash. Although textile traditions do vary from state to state, the most dramatic regional differences are visible in the sari, India's most iconic garment. Even if you don't want to purchase a sari, it's interesting to see how the borders, coloring, and draping styles change from one region to another.

SPICES

From cardamom to cloves, aromatic spices seem to fill the air wherever you are in India. Head to a local spice market to stock up on turmeric or cumin seeds at a fraction of the price of grocery stores back home—most merchants will even grind the spices for you on the spot. Be sure to bring back some garam masala, as well, a basic blend of ground spices used in many Indian dishes. The ingredients can vary slightly but usually include cloves, peppercorns, cumin, cardamom, star anise, and coriander seeds. A *masala dabba* is a traditional, round spice holder that has two lids and fits several smaller tins of spices inside, along with one or more spice spoons. These are good souvenirs, too, with or without spices included.

SOAPS AND BEAUTY PRODUCTS

With its history of ayurveda, or holistic medicine, that dates back thousands of years, India has always espoused the use of natural beauty products. Look for specialty brands like Forest Essentials, Kama Ayurveda, and Himalaya Herbals (found at local pharmacies and chemists shops). Popular ingredients and herbs include rose, sandalwood, neem (the leaves and bark from a tropical evergreen-like tree), and *khus-khus* (an Indian grass used as an exfoliant).

MINIATURE PAINTINGS

Scenes of courtship, palace living, and the pursuit of the arts are often portrayed in the miniature watercolor and oil paintings available throughout the country. You'll undoubtedly find framed miniatures like these in New Delhi and Mumbai, but the art of miniature painting originated in Udaipur, making it worthwhile to look for these paintings in Rajasthan.

BOOKS AND CDS

Whether you're in search of a copy of the Bhagavad Gita or just the latest mystery novel, English-language bookstores are ubiquitous in India's big cities. Many have generous selections of Indian fiction, so it's easy to pick up works by authors like Vikram Seth, William Dalrymple, Rohinton Mistry, and others for a fraction of the price you'd pay Stateside. For Bollywood or Indian instrumental CDs, you might not need to look farther than the bookstores as well, as many have extensive music sections.

ANTIQUES AND CARPETS

From rosewood furniture to ornate carpets, some people come to India specifically to search for top-notch furnishings at deep discounts. Since stores and dealers vary so greatly, though, it's best to employ a degree of caution when making big-ticket purchases. Getting an unbiased expert to come with you, or asking for recommendations from a concierge, can help.

SHOES AND LEATHER GOODS

In general, you'll find more variety than you can choose from when it comes to sandals and shoes. From the classic Kohlapuri *chappal,* a thonglike flat sandal with a toe strap, to more modern wedge-heel and peep-toe sandals and shoes, Indians just love their footwear!

Compared to street stalls, shoe chains like Metro and Catwalk in Mumbai and Delhi stock products of better quality and durability at reasonable rates. For other leather goods, such as wallets and purses, start by exploring the government-run emporiums or consider department stores like Shoppers Stop, which has more than a dozen locations across the country.

CONTEMPORARY CLOTHING

Although India's textile traditions continue to be preserved in provinces across the country, its modern fashion industry continues to grow. Designers are moving forward to bring an Indian eye and aesthetic to modern-day silhouettes and garments. Several of them, including Manish Arora, Ashish N Soni, and Sabyasachi Mukherjee, have shown at international fashion weeks in Milan and New York. Shopping complexes such as Khan Market in New Delhi and the Courtyard in Mumbai are full of chic boutiques stocking chiffon and organza dresses, A-line skirts with delicate touches of embroidery, and accessories adorned with Indian fabrics or trimmings. Increasingly, many Indian designers are also drawing on endangered traditional techniques and more eco-friendly weaving methods and incorporating them into their modern aesthetic.

A miniature painting

INDIAN DANCE, MUSIC, AND PERFORMING ARTS

The appreciation of beauty, combined with a love of celebration and worship, is evident throughout India, especially in the realm of the performing arts.

(top left) Young girls practicing a traditional dance; (top right) A music performance at Mumbai's National Centre for the Performing Arts; (bottom right) An Indian music and dance performance

Centuries of different cultural influences and religious traditions make for a rich array of delights when it comes to the performing and visual arts. Ancient styles and themes continue to flourish alongside growing contemporary movements, and there are also varieties of performing arts that bring together features from throughout the ages.

Whether you choose to attend a formal dance or music performance, go to a Bollywood film, happen upon a street musician, or find yourself in the midst of a religious celebration, experiencing the various manifestations of Indian culture will bring you closer to understanding the Indian way of life.

Mumbai's National Centre for the Performing Arts is a particularly good place to see live performances, although there are all sorts of formal and informal venues throughout the country.

RAMLILA

If you're in North India during the Navratri festival (see Holidays), try to see part of a Ramlila (literally, "Ram's play"). Actors—traditionally men and boys—wearing gaudy costumes and fake mustaches, dramatize the story of Ram, Prince of Ayodhya, who must fight the demon Ravana to rescue his kidnapped wife Sita. Some performances are makeshift, but others are 100-year-old institutions.

MUSIC

Music is fundamental to Indian life, and it's almost impossible to walk from one end of a street to another without hearing an old Hindi film song crackling from a radio or the thumping bass of a gangster rap Bhangra mash-up from a passing car. Beyond this, however, there is a rich tradition of classical Indian music. Classical music is divided into Hindustani (predominately from North and Central India and heavily influenced by Persian traditions), and Carnatic (the melodic, formal tradition of the south). There is also a lively tradition of folk music, ranging from classical deviations to lusty rural songs about everything from the monsoons to migrant life. Non-classical music can be boisterous—like Punjabi Bhangra—or steeped in refined sentimentality—like Bengali Rabindrasangeet (based on Rabindranath Tagore's lyrical works). Contemporary music ranges from Bollywood film music to Hindi (and other language) pop, rap, and hip-hop. In bars and clubs in the cities, it's not uncommon to find electronic music DJs, heavy-metal bands, and classically trained fusion artists.

DANCE

Hand in hand with music is classical dance, of which there are a number of schools. Performances are enhanced by unusual and colorful costumes. Among dance performances to look for are the silk-clad and jewel-ornamented

dancers of the Bharatnatyam, Kuchipudi, and Mohiniyattam styles, which were once performed in temples; the exacting beat-driven Kathak, which evolved in royal courts; the grotesque and gorgeous makeup and wide skirts of Kathakali from Kerala; and gracefully delicate Manipuri from the northeast.

FILM

With such strong traditions of music and movement in Indian culture, it's not surprising that song and dance come together in Indian cinema. From the early days of sugar-sweet love songs and jaunty, jazzy numbers, Hindi films have absorbed and transformed many influences over the years, and these days the cinema produces endless pop and R&B-flavored film music. Independent cinema, once influenced by the New Wave movement of the 1950s and 1960s, continues to exist in the shadow of Bollywood but has also seen recent growth in experimental efforts and documentaries.

THEATER

Theater is also important, and you might see troupes who perform special street plays on religious occasions or public service plays on issues like child labor or female infanticide. Folktales told through puppetry and the Western-style staging of Indian and international playwrights' works are also on the agenda.

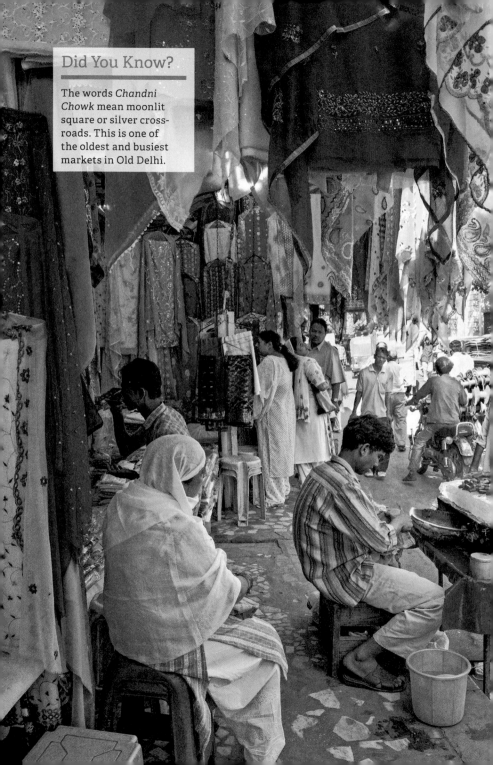

Chapter 4

DELHI

Updated by
Malavika
Bhattacharya

4

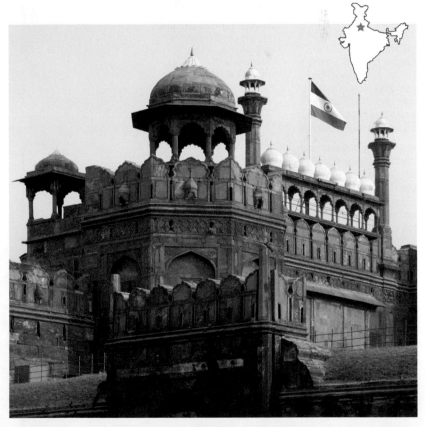

⊙ Sights	🍴 Restaurants	🛏 Hotels	🛍 Shopping	🍸 Nightlife
★★★★★	★★★★★	★★★★★	★★★★★	★★☆☆☆

WELCOME TO DELHI

TOP REASONS TO GO

★ **The Mughal Capital:** Delhi has a wealth of Mughal architecture—including Lal Qila (the Red Fort), Humanyun's Tomb, and Jama Masjid—that's survived for 450 years.

★ **Remnants of the Raj:** The British may have left in 1947, but colonial architecture still dominates Central Delhi, popularly known as Lutyens' Delhi: beautiful villas and large avenues lined with trees make this one of the most peaceful areas in the city.

★ **Shopping Nirvana:** From Western designer duds to beautiful silk Indian saris, there's an incredible selection of ready-to-wear and custom-made clothing in Delhi's variety of malls, shopping centers, and street markets.

★ **Taste of India:** Delhi is known as the unofficial food capital of India. From the best Mughlai cuisine (tandoori chicken done right) to tantalizing street food and international fare, you'll find kebabs and more around every corner.

India's capital radiates from the broad avenues of its British-built center, its sprawl circumscribed by several concentric roads.

1 Old Delhi. Anchored by Lal Qila (the Red Fort) and Jama Masjid, India's largest mosque, the walled Old City (originally called Shahjahanabad) provides the best glimpse into the city's treasured Mughal past, with a chaotic mix of colors and scents that stir the senses. Narrow, winding lanes branch off the main avenue, Chandni Chowk, crowded with wholesale markets, ancient shops, hidden monuments, and crumbling *havelis* (mansions).

2 Central Delhi. With the India Gate memorial at its heart, the capital is now home to government buildings, parks, upscale markets, and the low-lying bungalows of the country's most powerful citizens.

3 South Delhi. The suburbs to the south of Central Delhi include residential communities, markets, and commercial districts along with some of the oldest monuments in the capital, lovely parks, and charming locales such as Hauz Khas Village.

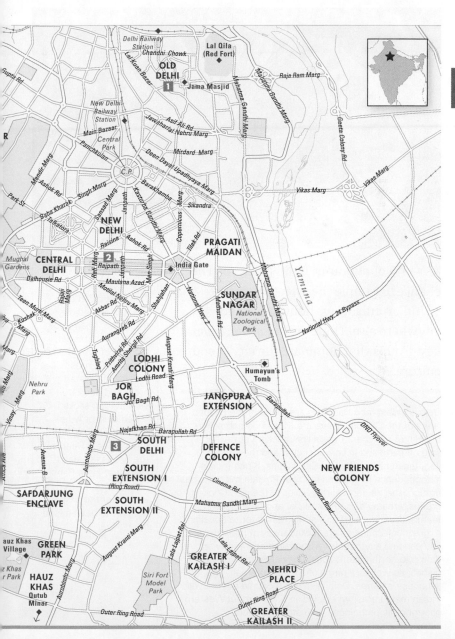

EATING WELL IN DELHI

Mango kulfi

As a city of migrants, Delhi gives you the chance to sample the sweeping range of Indian cuisine without having go anywhere else. There are, however, several key groups that dominate the city's food culture.

Delhi's oldest food traditions are found in the chaotic lanes of the Old City. There are Muslim kebab sellers; the Hindu merchant class's lip-smacking street food, sold off carts and in corner shops; and the simple vegetarian fare of the Old City's Jains. Since India's independence in 1947, an influx of Punjabi migrants has brought that region's earthy flavor to the city. Cooked greens, creamy dals, thick lassis, and hearty breads feature prominently. Local spots that cater to specific migrant communities are tucked away in markets, and you can find anything from South Indian vegetarian diners to northeastern spots specializing in spicy pork dishes, as well as a range of Afghani, Korean, and Japanese eateries. Delhi also has a couple of "nouvelle" Indian restaurants, where Indian flavors meet Western gastronomic techniques with striking results.

OLD DELHI

The walled Old City is a maze of edible treasures. Khari Baoli, the spice market at the end of Chandni Chowk, is a must-visit. Piles of twisted roots and dried fruit sit between sacks of red chilli powder, yellow turmeric, and other spices. Nearby, the wholesale paan market at Naya Bans carries everything necessary for the preparation of the betel-based digestive.

DAL MAKHANI

A Punjabi staple, **dal makhani** (also known as *kaali dal*, or *maa ki dal*) is a nearly ubiquitous lentil stew, served by humble villagers and in superluxe hotel restaurants. Black urad beans and red kidney beans are tempered with a fry-up of garlic, ginger, tomato, and spices and ideally slow-cooked overnight on a coal fire. The dal is often finished with generous amounts of butter or cream.

PARATHA

Served with spicy achhaar pickles and yogurt, and topped with a dollop of butter, a **paratha** is a meal in itself. Whole wheat flour dough is rolled with oil before being panfried to create a flaky flatbread. The dough can be stuffed with anything; some fillings include radish, cauliflower, and sweet milk solids. "Mughlai" parathas include egg and are thicker. In Old Delhi, visit Gali Paranthe Wali, a lane dedicated to this Punjabi bread.

KULFI

As early as the 16th century, Mughal emperors enjoyed the frozen dessert called **kulfi**. The Indian version of ice cream, standard kulfi is a mixture of milk solids (*khoya*) or cream, sugar, and pistachios—which are frozen in a conical metal or clay container sealed with dough. Kulfi is eaten as is, or with

A bowl of nihari stew

starch vermicelli noodles (*faloodeh*). Besides flavors like pistachio and rose, Old Delhi *kulfiwallas* make fruit-flavored kulfis, sometimes frozen inside hollowed-out fruit, like mangoes.

NAGORI HALWA

Not well-known but quintessentially Delhi, the **nagori halwa** breakfast is found almost exclusively in the Old City. It's a combination of three elements: small crisp breads made of deep-fried wheat and semolina flour; a mushy potato curry packed with fiery and warming spices; and a bit of *halwa*—a sweet preparation of semolina roasted in ghee and mixed with water. It's best eaten mixed all together for a delicious hot, sweet, and spicy combination.

NIHARI

Easily the most coveted dish from Old Delhi, **nihari** is a buffalo (since beef is not eaten) or goat stew cooked overnight in a virtual swimming pool of ghee. More scorching than the city's summer sun, nihari is usually eaten in the morning, especially in the foggy winter months. Legend has it that when Shah Jahan settled Delhi his doctor deemed the Yamuna River's water unfit for consumption; this firecracker of a dish, however, was believed to kill the germs.

Aloo paratha (bread with potatoes in it)

DELHI'S HOLY SITES

At Hazrat Nizamuddin Dargah

Brash, corrupt, political—the capital of India doesn't have a particularly spiritual reputation, yet Delhi, as the recurring seat of empires with vested religious and cultural interests, is a veritable melting pot of religiously significant sites.

Because the walled city of Old Delhi was divided into religious ghettos when it was first built by the Emperor Shah Jahan, it is home to a great variety of religious sites: the area is dotted with domes and spires of mosques, dozens of Hindu shrines to Shiva, the bustling Sisganj Gurdwara (an important Sikh site), and peaceful, marble-clad Jain temples.

Beyond Old Delhi, Sufi saints still draw thousands of visitors to their graves. Churches and cemeteries testify not only to the continued presence of South Indian Christians in Delhi, but also to the city as a place where scores of British lived and died. Among other things, you can also find Buddhist monasteries and Bengali temples in this city.

HANUMAN MANDIR

In the thick of things near Connaught Place is **Hanuman Mandir.** Said to have mythic origins, the temple was constructed over the 16th and 17th centuries. Note the crescent-moon finial, typically associated with Islam. The surrounding area can be overwhelming, with beggars dressed as the monkey god worshipped here, women painting henna tattoos, and Delhi's best bangle market.

AKSHARDHAM TEMPLE

One of the newest additions to Delhi's spiritual scene is **Akshardham temple**: a theme park of polytheistic Hinduism. Despite criticism over its environmentally dubious location (a sprawling 90 acres on the Yamuna riverbank), this bulwark of pink sandstone and Italian marble—possibly the largest Hindu temple in the world—is undeniably dramatic. Set in landscaped gardens with a musical fountain, the temple incorporates traditional hand-carving and craftsmanship as well as a peacock-boat ride through dioramas of Indian history and mythology, and an IMAX film about the sect's founder.

HAZRAT NIZAMUDDIN DARGAH

In many ways the still-beating heart of spirituality in central Delhi is the mausoleum of saint Nizamuddin Auliya of the Sufi Chishti order. At **Hazrat Nizamuddin Dargah** evenings are enlivened by a troupe of qawwals (who sing Sufi devotional music) and the distribution of food. You'll have to leave your shoes outside (tip a rose-petal seller a few rupees to keep them safe).

JAMA MASJID

India's largest mosque, **Masjid-i-Jahan-Numa** ("world-showing mosque") as it is properly named, is a welcoming

The Bahá'i House of Worship (Lotus Temple)

space with a well-loved, worn-in feel. Visitors are welcome any time except during prayers, and it is advisable to cover your head as a sign of respect. Climb the minaret for an incredible view of the city and note the north gate's reliquary, which houses a beard hair and footprint of the Prophet Muhammad and an antique Koran.

SIS GANJ SAHIB GURDWARA

Right on Chandni Chowk itself is the Sikh **Sis Ganj Sahib Gurdwara.** It was on the site of this bustling *gurdwara* (temple) that the ninth Sikh leader, Guru Tegh Bahadur, was beheaded on order of the Mughal emperor Aurangzeb in 1675. To learn more about Sikh martyrs, visit the gloriously kitsch Bhai Mati Das Bhai Sati Das Bhai Dyala Museum of Sikh history across the street. Delhi's grandest gurdwara, Bangla Sahib near Connaught Place, has gleaming golden domes that reflect in its large pond of holy water.

BAHA'I HOUSE OF WORSHIP

The Lotus Temple, as the **Baha'i House of Worship** is also known, is probably Delhi's most iconic modern holy site and one of the most visited places in the world—designed by the Canadian architect Fariborz Sahba, it was built in 1986.

The Akshardham Temple

Delhi is the best place to experience all that brings people to India: history, culture, food, spirituality, madness, mystery. Spend a day amid its lived-in splendor, and you'll realize why so many battles have been fought over it. Here are the extremes that make India so compelling. Old Delhi's Mughul glory, Central Delhi's European grandeur, West Delhi's Punjabi opulence, and South Delhi's bars, boutiques, and massive houses—all come together with the poor, the pollution, and overpopulation.

Modern Delhi has its foundation on a city base that has been around for centuries. Various monuments lie scattered across the region, revealing the numerous empires that have invaded Delhi and made it their home. Of these, the Mughals and British have left the deepest mark.

The city has grown exponentially over the years and continues to do so to accommodate the expanding population, currently estimated at more than 16 million, within a little less than 1,554 square km (600 square miles). It's part of the larger National Capital Region (NCR), which includes neighboring state suburbs like Ghaziabad, Faridabad, Noida, Greater Noida (all across the border in Uttar Pradesh), and Gurgaon (in Haryana). The latter is known in particular for its call centers and gleaming malls, which feed the consumer craze of India's rapidly expanding middle class.

In Delhi the different versions of modern India all coexist, and its contradictions quickly become abundantly clear to visitors. Newly minted junior executives ride in chauffeured, air-conditioned comfort as scores of children beg and hawk magazines in the streets.

EXPLORING DELHI'S SITES

Most of sprawling Delhi is best navigated on wheels—hire a car, taxi, or auto-rickshaw to get around. In contrast, the narrow lanes of Old Delhi are a walker's delight, though you can hop on a cycle rickshaw if you get tired. Most people speak workable English, so don't assume there will be an insurmountable language barrier.

The challenge Delhi presents is to find areas—beyond the Old City—in which walking is a viable mode of exploration. One of these areas is the central British-built commercial hub, Connaught Place. "CP" is a tourist magnet for its travel agent bucket shops, restaurants, and shops, as well as proximity to a number of midrange and budget hotels. It's also the location of Delhi's main metro station and can be a pleasant area to meander along colonnaded circles, or people-watch in the central park. There are plenty of shopping options nearby, including the street market, Janpath, where everything from brightly colored kolhapuri slippers to designer overstock to incense and natural soaps can be found. Keep in mind that even though it's commonly referred to as Connaught Place, the name was officially changed to Rajiv Chowk, which is what you'll see on metro stops and maps.

Around the hubs of Connaught Place and India Gate is the British-built city. This is the seat of the Indian government, with Rashtrapati Bhavan (the Presidential Palace), the North and South Secretariats, Sansad Bhavan (Parliament House), and India Gate (a monument to British Indian Army soldiers killed in World War I and the Afghan wars) within a tight radius. Getting ice cream at India Gate's huge lawns or boating in the ornamental canals here are "very Delhi" things to do. Many museums are nearby, including the National Gallery of Modern Art and the National Museum.

Also here are the palatial residences of the affluent and lavish government bungalows. Khan Market, one of Asia's most expensive retail locations, is perfectly at home in this setting. It's also the place where Delhi's expats feel most at home, with its coffee shops and multiple ATMs. Down the road is Delhi's green lung, Lodhi Gardens, and several cultural centers, including the elite's mainstays, the India International Centre and the India Habitat Centre (performances are pretty much on tap, especially in winter).

The mostly residential areas of South Delhi, West Delhi, North Delhi, and East Delhi (across the Yamuna) all have their own flavor, but visitors are most likely to venture into the neighborhoods, markets, and monuments of the first, roughly defined as south of Lodhi Road. In between semigated colonies are a good mix of urban villages, hectic alleyways, posh markets, and office complexes. Some of the city's oldest monuments can be found here, as well as some of its newest monuments to modernity: the massive malls squatting southward, en route to megasuburb Gurgaon. The hippest of Delhi's hot spots though, is not a mall, but a gentrified urban village—Hauz Khas Village—with boutiques and trendy restaurants nestled atop each other along narrow alleys, next to a 13th-century reservoir and several Sultanate ruins.

Among the attractions throughout Delhi are several temples. Be respectful when you visit, as most are ongoing houses of worship. A type of food offering called prasad is given to devotees in many of them. Part of a religious ritual, this sweet item is offered first to a deity and then given in that deity's name to anyone who comes through the temple; it is accepted with the right hand.

NIGHTLIFE IN DELHI

Delhi's nightlife is in a constant state of flux, and among the growing set of young people who can afford it, the scene is intense. Various kinds of watering holes are on offer, with the lounge bar emerging as the most successful formula. Though Delhi doesn't rival the cosmopolitan feel of Mumbai, it seems as if a new lounge opens here every week. That said, the city's somewhat stodgy reputation is still partly deserved: all the major hotels have bars, but most are better suited for a collective nap with a few tired foreigners than a night of Indian camaraderie; they still shut by midnight and many nightclubs close not much later, though there are a few all-night venues.

Hotel bars come in two stripes: those that aim for a British Raj look and an older, quieter clientele, or raucous, late-night dance clubs. Due to high taxes on alcohol, especially imported brands, drinks prices come close to those in London and New York. Those in search of late-night dancing and drinking sometimes head for the suburbs or five-star hotels, which can stay open later.

The disco scene has undergone a transformation in recent years. Select places attract top international DJs and charge cover prices to match. Slowly, electronic dance music is overtaking drunk renditions of classic rock and Bollywood favorites at most places. Overly casual attire (shorts, T-shirts, sandals on men) is typically frowned on, and closing times tend to vary with the mood of the city government that month.

Most bars and clubs are concentrated in the Central and South Delhi enclaves. Old Delhi has little to offer in this department.

PERFORMING ARTS IN DELHI

Delhi is India's cultural hub, with performers from all over the country heading to the capital to cultivate their national audience. Painting, music, dance, theater, and, of course, film are all well represented. The large and modern India Habitat Centre has the best combination of all of the above; on any given evening, it hosts several good programs. The only problem is that publicity is nonexistent, so you must be persistent to find out what's happening— ⊕ www.delhievents. com is a reliable source of information on cultural events. Failing that, the daily newspapers, especially the *Times of India* and the *Hindustan Times,* are also good sources. The staff at your hotel may be able to help, too.

Delhi's art scene is extremely dynamic. Contemporary Indian painting—which often blends traditional Indian motifs with Western techniques—is blossoming, but if you're looking to buy, bargains are hard to come by. Private galleries have mushroomed, and art prices have skyrocketed. Most galleries are quite small, so if you want a broad view of what's happening, hire a car or taxi for an afternoon of gallery-hopping. Authenticating any major purchases is advisable. Visit ⊕ in.blouinartinfo.com for exhibit details and artist profiles. Many galleries are closed on Sunday. Hauz Khas Village has a cluster of galleries.

Popular films are easily the biggest influence on contemporary Indian culture, and understanding the country and its eccentricities can be much easier if you've watched a few of the standard stars. India's Mumbai-based film industry, known as Bollywood, produces more films annually than any other country in the world. Most Bollywood films last longer than three hours and are in Hindi, but anyone can get the gist—most are romantic musicals, with dollops of family drama and occasionally a violent villain. Delhi cinemas show all the latest Hindi movies plus the current Hollywood films—the latter are screened mainly at multiplex theaters in the malls at Saket and Vasant Kunj. To find out what's playing, check listings in the magazine section of any daily newspaper. If your movie of choice is a hot new release, consider buying tickets a day in advance; your hotel can help, and tickets can often be bought online.

Art films from all over the world are shown at various cultural institutes; events websites, such as ⊕ www. delhievents.com, ⊕ www.bpbweekend. com, and ⊕ www.bookmyshow.com carry schedules for local film festivals and other screenings.

India has an ancient dramatic tradition, and *nautanki* plays, which combine drama, comedy, and song, are still held in many villages. Delhi has an active theater scene in both English and Hindi, with many shows locally written, produced, and performed. Most run only for one weekend and don't travel afterward, so they can seem a bit unpolished even when they're fundamentally good.

And great musicians and dancers are always passing through Delhi. Most performances are free, but tickets ("passes") are sometimes required for high-demand performers. For many of them, however, it's enough to show up at the venue an hour or so in advance to get free tickets from the organizers. You can also visit Bookmyshow.com to book tickets for many cultural events.

SHOPPING IN DELHI

Delhi is a shopping center for goods from all over India, making it the best place to stock up on gifts and souvenirs. Bargaining is often appropriate—and almost mandatory. A good rule of thumb: when the price is written down, it's probably fixed; when you have to inquire about the price, it's negotiable.

Old Delhi is an endlessly interesting place to shop, admittedly more for the experience than for what you'll take away. The sidewalks of Chandni Chowk are lined with clocks, baby clothes, tacky toys, blankets, and much more; the shops on Dariba Kalan are filled with silver and gold jewelry. Stalls behind the Jama Masjid sell metalware and utensils, and one street specializes in stationery, especially Indian wedding invitations. Kinari Bazaar glistens with Hindu wedding paraphernalia. Khari Baoli, west of Chandni Chowk toward Lahori Gate, is renowned for its wholesale nuts, spices, and Indian pickles and chutneys.

India has one of the world's foremost Oriental rug industries, and there are carpet vendors all over Delhi. Unfortunately, carpet sellers are a notoriously dishonest crowd. In addition to being obnoxiously pushy, they are likely to sell you inauthentic merchandise at colossally inflated prices and then deny it later. There are some exceptions to this rule, but they tend to sell out of their homes

rather than upscale showrooms—so call before you go.

Clothes shopping is one of Delhi's great pleasures. *Khadi,* the hand-spun, handwoven cotton that Gandhi turned into a nationalist symbol during the Independence movement, has made a roaring comeback and is now worn by many Delhi women during the long, hot summer. You can experience khadi in a *salwar-kameez*—the classic North Indian ensemble of long tunic and loose pants, also popular in a variation called the *kurta-churidar*—and in Western-style tops and skirts. Some Indian fabrics can fade or bleed easily, so it's always a good idea to wash clothes first before wearing.

If you find yourself shopping for a sari, savor the experience of learning about this amazing handicraft. Silks and attractive cotton saris are sometimes sold at Dilli Haat market, depending on which vendors have set up shop that week. Silks are sold en masse at upscale stores in South Extension, Greater Kailash I, and Connaught Place, but the highest thumbs-up go to Kalpana and Padakkam.

For crafts and curios, Delhi's fixed-price government emporiums near Connaught Place offer good values to travelers with limited time. They're also conveniently open seven days a week. The best market for fine curios and antiques is in the exclusive leafy neighborhood of Sundar Nagar. In addition to the shops listed here, a few shops on the southern (right-hand) side of the market have collections of old optical instruments.

Jewelry is another popular item on visitors' shopping lists. India consumes more gold annually than any other country in the world, mainly because gold is an essential part of a bride's trousseau. With Delhi's upper middle class spending ever more money, and now chasing such Western fancies as diamonds and platinum, jewelry is big business here. The flashiest jewelry stores are clustered

4

Delhi

in South Extension, Greater Kailash I, and Connaught Place, offset by a handful of older shops in Sundar Nagar. Indian gold is 22 karat, and some Westerners tend to find its bright-yellow tone a bit too flashy. For a gold Indian piece in a subtler antique style, stroll through the market in Sundar Nagar. Hit the glitzier stores for the princess look. Indian jewelers as a group have been accused of adulterating their gold, but alas, you as a consumer will have no way to determine the content of each piece. Old Delhi is packed with jewelry and curio shops, though you have to search harder for fine designs. Stroll Dariba Kalan for the best selection of silver and gold.

As the center of India's English-language publishing industry, and, arguably, India's intellectual capital, Delhi has something of a literary scene. For those with hard currency, Indian books are great bargains, including lower-price local editions of titles published abroad. If you'll be in Delhi for a while, hunt down the elusive but excellent *Old Delhi: 10 Easy Walks,* by Gaynor Barton and Laurraine Malone (New Delhi: Rupa, 1997)—these painstakingly detailed routes are fascinating and manageable. The top hotels have small bookshops, but Khan Market has several of the capital's best.

Most shops are open six days a week, as each neighborhood's market area closes one day a week, usually Sunday, Monday, or Tuesday. Most shops in Old Delhi are closed on Sunday.

Planning

MAKING THE MOST OF YOUR TIME
The best way to cover a lot of ground in Delhi is to hire a car, especially if you're on a limited schedule. Avoid tackling Old Delhi on your first day if you've never been to India before—its startling chaos can be overwhelming. Starting with New Delhi will also give you a

better idea of the aesthetic and cultural dichotomy between the two areas. A drive through the graceful avenues of the British capital will ease you gently into the capital, but don't let it lull you into a state of pleasant, orderly inertia. The rest of the city requires that all your senses be in working order. Depending on your interests, visit South and Central Delhi's monuments (Humayun's and Safdarjang's tombs, the Qutub Minar, Lodhi Gardens, Hazrat Nizamuddin Dargah), some sites commemorating the leaders of India's independence movement (the Nehru Museum or Gandhi Smriti), a museum, or a temple or *gurdwara* (Sikh temple). When you're ready, plunge into Old Delhi—explore the Lal Qila (Red Fort) and the stunning Jama Masjid, then venture into Chandni Chowk. Make sure to eat at the famous Gali Paranthe Wali and the restaurant Karim's.

The Red Fort and most museums are closed on Monday, and the Jama Masjid is closed to non-Muslims on Friday.

WHEN TO GO
HIGH SEASON: MID-NOVEMBER–MARCH
The most popular time to visit is during peak festive season, when cool temperatures (near-freezing at times) get people out of their homes, wrapped in shawls on the street, huddled around charcoal braziers at lawn parties, clutching hot kebab rolls in their hands. This is also peak cultural season; calendars are packed with music, dance, theater, and more. It does get cold though, and Delhi is especially foggy around New Year's, so try not to schedule any night driving around then. Delhi's February sun has its own charming character, and seasonal trees turn the city into a riot of colors in the late winter.

LOW SEASON: MAY TO MID–AUGUST
The heat is intense from April until the monsoons arrive in July, after which rain and intense humidity add to the misery. Air-conditioning is a staple, and there's

Dressing the Part

Many traveling women (and a few traveling men) are inspired to buy an Indian outfit to wear for all or part of their trip. Here's a primer:

Traditional Wear

The traditional North Indian women's ensemble of a long tunic over loose pants is known as a salwar-kameez. Today it is equally common in a variation called the kurta-churidar. The word *kameez* is a general term meaning "shirt," whereas kurta/kurti specifies a traditional Indian tunic worn by men or women, respectively. The pants worn beneath women's kurtas take two forms: the *salwar,* which is very loose, with only a slight tapering at the ankle, and the *churidar,* which is usually loose in the thigh but tight along the calf, bunched up near the ankle like leggings. Presently the churidar is in greater vogue than the salwar, and true fashionistas now wear very short (above the knee) kurtas over thigh-tight churidars, a look with a Western element: it favors skinny women. Most women opt for knee- or calf-length kurtas.

The outfit is usually finished with a matching *dupatta* or *chunni,* a long scarf draped over the chest with the ends dangling in back, traditionally 6 feet long and 3 feet wide. These days you're free to drape the dupatta however you like; slinging it back from the neck, or even forward from the neck (Western-style), gives the outfit a modern twist. Just beware of dupattas made of stiff or starchy fabric—no matter how beautiful they look, you will probably find them unwieldy. A dupatta is particularly useful in places like Old Delhi and Nizamuddin, where you can pull it over your head as a kerchief if you feel too conspicuous.

Where to Buy It

You won't have to invest much in any of these items; at Fabindia or Dilli Haat you can buy a smart trio of kurta, churidar or salwar, and dupatta for US$25–US$50. Another option at Dilli Haat and some fabric stores is to buy uncut "suit fabric," a smartly matched set of three pieces of fabric meant to be sewn into the full regalia. If you buy suit fabric, simply take it all to a tailor (ask any market merchant to suggest one; most are holes-in-the-wall), allow him to measure you, tell him what kind of neckline you fancy and whether you want a churidar or salwar, and come back for your custom-made "suit." This can take a few days, but the tailoring costs about US$10 and these ensembles are very attractive.

Muted or Jewel Tones?

Men's kurtas are traditionally paired with a churidar or with loose, straight-legged "pajamas." Most urban Indian men wear Western shirts and trousers, but Delhi's politicians keep the white cotton kurta-pyjama and the more formal *dhoti* (a bunchy wrap skirt) alive and kicking. Formal silk kurta-churidars are trotted out only for weddings.

Many Western women who buy salwar-kameez choose muted colors, perhaps on the premise that light skin tones need light fabric tones. Unfortunately, muted colors often make Westerners look washed-out and even more "foreign." Be bold! Women of all complexions are flattered by the jewel tones of many Indian clothes.

plenty to do indoors, from museums to malls, so don't let the outside stickiness deter you. Unfortunately, the rains shut the city down because of improper drainage, and the already intense traffic takes a turn for the worse, with people stuck on roads for hours on end.

SHOULDER SEASON: SEPTEMBER AND OCTOBER AND MARCH AND APRIL

Autumn and early spring bring mild, sunny days and the tourist crowds are thinner than in winter. Temperatures are comfortable, though a light sweater may come in handy in the evenings closer to the cold months.

GETTING HERE AND AROUND

AIR TRAVEL

All flights arrive and depart from Delhi's Indira Gandhi International Airport, along the southwestern edge of the city. It has separate domestic and international terminals that are quite a few miles apart, though connected by a free shuttle bus every 20 minutes.

AIRPORT TRANSFERS

The airport is about a 45-minute drive from Delhi's center in light to moderate traffic (i.e., before 9 am or after 8 pm).

Major hotels provide airport transfers, otherwise taking a cab is your best bet. To avoid being overcharged, use the prepaid taxi service from a counter near the exit. Unfortunately, hucksters have set up similar services; ignore them. Your destination determines the fare, to which a small fee for each piece of luggage is added. Pay in advance at the counter, then take the receipt and exit. When you get outside, people might try to help you with your luggage; ignore them also, and make sure they do not touch your things. Wheel your luggage down the ramp toward the black taxis with yellow tops, at which point the drivers will appear. If your receipt contains a taxi number, use that cab; if not, the drivers will decide among themselves who should take you. Tell the driver where you're going, and

hold on to the receipt until you arrive. Tips are not expected unless they help with your luggage.

BUS TRAVEL

You're best off avoiding bus travel in Delhi: public buses are generally dirty, crowded, and unpleasant.

CAR TRAVEL

Hiring a car and driver is the best way to see the most of this sprawling city, especially for those with a limited amount of time. Most hotels can arrange a car, but they will also charge a premium for the service. Reputable travel agents do the same for less money (budget Rs. 1,000 or more per day for a basic car with air-conditioning and an English-speaking driver, for travel in Delhi only). Tip in advance if you want some extra-deferential, but exceedingly helpful service.

METRO TRAVEL

The city's metro, which came into service in 2002, is air-conditioned, reliable, and state-of-the-art. With new stations and lines opening for service every few months, subway service is rapidly changing the face of the city. It's an inexpensive (starting at Rs. 10 per one-way trip) and convenient way to move between Connaught Place (Rajiv Chowk station), Lutyens' Delhi (Central Secretariat station), and Old Delhi (Chandni Chowk and Chawri Bazaar stations). For example, getting to Old Delhi from CP is three stops and takes about 15 minutes. There are currently eight lines—red, yellow, blue, green, violet, magenta, pink, and the airport express, which links the airport with the centrally located New Delhi stop, which is close to the New Delhi railway stop. The fare for the airport express is Rs. 60. Maps are available at the official tourist office and often at your hotel concierge desk. The Rajiv Chowk station is massive; ask for directions as you go.

TAXI AND AUTO-RICKSHAW TRAVEL

Apart from a hired car, the best way to get around New Delhi is by black-and-yellow taxi or radio cab service, which includes the use of Uber. Most hotels and restaurants will gladly call you a cab, and major markets and tourist attractions usually have a taxi stand. Most drivers speak a little English. ■TIP➔ **Tell the driver where you want to go and make sure he turns on the meter before you set off.** If he insists the meter is broken, get out of the car and find another cab. Most taxi drivers are honest, so it's not worth dealing with one who isn't.

The ubiquitous green-and-yellow auto-rickshaws are a good way to see the city from a different angle. But they aren't for the faint of heart, as the drivers zip through traffic at breakneck speed. The three-wheeled auto-rickshaws, often just called "autos" in India, are half the price of taxis and roughly half as comfortable—except in summer, when the open-air breeze keeps you cool while taxis trap the heat horrendously. The problem is that auto-rickshaw drivers refuse to use their meters (here they really often are broken, as the drivers deliberately break them), and if you look even remotely new to Delhi they will quote absurdly high fares. A trip around the corner should cost about Rs. 30, and a trip across the city should never cost more than Rs. 200. Government-run booths for prepaid auto-rickshaws can be found at Connaught Place, Basant Lok, Dilli Haat, and the Community Centre in Saket, among other places. Try to have exact change, as many drivers will claim to have none, and discussion is difficult, as most do not speak English.

In Old Delhi and a few other neighborhoods you can still hire a cycle-rickshaw. It's a great way to cruise Chandni Chowk, explore the maze of narrow lanes, and get from one sight to the next. A short one-way trip costs Rs. 30; work out a higher fare, up to Rs. 200, if you want to ride around for longer.

TRAIN TRAVEL

Delhi is the major hub for India's northern rail system, with five train stations. Most arrive at New Delhi Station, within walking distance of Connaught Place; Hazrat Nizamuddin, from which trains leave for Agra and points south; or Old Delhi Station. With luggage in tow and crowded streets, consider taking a taxi or auto-rickshaw to your hotel. Note that traveling by train in India is much different than in the United States or in Europe, in part due to the sheer number of travelers. Terminals are chaotic, and it can be unclear and confusing to determine when and from where your train is scheduled to leave. Trains are often also crowded and delayed. Your best bet, if you choose this means of travel, is to factor in plenty of extra time and a lot of patience. All stations have prepaid taxi and auto-rickshaw stands, though these can get quite busy.

EMERGENCIES

Most hotels have physicians on call. For emergencies, go to Indraprastha Apollo Hospital, Delhi's premier private hospital, southeast of town, or ask at your hotel. From there you can call Meera Rescue if international evacuation is necessary; *do not* go to a government hospital. The conditions at government hospitals are not up to par; they are overcrowded and treatment is often delayed. In a grave emergency, contact your embassy.

Although not equipped for trauma, the Max Medcentre—in conjunction with Harvard Medical International, one of India's major pharmaceutical companies—runs a first-rate clinic open daily from 8 am to 8 pm. Its hospital in Saket can treat complicated ailments and has many specialists. Many of the physicians are American-trained, and there's a 24-hour pharmacy on-site. The East–West Medical Centre is also a great resource for travelers, with ambulance service and regional evacuation, though it has no pharmacy.

CONTACTS East–West Rescue ✉ *38 Golf Links, New Delhi* ☎ *11/2469–9229, 11/2469 8865* ⊕ *www.castwestrescue.com.* **Indraprastha Apollo Hospital** ✉ *Mathura Rd., Sarita Vihar, New Delhi* ☎ *11/2682–5555, 11/2692–5858* ⊕ *www. apollohospdelhi.com.* **Max Multi Speciality Centre** ✉ *N–110 Panchsheel Park, New Delhi* ☎ *11/4609–7200* ⊕ *www. maxhealthcare.in.* **Meera Rescue** ✉ *112 Jor Bagh, New Delhi* ☎ *11/2465–8075, 11/2465–3170* ⊕ *www.meera-rescue. com.*

24-HOUR PHARMACIES Max Super Specialty Hospital ✉ *2 Press Enclave Rd., Saket, New Delhi* ☎ *11/2651–5050* ⊕ *www.maxhealthcare.in.* **New Delhi Medicos** ✉ *K–176, Old RK Ashram Marg, near RML Hospital, New Delhi* ☎ *11/6500–5705.*

RESTAURANTS

Restaurants are generally open daily 12:30 to 3 for lunch and 7:30 to 11 for dinner. You can assume that all restaurants serve alcohol unless we indicate otherwise. However, imported liquor is extremely expensive—inquire before you imbibe. Expect a 20% tax on your food and beverage bill.

HOTELS

Unless otherwise specified, you can expect private bath, phone, and TV in your room. Be sure to reserve in advance for stays between October and February, as even the largest hotels fill up. Rates are dynamic and fluctuate widely by season. Unless indicated, prices listed are not inclusive of taxes, which are an additional 18% or 28%.

Hotel reviews have been shortened. For full information, visit Fodors.com.

What It Costs

	$	$$	$$$	$$$$
RESTAURANTS				
	under Rs. 500	Rs. 500–Rs. 1,000	Rs. 1,001–Rs. 1,400	over Rs. 1,400
HOTELS				
	under Rs. 6,000	Rs. 6,000–Rs. 9,000	Rs. 9,001–Rs. 13,000	over Rs. 13,000

INTERNET, MAIL, AND SHIPPING

Internet facilities can be found in most major markets, but they are often holes-in-the-wall with a handful of grimy, outdated terminals. Coffee-shop chains and some larger bookstores often have Wi-Fi hot spots available.

One centrally located post office is on the roundabout just southwest of Connaught Place. Hotels usually have mailing facilities, too. DHL outlets are available around the city, but you'll pay a premium—possibly as much as your own plane ticket—to ship anything heavy to the West (just sending documents will cost you at least US$60). Use Speed Post at the main post office, which is a fraction of the price and usually reliable. Be prepared to wait (and then wait some more).

POST OFFICES Main Post Office ✉ *Gol Dak Khana, Baba Kharak Singh Marg, Connaught Pl., New Delhi* ⊕ *www.indiapost. gov.in.*

VISITOR INFORMATION

The Government of India Tourist Office south of Connaught Place is open weekdays 9 to 6 and Saturday 9 to 2, but it doesn't have anything a decent hotel can't offer. Its airport counters are open for major flight arrivals, and its train-station counters are open 24 hours.

CONTACTS Government of India Tourist Office ✉ *88 Janpath, Connaught Pl., New Delhi* ☎ *11/2332–0005* ⊕ *www.tourism. gov.in.*

Delhi's India Gate is similar to the Arc de Triomphe in Paris.

Central Delhi

Sometimes also called Lutyens' Delhi after the British urban planner and architect who was largely responsible for its design, Central Delhi houses the government center and the broad, imperial streets of power. Also sometimes referred to as "New Delhi" (as opposed to Old Delhi, Shah Jahan's pre-British city), it begins around Connaught Place and extends about 6 km (4 miles) south. Most sights are south of Connaught Place.

Sights

Akshardham Temple Complex

RELIGIOUS SITE | Rising over the traffic jams of National Highway 24 on the way to Noida lies a massive, 100-acre temple complex. Completed in November 2005, the pink-stone religious emporium pays tribute to Bhagwan Swami Narayan (1781–1830), the founder of a worldwide spiritual movement that claims a million devotees. An architectural marvel built over five years and without using steel, the elaborate main temple and its soaring domes and 20,000 carved figures only appear ancient. This gleaming complex includes a giant movie theater and a 14-minute boat ride that is quite an experience. Whisking the visitor through 10,000 years of Indian culture, the ride could be mistaken for something straight out of Disney World—Indian style! Just viewing the exhibits takes at least two hours. Admission lines can be lengthy, so allow plenty of time. Security is airtight. **All bags, electronics (including mobile phones and cameras), and tobacco products are banned, so check them in or leave them at the hotel or in the car before you get in line.** Exhibitions tend to shut an hour before the complex itself; the food court provides decent, cheap vegetarian meals and snacks for those who opt to spend the day. ✉ *Noida Mor, National Hwy. 24, Central Delhi* ☎ *11/4344–2344* ⊕ *www.akshardham.com* ✆ *Free; exhibitions Rs. 170* ☾ *Closed Mon.* Ⓜ *Akshardham.*

Some Delhi History

The ancient epic *Mahabharata* places the great town of Indraprastha on the banks of the Yamuna River, perhaps in what is now Delhi's Old Fort. Late in the first millennium AD, Delhi became an outpost of the Hindu Rajputs, warrior kings who ruled what's now Rajasthan. It was after 1191, when Mohammad Ghori of Central Asia invaded and conquered, that the city first acquired its Islamic flavor. Other Afghan and Uzbek sultanates handed Delhi back and forth over the next 300 years, until the mighty Mughals settled in. Beginning with the invasion of Babur in 1526, the Mughals shifted their capital between Delhi and Agra until 1858, leaving stunning architecture at both sites, including the buildings at what's now known as Old Delhi.

The British Arrive

The fall of the Mughal Empire coincided with the rise of the British East India Company, first in Madras (modern-day Chennai) and Calcutta and eventually throughout the country. When several of Delhi's Indian garrisons rose up against their Company employers in 1857, the British suppressed them, moved into the Red Fort, and ousted the aging Mughal emperor. In 1911, with anti-British sentiment growing in Calcutta, they moved their capital from Calcutta to Delhi—the ultimate prize, a place where they could build a truly imperial city that would dwarf the older ones around it. Architect Sir Edwin Lutyens was hired to create New Delhi, a majestic sandstone government complex surrounded by wide, leafy avenues and traffic circles, in contrast to Old Delhi's hectic lanes.

Independence and Upheaval

When India gained independence on August 15, 1947, with Jawaharlal Nehru the first prime minister, the subcontinent was partitioned into the secular republic of India and the Muslim nation of Pakistan, which was further divided into West Pakistan (now Pakistan) and East Pakistan (now Bangladesh). Trapped in potentially hostile new countries, thousands of Muslims left Delhi for Pakistan while millions of Hindu and Sikh refugees streamed in—changing Delhi's cultural overtone almost overnight from Persian to Punjabi.

Liberalization and Flux

Since Prime Minister Rajiv Gandhi (grandson of Nehru) and his successor, Narasimha Rao, began to liberalize India's planned economy in the late 1980s and early 1990s, Delhi has experienced tremendous change. Foreign companies have arrived and hired locals for white-collar jobs, residential enclaves and shopping strips have sprouted in every crevice, and land prices have skyrocketed. Professionals seeking affordable living space now move to the suburbs and drive into town, aggravating the already substantial pollution problem. At the same time, North Indian villagers still come here in search of work and build shanties wherever they can, sometimes in the shadows of forgotten monuments. It is they—Rajasthani women in colorful saris digging holes with pickaxes, men climbing rickety scaffolds in saronglike *lungis*—who build new homes for the affluent. Many Delhiites say, with a sigh, that their city is in a perpetual state of flux.

Jantar Mantar

OBSERVATORY | This odd grouping of what might seem like random modern sculptures is actually a huge sundial and open-air observatory. One of five such installations built by the Maharaja Sawai Jai Singh II of Jaipur in the early 18th century (the one in Jaipur is the best preserved), Jantar Mantar is an interesting place to wander, though better understood with a good guide. The Samrat Jantar, the sundial, is the largest structure here, at 90 feet. The Hindu Chhatri, a small domed building, can tell when the monsoons are coming in and whether the weather will change. The Jai Prakash shows the sun's position at the time of the equinox. The Ram Yantra consists of two large buildings, both with open tops: they're used, together, to measure the altitude of stars. The Mishra Yantra consists of five instruments, which are used to measure the shortest and longest days of the year. ✉ Sansad Marg, Connaught Pl., Central Delhi ☎ 11/2336–5358 ☎ Rs. 100 Ⓜ Patel Chowk.

★ **Lutyens' Delhi**

HISTORIC SITE | Rajpath—the broadest avenue in the city—leads to Delhi's British capital: Sir Edwin Lutyens' imperial city, built between 1914 and 1931 in a symbolically heavy-handed design after the British moved their capital from Calcutta to Delhi in 1911.

Starting from India Gate, at the lowest and eastern end of Rajpath, nearby land was allocated to numerous princely states, each of which built small palaces, such as the **Bikaner House** (now the Rajasthan tourism office) and **Jaipur House** (now the National Gallery of Modern Art). It might be said that this placement mirrored the British sentiments toward the princes, who lost much of their former power and status during the British Raj. Here, too, are the state Bhavans (houses), where you can taste the cuisine of each state.

Moving up the slowly inclining hill at the western end of the avenue, you also move up the British ladder of power, a concept inherent in the original design. First you come to the enormous **North and South Secretariats,** facing each other on Rajpath and reflecting the importance of the bureaucracy, a fixture of Indian society since the time of British rule. Identical in design, the two buildings have 1,000 rooms and miles of corridors.

Directly behind the North Secretariat is the Indian parliament house, **Sansad Bhavan,** a circular building in red and gray sandstone, encompassed by an open colonnade. Architecturally, the Indian design is meant to mirror the spinning wheel that was the symbol of Mahatma Gandhi, but the building's secondary placement, off the main avenue, may suggest the attitude of the British toward the Indian legislative assembly.

At the top of the hill is the former Viceroy's House, now called **Rashtrapati Bhavan,** where the president of India (not the prime minister) resides. It was built in the 20th century, but the building's daunting proportions seem to reflect an earlier, more lavish time of British supremacy. The Bhavan contains 340 rooms, and its grounds cover 330 acres. The shape of the central brass dome, the palace's main architectural feature, reflects that of a Buddhist *stupa* (shrine). The execution of Lutyens' design has a flaw: the entire palace was supposed to fill the vista as you approach the top of the hill, but the gradient is too steep, so only the dome dominates the horizon. Just a few years after the imperial city was completed, the British packed up and went home, and this lavish architectural complex became the grand capital of newly independent India.

Permission to enter Rashtrapati and Sansad Bhavan is almost impossible to obtain; unless you have contacts in high places, you'll have to satisfy yourself with a look at the poshest address in

4

Delhi CENTRAL DELHI

town from outside. ■TIP→ Parts of the Rashtrapati Bhavan, including the extensive gardens, are accessible to the public on prebooked tours, which are fully booked out much in advance. Book online and if you do get tickets, carry your passport. Heavy security is in place (no bags or cell phones, for instance).

For an experience of imperial Delhi, stop for tea at the Imperial Hotel on Janpath; for a glimpse of Delhi's contemporary elite, browse at Khan Market. A stroll through Lodhi Gardens is a relaxing break and Habitat World or the India International Centre are good bets if you have a taste for culture. ⊠ Central Delhi ⊕ www.rashtrapatisachivalaya.gov.in/rbtour ☎ Tours, Rs. 50 ⊗ Closed. Mon.–Wed. Ⓜ Central Secretariat.

National Crafts Museum
MUSEUM | Designed by the Indian architect Charles Correa, this charming museum near the Purana Qila houses thousands of artifacts and handicrafts. You're greeted outside by playful terra-cotta sculptures from Tamil Nadu. Inside, the annotations are sketchy, but the collection is fascinating. Items in the Folk and Tribal Art Gallery, including some charming toys, illustrate village life throughout India. In one courtyard you'll see a giant wooden temple car (cart), built to carry deities in festive processions; one of the adjacent buildings contains a lavishly decorated Gujarati haveli. The Courtly Crafts section suggests the luxurious lives of India's former royalty, and the entire upper floor is a spectacular showcase of saris and textiles. In the village complex out back, craftspeople demonstrate their skills and sell their creations in replicas of village homes. The museum shop is one of the best in Delhi, with high-quality art books and crafts. The in-house restaurant, Café Lota, serves regional highlights from all over the country. ⊠ Bhairon Rd., off Mathura Rd., opposite Pragati Maidan, Central Delhi ☎ 11/2337–1641 ⊕ www.

nationalcraftsmuseum.nic.in ☎ Rs. 200 ⊗ Closed Mon. Ⓜ Pragati Maidan.

National Museum
MUSEUM | The facade of this grand building imitates Lutyens' Presidential Palace: a sandstone dome is supported by classical columns of brown sandstone on a red-sandstone base. When you enter, you'll see a 13th-century idol—from the Konark Sun Temple in Bhubaneswar—of Surya, the sun god, standing beneath the dome. Such a statue is emblematic of the National Museum's strength—it showcases ancient, mainly Hindu, sculptures. An entire room is dedicated to artifacts from the Indus Valley Civilization, circa 2,700 BC; others display works from the Gandharan, Chandela, and Chola periods. Besides sculpture, also on exhibit are jewelry, painting, musical instruments, coins, carpets, and weapons, including Shah Jahan's sword. Be sure to pick up a brochure to help you navigate, and get the audio guide, included in ticket rates, which is also worth a listen. ⊠ Janpath and Rajpath, near India Gate, Central Delhi ☎ 11/2301–9272 ⊕ www.nationalmuseumindia.gov.in ☎ Rs. 650 ⊗ Closed Mon. Ⓜ Central Secretariat.

Nehru Memorial Museum
MUSEUM | This colonial mansion, also known as Teen Murti Bhavan, was originally built for the commander of the British Indian Army. When the Viceroy's residence, Rashtrapati Bhavan (at the other end of South Avenue), became the home of India's president, India's first prime minister, Jawaharlal Nehru, took up residence here. Those interested in the Independence movement should not miss this landmark or the nearby Gandhi Smriti. Nehru's yellow mansion is fronted by a long, oval-shape lawn; out back there's a tranquil flower garden. Inside, several rooms remain as Nehru left them, and extensive displays chronicle Nehru's life and the Independence movement. Move through the rooms in order: one by

one, photographs, newspaper clippings, and personal letters tell the breathtaking story of the birth of the world's largest democracy. On your way out, stop and see the 14th-century hunting lodge next to the Nehru Planetarium. (The latter, good for children, has shows in English at 11:30 am and 3 pm.) ✉ *Teen Murti Marg, Central Delhi* ☎ *11/2301–7587* 🌐 *www.nehrumemorial.nic.in* 🎟 *Free; planetarium Rs. 50* 🕒 *Closed Mon.* [M] *Lok Kalyan Marg.*

Purana Qila (*Old Fort*)
ARCHAEOLOGICAL SITE | India's sixth capital was the scene of a fierce power struggle between the Afghan Sher Shah and Humayun, son of the first Mughal emperor, Babur, in the 16th century. When Humayun started to build his own capital, Dinpanah, on these grounds in the 1530s, Sher Shah forced the emperor to flee for his life to Persia. Sher Shah destroyed what existed of Dinpanah to create his own capital, Shergarh. Fifteen years later, in 1555, Humayun returned and seized control, but he died the following year, leaving Sher Shah's city for others to destroy.

Once you enter the massive Bara Darwaza (Main Gate), only two buildings are intact. The **Qila-i-Kuhna Masjid,** Sher Shah's private mosque, is an excellent example of Indo-Afghan architecture in red sandstone with decorative marble touches. The **Sher Mandal,** a two-story octagonal tower of red sandstone and white marble, became Humayun's library and ultimately his death trap: hearing the call to prayer, Humayun started down the steep steps, slipped, and fell to his death. Excavated antiques are on display in a small museum. ✉ *Mathura Rd., near Pragati Maidan, Central Delhi* 🎟 *Rs. 200* [M] *Pragati Maidan.*

🍴 Restaurants

The All American Diner
$ | **DINER** | This is the city's best-known faux-1950s diner, complete with old advertisements on the wall and Elvis music on the hi-fi. Take one of the red-leather booths and get ready for standard, but high-quality, diner fare, such as whopping burgers and hearty steaks. **Known for:** great all-day breakfasts; old-school jukebox; garden-side outdoor seating. [$] *Average main: Rs. 450* ✉ *India Habitat Centre, Lodhi Rd., Central Delhi* ☎ *11/4366–3333* 🌐 *www.habitatworld.com.*

Bengali Sweet House
$ | **INDIAN** | **FAMILY** | This is a classic spot for evening *golgappa* outings. Also on offer are other Delhi snack staples: *chole bhatura* (also known as *chana bhatura*—spicy chickpeas with fried, airy puri bread), stuffed parathas, paneer fritters, and *raj kachori* (spicy *chaat* bowl with assorted fillings).**Known for:** milk-based Indian sweets; local favorite; pocket-friendly eats. [$] *Average main: Rs. 170* ✉ *30–33 Bengali Market, near Connaught Pl., Central Delhi* ☎ *11/2331–9224* 💳 *No credit cards* [M] *Mandi House.*

Bikanervala
$ | **INDIAN** | This is a reliable place for typical street food in an indoor, seated setting. Apart from chaat and snacks like kachori and *dhokla*, options include North Indian *thali* meals and South Indian food.**Known for:** vegetarian food; quick, self-service; family vibe. [$] *Average main: Rs. 160* ✉ *Rajiv Gandhi Handicraft Bhavan, Baba Kharag Singh Marg, 1st fl., Connaught Pl., Central Delhi* ☎ *97177–01177 mobile* 🌐 *www.bikanervala.com* [M] *Rajiv Chowk.*

Bukhara
$$$$ | **NORTH INDIAN** | Served amid stone walls, rough-hewn dark-wood beams, copper urns, and blood-red rugs, Bukhara's menu hasn't changed in years, and its loyal clientele wouldn't have it any

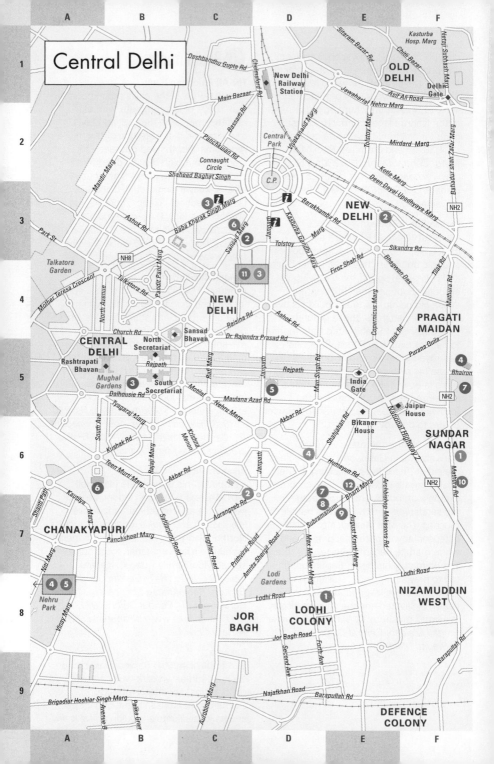

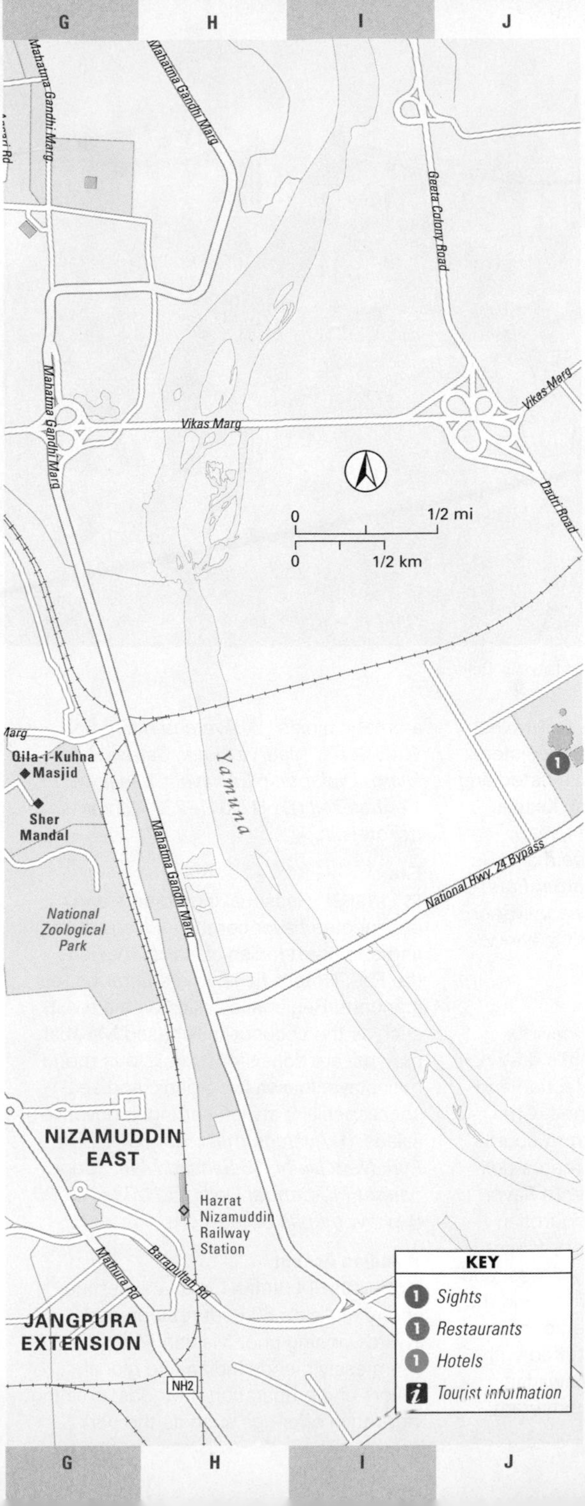

G H I J

Sights ▼

1 Akshardham Temple Complex **J5**
2 Jantar Mantar...................... **C3**
3 Lutyens' Delhi **B5**
4 National Crafts Museum........... **F5**
5 National Museum.................. **D5**
6 Nehru Memorial Museum........ **A6**
7 Purana Qila......................... **F5**

Restaurants ▼

1 The All American Diner **D8**
2 Bengali Sweet House **E3**
3 Bikanervala......................... **C3**
4 Bukhara............................. **A8**
5 Dum Pukht......................... **A8**
6 Fire **C3**
7 Khan Chacha....................... **E6**
8 Latitude 28......................... **E7**
9 Mamagoto.......................... **E6**
10 Nathu's Sweets **F6**
11 San Gimignano..................... **D3**
12 Yellow Brick Road **E6**

Hotels ▼

1 Ahuja Residency.................... **F6**
2 The Claridges, Delhi............... **C7**
3 The Imperial....................... **D3**
4 Taj Mahal **D6**

4

Delhi CENTRAL DELHI

Mahatma Gandhi Marg · Geeta Colony Road · Vikas Marg · Dadri Road · Vikas Marg

0 1/2 mi
0 1/2 km

Qila-i-Kuhna ◆Masjid
◆ Sher Mandal
National Zoological Park
Yamuna
National Hwy. 24 Bypass
NIZAMUDDIN EAST
Hazrat Nizamuddin Railway Station
JANGPURA EXTENSION
Mathura Rd · Barapullah Rd
NH2

KEY
1 *Sights*
1 *Restaurants*
1 *Hotels*
🛈 *Tourist information*

A view of the government buildings at Lutyens' Delhi

other way. The cuisine of the Northwest Frontier, now the Pakistan–Afghanistan border, is heavy on meats, marinated and grilled in a tandoor (clay oven). **Known for:** dal bukhara; murgh malai kabab; extensive wine list. $ *Average main: Rs. 2195* ⊠ *ITC Maurya Hotel, Sardar Patel Marg, Diplomatic Enclave, Chanakyapuri, Central Delhi* ☎ *11/2611–2233* ⊕ *www. itchotels.in.*

★ Dum Pukht

$$$$ | **NORTH INDIAN** | Like the *nawabi* (princely) culture from which it's drawn, this restaurant has a food selection and style that are subtle and refined. Chef Imtiaz Qureshi, descended from court cooks in Avadh (Lucknow), creates delicately spiced meals packed with flavor: *dum ki khumb* (button mushrooms in gravy, fennel, and dried ginger), *kakori kabab* (finely minced mutton, cloves, and cinnamon, drizzled with saffron), and the special *raan-e-dumpukht* (a leg of mutton marinated in dark rum and stuffed with onions, cheese, and mint).**Known for:** royal decor; award-winning restaurant;

aromatic biryani. $ *Average main: Rs. 1845* ⊠ *ITC Maurya Hotel, Sardar Patel Marg, Diplomatic Enclave, Chanakyapuri, Central Delhi* ☎ *11/2611–2233* ⊕ *www. itchotels.in.*

Fire

$$ | **INDIAN** | Seasonal ingredients and unexpected flavor combinations update and transform Indian classics, making the Park Hotel's flagship restaurant a real standout. Regional classics with a twist, such as the coconut-milk-based Malabar prawns, are consistently delicious menu mainstays. **Known for:** organic and seasonal specials; stylish setting; innovative salads. $ *Average main: Rs. 595* ⊠ *The Park New Delhi, 15 Sansad Marg, Connaught Pl., Central Delhi* ☎ *11/2374–3000* ⊕ *www.theparkhotels.com.*

★ Indian Accent

$$$$ | **MODERN INDIAN** | In a luxe setting at one of Asia's 50 best restaurants, award-winning chef Manish Mehrotra seamlessly blends Indian and global flavors and preparation methods, creating innovative offerings such as the pork

belly tikka. Choose the chef's tasting menu for six wildly modern dishes created with typically Indian ingredients and paired with complementing wines. **Known for:** top-notch service; innovative presentation; tandoori bacon prawns. [$] *Average main: Rs. 1500* ✉ *The Lodhi, Lodhi Rd., Central Delhi* ☎ *11/6617–5151* 🌐 *www.indianaccent.com.*

Khan Chacha

$ | **NORTH INDIAN** | Hot-off-the-grill kebabs are the specialty at this small, self-service eatery tucked into an upper level in Khan Market's busy lanes. Expect melt-in-the-mouth mutton, chicken, and *paneer tikka roomali* rolls in a no-frills setting.**Known for:** seekh kebabs; quick service; local hangout. [$] *Average main: Rs. 245* ✉ *50 Khan Market, 1st fl., middle lane, Central Delhi* ☎ *11/4368–0449* [M] *Khan Market.*

★ **Latitude 28**

$$ | **ECLECTIC** | One of Delhi's prettiest, hippest cafés, Latitude 28 is the place to go if you want to relax over a thoughtful meal, cold beer, or specialty tea. Celebrity chef Ritu Dalmia has put together a playful mix of comfort food from around the world and quirky takes on regional staples from around India. **Known for:** artsy decor; market views; healthy salads. [$] *Average main: Rs. 690* ✉ *9 Khan Market, Central Delhi* ☎ *11/2462–1013* 🌐 *divarestaurants.com/latitude.*

Mamagoto

$ | **ASIAN** | Japanese for "play with your food," cheery Mamagoto, hidden behind a yellow door in the middle lane of Khan Market, is indeed a fun place for a low-key meal. This is a great spot to have a couple of cocktails and share several Pan-Asian dishes. **Known for:** innovative small plates; kitschy decor; truffle oil dumplings. [$] *Average main: Rs. 400* ✉ *53 Khan Market, first fl., middle lane, Central Delhi* ☎ *11/4516–6060* 🌐 *www.mamagoto.in* [M] *Khan Market.*

Nathu's Sweets

$ | **INDIAN** | **FAMILY** | This city institution with several branches offers quick-service vegetarian snacks and meals in a clean, fuss-free setting. There's a very wide selection of breads and sweets, with more than a dozen options in parathas alone; go for the ones filled with mint or cauliflower. **Known for:** Persian origin sohal halwa sweet; flaky kachoris; papri chaat. [$] *Average main: Rs. 220* ✉ *2 Sundar Nagar Market, Central Delhi* ☎ *11/2435–2435* 🌐 *www.nathusweets.com.*

San Gimignano

$$$ | **ITALIAN** | Delhi's most rarefied Italian restaurant is known for its playful, sensuous dishes, relying heavily on black olives, Parmesan cheese, and fresh local produce, and for its excellent service. The small wood-panel rooms are inviting; in winter you can dine on a terra-cotta patio in the fabulous garden. **Known for:** award-winning Italian food; extensive wine list; varied vegetarian options. [$] *Average main: Rs. 1225* ✉ *Imperial Hotel, Janpath, Connaught Pl., Central Delhi* ☎ *11/4111–6608* 🌐 *www.theimperialindia.com.*

Yellow Brick Road

$$ | **INTERNATIONAL** | Delhi's insomniacs love this super-bright, tiny 24-hour coffee shop with blinding-yellow striped wallpaper, vintage French-colonial posters, and distressed-yellow tables. The extensive menu features everything from tandoori to Thai, along with several vegetarian choices and a decent bar menu. **Known for:** all-day breakfasts; cheery vibe; late-night comfort food. [$] *Average main: Rs. 895* ✉ *Vivanta by Taj Ambassador Hotel, Subramaniam Bharti Marg, near Khan Market, Sujan Singh Park, Central Delhi* ☎ *11/6626–1000* 🌐 *www.tajhotels.com* [M] *Khan Market.*

Hotels

★ Ahuja Residency

$$ | **B&B/INN** | Hospitality and attention to detail are second to none at this little-known guesthouse, Delhi's only combination of style and affordability. **Pros:** immaculate, clean, and neat; well-located close to Lutyens' Delhi sights; homely, freshly cooked meals. **Cons:** reservations difficult to get; bathrooms have showers only; can be hard for taxis to locate. [$] *Rooms from: Rs. 7000* ✉ *193 Golf Links, Central Delhi* ☎ *11/2462–2255* 🌐 *www.ahujaresidency.com* 🛏 *9 rooms* 🍴 *Free Breakfast* [M] *Khan Market.*

The Claridges, Delhi

$$$$ | **HOTEL** | In 1950, three years after Independence, an Indian family was talked into building a hotel with a British aesthetic, and the result was a winner: tasteful yet unpretentious, in a central yet quiet location. **Pros:** Sevilla, the Mediterranean eatery, gets high marks; excellent pool; the specialty vodka bar, Aura, is a rarity in the city. **Cons:** rooms near the nightclub can be noisy; food and drinks are expensive; some rooms' bathrooms are quite small. [$] *Rooms from: Rs. 15000* ✉ *12, Dr APJ Abdul Kalam Rd., Central Delhi* ☎ *11/3955–5000* 🌐 *www.claridges.com* 🛏 *131 rooms* 🍴 *Free Breakfast* [M] *Lok Kalyan Marg.*

★ The Imperial

$$$$ | **HOTEL** | Easily the most appealing hotel in Delhi, with a driveway lined by soaring king palms, the luxurious Imperial offers unparalleled service and location. **Pros:** top-notch restaurants and bar; special rooms and a floor for single-women travelers; good spa. **Cons:** very expensive; standard rooms on the small side; outdoor pool not heated in winter. [$] *Rooms from: Rs. 22500* ✉ *Janpath, south of Tolstoy Marg, Connaught Pl., Central Delhi* ☎ *11/2334–1234* 🌐 *www.theimperialindia.com* 🛏 *235 rooms* 🍴 *Free Breakfast.*

★ Lodhi Hotel

$$$$ | **HOTEL** | An exclusive hotel at an exclusive address, the Lodhi Hotel is over-the-top luxury all the way, starting with the private pool nestled on the balcony of most of the rooms. **Pros:** luxurious to the hilt; next door to Khan Market and close to Lodhi Garden; great spa. **Cons:** staff can be hard to find when you need them; exorbitantly expensive; service can feel impersonal. [$] *Rooms from: Rs. 26450* ✉ *Lodhi Rd., Central Delhi* ☎ *11/4363–3333* 🌐 *www.thelodhi.com* 🛏 *111 rooms* 🍴 *No meals.*

★ Taj Mahal

$$$$ | **HOTEL** | The Taj Mansingh, as it's locally known, is Delhi's premier social hotel, with nightly cocktail affairs, cultural events, and occasional society weddings drawing the glitterati. **Pros:** centrally located in Lutyens' Delhi; popular with business travelers and celebrities, and the service is correspondingly slick; excellent dining options, including Varq and Wasabi by Marimoto. **Cons:** rooms on the small side; very expensive in the high season; outdoor pool is very cold in winter. [$] *Rooms from: Rs. 15000* ✉ *1 Mansingh Rd., Central Delhi* ☎ *11/6656–6162* 🌐 *www.tajhotels.com* 🛏 *292 rooms* 🍴 *Free Breakfast* [M] *Lok Kalyan Marg.*

Nightlife

Agni

DANCE CLUBS | Named for the Vedic fire god, the swanky Agni, in the Park Hotel, attracts Delhi's party crowd, playing electronic interspersed with pop, hip-hop, and Bollywood hits. The door staff can be selective. ✉ *The Park Hotel, 15 Parliament St., near Connaught Pl., Central Delhi* ☎ *11/2374–3000* 🌐 *www.theparkhotels.com.*

Aqua

PIANO BARS/LOUNGES | As the name suggests, Aqua is a giant outdoor space focused on a large swimming pool surrounded with lovely cabanas. It's got a well-heeled, more sedate crowd, especially when compared to its crazy next-door neighbor, Agni. ⊠ *The Park Hotel, 15 Parliament St., Connaught Pl., Central Delhi* ☎ *11/2374–3000* ⊕ *www.theparkhotels.com.*

1911

PIANO BARS/LOUNGES | The large bar here is a classic watering hole decked out the way it looked in the years leading up to the end of the Raj. The drink menu is massive, and lounge music keeps the vibe contemporary. ⊠ *Imperial Hotel, Janpath, Connaught Pl., Central Delhi* ☎ *11/2334–1234, 11/4150–1234* ⊕ *www.theimperialindia.com.*

Rick's

BARS/PUBS | The booze selection is hard to beat at this magnet for Delhi's beautiful people. It features an extensive whisky selection, accompanied by snacks that are Southeast Asian. Go before 9 pm if you want a seat. ⊠ *Taj Mahal Hotel, 1 Mansingh Rd., Central Delhi* ☎ *11/2302–6070* ⊕ *www.tajhotels.com* Ⓜ *Khan Market.*

🎭 Performing Arts

Art Heritage

ART GALLERIES—ARTS | Part of the Triveni Kala Sangam cultural institute, with several galleries and performance spaces, Art Heritage has some of the finest exhibits in town. ⊠ *Triveni Kala Sangam, 205 Tansen Marg, Mandi House, near Connaught Pl., Central Delhi* ☎ *98186–96193* ⊕ *www.artheritagegallery.com* Ⓜ *Mandi House.*

Dhoomimal Gallery

ART GALLERIES—ARTS | This large gallery that focuses on older contemporary and emerging artists is centrally located and worth a visit even though it's a bit chaotic. ⊠ *G–42 and A–8 Connaught Pl., Central Delhi* ☎ *11/4151–6056* ⊕ *www.dhoomimalgallery.com* Ⓜ *Rajiv Chowk.*

Kamani Auditorium

DANCE | This long-standing venue for Indian classical music and dance is also a good place to sample Delhi's vibrant student-theater scene. ⊠ *1 Copernicus Marg, Mandi House, Central Delhi* ☎ *11/4350–3351* ⊕ *www.kamaniauditorium.org* Ⓜ *Mandi House.*

Lalit Kala Akademi

ART GALLERIES—ARTS | This government-run gallery in a large 1950s building shows several exhibits at once, usually of varying quality. ⊠ *Rabindra Bhavan, 35 Ferozeshah Rd., near Connaught Pl., Central Delhi* ☎ *11/2300–9200* ⊕ *www.lalitkala.gov.in* Ⓜ *Mandi House.*

PVR Plaza

FILM | ⊠ *H Block, Connaught Pl., Central Delhi* ⊕ *www.pvrcinemas.com* Ⓜ *Rajiv Chowk.*

Shri Ram Centre for Performing Arts

CULTURAL TOURS | A constant stream of plays and dance performances in both Hindi and English are staged here, some for one day only. ⊠ *4 Safdar Hashmi Marg, near Connaught Pl., Central Delhi* ☎ *11/2371–4307* ⊕ *www.shriramcentre.org* Ⓜ *Mandi House.*

Triveni Kala Sangam

ART GALLERIES—ARTS | In addition to the galleries at Art Heritage, regular dance performances and classes take place here. There's also a cozy cafeteria where you can retire afterward for a relaxed tea and *paranthas* amid lush greenery. ⊠ *205 Tansen Marg, near Connaught Pl., Central Delhi* ☎ *11/2371–8833* ⊕ *www.trivenikalasangam.org* Ⓜ *Mandi House.*

🛍 Shopping

BAZAARS AND MARKETS
Connaught Place

OUTDOOR/FLEA/GREEN MARKETS | Open every day but Sunday from about 10 to 7:30, this is the former commercial district of the British Raj. Pillared arcades and a wheel-shaped layout make it a pleasant place to stroll, especially the inner circle, though you have to get used to the intermittent entreaties of hawkers and beggars. Shops run the gamut from scruffy to upscale. Beneath the green park at the center of Connaught Place is **Palika Bazaar,** a cheap underground market with all the charm of a Times Square subway station—avoid it; it's a favorite haunt of pickpockets and many shopkeepers are dishonest. ⊠ *Central Delhi.*

Khan Market

SHOPPING NEIGHBORHOODS | Though it's not cheap, this is one of the capital's most pleasant and popular markets, with dozens of fine shops selling books, drugs, ayurvedic cosmetics, clothing, home decorations, imported magazines, and imported foods. The crowd is thick with expats and Delhi intelligentsia, bureaucrats, and politicians. While the shops are closed on Sunday, restaurants and bars are open. ⊠ *Sujan Sing Park N, Central Delhi* Ⓜ *Khan Market.*

Santushti Shopping Complex

SHOPPING CENTERS/MALLS | Open every day but Sunday from 10 to 6 or 7, this collection of posh and arty boutiques is scattered around a small, quiet garden across from the Ashok Hotel in the Diplomatic Enclave. Prices can approach those in the West, but this is a relaxing place to stroll and browse. Clothing is the main draw, followed by home furnishings, jewelry, leather, and ayurvedic beauty products. The quaint Diggin café serves good Mediterranean food. ⊠ *Chanakyapuri, Central Delhi* Ⓜ *Lok Kalyan Marg.*

BOOKS
Bahri Sons

BOOKS/STATIONERY | This place is stuffed to the ceiling with dusty nonfiction, particularly academic history, politics, and Indian heritage, as well as a good amount of fiction titles. ⊠ *Khan Market, Subramaniam Bharti Marg, opposite main entrance, Central Delhi* ☎ *11/2469–4610* ⊕ *www. booksatbahri.com* Ⓜ *Khan Market.*

The Bookshop

BOOKS/STATIONERY | This shop is strong on literary fiction, including hot new titles from abroad. ⊠ *13/7 Jor Bagh, Main Market, Central Delhi* ☎ *11/2469–7102* Ⓜ *Jor Bagh.*

Faqir Chand & Sons

BOOKS/STATIONERY | This bookstore carries a fair number of coffee-table books. ⊠ *15A Khan Market, Central Delhi* ☎ *11/2461–8810* Ⓜ *Khan Market.*

★ Full Circle

BOOKS/STATIONERY | Spirituality, self-help, and coffee-table books are the specialty at this bookshop with an attached café. ⊠ *23 Khan Market, Central Delhi* ☎ *11/2465–5641* ⊕ *www.fullcirclebooks. in* Ⓜ *Khan Market.*

CLOTHING
Banaras House

CLOTHING | This store sells the rich brocaded silks of Varanasi. ⊠ *N–13 Connaught Pl., Central Delhi* ☎ *11/2331–4751* Ⓜ *Rajiv Chowk.*

★ Fabindia

CLOTHING | An India institution, this emporium is stuffed with block-printed kurtas, salwars, churidars, dupattas, Western tops, and skirts in subtle colors for trendy Delhiites, their moms and dads, expats, and tourists. Quality can vary. Avoid Saturday, when the place is a madhouse and it's difficult to get your hands on the stock. There are also branches in Khan Market, the Delhi airport, Green Park, a mall in Vasant Kunj, Greater Kailash and elsewhere. ⊠ *Hamilton House, A 1, Connaught Pl., Central Delhi* ☎ *11/4304–8295* ⊕ *www.fabindia.com* Ⓜ *Rajiv Chowk.*

Kalpana

CLOTHING | Like an upscale version of the Dilli Haat market, Kalpana has exquisite traditional saris from all over India plus gorgeous Kashmiri shawls. ⊠ *F–5 Connaught Pl., Central Delhi* ☎ *11/4362– 3738, 11/6472–3772* Ⓜ *Rajiv Chowk.*

Kanika

CLOTHING | Beautiful, if somewhat pricey, salwar-kameez sets in contemporary cuts of traditional fabrics are sold here. ⊠ *M–53 Connaught Pl., Central Delhi* ☎ *11/4151–7907* Ⓜ *Rajiv Chowk.*

Khanna Fabrics

CLOTHING | This is a good place for handsome salwar-kameez, some hand-embroidered, and raw fabric sets in great colors and patterns at good prices. The in-house tailor can create a salwar-kameez in as little as four hours starting at Rs. 600. ⊠ *D–6 Connaught Pl., Central Delhi* ☎ *11/2341–1929* Ⓜ *Rajiv Chowk.*

Tulsi

CLOTHING | The supple garments and home furnishings here are made of handwoven silk, linen, and cotton. ⊠ *19 Santushti Shopping Complex, Chanakyapuri, Central Delhi* ☎ *11/2687–0339* ⊕ *www.tulsionline.in* Ⓜ *Lok Kalyan Marg.*

CRAFTS AND CURIOS
Bharany's

CRAFTS | Specializing in jewelry, this store also sells rare old shawls and wall hangings from all over India. ⊠ *14 Sunder Nagar Market, Central Delhi* ☎ *11/2435–8528* ⊕ *www.bharanys.com.*

★ Central Cottage Industries Emporium

CRAFTS | Purchase crafts from all over the country at this fixed-price, government-run shop; it will ship items abroad too. Even if you don't buy anything here, it's a good place for getting an idea of the upper bounds of prices before you go bargaining elsewhere. ⊠ *Jawahar Vyapar Bhavan, Janpath, opposite Imperial Hotel, near Connaught Pl., Central Delhi* ☎ *11/2332–3825* ⊕ *www.cottageemporium.in* Ⓜ *Janpath.*

Curio Palace

CRAFTS | There's an overwhelming array of silver and brass curios here, with much of the brass oxidized for an antique look. ⊠ *17 Sunder Nagar Market, Central Delhi* ☎ *11/2435–8929* ⊕ *www.curiopalace.com.*

★ Happily Unmarried

GIFTS/SOUVENIRS | This lighthearted store carries products like an ashtray shaped like a *sandaas* and an Indian-style squat toilet. Also fun are wine-bottle stoppers shaped like old-fashioned water pumps and CD stackers in cylindrical tiffin carriers. ⊠ *Bombay Life Bldg., N35–A Connaught Pl., Outer Circle, Central Delhi* ☎ *11/2331–3326* ⊕ *www.happilyunmarried.com.*

India Arts Palace

CRAFTS | This is an absolute hurricane of Indian ephemera, with dangling colored lanterns, Hindu icons, cute animal curios, drawer pulls, and so forth. ⊠ *33 Sunder Nagar Market, Central Delhi* ☎ *11/4354–6861.*

La Boutique

CRAFTS | This shop pleases the eye with painted wooden items from Rajasthan, plus Hindu and Buddhist icons and other curiosities. ⊠ *20 Sunder Nagar Market, Central Delhi* ☎ *11/2435–0066* ⊕ *www.laboutiqueindia.com.*

Ladakh Art Gallery

CRAFTS | Distinctive silver items and small Hindu icons are offered by this gallery. ⊠ *34 Sunder Nagar Market, Central Delhi* ☎ *11/2435–5424.*

★ State Emporiums

CRAFTS | The many state emporiums, strung out over three blocks, can keep you busy for hours: the Kashmir store specializes in carpets, Karnataka in sandalwood, Tripura in bamboo, and so on. The prices are all fixed. ⊠ *Baba Kharak Singh Marg, near Connaught Pl., Central Delhi* Ⓜ *Rajiv Chowk.*

HOME FURNISHINGS
Good Earth

HOUSEHOLD ITEMS/FURNITURE | Geared to the sophisticated shopper, Good Earth has shops in several Indian cities and sells items like jewel-toned, pop-art cushion covers and other high-end home accessories, including linens, pottery, and brass. In Delhi, there's also a Good Earth store in the Select Citywalk Mall in Saket. ⊠ *Khan Market, 9 ABC, Central Delhi* ☎ *11/2464–7175* ⊕ *www.goodearth.in* Ⓜ *Khan Market* ⊠ *3rd fl. Select City Walk Mall, S–06, A–3 District Centre, Saket, South Delhi* ☎ *11/4053–4567* ⊕ *www. goodearth.in.*

Neemrana Shop
HOUSEHOLD ITEMS/FURNITURE | This upscale shop has some beautiful India-inspired women's clothing, men's kurtas, and household gifts at nearly Western prices. ⊠ *26A Khan Market, Central Delhi* ☎ *11/4358–7183* ⊕ *www.neemranahotels.com* Ⓜ *Khan Market.*

Play Clan
STORE/MALL | The design collective (also in several other Indian cities) has collaborated with the likes of Paul Smith. Popular items include cushion covers and totes with maps of Indian locales, Mughal-ruler playing cards, and T-shirts (they even add custom kitsch to Converse shoes). There's another branch in Khan Market. ⊠ *17 Meher Chand Market, Lodhi Rd., Central Delhi* ☎ *11/2464–4393* ⊕ *www. theplayclan.com* Ⓜ *Jor Bagh.*

JEWELRY
Ivory Mart
JEWELRY/ACCESSORIES | Reproductions of antique *kundan* jewelry, in which several gems are set in a gold-outlined design, are a specialty here, and there's a huge selection of lovely necklaces in updated traditional styles. ⊠ *F–22 Connaught Pl., Central Delhi* ☎ *11/2331–0197* ⊕ *www. ivorymartjewellers.com* Ⓜ *Rajiv Chowk.*

Mayur Jewellers
JEWELRY/ACCESSORIES | Beautiful silver and gold jewelry, especially necklaces, is in tasteful traditional styles, including gemstone wedding sets. ⊠ *4 Sunder Nagar Market, Central Delhi* ☎ *11/2435–8664.*

Mehrasons
JEWELRY/ACCESSORIES | This store with branches across Delhi has an immense selection of gold and diamond jewelry, along with loose gemstones and a pricey

range of *polki kundan* sets. ⊠ *68 Janpath, near Connaught Pl., Central Delhi* ☎ *11/4567–0700* ⊕ *www.mehrasonsjewellers.com* Ⓜ *Rajiv Chowk.*

Roopchand Jewellers
JEWELRY/ACCESSORIES | Some eye-popping regal pieces in antique styles are among the offerings here. ⊠ *C–13 Connaught Pl., Central Delhi* ☎ *11/2341–1709* Ⓜ *Rajiv Chowk.*

MUSIC
Mercury
MUSIC STORES | It looks ordinary, but Mercury is a good place to pick up LPs, Indian classical music, and *ghazals* (Urdu-language love songs). ⊠ *20 Khan Market, Central Delhi* ☎ *11/2469–0134* Ⓜ *Khan Market.*

TEA AND COFFEE
Asia Tea House
FOOD/CANDY | Next door to Mittal, Asia Tea House sells fine teas and tea paraphernalia. ⊠ *12 Sunder Nagar Market, Central Delhi* ☎ *11/2435–0115.*

★ **Mittal Tea Store**
FOOD/CANDY | Stuffed to the ceiling with Indian teas, herbs, and spices, this teahouse has a charming owner, Vikram Mittal, who will tell you everything you ever wanted to know about tea. Another branch is on Barakhamba Road. ⊠ *12 Sunder Nagar Market, Central Delhi* ☎ *11/2435–8588* ⊕ *www.mittalteas.com.*

Old Delhi and Nearby

Old Delhi (6 km [4 miles] north of Connaught Place), or Purani Dilli, is also called by its original name of Shahjahanabad, for the emperor, Shah Jahan, who built it. The havelis that line the gullies are architecturally stunning but irreversibly crumbling. Old Delhi's monuments—the Jama Masjid and the Red Fort that anchors the Old City—are magnificent, and the main artery, Chandni Chowk, should not be missed. It's a convenient metro ride to the Old City from Connaught Place.

Old Delhi is crowded and hectic, and the roads and footways are poorly maintained. It's best to chalk up all the bustle to added charm and just immerse yourself in the experience. It's one of the most incredible places to shop and eat, with lots of specialty markets crowding the area on both sides of Chandni Chowk (literally the "silver crossroad" but also meaning moonlit market or square). Kinari Bazaar and Katra Neel are two others, and are a tight squeeze with their maze of alleys. Gorgeous, intricately embroidered fabrics and appliqué materials, lace, bangles, spices, herbs, and Indian sweets can be found in all of them. Watch out for Khari Baoli, Asia's largest spice market, toward the western end of Chandni Chowk (after Fatehpuri Masjid). You'll smell it before you see it.

Jama Masjid is the principle mosque in Old Delhi, and was built by Shah Jahan as well. It's the largest mosque in India, a colossal structure beautifully constructed out of red sandstone. The courtyard of the mosque can be reached from the east, north, and south gates by three flights of steps, all of which have religious significance. The northern gate has 39 steps, the southern side has 33 steps, and the eastern gate, which was once the royal entrance that Shah Jahan and his entourage used, has 35 steps. Arched colonnades and minarets surround the mosque itself, which rests on a platform. Apparently, the courtyard can hold up to 25,000 devotees.

The Red Fort, or Lal Qila, is another Old Delhi institution, and was also built by Shah Jahan as the main residence of the royal family. It's an important top attraction, and combines Indo-Persian architecture to perfection.

If you find yourself daunted by the throngs of people or just need a break after a few hours, try a cycle-rickshaw

tour: for about Rs. 100 you can be carted around in a cycle-rickshaw (which seats two slim people) for about an hour. The rickshaw- *wallahs* (drivers) in front of the Red Fort are serious bargainers, but they know the city well, and many can show you places you wouldn't discover on your own.

The variety of traditional Indian food that can be found in Old Delhi is heavenly. Try the kulfi (a flavored frozen milk dessert) at places like Lala Dulichand, which serves the treat inside fruit. The *aam* (mango) and *anjeer* (fig) versions are to die for. Karim's, a restaurant right around the Jama Masjid, is another stop. Make sure you have cash on hand, because many of the smaller shops and stalls don't have credit card machines.

 Sights

★ Chandni Chowk

NEIGHBORHOOD | This was Delhi's former imperial avenue, where the Mughal emperor Shah Jahan rode at the head of his lavish cavalcade. That scene is hard to picture today, as bicycles, freight carts, cows, auto-rickshaws, and pedestrians create a breathtaking bazaar. It runs from the Red Fort into the walled city, functioning as a major, if congested, artery. As in the days of the Mughals, commerce is everywhere: astrologers set up their charts on the pavement; shoemakers squat and repair sandals; sidewalk photographers with old box cameras take pictures for a small fee; medicine booths conceal doctors attending to patients; and oversize teeth grin from the windows of dentists' offices. Peer through a portico, and you might see men getting shaved, or silver being hammered into paper-thin edible sheets. While the scenes may seem archaic, the shopping is exactly where it's supposed to be, so make sure you carry cash (safely tucked about your person). The stores in tinsel-filled Kinari Bazaar and Dariba Kalan, with its jewelry and gemstones,

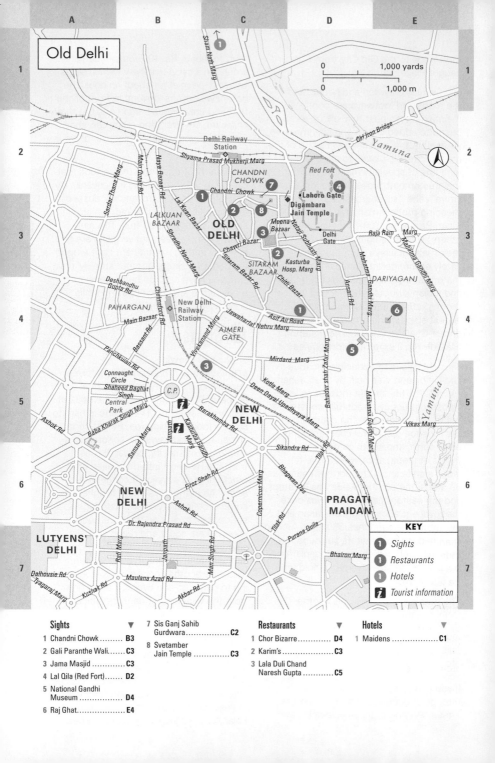

Old Delhi

0 — 1,000 yards
0 — 1,000 m

Yamuna

Old Iron Bridge

Delhi Railway Station

Shyama Prasad Mukherji Marg

CHANDNI CHOWK

Chandni Chowk

Red Fort

Lahore Gate
Digambara Jain Temple

LALKUAN BAZAAR

OLD DELHI

Meena Bazaar

Delhi Gate

Raja Ram Marg

Chawri Bazaar

Kasturba Hosp. Marg

SITARAM BAZAAR

DARIYAGANJ

Deshbandhu Gupta Rd

PAHARGANJ

New Delhi Railway Station

Main Bazaar

AJMERI GATE

Jawaharlal Nehru Marg

Asif Ali Road

Mirdard Marg

Kotla Marg

Deen Dayal Upadhyaya Marg

Connaught Circle
Shaheed Baghat Singh
Central Park

C.P.

Barakhamba Rd

NEW DELHI

Sikandra Rd

Vikas Marg

Yamuna

NEW DELHI

Firoz Shah Rd

Ashok Rd

PRAGATI MAIDAN

LUTYENS' DELHI

Dr. Rajendra Prasad Rd

NEW DELHI

Purana Qila

Bhairon Marg

Dalhousie Rd

Maulana Azad Rd

Akbar Rd

KEY

- 1 Sights
- 1 Restaurants
- 1 Hotels
- i Tourist information

Sights ▼

1 Chandni Chowk B3
2 Gali Paranthe Wali C3
3 Jama Masjid C3
4 Lal Qila (Red Fort) D2
5 National Gandhi
   Museum D4
6 Raj Ghat E4

7 Sis Ganj Sahib
   Gurdwara C2
8 Svetamber
   Jain Temple C3

Restaurants ▼

1 Chor Bizarre D4
2 Karim's C3
3 Lala Duli Chand
   Naresh Gupta C5

Hotels ▼

1 Maidens C1

Outside the Jama Masjid

may make you want to empty your wallet. Also, lining just about every alley are the famous *halwais*, a group of sweets makers selling staples such as fried orange *jalebis*. ✉ *East–west artery from Red Fort 1½ km (1 mile) west to Fatehpuri Masjid, Old Delhi* ☾ *Most shops closed Sun.* Ⓜ *Chandni Chowk.*

Gali Paranthe Wali
NEIGHBORHOOD | This narrow, festive lane is filled with shopkeepers selling fabric and saris, including the well-known Ram Chandra Krishan Chandra's, where young brides choose their red-and-gold finery. The lane is named for its other industry: the fabulous paranthas (fried flatbreads) that are sold here in no-frills open-air eateries. Stuffed or served with a variety of fixings, such as radishes, soft cheese, and seasonal vegetables, paranthas are delicious. The parantha makers moved into this lane in the 1870s, even though a couple of its original sari and jewelry shops still dot the lane. The three oldest and most famous of these parantha makers are Pandit Gaya Prasad Shiv Charan

(established in 1872), Pandit Kanhaiyalal & Durga Prasad Dixit (1875), and Pundit Baburam Devidayal Paranthe Wali (1889). A few kitchens have seating, making them excellent places to refuel while looking at photos of famous statesmen doing the same. ✉ *South off Chandni Chowk, en route to Kinari Bazaar, Old Delhi* Ⓜ *Chandni Chowk.*

★ Jama Masjid
RELIGIOUS SITE | An exquisite statement in red sandstone and marble, India's largest mosque was the last monument commissioned by Shah Jahan; it was completed in 1656 after six years of work by 5,000 laborers. Three sets of broad steps lead to two-story gateways and a magnificent courtyard with a square ablution tank in the center. The entire space is enclosed by pillared corridors, with domed pavilions in each corner. Thousands gather to pray here, especially on Friday.

With its onion-shaped dome and tapering minarets, the mosque is characteristically Mughal, but Shah Jahan added an innovation: the stripes running up and down the marble domes and minarets. Climb the south minaret to see the domes up close, and to see how finely the mosque contrasts with the commercial streets around it. Look into the prayer hall (you can only enter after a ritual purification at the ablution tank) for the pulpit carved from a single slab of marble. In one corner is a room where Shah Jahan installed the marble footprints of the Prophet Mohammed. Each of the arched colonnades has black-marble inscriptions inlaid in white marble that relate the history of the building.

If you're feeling hungry, the restaurant Karim's is in the shadow of the Jama Masjid. The site is closed to non-Muslims from noon–1:30 pm and during prayer hours. ⊠ *4½ km (3 miles) north of Connaught Pl., across from Red Fort, Old Delhi* ⌐ *Free; from Rs.100* Ⓜ *Chawri Bazaar, Chandni Chowk.*

★ Lal Qila (Red Fort)

HISTORIC SITE | Named for its red-sandstone walls, the Red Fort, near the Yamuna River in Old Delhi, is the greatest of Delhi's palace cities. Built by Shah Jahan in the 17th century, Lal Qila recalls the era of Mughal power and magnificence—imperial elephants swaying by with their mahouts (elephant drivers), a royal army of eunuchs, court ladies carried in palanquins, and other vestiges of Shah Jahan's pomp. At its peak, the fort housed about 3,000 people. After the Indian Mutiny of 1857, the British moved into the fort, built barracks, and ended the grand Mughal era; eventually the Yamuna River changed course, so the view from the eastern ramparts is now a busy road. Still, if you use your imagination, a visit to the Red Fort gives an excellent idea of what a fantastic city Shahjahanabad was.

The view of the main entrance, called **Lahore Gate,** flanked with towers facing Chandni Chowk, is unfortunately blocked by a barbican (gatehouse), which the paranoid Aurangzeb added for his personal security—to the dismay of Shah Jahan, his father. From his prison, where he was held captive by his power-hungry son, Shah Jahan wrote, "You have made a bride of the palace and thrown a veil over her face."

Once you pass through Lahore Gate, continue down the **Chhatta Chowk** (Vaulted Arcade), originally the shopping district for the royal harem and now a bazaar selling rather less regal goods. From the end of the arcade you'll see the **Naubat Khana** (Welcome Room), a red-sandstone gateway where music was played five times daily. Beyond this point, everyone but the emperor and princes had to proceed on foot. Upstairs, literally inside the gateway, is the Indian War Memorial Museum (open Tuesday–Sunday 10–5; no extra charge), with arms and military regalia from several periods.

An expansive lawn leads to the great **Diwan-i-Am** (Hall of Public Audience)—you have now entered the Delhi of Shah Jahan. Raised on a platform and open on three sides, the hall is studded with some of the most emblematic arches in the Mughal world. In the center is Shah Jahan's royal throne, once surrounded by decorative panels that sparkled with inlaid gems. (It was stolen by British soldiers after the Indian Mutiny, but some of the panels were restored 50 years later by Lord Curzon.) Watched by throngs of people from the courtyard below, the emperor heard the pleas of his subjects; the rest of the hall was reserved for rajas and foreign envoys, all standing with "their eyes bent downward and their hands crossed." High above them, wrote the 17th-century French traveler François Bernier, under a pearl-fringed canopy resting on golden shafts, "glittered the dazzling figure of the Grand Mughal, a figure to strike terror, for a frown meant death."

Behind the Diwan-i-Am, a row of palaces overlooks the now-distant river. To the extreme right is the Mumtaz Mahal, now the **Red Fort Museum** (open Tuesday–Sunday 10–5; no extra charge), with numerous paintings and relics from the Mughal period, some in better lighting than others.

Heading back north, you'll come next to the **Rang Mahal** (Painted Palace), once richly decorated with a mirrored ceiling that was dismantled to pay the bills when the treasury ran low. Home of the royal ladies, the Rang Mahal contains a cooling water channel—called the Canal of Paradise—that runs from the marble basin in the center of the floor to the rest of the palace and to several of the others. You can't enter this or any of the palaces farther ahead, so you must peer creatively from the side.

The emperor's private **Khas Mahal** has three sections: the sitting room, the "dream chamber" (for sleeping), and the prayer chamber, all with lavishly carved walls and painted ceilings still intact. The lovely marble screen is carved with the Scale of Justice—two swords and a scale that symbolize punishment and justice. From the attached octagonal tower the emperor Muthamman Burj would appear before his subjects each morning or watch elephant fights in the nearby fields.

The **Diwan-i-Khas** (Hall of Private Audience) was the most exclusive pavilion of all. Here Shah Jahan would sit on his Peacock Throne, made of solid gold and inlaid with hundreds of precious and semiprecious stones. (When Nadir Shah sacked Delhi in 1739, he hauled the famous throne back to Persia. It was destroyed a few years later after Nadir Shah's assassination.) A Persian couplet written in gold above a corner arch sums up Shah Jahan's sentiments about his city: "If there be a paradise on Earth—It is this! It is this! It is this!"

The **Royal Hammam** was a luxurious three-chamber Mughal bath with inlaid-marble floors. The fountain in the center supposedly had rose-scented water. Sometimes called a Turkish bath, the hammam is still used in many Muslim cultures. Peek through the windows for a look.

Next door to the hammam is the **Moti Masjid** (Pearl Mosque), designed by Aurangzeb for his personal use and that of his harem. The building is now closed, but the prayer hall is inlaid with *musalla* (prayer rugs) outlined in black marble. Though the mosque has the purity of white marble, some critics say its excessively ornate style reflects the decadence that set in late in Shah Jahan's reign.

Beyond the mosque is a typical Mughal *charbagh,* or four-section garden. Stroll through this quieter part of the fort to see some small pleasure palaces including the Zafar Mahal, decked out with carved sandstone *jalis* (screens) and once surrounded by water.

There has been a sound-and-light show at the venue in both Hindi and English with an additional cost of Rs. 80; however, at the time of this writing it was suspended for upgrading. ⊠ *Netaji Subhash Marg, eastern end of Chandni Chowk, Old Delhi* ⊠ *Rs. 500* ⊗ *Closed Mon.* Ⓜ *Chandni Chowk.*

National Gandhi Museum

MUSEUM | Run by a private foundation, this museum across Raj Ghat houses a great many photographs, a display of spinning wheels with some information on Gandhi's khadi (homespun cotton) crusade, and some of the Mahatma's personal effects, including the blood-stained dhoti he was wearing at the time of his murder. The tiny art gallery has a poignant wooden sculpture, made by a South African, of Gandhi in a pose suggesting Jesus's Crucifixion. A film on Gandhi's life is shown on weekends at 4. ⊠ *Rajghat, Ring Rd., Old Delhi* ☎ *11/2331–0168* ⊕ *www.gandhimuseum. org* ⊠ *Free* ⊗ *Closed Mon.*

4

Delhi OLD DELHI AND NEARBY

The Raj Ghat memorial to Mahatma Gandhi

Raj Ghat

MEMORIAL | After Mahatma Gandhi was shot and killed by a Hindu fanatic on January 30, 1948, his body was cremated on the banks of the Yamuna River; the site is now a national shrine called Raj Ghat, where tourists and pilgrims stream across the peaceful lawn to pay their respects to the saintlike "Father of the Nation." At the center of a large courtyard is a raised slab of black marble adorned with flowers and inscribed with Gandhi's final words, "Hai Ram!" (Oh, God!). An eternal flame burns at its head. The sandstone walls enclosing the shrine are inscribed with passages written by Gandhi, translated into several tongues including Tamil, Malayalam, Nepali, Urdu, Spanish, Arabic, and Chinese. Near Raj Ghat are the cremation sites of other leaders, including two other assassinated heads of state, Indira Gandhi and her son Rajiv (no relation to Mohandas). ⊠ *Raj Ghat, near Red Fort, Old Delhi* 🎫 *Free.*

Sis Ganj Sahib Gurdwara

RELIGIOUS SITE | Old Delhi's most famous Sikh shrine is a restful place to see one of North India's emblematic faiths in practice. Built at various times between 1784 (when the Sikhs conquered Delhi) and the 20th century, it marks the site where the Mughal emperor Aurangzeb beheaded Guru Teg Bahadur in 1675, when the guru refused to convert to Islam. It's a gory story, but before his body could be quartered and displayed to the public as an example, it was stolen by disciples. He was cremated by his son, Guru Gobind Singh, the 10th and last great Sikh guru. As in any gurdwara (Sikh temple), sections of the *Guru Granth Sahib* scripture are chanted continuously; depending on the season, you might also find decorations of tinsel, colored foil, and blinking lights. Leave your shoes at the entrance, and cover your head before entering. If you don't have a head covering, you can don one of the scarves that are provided for free. If you have any questions about Sikhism or the shrine after your visit, stop into the friendly information office to the left of the entrance to hear legends and symbols unfold. ✉ *Chandni Chowk, Old Delhi* 🎫 *Free* Ⓜ *Chandni Chowk.*

Svetamber Jain Temple

RELIGIOUS SITE | Properly called the Indraprastha Tirth Sumatinatha Jain Svetamber Temple, this splendid house of worship is painted head to toe with finely rendered murals and decorations covering the walls, arches, and ceilings. Reflecting the building's surroundings, some of the artwork shows Mughal influence. Look inside the silver doors of the shrine to Sumatinatha—the fifth of Jainism's 24 *Tirthankaras* (perfect souls)—to see some incredible original painting finished with gold leaf.

As interesting as the temple itself is the street it's located on. It's called Naughara Gali, which directly translates into Nine Houses Street (they date back to the late 18th century). Owned mainly by jewelers, this gated cul-de-sac somehow shuts out all the noise and chaos of the Old City. It's peaceful and charming and each of the houses is brightly painted in shades of pink and blue with floral motifs drawn intricately over the doorways. *It is closed in the afternoons, though if you knock, you may be allowed entrance.* ✉ *Naughara Gali, Kinari Bazaar, Old Delhi* ☎ *11/2327–0489.*

🍴 Restaurants

★ Chor Bizarre

$ | **NORTH INDIAN** | Delhi's best-known Kashmiri restaurant is also one of its most beautiful, an art deco enclave with a tile floor, a spiral staircase leading nowhere, and antique furniture and mirrors from various *chor* ("thieves'") bazaars. Kashmiri food, which is milder than many Indian regional cuisines, is exemplified by mutton *yakhni* (in a sauce of yogurt, cardamom, and aniseed) and mutton *mirchi korma* (in cardamom and clove gravy). **Known for:** old-world charm;

fragrant Kashmiri kahwa tea; pocket-friendly cocktails. Ⓢ *Average main: Rs. 495* ✉ *Hotel Broadway, 4/15A Asaf Ali Rd., just outside Old Delhi, near Delhi Gate, Old Delhi* ☎ *11/4366–3600* ⊕ *www. chorbizarre.com.*

Karim's

$ | **NORTH INDIAN** | This is an Old Delhi institution dating to 1913, and here, mutton (which generally means goat in India) is king, especially in thick, rich gravies, accompanied by tandoor breads. The no-frills decor belies its atmospheric charm, highlighted by the large cauldrons of meaty concoctions and smoking kebabs on spits that are on display in an open kitchen. **Known for:** mutton qorma; typical Old Delhi vibe; deft, fuss-free service. Ⓢ *Average main: Rs. 385* ✉ *Gali Kababian, near Jama Masjid, Old Delhi* ☎ *11/2326–9880, 11/2326–4981* 🚫 *No credit cards* 🕐 *Closed daylight hrs during Ramadan* Ⓜ *Chawri Bazaar.*

★ Lala Duli Chand Naresh Gupta

$ | **INDIAN** | A Delhi summer isn't complete without one of the famous kulfis— the frozen milk–based treats similar to ice cream made here. What makes this spot unique is that you'll get your kulfi served in the fruit that it's flavored with: order apple, for instance, and you'll get an apple (it looks like a frozen candy apple) that splits open to reveal the delicious kulfi inside. **Known for:** exotic fruit flavors; people-watching; matka (earthen pot) kulfi. Ⓢ *Average main: Rs. 50* ✉ *Bazaar Sita Ram, 934 Kucha Pati Ram, Old Delhi* ☎ *11/2323–7085* 🚫 *No credit cards* Ⓜ *Chawri Bazaar.*

🏨 Hotels

Maidens

$$ | **HOTEL** | Run by the Oberoi group, this is one of the city's oldest hotels, occupying a classic Raj building, with high-arched windows, deep verandas, grand old trees, pleasant lawns, and a quirky interior with huge rooms and bathrooms.

Pros: coffee shop has a nice patio and an English feel, especially when British tour groups are in residence; renovations have brightened up the rooms; add on free breakfast for a slightly higher room rate. **Cons:** even with the metro, you are removed from the rest of the city; food and beverage options are limited; a long drive from the airport. $ *Rooms from: Rs. 6500* ✉ *7 Sham Nath Marg, Civil Lines* ☎ *11/2388–5700* 🌐 *www.maidenshotel.com* 🛏 *54 rooms* 🍴 *No meals* [M] *Civil Lines.*

Shopping

Multan Enamel Mart
JEWELRY/ACCESSORIES | Along with other stores in the area, Multan Enamel Mart sells old and new silver jewelry and curios by weight. ✉ *No. 246–247 Dariba Kalan, Old Delhi* ☎ *11/2324–2725* [M] *Chandni Chowk.*

Ram Chandra Krishan Chandra
CLOTHING | This venerable shop has several rooms full of traditional silks. ✉ *976–978 Chandni Chowk, Gali Parathe Wali, Old Delhi* [M] *Chandni Chowk.*

Shivam Zari Palace
CRAFTS | In Old Delhi, Shivam Zari Palace and its neighbors sell inexpensive Hindu wedding paraphernalia such as turbans, fabric-covered boxes, *torans* (auspicious door hangings), tiny brass gods, and shiny bric-a-brac. ✉ *2178 Kinari Bazaar, Old Delhi* ☎ *11/2327–7617* [M] *Chandni Chowk.*

Singh Copper & Brass Palace
CRAFTS | Several dusty floors here are filled with brass, copper, and wood artifacts. ✉ *1167 Chah Rahat Gali, near Jama Masjid, Old Delhi* ☎ *11/2326–6717* [M] *Chandni Chowk.*

South Delhi

South Delhi, the older suburbs and colonies of the new city, has monuments even older than those in Old Delhi, including the Qutub Minar, Kauz Khas, and numerous pre-Mughal tombs, some of which lie abandoned in the midst of contemporary houses and apartments.

Along with a mix of government-built apartments, posh mansions and "farm-houses" of the elite, and refugee colonies from the 1950s, South Delhi also has the more recent addition of malls, particularly in Saket and Vasant Kunj. There is also plenty of soul and tradition. Getting in some quiet meditation at the Lotus Temple is a must. The incredible urbanized villages of Hauz Khas and Shahpur Jat may turn up anything from vintage Bollywood posters to beautifully beaded slippers. Visit Nizamuddin East for a Sufi music performance that may transport you to a spiritual plane. Most destinations in South Delhi are now accessible by the Delhi metro, including its wealth of restaurant and bars, many of which are packed on weekends.

Sights

Baha'i House of Worship (The Lotus Temple)
RELIGIOUS SITE | The lotus flower is a symbol of purity and spirituality throughout India, and Delhi's Baha'i Temple celebrates this in a unique architectural way. Designed by Fariborz Sahba, an Iranian-born Canadian architect, and completed in 1986, the building incorporates the number nine—the highest digit and, in the Baha'i faith, a symbol of unity. The sleek structure has two layers: nine white marble-covered petals that point to heaven, and nine petals that conceal the portals. From a short distance it looks like a fantastic work of origami. The nine pools outside signify the green leaves of the lotus and cool the starkly elegant, usually silent marble interior. The interior

The gardens leading up to the Lotus Temple, also known as the Baha'i House of Worship

conforms to that of all Baha'i houses of worship: there are no religious icons, just copies of the Holy Scriptures and wooden pews. The road to the temple passes through a colorful temple bazaar connected to the nearby Kalkaji Mandir. ✉ *Lotus Temple Rd., Bahapur, Kalkaji, South Delhi* ☎ *11/2644–4029* ⊕ *www. bahaihouseofworship.in* ✉ *Free* ⊙ *Closed Mon.* Ⓜ *Kalkaji Mandir.*

Chhattarpur Temples

RELIGIOUS SITE | If you're on your way south to Agra or Jaipur, drive a few miles beyond the Qutub Minar on Mehrauli Road and check out this massive Hindu temple complex. It's a mishmash of styles, but the unifying factor—from the huge dome over the Shiva lingam to the 92-foot statue of the monkey god Hanuman—is its flashy and elaborate architecture, done in so-called Punjabi Baroque. It's quite a sight to take in: these huge temples looming on either side of the road. You can go inside even if you're not Hindu; just enter through the sanctum with the devotees and be

respectful and quiet while they show their respect to the idols. Many gods and goddesses are represented, but the inner sanctum is dedicated to Adhya Ma Kat- yan, a mother goddess. Hymns are sung all night during full moons. Make sure you're dressed modestly, and be ready to take off your shoes. ✉ *Chhattarpur Rd., Chhattarpur, South Delhi* ☎ *11/2680–2925* ⊕ *www.chhattarpurmandir.org* ✉ *Free* Ⓜ *Chhattarpur.*

Hauz Khas Village

NEIGHBORHOOD | The road south to the urban village of Hauz Khas is lined on both sides by ancient stone monuments, and the entire village is dotted with domed structures—the tombs of minor Muslim royalty from the 14th to the 16th centuries. At the end of the road is the tomb of Firoz Shah Tughlaq, who ruled Delhi in the 14th century. Hauz Khas means "Royal Tank," referring to the artificial lake visible from Firoz Shah's pillared tomb. The tank was actually built a century earlier by Allauddin Khilji as a water source for his nearby fort, then

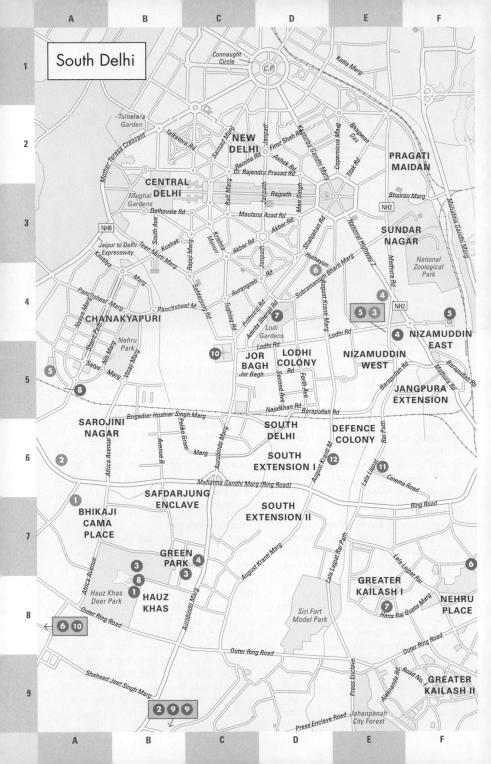

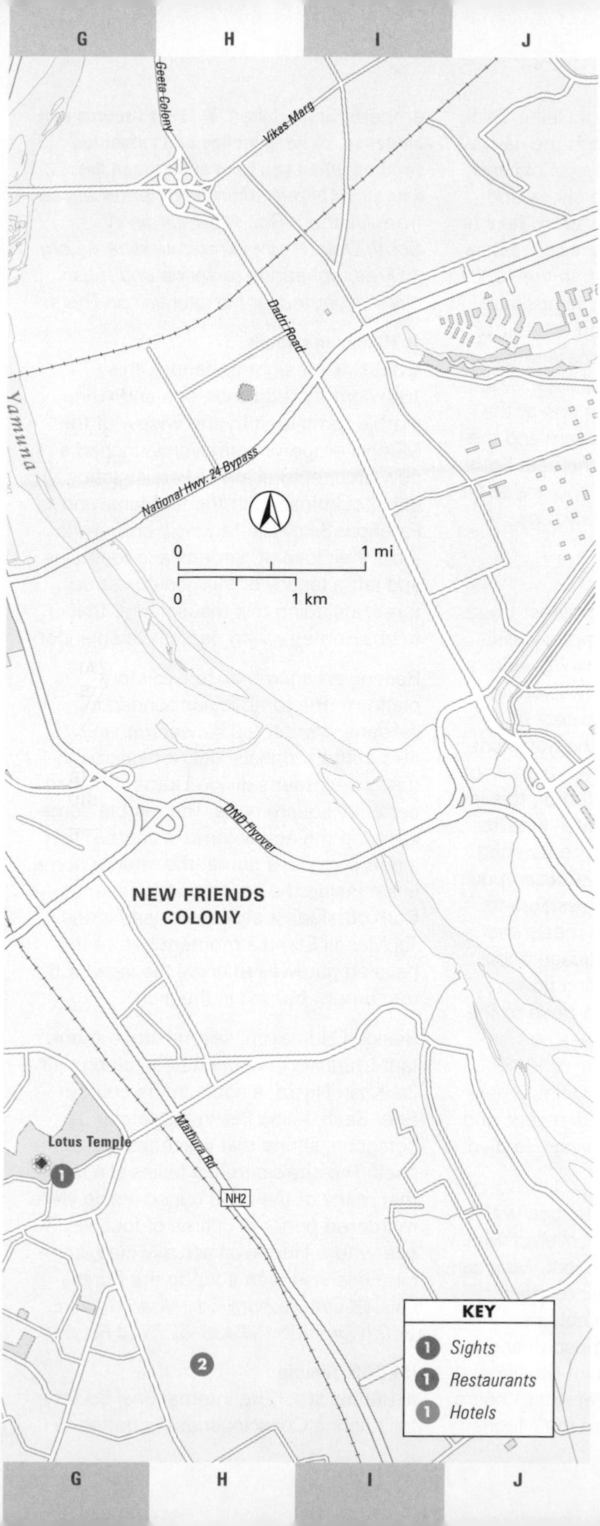

Sights ▼

1 Baha'i House of Worship
  (The Lotus Temple) **G8**
2 Chhattarpur Temples **B9**
3 Hauz Khas Village **B7**
4 Hazrat Nizamuddin
  Dargah **E4**
5 Humayun's Tomb **F4**
6 ISKCON Temple **F7**
7 Lodhi Gardens **D4**
8 National Rail
  Museum **A5**
9 Qutub Minar **B9**
10 Safdarjung's Tomb **C5**

Restaurants ▼

1 Coast Cafe **B8**
2 Diva Italian **H9**
3 Evergreen Sweet House **C8**
4 Gung the Palace **C7**
5 Indian Accent **E4**
6 Kainoosh **A8**
7 Moti Mahal Deluxe **E8**
8 Naivedyam **B8**
9 Olive Bar & Kitchen **B9**
10 Punjabi By Nature **A8**
11 Sagar Ratna **E6**
12 Swagath **E6**

Hotels ▼

1 Hyatt Regency **A7**
2 ITC Maurya **A6**
3 Lodhi Hotel **E4**
4 The Oberoi **E4**
5 Taj Palace **A5**
6 Vivanta by Taj
  Ambassador Hotel **D4**

4

Delhi SOUTH DELHI

NEW FRIENDS
COLONY

Lotus Temple

0 —— 1 mi
0 —— 1 km

KEY

① Sights
① Restaurants
① Hotels

called Siri (the second city of Delhi). Back in the village, wander through the narrow lanes to experience a medley of old and new structures—expensive shops and art galleries in a medieval warren. **Take in the lake view with sundowners at a rooftop bar such as Hauz Khas Social.** In the 1980s Hauz Khas was designated an upscale tourist destination, but of late it's better known as a tightly packed maze of bars, designer boutiques, and start-ups. After exploring, stop for a meal at one of the village's restaurants: Naivedyam and the Coast Café serve some of the best South Indian food this side of the country. ⊠ *Off Aurobindo Marg, Hauz Khas Village, South Delhi* Ⓜ *Green Park.*

Hazrat Nizamuddin Dargah

MEMORIAL | One of Delhi's greatest treats is hearing devout Sufis sing *qawwalis,* ecstatic devotional Muslim songs with a decidedly toe-tapping quality. Evenings from around 7:45 to 8:30, except on Thursday, the followers of the Sufi saint Hazrat Nizamuddin Aulia often gather to sing in front of his *dargah* (tomb); this is one of the best places to catch a performance. To get here, follow the twisting lanes in the bazaar section of Nizamuddin West—you'll pass open-air restaurants serving simple meat-based meals and tiny shops selling Urdu-language books. When you see vendors selling flowers and garlands, you're getting close to the dargah. Nizamuddin, who was born in Bukhara (now in Uzbekistan) in 1238, later fled with his family to Delhi, where he became an important Sufi mystic and attracted a dedicated following. He died in 1325.

The tomb, built in 1562, is topped with an onion-shaped dome and is covered with intricate painting and inlay work. Men can enter the shrine to pay their respects; women must peer in from outside. The tomb is flanked by a mosque and the graves of other important Muslims, including the great Sufi poet Amir Khusro and Jahanara, a daughter of the Mughal

emperor Shah Jahan. ■**TIP➔ Crowds can be dense, so keep money and valuables secured when you're in and around the dargah.** ⊠ *Nizamuddin Basti, enter bazaar from Mathura Rd., Nizamuddin W, South Delhi* ⊕ *www.nizamuddinaulia.org* ⊠ *Free, donations to shrine and musicians accepted* ☞ *No qawwali on Thurs.*

★ Humayun's Tomb

MEMORIAL | A sight to behold, this 16th-century red sandstone and white marble tomb built by the widow of the Mughal emperor Humayun launched a new architectural era of Persian influence, culminating in the Taj Mahal and Fatehpur Sikri. The Mughals brought to India their love of gardens and fountains and left a legacy of harmonious structures, including this mausoleum, that fuse symmetry with decorative splendor.

Resting on an immense two-story platform, the tomb is surrounded by gardens intersected by water channels in the Mughals' beloved charbagh design—gardens divided into four (*char*) perfectly square parts. The marble dome covering the actual tomb is another first: a dome within a dome (the interior dome is set inside the soaring dome seen from outside), a style later used in the Taj Mahal. Stand a moment before the beveled gateway to enjoy the view of the monument framed in the arch.

Besides Humayun, several other important Mughals are buried here, along with Isa Khan Niyazi, a noble in the court of Sher Shah—who lies in the fetching octagonal shrine that precedes the tomb itself. The site's serenity belies the fact that many of the dead buried inside were murdered princes, victims of foul play. To see where Humayun actually died, combine this visit with a trip to the Purana Qila. ⊠ *Off Mathura Rd., Nizamuddin E, South Delhi* ☎ *11/2435–5275* ⊠ *Rs. 500.*

ISKCON Temple

RELIGIOUS SITE | The International Society for Krishna Consciousness is better

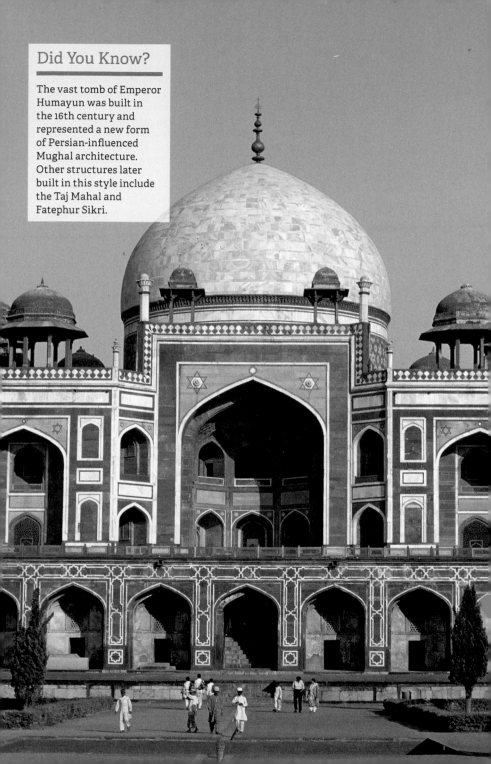

known as the Hare Krishna sect, and despite the 1960s association they are very much alive and kicking. In the 1990s ISKCON erected enormous, gleaming Krishna temples in several Indian cities, and these offer a unique glimpse into the remaining pockets of international Hinduism, with shaven-headed foreigners in saffron robes mingling with Indian colleagues, devotees, and tourists. Built impressively on a rock outcropping near a residential market, Delhi's temple is an amalgam of architectural styles: Mughal, Gupta, and the flashy Delhi style jokingly called Punjabi Baroque. The sanctum contains three idols—Balram Krishna, Radha-Krishna, and Laksman (along with Rama and Sita)—each representing a different incarnation of Lord Krishna. The art gallery behind the idols must be viewed in a clockwise direction, as this *parikrama* (revolution) is the only appropriate way to move around the gods. At the Vedic Museum art displays and sound-and-light shows (even a robotics display) enact the *Bhagavad Gita* scriptures and the ancient epic, the *Mahabharata. ISKCON's temples are by far the cleanest in India, and very welcoming to visitors.* ⊠ *Sant Nagar Main Rd., east of Kailash, South Delhi* ☎ *11/2623–5133* ⊕ *www.iskcondelhi.com* ⊠ *Free* Ⓜ *Nehru Place.*

★ **Lodhi Gardens**

GARDEN | After the Mughal warrior Timur (aka Tamerlane) ransacked Delhi at the end of the 14th century, he ordered the massacre of the entire population as retribution for the murder of his soldiers. As if in unconscious response to this horrific act, the subsequent Lodhi and Sayyid dynasties built no city, only a few mosques and some mausoleums and tombs, the latter of which stand in what is now a delightful urban park. Winding walks cut through landscaped lawns with trees and flowers, past schoolboys playing cricket, politicians taking in some air, friends and lovers relaxing in the greenery, and parrots squawking.

Lodi–The Garden Restaurant is a good place to get a meal after an evening walk. Near the southern entrance on Lodhi Road is the dignified mausoleum of Mohammed Shah, third ruler of the Sayyid dynasty, and some members of his family. This octagon, with a central chamber surrounded by verandas carved with arches, is a good example of the architecture of this period. Near the road is the open-air National Bonsai Park, with some nice specimens of the trees. The smaller, equally lovely octagonal tomb of Sikandar Lodhi in the park's northwestern corner, has an unusual double dome. ⊠ *Lodhi Rd., southeast of Khan Market, South Delhi* Ⓜ *Jor Bagh.*

National Rail Museum

MUSEUM | FAMILY | This large, mostly outdoor museum is a glimpse into the largest railroad system in the world. The 10-acre grounds are home to 75 authentic locomotives, bogies (railway cars), royal saloon cars, and even a working roundabout (a device that turns rail cars). Parked behind glass is the *Fairy Queen*; built in 1855, it's the oldest running steam engine in the world. Inside the museum are displays that discuss the history of India's rail system. The museum is good not only for train buffs but also children, who love riding the tiny train that circles the grounds. ⊠ *Nyaya Marg, off Shanti Path, Chanakyapuri, South Delhi* ☎ *11/2688–1826, 11/2688–0939* ⊕ *www.nrmindia.com* ⊠ *Weekdays Rs. 50, weekends Rs. 100* ⊘ *Closed Mon.*

Qutub Minar

RELIGIOUS SITE | Named for the Muslim sultan Qutab-ud-din Aibak, this striking tower is 238 feet high, with 376 steps, and the tallest stone tower in India. Qutub-ud-din Aibak began construction in 1193; his son-in-law and successor, Iltutmish, added three more stories, while Firoz Shah Tughlak added the fifth. The result is a handsome sandstone example of Indo-Islamic architecture,

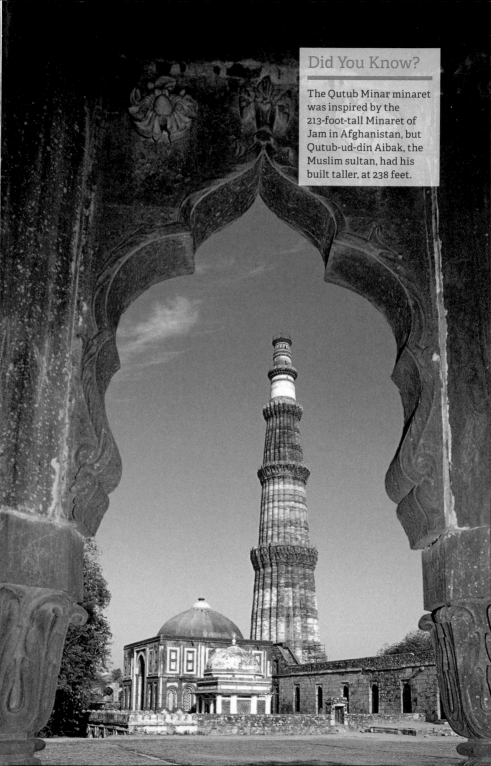

with terra-cotta frills and balconies. At its foot lies the **Quwwat-ul-Islam Masjid,** the first mosque in India. The Muslims erected the mosque in the 12th century after they defeated the Hindu Chauhan dynasty—they built it on the site of a Hindu temple and used pillars and other materials from 27 demolished Hindu and Jain shrines. (Which explains why you see Hindu and Jain sculptures in the mosque.) The mosque is also famous for a 24-foot-high, 5th-century iron pillar, inscribed with six lines of Sanskrit. According to legend, if you stand with your back to the pillar and can reach around and touch your fingers, any wish you make will come true. (Unfortunately, it's now fenced off.) ✉ *Aurobindo Marg, near Mehrauli, South Delhi* 🎫 *Rs. 500* [M] *Qutub Minar.*

Safdarjang's Tomb
MEMORIAL | Delhi's last great garden tomb, built in 1754 for the prime minister of the emperor Mohammad Shah, is pleasantly located in the center of town. With its marble oversize dome and minarets, it can't compete with Humayun's resting place, but the finials and other details have a distinctly Mughul fineness, and the charbagh (four-section garden, which is a typical Mughal style) is a peaceful place to listen to the birds chirp. The site would be lovelier if water still ran through the four large channels in the gardens, but you have to imagine that part to complete the 18th-century scene. ✉ *Aurobindo Marg at Lodhi Rd., Jor Bagh, South Delhi* 🎫 *Rs. 200* [M] *Jor Bagh.*

🍴 Restaurants

Coast Cafe
$$ | **SOUTH INDIAN** | This is one of the few places in Delhi where you can sample the cuisine of India's west coast, famous for its lush and bold flavors, heavy on coconut-milk curries. Well-lit, spacious, and designed for a laid-back evening, with wicker chairs, winding staircase, arches, balconies, and terrace windows, the leafy outdoor space here is particularly charming on winter afternoons. **Known for:** sweet and spicy prawn moilee; vegetables flavored with kokum, a sour fruit native to the west coast; stylish vibe. [$] *Average main: Rs. 580* ✉ *Above OGAAN, H2 Hauz Khas Village, South Delhi* ☎ *11/4160–1717.*

★ Diva Italian
$$ | **ITALIAN** | Count on this award-winning, popular joint for delicious pizza and pasta—most of Delhi does—but if you're looking for something more substantial, mains like pan-seared lamb chops are also excellent, so make sure to ask about the daily specials. With classy interiors and attentive service, the setting is suited to a wine-soaked lunch or cozy dinner for two. **Known for:** celebrity chef Ritu Dalmia; extensive wine list; decadent desserts. [$] *Average main: Rs. 930* ✉ *M–8A M Block Market, Greater Kailash 2, South Delhi* ☎ *11/4163–7858* 🌐 *www.divarestaurants.com.*

Evergreen Sweet House
$ | **INDIAN** | A large and fuss-free air-conditioned space with quick service, this is a well-known stop in south Delhi for street food like chole bhatura (spicy chickpeas and puffy fried bread) and vegetarian thalis (combination platters). Plastic tables are always crammed with office goers, expats, tourists, and students looking for a tasty and pocket-friendly meal. **Known for:** idli-vada and South Indian food; gulab jamun sweets; people-watching. [$] *Average main: Rs. 160* ✉ *Green Park Market, S–29 and 30, South Delhi* ☎ *11/2651–4646* 🌐 *www.evergreensweethouse.com* [M] *Green Park.*

Gung the Palace
$$$ | **KOREAN** | Set over three floors and a basement, the main gathering place for New Delhi's large population of Korean expats is luxuriously furnished with a combination of sunken tables and little booths, though there are several standalone tables for those uncomfortable or unable to use traditional Korean seating.

This remains one of the city's few places to sample a range of Korean grills and noodle soups. **Known for:** Korean soju; barbecued pork ribs; buzzing vibe. [$] *Average main: Rs. 1000* ✉ *D 1–B, Green Park, South Delhi* ☎ *11/4608–2663.*

Kainoosh

$$ | **MODERN INDIAN** | Low-hanging lamps and delicate latticed screens set the refined mood at this upscale Indian restaurant where the extensive menu excels in its Mughlai offerings. All the lamb options are excellent, as is the okra and anything with lentils (dal). **Known for:** spicy Rajasthani-style lal maas; classic Indian drinks like aam panna; raan (leg of lamb). [$] *Average main: Rs. 775* ✉ *DLF Promenade Mall, Nelson Mandela Marg, ground fl., Vasant Kunj, South Delhi* ☎ *95607–15533mobile.*

Moti Mahal Delux

$$ | **NORTH INDIAN** | **FAMILY** | An easily accessible South Delhi outpost of the iconic Old Delhi Moti Mahal, this old-fashioned family restaurant serves Punjabi and North Indian comfort food in an old-school dining room–style setting. Loyal customers continue to flock here for the tandoori kebabs and prompt service. **Known for:** butter chicken; dal makhani; old-world vibe. [$] *Average main: Rs. 735* ✉ *M–30 Greater Kailash I, South Delhi* ☎ *11/2924–0480* 🌐 *www.motimahal.in* ⊗ *Closed Tues.*

Naivedyam

$ | **SOUTH INDIAN** | **FAMILY** | This dark, soothing restaurant, with South Indian decor and gold-embossed paintings designed by artisans from the Tamil Nadu town of Thanjavur, specialzes in Udupi food, a vegetarian cuisine from a town near Mangalore. South Indian staples like *uthappams* and *idlis* are served in traditional style, on a banana leaf.**Known for:** rava masala dosa; spicy rasam pepper soup; mysore pak sweets. [$] *Average main: Rs. 160* ✉ *1 Hauz Khas Village, South Delhi* ☎ *11/2696–0426* 🌐 *www.naivedyamrestaurants.in.*

Olive Bar & Kitchen

$$$$ | **MEDITERRANEAN** | In the shadow of the Qutub Minar, this sprawling Mediterranean restaurant with elegant white-on-white decor is reminiscent of Santorini. Delhi's most fashionable congregate here for a sumptuous Sunday brunch, and it's one of the best spots for French cheese platters, hearty Italian soups, and hand-rolled pastas. **Known for:** sangrias and cocktails; stylish vibe; braised lamb chops. [$] *Average main: Rs. 1595* ✉ *Haveli 6, One Style Mile, Kalkadass Marg, near Qutub Minar, Mehrauli, South Delhi* ☎ *11/2957–4444* 🌐 *www.olivebarandkitchen.com.*

Punjabi by Nature

$$ | **NORTH INDIAN** | In a tony shopping mall, with dimly lit interiors, this popular restaurant draws large groups with its innovative twists on hearty Punjabi classics. For a wide sampling, order a range of chicken, mutton, fish, and vegetarian small plates. **Known for:** innovative Indian-flavored cocktails; golguppa shots; butter chicken. [$] *Average main: Rs. 595* ✉ *Ambience Mall, T 305, 3rd fl., Nelson Mandela Rd., Vasant Kunj, South Delhi* ☎ *80102–56256 mobile* 🌐 *www.punjabibynature.in.*

Sagar Ratna

$ | **SOUTH INDIAN** | This no-frills vegetarian family joint bustles nonstop, serving up South Indian dishes like crispy *dosas* (rice-batter crepes) and fluffy idli (rice cakes) with fresh coconut chutney and hot *sambar* (lentil soup). A long-standing favorite since the '80s, this neighborhood market delivers quick service and attracts a steady stream of locals looking for a pocket-friendly bite.**Known for:** classic masala dosa; filter coffee; South Indian thali meal. [$] *Average main: Rs. 180* ✉ *18 Defence Colony Market, South Delhi* ☎ *11/2433–3110* 🌐 *www.sagarratna.in* [M] *Lajpat Nagar.*

Swagath

$$ | **SOUTH INDIAN** | **FAMILY** | Delhi's original Mangalorean restaurant—specializing

in seafood from the western coast between Goa and Kerala—is outstanding for seafood served in prim, softly lit dining rooms with good service. Choose your sauce, then decide between fish, prawns, or crab, and mop up your food with *appam* or *neer dosa,* soft South Indian rice breads. **Known for:** fish in coconut-flavored gassi gravy; spicy Chettinad cuisine; prompt, warm service. $ *Average main: Rs. 655* ⊠ *14 Defence Colony Market, South Delhi* ☎ *11/2433–0930* ⊕ *www.swagath.in* Ⓜ *Lajpat Nagar.*

Hotels

Hyatt Regency
$$$ | HOTEL | For its size and range of amenities, the Hyatt has a surprisingly homey feel. **Pros:** the shopping arcade is easily the best in Delhi, with dozens of shops selling jewelry, handicrafts, Kashmiri carpets and more; the pool may take top honors, too; its terrific China Kitchen restaurant. **Cons:** service can be impersonal; some of the rooms can feel a bit old; pool is on the small side. $ *Rooms from: Rs. 10250* ⊠ *Ring Rd., Bhikaji Cama Pl., South Delhi* ☎ *11/2679–1234* ⊕ *www.hyatt.com* ⟿ *507 rooms* ᵀ�O∣ *No meals.*

★ ITC Maurya
$$$$ | HOTEL | A favorite with executives and dignitaries, the Maurya works hard to style itself as the swankiest hotel in Delhi, and the whole place buzzes with importance. **Pros:** knockout restaurants draw as many locals as travelers, especially the famous Bukhara and Dum Pukht; pool and gym are best-in-class; business services get top marks. **Cons:** Wi-Fi is chargeable; far from most major sites; chattering tour groups can dominate the atmosphere. $ *Rooms from: Rs. 15000* ⊠ *Sardar Patel Marg, Diplomatic Enclave, Chanakyapuri, South Delhi* ☎ *11/2611–2233* ⊕ *www.itchotels.in* ⟿ *437 rooms* ᵀO∣ *Free Breakfast.*

★ The Oberoi
$$$$ | HOTEL | After a nearly two-year, multimillion-dollar refurbishment, the beloved hotel reopened in 2018 in a fresh new avatar though still retaining much of its classic Indian charm; highlights of the change include more spacious rooms and technological upgrades. **Pros:** fabulous views from the rooftop bar; top-notch service; air purifiers throughout, for clean air in a polluted city. **Cons:** extremely expensive; service at the restaurants can be quite slow; spa can be quite busy, book in advance. $ *Rooms from: Rs. 14500* ⊠ *Dr. Zakir Hussain Rd., next to Delhi Golf Club, South Delhi* ☎ *11/2436–3030* ⊕ *www.oberoihotels.com* ⟿ *220 rooms* ᵀO∣ *No meals.*

★ Taj Palace
$$$$ | HOTEL | Facilities are top-notch in this giant, boomerang-shape hotel with first-rate business services and good leisure amenities. **Pros:** business services are best-in-class; the pool-view Blue Bar is among the city's finest spots for a drink; luxurious Jiva spa on-site. **Cons:** far from some tourist sites; in high season you'll battle package-tour crowds; dynamic pricing means high season can be expensive. $ *Rooms from: Rs. 14680* ⊠ *2, Sardar Patel Marg, Diplomatic Enclave, Chanakyapuri, South Delhi* ☎ *11/2611–0202* ⊕ *www.tajhotels.com* ⟿ *403 rooms* ᵀO∣ *Free Breakfast* Ⓜ *Dhaula Kuan.*

Vivanta by Taj Ambassador Hotel
$$$$ | HOTEL | In an exclusive 1930s neighborhood dripping with late-Raj charm, this quiet Taj Group hotel's service is heartwarmingly friendly. **Pros:** cheery Yellow Brick Road is a popular 24-hour restaurant; next door to Khan Market and close to Lodhi Garden; service is warm and friendly. **Cons:** not as up-to-date as other, similarly priced properties; lacks the regal splendor of signature Taj properties; pool under renovation (at the time of writing). $ *Rooms from: Rs. 16275* ⊠ *Subramaniam Bharti Marg, near Khan*

Market, Sujan Singh Park, South Delhi ☎ 11/6626–1000 ⊕ www.tajhotels.com ⊷ 88 rooms ⏧ Free Breakfast Ⓜ Khan Market.

Nightlife

BARS AND PUBS
Blue Bar
PIANO BARS/LOUNGES | This sophisticated spot is ideal for a well-made cocktail, either in the small indoors section or alfresco on large couches with pool views. Expect to rub shoulders with international business travelers and the city's most affluent people. ⊠ Taj Hotel Diplomatic Enclave, 2 Sardar Patel Marg, Chanakyapuri, South Delhi ☎ 11/2611–0202 ⊕ tajhotels.com.

Golf Bar
PIANO BARS/LOUNGES | At the dark and publike Golf Bar, you're sure to hear cheesy pop and rock hits from the '80s onward (think wedding reception). Some nights it's just elderly gentlemen sipping whiskey sodas on leather couches, while other nights you may stumble on a party in full swing. ⊠ ITC Maurya Hotel, Sardar Patel Marg, Diplomatic Enclave, Chanakyapuri, South Delhi ☎ 11/2611–2233 ⊕ www.itchotels.in.

Polo Lounge
PIANO BARS/LOUNGES | While very much a hotel bar, this place can be very lively. The wood-panel room has a curved bar, a leather sofa, a library with newspapers, an oddball collection of books, and sports channels playing on TV. It's known for its collection of vintage single malts and live jazz. ⊠ Hyatt Regency, Ring Rd., Bhikaji Cama Pl., South Delhi ☎ 11/6677–1314 ⊕ www.hyatt.com.

MUSIC CLUBS
Hard Rock Café
BARS/PUBS | This venue obviously isn't especially India, but it does sometimes book some interesting bands (call for the weekly performance schedule). If you're homesick for the States, come here for a plate of nachos, washed down with a margarita or two. ⊠ M-110 DLF Place Mall, 1st fl., District Centre, Saket, South Delhi ☎ 11/4715–8888 ⊕ www.hardrock.com/cafes/new-delhi Ⓜ Malviya Nagar.

The Piano Man Jazz Club
PIANO BARS/LOUNGES | With live performances every night and an eclectic roster of local and international musicians, this tiny jazz bar with wood-and-brick interiors draws the capital's creative types. ⊠ B–6, Safdarjung Enclave Market, South Delhi ☎ 11/4131–5181 ⊕ www.thepianoman.in.

WINE BARS
★ Perch Wine & Coffee Bar
WINE BARS—NIGHTLIFE | This sophisticated spot goes from an entrepreneur-populated coffee shop in the day to a chic wine bar in the evening, where expats and Delhi's most fashionable congregate. ⊠ 18A, Basant Lok Market, Vasant Vihar, South Delhi ☎ 83739–76637mobile.

 Performing Arts

Discover DAG
ART GALLERIES—ARTS | A substantial collection of paintings by Old Masters and contemporary artists can be seen here; it often hosts comprehensive historical art exhibitions. ⊠ 11 Hauz Khas Village, South Delhi ☎ 11/4600–5300 ⊕ www.discoverdag.com ⊗ Closed Sun.

Gallery Espace
ART GALLERIES—ARTS | This small but remarkable space features both new and canonical artists, sometimes mixed together in edgy theme shows. ⊠ 16 Community Centre, New Friends Colony, South Delhi ☎ 11/2632–6267 ⊕ www.galleryespace.com.

Habitat World
ART GALLERIES—ARTS | The various exhibition spaces here showcase painting, sculpture, Indian craft, and creativity of every kind. The main Visual Arts Gallery is just inside Gate 2. ⊠ India Habitat Centre,

Classic Chaats

No trip to India is complete without some Indian snack food. The most popular street foods are *papri chaat* (fried wafers piled high with potatoes, chickpeas, yogurt, and chilli powder), *chole bhatura* (also known as chana bhatura—spicy chickpeas with fried, airy *puri* bread), and *golgappas* (fried dough in a hollow golf-ball shape, which you fill with a spicy mixture of potatoes, chickpeas, tamarind, and coriander sauce), *pakoras* (battered and fried vegetables, cheese, or chicken), and the Mumbai delicacy known as *bhel puri* (spicy rice with bits of onion). The best places to nosh on these snacks, other than in the by-lanes of Old Delhi, are in neighborhood markets. Here are a few recommendations in Central and South Delhi.

The **Bengali Sweet House** (*27–37 Bengali Market, near Connaught Pl., Central Delhi Mandi House*) is a classic spot for evening golgappa outings.

At **Bikanervala** (*Rajiv Gandhi Handicraft Bhavan, Baba Kharak Singh Marg, 1st fl., near Connaught Pl., Central Delhi*) you can sample such Gujarati snacks as *khandvi*, which is a delicious panfried snack made from

a seasoned batter of chickpea flour and buttermilk, then cut into rolls and sprinkled with coconut and coriander; and *dhokla*, which is a savory, fluffy, steamed cake made with chickpea flour, mustard seeds, and an inch of sugar and topped with coriander leaves.

Nathu's (*2 Sundar Nagar Market, Central Delhi www.nathusweets.com*) is the perfect place to kick back after shopping for high-end souvenirs, with its robust Indian sweets and pleasant seating area. The nearby **Sweets Corner** supplies the fried stuff outdoors.

Under a charming tin ceiling at the **Evergreen Sweet House** (*S–30 Green Park Market, South Delhi Green Park*), a large crowd stuffs itself with chole bhatura and vegetarian *thalis* (combination platters).

Prince Paan Box (*M-Block Market, eastern corner, Greater Kailash-1, South Delhi*) is where you will find one of Delhi's most popular *paanwallahs* (paan sellers), attracting a crowd at all hours. It's also known, of course, for its paan, betel-nut leaves wrapped around various ingredients. There's no seating here.

Lodhi Rd., South Delhi ☎ *11/2468–2001* ⊕ *www.indiahabitat.org* Ⓜ *Jor Bagh.*

India Habitat Centre
CULTURAL FESTIVALS | Several cultural events, from classical Indian dance performances to film and photo festivals take place at this performing arts center nearly every evening. It's also a regular venue for local theater troupes. ⊠ *Lodhi Rd., Lodhi Institutional Area, South Delhi* ☎ *11/2468–2001* ⊕ *www.indiahabitat.org.*

India International Centre
CULTURAL FESTIVALS | This established performance space near the Habitat Centre holds events from poetry readings to documentary film festivals. It's the place to witness the capital's famed love of high art. ⊠ *40 Max Mueller Marg., Lodhi Estate, South Delhi* ☎ *11/2461–9431* ⊕ *www.iicdelhi.nic.in.*

Nature Morte
ART GALLERIES—ARTS | This is one of the most cutting-edge art and photography

galleries in town. ✉ *A–1 Neeti Bagh, opposite Kamla Nehru College, Neeti Bagh, South Delhi* ☎ *11/4068–7117* ⊕ *www.naturemorte.com.*

PVR Anupam

FILM | ✉ *Community Centre, Saket, South Delhi* ⊕ *www.pvrcinemas.com* Ⓜ *Malviya Nagar.*

The Stainless

ART GALLERIES—ARTS | One of the more experimental galleries in Delhi, this space welcomes designers, architects, artists, and sculptors to display their work, and there is a permanent collection of stainless-steel installations. ✉ *Mira Corporate Suites Complex, 1–2 Old Ishwar Nagar, Mathura Rd., Okhla Crossing, South Delhi* ☎ *11/4260–3167* ⊕ *www.thestainless.in.*

Vadehra Art Gallery

ART GALLERIES—ARTS | Respected for its permanent collection of 20th-century masters, this is also one of Delhi's best galleries for contemporary, established artists. There are two locations. ✉ *D–40 and D–53 Defence Colony, South Delhi* ☎ *11/2462–2545* ⊕ *www.vadehraart.com* Ⓜ *Lajpat Nagar.*

● Shopping

BAZAARS AND MARKETS
★ **Dilli Haat**

OUTDOOR/FLEA/GREEN MARKETS | This government-run food and crafts bazaar invites artisans from all over the country to sell their wares directly. More than 60 do so at any given time; the vendors rotate every two weeks according to changing themes such as handicrafts, textiles, or Rajasthani goods. Constants include Kashmiri shawls, Lucknavi *chikan* (white embroidery on pastel cotton), woodwork, pottery, cotton dhurries, and simple children's toys. Stalls serve regional food from around the country, providing shoppers with a rare opportunity to sample Goan fish curry, Bengali

fish in mustard sauce, and Kerala chicken stew outside their states of origin. ✉ *Aurobindo Marg, South Delhi* ☎ *11/2611–9055, 11/2611–9055* ⊕ *www.dillihaat.net.in* ☞ *Admission Rs. 20* Ⓜ *INA Market.*

Hauz Khas Village

SHOPPING NEIGHBORHOODS | In the narrow medieval alleys of South Delhi's Hauz Khas Village, boutiques and shops in converted old homes sell crafts, curios, jewelry, artisanal furniture, and clothing (mostly glitzy Indian wear). Design stores include places like House of Blondie. The back alley also has fun vintage stores where you can find movie posters from Hollywood and Bollywood films. Most stores are open every day but Sunday from 10:30 to 6 or 7. The village is also dotted with bars and restaurants. ✉ *New Delhi.*

INA Market

OUTDOOR/FLEA/GREEN MARKETS | Across the street from Dilli Haat, this colorful market is one of Delhi's most exciting food bazaars, with shops full of imported packaged foods giving way to a covered fruit-and-vegetable market complete with coolies (porters) ready to carry your choices in a basket while you shop. Dry-goods merchants sell spices, nuts, and Indian salty snacks. Meat and seafood are prepared and sold on a muddy lane in back. ✉ *Aurobindo Marg, South Delhi* Ⓜ *INA Metro Station.*

BOOKS
CMYK

BOOKS/STATIONERY | Come here for art and design books, and perhaps one of the occasional cultural events (check the website or drop in for a schedule). ✉ *M–75, Greater Kailash II Market, 1st fl., South Delhi* ☎ *11/2921–1881* ⊕ *www.cmykbookstore.com.*

CARPETS
Carpet Cellar

HOUSEHOLD ITEMS/FURNITURE | This store has a vast selection of tribal and Mughal-print carpets and handwoven dhurries.

1 Anand Lok, August Kranti Marg, South Delhi ☎ *11/4164–1777* ⊕ *www. carpetcellar.com.*

Janson's Carpets

HOUSEHOLD ITEMS/FURNITURE | Jasim Jan, of Janson's Carpets, delivers exactly what he describes—carpets old and new, silk and wool, Persian and tribal—and at fair (not cheap) prices. *⊠ A–14 Nizam-uddin E, South Delhi* ☎ *11/2435–5615, 98111–29095 cell phone* ⊕ *www.janson-scarpets.com.*

CLOTHING

Kilol

CLOTHING | Some of the most stunning salwar-kameez fabric sets in India are available here, with color-drenched crêpe dupattas topping off soft, block-printed cottons. They're stacked on shelves upstairs. *⊠ N–4 N Block Market, Greater Kailash I, South Delhi* ☎ *11/2924–3388* ⊕ *www.kilol.com.*

L'Affaire

CLOTHING | Flamboyant party wear and hand-loomed saris at prices to match; there's another branch at Select Citywalk mall in Saket. *⊠ M–59 M Block Market, Greater Kailash I, South Delhi* ☎ *11/2923–9974* ⊕ *www.laffaire.net.*

Nalli

CLOTHING | This is a Chennai-based chain specializing in gold-trimmed silks from the Tamil town of Kanchipuram. The South Extension location is larger than the Connaught Place one. *⊠ D–2, South Extension II, South Delhi* ☎ *11/2626–9924* ⊕ *www.nalli.com* ⊠ *P–7/90 Connaught Pl., Central Delhi* ☎ *11/2374–7154* ⊕ *www.nalli.com* Ⓜ *Rajiv Chowk.*

JEWELRY

Cottage of Arts & Jewels

CRAFTS | This subterranean treasure trove is a musty jumble of old prints, photos, maps, curios, and junk. *⊠ 50 Hauz Khas Village, South Delhi* ☎ *98995–01934mobile.*

Hazoorilal

JEWELRY/ACCESSORIES | From bangles to necklaces to earrings and more, the jewelry here has fairly modern designs. *⊠ M–44 M Block Market, Greater Kailash I, South Delhi* ☎ *11/4173–4567* ⊕ *www. hazoorilaljewellers.com.*

SIDE TRIPS FROM DELHI

Updated by
Margot Bigg

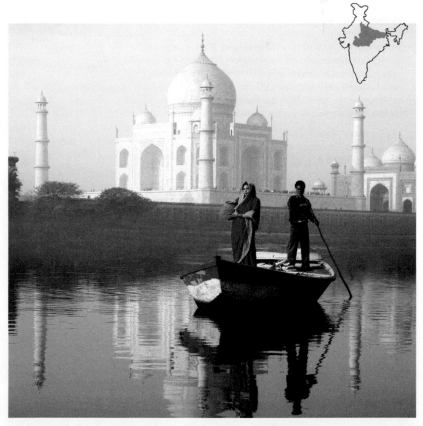

👁 Sights	🍴 Restaurants	🛏 Hotels	🛍 Shopping	🍸 Nightlife
★★★★★	★★★★☆	★★★★☆	★★★☆☆	★☆☆☆☆

WELCOME TO
SIDE TRIPS FROM DELHI

TOP REASONS TO GO

★ **Fatehpur Sikri:** Easily visited in conjunction with the Taj Mahal, this UNESCO World Heritage site, the former Mughal capital, is astounding for its prescient urban planning and architecture.

★ **Khajuraho:** The temples of Khajuraho, built between the 9th and 10th centuries, are famous for their exquisite sculptures, especially the erotic ones; it is also a UNESCO World Heritage site.

★ **The Taj Mahal:** One of the most iconic sites in the world, the Taj is even more enchanting in real life; the minute detail is awe-inspiring.

★ **Varanasi:** Among the oldest and holiest cities in the world, Varanasi is unlike anywhere else you'll go; it can be quite a culture shock, because it is very intense and dirty, but it's a truly awesome, unforgettable experience. Nearby Sarnath is the site of the Buddha's first teachings.

The places covered here may be the most awe-inspiring region of this tremendous country, and if you plan to visit India only once in your lifetime, this is the place to go, tourist traps and all.

1 Agra. Home to the over-the-top Taj Mahal, Agra is the architectural heart of North Central India.

2 Fatehpur Sikri. The abandoned fortress-city of Fatehpur Sikri is an easy day trip from Agra.

3 Khajuraho. Khajuraho is home to impressive temples built by the Chandelas.

4 Varanasi. The Ganges flows through this sacred city, which is one reason why thousands of *sadhus* (holy men) and pilgrims flock to it all year round.

5 Sarnath. The historic home of Buddhism, Sarnath is an easy day trip from Varanasi.

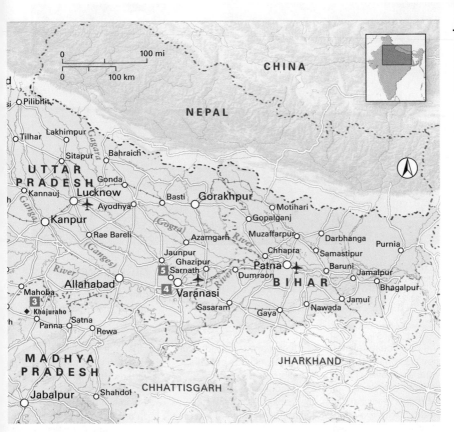

EATING WELL ON DELHI SIDE TRIPS

Paan ingredients in a betel leaf

The Awadh region has a vibrant culinary history that arose from the royal courts of the Muslim Nawabs who ruled the area.

The often quite refined dishes that make up Awadhi cuisine are reminiscent of the Mughal traditions of Delhi, Agra, and Kashmir and the Nawabi cuisine of Hyderabad, but they remain distinct. Awadhi *bawarchis* and *rakabdars* (cooks and specialty cooks) are most often credited with inventing the "*dumpukht*" style of sealing ingredients like rice, spices, and meat in an earthen pot and slow cooking them.

Agra's better hotels offer a taste of nonvegetarian Awadhi food, but in the part of Varanasi near the Ganges you'll mostly find just simple vegetarian restaurants and international backpacker-friendly cafés. The city's importance as a Hindu holy site has led to the popularization of bland, "*sattvik*" food, made by using vegetarian ingredients deemed conducive to meditation and avoiding others, such as onions and garlic, deemed too stimulating.

DIGESTIVE AID

Chewed as a digestive all over India, **paan** is a slightly intoxicating slug of areca nut and other ingredients wrapped in a betel leaf. It often includes varieties of tobacco, which can be left out on request. Paan can also include chutneys, spices, and sweets. Every *paanwallah* (paan vendor) has his own way of doing things. Beginners should ask for a sweet or "*mitha*" (no tobacco) paan.

PETHA

Petha is Agra's most famous sweet. Usually white and slightly translucent, this somewhat gelatinous confection is made from boiled and sweetened winter melon. There's also a yellow saffron-infused version called *angoori petha*. The sweet varies in consistency from soft and syrup filled to crunchy and nearly crystalline. Petha is sold by weight in cardboard boxes all over Agra, and comes in many flavors, such as rose, paan (betel), and coconut.

Petha

LITTI CHOKHA

Litti chokha is especially common in eastern Uttar Pradesh. Similar to Rajasthan's *batti* (and sometimes referred to by that name), the *litti* is a tough ball of baked dough made of *sattu,* a roasted flour particular to the region that's made from chickpeas. Around Varanasi and farther afield, you may see stalls serving litti with *chokha*—a vegetable accompaniment of eggplant, potato, or tomato.

MALLAIYO

One of the more fussy foods you may find in Varanasi is a yellow dairy dessert called **mallaiyo.** Like the version of the dish found in Delhi (where it's called *daulat ki chaat*), *mallaiyo* is an airy, saffron-scented concoction that magically melts away on your tongue.

Traditionally, this is a winter morning sweet: to prepare it, milk has to be thickened and allowed to foam, then set overnight. The foam is then skimmed off and sold as mallaiyo.

KAKORI KEBABS

Tender, melting morsels of meat called **kakori kebabs** are a common menu item in Uttar Pradesh. You can try these kebabs at restaurants in Agra, especially those that serve Awadhi food. Minced twice and tenderized with *papain* (from raw papaya), this delicately spiced dish is typically eaten with a large, very thin and soft *roomali roti* ("handkerchief" bread).

DUMPUKHT BIRYANI

An elaborate dish that originated in the royal Awadhi court, **dumpukht biryani** consists of rice and meat suffused with aromatic spices. Half-cooked lamb (or other meat) and rice are layered in a clay pot, which is then sealed with dough and slow-cooked over low heat. Although you won't find *dumpukht biryani* in vegetarian Varanasi, it's well worth sampling at one of Agra's restaurants.

Dumpukht biryani in a clay pot

Grand tales of love and loss, and myth and legend, come to life in this section of the Hindi heartland, anchored by Agra, home of the stunning Taj Mahal; Varanasi, one of the world's oldest and holiest (and most chaotic) cities; and Khajuraho—a sleepy, unforgettable temple town dating back around a thousand years. In this spiritually rich, highly diverse, and deeply historical part of North India, surrounded by Mughal magnificence and houses of worship, it's quite possible to believe you're in the home of the gods.

Agra was a seat of the Mughals' power, and their legacy remains (partially intact) for us to marvel at. Dominated by Muslim influences in culture, art, architecture, and cuisine, the city is a testament to the beauty and grandeur of Mughal aesthetics, most notably in the form of the Taj Mahal and Fatehpur Sikri.

Some 440 km (273 miles) southeast of Agra, in the northern part of Madhya Pradesh, the sleepy village of Khajuraho predates the Mughals. Khajuraho was founded at the end of the classical age of Hindu civilization, and is home to stunning Hindu and Jain temples that are famous for their erotic, often explicit sculpture. Excavations here have also uncovered a long-forgotten complex of Buddhist temples.

According to legend, Varanasi was founded by the Hindu god Shiva, and it's said to be one of the oldest populated cities in the world—about 3,000 years old. In many ways, the city (still sometimes called by its Raj-era name, Benares), in southwestern Uttar Pradesh, is the antithesis of Khajuraho. Varanasi teems with pilgrims, hospice patients, mourners, ascetics, priests, Hindu pundits, and international citizens of many religions. Its famous *ghats* (wide stone stairways leading down to the Ganges) are both key religious sites and secular promenades. Writer Mark Twain explained its charm perfectly. He said it is "older than history, older than tradition, older even than legend and looks twice as old as all of them put together." Hindus believe that a person who dies here will gain *moksha* (salvation and freedom from the cycle of birth and rebirth). Sarnath, on the outskirts of Varanasi, is where the Buddha is said to have preached his first sermon after his enlightenment. The ruins and temples here draw Buddhist pilgrims from all over the world.

Agra and Varanasi are at opposite ends of Uttar Pradesh. Both lie on the Gangetic plain, also known as the Northern Plain, which stretches across most of northern India. The countryside in both areas is similar: a dry landscape planted with sugarcane, mustard, and wheat in winter. In Khajuraho, 418 km (260 miles) south-east of Agra—sort of midway, but south, between Agra and Varanasi—you'll get a good sense of the natural environment, because it's an uncongested area. The monsoon hits harder to the east, around Varanasi, so the terrain there is a little more lush.

Planning

WHEN TO GO
HIGH SEASON: MID-OCTOBER TO MARCH
The weather during these months is cool and nice, but hotels tend to charge premium rates. December and January are the best times to visit, but it can get relatively cold, with temperatures dropping to 40°F. Remember to pack some warm clothes. While it's the best time of year for outdoor sightseeing, you're trading the sun for much higher prices and unbelievable amounts of foot traffic. The weather from early February to mid-March is wonderfully temperate.

LOW SEASON: APRIL TO AUGUST
If you decide to go to Agra from April to early July, even Indians might look at you as if you're crazy. There's no denying that this region is at its hottest then, making sightseeing in Agra and Khajuraho, which involves hours in the sun, borderline unbearable, especially while looking at the red sandstone monuments, which radiate heat. Temperatures will be well above 100°F, with monsoon showers picking up toward the end of July and continuing through August. Temperatures during this period will be in the 80s, rain is intermittent, and hotel rates go down, so this is a good time to get a deal.

SHOULDER SEASON: SEPTEMBER TO MID-OCTOBER
During this period the weather just begins to cool, and while you might still be unlucky enough to catch a shower or two, it is a great time to visit. Some hotels still give discounts for off-peak season.

PLANNING YOUR TIME
It's a good idea to take an express train to **Agra** to avoid Delhi traffic. To see the Taj and related sights without being completely rushed, plan on spending at least one night in Agra.

The ancient city of **Fatehpur Sikri** is an easy day trip from Agra. The drive takes about 45 minutes.

Khajuraho is located halfway between Agra and Varanasi. The best way to visit is to fly here either on your way to or from Varanasi. Plan to spend two days exploring the Chandela temples.

Varanasi requires at least two days. The best option is to fly from Delhi, perhaps stopping in Khajuraho.

Sarnath is an easy day trip from Varanasi. Plan to spend half a day here.

GETTING HERE AND AROUND
AIR TRAVEL
The flight connecting Delhi with **Agra and Fatehpur Sikri** is just 40 minutes, but it's easier and more cost-effective to take the train.

Khajuraho Airport is 7 km (4 miles) from town; the taxi ride costs about Rs. 700.

Bhabatpur, the nearest airport to **Varanasi and Sarnath**, is a 45-minute drive, from most hotels in Varanasi. The airport is about 23 km (14 miles) from the Cantonment area, or 30 km (19 miles) from the riverfront area. A taxi costs about Rs. 100 (air-conditioned) to the Cantonment area, or about Rs. 1,100 into the city proper.

Air India operates direct flights from Varanasi to Agra. From Agra, there's an Air India flight to Khajuraho. The Varanasi airport is connected by air from Delhi, with flights by Air India, Vistara, SpiceJet, and Indigo.

AUTO-RICKSHAW AND TAXI TRAVEL

Auto-rickshaws and taxis are a cheap, convenient option for getting around in all the big cities, and can also be hired for an entire day of sightseeing. Be prepared to bargain, though.

Fares for an auto-rickshaw ride, especially one in **Agra**, depend on several factors, including how wealthy you look, how far you want to go, how many times you want to stop, the time of day, and whether it's raining. You can generally expect to pay about Rs. 800 for a half day, and Rs. 1,200 for a full day. If you're not comfortable with the price you're given, look for another auto-rickshaw, and if you don't want to haggle, take a metered taxi or book a car. Taxis can take you to nearby **Fatehpur Sikri**.

In **Khajaraho**, taxis are available, but the temples are best explored by foot or rickshaw.

Auto-rickshaws are a fast way to scoot through crowded city streets, but the fumes from other automobiles can be horrendous at busy times. In **Varanasi and Sarnath**, an auto-rickshaw from the Cantonment area to the ghats costs around Rs. 200. When traffic is heavy, take an air-conditioned taxi with the windows closed, especially if you're coming from one of the hotels far from the ghats. Ask your hotel or the tourist office for the going rate, and agree on a fare in advance.

BUS TRAVEL

Traveling to these cities via bus is the cheapest option, but it's only for the truly adventurous, because local schedules are difficult to come by and service is spotty. If you're taking off from Delhi, the bus stations are large and can be chaotic and hard to deal with. You can book a seat on a private, air-conditioned bus for travel between the cities through any local travel agent. Traveling from Delhi to **Agra and Fatehpur Sikri** by bus is an easy and short trip, but bus travel to **Khajuraho, Varanasi, and Sarnath** might require overnights and transfers. It's not recommended.

Within cities, local bus lines are the only form of public transportation. In general, they are too crowded and difficult to use for the average foreign visitor.

CAR TRAVEL

The Yamuna Expressway has reduced driving time from Delhi to **Agra** to 2½ hours, making driving a convenient but somewhat pricey option. Taking the train—just a three-hour commute—is a good alternative.

Hire a car and driver through your hotel or tour operator; UP Tours, the government of Uttar Pradesh's tour arm ; the Madhya Pradesh State Tourism Development Corporation; or a recommended local travel agent.

For trips to Agra from Delhi, contact Dhanoa Tours and Travels (listed below). Rates start around Rs. 10,000 for a day trip, depending on the size of the vehicle. The price includes tax, a driver, and a guide. Expect to pay about Rs. 100 extra for a worthwhile detour to **Fatehpur Sikri**. Fatehpur Sikri is a 45-minute drive from Agra and an easy day trip.

Prices in Agra are generally Rs. 9–Rs. 10 per km. A non-air-conditioned car for four hours or 40 km (25 miles) should cost about Rs. 1,400–Rs. 1,600—the minimum charge. For overnight excursions, add a halt charge of at least Rs. 600. The standard charge for a trip to Fatehpur Sikri is Rs. 2,800, but prices are always negotiable. You can hire a taxi at the train station under a fixed-rate system. *If you'd prefer not to be taken to the driver's choice of stores, restaurants, or hotels (where he gets a commission), say so firmly up front.*

Khajuraho is about a six-hour drive from Varanasi, 6½ hours from Agra, and more than nine hours from Delhi.

In Khajuraho, a hired car can be convenient if you want to wander outside town or can't walk the 3 km (2 miles) to the most distant temples. An air-conditioned car should cost about Rs. 1,000 for four hours and up to 40 km (25 miles). You can hire a taxi for about Rs. 8–Rs. 10 per km.

Varanasi is a maze of streets and alleys, making car travel difficult. The best way to see the city is on a boat tour of the Ganges River.

Sarnath is an easy half-day trip from Varanasi. You can ask your hotel or tour operator for a car and driver.

CONTACTS Dhanoa Tours and Travels ✉ *Dharam Marg, near Malcha Marg Market, Chanakyapuri, Central Delhi* ☎ *011/2688–6051, 981/005–8913.* **Touraids Travel Service** ✉ *Behind Hotel Trident, Agra* ☎ *0562/223–0741, 931/910–0644* ⊕ *www.touraidsi.com.*

CYCLE-RICKSHAW TRAVEL

Cycle-rickshaws should cost no more than Rs. 100 per hour in **Agra** or **Khajuraho**. They're a particularly pleasant way to get around Khajuraho, especially to the outlying temples. Distances are long in **Varanasi**, so a cycle-rickshaw is better for a leisurely roll through the Old City (it frees you from fighting the crowds) than for cross-town transportation. A trip from the Cantonment to the ghats should cost about Rs. 100. If you hire a cycle-rickshaw for the day, agree on the price in advance and expect to pay about Rs. 400.

TRAIN TRAVEL

Train service is superb, as the region is connected by several local and express trains originating in Delhi and other major cities, and taking the train to **Agra** is a good option. If you're going by train to **Khajuraho**, one good option is to take the UP Sampark Kranti Express, which comes in from Delhi H. Nizamuddin Station to Khajuraho three times a week (Tuesday, Friday, and Sunday). There are trains available from **Delhi** to **Varanasi**, but distances are long and trips might require an overnight or transfer. Flying is much more convenient. *For more info about train travel, see the Travel Smart chapter.*

TOURS

UP Tours (Uttar Pradesh's state tour agency) has a vast offering of tours, including Buddhist circuit tours and a daily guided bus tour (except Friday) of Fatehpur Sikri, Agra Fort, and the Taj Mahal for Rs. 2,850 per person (this covers transportation, a guide, and admission fees, including the Rs. 1,000 admission to the Taj); a half-day tour of Agra alone is Rs. 1,900. For a personal guide, ask your hotel or contact the nearest India Tourism office.

CONTACTS Kamalan Travels ✉ *508, Hemkunt House, 6 Rajendra Pl., Delhi* ☎ *11/2573–0256* ⊕ *www.kamalan.travel.* **Outbound Travels** ✉ *216A/11 Gautam Nagar, 3rd fl., South Delhi* ☎ *011/4164–0565* ⊕ *www.outboundtravels.com.*

VISITOR INFORMATION

If you are planning your trip from New Delhi, the India Ministry of Tourism's office on Janpath is worth a visit.

You can pick up maps and information about approved guides at the India Ministry of Tourism offices in Agra, Khajuraho, and Varanasi's Cantonment, and at an information desk at Varanasi's airport. The Madhya Pradesh State Tourism Development Corporation, one of India's better state tourist offices, has friendly staff and information on Khajuraho.

The Uttar Pradesh State Tourism Development Corporation arranges tours and cars in Agra. The New Delhi office (centrally located near the Imperial Hotel) has maps, brochures, and information on approved guides. The best information at Varanasi's Uttar Pradesh State Tourism office is in Hindi, but the staff can still help you, and there's a satellite desk at the train station.

TOURIST OFFICES India Ministry of Tourism ✉ *88 Janpath, Connaught Place* ☎ *011/2332–0005* ⊕ *www.incredibleindia. org.* **Madhya Pradesh State Tourism Corporation** ✉ *Near Circuit House, Khajuraho* ☎ *768/627–4051* ✉ *At airport, Khajuraho* ⊕ *www.mptourism.com.* **Uttar Pradesh Tourist Office** ✉ *Chandralok Bldg., 36 Janpath, Central Delhi* ☎ *11/2332–2251* ⊕ *www.uptourism.gov.in* ✉ *Rahi Tourist Bungalow, Sarnath* ☎ *542/259–5965.*

RESTAURANTS

Restaurants on this route generally serve kebabs and other grilled meats, *biryanis* (rice casseroles), and the rich almond-and-saffron-scented concoctions of Mughlai (Mughal-style) cuisine. Most hotels offer a menu of Indian (with choices from various regions), continental, Chinese (adapted for Indian tastes), and sometimes Thai or Japanese dishes; Khajuraho has several Italian restaurants. Small places in villages along the way have simple local vegetarian dishes that are often delicious and almost always cheap. Also keep an eye out for South Indian joints, where you can get a delicious spiced-potato-filled *masala dosa* (crisp rice crepe) for Rs. 100 or less. Most restaurants are open from 7 to 10 for breakfast, noon to 3 for lunch, and 7:30 to 11 for dinner; high-end hotels often have 24-hour restaurants, often billed as "coffee shops" (though they generally serve full meals).

HOTELS

Most of India's major high-end hotel groups are represented in this region, often with room rates on par with what one might find in Europe or North America. An increasing number of four-star hotels aimed primarily at Indian business travelers are also popping up across northern India; these tend to offer comfortable amenities at much more reasonable prices. Boutique hotels and budget guesthouses are also an option, particularly for those not only on a budget but also for travelers who prefer a bit more of a simple, yet authentic, experience. *Hotel reviews have been shortened. For full information, visit Fodors.com.*

What It Costs			
$	$$	$$$	$$$$
RESTAURANTS			
under Rs. 300	Rs. 300– Rs. 499	Rs. 500– Rs. 700	over Rs. 700
HOTELS			
under Rs. 4,000	Rs. 4,000– Rs. 5,999	Rs. 6,000– Rs. 10,000	over Rs. 10,000

Agra

200 km (124 miles) southeast of Delhi.

Agra is synonymous with that monument of love: the stunning Taj Mahal. The city is crowded and congested, but once you lay eyes on the dazzling marble monument, inlaid with precious stones, shrouded in tales of romance and valor, even an arduous journey to get here feels worth it. Imagine walking down an avenue of stores selling tiny replicas of the Taj Mahal, with guides and hawkers vying for your attention, and then passing through a massive doorway and seeing the Taj Mahal in all its splendor. It's a magical moment.

It's safe to say that this sprawling city of nearly 1.5 million inhabitants would not be on many tourists' maps if it weren't

North Central's Festivals

Agra's Taj Mahotsav (10 days, in February) is a festival celebrating the arts, crafts, and culture of North India. The Khajuraho Festival of Dance (a week, usually between late February and March) is geared primarily to visitors. It's a spectacular event that attracts classically trained dancers from all parts of the country, who perform against a magnificently floodlighted backdrop of the temples.

In Varanasi there's a major religious festival practically every week, but their dates shift every year (check ⊕ *www.incredibleindia.org* for upcoming dates). Varanasi's great bathing days, when thousands stream down the ghats into the Ganges, include Makar Sankranti (January), the full moon of the Hindu month Kartik

(October or November), and Ganga Dussehra (May or June). Durga Puja (September or October) ends with the city's large Bengali community marching to the river at sunset to immerse large mud-daubed images of the goddess Durga. The Bharat Milap festival, held in October or November, occurs the day after the major Hindu festival of Dussehra. It marks Lord Rama's return from exile (from the epic *Ramayana*). It's held in Nati Imli in Varanasi.

Buddhists from Tibet and all over Asia celebrate their festivals in Sarnath. The Buddha Jayanti is celebrated on a full moon day in April or May. It honors the Buddha's birth anniversary as well as his day of enlightenment.

for the Taj Mahal, but other amazing sights are also nearby. You can drive to the old fortress city of the Mughals, Fatehpur Sikri, as well as Agra's fort, where the emperor who had the Taj built was imprisoned near the end of his life.

In this Mughal stronghold every successive emperor added something new to prove his cultural sensibilities and his power. Under the Mughal emperor Akbar (1542–1605) and his successors Jahangir (1605–27) and Shah Jahan (1628–58), Agra flourished. However, after the reign of Shah Jahan's son Aurangzeb (1658–1707) and the gradual disintegration of the empire, the city passed from one invader to another before the British took charge early in the 19th century. The British, particularly Governor General Lord Curzon (in office 1898–1905), did much to halt and repair the damage inflicted on Agra's forts and palaces by raiders and vandals.

Much of Agra today may be crowded and dirty, and some of the Mughal buildings are irrevocably scarred. But the government has taken steps to protect the city's most important site from pollution, closing the streets around the Taj Mahal to gas-fueled vehicles (visitors are ferried from a remote parking lot by battery-powered buses) and relocating small factories and fire-burning shops away from the area. Still, Agra's monuments remain strewn like pearls in ashes, evoking that glorious period in Indian history when Agra was the center of the Mughal empire.

■ TIP➔ Opening hours change constantly; inquire in advance at your hotel or the Uttar Pradesh State Tourist Office.

GETTING AROUND
It's a good idea to spend at least one night in Agra and start tackling the sights early in the morning, if only because you'll get a couple of hours in before the hot sun begins to bear down. It's true

A Good Tour

Assuming you see the Taj Mahal first thing in the morning (and that's certainly not mandatory), it's easy to take leisurely drives to the rest of the sights and be ready to unwind by early evening. Drive 5 km (3 miles) north of the Taj Mahal—about a 20-minute drive on a congested road—to **Itimad-ud-Daulah's Tomb** and then 8 km (5 miles) northwest—about a half-hour drive, with traffic—to **Akbar's Tomb.** (Also known as Sikandra for the town it's in, this monument is often overlooked, but it's an impressive sight that's well worth a stop.) From here it's a 12-km (7-mile), or 45-minute, drive northeast to **Agra Fort**, where it's easy to spend an hour or more. If you have the time and energy, drive southwest for an hour (37 km [23 miles]), to **Fatehpur Sikri.**

If you're day-tripping from Delhi with a car and driver, it's wise to leave town by 5 am to avoid morning traffic. You can see Akbar's Tomb and Itimad-ud-Daulah's Tomb on the way and still make it to the Taj before noon. Spend the afternoon visiting the Agra Fort or Fatehpur Sikri before heading back to Delhi.

Timing
The period between mid-September and the end of March is ideal for visiting. Pack a jacket or sweatshirt if you plan to visit during the chilly months of December or January.

It's a lot to do all of Agra's main attractions in a day trip from Delhi, unless you really just want to see the Taj Mahal. To avoid feeling rushed, consider spending a night or two in Agra and slowing your pace down.

Essentials
Government-approved tourist guides can be found through the local tourist offices and at the entrances to most major attractions.

CONTACTS Uttar Pradesh Tourist Office ✉ *64 Taj Rd., UP Tourist Office* ☎ *562/222–6431* ⊕ *www.uptourism. gov.in.*

that the Taj at sunrise is glorious, but if you happen to sleep in, don't worry. Hotels and tour guides tend to make a big deal about the best times of day to see the Taj Mahal, but this legendary mausoleum is spectacular whenever you choose to visit—so don't feel despondent if you arrive at noon as opposed to sunrise or sunset. (A midday visit, however, *would* be the worst time to forget your sunglasses.) Keep in mind that the Taj Mahal can get extremely crowded at all hours of the day, so don't assume that an early start will necessarily save you from the relentless foot traffic.

The fastest way to drive to Agra from Delhi is via the Yamuna Expressway, or you can take the other, more historic route, which follows the Grand Trunk Road—a royal route established by India's Mughal emperors in the 16th and 17th centuries, when their capital alternated between Delhi, Agra, and Lahore (now in Pakistan). If you get an early start, you can see Agra's sights in one very tiring day: start at Akbar's Tomb, 10 km (6 miles) north of Agra, then move on to Itimad-ud-Daulah's Tomb, the Taj Mahal, and Agra Fort.

Sights

★ Agra Fort
MILITARY SITE | A succession of Mughal emperors lived within the red sandstone walls of this World Heritage site, and it

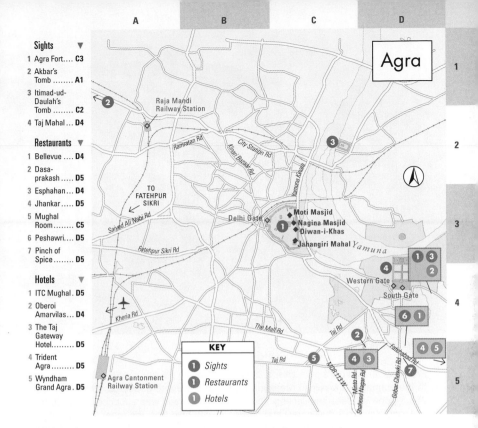

KEY

① Sights
① Restaurants
① Hotels

was from here that they governed the country. As with similar Mughal facilities in Delhi and Lahore, the word "fort" is misleading: the complex is really a forti-fied palace, containing royal apartments, mosques, assembly halls, a dungeon, and the largest state treasury and mint—the entire cityscape of an imperial capital. A massive wall 2½ km (1½ miles) long and 69 feet high surrounds the fort's roughly triangular shape. With the Yamu-na River running at its base, the fort was also protected by a moat and another wall, presenting a daunting barrier to anyone hoping to access the treasures within.

The structure was originally a brick fort, and Ibrahim Lodi held it for nine years until he was defeated and killed in the battle of Panipat in 1526. The Mughals captured the fort along with masses of treasure, which included one of the most famous gems in the world, the Koh-i-Noor diamond. The emperor Babur stayed in the fort in the palace of Ibrahim, while Humayun was crowned here in 1530. Emperor Akbar decided to make it his capital when he arrived in Agra in 1558. He rebuilt it with red sandstone from the Barauli area in Rajasthan, and the whole process took eight years. The architecture of the current fort reflects the collective creative brilliance of Akbar, his son Jahangir, and grandson Shah Jahan.

The fort's entrance is accessible through the Amar Singh Gate (also called the Lahore Gate, for the city in modern-day Pakistan that it faces). It was named for Amar Singh Rathore, a legendary general who served the Mughals. North of this entrance sits the fort's largest private residence, the **Jahangiri Mahal,** built by Jahangir as a harem, mainly for his

Agra's massive fort

Rajput wives. (Akbar's own palace, closer to the entrance, is in ruins.) Measuring 250 feet by 300 feet, the Jahangiri Mahal juxtaposes *jarokhas* (balconies) and other elements of Hindu architecture with pointed arches and other Central Asian influences imported by the Mughals. The palace's central court is lined with two-story facades bearing remnants of the rich, gilded decoration that once covered much of the structure.

After Jahangir's death in 1628, Shah Jahan assumed the throne and started his own buildings inside the fort, often tearing down those built by his father and grandfather and adding marble decorations (it is said that he was partial to the material). The **Anguri Bagh** (Grape Arbor) shows the outlines of a geometric garden built around delicate water channels and chutes. The 1637 **Khas Mahal** (Private Palace) is an early masterpiece of Shah Jahan's craftsmen. The central pavilion, made of white marble, follows the classic Mughal pattern: three arches on each side, five in front, and two turrets rising out of the roof. Of the two

flanking pavilions where Shah Jahan's two daughters resided, one is of white marble and was supposedly decorated with gold leaf; the other is made of red stone. The arched roofs of all three pavilions are stone interpretations of the bamboo architecture of Bengal. In one part of the Khas Mahal a staircase leads down to the palace's "air-conditioned" quarters—cool underground rooms that were used in summer. It's famous for its paintings on marble.

The octagonal tower of the **Mussaman Burj** has fine inlay work and a splendid view down the river to the Taj Mahal. This is where Shah Jahan is said to have spent the last seven years of his life, imprisoned by his son Aurangzeb but still able to look out on his greatest monument, the Taj Mahal. He may have built the tower for his wife Mumtaz Mahal (for whom he also built the Taj Mahal). On the northeastern end of the Khas Mahal courtyard stands the **Sheesh Mahal** (Palace of Mirrors), built in 1637 as a bath for the private palace and dressing room for the harem. Each of the two chambers contained a bathing tank fed by marble channels.

The emperor received foreign ambassadors and other dignitaries in the **Diwan-i-Khas** (Hall of Private Audience), built by Shah Jahan in 1636–37. Outside, the marble throne terrace holds a pair of black and white thrones. The black throne, carved from a single block of marble, overlooks the Yamuna and, according to the inscription, was used by Shah Jahan; the white throne is made of several marble blocks and was his father's seat of power. Both thrones face the **Machhi Bhavan,** an enclosure of fountains and shallow pools, and a number of imperial offices.

To the empire's citizens and to the European emissaries who came to see these powerful monarchs, the most impressive part of the fort was the **Diwan-i-Am** (Hall of Public Audience), set within a large quadrangle. This huge, low structure rests on a 4-foot platform, its nine cusped Mughal arches held up by rows of slender supporting pillars. Here the emperor sat and dispensed justice to his subjects, sitting on the legendary Peacock Throne, now lost.

Northeast of the Diwan-i-Khas is the **Nagina Masjid,** a private mosque raised by Shah Jahan for the women of his harem. Made of white marble and walled in on three sides, it has typical cusped arches, a marble courtyard, and three graceful domes. While in the Nagina Masjid, royal ladies could buy beautiful items from tradesmen who set up a temporary bazaar for them in front of its balcony. Nearby is the lovely **Moti Masjid,** a perfectly proportioned pearl mosque (*moti* means pearl) built in white marble by Shah Jahan. ⊠ *Yamuna Kinara Rd.* ⊕ *www.agrafort.gov.in* 🖾 *Rs. 550.*

Akbar's Tomb

MEMORIAL | Akbar's resting place, in what's now the small town of Sikandra, was begun by the emperor himself in 1602 and completed after his death by Jahangir. Topped with white marble and flanked by graceful minarets, this mausoleum of rough red sandstone sits in a typical Mughal garden called a *charbagh*—four quadrants separated by waterways. The garden, however, is not well tended, and Jat raiders (who invaded Agra after the fall of the Mughal empire) destroyed much of the gold work that once adorned the tomb, though the British partially restored it. In a domed chamber three stories high, the crypt is inscribed with the 99 names of Allah, plus the phrases *Allah-o-Akbar* (God is great) at the head and *Jalla Jalalahu* (Great is His glory) at the foot. It's a charming spot to visit; you'll spot many langurs (long-tailed monkeys) and deer in the gardens. Akbar had originally meant this to be the official resting place for the Mughals, but it didn't turn out that way: only two of his daughters are buried here. ◼ TIP→ **You can actually see the tomb's enormous gateway, topped with bright tilework, from the train from Delhi— look out the left window 10 or 15 minutes before the train is due to reach Agra.** ⊠ *10 km (6 miles) north of Agra on Grand Trunk Road to Delhi, Sikandra* 🖾 *Rs. 210.*

★ Itimad-ud-Daulah's Tomb

MEMORIAL | The empress Nur Jahan (Jahangir's favorite wife) built this small, gorgeous tomb for her father, Mirza Ghiyas Beg (pronounced Baig), a Persian nobleman who became Jahangir's chief minister. Beg was also the grandfather of Mumtaz Mahal, the wife of the emperor Shah Jahan. The monument, one of Agra's loveliest, was supposedly built by workers from Persia. The tomb incorporates a great deal of brown and yellow Persian marble and marks the first use of Persian-style marble inlay in India—both features that would later characterize the style of Shah Jahan. Particularly in its use of intricate marble inlay, this building was a precursor of, and very likely an inspiration for, the Taj Mahal (for this reason it has earned the somewhat goofy nickname of the "Baby Taj"). The roof is

Taj Mahal Visting Tips

Hours: The Taj is open Saturday to Thursday, from sunrise to sunset. It's closed on Friday. The Taj Mahal museum is open Saturday to Thursday 10 am to 5 pm.

Admission: Rs. 1,000

Best time to visit: Many people say that sunrise or sunset is the best time to see the Taj Mahal, for the glorious colors. Though the Taj Mahal is glorious any time of day, midday is probably the worst time to visit because of the bright sun reflecting off the white marble (bring your sunglasses). By all means, go early to beat the heat, but don't count on having the place to yourself, as there are almost always crowds at the Taj Mahal.

Night Viewing: The Taj is open for viewing five nights per month, on the full moon and two nights before and after, except Friday and during Ramadan. Limited numbers of tickets are sold one day in advance (your hotel might be able to arrange tickets for you), for a half-hour visit between 8:30 pm and 12:30 am. Admission price is the same as during regular hours. It's a romantic way to see the Taj but definitely not a substitute for a daytime visit. Taj Ganj, Taj Rd. www.tajmahal.gov.in

To buy night-view tickets: Archaeological Survey of India. Agra Circle, 22 The Mall, Agra (10 am to 6 pm). 562/222–7261 or 562/222–7262

arched in the style of Bengali terra-cotta temples, and the minarets are octagonal, much broader than the slender cylinders of the Taj Mahal—in its fine proportions this mausoleum almost equals that masterpiece. Inside, where the elegant decoration continues, the central chamber holds the tombs of Itimad-ud-Daulah and his wife; other relations are buried in adjacent rooms. Most travelers to Agra never see this place, but its beauty and tranquillity are extraordinary, and its well-maintained gardens make it a wonderful place to pause and reflect. ⊠ *5 km (3 miles) north of Taj Mahal on left bank of Yamuna River* ⚄ *Rs. 210.*

★ Taj Mahal

MEMORIAL | The tale of love and loss that supposedly sparked the existence of the Taj Mahal (literally, the "Crown Palace") sometimes seems as incredible as the monument's beauty. It is said that Shah Jahan fell in love with his favorite wife, Arjuman Banu, at first sight, and went on to revere her for her generosity, intelligence, and the 14 children she

bore. She became his *Mumtaz Mahal* (the Exalted of the Palace), and her love for him was apparently just as great—on her deathbed, or so the legend goes, she begged the king to build a monument so beautiful that the world would never forget their love. Five months later, a huge procession brought Mumtaz Mahal's body to Agra, where Shah Jahan began the process of honoring her request.

Indeed, it's difficult to imagine a grander gesture throughout history, but the design, execution, and end result is what truly makes the Taj Mahal a must-see. It took 20,000 laborers 17 years (starting in 1632) to complete the vast tomb of white marble on the banks of the Yamuna River, making it the most stunning example of the elaborate aesthetic world that the Mughals created in India.

The Taj Mahal stands at the end of a large, four-quartered garden, or charbagh, symbolizing paradise, extending about 1,000 feet in each direction from a small central pool. You enter the grounds through a huge sandstone gateway emblazoned with an inlaid Koranic inscription. Ahead, facing the long reflecting pool, the Taj Mahal stands on two bases, one of sandstone and, above it, a marble platform measuring 313 square feet and worked into a chessboard design. A slender marble minaret stands at each corner of the platform, blending so well into the general composition that it's hard to believe each one is 137 feet tall. The minarets were built at a slight tilt away from the tomb so that, in case of an earthquake, they'd fall away from the building. Facing the Taj Mahal from beneath its platform are two majestic sandstone buildings, a mosque on the left and its mirror image (built purely for symmetry) on the right. Behind the tomb, the Yamuna winds along its broad, sandy bed.

The tomb's central archway is deeply recessed, as are the smaller pairs of companion archways along the sides and the beveled corners of the 190-square-foot structure. The Taj Mahal's most extraordinary feature is its onion dome, crowned by a brass finial mounted in a scalloped ornament, which is an inverted Hindu motif of the lotus. The dome uses the Central Asian technique of placing a central inner dome, in this case 81 feet high, inside an outer shell to attain the extraordinary exterior height of 200 feet; between the two is an area nearly the size of the interior hall itself. Raising the dome above the minarets was the builders' great stroke of genius. Large *chattras* (umbrellalike domes), another feature borrowed from Hindu design, balance the dome.

Inside the mausoleum, the changing light creeps softly in through marble screens that have been chiseled like silver filigree. Look closely at the tiny flowers drawn in inlaid semiprecious stones and the detailed stonework on each petal and leaf. The work is so fine that not even a magnifying glass reveals the tiny breaks between stones, yet a single 1-inch

flower on the queen's tomb has 60 pieces. Directly under the marble dome lie the tombs of Mumtaz Mahal and Shah Jahan, surrounded by a *jali* (latticed) screen carved from a single block of marble, with a design as intricate as lace. In the center of the enclosure, diminishing rectangles lead up to what looks like a coffin; in fact, both Mumtaz Mahal and Shah Jahan are buried in a crypt below these tombs in deference to the Islamic tradition that no one should walk upon their graves. After his death, Shah Jahan was buried next to his wife by his son Aurangzeb, upsetting the perfect symmetry, most likely a cost-cutting measure that forms an ironic postscript to the munificence of Shah Jahan. But it's fitting that the emperor lies in perpetuity next to his favorite wife.

In early morning, the pale rays of the sun give the marble of the Taj Mahal a soft pink luster; at sunset the west side of the monument turns lemon yellow, then pumpkin orange. Once the sun goes down, the marble is pure white against a black sky.

The small **Taj Mahal Museum** stands near the mosque to the left of the Taj. It holds Mughal memorabilia and provides some historical background to the Taj, as well as paintings of the famous couple, manuscripts, letters, and a display of precious stones used in the construction of the Taj. ⌧ *Taj Ganj, Taj Rd.* ☎ *562/233–0498* ⊕ *www.tajmahal.gov.in* ⌦ *Rs. 1000* ☉ *Closed Fri.*

 Restaurants

★ Bellevue

$$$$ | INDIAN | This airy indoor restaurant looks out on the Oberoi's gardens, with beautiful views of the Taj Mahal in the distance. Decor is stylish, with chic brown-and-white tile floors, plush turquoise booths, and dusky wooden tables and chairs. **Known for:** Indian cuisine; Taj Mahal views; sleek interiors. $ *Average*

Continued on page 158

THE TAJ MAHAL

Described as an "elegy in marble," the Taj Mahal is an epic monument to Emperor Shah Jahan's beloved wife. Seeing the magnificent structure in person reveals the minute details of its decoration and its construction, and the incredible symmetry of the elements.

The Taj Mahal is one of the most recognizable, most reproduced images in the world, and the tale of love and loss that sparked its creation is almost as incredible as the monument's beauty. It was built by the fifth Mughal emperor, Shah Jahan, in memory of his third but favorite wife, who was called his Mumtaz Mahal (the Jewel of the Palace). As the legend goes, she asked him to build her a monument so beautiful that the world would never forget their love. She died after giving birth to their thirteenth child, and six months after her death a huge procession brought Mumtaz Mahal's body to Agra, where Shah Jahan began the process of honoring her request with the Taj Mahal. Construction of the monument began in about 1632, and it took 20,000 laborers a period of about 17 years to complete the vast, bejeweled, white marble tomb on the banks of the Yamuna River. The building's perfect proportions, scale, and exquisite detail make it a vision unlike anything else. It was made a UNESCO World Heritage site in 1983.

Up close the intricately crafted and colorful detail of the building is apparent, but from far away, the magnificent structure appears all white—though depending on the sun and the time of day it takes on different hues. At sunrise it takes on a pinkish hue; at sunset it's a lemon yellow, then orange. Once the sun goes down, the marble is pure white against a black sky.

(top) An artist's rendition of Mumtaz Mahal
(right) The reflecting pool leading up to the Taj Mahal is a typical element of Islamic gardens and courtyards

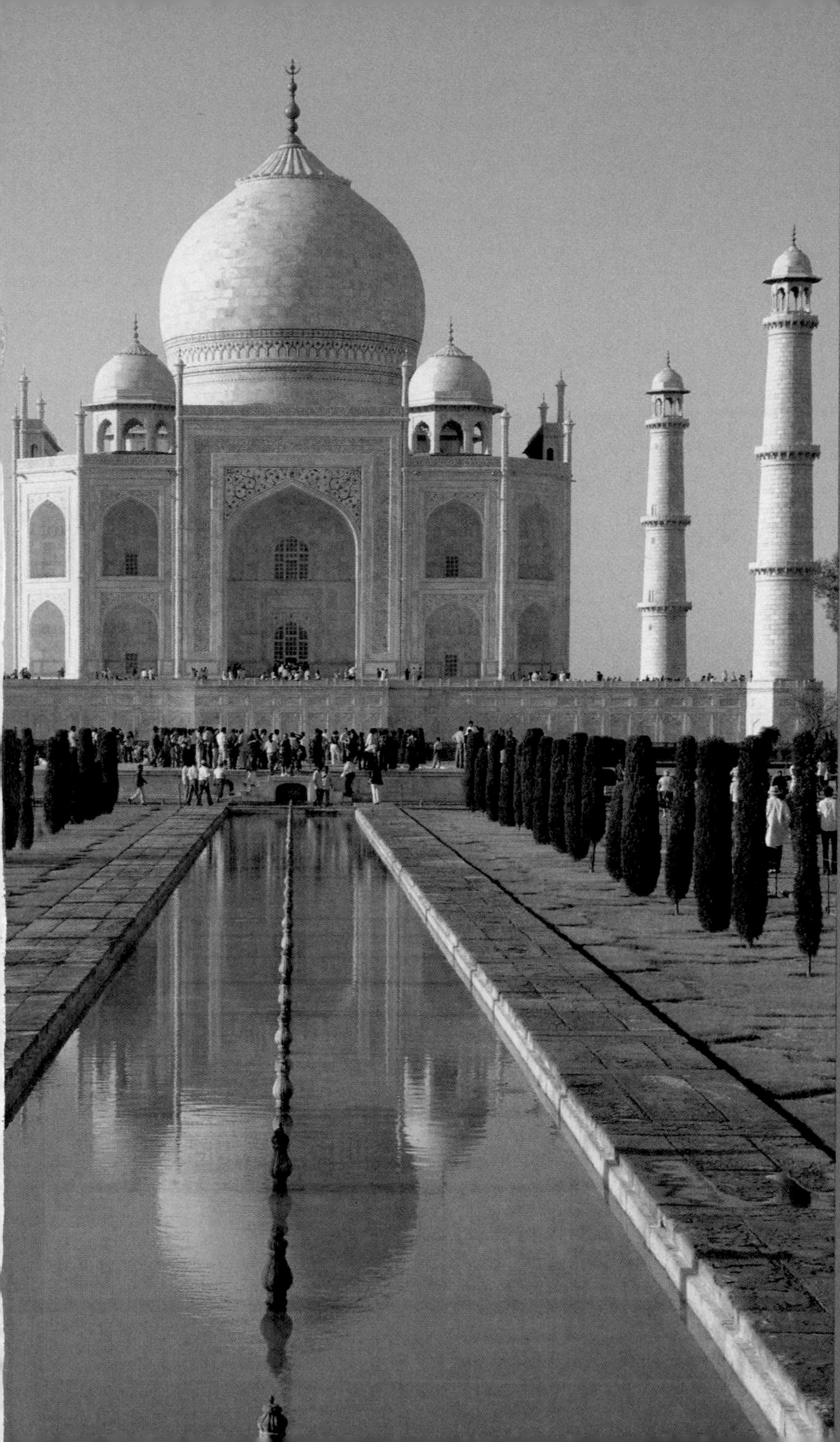

THE OUTER TAJ

ENTRANCE
You enter the grounds through a huge sandstone gateway boldly emblazoned with an inlaid Koranic inscription.

THE GARDENS
The Taj Mahal stands at the end of a large garden that is divided into four sections by pools of water. Midway between the entrance and the Taj is a large pool, called the Lotus pool because of its lotus-shaped water spouts. The water reflects the Taj, and standing in front of the lotus pool makes for a popular photo op.

The garden in front of the Taj is said to symbolize Paradise, because Islamic texts of the period describe Paradise as a garden of abundance with four rivers separating it into four quadrants.

THE TOMB
The 190-square-foot central marble building, the mausoleum or pavilion, is the focus of the structure, and it stands on two bases: sandstone on the bottom level, and marble on the top (measuring 313 square feet) that has been worked into a chessboard design.

The mausoleum's central archway is deeply recessed, as are the smaller pairs of companion archways along the sides and the beveled corners of the 190-square-foot structure.

Behind the main pavilion, the Yamuna River winds along its broad, sandy bed.

THE DOME
The Taj Mahal's most extraordinary feature is its onion-shaped dome, crowned by a brass finial

(top left) Emperor Shah Jahan standing on a globe (top middle) Entrance to the Taj Mahal (top right) Interior of the mosque (bottom left) The Taj Mahal in early morning (bottom middle) An artist's drawing of the Taj Mahal (far right top) The lotus pool (far right bottom) Map of the Taj

mounted in a scalloped ornament: an inverted Hindu motif of the lotus. The dome uses the Central Asian technique of placing a central inner dome, in this case 81 feet high, inside an outer shell to attain the extraordinary exterior height of 200 feet; between the two is an area nearly the size of the interior hall itself.

MINARETS

There are four slender, marble minarets—one at each corner of the Taj platform. They blend so well into the general composition that it's hard to believe each one is over 130 feet tall. The minarets were built at a slight tilt away from the tomb so that, in case of an earthquake, they'd fall away from the building.

MOSQUES

On opposite sides of the Taj Mahal are two majestic sandstone buildings: on the left is a mosque; the one on the right is believed to have been built as a mirror image, for symmetry, but may also have been used as a guesthouse.

MUSEUM

The small Taj Mahal Museum stands near the mosque to the left of the Taj. It contains Mughul memorabilia and provides some historical background

to the Taj, as well as paintings of the famous couple, manuscripts, letters, and a display of precious stones used in the construction of the Taj.

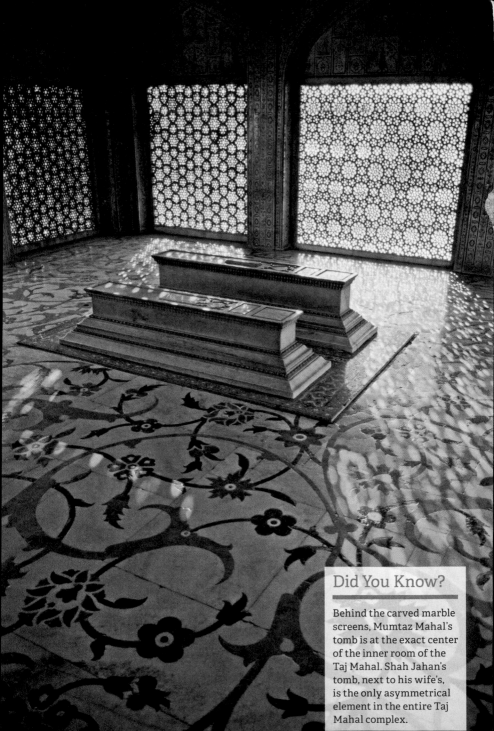

Did You Know?

Behind the carved marble screens, Mumtaz Mahal's tomb is at the exact center of the inner room of the Taj Mahal. Shah Jahan's tomb, next to his wife's, is the only asymmetrical element in the entire Taj Mahal complex.

INSIDE THE MAUSOLEUM

The Taj Mahal is a glorious example of the refined aesthetics of the Mughals. In addition to the magnificent architecture of the buildings and the layout of the gardens, the mausoleum itself, likened to a jeweled box, showcases a range of art forms. One of the recurring motifs throughout the Taj are the many flower forms: flowers were believed to symbolize paradise on earth.

Carved marble screen

CARVED MARBLE SCREENS
Directly under the marble dome lie what look like the coffins of Mumtaz Mahal and Shah Jahan (photo at left), surrounded by a screen chiseled from a single block of marble, with latticework as intricate as lace. In fact, however, both are buried in a crypt below, in deference to the Islamic tradition that no one should walk upon their graves.

Crypt

CRYPT
Visitors are no longer allowed to go downstairs to the main crypt area (photo at right), where the bodies of Mumtaz Mahal and Shah Jahan are buried, because of the vandalism that has occurred over the years.

INLAY WORK
Pietra dura, a type of mosaic work, is believed to have originated in Italy and later imported to Asia. It makes use of colorful, cut stones set in marble to create images. The intricate designs in the Taj use semiprecious stones including agate, carnelian, coral, jasper, lapis lazuli, malachite, tiger's eye, and turquoise, set in different shades of marble, sandstone, and slate. Look closely at the tiny flowers and detailed stonework on each petal and leaf in the Taj. The work is so fine that not even a magnifying glass reveals the tiny breaks between stones, yet a single one-inch flower on the queen's tomb has 60 pieces.

Inlay work

CARVED RELIEF WORK
Panels of carved flowers, foliage, and vases decorate the lower parts of the walls inside the mausoleum.

Carved relief work

CALLIGRAPHY
Inlaid calligraphy of black marble ornaments the undecorated surfaces of the mausoleum. The banner-like inscriptions on the arches are passages from the Koran.

Calligraphy

main: Rs. 1800 ⊠ The Oberoi Amarvilas, Taj East Gate Rd. ☎ 562/223–1515.

Dasaprakash

$ | **SOUTH INDIAN** | **FAMILY** | The light and spicy South Indian vegetarian dishes served at this casual town favorite are a nice change from Agra's usual rich Mughlai fare. The food is excellent and service is fast at this casual, reliable, chain eatery. **Known for:** South Indian dosas and idlis; vegetarian thalis (combo platters); ice creams and floats. $ Average main: Rs. 250 ⊠ 9 Fathehabad Rd. ☎ 562/223–0089 ⊕ www.dasaprakash.in.

Esphahan

$$$$ | **NORTH INDIAN** | Situated just past The Oberoi Amarvilas's illuminated Mughal-style courtyard and grand marble lobby, this intimate den celebrates local craftsmanship, with square pillars of red sandstone and white marble and carved wooden screens. Through the glass wall of the kitchen you can watch the chefs at work, while live instrumental music, including performances on the dulcimer-like *santoor*, adds to the mood throughout the week. **Known for:** elegant ambience; rich Lucknowi leg of lamb; tandoori prawns marinated in citrus-infused yogurt. $ Average main: Rs. 1800 ⊠ The Oberoi Amarvilas, Taj East Gate Rd. ☎ 562/223–1515 ⊙ No lunch.

Jhankar

$$$$ | **INDIAN** | Occupying an elegant, airy space that opens out to the lobby of the Taj Gateway Hotel, Jhankar serves excellent Mughlai dishes every day at dinnertime. Flavors are subtle and distinct; many herbs and vegetables come from the kitchen garden. **Known for:** regular live dance performances; aloo dum chutneywale (potatoes in mint and coriander chutney); magazi murgh korma (chicken in a yogurt and cashew sauce). $ Average main: Rs. 1500 ⊠ Taj Gateway Hotel, Fatehabad Rd., Taj Ganj ☎ 562/223–2400 ⊕ gateway. tajhotels.com/en-in/fatehabad-road-agra/ restaurants/jhankar.

Mughal Room

$$$$ | **INDIAN** | The panoramic view from a wall of windows takes in both the Taj Mahal and the Fort, while evening live *ghazals* (Urdu love song) performances set the mood for rich Mughlai dishes served here. A ceiling of faux twinkling stars floats over an interior of rich reds, with brass trays hanging on walls and tables set with silver goblets. **Known for:** kabuli naan (flatbread stuffed with cheese and raisins); murg malia tikka (spicy, cream-marinated baked chicken); live kitchen displays. $ Average main: Rs. 900 ⊠ Hotel Clarks Shiraz, 54 Taj Rd., top fl. ☎ 562/222–6121to 6127.

★ Peshawri

$$$$ | **INDIAN** | Rustic wood tabletops resting on tree-trunk bases, plush, bright-orange seat cushions, and hammered copper plates and goblets create a dark, romantic mood, complemented by the simple, delicious barbecue cuisine of the North West Frontier area in present-day Pakistan and Afghanistan. All kinds of meats are freshly prepared over open flames and served with rich, aromatic sauces, with plenty for vegetarians, and guests are encouraged to eat with their hands. **Known for:** rich, slow-cooked buttery dal; heavy slow-roasted meat dishes; rustic-chic ambience. $ Average main:

Rs. 2200 ✉ ITC Mughal Hotel, Taj Ganj ☎ 562/402–1700.

Pinch of Spice
$$ | **NORTH INDIAN** | This sleek, modern restaurant is decorated in rich shades of purple, beige, and orange, and lighted by glittering glass chandeliers. The five-page menu includes Chinese and European dishes, but the North Indian cuisine is what makes the restaurant so popular with domestic visitors. **Known for:** rich North Indian food; paan shots (spiced breath freshener drinks served after meals); crowded and lively atmosphere. Ⓢ Average main: Rs. 400 ✉ 1076/2, Fatehabad Rd. ✢ Opposite Hotel ITC Mughal ☎ 0562/404–5252 ⊕ www. pinchofspice.in.

Hotels

ITC Mughal
$$ | **RESORT** | **FAMILY** | Set within 36 acres of lush gardens with a miniature lake, this brick and marble hotel is one of Agra's largest, and its size can be daunting. **Pros:** extensive activities for kid; huge, opulent spa; elegant rooms. **Cons:** large and difficult to navigate; breakfast not included; can feel impersonal. Ⓢ Rooms from: Rs. 5500 ✉ Fatehabad Rd., Taj Ganj ☎ 562/402–1700 ⊕ www. itchotels.in ⇋ 233 rooms |◯| No meals.

★ Oberoi Amarvilas
$$$$ | **RESORT** | One of India's best resorts emulates the opulent lifestyle of the Mughal emperors, and each room has a breathtaking view of the Taj Mahal. **Pros:** gorgeous views; flawless service; free rides to the Taj Mahal and guide services. **Cons:** extremely high room rates; Internet not included; food is expensive. Ⓢ Rooms from: Rs. 42000 ✉ Taj East Gate Rd. ☎ 562/223–1515 ⊕ www.oberoihotels.com/hotels-in-agra-amarvilas-resort ⇋ 110 rooms |◯| No meals.

The Taj Gateway Hotel
$$$ | **HOTEL** | **FAMILY** | A good, though distant, view of the Taj Mahal from some rooms and the rooftop make this hotel a popular choice. **Pros:** views of the Taj Mahal from some rooms; a dedicated yoga channel in every room; live evening entertainment including puppet shows. **Cons:** can get crowded; removed from the Taj Mahal; standard rooms lack local character and feel corporate. Ⓢ Rooms from: Rs. 6000 ✉ Fatehabad Rd., Taj Ganj ☎ 0562/660–2000 ⊕ www.tajhotels.com ⇋ 100 rooms |◯| No meals.

Trident Agra
$$ | **HOTEL** | **FAMILY** | Built around a large garden courtyard with fountains, a soothing expanse of green lawn, and a pool, this place is a real oasis in Agra. **Pros:** wheelchair-accessible rooms; kid-friendly cozy tent stocked with a PS3, games, and movies; live entertainment and henna every evenings. **Cons:** room decor lacks local charm; restaurant gets crowded at mealtimes; too far to walk to the Taj Mahal. Ⓢ Rooms from: Rs. 5000 ✉ Fatehabad Rd. ☎ 562/223–5000 ⊕ www.tridenthotels.com ⇋ 135 rooms |◯| No meals.

Wyndham Grand Agra
$$$$ | **RESORT** | **FAMILY** | A night at this large estate feels a bit like staying in a Mughal palace, with sweeping beige and white marble arches, manicured gardens, gurgling fountains, and elaborate rooms. **Pros:** five restaurants offer plenty of dining options; largest pool in Agra; regular evening entertainment, with music, dance, and puppetry. **Cons:** rooms are far from the lobby; huge property and can feel impersonal; service can be slow. Ⓢ Rooms from: Rs. 12000 ✉ 7th Mile Stone, Fatehabad Rd. ☎ 562/223–7000 ⊕ www.wyndhamgrandagra.com ⇋ 148 rooms |◯| Free Breakfast.

Shopping

Tourist shops are generally open daily from 10 to 7:30. Many Agra shops sell hand-knotted dhurries and other rugs, jewelry made from precious and semiprecious stones, brass statues, and marble inlays that continue the form and motifs seen in the city's great monuments. Resist drivers and touts who want to take you to places offering special "bargains"; they receive big commissions from shopkeepers, which you pay in the inflated price of the merchandise. Beware, too, of soapstone masquerading as marble: this softer, cheaper stone is a convincing substitute, but you can test it by scraping the item with your fingernail—Indian marble won't scrape. Finally, for what it's worth, local lore has it that miniature replicas of the Taj Mahal bring bad luck.

Ganeshi Lall and Son

JEWELRY/ACCESSORIES | This reliable, family-owned jeweler, established in 1845, retails precious and semiprecious gold and silver jewelry. They specialize in older pieces and also create new ones. Past clients have included Prince Charles and Jacqueline Kennedy Onassis. ⊠ *Hotel ITC Mughal, Fatehabad Rd.* ☎ *562/233–0181* ⊕ *www.ganeshilall.com.*

Kohinoor

JEWELRY/ACCESSORIES | This company has been designing jewelry using cut and uncut emeralds and other precious stones since 1862; a special "connoisseur's room" with unique pieces is open only by appointment. Don't miss the little museum display of fantastic 3-D *zardoji* (embroidered paintings). Some have been encrusted with gems by the master of the technique. ⊠ *Fatehabad Rd.* ☎ *0562/223–0027, 0562/223–0028* ⊕ *www.kohinoorjewellers.com.*

Munshi Ganeshi Lal & Son

CRAFTS | This three-room emporium stocks *zardozi* (embroidery), traditional jewelry, and marble inlay work. A large room on the upper floor is dedicated to antique-style gold and silver jewelry inlaid with precious stones. The basement doubles up as a workshop for marble inlay tables, plates, and other items. ⊠ *194 Fatehabad Rd.* ☎ *0562/233–0168* ⊕ *www.mglagra.com.*

The Marble Mecca

The Taj Mahal's marble may have come from the mines of Makrana, a small Rajasthani village 400 km (250 miles) to the west that's renowned for its marble supply. The artisans creating marble inlay in Agra today are likely using Makrana marble, and they're believed to be descendants of those who mined the marble or did the inlay work on the Taj.

Oswal Exports

CRAFTS | Excellent examples of inlaid white, pink, green, and black marble are produced here; you can watch daily demonstrations as artisans work on marble and also learn their techniques. Handicrafts, jewelry, and textiles are also available. ⊠ *30 Munro Rd., Sadar Market* ☎ *562/222–5710, 562/222–5712.*

Subhash Emporium

CRAFTS | This was the first store to revive Agra marble work in the 1960s. Ask to see some of the masterpieces in the private gallery to give you a better perspective on quality. ⊠ *18/1 Gwalior Rd.* ☎ *562/326–0604* ⊕ *www.marbleemporium.com.*

U.P. Handicrafts Palace

GIFTS/SOUVENIRS | Stunning marble-inlaid tabletops in every size, some with latticework, are on display in this massive showroom of marble collectibles. At the demo workshop outdoors, you can watch craftsmen work and paint on marble. Other pieces include vases, decorative elephants, and plates. ⊠ *Fatehabad Rd., next to Munshi Ganeshi Lal & Son* ☎ *0562/400–1601, 562/223–2661 to 2663* ⊕ *www.upcraftspalace.com.*

One of the red sandstone buildings at Fatehpur Sikri

Fatehpur Sikri

37 km (23 miles) southwest of Agra.

The capital of the Mughal Empire for only 14 years (from 1571 to 1585), the majestic red sandstone buildings of the now uninhabited fortified city of Fatehpur Sikri are remarkably well preserved, and showcase elegant architecture and an inspired sense of planning.

In a sense, Fatehpur Sikri was built on faith: in 1569, so the story goes, the Mughal emperor Akbar was driven to despair because he didn't have a male heir. He made a pilgrimage to visit the Sufi mystic Salim Chisti, who blessed him. The blessing evidently worked, as Akbar had a son within the next year, naming him Salim (the future emperor Jahangir) in honor of the saint. Two years later, Akbar began building a new capital in Chisti's village of Sikri, later renaming it Fatehpur Sikri (City of Victory) after a great triumph in Gujarat. Standing on a rocky ridge overlooking

the village, Fatehpur Sikri originally had a circumference of about 11 km (7 miles). Massive walls and seven gates enclosed three sides, and a lake (now dried up) protected the fourth. When the British came to Fatehpur Sikri in 1583 to meet Akbar, they were amazed to see a city that exceeded contemporary London in both population and grandeur—with more rubies, diamonds, and silks than they could count.

What remains is a beautiful cluster of royal dwellings on the top of the ridge, landscaped with lawns and flowering borders. The structures elegantly blend architectural styles from Persia as well as Akbar's various Indian holdings, a reflection of the synthesizing impulse that characterized the third and greatest of the Mughal emperors. Also notable is how Akbar synthesized Muslim and Hindu beliefs here. The magnificently carved Brahma pillar is testament to his stand on communal harmony. Akbar ruled here for only 14 years before moving his capital—perhaps in pursuit of water, but more likely for political reasons—to Lahore and

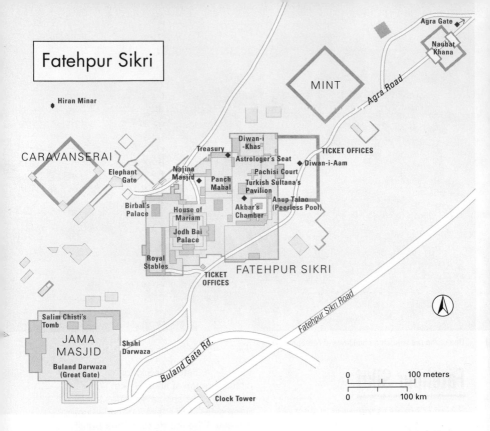

Fatehpur Sikri

then eventually back to Agra. Because it was abandoned and never resettled, the city was not modified by later rulers, and thus is the best reflection of Akbar's aesthetic and design philosophies. Fatehpur Sikri now stands as an intriguing ghost town, reflecting a high point in India's cultural history.

GETTING HERE AND AROUND

To reach Fatehpur Sikri from Agra, hire a car and driver or join a tour. The drive takes about an hour. There are ticket offices at the Jodh Bai Palace entrance, Diwan-i-Aam.

TIMING

Fatehpur Sikri is best visited early in the morning. Set out from Agra by about 6:30 am to avoid traffic. You'll be done well before 11 am, which is when the heat begins to really kick in. Plan to spend at least two or three hours wandering

the grounds. Wear good walking shoes; there's a lot of ground to be covered here.

 Sights

Fatehpur Sikri

BUILDING | The usual starting point for exploring Fatehpur Sikri is the Buland Darwaza (Great Gate) of the **Jama Masjid**, near the parking lot, but the cluster of hawkers and guides nearby can be unrelenting. If you arrive by car, you can avoid this minor annoyance by asking to be dropped at the subsidiary entrance at the northeastern end of the city, **Agra Gate**, where the following self-guided tour begins (ask your driver to pick you up at the exit at the Buland Darwaza, or "Great Gate").

Approach the Fatehpur Sikri complex, and walk through the **Naubat Khana,** a gate that was manned by drummers and musicians during imperial processions. Just ahead on the right is the **Mint,** a workshop that may have minted coins.

Next, a few steps from an archaeological museum is the **Diwan-i-Aam** (Hall of Public Audience), a large courtyard 366 feet wide by 181 feet long with colonnades on three sides. Ahead is the balcony where the emperor sat on his throne to meet subjects or observe celebrations and other spectacles. Through chiseled marble screens, the women of the court would watch as Akbar, the empire's chief justice, handed down his decisions: it's said that those condemned to die were impaled, hanged, or trampled under the feet of an elephant. What looks like a square two-story building with domed cupolas at each corner is the **Diwan-i-Khas** (Hall of Private Audience). Inside it's actually one tall room where Akbar sat on an elaborate elevated platform and, it's thought, conducted meetings with his ministers. Supported by a stone column topped with a giant lotus flower intricately carved in stone, it's connected by causeways to four balconies with window seats on which the ministers sat. The throne's position is thought to have symbolized the center of the world or, alternatively, the one god sought by several major religions; it also may have had a practical side, shielding the emperor from would-be assassins.

Across from the hall is the **Treasury**, also known as **Ankh Michali** (Hide and Seek), said to be named for Akbar's playful habit of playing the game with his harem inside the broad rooms and narrow passageways. The deep recesses in the walls, though, suggest that it may have been used as a treasury. Adjacent is the **Astrologer's Seat,** a platform where Akbar's royal astrologer sat. Pass through the courtyard paved with a board on which Akbar played *pachisi* (an early form of parcheesi that used slave girls as pieces), into the pavilion centered by the **Anup Talao** (Peerless Pool), a square pool

with a central platform, connected by four bridges. Below the basement of the pavilion is an excavated underground palace whose entrances cleverly concealed it until archaeologists, led by reports from Akbar's day, discovered it. The emperor would come to these rooms, constructed at the center of a water-filled tank, to escape the summer heat. Unearthed within them was the 12-foot-high stone bowl (now displayed on the pavilion) used to store water transported from the Ganges—the only water Akbar would drink. At the edge of the pool is the **Turkish Sultana's Pavilion,** a charming structure covered with elaborate Persian carvings in floral and zigzag patterns. It is said to have been the home of the emperor's Turkish wife, but was more likely a place to relax by the pool and have a quiet conversation. Separated from the sultana's pavilion as well as from the official buildings of the palace by the Anup Talao are Akbar's private chambers.

The Imperial Harem, where the women of Akbar's household resided, consists of several buildings connected by covered passages and screened from view of the more public areas. The **Panch Mahal** is a breeze-catching structure with five (*panch* in Hindi) arcaded stories, each smaller than the one below. Its 176 columns are carved with tiny flowers or other motifs (no two of the first floor's 56 columns have the same design). As Fatehpur Sikri's tallest building, it affords grand views of the city and the surrounding landscape from its upper stories. When the women prayed, they did so behind the screened arches of the**Najina Masjid** (Small or Jewel Mosque), behind the Panch Mahal across a small garden. The largest residence in the complex is the Gujarati-influenced **Jodh Bai Palace,** more properly called Principal Haram Sara, because behind its eunuch-guarded entrance lived a number of the emperor's wives rather than just that of his Hindu wife, Jodh Bai. The **Hawa Mahal** (Palace of the Winds) is a cool vantage point from which women could peek out at the court unseen from beautifully carved stone screens.

The **House of Mariam** (on a diagonal between Jodh Bai's Palace and the Panch Mahal) is the home of either Akbar's Christian wife or, more likely, his mother. Look for the faded paintings of horses and elephants on the exterior walls. Some of the brackets supporting the eaves are carved with scenes from mythology. **Birbal's Palace,** which sits a few yards northwest of Jodh Bai's Palace and the Hawa Mahal, was named for the emperor's playfully irreverent Hindu prime minister. Because it's unlikely that he would have lived inside the harem, the Archaeological Survey of India ascribes it to Akbar's two senior wives. The palace's ornamentation makes use of both Hindu and Islamic motifs.

The big open colonnade behind the harem is known as the **Royal Stables** because the stalls were once thought to have housed elephants and horses; however, it is more likely that it was the quarters of the serving women, and that the open stalls were enclosed by curtains tied to the stone rings once thought to have tethered the animals. At the edge of the city complex, by Sikri Lake, you should be able to see the **Hiran Minar** tower, decorated with six-pointed stars and hexagons, from which elephant tusks protrude (the originals have been replaced with stone tusks). If it's open, there are 53 steps that take you to the top of the tower, from where you have a bird's-eye view of Fatehpur Sikri.

Follow the path down to the east gate of the **Jama Masjid** (Imperial Mosque); built around 1571 and designed to hold 10,000 worshippers, it's still in active use. Note the deliberate incorporation of Hindu elements in the design, especially the pillar decorations. The **Shahi Darwza** (Emperor's Gate) is on the eastern side of the mosque; only the emperor and his courtiers were allowed to pass through

Want a Boy?

Many people believed that Salim Chisti, the famous Sufi saint, could perform miracles. Women of all faiths still come to his tomb to cover it with cloth and tie a string on the marble latticework in hopes of giving birth to a son.

this gate. The sandstone gateway is fully carved in geometrical design, and has two arches, one on top of the other; a lotus-bud motif runs through the smaller arch.

In the courtyard of the Jama Masjid (opposite the Buland Darwaza) lies **Salim Chisti's tomb,** surrounded by walls of marble lace, each with a different design. Begun upon the saint's death in 1571 and finished nine years later, the tomb was originally faced with red sandstone, but was refinished in marble by Jahangir, the heir Akbar's wife bore after the saint's blessing. From here you can cross the courtyard and exit through the imposing Buland Darwaza. Tombs of those people lucky enough to be buried by the revered saint are in this area. And here is the **Buland Darwaza** (Great Gate), at the southwestern end of the city. The beautiful inscription etched on it translates to "The world is but a bridge, pass over but build no houses on it." With its beveled walls and inset archways, the southern gate rises 134 feet over a base of steps that raise it another 34 feet, dwarfing everything else in sight. Akbar built it after conquering Gujarat, and it set the style for later gateways, which the Mughals built habitually as symbols of their power.

The various upper stories of Fatehpur Sikri are now closed to visitors because of the proliferation of graffiti. ⊠ *Fatehpur Sikri* 🖃 *Rs. 500.*

Khajuraho

*395 km (245 miles) southeast of Agra;
379 km (235 miles) southwest of
Varanasi.*

The UNESCO World Heritage site temples of Khajuraho are known for their carved erotic images, but they are also examples of the advanced architectural styles of the Chandela kings. The soaring *shikharas* (spires) of the temples are meant to resemble the peaks of the Himalayas, the abode of Lord Shiva. The spire of each temple rises higher than the one before it, as in a range of mountains that seems to draw near the heavens. Designed to inspire the viewer toward the highest human potential, these were also the builders' attempts to reach upward, out of the material world, to *moksha,* the final release from the cycle of rebirth. It's definitely worth a visit here, though getting to Khajuraho is not easy.

This small rural village in the state of Madhya Pradesh was the religious capital of the Chandelas, one of the most powerful Rajput dynasties of Central India, from the 10th to 12th century. They built 85 temples here, 22 of which remain to give a glimpse of a time when Hindu art and devotion reached its apex. When the dynasty eventually succumbed to invaders, Khajuraho's temples lapsed into obscurity until their rediscovery by the British explorer Captain T.S. Burt in 1838.

During the Chandelas' rule, the temples' royal patrons were rich, the land was fertile, and those at the top lived the good life, trooping off to hunts, feasts, and theater, music, and dance performances. This abundance was the perfect climate for creativity, and temple-building emerged as the major form of expression. There were no strict boundaries between the sacred and the profane, no dictates on acceptable deities: Shiva, Vishnu, Brahma, and the Jain saints were all lavishly honored here. Among other things, Khajuraho represents an incredible testament of the strength of human devotion and faith.

Excavations have also uncovered a complex of Buddhist temples. Despite the interest in heaven, the real focus was Earth, particularly the facts of human life. Here, immortalized in stone, virile men and voluptuous women cavort and copulate in the most intimate, erotic, and sometimes bewildering postures. Khajuraho represents the best of Hindu temple sculpture: sinuous, twisting forms, human and divine, pulsing with life, tension, and conflict. But its Buddhist side is more serene.

A number of sculptural motifs run through the temples. Certain gods, for instance, have directional positions: elephant-headed Ganesh faces north; Yama, the god of death, and his mount, a male buffalo, face south. Other sculptures include the *apsaras* (heavenly maidens), found mainly inside, and the Atlas-like *kichakas,* who support the ceilings on their shoulders. Many sculptures reflect everyday activities, such as a dance class, and there are sultry *nayikas* (mortal women) and plenty of *mithunas* (amorous couples). The scorpion appears as an intriguing theme, running up and down the thighs of many female sculptures as a kind of erotic thermometer.

Of the extant temples, all but two were made from sandstone mined from the banks of the River Ken, 30 km (19 miles) away. The stone blocks were carved separately, then assembled as interlocking pieces. Though each temple is different, all observe precise architectural principles of shape, form, and orientation and contain certain essential elements: a high raised platform, an *ardh mandapam* (entrance porch), a *mandapam* (portico), an *antrala* (vestibule), and a *garbha griha* (inner sanctum). Some of the larger temples also have a walkway around the inner sanctum, a *mahamandapam* (hall), and subsidiary shrines at each corner of the platform, making a complete *panchayatana* (five-shrine complex).

No one knows why erotic sculptures are so important here, though many explanations have been suggested. The female form is often used as an auspicious marker on Hindu gateways and doors, in the form of temple sculptures as well as domestic wall paintings. In the late classical and early medieval periods, this symbol expanded into full-blown erotic art in many places, including the roughly contemporary sun temple at Modhera, in Gujarat, and the slightly later one at Konark, in Odisha. A common folk explanation is that the erotic sculptures protect the temples from lightning; and art historians have pointed out that many of the erotic panels are placed at junctures where some protection or strengthening agent might be structurally necessary. Others say the sculptures reflect the influence of a Tantric cult that believed in reversals of ordinary morality as a religious practice. Still others argue that sex has been used as a metaphor: the carnal and bestial sex generally shown near the bases of the temples represents uncontrolled and baser human appetites. They're metaphors of leaving bodily desires behind, to follow a spiritual path. Conversely, the couples deeply engrossed in each other, oblivious to all else, represent a divine bliss, the closest humans can approach to God.

GETTING HERE AND AROUND

Khajuraho is so small that bicycles, cycle-rickshaws, and walking are the best available options for getting around, rather than taxis or auto-rickshaws. For Rs. 70–Rs. 100 you can **rent a bicycle** for the day from one of the many places across from the bus stand, behind the museum, and from some hotels. It's a great way to get around this relatively traffic-free town and to explore the small streets of Khajuraho village, the old residential area near the Eastern Group of temples that teems with shops, animals, and children.

Evening Entertainment

Sound-and-Light Show This popular 50-minute extravaganza, narrated in Hindi and English, traces the story of the Chandela kings and the temples from the 10th century to the present. The exact showtime varies based on sunset, so confirm it with your hotel or the tourist office. Buy tickets at the tourism office. ⊠ *Western Group* ⊕ *www.mptourism.com* 🎟 *Rs. 700.*

Entrepreneurial boys will gladly guide you around for a small sum.

TIMING
Dance Festival

FESTIVAL | In late February or early March, Khajuraho holds an annual, weeklong dance festival, set in part against the backdrop of the temples. This superb event attracts some of the country's best performers. Contact the tourist office for more information. ⊠ *Khajuraho.*

ESSENTIALS
Madhya Pradesh Tourism

For maps, information brochures, and seeing about arranging a hired car, contact the MP Tourist Office. ⊠ *Near Circuit House* 🕾 *768/627–4051* ⊕ *www.mptourism.com.*

Sights

WESTERN GROUP OF TEMPLES

Most of the Western Group of temples, the richest and largest group, are inside a formal enclosure whose entrance is on Main Road, opposite the State Bank of India. Although the rest of the town's temples are always accessible and free, these are open daily only from sunrise to sunset and have an admission charge of Rs. 500 (free for children under 15). The first three temples, though considered part of the Western Group, are at a slight distance from the enclosure.

To actually enter the temples, you'll need to leave your shoes outside. The stone steps get really hot on summer afternoons—bring along a fresh pair of socks to wear so you don't burn your feet.

Chausath Yogini Temple

ARCHAEOLOGICAL SITE | The oldest temple at Khajuraho is set on a granite outcrop southwest of the Shivsagar Tank, a small artificial lake. It may have been built as early as AD 820. It's dedicated to Kali (a form of the goddess Durga, Slayer of Demons), and its name refers to the 64 (*chausath*) female ascetics (*yogini*) who serve this fierce goddess in the Hindu pantheon. A little more than half that number have survived. Unlike its counterparts, which are made of pale, warm-hued sandstone, this temple is made of granite. ⊠ *Khajuraho.*

Lalguan Mahadeva

ARCHAEOLOGICAL SITE | Lying in ruins, with the original portico missing, this Shiva temple is 600 meters west of Chausath Yogini. It is historically significant because it was built of both granite and sandstone, marking the transition from Chausath Yogini to the later temples. ⊠ *Khajuraho.*

Matangesvara Temple

ARCHAEOLOGICAL SITE | Just outside the boundary of the Western Group stands this temple, which has its own gate to the left of the entrance. It's the only one still in use here; worship takes place in the morning and afternoon. The lack of ornamentation, the square construction, and the simple floor plan date this temple to the early 10th century. It has large bay windows, a projecting portico, and a ceiling of overlapping concentric circles. An enormous lingam (a phallic symbol associated with Shiva), nearly 8½ feet tall, is enshrined in the sanctum. ⊠ *Khajuraho.*

Archaeological Museum

MUSEUM | Across the street from Matangesvara Temple, this museum displays exquisite carvings and sculptures that archaeologists have recovered from the temple sites. The three galleries attempt to put the works into context, according to the deities they represent. ⊠ *Main Rd.* ☎ *768/627–2320* ⊠ *Rs. 5* ⊘ *Closed Fri.*

Varaha Temple

ARCHAEOLOGICAL SITE | Just inside the main entrance gate, to your left, next to a small Lakshmi temple, is this beautiful temple dedicated to Vishnu's Varaha avatar (his incarnation as a boar). It was built circa 900–925. Vishnu assumed this form in order to rescue the earth after a demon had hidden it in the slush at the bottom of the sea. In the inner sanctum, all of creation is depicted on the massive and beautifully polished sides of a stone boar, which in turn stands on the serpent Shesha. The ceiling is carved with a lotus relief, which represents the flowering of the crown chakra, the spiritual center. ⊠ *Khajuraho.*

Lakshmana Temple

ARCHAEOLOGICAL SITE | Across from the Varaha Temple stands this temple dedicated to Vishnu. It is the only complete temple remaining. Along with Kandariya Mahadeva and Vishvanath, this edifice represents the peak of achievement in North Indian temple architecture. All three temples were built in the early to mid-10th century, face east, and follow an elaborate plan resembling a double cross, with three tiers of exterior sculpture on high platforms. The ceiling of the portico is carved with shell and floral motifs. The support beam over the entrance to the main shrine shows Lakshmi, goddess of wealth and consort of Vishnu, with Brahma, Lord of Creation, on her left and Shiva, Lord of Destruction, on her right. Around the exterior base are some of Khajuraho's most famous sculptures, with gods and goddesses on the protruding corners, erotic couples or groups in the recesses, and apsaras

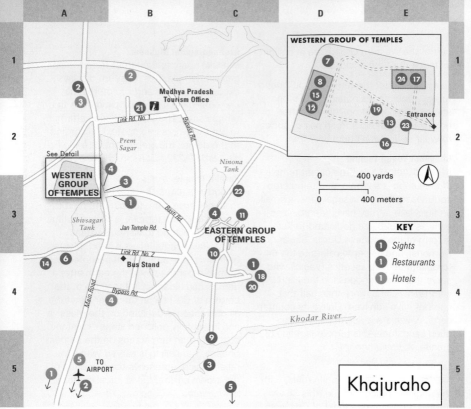

Khajuraho

and *sur-sundaris* (apsaras performing everyday activities) in between. Along the sides of the tall platform beneath the temple, carvings depict social life, including battle scenes, festivals, and more X-rated pursuits. According to the inscription on the Lakshmana Temple, it was built by King Yasovarman. The whole temple was built to house an image of Vishnu given him by his Pratihara overlord, Devapala. This image (it can still be seen here) was originally brought over from Tibet. ⊠ *Khajuraho.*

★ Kandariya Mahadev

ARCHAEOLOGICAL SITE | This temple, which lies west of the Lakshmana, is the tallest and most evolved temple in Khajuraho in terms of the blending of architecture and sculpture, and one of the finest in India. Probably built around 1025–50 by King Vidyahara (the greatest of the Chandela kings), it follows the five-shrine design. Its central spire, which towers 102 feet above the platform, is actually made up of 84 subsidiary towers built up in increments. The feeling of ascent is repeated inside, where each succeeding portico rises a step above the previous one, and the inner sanctum is higher still; dedicated to Shiva (Mahadev is another name for Shiva), this inner sanctum houses a marble lingam with a 4-foot circumference. Even the figures on this temple are taller and slimmer than those elsewhere. The rich interior carving includes two beautiful *toranas* (arched doorways). Outside, three bands of sculpture around the sanctum and transept bring to life a whole galaxy of Hindu gods and goddesses, mithunas, celestial handmaidens, and lions. ⊠ *Khajuraho.*

Devi Jagdamba Temple

ARCHAEOLOGICAL SITE | This temple was originally dedicated to Vishnu, as indicated by a prominent sculpture over the sanctum's doorway. It now honors Parvati, Shiva's consort, but because her image is black—a color associated with Kali—it's also known as the Kali Temple. From the inside, its three-shrine design

Don't Miss the Details

It's well worth hiring a guide, for the Western Group at least, who can point out the more quirky aspects. The number of carvings can seem overwhelming, but keep an eye out for work into which the carvers injected their own views of life, often with a sense of humor. In the Western Group's Lakshmana temple, there is an elephant turning his head and laughing at the couple having sex beside him. In another carving a man has covered his face in embarrassment, but he's still peeping through his fingers at what's going on nearby.

makes the temple appear to be shaped like a cross. The third band of sculpture has a series of erotic mithunas, considered some of the finest sculpture of this type in all of Khajuraho. The ceilings are similar to those in the Kandariya Mahadev, and the three-headed, eight-armed statue of Shiva is one of the best cult images in Khajuraho. ⊠ *Khajuraho.*

Mahadeva Temple

ARCHAEOLOGICAL SITE | Sharing the platform with the Kandariya Mahadev and the Devi Jagdamba, this small temple is mostly in ruins. Now dedicated to Shiva, it may originally have been a subsidiary temple to the Kandariya, probably dedicated to Shiva's consort. In the portico stands a remarkable statue of a man caressing a mythical horned lion. ⊠ *Khajuraho.*

Chitragupta Temple

ARCHAEOLOGICAL SITE | This temple that's just north of the Devi Jagdamba also resembles it in construction. In honor of the presiding deity, the sun god Surya, the temple faces east, and its cell contains a 5-foot-tall image of Surya complete with the chariot and seven horses that carry him across the sky. Surya also appears above the doorway. In the central niche south of the sanctum is an image of Vishnu with 11 heads; his own face is in the center, and the other heads represent his 10 main incarnations. Sculptural scenes of animal combat, royal processions, masons at work, and joyous dances depict the lavish country life of the Chandelas. It also has an ancient three-story stepped tank (water reservoir). ⊠ *Khajuraho.*

Vishvanath Temple

ARCHAEOLOGICAL SITE | Two staircases lead up to this temple, the northern one flanked by a pair of lions and the southern by a pair of elephants. The Vishvanath probably preceded the Kandariya, but here only two of the original corner shrines remain. On the outer wall of the corridor surrounding the cells is an impressive image of Brahma, the three-headed Lord of Creation, and his consort, Saraswati. On every wall the female form predominates, portraying some women's 10th-century occupations: writing a letter, holding a baby, applying makeup, or playing music. The nymphs of paradise are voluptuous and provocative, the erotic scenes robust. An inscription states that the temple was built by Chandela King Dhanga in 1002. The temple sits on a terrace to the east of the Chitragupta and Devi Jagdamba temples. ⊠ *Khajuraho.*

Nandi Temple

ARCHAEOLOGICAL SITE | This simple temple, which faces Vishvanath, houses a monolithic statue of Shiva's mount, the massive and richly harnessed bull Nandi. ⊠ *Khajuraho.*

Parvati Temple

ARCHAEOLOGICAL SITE | The small and heavily rebuilt temple, near Vishvanath, was originally dedicated to Vishnu. The present icon is that of the goddess Ganga (a representation of the river Ganges) standing on her mount, the crocodile. ⊠ *Khajuraho.*

State Museum of Tribal and Folk Arts

MUSEUM | There's an excellent collection here, consisting of more than 500 artifacts of terra-cotta, metal, and wood crafts, paintings, jewelry, and masks from all over Madhya Pradesh and the Bastar region (known for tribal crafts) in the neighboring state of Chhattisgarh. ⊠ *Chandela Cultural Complex, Rajnagar Rd.* ☎ *768/627–4051* ⊠ *Free* ☉ *Closed Mon.*

EASTERN GROUP OF TEMPLES

Scattered around the edges of the old village of Khajuraho, the Eastern Group of temples includes three Brahma and four Jain temples. Their proximity attests to the religious tolerance of the times in general and the Chandela rulers in particular.

Vamana Temple

ARCHAEOLOGICAL SITE | The late-11th-century Vamana Temple, the northernmost one in the Eastern Group, is dedicated to Vishnu's dwarf incarnation (though the image in the sanctum looks more like a tall, sly child). The sanctum walls show unusual theological openness, depicting most of the major gods and goddesses; Vishnu appears in many of his forms, including the Buddha, his ninth incarnation. Outside, two tiers of sculpture are concerned mainly with the nymphs of paradise, who strike charming poses under their private awnings. The pretty view from this temple includes barley fields. ⊠ *Khajuraho.*

Javari Temple

ARCHAEOLOGICAL SITE | Small and well-proportioned, this temple is just south of the Vamana and roughly contemporary with it. It has a simplified three-shrine design: the two main exterior bands of sculpture bear hosts of heavenly maidens. It's also dedicated to Lord Vishnu. ⊠ *Khajuraho.*

Carvings on the Kandariya Mahadev

Brahma Temple

ARCHAEOLOGICAL SITE | This granite-and-sandstone temple, one of the earliest here (circa 900), is probably misnamed. Although Brahma is a member of the triad of Hinduism's great gods, along with Shiva and Vishnu, he rarely gets a temple to himself. (The only other famous Brahma Temple is at Pushkar, in Rajasthan.) It differs in design from most of the other temples here, particularly in the combination of materials and the shape of its spire. Nearby is Ninora Tal, one of the largest tanks in Khajuraho. ⊠ *Khajuraho.*

Ghantai Temple

ARCHAEOLOGICAL SITE | All that's left of the temple here are its pillars, festooned with carvings of pearls and bells. Adorning the entrance are an eight-armed Jain goddess, Chakreshvari, riding the mythical bird Garuda and a relief illustrating the 16 dreams of the mother of Mahavira, the founder and greatest figure in Jainism and a counterpart to the Buddha. The temple sits south of the Vamana, Javari,

and Brahma temples, toward the Jain complex. ⊠ *Khajuraho.*

Adinath Temple

ARCHAEOLOGICAL SITE | The late-11th-century Adinath Temple, a minor shrine, is set in a small walled compound southeast of the Ghantai temple. Its porch and the statue of the Tirthankara (literally, Ford-Maker, a figure who leads others to liberation) Adinatha are modern additions. Built at the beginning of the Chandelas' decline, this temple is relatively small, but the spire and base are richly carved. ⊠ *Khajuraho.*

Parsvanath Temple

ARCHAEOLOGICAL SITE | This temple was built in the mid-10th century during the reign of King Dhangadeva. It is the largest and finest in the Eastern Group's Jain complex and holds some of the best sculpture in Khajuraho, including images of Vishnu. In contrast to the intricate calculations behind the layout of the Western Group, the plan for this temple is a simple rectangle, with a separate spire in the rear. Statues of flying angels

and sloe-eyed beauties occupied with children, cosmetics, and flowers adorn the outer walls. The stone conveys even the texture of the women's thin garments. ✉ *Khajuraho.*

Shantinath Temple

ARCHAEOLOGICAL SITE | Set within the walled Jain temple complex alongside the Adinath and Parsvanath temples, the Shantinath Temple is a collection of small, early-11th-century shrines. Though remodeled extensively, it still contains some old Jain sculptures. The main draw is the 12-foot idol of Lord Shantinath in the inner sanctum. ✉ *Khajuraho.*

SOUTHERN GROUP OF TEMPLES

The Southern Group, the smallest, includes two impressive temples from the 12th century. They are the Chaturbhuja Temple (which has a massive, carved image of Vishnu) and the Duladeo Temple, one of the last temples of the Chandela era.

Duladeo Temple

ARCHAEOLOGICAL SITE | Though built in the customary five-shrine style, this 12th-century temple looks flatter and more massive than most Khajuraho shrines. About 900 yards south of the Eastern Group's Ghantai, it stands near the Khudar rivulet. Probably the last temple built in Khajuraho, the Duladeo lacks the usual ambulatory passage and crowning lotus-shaped finials. Here, too, in this temple dedicated to Shiva, eroticism works its way in, though the amorous figures are discreetly placed. ✉ *Khajuraho.*

Bijamandala Temple

ARCHAEOLOGICAL SITE | As part of continuing explorations since 1999, the largest temple yet—4 meters longer than the Kandariya Mahadeva—has been partially unearthed. On the Bijamandala you can see multiple tiers of beautifully carved moldings and a Shiva lingam placed on a marble pedestal. Images of Vishnu and Brahma have been found as well, and it also houses a lovely image of Saraswati. Archaeologists surmise that the temple, begun in the late 10th or early 11th century and between the Duladeo and the Chaturbhuj, may never have been completed, judging by the remains and unfinished statues found on the site. ✉ *Khajuraho.*

Chaturbhuj Temple

ARCHAEOLOGICAL SITE | This small 12th-century temple, nearly 3 km (2 miles) south of Duladeo, is often ignored given its distance from the main complex. It has an attractive colonnade entrance and a feeling of verticality thanks to its single spire. Inside, its impressive four-armed image of Vishnu in a sunken sanctum, may be the single most striking piece of sculpture in Khajuraho. The exterior sculpture here is not nearly as impressive as other examples in the area, but the temple is definitely the best place in Khajuraho to watch the sun set. In the north corner there is a rare image of the goddess Narsimhi, who has a lion's face and a human body. ✉ *Khajuraho.*

🍴 Restaurants

Bella Italia

$ | **ITALIAN** | Though simple and no-frills, this rooftop restaurant, with plastic tables and chairs and just a few potted plants is a longtime traveler favorite. The food here is the main draw, with Italian cuisine that many foreign guests find a welcome respite from the area's ubiquitous spicy curry dishes. **Known for:** thin-crust pizzas; house-made pastas; Nutella crepes topped with ice cream. [$] *Average main: Rs. 250* ✉ *Jain Temple Rd.* ☎ *89621–59510* 💳 *No credit cards.*

Blue Sky Restaurant

$ | **INTERNATIONAL** | Across from the Vishvanath and Nandi temples, Blue Sky serves decent food, but it's the views here that draw in the crowds. The entire Western Group of temples is visible from the second-floor and rooftop terraces, and dinnertime guests can see the sound-and-light show from their tables.

Known for: international cuisine, including some Japanese items; good variety of breakfast items; stellar views of the Western Group of temples. [$] *Average main: Rs. 200* ✉ *Main Rd., near Western Group of Temples* ☎ *94251–43803* 💳 *No credit cards.*

Maharaja Cafe

$ | **INTERNATIONAL** | A spiral staircase leads up to this indoor, air-conditioned restaurant with cheery bright curtains on a rooftop. The Maharaja Cafe overlooks a *maqbara* (domed memorial) to the left and the Western Temples to the right; there's a wooden platform with outdoor seating offering great views of the sights and market below.**Known for:** rich pastas and curries; tandoori chicken dishes; friendly and attentive service. [$] *Average main: Rs. 250* ✉ *Opposite Western Group of Temples* ☎ *83490–17939* 💳 *No credit cards.*

★ **Raja Café**

$$ | **INTERNATIONAL** | This charming, two-story restaurant just across the road from the Western Temples (there are stunning views from the terrace) serves a mix of Indian and continental fare. It has a distinctly European aesthetic, with an open courtyard, where marble-top tables are shaded by an enormous neem tree and overhanging branches of bougainvillea, and a small indoor section that is air-conditioned (the summer heat can be quite punishing). **Known for:** crostinis with Swiss cheese; European-style pastries; wood-fire pizzas. [$] *Average main: Rs. 350* ✉ *Opposite the Western Temples* ☎ *7686/272–307* 🌐 *www.rajacafe.com.*

Hotels

Hotel Clarks Khajuraho

$$$ | **HOTEL** | A 10-minute drive from the main group of temples, this is a clean and tastefully decorated hotel, and though it lacks personality, it does have an excellent range of sport and leisure options, including swimming, cricket, badminton, tennis, and jogging. **Pros:** large fitness center; on-site spa; gorgeous pool. **Cons:** Wi-Fi not included; can be noisy during Indian wedding season; average food. [$] *Rooms from: Rs. 6500* ✉ *Near Airport Rd., between airport and temples, off main road* ☎ *7686/274–038, 7686/274–056, 7686/274–421* 🌐 *www.hotelclarks.com/khajuraho* 🛏 *100 rooms* 🍴 *No meals.*

Hotel Tourist Village

$ | **HOTEL** | **FAMILY** | Affordable and charming, this quaint hotel, run by the Madhya Pradesh Government, is built in the style of a "traditional village," and although it's a 10-minute walk from the bustle and noise of the main road, it feels much more remote. **Pros:** quiet, relaxing ambience; economical; resident bunnies and chickens are a hit with kids. **Cons:** white fluorescent lights in the rooms detract from the village charm; rooms are basic and worn; menu options are limited. [$] *Rooms from: Rs. 2500* ✉ *Near Vidhyadhar Colony* ☎ *7686/274–062* 🌐 *www.mptourism.com* 🛏 *11 rooms* 🍴 *Free Breakfast.*

Lalit Temple View Khajuraho

$$$ | **HOTEL** | As the closest hotel to the temples, the Lalit has a great view of them—one you can enjoy while lounging in the manicured garden, sipping cocktails next to the pool. **Pros:** a five-minute walk from the main temples; food available 24 hours; kids' playground on-site. **Cons:** room rates are high; only some rooms have temple views; expensive food and bottled water. [$] *Rooms from: Rs. 8000* ✉ *Opposite Circuit House* ☎ *7686/272–111* 🌐 *www.thelalit.com/the-lalit-khajuraho* 🛏 *47 rooms* 🍴 *No meals.*

Radisson Hotel Khajuraho

$$ | **HOTEL** | Luxurious and modern, this hotel situated just a kilometer from the Western Temples has a lively restaurant and lovely surroundings—the pool, one of the deepest in Khajuraho at 9 feet, is surrounded by undulating landscaped gardens, so you can always hear

birdsong. **Pros:** lots of on-site amenities; free Wi-Fi; lovely, deep pool. **Cons:** feels like a big-city hotel, with little local charm; rooms are lackluster; slow service in restaurant at times. $ *Rooms from: Rs. 5500* ✉ *Bypass Rd.* ☎ *7686/272-777* ⊕ *www.radisson.com/khajurahoin* ⤳ *94 rooms* ❘O❘ *No meals.*

★ **Ramada Khajuraho**

$$ | **HOTEL** | The expansive lawns of this 14-acre property feature a lovely walking track, a rose garden, and an organic kitchen garden, while inside the hotel all is grand and cool white-marble elegance. **Pros:** a lot of bang for your buck compared with others in town; discounts available; friendly and attentive staff. **Cons:** fees for Wi-Fi after first device; no views of temples; swimming pool is small. $ *Rooms from: Rs. 4500* ✉ *Airport Rd.* ☎ *768/272-302* ⊕ *www.ramadakhajuraho.com* ⤳ *85 rooms* ❘O❘ *No meals.*

 # Shopping

Numerous shops around the Western Group of temples sell curios, including cheeky takes on Khajuraho's erotic sculptures, as well as tribal metalwork.

Chandela Emporium

CRAFTS | This expansive stores stocks local handicrafts, miniature wood paintings, brass sculptures, and jewelry. The textiles are particularly impressive: there's a huge collection of scarves, saris, and clothing in silks and cottons, with traditional Indian prints. ✉ *Opposite Pahil Batika* ☎ *768/627-4077.*

Kandaryia Shilpgram

CRAFTS | This large crafts shop, with woodwork, handicrafts, jewelery, and silks, is owned by the Agra marble-inlay maker Oswal. It's associated with a government project that hosts craftspeople from all over India for residences during peak travel season; you can watch the artisans at work as you shop. ✉ *Bamitha Rd., near Jhankar Hotel* ☎ *768/627-4125.*

Side Trips from Khajuraho

If you have time, take an extra day to explore and picnic in the beautiful countryside around Khajuraho.

Gharial Sanctuary

NATURE PRESERVE | Drive or bike to the Gharial Sanctuary on the Ken River, 28 km (17 miles) away; the park was set up to protect the slender-snouted crocodile and has some lovely waterfalls. The Madhya Pradesh Tourism office has information about renting a jeep, and can provide directions. ✉ *Gharial Sanctuary* ☉ *Closed during monsoon.*

Panna National Park

NATURE PRESERVE | Open October through June, Panna National Park is ideal for viewing wildlife such as antelope, deer, and all kinds of monkeys; if you come for one of the twice-daily safaris (departing early morning and midafternoon), you may see one of the 27 elusive tigers in the Panna Tiger Reserve. The best viewing season is January through March. ✉ *31 km (19 miles) southeast of Khajuraho* ⊕ *pannatigerreserve.in* 🎫 *Rs. 250* ☉ *Closed July–Sept.*

Varanasi

406 km (252 miles) east of Khajuraho; 765 km (474 miles) southeast of Delhi.

A visit to Varanasi, also known as Benaras or Benares, or as Kashi (meaning "resplendent with light"), is an experience unlike any other. This is the epitome of a holy city, inundated with religious pilgrims and sacred cows, yet it is also a city firmly grounded in the commerce and reality of day-to-day existence. A visit here is thrilling but exhausting, and never boring.

Along the left bank of the Ganges, a river believed by Hindus to hold the power of salvation in every drop, Varanasi is one of the most sacred places in the world, considered by many to be the spiritual heart of India. Every year the city welcomes millions of pilgrims for whom the water—physically fouled by the pollution of humans both living and dead—remains spiritually pristine enough to cleanse the soul.

About 90 ghats, or steps, line this 6-km (4-mile) stretch of the Ganges, wedding the holy river to the chaotic city above it—a maze of streets and alleys crammed with derelict palaces, homes, and about 2,000 temples and shrines (most of these holy sites are open only to Indians, however). Here you'll see funeral processions, cows and goats munching on whatever they can find, and, especially near the Golden Temple (Kashi Vishvanath) and centrally located Dashashvamedh Ghat, assertive hawkers and phony guides.

The most essential thing to do in Varanasi is to take a boat ride along the Ganges, preferably at dawn or sunset, to see the ghats and the rituals being performed—it's also a peaceful respite from the chaos of the city.

Sarnath, just a few kilometers north of Varanasi, is a peaceful park and the historic center of the Buddhist world, where the Buddha preached his first sermon, revealing the Eightfold Path that became the central tenets of Buddhism. It is an easy, and fairly peaceful, place to visit.

GETTING ORIENTED

Varanasi is on the west bank of the Ganges, which is intersected by two smaller rivers: the Varana, to the north, which winds by the Cantonment area (often abbreviated as Cantt) and joins the Ganges near Raj Ghat, and the Asi, a small stream in the south. The ghats stretch along the river from Raj Ghat in the north to Assi Ghat in the south; beyond Assi is the university, across the river from Ramnagar Fort and Palace. The city itself spreads out behind the ghats, where there are smaller hotels and restaurants; the larger chain hotels are in the Cantonment area, about 20 minutes from the river by auto-rickshaw.

Traditionally, Varanasi is divided into three sections named after important temples to Shiva. Omkareshvara is the namesake temple in the northern section, which is probably the oldest area but is now impoverished and seldom visited by pilgrims. The central section is named after Kashi Vishvanath, the famous "Golden Temple." Vishvanath itself means "Lord of the Universe," one of Shiva's names, and there are many Vishvanath temples. The southern area, the Kedar Khand, is named for Kedareshvara, a temple easily spotted from the river thanks to the vertical red and white stripes painted on its walls, a custom of the South Indian worshippers who are among the temple's devotees.

GETTING AROUND

Varanasi is a chaotic place, and although you can certainly find your own way around, you might want to hire a guide for your first day to help you get oriented: guide fees start from Rs. 1,600 for a half-day or Rs. 2,000 for an eight-hour full day, depending on how many people are in your party. You can book a guide through your hotel, or through the Indian tourism office. A guide will also know which temples and mosques are open to foreigners and/or non-Hindus, as many are not.

Out on your own, walking is your best bet within the old city, and if your feet get tired, or you get lost, take an auto- or cycle-rickshaw.

ESSENTIALS
India Ministry of Tourism
You can also find an official tourist counter at the airport. ✉ *15B The Mall* ☎ *0542/250–1784* ⊕ *www.incredible-india.org.*

Sights

Bharat Kala Bhavan Museum
MUSEUM | No one interested in Indian art should miss this museum on the campus of Banaras Hindu University. The permanent collection includes brocade textiles,

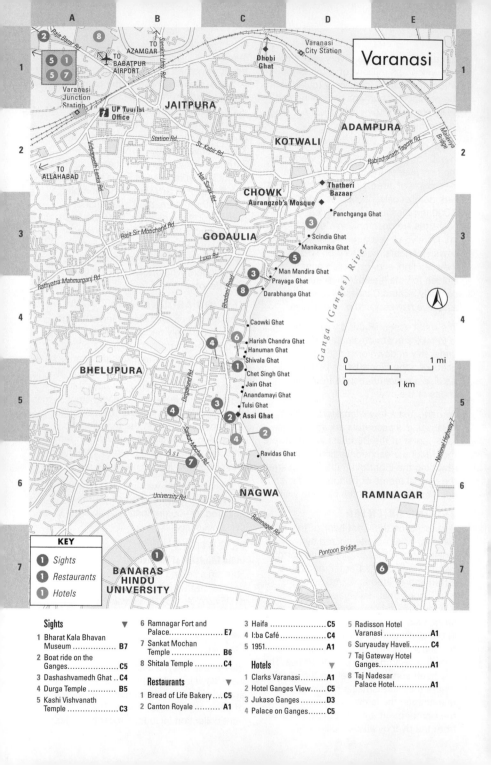

excellent Hindu and Buddhist sculptures, and miniature paintings from the courts of the Mughals and the Hindu princes of the Punjab hills. One sculpture with particular power is a 4th-century Gupta-dynasty frieze depicting Krishna (an incarnation of Vishnu) holding up Mt. Govardhan to protect his pastoral comrades from the rain. Have your car or rickshaw wait for you, as transportation can be hard to find on the university's sprawling campus. It's a good idea to go with a guide, since the upkeep of the museum is a bit haphazard and you might need someone who knows his way around and can turn the lights on. ✉ *Banaras Hindu University, Lanka* ☎ *542/230–7621* ⊕ *www.bhu.ac.in* ▣ *Rs. 250* ⊗ *Closed Sun.*

★ Boat ride on the Ganges

TOUR—SIGHT | The quintessential Varanasi experience is a boat ride along the Ganges. The most popular place to hire a boat is at Dashashvamedh Ghat—essentially in the middle of Varanasi, and convenient if you're staying near the water—or at Assi Ghat, the southernmost end of the ghats. It's a good idea to arrange your boat trip the afternoon before, then get up and meet your boatmen early the next morning so that you can be out on the water as the sun comes up. Rates are negotiable, but it should cost about Rs. 125 per person for an hour, or Rs. 500 for a private boat. If you are traveling to Varanasi between July and September, check with the Ministry of Tourism Office first, as boat rides are sometimes prohibited during monsoons for safety reasons. Probably the most popular routes are any that take you past Manikarnika, the main "burning" ghat, though the people and their rituals might be more sightworthy than the ghats themselves.

These are some of the landmarks that you'll see along the way.

Panchganga Ghat. Down below Aurangzeb's Mosque, this is an important bathing point. It's the mythical meeting place of the five sacred rivers, and images of the river goddesses are displayed here.

Aurangzeb's Mosque. The Alamgir Mosque, known as Aurangzeb's Mosque, was built by the Mughal emperor Aurangzeb over the remains of the Hindu temple that had previously stood here—when he conquered Banaras, he had ordered the destruction of all temples. The mosque's dramatic vantage point overlooking the Ganges gives it a prominent place on the skyline. The mosque is closed to non-Muslims.

Manikarnika Ghat. This is Varanasi's main burning ghat. At the top of Manikarnika's steps is a small, deep pool, or *kund,* said to have been dug by Vishnu at the dawn of creation and thus to be the first *tirtha*—literally, "ford," and figuratively a place of sacred bathing. Shiva is said to have lost a jeweled earring (*manikarnika*) as he trembled in awe before this place, one of the holiest sites in Varanasi.

Kashi Vishvanath Temple (Golden Temple). This temple, with its gold-plated spire, is easy to spot on the skyline. It's the most sacred shrine in Varanasi.

Chausath Yogini Temple. Just north of Dashashvamedh Ghat, Chausath Yogini is at the top of a particularly steep set of steps by the ghat of the same name. Originally devoted to a Tantric cult that is also associated with an important ruined temple at Khajuraho, it's now dedicated to Kali (the goddess most popular with Bengalis), known here simply as "Ma"—Mother. The worshippers are mainly white-sari-clad widows from Varanasi's Bengali quarter; in the early morning you'll see them coming for the *darshan* (vision) of Kali after bathing in the Ganges.

Dashashvamedh Ghat. This is one of the busiest ghats, and a good starting place for a boat ride. Every evening at sunset the Ganga Arti prayer ceremony

Continued on page 186

VARANASI

Also known as Kashi (City of Light) or Kashika (Shining One), Varanasi is one of the holiest cities on earth: there are more than 700 temples and countless shrines here—though none of these are more holy than the Ganges River itself.

Each drop of Ganges water is believed to hold the power of salvation: immersing oneself in it is said to cleanse one not just of sins in this life, but of all the sins of past lives, too. As a result, millions of pilgrims come to this city every year to take part in ritual cleansing. Dying here and being cremated is believed to give instant enlightenment and freedom from the cycle of rebirth.

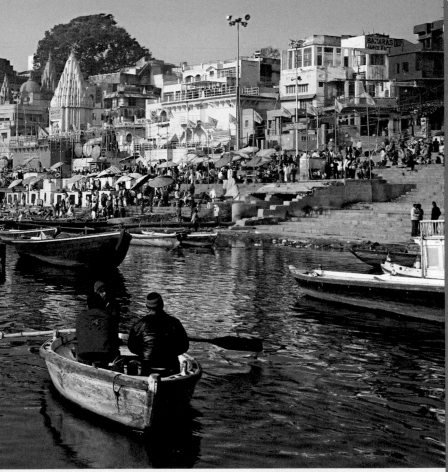

While the water here might be spiritually pure, the Ganges is also one of the dirtiest bodies of water in the world, and drinking it or bathing in it carries the risk of infection. To get the full experience of the river (without actually going in), take a boat ride, preferably as the sun comes up in the morning. From this vantage point you'll see not only the various *ghats* (stairs down to the river) but also the daily rituals and prayers that are a part of this incredible city: everything from elderly men sitting cross-legged in prayer or meditation, to young men exercising, people washing clothes, and various and sundry people and animals bathing.

Above, Dashashvamedh ghat on the banks of the Ganges River, in Varanasi.

ALONG THE GANGES

Roughly 85 ghats line the west bank of the Ganges, stretching out over about 6 km (4 mi); each has a different historical or ritual significance.

Chet Singh Ghat

Dashashvamedh Ghat

Chausath Yogini Temple

Dashashvamedh Ghat Prayaga Ghat

Darabhanga Ghat

Caowki Ghat

Lali Ghat

Harish Chandra Ghat

Hanuman Ghat

Shivala Ghat

Chet Singh Ghat

Jain Ghat

Bhadani Rd.

Pandit Manmohan Malviya Rd.

Durga Temple (Monkey Temple)

Anandamayi Ghat

Sankat Mochan Temple

Tulsi Ghat

Assi Ghat

> **Dashashvamedh** is one of the busiest ghats along the Ganges. This is a good place to hire a boat (*see full listing*).

Assi Ghat. This southernmost ghat marks the place where the Assi River and the Ganges meet.

On the eastern side of the river is the **Ramnagar Fort and Palace** (*see full listing*).

Durga Temple (aka Monkey Temple). Inland and a short walk from Assi Ghat, the monkey temple is recognizable by its mulitiered spire (*see full listing*).

Tulsi Ghat. This ghat was named for Tulsi Das, the great 16th-century Hindu poet who wrote the epic Ramcharitmnanas while he was in Varanasi; the poet's house and temple are close by as well. Legend has it that the manuscript fell into the water and did not sink, but floated instead, and was saved. Cultural activities often take place at this ghat.

Anandamayi Ghat. This ghat is named after the Bengali (female) saint Anandamayi Ma who died in 1982. The ashram that she founded here attracts thousands of devotees.

Jain (Bachraj) Ghat. Previously part of the adjoining ghat, the Jains made this their own in the early 20th century. The Jain temple here is quite impressive.

Chet Singh Ghat. The reddish color of the fort at Chet Singh ghat stands out, although you won't see many bathers here because it's said that the currents here are dangerous. The ghat is historically notable as being the spot where the maharaja of Varanasi was defeated by the British in the mid 1800s.

Shivala Ghat. Built in 1770 by Chet Singh, the maharaja of Varanasi, the ghat has a large mansion and temple.

Hanuman Ghat. Legend has it that this ghat was built by Lord Ram (the original name was Ramesvaram ghat), and that the ghat is dedicated to his favorite disciple: Hanuman. Because Hanuman is a symbol of strength, you can often see local wrestlers and body builders here.

Harish Chandra Ghat. This cremation ghat has been modernized and has an electric crematorium. It's also known as Adi Manikarnika, which means "original creation ground."

Lali (Dhobi) Ghat. *Dhobis* (washer men and women) do early morning laundry here, beating the clothes against the stones in the river.

Caowki Ghat. A huge ficus tree at the top of the steps makes this ghat recognizable. Under the tree

Ganga Ghats

Along the Ganges

Offering to the Gods

KEY

▰	*Ghats*
⬯	*Mosques*
⛩	*Temples*
⛵	*Boats*

Man Mandira Ghat · Nepali Ghat · Manikarnika Ghat · Vishvanath Temple · Scindia Ghat · Aurangzeb's Mosque · Panchganga Ghat

Ganges River

Manikarnika Ghat

many stone figures of snakes are arranged.

Darabhanga Ghat. You can recognize this ghat by the Greek-style pillars.

Chausath Yogini Temple. A steep set of stairs leads from the Chausath Yogini ghat to the temple of the same name. Originally devoted to a Tantric cult that is also associated with an important ruined temple at Khajuraho, it's now dedicated to Kali (the goddess most popular with Bengalis), known here simply as "Ma"—Mother. The worshippers are mainly white-sari-clad widows from Varanasi's Bengali quarter; in the early morning you'll see them coming for the *darshan* (vision) of

Kali after bathing in the Ganges.

Prayaga Ghat. This ghat marks the location where the Ganges, the Yamuna, and the invisible Sarasvati rivers all come together. The temple is not often used, however, except by boatmen, who store their boats here.

Man Mandira Ghat. Maharajah Jai Singh, of Jaipur, built his palace here, along with one of his 5 observatories (the most famous is the Jantar Mantar in Jaipur).

Vishvanath (Golden) Temple. With its gold-plated spire, this temple is easy to spot on the skyline. It's the most sacred shrine in Varanasi *(see full listing).*

Nepali Ghat. One of the more prominent ghats, Nepali has a golden lion outside a pagoda-like temple, built by the royal

family of Nepal. Many Nepalese live in the area.

Manikarnika Ghat. Varanasi's main burning ghat is a focal point for most trips along the river, and the traditional funeral pyres burn 24 hours a day. Boats keep a distance, out of respect, but you can still see the fires. At the top of Manikarnika's steps is a small, deep pool, or *kund,* said to have been dug by Vishnu at the dawn of creation and thus to be the first *tirtha*—literally, "ford," and figuratively a place of sacred bathing. Shiva is said to have lost a jeweled earring *(manikarnika)* as he trembled in awe before this place, one of the holiest sites in Varanasi.

Scindia Ghat. This ghat is notable for its ornate temple, which was so heavy that

it collapsed into the river and is now partially submerged.

Aurangzeb's Mosque. The Alamgir Mosque, known as Aurangzeb's Mosque, was built by the Mughul emperor Aurangzeb over the remains of the Hindu temple that had previously stood here. When Aurangzeb conquered Banaras, he had ordered destruction of all temples. The mosque's dramatic vantage point overlooking the Ganges gives it a prominent place in the skyline. The mosque is closed to non-Muslims.

Panchganga Ghat. Below Aurangzeb's Mosque, this is an important bathing point. It's the mythical meeting place of the 5 sacred rivers and images of the river goddesses are displayed here.

Ramnagar Fort

Saris draped on the stairs to dry

PRACTICAL MATTERS (FAQ)

Where can I hire a boat? The most popular place to hire a boat is at Dashashvamedh Ghat—essentially in the middle of Varanasi, and convenient if you're staying near the water. You can also hire one at Assi Ghat, the southernmost end of the ghats. It's a good idea to arrange your boat trip the afternoon before, then get up and meet your boatman early the next morning so that you can be out on the water as the sun comes up.

How much will it cost? Rates are negotiable, but it should cost about Rs. 100–150 for a one-hour trip.

Where do I want to go? The most popular routes are any that take you past the Manikarnika cremation ghat, the main burning ghat. In general, though, the people and their rituals are more sightworthy than the ghats themselves.

When should I go? The best time to be on the river is as the sun comes up in the morning, when people and pilgrims are getting ready to start the day.

At morning prayer

A *sadhu* (holy man)

Crowds bathing in the sacred Ganges

Morning traffic on the Ganges

A painting on a temple wall

Climbing the steep ghat stairs

A *puja* offering to the Gods

Darabhanga Ghat

ceremony

GANGA ARTI

Take a boat ride on the Ganges at sunrise, but come back to the water's edge in the evening, as the sun goes down for *Ganga Arti* (*arti* means prayer), at Dashashvamedh Ghat. The steps fill with people singing Vedic hymns, lighting lamps, and praying along with the priests. It can get very crowded, so you might even want to hire another boat so that you can witness the whole scene from the water, without dealing with the crush on the ghat.

is performed here, with the steps filling with priests and people praying.

Dhobi Ghat. At this ghat south of Dashashvamedh, *dhobis* (washer men and women) do early morning laundry by beating it against stones in the river.

Durga Temple (aka Monkey Temple). Inland and a short walk from Assi Ghat, it's recognizable by its multitiered spire.

On the eastern side of the river you can see the **Ramnagar Fort and Palace**.

Assi Ghat. The southernmost ghat, marking the place where the Assi River and the Ganges meet, has a pipal tree with a lingam. ⊠ *Varanasi.*

★ **Dashashvamedh Ghat**

BUILDING | At roughly the midway point of Varanasi's ghats, this is a convenient and popular spot, always busy with hawkers and pilgrims, and a good place to hire a boat. It's one of the holiest ghats, the site of ancient sacrificial rite: the name literally means "10-horse sacrifice."
Ganga Arti is an *arti* (prayer ceremony) performed at Dashashvamedh Ghat every night at sunset. Priests clad in saffron and white robes blow conch shells and perform a synchronized ritual with *diyas* (lamps), flowers, and incense. The steps fill with people singing Vedic hymns, lighting lamps, and praying along with the priests; if you're out on a boat at this time, you can take in the whole scene without having to deal with the crush on the ghat itself. ⊠ *East of Godaulia Crossing, Chowk.*

Durga Temple

RELIGIOUS SITE | This 18th-century shrine, dedicated to the goddess Durga, Shiva's consort, stands beside a large, square pool of water due west about 1 km from Assi Ghat. The multilevel spire (five lower ones, and one on top) symbolizes the belief that the five elements of the world (earth, air, water, fire, and ether) merge with the Supreme. The shrine is also called the Monkey Temple because there are monkeys everywhere, and they'll

steal anything (keep all food and water out of sight). ⊠ *Durgakund Rd.*

Kashi Vishvanath Temple

RELIGIOUS SITE | Known as the Golden Temple because of the gold plate on its spire—a gift from the Sikh Maharaja Ranjit Singh of Punjab in 1835—this is the most sacred shrine in Varanasi. It's dedicated to Shiva, whose pillar of light is said to have appeared on this spot. Foreigners are only admitted through Gate 2, and are required to bring passports and register prior to entering. Various forms of the arti prayer ceremony are performed outside at 2:30 am, 11:30 am, 7:30 pm, and 11:30 pm, though times can change depending on the season, so it's best to confirm directly. It's located in the Old City above the Ganges, between Dashashvamedh and Manikarnika ghat; to get here, walk from Dashashvamedh Road down the relatively broad, shop-lined lane (Vishvanath Gali, the main sari bazaar) to Vishvanath Temple. The lane turns sharply right at a large idol of the elephant-head god Ganesh, then passes the brightly painted wooden entrance to the 1725 **Annapurna temple** (Annapurna was Vishvanath's consort), on the right. On the left, look for the silver doorway, which is usually manned by a police officer—this is the entrance to the Kashi Vishvanath Temple. The present temple was built by Rani Ahalyabai of Indore in 1776, near the site of the original shrine, which had been destroyed by the emperor Aurangzeb. Nearby is the **Gyanvapi Mosque,** built by Mughal emperor Aurangzeb after he destroyed the temple that stood here; the building's foundation and rear still show parts of the original temple. As a result of Hindu revivalist attempts to reconsecrate the site of the former temple, the area is usually staffed with police and fenced with barbed wire. It's normally very sedate, however, and is an important starting point for Hindu pilgrims. Nonpilgrims aren't allowed into the inner sanctum. ⊠ *Vishvanath Gali.*

The Economics of Burning

Public cremation is the norm for Hindus throughout India, but the spiritual implications of being cremated in Varanasi make dying here an especially celebratory occasion. The idea is that because the Ganges is so holy, a spiritual cleansing in this water means easier achievement of moksha, *the* release from the cycle of rebirth. In Varanasi bodies are wrapped in silk or linen—traditionally white for men, red or orange for women—and carried through the streets on bamboo stretchers to the smoking pyres of the burning ghat. Then, after a brief immersion in the Ganges and a short wait, the body is placed on the pyre for the ritual that precedes the cremation. Funeral parties dressed in white, the color of mourning, surround the deceased. **Photographing funeral ghats is strictly forbidden,** but you are allowed to watch.

While Hindus believe dying in Varanasi will get them closer to achieving purification and moksha, there are still obstacles to achieving the ultimate release from the cycle of rebirth, and money is the most common problem. A proper wood cremation ceremony, even in one's hometown, involves basic **expenses that much of India's poor majority**

simply cannot afford. The most expensive aspect is the wood itself, though there are plenty of other required supplies for the rituals, including ghee (clarified butter), sandalwood powder, cloth to prepare the body, and a tax to be paid, too. Add to that the cost of traveling to Varanasi, and the prospect of honoring the dead at the bank of the Ganges becomes financially daunting.

To help with cost, traditional funeral pyres share space at the burning ghat with Varanasi's one electric cremation center. Burning a body here costs a fraction of the cost of wood cremation, though still expensive by Indian standards. A lack of money, in fact, is probably the best explanation for a body drifting by during a boat ride on the Ganges. It's unlawful to offer dead bodies to the river now, except in a handful of cases—a pregnant woman, a child younger than five, someone with smallpox, someone who has been bitten by a cobra, or a holy man. Hindus believe that **gods live inside these bodies,** so they can't be burned. But in the absence of money for a cremation, poor relatives often have no other choice but to break the law if they want to honor the dead in the holiest of waters.

Ramnagar Fort and Palace

CASTLE/PALACE | Across the Ganges from the river ghats is the 17th-century, red sandstone palace of the Maharaja of Varanasi, who still lives here (if the flag is up, he's in residence) and performs ceremonial and charitable functions. Inside, there are some interesting collections—stop at the Durbar Hall and the Royal Museum—but the place is sadly run-down and the objects are not well maintained. It's sort of fascinating, though, to see the state of decay: a case full of beautiful black musical instruments, for example, is so completely white with dust and the case so covered with grime that it's almost impossible to see anything, and the royal costumes are ratty. Still, there are palanquins and howdahs in ivory, goldplate, or silver (completely tarnished); old carriages and cars; furniture; portraits of maharajas; and arms from Africa, Burma, and Japan. The palace was built to resist the floods of the monsoon, which play havoc with the city side of the river. (It should cost about Rs. 1,200 to take a taxi here and have him wait for an hour or two; negotiate beforehand.) Note that the fort is closed to visitors during monsoon season if the weather is bad. ✉ *End of Pontoon Bridge, off Ramnagar Rd.* ☎ *542/250–5033 tourism office* 🎫 *Rs. 150.*

Sankat Mochan Temple

RELIGIOUS SITE | One of Varanasi's most beloved temples—as well as one of its oldest—Sankat Mochan (Deliverer from Troubles) was built in the late 16th century. Though the city has encroached all around it, the building still stands in a good-size, tree-shaded enclosure, like temples elsewhere in India. (Most temples in Varanasi are squeezed between other buildings.) Although most of the city's major shrines are dedicated to Shiva or various aspects of the mother goddess, Sankat Mochan belongs to Hanuman, the monkey god, revered for his dedicated service to Rama, an incarnation of Vishnu whose story is told in the *Ramayana*. The best time to see Sankat Mochan is early evening, when dozens of locals stop for a brief visit at the end of the workday, and on Tuesday and Saturday—days sacred to Hanuman—when worshippers come in large numbers to pay their respects. ✉ *Durgakund Rd.*

Shitala Temple

RELIGIOUS SITE | This unassuming but very popular white temple near Dashashvamedh Ghat is dedicated to Shitala, the goddess of smallpox, who both causes and cures the disease. Despite the eradication of smallpox, Shitala is still an important folk goddess in North India. ✉ *Shitala Ghat.*

🍴 Restaurants

Bread of Life Bakery

$$ | **CAFÉ** | Handily located behind the Shivala Ghat, this is an impressive haven for homesick Western palates and a great place for breakfast after a morning boat ride. All profits of the café and the art gallery upstairs go to charities, or are used for the employees' education. **Known for:** pancakes with real maple syrup; rich desserts, including eclairs and cakes; savory international lunch items. [$] *Average main: Rs. 300* ✉ *B-3/322 Shivala* ☎ *542/227–5012* 💳 *No credit cards.*

Canton Royale

$$$ | **ECLECTIC** | Behind the colonial facade of the Surya Hotel, the Canton Royal is a simple but elegant restaurant, with vaulted ceilings, statues, and framed pictures of Benarasi royalty. The menu is eclectic, spanning European, Mediterranean, Mexican, and Chinese, but the Indian is the best. **Known for:** tandoori chicken; Varanasi specialties; alfresco dining in the garden. [$] *Average main: Rs. 500* ✉ *Surya Hotel, S-20/51A-5 The Mall* ☎ *542/250–8465, 542/250–8466* 🌐 *www.hotelsuryavns.com.*

Haifa

$$ | **MIDDLE EASTERN** | Situated at the lobby level of Hotel Haifa, this restaurant's specialty is Middle Eastern food. It's basically a long room with nondescript tables and lots of tourists flowing in and out—and no wonder, because it's incredibly cheap and the only place in town to sample freshly made Middle Eastern treats. **Known for:** Middle Eastern "thalis" (meze); Chinese food; reasonable prices. [$] *Average main: Rs. 350* ✉ *B-1/107 Assi Ghat, Varanasi* ☎ *542/231–2960.*

★ I:ba Café

$$ | **ASIAN FUSION** | At this unexpected oasis away from the chaos of the ghats, you can find good Japanese food and great cold coffee, perfect after a hot walk. Dark wood accents, warm yellow lights, and pleasing jazz music set a stylish scene—cane "tikki roofs," cozy floor couches, dangling bells, dry corn husks. **Known for:** chicken gyoza; authentic ramen dishes; Thai, Korean, and Japanese food. [$] *Average main: Rs. 350* ✉ *B3/335B, Shivala* ☎ *542/227–7523.*

1951

$$$$ | **ECLECTIC** | Situated in the plush Clarks Hotel, this upmarket restaurant that's decorated in tones of white and dark wood is best for its Indian food, though there are plenty of fusion and multicuisine choices on the menu. The chef cooks up innovative items in the lively kitchen, with vegetarian and meat-based dishes available. **Known for:** elegant ambience; Indian-international fusion fare; locally inspired Banarasi thalis. [$] *Average main: Rs. 800* ✉ *Clarks Varanasi Hotel, The Mall, Cantt* ☎ *542/250–1011.*

Hotels

There are two options in Varanasi: you can stay near the water, where most of the lodgings are smaller and right in the midst of the action; or you can stay in the Cantonment area, about a 20-minute rickshaw ride away, where the more established, larger hotels are located. The latter area has less character, but it's definitely quieter and less chaotic.

WATERFRONT

Hotel Ganges View

$$ | **B&B/INN** | Still the residence of a well-to-do family, this guesthouse has small, beautiful rooms with quirky charm, and classical Indian concerts are often held here. **Pros:** the veranda is the best place in town to watch pilgrims and tourists; on-site tour and boat-ride bookings; elegant rooms, many with four-poster beds. **Cons:** it's pretty noisy, particularly in rooms without a/c; narrow stairs to the front door make access difficult; fills up fast. [$] *Rooms from: Rs. 5000* ✉ *Assi Ghat* ☎ *542/231–3218, 542/329–0289* 🌐 *www.hotelgangesview.co.in* 🛏 *15 rooms* 🍴 *Free Breakfast.*

Jukaso Ganges

$$$ | **HOTEL** | Accessed by boat from the nearby Dasaswamedh Ghat, this stunning sandstone heritage hotel on the Ganges is perfect for a romantic getaway or a personal retreat. **Pros:** excellent river views; complimentary transfer to Dasaswamedh Ghat to watch the Ganga Arti prayer ceremony; yoga and meditation room. **Cons:** boat access impossible during monsoon, and it's quite a trek overland; monsoon can flood the lobby; limited menu options. [$] *Rooms from: Rs. 10000* ✉ *CK 1/14 Patni Tola Chowk, between Mehta Hospital and Bhosle Ghat* ☎ *542/240–6667 to 6668* 🌐 *jukaso.co.in* 🛏 *15 rooms* 🍴 *Free Breakfast.*

Palace on Ganges

$$$ | **HOTEL** | In this century-old building on Assi Ghat, rooms are styled after Indian states—Gujarat (brightly colored drapes studded with mirror work), Rajasthan (elaborately carved doors and furnishings), and Assam (lots of bamboo). **Pros:** magnificent view from the rooftop; library well stocked with cultural and history books; great food. **Cons:** you'll have to climb a flight of stairs just to get to the front door; rooms with a view are overpriced; power cuts. [$] *Rooms from: Rs. 7000* ✉ *B-1/158 Assi Ghat, Varanasi* ☎ *542/231–4304 to 05* 🌐 *www.palaceonganges.com* 🛏 *24 rooms* 🍴 *Free Breakfast.*

Suryauday Haveli

$$$$ | **HOTEL** | Built in the style of a traditional Nepali courtyard by the royal family of Nepal and once frequented by the king of Nepal and his guests, this boutique hotel sits directly on the banks of the Shivala Ghat. **Pros:** complimentary boat ride to Dashashwamedh Ghat in the evening to watch the Ganga Arti prayers; luxurious rooms; excellent service. **Cons:** windows in all the rooms are a bit small; a long, narrow flight of stairs to reach the main entrance; expensive. [$] *Rooms from: Rs. 15000* ✉ *B–4/25 Shivala Ghat, Nepali Kothi* ☎ *542/654–0390, 542/227–6820, 80/4130–6352 reservations*

🌐 *www.suryaudayhaveli.com* 🛏 *14 rooms* 🍴 *Free Breakfast.*

CANTONMENT

Clarks Varanasi

$$$ | **HOTEL** | With upscale amenities amid lots of greenery, Clarks makes a good choice for a quiet stay. **Pros:** a 24-hour coffee shop/restaurant; sprawling lawns; well-stocked shopping arcade. **Cons:** removed from the unique hustle and bustle of Varanasi; rooms and facilities are worn and tired; Wi-Fi costs extra. [$] *Rooms from: Rs. 7500* ✉ *The Mall, Cantt* ☎ *542/250–1011 to 1020* 🌐 *www.clarkshotels.com* 🛏 *103 rooms* 🍴 *Free Breakfast.*

★ **Radisson Hotel Varanasi**

$$$ | **HOTEL** | Plush and always lively, this hotel in the relatively noise-free Cantonment is a favorite for its luxurious settings and well-maintained and upscale amenities. **Pros:** free Wi-Fi throughout the property; good breakfast buffet at the cheerful East-West restaurant; decent fitness center and spa facilities. **Cons:** pool is rather small; view from rooms is nothing special; generic, business-hotel feel. [$] *Rooms from: Rs. 6400* ✉ *The Mall, Cantt* ☎ *542/250–1515* 🌐 *www.radisson.com/varanasi-hotel-up-221002/indvaran* 🛏 *116 rooms.*

Taj Gateway Hotel Ganges

$$$ | **HOTEL** | Rooms at the Gateway are modern, done in soft colors with brass-accented furniture and eclectic Indian art, and most are spacious. **Pros:** lots of space to take peaceful walks without fear of being run over in this crowded city; poolside barbecue in winter; lovely pool on grassy grounds. **Cons:** a tour-group magnet; rooms lack local charm; impersonal ambience. [$] *Rooms from: Rs. 8000* ✉ *Nadesar Palace Grounds* ☎ *542/666–0001 to 0019* 🌐 *www.tajhotels.com* 🛏 *130 rooms* 🍴 *No meals.*

★ **Taj Nadesar Palace Hotel**

$$$$ | **RESORT** | This restored heritage palace provides the most luxurious accommodations in Varanasi, as it did in its heyday, when guests of the Maharaja of Benaras included Queen Elizabeth, Lord Mountbatten, Jawaharlal Nehru, and the king of Persia. **Pros:** extraordinarily luxurious grounds and rooms; attentive, pampering service; spa with ayurvedic treatments. **Cons:** extremely expensive; Wi-Fi not included in all packages; rooms get outside noise. [$] *Rooms from: Rs. 22000* ✉ *Off Raja Bazar Rd., Cantt* ☎ *542/666–0002, 542/250–3016* 🌐 *taj.tajhotels.com/en-in/taj-nadesar-palace-varanasi* 🛏 *10 rooms* 🍴 *No meals.*

Shopping

The city's shops are open generally from 10 to 8; the larger shops close on Sunday, but the street sellers and smaller shops are open daily. One of India's chief weaving centers, Varanasi is famous for its silk-brocade saris, which start at around Rs. 2,000. Some saris are still woven with real gold and silver threads, though in most noncustom work the real thing has been replaced by artificial fibers.

Weaving is typically a family business, and most weavers are Muslims who belong to the Ansari community. Kamalan Travels (*see* Tours) organizes visits to the traditional silk houses, where you can interact with weavers and watch them weave silk using foot-powered looms.

Cottage Industries Exposition

TEXTILES/SEWING | Come here for excellent Varanasi weaves in silk and cotton, a vast rug room, plus brass wares and Kashmiri embroidered shawls. Everything is expensive. ✉ *Mint House, Nadesar, across from the Taj* ☎ *542/250–7626.*

Thatheri Bazaar

GIFTS/SOUVENIRS | Among the brass vendors, on a small lane 50 meters north of the Chowk, some shops sell silks and woolens to a local crowd. ✉ *Varanasi.*

Dhamekh Stupa rises from the ruins in Sarnath.

Todarmal (who later became a governor under Akbar's rule), built an octagonal tower to commemorate the visit of Emperor Humayun, the father of Emperor Akbar. The event is recorded in Arabic in a stone tablet above the doorway on the north side. ✉ *Sarnath.*

Dhamekh Stupa

MEMORIAL | Dappled with geometric and floral ornamentation, the stone-and-brick Dhamekh Stupa is the largest surviving monument in Sarnath, at 143 feet in height and 92 feet in diameter at the base. Built around 500 AD, Dhamekh is thought to mark the place where the Buddha delivered his sermon, though excavations have unearthed the remains of an even earlier stupa of Mauryan bricks of the Gupta period (200 BC). An Ashoka pillar with an edict engraved on it stands near the stupa. ✉ *Sarnath.*

Mulagandha Kuti Vihar Temple

RELIGIOUS SITE | Built in 1931 by the Mahabodhi Society, the temple joins the old foundations of seven monasteries. The walls bear frescoes by a Japanese artist, Kosetsu Nosu, depicting scenes from the Buddha's life, and relics of Sakyamuni Buddha are enshrined here. On the anniversary of the temple's founding—the first full moon in November—monks and devotees from all parts of Asia **assemble her**e. The temple is behind a separate gate just outside the park. ✉ *Sarnath.*

Sarnath Archaeological Museum

MUSEUM | At the entrance to this excellent museum is Ashoka's Lion Capital, moved here from its original location in the park. The museum represents the oldest site in the history of India's Archaeologial Survey. Other beautiful sculpture is here as well, including lots of Buddhas; still more of Sarnath's masterpieces are in the National Museum, Delhi, and the Indian Museum, Kolkata. ✉ *Ashoka Marg at Dharmapal Marg* ☎ *542/259–5095* ⊕ *www.sarnathmuseu-masi.org* ✉ *Rs. 5* ☉ *Closed Fri.*

Vishvanath Gali

CLOTHING | Most hotels sell silk-brocade saris in their shops, but the main bazaars for silks and saris are in Vishvanath Gali—the lane leading from Dashashvamodh Road to the Kashi Vishvanath Temple, where the customers are mainly pilgrims and tourists. Try to go early—it gets quite crowded in the afternoon. ⊠ *Varanasi.*

Performing Arts

Nagari Natak Mandal

FESTIVALS | Music and dance performances during November's Ganga Mahotsav festival are held here. Concerts of some of Varanasi's—and India's—best musicians are also infrequently hosted here throughout the year. Ask your hotel to check the local Hindi newspaper, *Aj,* for events while you're in town, or check the English-language papers and websites yourself. ⊠ *Kabir Chowra* ☎ *542/221–4855* ⊕ *www.nnmkashi.org.*

Sarnath

11 km (7 miles) north of Varanasi.

Sarnath is where the historical Buddha, Siddhārtha Gautama (ca. 563–ca. 483 BC) first taught the Buddhist dharma. In 528 BC, about five weeks after having attained enlightenment at Bodh Gaya, he came to Sarnath and preached his first sermon (now called Dharma Chakra Pravartan, or Set in Motion the Wheel of Law) in what is today Sarnath's Deer Park.

Legend has it that the Buddha was incarnated as King of the Deer in the deer park—the name "Sarnath" comes from Saranganath, which means "Lord of the Deer." In the Deer Park you can buy some carrots for a few rupees and feed the current denizens.

When the Buddha arrived at Sarnath, he revealed his Eightfold Path, which is meant to lead to the end of sorrow and the attainment of enlightenment. Three hundred years later, in the 3rd century BC, the great Mauryan emperor Ashoka arrived in the area; he was a convert to Buddhism and had made it the state religion. In Sarnath he had several stupas (large, mound-shape reliquary shrines) built, along with a pillar with a lion capital that was adopted by independent India as its national emblem—it's called the Ashoka pillar. The wheel motif under the lions' feet represents the *dharma chakra,* the wheel (*chakra*) of Buddhist teaching (*dharma*), which began in Sarnath. The chakra is replicated at the center of the Indian national flag.

Sarnath reached its zenith by the 4th century AD, under the Gupta dynasty, and was occupied into the 9th century, when Buddhist influence in India began to wane. By the 12th century Sarnath had more or less fallen to Muslim invaders and begun a long decay. In 1836 Sir Alexander Cunningham started extensive excavations here, uncovering first a stone slab with an inscription of the Buddhist creed, then numerous other relics. It was then that the Western world realized that the Buddha had been an actual person, not a mythical figure. Most of the sites are in a well-manicured park behind a gate (admission is Rs. 100).

GETTING HERE AND AROUND

Sarnath is an easy taxi or auto-rickshaw ride from Varanasi; be prepared to bargain. A round-trip taxi from the Cantonment area should take around 45 minutes and cost between Rs. 2,500 and Rs. 3,000.

⊙ Sights

Chaukhandi Stupa

MEMORIAL | The first monument you come to in Sarnath, on the left-hand side of Ashoka Marg on the way to the park, is this Buddhist shrine that is believed to have originally been a terraced temple during the Gupta period (the 4th to 6th century). Govardhan, the son of Raja

Chapter 6

RAJASTHAN

Updated by Kristin
Amico

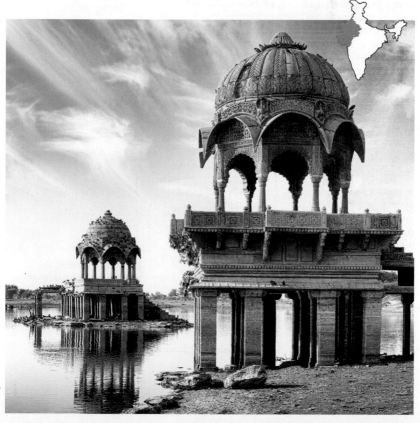

👁 **Sights**
★★★★★

🍴 **Restaurants**
★★★★★

🛏 **Hotels**
★★★★★

🛍 **Shopping**
★★★★★

🍸 **Nightlife**
★★★★★

WELCOME TO RAJASTHAN

TOP REASONS TO GO

★ **Appreciate Jaipur's pink architecture:** Dusty-pink Jaipur is the gateway to Rajasthan's beautiful palaces, forts, culture, and food.

★ **Marvel at the diversity of Rajasthan's landscapes:** You can travel from the golden sand dunes in Jaisalmer to Udaipur's lovely Lake Pichola, which is set against the Aravali Mountains.

★ **Admire the massive Mehrangarh Fort:** Standing dramatically on a hill, this massive fort is one of Jodhpur's most imposing treasures.

★ **Make a palace your home:** Spend a night in one of the many opulent palaces and forts that have been converted into heritage hotels around Rajasthan and experience Rajput grandeur.

★ **Go on a shopping spree:** Hopefully, there's room in your suitcase for the jewelry, clothes, fabric, carpets, leather-bound journals, silver, and everything else that has caught your eye—or buy an extra bag to hold your goodies.

The largest state in India, Rajasthan is in the northwestern part of the country, sharing a border with Pakistan. The hot, dry northwest region is dominated by the Thar Desert; the milder south is known for its lakes and greenery.

1 Jaipur. The modern and ancient worlds collide in Rajasthan's bustling capital.

2 Ranthambhore National Park. This national park is your best chance of seeing a tiger in the wild.

3 Bharatpur. Bharatpur was the capital of the Jat Kingdom.

4 Pushkar. People flock to Pushkar for the world-famous Puskar Camel Fair.

5 Udaipur. With the Lake Palace floating in the middle of Lake Pichola, the White City is charming and serene.

6 Ranakpur. Northwest of Udaipur, Ranakpur is known for its Jain temples.

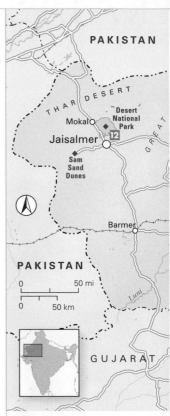

7 Kumbhalgarh. This mountaintop fort is home to the second-largest wall in the world.

8 Mount Abu. This popular hill station was once a summer escape for royalty.

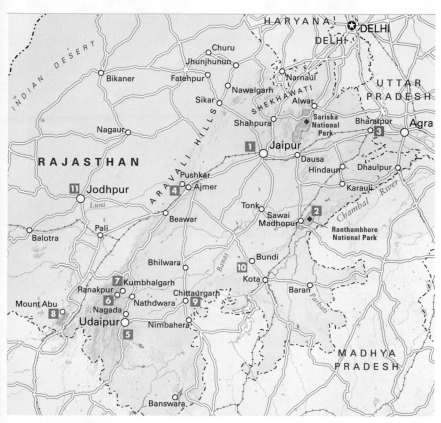

9 Chittaurgarh. The medieval citadel of Chittaurgarh is famous for its enormous fort.

10 Bundi. The town of Bundi is home to more than 50 stepwells.

11 Jodhpur. The blue houses in the Old City here contrast with the desert landscape and the regal Mehrangarh fort.

12 Jaisalmer. The Golden City is synonymous with its majestic fort, and a visit here just isn't complete without a safari, or a visit to the Sam Sand Dunes.

EATING WELL IN RAJASTHAN

Creamy safed maas

A major part of Rajasthan is also known as Marwar (literally "the land of dead" because not much grows there), and traditional cuisine revolves around the robust plants of the desert and the scarcity of water.

The lack of fresh green vegetables led to the use of gram (chickpea) and millet flour and the development of dry, long-lasting foods, and because water was scarce, many dishes were cooked in ghee (clarified butter) or milk, making them quite rich. Food tends to be heavily spiced, too, perhaps for preservation. The area was predominantly Hindu and Jain—both vegetarian religions—but besides the restrictive but rich meat-free cuisine, the ruling Rajputs were avid hunters and contributed a variety of game dishes, many heavily influenced by the Mughals.

Authentic *thali* meals (with a variety of different dishes) are usually available at casual eateries and offer a taste of Marwari home cooking.

COOKING SCHOOL

There are several places In Udaipur and Jaipur where travelers can pick up the basics of Rajasthani cooking: **Spice Box** (⊕ *www.spicebox.co.in*); **Hotel Krishna Niwas** (⊕ *www.cooking-classesinudaipur.com*); **Shashi Cooking Classes** (⊕ *www.shashicookingclasses.blogspot.com*); **Jaipur Cooking Classes** (⊕ *www.jaipurcooking-classes.com*).

LAAL MAAS

A dish fit for Rajasthani royalty, **laal maas** (literally "red meat") is the state's best-known nonvegetarian entrée. This spicy dish is usually made with goat, marinated in ginger, garlic, and yogurt, then cooked in ghee with red chilli powder. It's sometimes confused with a similar dish called *jungli maas* (wild meat), which is more of a confit, and probably originated on hunting trips where only basic, nonperishable ingredients were available.

Gatte ki sabzi

SAFED MAAS

The yin to *laal maas*'s yang, **safed maas** or "white" meat is another goat or lamb main dish—creamy white and wonderfully fragrant. The parboiled meat is massaged with yogurt before being sautéed in a fry-up of ghee, onion, ginger, garlic, cardamom, cloves, cinnamon, white peppercorn, and red pepper seeds. The meat is then finished with a paste of poppy seeds, cashew, almond, milk solids (*khoya*), and a hint of saffron or rosewater.

A true desert dish, **dal baati churma** is a staple of Rajasthani cuisine. The rustic *baati* is a ball of unleavened bread made of wheat, semolina, and ghee. Traditionally, these are cooked on coals to form a firm, slightly squashed sphere, which may be stuffed with

peas and other fillings. Baati is eaten with a hot mixed-lentil dal.

GATTE KI SABZI

One of Rajasthan's vegetable substitutes, *gatte* are sausage-shape gram-flour dumplings that are spiced and then boiled. Gatte can be eaten in a variety of ways, but the most typical dish is **gatte ki sabzi,** in which the dumplings are fried before they're mixed into a curry of yogurt, with a little more gram flour for thickening, and some mild spices. If you like this, try curry dishes made from pappadams or *mangodi* (sun-dried ground-lentil dumplings).

GHEVAR

One of the most eye-catching of Indian sweets, **ghevar,** which look like halved bagels with the cratered surface of an English muffin, can be seen stacked up on confectionery shelves. Crispy, with a slightly soft interior, the ghevar is made from batter that gets its texture from the bubbling heat of the ghee in which it is deep-fried. The crisp golden disc is then soaked in syrup flavored with the fresh-tasting screwpine flower essence (*kewra*) and sometimes topped with silver leaf, spice, and nuts.

Ghevar, a popular sweet

6

Rajasthan EATING WELL IN RAJASTHAN

CAMELS: SHIPS OF THE DESERT

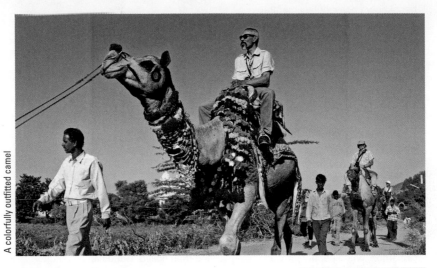

A colorfully outfitted camel

Taking a camel ride in the Thar desert is one of the most unforgettable experiences of a trip to India. If you can, start off before sunrise, so that you can watch the sun come up over the sand dunes.

Camels are an indispensable part of the local landscape and economy in Rajasthan, and you'll see them wherever you go in the state—approximately half a million camels live here. Apart from pulling loads (and that includes tourists on safaris), camels are also highly valued for their milk, meat, hair, leather, and even their droppings (used for fertilizer and dried for cooking fuel).

Camel owners usually dress their animals with flair: red, green, and gold saddle covers and tasseled bridles are signs of the well-dressed camel. They're also rather gentle creatures—contrary to popular belief—and you'll no doubt form a bond with yours.

Be sure to book through a reputable source to ensure that the camels are treated well and not overworked.

DESERT SUPERFOOD

Camel milk is rich in nutrients, and is a common food source for desert people worldwide. In India's desert regions the milk is consumed regularly, and a few enterprising people—Saras Dairy, for instance—even create camel-milk ice cream. Fans claim that it's easier to digest than cow's milk, but some travelers have reported tummy aches after consuming camel-milk products.

WHERE TO GO ON SAFARI?

It's easy to book a camel safari once you're in Rajasthan: Jaisalmer is the most popular place to take a safari, but other destinations like Pushkar and Jodhpur are good, too. You can choose to go for anything from several hours to several days. On a day trip, your guide will probably take you through a local village, maybe stopping for something to eat.

SIMPLE OR LUXURY

Overnight safaris range from simple and inexpensive—a one-night trip to a local campsite—to luxury glamping excursions. A lower-end, one-night safari will cost from around Rs.1,500, which includes a camel, a guide, a cot under the stars, and a basic dinner of dal and rice. Higher-end tours cost at least twice as much, and include more comfortable tented accommodations, multicourse meals, and even a jeep service to carry supplies and luggage between campsites. Water is not always included, so check to see if you need to pack your own.

WHAT TO BRING?

It's important to come prepared. The desert sun is very strong, so wear sunglasses, a brimmed hat, and high-power sunscreen even if you don't generally get sunburned. Long-sleeved shirts and

Sunset in the Thar Desert

full-length trousers are also a must—both for sun protection and to stop your legs from chafing. Wear solid shoes or boots with socks to avoid bites from small insects that live in the sand. Pack a scarf to protect your face in case of a sandstorm.

WHEN?

Overnight camel safaris typically run from late August to mid-April; in May, June, and July temperatures in the Thar Desert peak above 120 degrees, which is dangerously hot. Only male camels are used during the winter mating season, as adding females into the mix can cause the animals to bolt or even attempt mating, regardless of whether there's a rider on their back.

LEARNING TO RIDE

Although learning to ride a camel is easier than learning to ride a horse, it still takes a bit of getting used to. On short trips you might be tied to your guide's camel; on a longer trip, you will be taught to "drive" the camel yourself. Camel bridles are attached to pegs in the camel's nose, and camels are steered with reins. Camels have remarkably sensitive flanks, so a little practice and a few nudges with your legs is usually enough to get your steed to pick up the pace.

Camel safari

RAJASTHAN'S HOLY SITES

The Pushkar Brahma temple

Although Rajasthan is best known for its forts, palaces, and desert expanses, this huge state is also home to some of India's most awe-inspiring sacred sites.

The Jain temples in the southern part of Rajasthan are popular destinations; visitors marvel at the white-marble architecture and intricately carved designs that embellish the temple walls and pillars. The best-known Jain holy sites in the state include the temples at Ranakpur near Udaipur and at Dilwara in Mount Abu. There are also a number of significant Hindu temples in Rajasthan. Pushkar has one of the world's few temples dedicated to Brahmh, the god of creation in the Hindu trinity. The Eklingji temple complex near Udaipur was built by royalty and is dedicated to Shiva (the destroyer). Not everyone, however, feels the need to actually visit the Karni Mata temple at Deshnoke (popularly known as the Rat Temple among tourists) near Bikaner: it's known as an abode for thousands of rats, which are considered sacred. A popular Muslim pilgrimage site is just outside Pushkar, in Ajmer: Dargah Sharif is the shrine of Sufi saint Khwaja Moinuddin Chisti, and is among the most important pilgrimage sites for South Asian Muslims.

SWASTIKAS

Visitors to Rajasthan are often shocked to see images of the swastika—a symbol associated with Nazism in the West—on walls, doorways, and temples. The swastika predates Hitler as a symbol of divinity and good fortune, and is sacred to Hindus, Buddhists, and Jains, who place it prominently in all of their temples and holy books. Hitler misappropriated the holy symbol, turning it on its side and making it into his party's logo.

DARGAH SHARIF

In Ajmer's Old Town, the white-marble Dargah Sharif is one of the finest examples of Mughal architecture in the state. This is the shrine of Hazrat Khwaja Moinuddin Chisti, a Sufi saint of Persian descent who is best known for his service to the impoverished. Chisti's shrine is sacred to Muslims and every year, pilgrims from across the subcontinent flock to Dargah Sharif to commemorate the Chisti's Urs, the anniversary of the saint's death.

Inside one of the Jain temples at Ranakpur

DILWARA TEMPLES

The five temples of Dilwara in Mount Abu attract Jain pilgrims from across the country and people of all faiths with an interest in art and architecture. Each temple is devoted to a different *tirthankar* (enlightened being who is repeatedly reborn to impart the knowledge he has gained) from the Jain faith. The pillars, arches, and domes represent some of the finest marble artisanship in the country.

RANAKPUR TEMPLE

Between Udaipur and Jodhpur, this magnificent Jain temple venerates the tirthankar Rishabha. The four sides symbolize the four directions and the interior features an almost mazelike series of 1,444-plus intricately carved marble pillars. There's also a small, much older temple, dedicated to the sun.

EKLINGJI TEMPLE COMPLEX

Eklingji village is famous for its 108-strong temple complex, the highlight of which is the 15th-century Shiva Temple (some parts date back to the 8th century). There's a unique four-sided, four-faced black-marble image of Shiva here.

PUSHKAR BRAHMA TEMPLE

It seems like there's a temple every few feet in Pushkar—many restrict access to foreigners and non-Hindus, but the most famous temple, the red-spired 14th-century Brahma Temple, allows people of all backgrounds. The town's lake is also a holy spot unto itself, and many of Pushkar's priestly residents earn a living performing *pujas* (ceremonies) at the shore.

KARNI MATA TEMPLE

Near Bikaner, the town of Deshnoke is home to the Karni Mata temple, dedicated to a 14th-century female sage who was believed to be an incarnation of the goddess Durga. The temple is best known, however, for its large population of rats, which some people estimate at being around 20,000. The rodents are considered sacred, and are fed by the temple's caretakers.

The main gate of the Karni Mata Temple

SHOPPING IN RAJASTHAN

Indian bangles at a market in Jodhpur

When it comes to shopping, Rajasthan has something for everyone. From elegant silk saris to kitschy wooden camels, there are goodies here for even the most frugal visitor.

Rajasthan is well known for its craftspeople, and each region has its own distinct specialties. Jaipur is at the hub of the state's tourism industry and has handicrafts from across the state, but it is most famous for its jewelry; if you want something with a local flair here, pick up a piece of blue pottery or a pair of emerald earrings. Jodhpur is a good place to shop for appliquéd cloth, glass bangles, mirrored, sequined bedspreads, and wood furniture. Udaipur is known for miniature paintings and marble work. In Jaisalmer it's camel leather—patchwork bed covers, shoes, purses, and even book covers are made from the desert animal's hide. Yellow sandstone statues are also popular here. The best deals can be found in local markets—large private emporia and shops in "craft villages" tend to mark their items up to recover the huge commissions they pay to travel agents, guides, and taxi drivers.

BUYER BEWARE

Every year, unsuspecting tourists fall prey to shady self-professed "gem dealers," who befriend foreign visitors and try to get them to transport gems back to their home countries. The victims are then asked to leave a deposit for the jewels, which are inevitably nothing more than tin and glass. Most tourists don't realize they've been scammed until they're thousands of miles away.

JEWELRY

Rajasthan has been known for its fine selection of jewelry for centuries, and you're sure to find something special, no matter what your budget. The state is a major exporter of precious and semiprecious gems, and good deals on precious jewelry abound—just make sure you buy from a reputable source. Popular purchases include glass bangles, silver anklets, rings, pendants, and *meenakari* (enamel) rings and bracelets. More traditional are the *kundan* pieces: elaborate gold and gem jewelry with designs dating from the Mughal era.

LEATHERWORK

Handcrafted leatherwork is popular in Rajasthan, and you can find purses, journals, and traditional slippers, or *jootis,* at bargain prices. Watch out for overly pungent leathergoods (sniff before you purchase), and if you do end up with something smelly, seal the item in a plastic bag along with some fabric-softener dryer sheets and baking soda.

PAINTINGS

Rajasthan is famous for paintings in the *phad, pichwai,* and miniature styles. The *phad* is a red, green, and yellow scroll depicting the life of a local hero; the dark and richly hued *pichwais,* hung in

Handmade leather shoes

temples, are cloth paintings depicting Lord Krishna in different moods. Miniature paintings are created using squirrel-hair brushes on paper, silk, marble, or bone, and usually depict wildlife and courtly scenes, or illustrations of religious stories and mythological themes.

POTTERY

Most people believe that blue pottery originated in Rajasthan, but it's actually of Turko-Persian origin and only emerged in India in the 18th century. The craft nearly went extinct, but was revived in the 1960s and 1970s. The name blue pottery is misleading—it's available in an array of colors.

TEXTILES

Bandhani (tie-dye) has its origins in this part of the country and you'll often find fabrics with one or two colors embellished with tiny white circles. Handmade block-printing is also popular, and is made by using wooden stamps to transfer natural dyes onto fabric. Detailed embroidery and appliqué, often featuring mirror work, are also popular.

Bandhani fabric

Steeped in tales of chivalry and romance, and famous for its striking desert landscape, massive forts, and fabulous palaces, Rajasthan represents, for many, quintessential India. With the legendary cities of Jaipur, Jodhpur, Udaipur, and Jaisalmer, built by the mighty Rajput warriors, and the indigenous tribal and artisan communities, Rajasthan is a unique combination of royal and tribal India.

The variety of Rajasthan's landscape is unparalleled: the region is packed with awe-inspiring forts, sparkling palaces, tranquil lakes and gardens, and exquisite temples and shrines. The crafts and folk art produced here are world-renowned. Once called Rajputana ("Abode of Princes"), this vast land consisted of more than 22 princely states before most of them were consolidated into modern Rajasthan in 1949. Each of the 22 states was ruled by a Rajput, an upper-caste Hindu warrior-prince, and the Rajputs were divided into three main clans: the Suryavanshis, descended from the sun; the Chandravanshis, descended from the moon; and the Agnikuls, who had been purified by ritual fire. When they were not fighting among themselves for power, wealth, and women, the Rajputs built the hundreds of forts, palaces, gardens, and temples that make this region so enchanting.

The Rajputs' contribution to cultural life in Rajasthan lives on to this day, and with the amalgam of so many states,

each with its rituals and ways of life, Rajasthan is extremely culturally diverse. Communities vary in everything from the colors of their sandstone buildings to the languages they speak—a local saying has it that you hear a new dialect every 4 km (2½ miles). Travelers will notice the brilliant colors of the local women's *lehangas* (long skirts with separate veils), designed to stand out against the starkness of the desert. Women also wear elaborate jewelry, and Rajasthani men are famous for their turbans—called *saafas*—which vary in style from region to region and caste to caste; the style of wearing high turbans with a tail is preferred by Rajputs, for instance, while *pagris* (compact turbans, often orange) are worn by businessmen. Even facial hair is unique in these parts: Rajputs, in particular, sport long, Salvador Dalí–like handlebar moustaches.

Although Rajasthan has many social problems, most notably widespread rural poverty, low literacy rates, and child marriages, its cities and people remain lively. Cultural festivals, crafts fairs, and religious gatherings take place throughout the year. With its bright colors and rich folk traditions, and the sheer variety of experiences it has to offer the traveler, Rajasthan easily earns its place as one of India's most popular tourist destinations.

Planning

WHEN TO GO
HIGH SEASON: OCTOBER TO FEBRUARY

The high season officially begins in October, though many tour groups begin arriving in August and September during the rains. Monsoon days can be quite hot between showers. The peak is November through mid-February when the weather is at its best, the days are perfect for sightseeing and evenings are pleasant—and can even be chilly in the desert areas. Temperatures rarely rise above the mid-80s, but the sun is still strong, so cover up if you're susceptible to sunburn. Many hotel rates are close to double those charged in low season, and monuments are crowded with group tours with the busiest periods being around Christmas and around Diwali when Indian tourists are holidaying. This is also when the Ranthambhore National Park is open and the winter migratory birds come to Bharatpur (Keoladeo Ghana) Bird Sanctuary.

LOW SEASON: MAY TO JULY

These summer months can be unbearably hot, with temperatures, particularly in desert cities like Jaisalmer and Jodhpur, at times soaring close to 120 degrees. It's almost impossible to endure a full day of sightseeing or be out in the sun for more than an hour or two. As a result, most hotels are vacant and offer great deals—often less than half their usual rates—and the monuments are close to deserted.

SHOULDER SEASON: AUGUST TO SEPTEMBER AND MARCH TO APRIL

As long as you don't mind the monsoon, this is not a bad time to visit. The weather is neither at its best nor its worst, and crowds can easily be avoided. However, hotel deals are not as highly discounted as in the low season, and the wildlife parks are closed.

GETTING HERE AND AROUND

Rajasthan is India's largest state, and if you try to cram too much into one trip you may find yourself spending more time on the road than at your destinations. It can be helpful to use a travel agent for advice on getting around— they're seemingly everywhere you look in the touristy parts of Rajasthan's major cities, and they can help you reserve train and bus tickets for a nominal fee, and most are happy to offer destination advice, though not always unbiased as far as accommodations are concerned.

AIR TRAVEL

There are domestic airports in Jaipur, Jodhpur, and Udaipur (there's also a new airport in Jaisalmer, but civilian flights are still suspended as of this writing). Popular domestic airline carriers to these three cities include Jet Airways, Air India, IndiGo, Go Air, and SpiceJet. Note that air connections *between* cities in Rajasthan are nonexistent and must be made via Delhi or Mumbai.

AIRPORTS AND TRANSFERS

Jaipur's Sanganer Airport is about 13 km (8 miles) south of town; a taxi into town costs about Rs. 250 if you call for a radio taxi, or Rs. 360 for a private non-a/c taxi and Rs. 400 for a private a/c taxi. Jodhpur's airport is 5 km (3 miles) from the city center; a taxi into town costs about Rs. 600. Udaipur's Dabok Airport is 25 km (16 miles) from the city center; the ride costs about Rs. 750. You can also book and pay for a car to pick you up from the airport online (⊕ *www.makemytrip.com* or ⊕ *www.savaari.com*).

BUS TRAVEL

If convenience and a cheap price are more important to you than a supercomfortable journey, travel by bus—but keep in mind that the quality of buses in India varies widely. The state-run Volvo buses are a good option for intercity travel. Some "tourist" buses end up picking up hitchhikers, so by the time you reach your destination people are sitting in the aisles and sometimes even on the roof. If you don't mind an adventure, or if you have no other choice, by all means take a bus. Otherwise, take a train (equally cheap) or rent a car and driver. The easiest way to get a bus ticket in advance is not from the bus stations, but from many of the private vendors in tourist areas. Your hotel reception or concierge might be able to help (for a fee).

CAR AND DRIVER TRAVEL

It's not cheap, but having a car and driver to yourself is highly efficient if you're short on time, as distances between points of interest are usually long, and direct trains can sometimes be hard to come by. It is also the best option if you plan to visit more than one city in Rajasthan. Plan to start early, when traffic on highways (and through toll plazas) is reduced, and so you are not traveling after dark. You can hire a car and driver through your hotel or a recognized travel agent—hiring through your hotel is usually more expensive, depending on the class of the hotel, because the hotel will tack on a finder's fee. Car rates are extremely variable so do shop around. An a/c sedan car and driver should cost about Rs. 15 to Rs. 17 per km (½ mile), not including tolls for a minimum of 250 km (155.3 miles) per day. An extra Rs. 200 to Rs. 300 per day is usually tacked on for overnight trips, and you should offer to pay for your driver's meal if you stop for one. A small tip at the end of the trip is customary if you are satisfied with the service provided. If you organize a car directly through the driver, it will be cheaper, but check the vehicle and driver out properly the day before you start. Expect to spend about Rs. 5,000 for a tour of the region from Delhi to Jaipur in a sedan a/c car with room for three passengers or about Rs. 6,500 in an a/c larger vehicle that can carry five passengers. Because the driver has to return to his point of origin, you pay the round-trip fare even if you're going one way. To hire a car for a day of city driving expect to pay Rs. 2,000 for eight hours or 80 km (50 miles), whichever comes first for an a/c sedan plus tips and money for the driver's lunch.

ROAD CONDITIONS

Aside from major national highways crossing through Rajasthan, the state highways are not in very good shape, and the going is slow: the Delhi–Jaipur Highway (NH–8) is well paved, but once you're off the highway the roads are full of potholes, and it takes a long time to travel even short distances. When calculating driving time, plan to cover 40 kph–50 kph (25 mph–31 mph) at best. That said, driving is an excellent way to see the Indian countryside and glimpse village life.

Jaipur is a five- to six-hour drive from Delhi on National Highway (NH) 8. This is a congested industrial road with a high accident rate, so prepare for a trying experience.

Road surfaces are rough in and out of Jodhpur, and the going is slow. Don't expect to average more than 40 kph (25 mph)—Jodhpur-Jaipur is a seven-hour drive, Jodhpur-Jaisalmer is a five-hour drive, and Jodhpur-Udaipur is a six-hour drive. Udaipur is on National Highway 8, one of the better roads, which links Mumbai and Delhi, but in sections is rough. Again, expect your road speed to top out at 40 kph (25 mph). Journeys between Udaipur and Jaipur take seven hours or more. The Jodhpur-Jaisalmer road is in very good condition and it is possible to do 50 kph–60 kph (31 mph–37.3 mph).

TAXIS AND AUTO-RICKSHAW TRAVEL

Taxis are unmetered in Jaipur, Jodhpur, and Udaipur, so ask your hotel for the going rate and negotiate with the driver before you set off (and in Jaipur use dial-a-cabs); hire one through your hotel or the RTDC's Tourist Information Center (*See Visitor Information, below, for contacts*). Depending on the distance to be covered, a taxi for half a day will cost about Rs. 900, and for a full day about Rs. 1,800. A full day usually equates to eight hours and 80 km (50 miles) within the city limits; a set sightseeing city tour may cost less.

Auto-rickshaws in Jaipur are metered, but the meters are hardly ever used. Insist on setting the price in advance and negotiate—settle for no more than Rs. 10 per km (½ mile). Auto-rickshaws in Jodhpur and Udaipur are unmetered, so agree on a price before departing. You can also hire an auto-rickshaw by the hour, for about Rs. 150 per hour. Note that all of these rates go up by 25% to 50% after 11 pm.

TRAIN TRAVEL

In Rajasthan if you want to travel overnight, it's safer and more comfortable to take the train than a bus or car. Trains offer classes of service for all budgets (seats and sleepers, a/c and non-a/c, reserved and unreserved). Trains do get crowded, though, during peak season, and you may want to investigate special "tourist quotas" that set aside seats for foreign travelers. Check with a travel agent rather than deal with the crowds and administrative chaos at the train station, and book as far ahead as possible. Book online at ⊕ *www.indianrail.gov.in.*

Trains are the best method of getting to Jaisalmer. The Shatabdi Express, an a/c chair-car train (the local term for a train carriage with only seats, no sleeping arrangements), travels every morning from New Delhi, departing at 6:05 am to arrive at Jaipur by 10:35 am. The Double Decker leaves Delhi S Rohilla station at

Prioritizing Your Time

Rajasthan is big—very big—with long stretches between the most popular destinations. If you have limited time, stay in one place and explore the surrounding area rather than rushing through all the highlights. If you have to choose one city to focus on, Udaipur is probably your best bet—it's the most enchanting and tourist-friendly of Rajasthan's four major tourist cities—but if you only have a couple of days, you may be better off sticking to Jaipur, which is closest to Delhi and Agra.

5:35 pm and reaches Jaipur at 10:05 pm. The Garib Nawaz Express leaves Delhi Cantt station at 1:35 pm and arrives at 7:05 pm on Monday, Wednesday, and Saturday. Daily trains connect Udaipur with Jaipur, Ajmer, Chittaurgarh, Ajmer (Pushkar), and Delhi. Trains also run out from Delhi to Jaisalmer and Jodhpur as well as Jodhpur to Jaisalmer, but they're significantly slower than the road routes. The famed Palace on Wheels is a luxury train that runs across the state, connecting major sights. If the train is running behind schedule, you might miss some sites.

TRAIN INFORMATION Indian Railway Catering and Tourism Corporation Ltd ☎ *755/393–4141* ⊕ *www.irctc.co.in.* **Palace on Wheels** ☎ *958/269–0401, 855/428–7555 U.S. and Canada* ⊕ *www. thepalaceonwheels.com.*

EMERGENCIES

If you need a doctor or a 24-hour pharmacy, ask at your hotel: they'll know the closest place and can send someone to get medicine, or find a doctor. There are emergency help lines and ambulance numbers for all major cities—108 is

Festivals in Rajasthan

The dates of most of Rajasthan's festivals are determined using the Hindu calendar, so timing varies from year to year.

Jodhpur's RIFF (Rajasthan International Folk Festival) and Jodhpur's Marwar Festival are usually in late October or November.

The Jaipur Literature Festival in January attracts authors from around the world and is considered one of the most vibrant book festivals in the world, given its size, location, and the number of people attending; speakers have ranged from the Dalai Lama to Amartya Sen, Oprah Winfrey, Michael Ondaatje, Orhan Pamuk, Pico Iyer, Gloria Steinem, V. S. Naipaul, Jhumpa Lahiri, Jonathan Franzen, Ved Mehta, William Dalrymple, and Tom Stoppard.

the emergency number for ambulance service in Rajasthan.

RESTAURANTS

Rajasthan's culinary traditions are heavily influenced by its desert setting and lack of a variety of fresh vegetables; in fact, in some parts of the state, sweets open the meal. Food tends to be highly spiced, perhaps for preservation. Instead of the rice and vegetables that are popular in regions with more rainfall, Rajasthani cuisine includes a lot of lentils, millets, and corn. *Restaurant reviews have been shortened. For full information, visit Fodors.com.*

HOTELS

The most opulent hotels in India—and perhaps in the world—are in Rajasthan. You can live like a king, waited on hand and foot, in one of several converted palaces, surrounded by glittering mirrored walls, tiger skins, and stained-glass windows. Rajasthan is also famous for Heritage Hotels, a group of castles, forts, and havelis (family homes) that have been converted to elegant accommodations. *Hotel reviews have been shortened. For full information, visit Fodors.com.*

What It Costs

	$	$$	$$$	$$$$
RESTAURANTS				
	under Rs. 300	Rs. 300–Rs. 499	Rs. 500–Rs. 700	over Rs. 700
HOTELS				
	under Rs. 4,000	Rs. 4,000–Rs. 5,999	Rs. 6,000–Rs. 10,000	over Rs. 10,000

TOURS

It's usually easiest to book tours through your hotel or a travel agent, although a few operators allow direct booking. Shop around—sometimes agents will try to undercut the competition by offering small discounts on their offerings: there are usually several agents next to each other on the same street, so you can go from one to another. Rajasthan Tourism Development Corporation also organizes city tours and excursions.

TOUR CONTACTS Karwan Tours ⊠ *Bissau Palace Hotel, outside Chandpol gate, near Saroj Cinema, Jaipur* ☎ *141/230–8103* ⊕ *www.karwantour. com.* **Le Passage to India** ⊠ *101 Ganpati Plaza, M.I. Road, Jaipur* ☎ *141/511–5415, 982/905–1387* ⊕ *www.lepassagetoindia.*

Dancers at Jaisalmer's Desert Festival

com ✉ *14/21 Lake Palace Rd., 1st fl., Udaipur* ☎ *029/4510–0422* ⊕ *www. lepassagetoindia.com* ✉ *Shop 04, Geeta Ashram Rd., Hanuman Circle, Jaisalmer* ☎ *299/225–0355* ⊕ *www.lepassagetoindia.com* ✉ *Airport Rd., Ratananda circle, opposite R.S.E.B. substation, Jodhpur* ☎ *291/251–0859* ⊕ *www.lepassagetoindia.com.* **Pink City Rickshaw Company** ☎ *735/795–3705* ⊕ *www.pinkcityrickshawcompany.com.* **Royal Desert Safaris** ✉ *Nachna Haveli, Gandhi Chowk, Jaisalmer* ☎ *299/225–2538, 299/225–1402* ⊕ *www.campsandsafaries.com.* **Savaari Car Rentals** ☎ *591/255–5600* ⊕ *www. savaari.com.* **Virasat Exeriences** ✉ *Om Niwas Hotel, E–23 Kaushalya Marg, Bani Park* ☎ *141/510–9090* ⊕ *www.virasatexperiences.com.*

VISITOR INFORMATION
Many hotels provide regional information and travel services. In Jaipur, Jodhpur, Udaipur, and Jaisalmer the Tourist Information Centers of the Rajasthan Tourism Development Corporation (RTDC) provide information, travel assistance, and guides and are open from 10 am to 6 pm. *Jaipur Vision* and the *Jaipur City Guide*, available in most hotels, are periodicals with visitor information and up-to-date phone numbers.

TOURIST OFFICES Rajasthan Tourism Development Corporation ✉ *Paryatan Bhawan, Khasa Kothi Hotel Campus, M.I. Rd., Jaipur* ☎ *141/511–0598, 141/515–5100* ⊕ *www.rajasthantourism.gov.in.*

PLANNING YOUR TIME
The ideal way to see Rajasthan is first to fly to Jaipur, Jodhpur, or Udaipur and then tackle nearby towns by train, bus, or private car. Ideally you should start at Jaipur, make your way around by car, and end up in Udaipur, from where you can fly to Mumbai or Delhi. Overnight train journeys between major cities in a/c sleeper coaches are a cheap way to travel without wasting too much time or money on hotel stays. For instance, you could also start in Jaipur and work your way to Udaipur, then to Jodhpur, Jaisalmer, and back to Delhi via Jodhpur.

EXPLORING RAJASTHAN

You could easily spend months in Rajasthan. The state's southwestern corner centers on Udaipur, a hilly town of palaces and artificial lakes, with the nearby hill station of Mount Abu, while central Rajasthan is anchored by Jodhpur, home to a glorious fort and the eye-catching blue houses, said to be of the Brahmin caste. Jaipur, the state capital, is in the east, toward Delhi. Western Rajasthan, largely given over to the Thar Desert, can best be explored from the golden city of Jaisalmer. In the northeast, between Jaipur and Delhi, the Shekhawati region is home to lovely painted havelis, the mansions of prosperous merchants. The southern and eastern regions also have a number of good wildlife parks.

Jaipur, the state capital, is worth a few days' visit: it's a delightful mixture of modernity and folk tradition. Don't be surprised to see camels pulling carts on the main streets, mingling with vehicular traffic. With its towering forts and impressive city palace, Jaipur is a good indicator of what to expect as you progress to interior Rajasthan. It's also a good base from which to visit other towns and parks in the region. The craft villages of Sanganer and Bagru, just outside Jaipur, are populated almost entirely by artisans, and you're free to stop in and watch them make fine paper and block-print textiles by hand. The Hindu pilgrimage town of Pushkar is known for its annual camel festival, held in November or sometimes slightly earlier. For an unusual experience, take a short overnight trip out of Jaipur to Bundi, as famous for its intricate stepwells and charming little lanes as it is for being one of Rudyard Kipling's former residences and the place that inspired him to write *Kim*. To escape civilization altogether, go bird-watching at Bharatpur's Keoladeo National Park or on a tiger safari at Ranthambhore (which may or may not result in spotting a tiger).

Romantic Udaipur, the major city here, warrants several days or more since the Aravali Hills and the Mewar region are home to several fascinating day-trip or overnight destinations, including the impressive medieval citadel of Chittaurgarh and the remarkable fort at Kumbalgarh. There are several famous temples and religious sites in the area, too, including the spectacular Jain Temples in Ranakpur and Mount Abu and the Shiva temple complex at Eklingji. An overnight trip is recommended for a visit to Mount Abu. Udaipur is a famous white marble center; make time to visit Bhuwana on the outskirts to purchase some wonderful carved marble handicrafts.

The stark, compelling beauty of the Thar Desert draws travelers to far-western Rajasthan—for good reason. Jaisalmer is a picture-perfect medieval city resplendent with golden homes and havelis and a towering citadel, which is an intriguing town in its own right, and is an excellent base for safaris into the desert and for day trips to the photogenic Sam Sand Dunes and Desert National Park. It is easily one of India's most unforgettable destinations, and well worth the journey to this farthest corner of the state.

Jaipur

261 km (162 miles) southwest of Delhi; 343 km (213 miles) east of Jodhpur; 405 km (252 miles) northeast of Udaipur.

There is a Rajasthani proverb that asks, *Je na dekhyo Jaipario, To kal men akar kya kario?* ("What have I accomplished in my life, if I have not seen Jaipur?").

Flanked on three sides by the rugged Aravali Hills, and celebrated for the striking, if somewhat run-down, pinkish buildings in the old part of the city, Jaipur is the capital of Rajasthan and these days a big city, modernizing very fast, and a good starting point for a trip through the region. It's a spirited place: a jumble of colorful Jaipuri natives attired in traditional clothes—*ghagharas* (skirts),

The Brave Rajputs

For centuries, Hindu Rajputs valiantly resisted invasion attempts by the Muslim Mughals. Their codes of battle emphasized honor and pride, and they went to war prepared to die. When defeat of their soldiers on the battlefield was imminent, the Rajput would perform the rite of *jauhar*, throwing themselves onto a flaming pyre rather than live with the indignity of capture. With the exception of the princes of Mewar, major Rajput states like Jaipur, Bikaner, Bundi, and Kota eventually gave up and built strong ties with the Mughals. The Mughal emperor Akbar was particularly skilled at forging alliances with the Rajputs; he offered them high posts in his court, and sealed the deal with matrimonial ties. Those kingdoms who sided with Akbar quickly rose in importance and prosperity.

"The Victory belongs to Akbar"

Raja Man Singh I of Jaipur was the first to marry his aunt to Akbar. As the emperor's brother-in-law and trusted commander in chief, Man Singh led Mughal armies to many victories, and both rulers benefited immensely. A traditional saying: *"Jeet Akbar ki, loot Man Singh ki"* translates as "The victory belongs to Akbar, the loot to Man Singh." The same people who initially sacrificed their lives to resist the Mughals quickly adapted.

A Golden Age

Skilled craftsmen from the Mughal courts were enticed to start craft schools, fomenting what would become a golden age of Indian art and architecture. The Mughals' influence in Rajasthan is still visible in everything from food to art and architecture, from intricate miniature paintings to the tradition of *purdah* (covering the head and face with a veil).

Decline

The beginning of the 18th century marked the decline of the Mughal period and the Rajputs. The incoming British took advantage of the prevailing chaos. The princes made treaties with the British in 1818 and were allowed to govern with a deceptive sovereignty. As a result, Rajasthan escaped overt colonization. The British introduced significant administrative, legal, and educational changes in Rajasthan, and exposed the Rajputs to new levels of excess. The British popularized polo (an old Asian game) and other equestrian sports, the latest rifles and guns, *shikar* (hunting) camps, Belgian glass, French chiffons, Victorian furniture, European architecture, and—eventually—fancy limousines. The influence extended to Rajput children: sons were sent to English universities, and daughters to finishing schools in Switzerland.

Defending the Raj

While the rest of India launched its struggle for independence, many Rajput princes ended up defending the Raj. Unwilling to give up their luxury and power, they did their best to suppress rebellion outside their own kingdoms by sending soldiers to help the British forces. When India became independent, the Rajput princes and kings merged their kingdoms into one state as part of the new nation, but they were allowed to keep the titles to their palaces, forts, lands, and other possessions.

complex turbans, and sturdy *jutis* (pointed shoes)—sidewalk shops overflowing with pottery and dyed or sequined fabric, and streets packed with camel carts, cycle-rickshaws, and wandering cows. The salmon-color Old City is where you'll spend most of your time: most of the sights you'll want to see are here, and it's full of appealing bazaars with colorful textiles and trinkets—look for *lac* (resin) bangles, steel utensils, and copper ornaments—and *mehendi* (henna) artists as well umpteen places to have snacks or tall glasses of lassi. Mirza Ismail (or M.I. Road as it's popularly known) is the main drag. It's a bit touristy and rather hectic in the Old City, so be prepared to deal with noise, chaos, and a lot of touts—and to bargain hard if you want to purchase something at one of the bazaars.

Jaipur was named after Maharaja Sawai Jai Singh II, an avid scientist, architect, and astronomer who founded the city in 1727 when he moved down from Amber, the ancient rockbound stronghold of his ancestors. It's known for being one of the first planned cities in the world. The city is rectangular in shape, and divided into nine blocks based on the principles of the ancient architectural treatise *Shilp Shastra*. Every aspect of Jaipur—streets, sidewalks, building height, and number and division of blocks—was based on geometric harmony, environmental and climatic considerations, and the intended use of each zone endures today, although the mad confusion tends to distort the planning of the city's forefathers. Part of the city is still enclosed in 20-foot-high fortified walls, which have eight gates.

GETTING HERE AND AROUND

Although you can fly to Jaipur, most people get here either by train or road. The train station and the city's main bus stand are less than half a mile apart, so if you don't have much luggage and need to transfer from a bus to train, or vice versa, you can easily walk from one to another.

Royalty Turns to Realty

After India's independence in 1947, the royal families of Rajasthan found it difficult to maintain their imposing forts and regal palaces without the special privileges they enjoyed under British rule. Now many of these beautiful palaces have been converted into five-star hotels—a creative way to maintain some of these historic sights while offering a taste of royal living to those who can afford it, be it only for a night.

To get around in the city, auto-rickshaws are your best bet, although prebooked cabs, though slightly more expensive, are hassle-free and air-conditioned; cycle-rickshaws are equally good for short distances especially in the Old City—just be sure to negotiate a fare before you climb aboard. Note that parts of the walled Pink City get very congested during rush hours, so you may find it easier to walk through this part of town.

TAXI COMPANIES Metro Cabs ☎ *141/424–4411* ⊕ *www.metrocabs.in.* **Ola Cabs** ⊕ *www.olacabs.com.*

TIMING

Two full days is enough to take in many of Jaipur's major sights, with a little bit of time left over for shopping. You could easily, however, extend your stay here to three or four days, and take day or overnight trips to smaller towns in the surrounding regions.

ESSENTIALS

TOURIST OFFICES Government of Rajasthan Tourist Office ✉ *Paryatan Bhawan, Khasa Kothi Hotel Campus, M.I. Rd.* ☎ *141/511–0598* ⊕ *rtdc.tourism.rajasthan.gov.in.*

Sights

Albert Hall Museum

MUSEUM | The oldest museum in Jaipur, inside the Ram Niwas Bagh, is worth a visit just for its breathtaking architecture—the sandstone-and-marble 19th-century Indo-Saracenic-style building was designed by Sir Samuel Swinton Jacob, the father of that movement that merged popular Indian and Victorian architecture of that era, and who was one of Rajasthan's great builders (he built the Rambagh Palace as well). Named in honor of Victoria's son Prince Albert (who became Edward VII) who came visiting shortly after it was built, the exteriors and gardens offer a glimpse of what the then–New Jaipur (completed circa 1887) was like. The museum's enormous collection includes folk arts, miniature paintings, textiles, pottery, traditional costumes, marble carvings, coins, musical instruments, ivory, and visual explanations of Indian culture and traditions. Avoid the weekends when it gets crowded with local tourists. The museum has night hours (7–10), when it's set aglow with twinkling lights and you can have access to the central part of the museum. ⊠ *In Ram Niwas Gardens, Adarsh Nagar* ☎ *141/257–0099* ⊕ *alberthalljaipur.gov.in* ⌦ *Rs. 300; night entrance, Rs. 100.*

★ Amber (Amer) Fort and Palace

CASTLE/PALACE | **FAMILY** | Surrounded by ramparts, this hulking but grandiose fortress is perched on a hill near the Maota Lake and grows more alluring as you approach it. There's a Persian inscription at Amer, added when it was completed, that reads: "Just as the heavens should always be laden with rain, so also this stately building, the foundation of the Maharaja's longevity and wealth, be preserved from any kind of damage."

And it has been preserved remarkably well. Raja Man Singh began building it in 1592; Mirza Raja Jai Singh and Sawai Jai Singh continued the construction over a period of 125 years. For centuries the fortress was the capital of the Kachhawah Rajputs, but when the capital shifted to Jaipur in the early 18th century, the site was abandoned. Although the fort is in ruins, the interior palaces, gardens, and temples retain much of their pristine beauty. Both the art and the architecture combine Rajput and Mughal influences in felicitous ways; the old rainwater harvesting and lifting systems have been renovated and are particularly worth a look. You approach the palace complex by walking up a sloping incline to the **Singh Pole** gate and **Jaleb Chowk,** the preliminary courtyard—or you can drive up from the rear end into Jaleb Chowk. Elephant rides are also offered up to the fort in the early morning; however, due to claims that the elephants are abused and that riding them causes lasting damage to their bodies, we do not recommend this option. The fort-palace attracts legions of tourists, especially during high season when Indians are also traveling (summer, Diwali, Independence Day, and the Christmas holidays) and sometimes the traffic volume is so high the traffic police close the roads to prevent further arrivals. You are best off exiting your hotel for Amer by 8:15 and reaching the fort entrance by 8:45 to beat the heat. You will then need to set aside just an hour to tour the fort. ■ **TIP→** **To get the most from your visit, pick up an audio guide at the ticket window.**

Two flights of stairs lead up from Jaleb Chowk; to start, skip the one leading to the Shiladevi Temple and take the one leading directly to the palace. In the next courtyard, the pillared **Diwan-i-Am** (Hall of Public Audience) contains alabaster panels with fine inlay work—the kind of craftsmanship for which Jaipur is famous. Typical of the Mughal period, the rooms are small and intimate, whereas the palace's successive courtyards and narrow passages are characteristically Rajput. In one corner is an interesting hammam (Turkish bath) area.

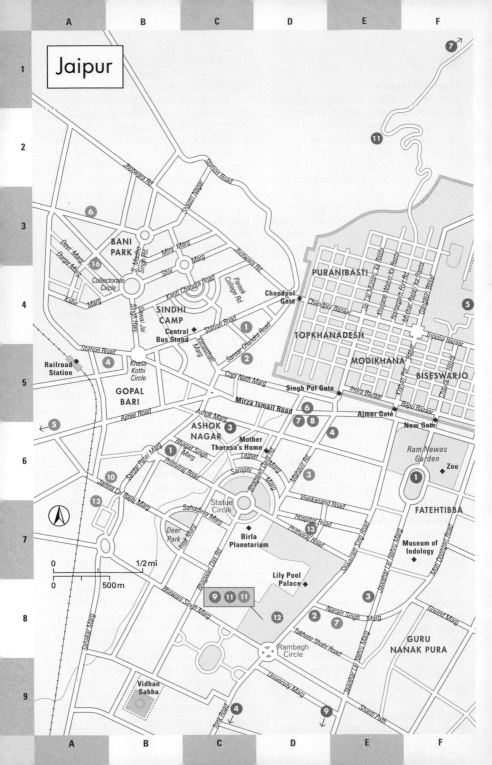

6

Man Sagar Lake

2 10 8 14 15

10

Jal Mahal

Amer Road

5

Samrat Gate

Zorawar Sing Gate

12

Gangapol Gate

KANWAR NAGAR

Govindji ka Temple

Moti Katra Bazaar

RAMACHANTRA COLONY

Hawa Mahal Bazaar

Chaura Nikas Road

8

6

Rampang Bazaar

Haldion ka Rasta

Surajpol Bazaar

GHST DARWAZA

Johari Bazaar

Ghat Darwaza Bazaar

Suraj Pol Gate

Sanganeri Gate

Agra Road

Rasta Balaji Ki Kothi

Bahar Ganj Ka Rasta

NH 8 Bypass Road

JANTA COLONY

Ghat Gate

ADARSH NAGAR

Adarsh Nagar Rd.

Ghat ki guni

12

Govind Marg

9

TO GALWAR BAGH

NH 8 Bypass Rd.

Sights ▼

1 Albert Hall Museum **F6**
2 Amber (Amer) Fort and Palace.... **I1**
3 Amrapali Museum **C6**
4 Chokhi Dhani **C9**
5 City Palace **F4**
6 Hawa Mahal **G4**
7 Jaigarh Fort **F1**
8 Jantar Mantar **G4**
9 Jawahar Kala Kendra **D9**
10 Kanak Vrindavan Gardens **I1**
11 Nahargarh Fort **E2**
12 Sisodia Rani ka Bagh **I7**

Restaurants ▼

1 Anokhi Cafe **B6**
2 Bar Palladio **D8**
3 Caffé Palladio **E8**
4 Indiana **E6**
5 Jal Mahal **H2**
6 Lassiwala **D5**
7 Natraj **D6**
8 Niros **D6**
9 Peshawri **D8**
10 Rainbow **I1**
11 Steam **D8**
12 Suvarna Mahal **D8**
13 Tapri **D7**

Hotels ▼

1 Alsisar Haveli **C4**
2 Arya Niwas **C5**
3 Diggi Palace **D6**
4 ITC Rajputana **A5**
5 Jai Mahal Palace **A6**
6 Mahal Khandela **A3**
7 Narain Niwas Palace **E8**
8 Neemrana Fort Palace **I1**
9 Oberoi Rajvilas **J7**
10 Pratap Bhawan Home Stay **B6**
11 Rambagh Palace, Jaipur **D8**
12 Samode Haveli **H3**
13 SUJÁN Rajmahal Palace **A7**
14 Tree of Life **I1**
15 Trident **I1**
16 Umaid Mahal **A3**

KEY

1 Sights
1 Restaurants
1 Hotels

G H I J

One of the elaborately carved and painted gates is known as **Ganesh Pol,** after the elephant god Ganesh. From a latticed corridor above it, the queen—always in purdah, or hiding—would await the king's return from battle and sprinkle scented water and flowers down upon him. Each room shows some vestige of its former glory, especially the **Sheesh Mahal** (Palace of Mirrors), with glittering mirror work on the ceiling. Narrow flights of stairs lead up to the lavish royal apartments, and beyond the corridors and galleries there you'll find the small, elegant **Char Bagh** garden. Take in the views of the valley, the palace courtyards, the formal gardens abutting the octagonal pool next to the lake, and the vast **Jaigarh Fort,** the ancient fortress on the crest of the hill above you. Also on the upper floor is **Jas Mandir,** a hall with filigreed marble *jalis* (screens) and delicate mirror and stuccowork.

On your way out, peek into the 16th-century **Shiladevi Temple** to the goddess Kali, with its silver doors and marble carvings. Raja Man Singh installed the image of the goddess after bringing it here from lower Bengal (now Bangladesh). Exit the palace by the gate near the temple, and just a few minutes down the road is the 16th-century **Jagat Shiromani** temple. Dedicated to Krishna, this exquisitely carved marble-and-sandstone temple was built by Raja Man Singh I in memory of his son. Amer village has several other old temples and buildings. Before you exit, within the fort there are a few legitimate government-run handicraft stores worth visiting—Rajasthali, Magical Creations, and Tribes. Avoid the handicraft shops in Amer village, even if your guide or driver recommends them. For a cool drink, stop at Coffee Cafe Day, also before the exit. ⊠ *Delhi Rd., 11 km (7 miles) north of Jaipur, Amber* ☎ *141/253–0844, 141/253–1042, 141/253–0293* ⊕ *www.rajasthantourism.gov.in* ⊠ *From Rs. 500.*

Amrapali Museum

MUSEUM | For those who love bling in all its forms and want to spend an hour or two developing Indian jewelry envy, the Amrapali Museum should rank high on your list. Opened in 2018, it was a labor of love 40 years in the making by Rajiv Arora and Rajesh Ajmera, founders of the Amrapali Jewelry shops. When the two started the business in 1978 they made it their mission to save family heirloom and tribal pieces from being melted down, as more owners were selling traditional jewelry for quick cash. More than 4,000 items from the 19th century to more modern times, including tea sets, silver tribal belts, and sparkling earrings that could easily be worn as statement pieces today, are on display. Looking for something to take home? The gift shop on the top floor sells vintage silver pieces, much like the ones on display, as well as contemporary offerings from the current Amrapali line. ⊠ *K–14/B, Ashok Rd., C-Scheme* ☎ *141/519–1100* ⊠ *Rs. 600.*

Chokhi Dhani

MUSEUM VILLAGE | About a 45-minute drive from Jaipur, this large replica cultural village includes a huge buffet meal in the admission price, consisting of pretty much every regional vegetarian dish you can imagine as well as a formidable selection of sugary desserts. Come hungry and expect to eat with other tourists, either sitting on benches or on the floor in a lantern-lit hut. If you are uncomfortable sitting on the floor, there is inside seating at chairs and tables in a/c comfort; however, prices are higher. Performance tents host a vibrant Rajasthani pageant—traditional dances, including the dramatic fire dance, folk singing, *katputli* (puppet shows), and juggling. Tipping is discouraged. You'll find plenty of vendors selling every type of Rajasthani tchotchke under the sun; salesmen can be irritatingly pushy. There's a less interesting hotel on-site, although not in authentic village style—it's much more luxurious—and its restaurant and bar,

The steep approach to the Amber Fort, and its situation amid the Aravali hills, made this an ideal stronghold for centuries of successive rulers before the capital was moved to Jaipur.

serving regular Indian fare, offer an alternative to the buffet. It gets very busy on weekends and holidays. ☒ *Tonk Rd.* ✛ *19 km (12 miles) south of Jaipur via town of Vatika*☎ *141/516–5000, 141/516–5015* ⊕ *www.chokhidhani.com* ✉ *From Rs. 700.*

★ City Palace

CASTLE/PALACE | The opulent complex of pavilions, courtyards, and chambers is one of the gems of Jaipur. Begun by Jai Singh II in 1727, wings were added by later maharajas. Start the tour with a visit to **Mubarak Mahal** (Guest Pavilion), built by Maharaja Madho Singh in the late 19th century. Now a museum, it's an ideal place to admire some of the royals' finest brocades, silks, and hand-blocked garments and robes, some dating back to the 17th century. **The armory** in the northwest corner of the courtyard has one of India's best collections of arms and weapons. The paints used on the beautiful, 18th-century ceiling are believed to have been made from crushed semiprecious stones. The Bhaggi Khana (carriage museum) offers a peek into the royal family's horse-drawn vehicles and palanquins. In the inner courtyard, through the gateway guarded by two stone elephants, is the art gallery, housed in the cavernous **Diwan-i-Am** (Hall of Public Audience). Built in the late 18th century, the building has a magnificent, vintage-1930s painted ceiling, rows of gray marble columns inside the courtyard, the second-largest chandelier in India, and two silver pots so large that they are mentioned in the Guinness Book of World Records. The art includes scores of miniatures from the Mughal and various Rajput schools, rare manuscripts, and 17th-century carpets from the Amber Palace. From the courtyard, enter a small hall on the left that leads to the **Pitam Niwas Chowk** (the square). Here's where to get up close to the four small gates (doorways), intricately painted to represent the four seasons and Hindu gods. They include the Peacock Gate, Green Gate, Rose Gate and Lotus Gate—they're smaller in person than they appear in photos but still striking. In busy months there's a line of people posing in front of each one. Look up to see the seven-story **Chandra Mahal** (Moon Palace). Built by Jai Singh II, it was the official residence of the last maharaja, "Bubbles" (a nickname bestowed on him by his British nanny because of the amount of Champagne that was consumed when he was born in 1931)—Lieutenant Colonel Sawai Bhawani Singh—who passed away in 2011; his family still lives on the upper floors. The ground floor, open to visitors, has sumptuous chandeliers and murals. A "Royal Grandeur" tour is available for Rs. 2,500, taking you close, but not quite into, the royal family's quarters and their guest rooms, including the grand **Sukh Niwas** (Hall of Rest), complete with stunning geometric archways painted in deep Wedgwood blue. Plan on two hours to tour the palace. The recently renovated **Baradari Restaurant** within the complex is a sleek, upscale eatery offering contemporary and traditional Rajasthani food, as well as alcoholic beverages. You don't need to pay admission to City Palace to enter the restaurant; it's become a trending spot with locals and visitors.

⚠ **Watch out for cons claiming that you need a guide to tour the palace—you don't. There are official guides available for Rs. 300 and audio guides for Rs. 200 in eight languages at the ticket window.** ✉ *Center of Old City, Pink City* ⊕ *Enter complex at Virendra Pole gate* 🎟 *Palace, from Rs. 500. Royal Grandeur tour, Rs. 2500.*

Hawa Mahal

CASTLE/PALACE | Jaipur's photogenic Palace of Winds was built by Maharaja Sawai Pratap Singh in 1799 so the women of the court (the *zenana*) could discreetly take in fresh air and watch the activity on the street below. Every story has semioctagonal overhanging windows, and each has a perforated screen. This curious five-story structure, named after the westerly winds that blow cool breezes through the 953 windows (or *jharokas*) is just one room wide, so the wind easily passes through the building and cools the interior. The building facade

What's with the Pink?

The buildings of Jaipur were originally colored yellow, which you can still see on the backs of the buildings. The capital, however, was painted pink (really more of a salmon color) when Prince Albert, consort of Queen Victoria, visited India in the middle of the 19th century. The idea stuck, and by law buildings in the Old City must still be painted pink. As a result Jaipur is commonly referred to as the Pink City.

has a delicate honeycomb design with close to 1,000 windows, and is fashioned from pink sandstone. Short on time? Skip a trip inside, and view the *mahal* from the outside, especially at sunrise or sunset, when it is most striking. **For best views, go to the touristy Wind View Cafe across the street, where you can buy a soda or snack and then snap a pic from the balcony.** ✉ *Sireh Deorhi Bazaar, Pink City* ☎ *141/261–8862* ⊕ *www.hawa-mahal. com* 🎟 *Rs. 50.*

Jaigarh Fort

ARCHAEOLOGICAL SITE | Originally the royal treasury, this dramatic-looking fort has large water tanks for storing rainwater channeled from the imposing Nahargarh. There are fantastic views of Jaipur from the watchtower. Star attraction of the fort is the Jaivana Tope, the largest wheeled cannon in the world, measuring more than 20 feet long and weighing in at around 50 tons. The mighty Jaivana was unsurpassed for power in its day; one of its cannon balls was found 35 km (22 miles) from here. This fort was responsible for the defence of Amer Fort (which is at a lower elevation) and its armory and museum showcases the weaponry it once had as well as photographs. Local lore has it

The Jantar Mantor Observatory in Jaipur

that when Indian prime minister Indira Gandhi ordered a search of the water tanks in 1976 a vast collection of gems and jewelry emerged. Guides are available at the entrance—an English-speaking one will charge about Rs. 200, but it's recommended to negotiate the fee down. For a small fee you can enter the fort by car to reach the top (where the cannon is) and save yourself a long, uphill walk. It's possible to drive from Jaigarh to Amber, but be sure to get a driver who knows the way through the narrow roads. ⊠ Off Amber Rd. ⊹ About 7 km (4 miles) from Jaipur ☎ 141/267–1848 ☞ Fort, from Rs. 100.

Jantar Mantar

OBSERVATORY | The scholarly Sawai Jai Singh II was well aware of European developments in the field of astronomy and wanted to create one of the world's finest observatories. He supervised the design and construction of five remarkable facilities in northern India, and Jantar Mantar is the largest and best preserved of the five. Built in 1726 out of masonry, marble, and brass, this observatory is neatly laid out and equipped with simple

solar instruments called yantras, which look like large, abstract sculptures, and are remarkably precise in measuring complex celestial data like time, the location of stars, angles of planets, and predicting forthcoming eclipses. Such accuracy was desired for creating astrological predictions. A guided tour is available for an additional Rs. 200, and guides will explain the history and how these devices work, as they're fascinating and, for nonscientists, somewhat complicated. **Avoid the observatory at noon, as it can be very hot.** ⊠ Tripoliya Bazaar, near entrance to City Palace, Pink City ☎ 141/261–0494 ☞ Rs. 200.

Jawahar Kala Kendra

ARTS VENUE | Jaipur's center for arts and crafts was founded by the state government with a specific vision: to create a space for understanding and experiencing culture and folk traditions. The center hosts regular theatrical, dance, and musical performances; check the website for schedules. It also holds regular classes on film, art, and traditional crafts. You can drop by the impressive modern building

Jaipur's Village Complexes

Rajasthan is a largely rural state, and the local villages still maintain unique lifestyles, with traditional entertainments and ways of life. It's a fascinating other world from what Westerners are used to. Travelers with little time and limited personal contact with the locals, though, aren't generally going to get invited to an authentic village to see how people really live—and language barriers can be an issue if you do. A popular alternative is to visit what is known as "village complexes," essentially artificial replicas of the real thing that feature souvenir stands, cultural entertainment programs, and regional cuisine. Popular with Indian and overseas tourists alike, these villages feel a bit like theme parks, but the cuisine and traditional entertainment is authentic, so they're quite worthwhile. A good one to visit when you're in Jaipur is Chokhi Dhani. Chokhi Dhani is a large, over-the-top complex that has a feast of local delicacies and entertainment included the admission price; of course, there also will be shopping opportunities. While these sites offer camel and elephant rides, they are not recommended due to the treatment of the animals.

to meet some of the locals who exhibit and perform here, or have a look at one of the rotating exhibits. ⊠ *Jawaharlal Nehru Marg, opposite Jhalana Institutional Area, Moti Dhungri* ⊕ *jawaharkalakendra.rajasthan.gov.in* ⊠ *Free.*

Kanak Vrindavan Gardens

GARDEN | This picturesque set of gardens and temples is just below the majestic Amber and Nahargarh forts and is nearly 300 years old. It was established by Jaipur maharaja Sawai Jai Singha. From here you can get a good look at the Jal Mahal Palace in Man Sagar Lake. The gardens also make a great picnic spot, especially on weekends if you like to people-watch. A few Bollywood films have been shot here, such as the famous romantic film *Lamhe.* ⊠ *Amber Rd., Man Sagar* ⊠ *Free.*

Nahargarh Fort

MILITARY SITE | The scenic hilltop location of Nahargarh Fort provides breathtaking views of Jaipur and its natural defenses. One of the main reasons to arrive here after doing a round of Jaigarh and Amer, a few kilometers away, is to take in the panoramic landscapes below. Initially built by Sawai Jai Singh in 1734, it was enlarged to its sprawling, present-day glory in 1885 by Sawai Madho Singh, who commandeered it as a lookout point. Cannons placed behind the walls recall the days when artillery was positioned against potential attackers below. During the 1857 revolt, several Britishers took refuge here. The palace of nine queens—with nine separate apartments for the wives of Maharaja Ram Singh—within the fort is also worth a short visit. The massive channels that carried rainwater from Nahargarh to Jaigarh Fort, a few miles away, where it was stored in large tanks as part of a rainwater harvesting system, can still be seen from the approach road. For best views of the city, a sunrise at the fort can't be missed. Alternatively, the lights at sunset give the fort a pretty glow. ⊠ *10 km (6 miles) north of Jaipur off Amber Rd.* ☎ *141/513–4038, 141/513–7686* ⊠ *Rs. 200.*

Sisodia Rani ka Bagh

CASTLE/PALACE | On Highway NH 11 that heads to Bharatpur and Agra stands one of many palaces built for the *ranis,* or queens, of Sawai Jai Singh II. Built in 1728, the palace, though not as opulent as it once was, still looks lovely against the backdrop of hills. The palace is furnished with murals illustrating hunting scenes and the romantic legend of Krishna and Radha, while the terraced Mughal gardens are dotted with fountains and frequented by prancing peacocks and monkeys. Stop by on your way down the Bharatpur-Agra road. It's often used as a reception site for local wedding parties. ✉ *8 km (5 miles) east of Jaipur on road to Bharatpur* 🎫 *Rs. 200.*

🍴 Restaurants

Visitors to Jaipur can choose from restaurant options as well as street food fare. Masala Chowk, which opened in 2018, brings together nearly two dozen street food vendors in a small square. The result is a lively area with food stalls and seating. You can find popular street food favorites such as *kulfi* (ice cream), *dosa* (thin pancake), omelets, samosa, and chai. It's on Ram Niwas Bagh, across from the Albert Hall museum and buzzes at night. There's a nominal fee (Rs. 10) to enter the food square.

Anokhi Cafe

$$ | CAFÉ | The Jaipur version of a Nordstrom Cafe, this little eatery, attached to the Anokhi store, has a relaxed air and is a perfect place for to rest limbs weary from sightseeing or shopping, enjoying a drink for as long as you like. Try the caramelized onion, goat cheese, and tomato pizza or opt for one of the freshly made salads (washed in filtered water); also among the selection are vegetarian sandwiches and pastas, and a variety of cold drinks (the ice cubes are safe to drink). **Known for:** light snacks; ice-cold drinks; vegetarian options. $ *Average main: Rs. 350* ✉ *2nd fl., KK Sq., 11 Prithviraj Rd., C-Scheme* 🕿 *141/400–7244* ⊕ *www. anokhi.com.*

★ Bar Palladio

$$$ | ITALIAN | With stunning blue walls and decorative details resembling the private rooms in City Palace, this cocktail lounge and restaurant on the expansive grounds of the Narain Niwas Palace Hotel makes for a leisurely retreat, where you can expect to brush shoulders with Jaipur's upwardly mobile, expats, and trendy tourists sipping whiskey on the candlelit patio late into the evening. Open for dinner and late snacks, Bar Palladio boasts traditional Italian favorites like homemade pasta and salads, as well as a classic cocktail menu. **Known for:** handmade pasta; classic cocktails; chic patio. $ *Average main: Rs. 500* ✉ *Narain Niwas Palace Hotel, Kanota Bagh, Narain Singh Rd.* 🕿 *141/256–5556* ⊕ *www.bar-palladio. com.*

★ Caffé Palladio

$$$ | MEDITERRANEAN | Popular with well-heeled locals, tourists, and expats for its lighter fare, Caffé Palladio has an airy space evoking a summer greenhouse and is perfect for lunch, an early dinner, or a tea break between sightseeing and shopping. From the Sicily-meets-Morocco menu, choose from small plates, pizza, pasta, salads, and sandwiches, or desserts like freshly made granita, ideal for hot weather. **Known for:** refined tagine; Roman-style pizza; popular lunch spot. $ *Average main: Rs. 600* ✉ *100 JLN Marg, Santha Bagh* 🕿 *141/256–3533* ⊕ *www.bar-palladio.com/caffe* ⊗ *Closed Tues.*

Indiana

$$$$ | INDIAN | A great spot for groups, this garden restaurant offers Indian, Chinese, and international cuisine as well as alcoholic drinks; crowds tend to be thin for lunch, but dinner is more crowded during high tourist winter months. The restaurant attracts tourists more for its open-air ambience and Rajasthani dances (nightly at 7 pm) than for the food, though the *lal maas* (spicy mutton) is a favorite. **Known for**: traditional Rajasthani entertainment; northern Indian food;

good for groups. $ *Average main: Rs. 900* ⊠ *J2–34 Mahaveer Marg* ☎ *141/236–2061, 141/236–2062.*

Jal Mahal

$$$$ | INTERNATIONAL | For a break after a morning of sightseeing at Jaipur's fortresses, go to this pretty restaurant in the Trident hotel to sample a mix of Indian and European fare—pastas, kebabs, salads, sandwiches—washed down with cold Indian beer, or try the grilled red snapper or the Rajasthani thali (traditional laal maas or spiced mutton), two of the best dishes on the menu. It also offers a sizeable breakfast buffet. **Known for:** large breakfast buffet with American and Indian staples; authentic Rajasthani specialties; wine by the glass or bottle. $ *Average main: Rs. 1100* ⊠ *Amber Fort Rd., opposite Jal Mahal* ☎ *141/267–0101* ⊕ *www.tridenthotels.com.*

Lassiwala

$ | CAFÉ | Across the street from Niros restaurant, under a green-and-white-striped awning, and on the periphery of a long chain of imposters, the real thing, Lassiwalla, can only be found under the sign "Kishan Lal Govind Narayan Agarwal"; it's so well-known that you may have to wait behind a line of locals waiting to get their daily serving of the sweet probiotic. Served in disposable red-clay cups, the delicious lassis come with a dash of hard cream on top and are available in medium and large sizes. **Known for:** creamy lassi (yogurt-based drink); early-morning opening; its long lines. $ *Average main: Rs. 60* ⊠ *M.I. Rd.* ✛ *Across from Niros.*

Natraj

$$ | INDIAN | The house specialties at this terrific place for Indian tea and dessert are *bundi ki laddu* (sugary, deep-fried chickpea-flour balls) and the *rasgulla* (cheese balls in a sugary syrup); other sweets include *ras malai* (sweet cheese dumplings smothered in cream), which melt in your mouth. Popular with locals for the thalis, this all-vegetarian

restaurant is also one of the few places open for breakfast—if you're in the mood for stuffed *paranthas* (whole-wheat flatbread) or *idlis* (South Indian steamed rice cakes). **Known for:** filling thali; vegetarian entrées; homemade dessert. $ *Average main: Rs. 400* ⊠ *6, M.I. Rd., just past Panch Batti* ☎ *141/237–5804.*

Niros

$$$$ | INTERNATIONAL | FAMILY | This bustling and often boisterous Jaipur institution with both inside and outside seating might be the most popular restaurant among the middle class, and it is the place to grab dinner before a Bollywood movie at the Raj Mandir Cinema around the corner. Dine on decent Indian and Chinese food (the range is extensive), as well as continental dishes; to drink, the options include beer and wine, and cold coffee topped with ice cream. **Known for:** chicken tikka masala; Chinese specialties; attracting locals and families. $ *Average main: Rs. 800* ⊠ *M.I. Rd., Panch Batti* ✛ *Next to Bank of Baroda* ☎ *141/237–4493, 141/221–8520* ⊕ *www.nirosindia.com.*

★ Peshawri

$$$$ | NORTH INDIAN | Considered one of the city's best (and most expensive) restaurants, Peshwari entices with melt-in-your-mouth, exquisitely spiced and marinated kebabs and other North-West Frontier foods; menu highlights include *paneer tikka, chicken makhani,* and the *dal bukhara,* served with an assortment of *rotis* and *naans.* The dining area has an outdoorsy, *dhaba* look—wood beams, shining copper platters, and pots hanging on the walls, with seating at log tables matched with stools. **Known for:** north Rajasthani meat curries; perfectly crisp flatbreads; upscale dining. $ *Average main: Rs. 2500* ⊠ *Palace Rd.* ☎ *141/510–0100* ⊕ *www.itchotels.in.*

Rainbow

$$ | SOUTH INDIAN | An upgraded dhaba (roadside eatery), this unprepossessing spot located on the way to Amer Fort is an attractive and convenient stop after a heavy morning of fort viewing. Air-conditioned and kept spotlessly clean by its house-proud and attentive owners, it serves North Indian specials; favorites include *palak paneer* (spinach with soft white cheese), garlic naan, *kadhi pakoda* (yogurt curry with chickpea dumplings), *achari aloo* (spiced potatoes), vegetable curry (stuffed potato dumplings in gravy) on its mostly vegetarian menu. **Known for**: vegetarian Indian dishes; busy with tour groups; clean and well maintained. [$] *Average main: Rs. 400* ✉ *72, Ramgarhmod, Amer Rd.* ✣ *Near post office* ☎ *141/267–2237.*

Steam

$$$ | **MEDITERRANEAN** | The pizzas and cocktails here are as memorable as the locale—the restaurant is located within an out-of-service steam engine; hop aboard and settle into an interior booth (a must in hot months) or dine on the Victorian-era platform. It's located on the grounds of the Rambagh Palace hotel, part of the Taj Hotel empire, and buzzes at night with locals and in-the-know travelers. **Known for:** pizza; cocktails; destination dining. [$] *Average main: Rs. 700* ✉ *Rambagh Palace, Bhawani Singh Rd.* ☎ *141/385–5700* 🌐 *www.tajhotels.com.*

★ Suvarna Mahal

$$$$ | **INDIAN** | Once the maharaja's throne room in the original palace, this grand hall within the Taj's Rambagh Palace Hotel—easily one of India's most elegant restaurants—has a soaring, frescoed ceiling,tapestry-covered walls, gold-plated silverware, and a staff eager to serve. It serves dishes from royal kitchens across India, from Punjab to Rajasthan, including both meat and vegetarian entrées; alcohol is available. **Known for:** laal maas (spicy lamb); dhundhar murg (chicken and mango curry); fine dining. [$] *Average main: Rs. 4500* ✉ *Rambagh Palace, Bhawani Singh Rd., Rambagh* ☎ *141/221–1919* 🌐 *www.tajhotels.com* ⏲ *No lunch* 👔 *Jacket and tie.*

Tapri

$ | **CAFÉ** | With several menu pages of tea varieties, coffee, and plenty of snacks—including samosa, pizza, and veggie options—Tapri is Jaipur's modern café where friends, ladies who lunch, and visitors come to spend a few hours relaxing while overlooking Central Park. The tea is served with a timer to ensure yours is steeped perfectly to your liking; the ice tea (you can order a whole pitcher) is perfect for blazing hot days. **Known for:** dozens of tea varieties; coffee; light meals. [$] *Average main: Rs. 200* ✉ *B4–E Prithviraj Rd., 3rd fl., C-Scheme* ✣ *Opposite Central Park* 🌐 *tapri.net.*

Hotels

★ Alsisar Haveli

$$$ | **HOTEL** | In the heart of the Old City, this gorgeous and opulent haveli—one of the most popular family-run heritage hotels in Jaipur—is a pretty and relatively quiet sanctuary with a popular pool, numerous courtyards, and elegant rooms featuring carved antique furniture, restored frescoes, crystal chandeliers, and hunting paraphernalia. **Pros:** good value; safaris can be arranged; spacious property close to historical sites. **Cons:** some rooms are dark; book in advance for high season; Wi-Fi can be spotty. [$] *Rooms from: Rs. 8000* ✉ *Sansar Chandra Rd., Chandpol* ☎ *141/236–4685, 141/510–7167, 141/510–7157* 🌐 *www.alsisarhaveli.com* 🛏 *45 rooms* 🍴 *No meals.*

Arya Niwas

$ | **HOTEL** | Trusted, reliable, comfortable, and probably the most efficient family-run hotel in Jaipur—and one of the best bets for a budget stay—the Arya Niwas has that ideal combination of convenience to the heart of the city and cushioning from its noise and chaos. **Pros:** centrally located; value for money; helpful staff and travel services. **Cons:** serves only vegetarian food and no alcohol; spotty Wi-Fi; bathrooms could be cleaner.

$ Rooms from: Rs. 2200 ✉ Sansar Chandra Rd., behind Amber Tower, off M.I. Rd. ☎ 141/407–3450, 141/407–3400 ⊕ www.aryaniwas.com ⇱ 91 rooms ⦿ Free Breakfast.

Diggi Palace

$$$ | HOTEL | In Jaipur's popular C-Scheme neighborhood (with hip coffee shops and boutiques), this palace, dating from the 18th century and retaining its regal ambience, is the venue for the famous Jaipur Literature Festival every January; the rest of the year it's a peaceful, intimate, and charming alternative to staying in the rowdy Old City. **Pros:** great value; walking distance to the Old City; lovely atmosphere. **Cons:** even the high-end rooms lack the opulence it could offer; Wi-Fi not in all rooms (but available in lobby); must book months in advance for literary festival. $ Rooms from: Rs. 6000 ✉ Shivaji Marg, Sawai Man Singh Rd., C-Scheme ☎ 141/237–3091 ⊕ www.hoteldiggipalace.com ⇱ 70 rooms ⦿ Free Breakfast.

ITC Rajputana

$$$ | HOTEL | Centrally located, this large and sumptuous ITC chain is a luxurious refuge from hectic downtown Jaipur. **Pros:** great dining options, especially the Peshawri; well priced; luxury feel without a five-star price tag. **Cons:** slightly impersonal; not a traditional Rajasthani environment; breakfast not included. $ Rooms from: Rs. 10000 ✉ Palace Rd., Gopalbari ☎ 0141/510–0100 ⊕ www.itchotels.in/hotels/jaipur/itcrajputana.html ttps://www.itchotels.in/hotels/jaipur/itcrajputana.html ⇱ 230 rooms ⦿ No meals.

Jai Mahal Palace

$$$$ | HOTEL | Rooms at this historic, Taj group–managed palace hotel are modern but plush, and many overlook 14 acres of lavish Mughal-style gardens. **Pros:** royal, historical environment; tented spas; large pool and fitness center. **Cons:** expensive; meals not always included; rooms near functions room can be noisy. $ Rooms from: Rs. 19000 ✉ Jacob Rd., Civil Lines ☎ 141/660–1111 ⊕ www.tajhotels.com ⇱ 106 rooms ⦿ No meals.

Mahal Khandela

$ | B&B/INN | The well-priced rooms—all with Rajasthani decor and period-style furniture—are the main reason for heading to this Bani Park haveli-hotel. **Pros:** value for money; central courtyard; pool. **Cons:** Bani Park is a few miles from the center of things; attracts families in high season and can be noisy; bathrooms show signs of wear and have low water pressure. $ Rooms from: Rs. 3500 ✉ D–219B, Bhaskar Marg, Bani Park ☎ 141/228–1748, 141/228–1749 ⊕ www.mahalkhandela.com ⇱ 27 rooms ⦿ Free Breakfast.

Narain Niwas Palace

$$$ | HOTEL | Built in 1928 by a commander for the Jaipur army as a vacation home, this sprawling heritage hotel, where peacocks strut through the expansive lawn, evokes visions of days past. **Pros:** year-round pool; spa services; bright, Rajasthani decor. **Cons:** some rooms and bathrooms show signs of age; Wi-Fi doesn't reach most rooms; breakfast buffet is bland. $ Rooms from: Rs. 8700 ✉ Narayan Singh Rd., Kanota Bagh ☎ 141/256–1291 ⊕ www.hotelnarainniwas.com ⇱ 37 rooms ⦿ No meals.

Neemrana Fort Palace

$$$ | RESORT | This 15th-century Rajput fort turned heritage hotel, set on 6 acres in the Aravali Hills between Delhi and Jaipur, is one of India's acclaimed retreats. **Pros:** lovely views and stunning sunsets; complimentary morning and afternoon tea with cookies; spa. **Cons:** original building full of stairs and steep ramps; can get crowded on weekends; no room service or TVs. $ Rooms from: Rs. 7500 ✉ Neemrana village, 150 km (94 miles) north of Jaipur, off NH–8 ☎ 1494/299–900, 149/424–6007, 11/4666–1666 ⊕ www.neemranahotels.com ⇱ 74 rooms ⦿ Free Breakfast.

★ Oberoi Rajvilas

$$$$ | **RESORT** | This fabulous 32-acre luxury retreat, 20 minutes outside Jaipur and set against a hilly backdrop, is a destination unto itself, whether you want to splurge on a private villa with its own pool, enjoy a spacious standard room, or revel in a romantic luxury tent with rich wood fittings on grounds that are home to hundreds of peacocks. **Pros:** large spa and beautiful pool; impeccable, personal service; lavish breakfasts. **Cons:** expensive; far from the airport; traffic jams hamper getting in and out of Jaipur for sightseeing. [$] *Rooms from: Rs. 55000* ✉ *Goner Rd., Babaji-ka-Mod, 18 km (11 miles) from Jaipur* ☎ *141/268–0101* 🌐 *www.oberoihotels.com* 🛏 *80 rooms* 🍴 *Free Breakfast.*

Pratap Bhawan Home Stay

$ | **B&B/INN** | Perfect for foodies, wildlife enthusiasts, and those who like to engage with locals, this cozy homestay, in the upscale C-Scheme residential area, is run by an energetic young couple, the Rathores—one a naturalist who runs wildlife tours, the other a food enthusiast who offers cooking and *rangoli* (a form of folk art) classes. **Pros:** warm, personal service from knowledgeable owners; home cooking; good value. **Cons:** simple, basic facilities; horns from nearby railroad can disturb light sleepers; book in advance during high season. [$] *Rooms from: Rs. 2800* ✉ *A–4 Pratap Bhawan, Jamnalal Bajaj Marg, C-Scheme* ☎ *98290–74354* 🌐 *www.pratapbhawan.com* 🛏 *4 rooms* 🍴 *Free Breakfast.*

Rambagh Palace, Jaipur

$$$$ | **HOTEL** | Set on 47 acres of lawns punctuated by arcaded patios with fountains, courtyards, long colonnades, and prancing peacocks, this wistfully romantic palace was one of the first in Jaipur to be converted into a heritage hotel and is one of the most classically elegant properties in India. **Pros:** lovely original indoor pool and newer outdoor pool; efficient, helpful service; excellent dining options. **Cons:** not within walking distance to the tourist sites; expensive; rooms above restaurant can be noisy. [$] *Rooms from: Rs. 50000* ✉ *Bhawani Singh Rd., Rambagh* ☎ *141/238–5700* 🌐 *www.tajhotels.com* 🛏 *100 rooms* 🍴 *Free Breakfast.*

★ Samode Haveli

$$$$ | **HOTEL** | Hidden amid the lanes of the Pink City, this stately and rambling heritage hotel built for a prime minister of the royal court in the mid-19th century preserves its Rajasthani character and harbors a few surprises, including elegant gardens and a beautiful open-air pool with poolside bar. **Pros:** charmingly decorated main dining room; huge rooms; grounds have swings for kids. **Cons:** fancier rooms are very expensive; vehicle access problematic during rush hours; rooms near mosque can be noisy. [$] *Rooms from: Rs. 21000* ✉ *Near Gangapole, Pink City* ☎ *141/263–2407, 141/263–2370, 141/263–1942* 🌐 *www.samode.com* 🛏 *39 rooms* 🍴 *Free Breakfast.*

★ SUJÁN Rajmahal Palace

$$$$ | **HOTEL** | This lavishly restored hotel has a long history of serving royalty (Queen Elizabeth once stayed here), though it's much more opulent now than it was in the 1960s. **Pros:** ideal for honeymoon or special splurge; expansive swimming pool; attention to detail and service. **Cons:** one of the most expensive hotels in Jaipur; need to book well in advance during high season; interior rooms can be a little dark. [$] *Rooms from: Rs. 35000* ✉ *Sardar Patel Marg, C-Scheme, Civil Lines* ☎ *11/4617–2700* 🌐 *sujanluxury.com/raj-mahal/index.htm* 🛏 *14 rooms* 🍴 *Free Breakfast.*

Tree of Life

$$$$ | **RESORT** | Nestled in the Aravali hills within an hour's drive of the city sights, this haven from the chaos of Jaipur offers secluded villa accommodations, spa treatments, and a chance to interact with the community. **Pros:** professional, personal service by owner and staff; stylish

and modern; yoga and cooking classes. **Cons:** 45-minute drive from Jaipur; not best suited to one-night stays; located in a small village, making food options limited. [$] *Rooms from: Rs. 18000* ✉ *Delhi–Jaipur Hwy., Kukas, Kacherawala* ☎ *1426/217–561, 1426/217–562* 🌐 *www.treeofliferesorts.com* 🛏 *13 rooms* 🍴 *Free Breakfast.*

Trident

$$$$ | **HOTEL** | While a stay at Trident—built to look like a rambling haveli 5 km (3 miles) from the center of town—does not offer the authentic royal experience, it does make for an interlude of gracious living. **Pros:** good location; close to Amer Fort but not too far from town; comfortable. **Cons:** service suffers in high season when this large hotel gets busy; decor is on the generic side; some rooms show signs of age. [$] *Rooms from: Rs. 11500* ✉ *Amber Fort Rd., opposite Jal Mahal* ☎ *141/267–0101* 🌐 *www.tridenthotels.com* 🛏 *134 rooms* 🍴 *Free Breakfast.*

Umaid Mahal

$$ | **HOTEL** | One of those faux havelis that abound in the Bani Park neighborhood, this small, comfortable hotel does a zealous job of re-creating old Rajasthani charm with colored glass windows, Mughal arches, ornate ceilings, mirror work, murals, old photographs and portraits, painted peacocks, turrets, and a giant entry arch. **Pros:** well priced; cheerful, eccentric decor; pool. **Cons:** it's not the real thing (not truly a heritage hotel); outside the city center; rooms facing the street can be noisy. [$] *Rooms from: Rs. 4500* ✉ *C–20/B–2 Bihari Marg, Bani Park* ☎ *931/450–3423, 141/220–1954* 🌐 *www.umaidmahal.com* 🛏 *35 rooms* 🍴 *Free Breakfast.*

Nightlife

Blackout

DANCE CLUBS | The rooftop bar and restaurant serves late lunches and dinner, and several nights a week the room is cleared of tables to create a dance floor. Come for pizza or Indian snacks, and stay for cold beers, cocktails, and either a DJ or performances by local musicians. There's a range of modern pop, hip-hop, and eclectic acts, and a the floor pulses with twenty- and thirtysomethings on dates and out with friends. ✉ *9th fl., Landmark Bldg., Golden Oak Hotel, C-Scheme* ☎ *992/811–6900.*

Polo Bar

BARS/PUBS | Sip a choice single malt or savor your cigar in an atmosphere rich in history. Rambagh Palace's Polo Bar is an extremely elegant place to have a drink—vistas of sweeping, peacock-dotted lawns and lots of old photographs that are testimony to Jaipur's long relationship with polo. There's a small fountain inside the bar, and a hand-picked selection of Cuban cigars available to purchase. ✉ *Rambagh Palace, Bhawani Singh Rd.* ☎ *141/238–5700* 🌐 *www.tajhotels.com.*

Performing Arts

Jawahar Kala Kendra

ART GALLERIES | Known simply as JKK, the Jawahar Kala Kendra complex houses art spaces, galleries, performance venues, a museum, and a modern café. In the afternoons you'll find visitors browsing the space, as well as remote workers and students who use as it as a co-working space given the speedy Wi-Fi. It's a good place to spend the afternoon like a modern Jaipur resident and a chance to take in the best example of modern architecture in the city. At night it buzzes with a lineup of activities. ✉ *2 Jawaharlal, Nehru Marg* ✣ *Opposite Commerce College* ☎ *141/270–6560* 🌐 *www.jkk.artandculture.rajasthan.gov.in.*

★ Rajmandir movie theater

FILM | This historic art deco movie theater is the place to experience Bollywood films and, in doing so, really soak in modern India. Widely visited by Indian and foreign tourists (the films are in Hindi without subtitles, but you get the gist of

the action even if you don't understand the language), Rajmandir is still constantly flooded with locals, who sing, cheer, and whistle throughout each film. Shows are usually at 12:30, 3:30, 6:30, and 9:30, but times may vary by 15 to 30 minutes, according to the length of the film. Tickets for popular new releases sell out quickly on weekends, but you can buy them in advance—your hotel reception or concierge should do this for you for a small fee. Expect a short intermission during longer films, and a long line at the restrooms during the break. ⊠ 16 Bhagwandas Rd., next to McDonald's, near Panch Batti ☎ 141/237–9372, 141/237–4694 ⊕ www.therajmandir.com ☒ From Rs. 200.

Ravindra Rang Manch

THEMED ENTERTAINMENT | In the heart of the city, surrounded by gardens, this theater and cultural organization hosts occasional dinner-and-dance programs. It also plays host to famous classical musicians and theater groups performing Indian classics and epics at the open-air amphitheater, especially during and around Indian festivals like Holi and Diwali. Most are free or with nominal charge; some are by invitation. Programs are listed in local newspapers. ⊠ Ram Niwas Gardens ☎ 141/261–9061.

Shopping

ARTS AND CRAFTS
Artchill
ART GALLERIES | This is Jaipur's leading gallery of contemporary art. There's a larger branch with an exhibit area of more than 5,000 square feet, in Amber Fort, with a wide-ranging collection of oil paintings, watercolors, and graphics by contemporary artists and sculptors. Open daily. ⊠ C 34 and 36 Rd. No. 1 ✛ Near Bais Godam Flyover, Bais Godam ☎ 141/403–4964 ⊕ www.artchill.com.

Khadi Ghar
GIFTS/SOUVENIRS | A good place to pick up practical gifts at reasonable prices, this national cooperative sells natural herbal soaps and shampoos, oils, incense, khadi textiles and clothing (the hand-spun and -woven fabric championed by Gandhi), leather goods, and handicrafts. Prices are fixed. ⊠ 320 M.I. Rd. ☎ 141/237–3745.

Khazana Walon ka Rasta
CRAFTS | Historically, this lane in the Old Pink City was devoted to marble statue cutters, though the area of late has become more generalized. You'll find a variety of clothing and jewelry vendors (accessible through Chandpol gate) scattered inside the area, too, but it's still a prime spot to watch stonecutters create artwork (big and small) in marble. Bargaining is recommended. ⊠ Chandpol.

P.M. Allah Buksh and Son
CRAFTS | Established in 1880 and still selling the finest hand-engraved, enameled, and embossed brassware—including oversize old trays, lamps, and historic armor—this is a great place to look for antique metalwork. ⊠ M.I. Rd., Panch Batti ☎ 141/401–2786.

Rajasthali
CRAFTS | If you have limited time and lots of gifts to buy or don't relish bargaining, head to this enormous, government-run emporium in the center of Jaipur. It overflows with crafts and textiles, including wooden pieces, puppets, jewelry, blue pottery, and scarves, though you might have to sift through a bewildering variety before you find what you want. Open from 11 am to 8 pm. **Be aware that sly salesmen and rickshaw drivers may try to take you to fake Rajasthali showrooms, which are privately run under the same name and charge exorbitant prices.** ⊠ M.I. Rd., opposite Ajmeri Gate ☎ 141/237–2974 ⊕ www.rajasthali.gov.in.

BEAUTY
Forest Essentials
SPA/BEAUTY | India's answer to L'Occitane is cheaper and has a wide range of ayurvedic as well as naturally made and herbal products, including fragrances, oils, creams, soaps, and skin and beauty

products. The night cream with saffron is a best seller, as is the saffron facial cleanser. ⊠ *341 M.I. Rd.* ☎ *141/402–9284* ⊕ *www.forestessentialsindia.com.*

CLOTHING AND TEXTILES

Anantaya

TEXTILES/SEWING | This modern Indian lifestyle brand combines contemporary aesthetics with traditional design. Find everything from linens and housewares to custom-made dhurries (woven rugs) and jewelry. Expect high-end boutique prices for pieces that might easily appear in the style section of glossy magazines. ⊠ *The Shops at Narain Niwas Palace* ☎ *141/406–8400* ⊕ *www.anantayadecor.com.*

★ Anokhi

TEXTILES/SEWING | This is a leading shop for fashionable clothing, mostly in cotton, some silk, with hand-block prints and paisley patterns—all of which will fit into your wardrobe back home. The selection includes both Indian and casual Western wear, and it has the prettiest *lehengas* (skirts) in the state. It has a great range of *kurtis* (short kurtas). You can also get beautiful bedspreads, quilts, and cloth bags here. After shopping, take a break at the attached café for a light bite or cold drink. Note: The store doesn't pay commissions to taxi drivers, which is why your driver might tell you the shop is closed or that they have a better deal for you. ⊠ *C–11, KK Sq., Prithviraj Rd., 2nd fl., C-Scheme* ☎ *141/400–7244, 141/400–7245* ⊕ *www.anokhi.com.*

Cottons

CLOTHING | Managed and staffed by women, Cottons carries attractive wardrobe staples for men and women, as well as small bags, quilts, and other decorative household items. ⊠ *Hari Bhawan, 4 Achrol House, Jacob Road, Civil Lines* ☎ *141/222–3870* ⊕ *www.cottonsjaipur.com.*

Fabindia

CLOTHING | This shop sells great cottons for men, women, children, and the home. They specialize in tailored pieces in vegetable dye prints. You can find men's tropical shirts, detailed dresses, or kurtas for both sexes, and they do saris as well as silks. Browse traditional pieces and modern garments that easily fit into your wardrobe back home. Prices for clothing begin at about Rs. 1,000. Open 10:30–10 daily. When you're done shopping, head upstairs to Tapri Tea House for a cuppa and lovely views of the city. ⊠ *B–4–E C-Scheme, opposite Gate 4, Prithviraj Rd.* ☎ *141/511–5997* ⊕ *www.fabindia.com.*

Jaipur Modern

CLOTHING | This hip boutique in the C-Scheme neighborhood carries well-known and up-and-coming designers from Jaipur and greater Rajasthan. Browse little summer dresses, elegant caftans, silk scarves, and oversized handbags that look just as fashionable in Rajasthan as they will carrying your laptop on the way to work. The attached café serves a full lunch and dinner menu. ⊠ *51 Dhuleshwar Garden* ☎ *141/411–2000* ⊕ *www.jaipurmodern.com.*

Krishna Textiles

TEXTILES/SEWING | A wide selection of Rajasthani-printed fabrics by the meter, bedcovers, shawls, pillow covers, and other items are the specialty of Krishna Textiles. Leather bags are also available. ⊠ *H–99C RIICO Industrial Area, Mansarovar* ☎ *141/401–9708.*

Mr Singh

CLOTHING | The modern atelier is a joint project between the owner of Bar Palladio and a craftsman trained in costume design. The chic tailor shop creates bespoke pieces (ranging from traditional wear to contemporary, romantic dresses) in a studio located in the lively Rajan Park district. Make an appointment to discuss design, fabric, and detailing, or bring your own fabric and have them craft one piece or an entire collection. The pricing is more expensive than tailor shops that a tour guide might suggest, but this house of design works with you

Shekhawati, Rajasthan's Open-Air Art Gallery

Known as Rajasthan's open-air art gallery because of the frescoes painted on the walls of ornate havelis in the region, Shekhawati—about 160 km (100 miles) from Jaipur or 200 km (124 miles) from Delhi—makes an intriguing stop on the way to Delhi or a day trip from Jaipur, provided one hits the road early. Influenced by the Persian, Jaipur, and Mughal schools of painting, Shekhawati's frescoes, many of which date back to the early 19th century, illustrate subjects ranging from mythological stories and local legends to hunting safaris and scenes of everyday life. You'll even find illustrated experiences with the British and cars or planes. The introduction of photography in 1840 gave Shekhawati's painters still more to work with.

Time-tested Techniques

The painters were called *chiteras* and belonged to the caste of *kumhars* (potters). Initially, they colored their masterpieces with vegetable pigments; after mixing these with lime water and treating the wall with three layers of a very fine clay, the chiteras painstakingly drew their designs on a last layer of filtered lime dust. Time was short, as the design had to be completed before the plaster dried, but the technique ensured that the images wouldn't fade.

Ornate Backdrops

The havelis themselves are quite spectacular, with courtyards, exquisitely latticed windows, intricate mirror work, vaulted ceilings, immense balconies, and ornate gateways and facades. They date from the British Raj, during which traditional overland trading routes to Central Asia, Europe, and China were slowly superseded by rail and sea routes. Only a handful of the havelis have survived—some have been restored by their owners, and a few have been converted into hotels. In **Sikar,** formerly the wealthiest trading center, look for the Biyani, Murarka, and Somani havelis. **Lachhmangarh** features the grand Char Chowk Haveli, particularly evocative of the prosperous Marwari lifestyle. In the village of **Churi Ajitgarh,** unusually erotic frescoes are painted behind doors and on bedroom ceilings in the Shiv Narain Nemani, Kothi Shiv Datt, and Rai Jagan Lal Tibrewal havelis. The frescoed temples of **Jhunjhunu** make for interesting comparisons: visit Laxmi Nath, Mertani Baori, Ajeet Sagar, and Qamrudin Shah Ki Dargah Fatehpur. Warrior-statesman Thakur Nawal Singh founded **Nawalgarh** in 1737, and the town has some of the best frescoes in Shekhawati, in the Aath, Anandilal Poddar, Jodhraj Patodia, and Chokhani havelis, as well as at the Roop Niwas Kothi hotel.

How to Visit

Hire a guide from Delhi or Jaipur, making sure they know the Shekhawati area; get an early start to make the most of your time, and be prepared to spend a lot of time driving from site to site, since the havelis are quite spread out. *The havelis listed above are the ones to prioritize.*

to create quality pieces that can be as simple as a kurta to a dress that would cost you three times the price in Paris boutique. ✉ *121 Gurunanakpura, Raja Park* ☎ *992/576–7636* ⊕ *www.bar-palladio.com/atelier.*

Salim's Paper

FACTORY | Whatever handmade paper you've seen back home may well have come from Salim's, a factory where you can see each step of the process. Some of the thick, beautiful papers are made with crushed flower petals; it's fun to see them thrown into the mixture of cotton and resin. At the showroom you can buy an enormous range of pretty paper products—gift bags, wrapping paper, gift tags, Christmas stars, albums, and gift boxes. ✉ *Gramodyog Rd.* ☎ *141/273–0222, 141/273–0444, 141/273–333* ⊕ *www.handmadepaper.com.*

Soma

TEXTILES/SEWING | Catering to the affluent and a design-loving tourist crowd, Soma is filled with vibrant colors. Here you'll find sustainably sourced (and extra-soft cotton) clothing for women and children, and decorative fabrics, including hand-painted white cloth lamp shades, as well as authentic block-printed goods for the home. One caveat: designs haven't been updated much in the last few years; if you shopped here on your last trip, you'll likely find the same items today. ✉ *Soma House, 2–B Girnar Extn, C-Scheme* ☎ *141/235–2391* ⊕ *www.somashop.com.*

Zari

CLOTHING | For exquisite but expensive formal wear, including lavish saris, embellished with *zari* (silver filigree embroidery), head here. The kurtis (short tunics) are also special. ✉ *10/11 Narayan Singh Circle, Tonk Rd.* ☎ *141/515–8500* ⊕ *www.zarijaipur.com.*

JEWELRY

Amrapali Jewels

JEWELRY/ACCESSORIES | This shop is a favorite among trendy and wealthy Indians for its whimsical silver and ornamental trinkets, as well as semiprecious stone artifacts. ✉ *M.I. Rd., Panch Batti* ✢ *Near Raj Mandir Cinema* ☎ *141/511–8215* ⊕ *www.amrapalijewels.com.*

Bhuramal-Rajmal Surana Showroom

JEWELRY/ACCESSORIES | For precious jewels, including gold ornaments, seek out this showroom, known worldwide for its kundan (a glasslike white stone) and *mina* (enamel) work. It has some reasonably priced silver jewelry featuring traditional patterns on contemporary styles. ✉ *368 J.L.N. Marg, Moti Dhungri* ☎ *141/257–0429, 141/257–0430* ⊕ *www.suranas.com.*

Chameli Market

JEWELRY/ACCESSORIES | If you're willing to bargain, head for this lane within the walls of the Old City to negotiate for silver and semiprecious jeweled ornaments, trinkets, and small toys. Know that some silver pieces may only be plated and you won't be able to verify the authenticity of stones. ✉ *Off M.I. Rd.*

Gem Palace

JEWELRY/ACCESSORIES | Shop here for Jaipur's best gems and jewelry, and a small collection of museum-quality curios, and you'll join the ranks of a royal clientele that includes Prince Charles and many members of Rajasthan's royal families. Even the princess of Jaipur, Maharani Gayatri Devi, might have been found here bargaining for a good deal. Prices range from US$25 to US$2 million. ✉ *M.I. Rd., Panch Batti* ☎ *141/237–3586* ⊕ *www.gempalace.com.*

Jaipur Jewellery House

JEWELRY/ACCESSORIES | This Johari Bazaar jeweler has an extensive and attractive collection of well-priced silver jewelry especially very unusual earrings with

A painted *haveli* in Shekhawati

semiprecious stones. They are very polite and patient and do not push you toward buying. Bargaining is the norm here. ✉ *81 Johari Bazaar* ☎ *889/041–9063* ⊕ *www.jaipurjeweleryhouse.com.*

Motisons

JEWELRY/ACCESSORIES | Less a shopping experience (the prices are high and so is the quality) and more a Jaipur experience, head here to see the kind of jewelry the city is known for. The showroom, in a phantasmagoric petal-shape modern mahal, has an enormous collection, including high-end pieces. It's considered one of the city's best addresses. The kundan jewelry is of particular interest. ✉ *110 Motisons Tower, Tonk Rd.* ☎ *141/416–0000* ⊕ *www.motisonsjewellers.com.*

POTTERY

Jaipur Blue Pottery Art Center

CERAMICS/GLASSWARE | A broad selection of Rajasthan's fetching blue pottery is available here, including a large selection of tiles, bathroom fittings, cups, plates, and decorative items such as cabinet knobs. Clay pots are made on the premises. ✉ *Amber Rd., near Jain Mandir* ☎ *141/263–0116* ⊕ *www.bluepottery.net.*

Neerja International

CERAMICS/GLASSWARE | The blue pottery here is particularly funky—the designer, owner Leela Bordia, has been at the forefront of the movement to keep the craft alive for more than three decades, and has exhibited all over the world. Her wares are made in nearby villages, helping to create jobs in rural areas. ✉ *1 Anand Bhawan, Jacob Rd., Civil Lines* ☎ *141/411–2609* ⊕ *www.neerjainternational.com.*

Ranthambhore National Park

161 km (100 miles) south of Jaipur.

Half of the world's endangered tiger population lives in India, and one of the national parks where the odds of seeing a tiger are much higher is Ranthambhore in eastern Rajasthan. Once a game reserve of the royal families of Jaipur and Karauli it was (mis)managed by their *shikar khaana* (hunting department). The 20th century saw India's tiger population decrease from an estimated 40,000 to 1,800, and areas like Ranthambore were the scene of exotic tiger hunts where the entire court showed up on as many as 40 elephants to slay prodigious amounts of big game. Today, Ranthambore, with its royal ruins and mixed vegetation—sand, scrub, grassland, hills—forms a dramatic background for tiger viewing and photography.

Sights

★ Ranthambhore National Park

NATIONAL/STATE PARK | If you want to see a tiger in the wild, Ranthambhore, in the Sawai Madhopur district and once the royal game reserve of the Maharaja of Jaipur, is the best park in Rajasthan to visit. The park (392 square km [151 square miles]) is part of the larger Ranthambhore Tiger Reserve which encompasses 1,334 square km (515 square miles) of rugged terrain bordered by the Chambal and Banas rivers and is home to a vast ecosystem of flora and fauna. To protect the fragile environment only a limited section of both the reserve and the park is open to visitors. Ranthambhore is noted for its tiger and leopard populations, although you still have only a 30% to 40% chance of seeing a large cat on any given expedition. The best time to see tigers is right before the monsoon, in summer, when the tigers emerge to

Tiger, Tiger

There are three national parks in the Delhi/Jaipur area. Ranthambhore (161 km [100 miles] south of Jaipur) is your best bet if tigers are your priority, but you'll still only have a 30% to 40% chance of seeing one. Keoladeo National Park in Bharatpur (150 km [93 miles] east of Jaipur, 55 km [34 miles] west of Agra) is mainly a destination for bird-watchers, though there are also some interesting flora and fauna. There is also Sariska, which is the closest park to Jaipur (110 km [68 miles]), but there are no tigers and it's not well run or worth a visit.

drink at small water holes—when it's dry and the water table is low, the tigers are forced out of hiding to quench their thirst. What you will definitely see are numerous peacocks, *sambar* (large Asian deer), *chital* (spotted deer), *chinkara* (gazelles), *nilgai* (blue bull or Asian antelope), wild boar, jackals, crocodiles, and often sloth bears.

Sighting a wild tiger in Ranthambhore is an exciting experience, even if you never come face-to-face with the king. First, of course, you will hear the jungle sounds that warn of a tiger's presence. Monkeys and peacocks scream loudly and the deer in the area become agitated and nervous. Ranthambhore became a national park in 1972 under the Project Tiger program, which was launched in an effort to save India's dwindling population of Bengal tigers. Sighting a leopard is much more difficult, as these cats live on high, inaccessible slopes and are extremely shy.

The park is run by the Indian government, and the rules are happily inflexible: you can only enter the park in an official government Jeep, and the Jeeps keep strict hours, daily from 6:30 or 7 am to 9:30

am, and 3 pm to 6 pm (the times may vary by 30 minutes during summer and winter months when the park opens later in the morning). Book a Jeep in advance, or online (though you must register on the website and book no more than 90 days in advance), or save yourself the hassle and book through your hotel (it's worth the service charge). Government regulations state that visitors must keep minimum distance of 20 meters from all wildlife (50 meters if you're in a vehicle) and that vehicles may only remain at a sighting point for up to 15 minutes. While the park is typically closed during mating season and monsoon season, July to early September, it's experimented with remaining partially open during this time in recent years. Check with your tour operator or hotel to confirm if you plan on visiting during this time.

You can also explore the surrounding region. The 10th-century **Ranthambhore Fort,** perched on a nearby hill, is one of Rajasthan's more spectacular military strongholds and where the reserve got its name. Dastkar, a craft-and-textile shop on the Ranthambhore Road, is run by a nongovernment legitimate cooperative organization.

The government-run heritage **Castle Jhoomar Baori** (12 rooms and two suites, Rs. 4,000–Rs. 7,500) offers the chance to spend a night near the animals, but little else. It can be booked through the Rajasthan Tourism Development Corporation website. A better option is to stay at one of the hotels along Ranthambhore Road and take a morning safari. The neighboring town of Sawai Madhopur has numerous hotels, but most are basic. ✉ *Ranthambhore National Park* ☎ *141/511–4768 Rajasthan Tourism Department* 🌐 *fmdss.forest.rajasthan.gov.in* 🎟 *Rs. 1650.*

Hotels

★ Oberoi Vanyavilas
$$$$ | **RESORT** | On the edge of the Ranthambore Tiger Reserve, this resort, one of the best in all of India, is ideal for those who want to "camp" in sheer luxury. **Pros:** natural surroundings and camping-like experience that doesn't skimp on luxury; service-oriented staff; less than 10 minutes from Ranthambhore park. **Cons:** expensive; book in advance; food is good but does not quite match the luxury setting. [$] *Rooms from: Rs. 61000* ✉ *Ranthambhore Rd., Sawai Madhopur* ☎ *746/222–3999* 🌐 *www.oberoihotels.com* 🕒 *Closed July–Sept. during monsoon season* 🛏 *25 tents* 🍴 *Free Breakfast.*

Ranthambhore Regency
$$$ | **RESORT** | This is the most comfortable midprice place on the Ranthambhore Road, 10 km (6 miles) from the park, in an elegant heritage-style building. **Pros:** friendly staff; local advice; pool. **Cons:** meals are buffet only; best to book weeks to months in advance during peak season; check with staff about timing of hot water. [$] *Rooms from: Rs. 8400* ✉ *Ranthambhore Rd., Sawai Madhopur* ☎ *7462/223–456* 🌐 *www.ranthambhor.com* 🛏 *75 rooms* 🍴 *Free Breakfast.*

Vivanta by Taj–Sawai Madhopur Lodge
$$$$ | **RESORT** | This small, intimate art deco lodge is convenient for those heading to the national park as well as being something of a destination in its own right. **Pros:** near the train station; just a 20-minute drive to the park; relaxing pool area. **Cons:** rooms are not particularly elegant or fancy; some packages include meals, while others do not; some rooms could use an update. [$] *Rooms from: Rs. 15000* ✉ *Ranthambhore Rd., Sawai Madhopur* ☎ *746/222–5155* 🌐 *www.vivantabytaj.com* 🛏 *48 rooms* 🍴 *No meals.*

Bharatpur

150 km (93 miles) east of Jaipur; 55 km (34 miles) west of Agra; 18 km (11 miles) west of Fatehpur Sikri.

Once the capital of a Jat kingdom, this town, which is very close to the border of Uttar Pradesh, is most famous for its proximity to the Bharatpur bird sanctuary, once a royal reserve, now renamed Keoladeo National Park. Bharatpur town has interesting bazaars, a fort, and several havelis in its vicinity.

Sights

Deeg

TOWN | Built in the 1730s, Deeg, which featured in *Siddhartha* (the 1972 film of Herman Hesse's novel) was the first capital of the Jat state and is known for its graceful palaces and gardens, complete with swings and ancient fountains. Indian families find this a charming location for a picnic. Check with your hotel about the condition of the fountains—mostly they are not working, and the lake is dirty. The Jal Mahal (water palace) has fountains that are run to musical accompaniment during certain days in August when the local fair is held. The 18th-century red-stone palace here was once used as a royal summer retreat and is rather arresting; it is surrounded by water. ⌂ *34 km (21 miles) north of Bharatpur* ☎ *946/073–9803, 0564/122–0215* 🖼 *Rs. 200.*

Keoladeo National Park

NATIONAL/STATE PARK | Founded by the Jat ruler Suraj Mal in 1733, the city of Bharatpur is famous for the Keoladeo National Park (also known as the Ghana Bird Sanctuary), once the duck-hunting forest of the local maharajas. This UNESCO World Heritage site is home to many mammals and reptiles—blue bulls (antelope), spotted deer, otters, and Indian rock pythons—but birds, especially waterbirds, are the main attraction. It's an ornithologist's dream—29 square km (10 square miles) of forests and wetlands with 400 species, more than 130 of which are resident year-round, such as the Saras crane, gray heron, snake bird (Indian darter), and spoonbill. In winter, birds arrive from the Himalayas, Siberia, and even Europe.

The best way to see the park is on foot or by boat (Rs. 200 per person, per hour, depending on boat type, though these are usually unavailable due to lack of rains even in the monsoon; check at entrance), but there are plenty of other options. The park's main artery is a blacktop road that runs from the entrance gate to the center. Surrounded by marshlands but screened by bushes, this road is the most convenient viewpoint for bird-watching and is also traveled by cycle-rickshaws (the best option; Rs. 100 per hour, Rs. 1,200 for the day, but drivers usually expect more, plus a tip of at least Rs. 50), bicycle (Rs. 60 per trip), and the park's electric bus (Rs. 200 per person). The rickshaw drivers, trained by the forest department, are pretty good at finding and pointing out birds. You can also rent a bicycle and head into more remote areas; just remember that most roads are unpaved. The excellent guides at the gate (Rs. 200 per hour; Rs. 250 for groups of five or more) are familiar with the birds' haunts and can help you spot and identify them.

Try to bring a bird guidebook: former royal-family member Salim Ali's *The Birds of India* is a good choice. The best time to see the birds is early morning or late evening, November through February; by the end of February, many birds start heading home. Stick around at sunset, when the water takes on a mirrorlike stillness and the air is filled with the calls of day birds settling down and night birds stirring.

A simple government-run restaurant at the Ashok RTDC offers decent Indian food, sandwiches, and drinks, but service is slow. ✉ *5 km (3 miles) south of city center* ☎ *5644/222–777* 🚻 *From Rs. 400.*

Lohagarh Fort

MILITARY SITE | In Bharatpur's Old City, this solid-looking fort, surrounded by a deep and wide moat, is also known figuratively as the Iron Fort, though it's built of mud. It has a colossal metal door that just might give you entryway envy. The structure might seem fragile, but it was tested and found invincible by a British siege in 1805. Armed with 65 pieces of field artillery, 1,800 European soldiers, and 6,000 Indian, sepoys did manage to win the battle, but they failed to break down the impregnable fort. There are palaces inside the fort and a museum that showcases wall paintings and pieces of sculpture and toys excavated nearby and dating from the 2nd century. The roads and trails leading to the fort are slippery during monsoon season. ✉ *Lohagarh Fort* ☎ *05644/228–185* 🚻 *Fort, free; museum, Rs. 50.*

Hotels

Laxmi Vilas Palace Hotel

$$$ | **HOTEL** | Rural and old-fashioned, this cozy, memorable heritage hotel is the best place to stay in the city and is still home to descendants of the former maharaja of Bharatpur. **Pros:** excellent value; impressive architecture; pool and gardens. **Cons:** lacks the luxury of fancier hotels in its category; slow service; food is average. 💲 *Rooms from: Rs. 7000* ✉ *Old Agra Rd., Kakaji Ki Kothi* ☎ *564/422–3523, 5644/223–523* 🌐 *www. laxmivilas.com* 🛏 *75 rooms and suites* 🍽 *Free Breakfast.*

Pushkar

146 km (90 miles) southwest of Jaipur.

With more than 500 temples, Pushkar is one of Hinduism's holiest sites and an interesting place to visit any time of year. The famous camel fair here is held in October or November. The focus of the town is its placid lake and the ghats, havelis, crumbling buildings, and temples, all whitewashed a splendid white, that edge the lake. Parts of the town have the vibe of a Rajasthani Varanasi and indeed this place is almost as sacred. But like many Indian towns Pushkar has several flavors. In its narrow car-free main bazaar, sadhus, tribals, hippies, the dreadlocked, backpackers, pilgrims, monkeys, beggars, and five-legged cattle (such birth deformities are considered lucky) vie for space with shops selling everything from religious paraphernalia to water bongs and chillams. Although goods from all over Rajasthan find their way to the bazaar, because Pushkar is such a holy city, no alcohol or meat can be sold here—some restaurants get around the alcohol restriction by serving beer in coffee mugs to their regular customers, but by no means should you count on being able to get anything alcoholic. Alcohol and nonvegetarian food is served in hotels located beyond the city limits. Pushkar's religious significance derives from the Vedic text, *Padma Purana,* which describes how the town was created: the Hindu god Brahma was looking for a place to perform the *yajna*—a holy ritual that involves placing offerings into a sacrificial fire for the fire god Agni—that would signify the beginning of the human age. He dropped a lotus from his hand, and Pushkar was where it struck the ground.

There are a few interesting types of handicrafts to shop for. Look for tiny wooden chests of drawers, wooden re-created antique telephones, trays, and other such knickknacks. Rajguru Emporium, opposite the Brahma temple, has a nice collection Pushkar crafts; bargain some.

GETTING HERE AND AROUND

Pushkar is best reached by road or by train via Ajmer (shuttle trains link Ajmer with Pushkar). The town is quite small, and everything worth seeing is in walking distance, or you can take an auto (negotiate the fare beforehand).

Sights

Bathing ghats (*flights of steps*)
RELIGIOUS SITE | Many of the marble bathing ghats on the holy Pushkar Lake—a must-visit if you want to see India's sacred sites—were constructed for pilgrims by royal families who wanted to ensure power and prosperity in their kingdoms throughout Rajasthan by appeasing the gods. It is believed that the waters of the lake are healing powers and that the water near different ghats have different powers. There are 52 ghats in all with various degrees of significance. When you pass an entrance to a ghat, be prepared for a priest (or 10) to solicit you by offering you a flower—he'll want you to receive a blessing, known as the "Pushkar Passport," and for you to give him a donation (or *dakshina*) in return upon completion of the ceremony (Rs. 100 is typical, or you can negotiate the sum when he approaches you). If you agree, he will lead you to the water's edge, say a prayer, and then ask you to recite a blessing in Sanskrit (you'll repeat after him). Then he'll paste a *tilak* (rice and colored powder dot) on your forehead and tie a religious red thread (denoting a blessing) to your wrist. Once you have the "passport," no other priest will approach you.

The ghats get extra busy during auspicious pilgrimage times, especially during the Kartik Purnima, the full moon during the Hindu month of Kartik, around November (also the time of the Pushkar Camel Fair). Thus there may be tens of thousands of people here bathing and getting blessings from local Brahmins. If you are claustrophobic, this might feel intense. The peaceful parts of the ghats can be accessed from the eastern shore of the lake, close to Sunset Café.

Be sure to follow etiquette, which includes taking off shoes and being respectful. ⊠ *Pushkar.*

Brahma Temple
RELIGIOUS SITE | In the center of town, not on the lake, this is one of India's most important temples in spite of its unimpressive architecture and more modern feel postreconstruction. Although many say it's the sole temple dedicated to Brahma in the world, in reality there are a few others; it's just that they are not considered authentic. The building is newer, but the shrine dates back to the 14th century. Pilgrims visiting the temple climb a long stairway into the walled area to take the blessings of the god—in the form of small sugar balls. There are varying versions of the legend concerning the temple, but most have to do with Brahma's wife Savitri, who was delayed in attending a special yajna or religious ceremony Brahma was carrying out. Impatient, Brahma married the goddess Gayatri (some say she was a milkmaid), and when Savitri found out, she put a curse on Brahma, declaring that the earth would forget him completely. She then relented, but said that Brahma could only be worshipped in Pushkar. Predawn and postsunset *aartis* (special rounds of worship) are held and are atmospheric. Shoes, bags, cameras, and video cameras are not allowed in the temple (do not try to take a photo with your phone)—it is best to leave everything in the car with your driver (if reliable) or back in your hotel, and deposit your shoes at the temple shoe stalls (for Rs. 20–Rs. 40). Mind your wallets and phones, and don't think of visiting the inner sanctum of the temple during festival times—there are thousands of others crowding to get inside—but if you're visiting at this time, you can view from afar. ⊠ *Pushkar.*

★ Camel Fair
FAIRGROUND | FAMILY | If you really want an experience, go to Pushkar during its renowned annual Camel Fair, the largest in the world. Every October or

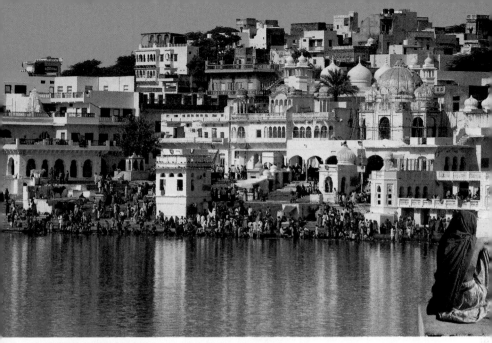

Looking out over Pushkar Lake

November—depending on the lunar calendar—during the full moon (Kartik Purnima), people flock here by the tens of thousands (if you don't love crowds, be prepared to feel overwhelmed) to see the finest camels parade around the fairground, edging the sand dunes, in colorful costumes. People come to buy, sell, and trade camels, and to race one camel against another, and it is a treat to see Rajasthanis, who already dress in bright colors, kitted out in their best. A good male camel goes for at least US$500, although some of the popular Marwari animals go for much more. Other types of livestock are also sold. In addition to the camel activities, there are cultural programs, cricket matches, competitions during the day, and all kinds of spontaneous music, dance, and folk performances in the evenings.

In recent years the festival has extended beyond the five days of camel trading (get here early to see the real traders in action), and the rest of the week-plus time has been packed with Indian and foreign tourists doing everything from snacking on cotton candy and playing fair games to taking camel rides out in the desert. Reserve a room far in advance—several months is best—and be prepared for street vendors and hawkers selling anklets, trinkets, and more to crowd you in hopes of making a sale. Several tented camps with modern conveniences also mushroom during the fair. *The website only goes live before the event.* ✉ *Pushkar* ⊕ *www.pushkar-camel-fair.com.*

Dargah Sharif

RELIGIOUS SITE | The shrine of the 13th-century Sufi saint Khwaja Moinuddin Chisty is in the heart of Ajmer, a city about 11 km (7 miles) southeast of Pushkar. The shrine is very significant for South Asian Muslims—visiting it means the chance to set your soul free eternally—and is visited by Muslims and non-Muslims alike. The busiest time is during Urs, the anniversary of the saint's death, which takes place during six days in the Islamic month of Rajab starting with the day of the full moon. The custom when you visit this shrine is to offer flowers, sugar balls, beads, and a *chaadar* (ornate scarf)—the beads and sweets will be blessed and given back to you. Sufiism is a more mystical and less austere aspect of Islam that is embraced vigorously in these parts.

Be prepared to deal with crowds and aggressive beggars on the street leading to the dargah whenever you visit. Ajmer itself isn't much of a destination, so most people bypass it on their way to Pushkar, then backtrack for a half-day visit to the shrine; the drive to Ajmer to Pushkar is scenic and descends through some minor hills offering views of Ajmer and its lake. The shrine is located at the end of a narrow lane and is not very accessible. Have the driver (if you have a car) park on the wider main road and hire a tuk tuk for Rs. 200 or so (let the driver negotiate a price, if possible) to take you to the dargah and back. Shoes, purses, rucksacks, cameras, and video cameras are not allowed in the dargah—it is best to leave those items in the car with your driver (if reliable) and deposit your shoes at the shrine shoe stalls (for Rs. 50, and you get a basket of flowers to offer inside). Mind your wallets and phones. Women and men need to cover their heads inside the shrine and must be dressed appropriately (no skirts, shorts, sleeveless tops). Don't think of visiting the inner sanctum of the dargah during the Urs festival, but do view from afar. There's a lot of rush on the weekends and during holidays, especially toward evening, and you can stop by to hear devotees banding together and sitting down in the couryard to sing *qawwalis*, lovely devotional Sufi music, from about 6 pm onward.

While you're here, the 19th-century **Nasi-yan Temple** is worth a visit as well. The detailed display depicting the Jain story of the world's creation inside the temple is mesmerizing. It's near Agra Gate, or just ask people how to find the Jain temple. ⊠ *Ajmer* ⊕ *www.dargahajmer.com.*

Savitri Temple

RELIGIOUS SITE | Make an early start to check out the Savitri Temple on a hill overlooking Pushkar Lake. The 1½ km- (1-mile) climb up the long flight of stairs leading up the hill takes between a half hour and an hour, and the outstanding view at sunrise is worth it. Alternatively, the ropeway (cable car) to the top takes 6 or 7 minutes and costs Rs. 80. **Be careful of menacing monkeys, which tend to grab anything edible; don't venture out to the temple if it is getting dark—it may be badly lit and dangerous.** ⊠ *Pushkar.*

🍴 Restaurants

Café Enigma

$ | ECLECTIC | This four-story, family-run restaurant is a good choice for continental cuisine (think veggie burgers and Israeli salads) as well as Indian classics, with spice levels suited to the Western palate; the pizzas and pastas are popular, too. It's also a good place for breakfast, as it usually stocks a few pastries from a nearby bakery, makes paranthas (potato-stuffed flatbreads) that are fresh and not too oily. **Known for:** homemade hummus; rooftop views; small snacks. $ *Average main: Rs. 200* ⊠ *Near Old Rangji Temple, Choti Basti* ☎ *998/344–1449* ▭ *No credit cards.*

Cafe Nature's Blessing

$$ | CAFÉ | This small café and bakery offers a range of healthy, light food, be it a tofu stir-fry or one of the interesting salads—all prepared to order. If you have had one too many naans or paneer-butter-ghee packed lunches, head here for a sandwich with homemade bread, cheesecake, or a healthy vegetarian or vegan meal. $ *Average main: Rs. 300* ⊠ *Panch Kund Rd.* ☎ *964/969–5538* ▭ *No credit cards.*

Laughing Buddha Cafe

$ | VEGETARIAN | The coffee at this tiny café is some of the best in Pushkar. Its petite menu features vegan and vegetarian entrées, cooked to order, including breakfast dishes and fresh salads, with proceeds going to fund local schools. **Known for:** vegetarian and vegan meals; salads; coffee. [$] *Average main: Rs. 200* ✉ *Main Market Rd.* ✥ *Near Gau Ghat* ☎ *810/734–3625.*

Out of the Blue

$$ | **INTERNATIONAL** | A favorite with backpackers, this quirky vegetarian restaurant in an old whitewashed-blue building near the Brahma Temple has chilled trance music in the background, and reasonably quick and attentive service. The lengthy menu has everything from pizzas, thalis, extensive breakfasts (fit for a king) with Italian espresso, 20 types of grilled sandwiches, 12 types of soup, many flavors of lassi (chocolate, rose, mixed fruit), pasta (a favorite is ravioli in sage sauce), Mexican favorites, and Israeli and Middle Eastern food like falafel, to crepes (vegetable, sweet, or salty) and apple pie. **Known for:** satisfying breakfast; rooftop dining; Italian coffee. [$] *Average main: Rs. 450* ✉ *Kapra Bazar* ☎ *978/408–9600* 💳 *No credit cards.*

Sunset Café

$$ | **INTERNATIONAL** | If you like to people-watch, this small terrace restaurant with lovely lake views is the place to be—expect to see an eclectic mash-up of dreadlocked backpackers, ornately adorned desert dwellers singing and dancing, and plenty of local priests eager to perform *pujas* (Hindu ceremonies). The menu mixes Indian (stuffed parathas or a thali), Italian (pizza, lasagna, bruschettas) and Mexican (enchiladas), though the international dishes aren't quite what you are used to back home; the veg sizzlers, lasagna, and banana pancakes are particularly popular here. **Known for**: lake views; light meals; vegetarian entrées. [$] *Average main: Rs. 450* ✉ *Parikrama Marg, next to Pushkar Palace, Choti Basti* ☎ *145/277–2382, 145/277–2725* 💳 *No credit cards.*

Hotels

Ananta Spa and Resorts

$$$ | **RESORT** | Spread across 9 acres, Pushkar's loveliest and most expensive hotel has an outdoorsy lodge feel and there are golf carts to get around. **Pros:** peaceful; not that far from the city but away from its bustle; full-service spa. **Cons:** 4 km (2½ miles) from the main town; expensive—during the Pushkar Fair rates more than triple; buffet food just okay. [$] *Rooms from: Rs. 9000* ✉ *Leela Sevri, Ajmer Pushkar Rd.* ☎ *145/305–4000* 🌐 *www.anantahotels.com* 🛏 *73 rooms* 🍴 *Free Breakfast.*

Gateway Hotel

$$$ | **HOTEL** | This eye-catching edifice in a delicate pink stone on a low hill is one of the first landmarks visible as you enter the outskirts of Pushkar town coming from Jaipur. **Pros:** nice pool; lovely ambience; well priced. **Cons:** far from town; rooms could be slightly more luxurious; hotel needs more facilities to keep guests busy. [$] *Rooms from: Rs. 7000* ✉ *Village Hokra, Pushkar Bypass, 10.8 km (6.7 miles) from town* ☎ *145/662–0000* 🌐 *gateway.tajhotels.com* 🛏 *88 rooms* 🍴 *No meals.*

Hotel Pushkar Palace

$$$ | **HOTEL** | In the best location in town, this charming, small palace, where all rooms open onto a pretty courtyard garden, sits above its own ghat (private stairs leading down to the lake) and has fabulous, panoramic views of Pushkar. **Pros:** lakeside location with great views; good food; safaris can be arranged. **Cons:** rooms could be cleaner; as elsewhere, room rates skyrocket during the Pushkar festival and all meals must be included at this time; lacks the polish and service of a luxury hotel. [$] *Rooms from: Rs. 7500* ✉ *Choti Basti, off Pushkar Bazaar (the main street)* ☎ *145/277–3001, 145/277–2401* 🌐 *www.hotelpushkarpalace.com* 🛏 *50 rooms* 🍴 *Free Breakfast.*

Evening falls at the Pushkar camel fair

Jagat Palace

$$$ | HOTEL | The bearded guard, brandishing a spear and offering a salute as you arrive, is a good indication of the style of service at this mildly eccentric haveli-style hotel, with a promising view of the dunes outside Pushkar from some parts of the property. **Pros:** pool; good value except during Pushkar Fair; elevator. **Cons:** slightly out of the city; service a bit slow; rooms and furniture show signs of age. $ *Rooms from: Rs. 7500* ✉ *Behind Ramdwara* ☎ *145/277–2001, 145/277–2401* ⊕ *www.hotelpushkarpalace.com* ⇗ *82 rooms* ○ *Free Breakfast.*

Master Paradise

$ | B&B/INN | This oversize pink bungalow is in a neat garden in the leafy Panch Kund road enclave of Pushkar, surrounded by hills. **Pros:** pool; close to the desert; well priced. **Cons:** 3 km (2 miles) from the main town; hot water can be problematic; rooms and bathrooms could use an update. $ *Rooms from: Rs. 2600* ✉ *Master Colony, Panch Kund Rd.* ☎ *145/277–3931, 145/277–3933* ⊕ *www.*

masterparadise.com ⇗ *63 rooms* ○ *Free Breakfast.*

Pushkar Resorts

$$$ | RESORT | The spirit of the countryside blends well with the comforts of resort living here, and guests can relax poolside under the shade of a palm tree in rustic environs, or wander the 32 acres, far from Pushkar's chaotic main bazaar, a 15-minute Jeep ride away. **Pros:** rooms with a view; nice pool; alcohol. **Cons:** need a car to get into town; some rooms allow smoking; Wi-Fi is spotty. $ *Rooms from: Rs. 6000* ✉ *Motisar Rd., Village Ganhera, outside Pushkar* ☎ *145/277–2944, 145/277–2945* ⊕ *www.sewara.com* ⇗ *40 rooms* ○ *Free Breakfast.*

Udaipur

405 km (251 miles) southwest of Jaipur; 335 km (207 miles) southeast of Jodhpur.

Romantic old-world charm, soothing lakes, and fairy-tale palaces are what draw so many visitors to Udaipur, known as the City of Lakes. It was founded in 1567, when, having grown weary of repeated attacks on the old Mewar capital of Chittaur—Chittaur is the historic name of the area, and Chittaurgarh literally means "the fort of Chittaur"—Maharana Udai Singh asked a holy sage to suggest a safe place for his new capital. The man assured Udai Singh that the new base would never be conquered if it was established on the banks of Lake Pichola, and thus was born Singh's namesake, Udaipur.

Despite being one of Rajasthan's largest cities, with a population of less than half a million people, modern Udaipur still feels like a small town. Added perks are the weather, which is balmy year-round except for a spot of summertime heat between April and mid-June, and the fact that the locals are extremely friendly. To enjoy this city's hospitality, book a stay in a palace or a haveli (the bigger the better). Five main gates lead into Udaipur's Old City: they are Hathi Pol (Elephant Gate) to the north; Kishan Pol to the south; Delhi Pol to the northeast; Chand Pol (Moon Gate) to the west; and Suraj Pol (Sun Gate) to the east.

Anchoring Udaipur's Old City are the famed City Palace and Lake Palace—the latter in the middle of Lake Pichola, and now a hotel run by Taj Hotels Resorts and Palaces. The Old City itself is built on tiny hillocks and raised areas, its lanes full of twists and turns, with plenty of charming little niches to be discovered. The major landmarks in the new section are Chetak Circle, Sukhadia Circle, and Sahelion Ki Bari gardens.

GETTING HERE AND AROUND
You can reach Udaipur by air from Delhi or Mumbai (not Jaipur) or by train (the superfast Shatabdi connects Udaipur and Jaipur) or by road. Most of Udaipur's top attractions are on the east shore of the lake, in the Old City, and if you stay near the Jagdish Temple or the City Palace, in the heart of the Old City, you'll be able to

reach most of the sites on foot. If you follow the main road downhill from the Jagdish Temple, you'll wind up at the Ghanta Ghar (clock tower)—the road continues north all the way to the city center in the newer, and far less enchanting, part of Udaipur. The easiest way to get from one side of the lake to the other is to cross the small bridge at Chand Pol, on the narrow northern edge. Auto-rickshaws are also widely available—don't pay more than Rs. 150 for a ride anywhere within the main city.

TAXI COMPANIES Ola Cab ☒ *Chetak Circle* ⊕ *www.olacabs.com.*

TIMING
While you can get through most of the sights if you stay here for only two days, three or four will give you time to explore the Old City's many winding lanes or take a day trip.

ESSENTIALS
TOURIST OFFICES Government of Rajasthan Tourist Office ☒ *Fateh Memorial, Suraj Pol* ☎ *294/241–1535* ⊕ *www.tourism. rajasthan.gov.in.*

Sights

Bagore ki Haveli
ARTS VENUE | FAMILY | It's fun to explore the many rooms and terraces of this elegant 18th-century haveli on Gangaur Ghat. It was built by a prime minister of Mewar. One-hour folk-dance performances are organized every evening at 7 in the outdoor courtyard (time may change, so check on arrival)—get there at least 30 minutes early for good seats. ☒ *Gangaur Ghat* ☎ *294/242–2567* ☒ *From Rs. 100.*

Bharatiya Lok Kala Mandal
MUSEUM | FAMILY | This folk-art museum displays a collection of puppets, dolls, masks, folk dresses, ornaments, musical instruments, and paintings. The museum hosts a 6 pm puppet show followed by traditional dancing. ☒ *Udaipur* ✛ *About 500 yds north of Chetak Circle, Panch*

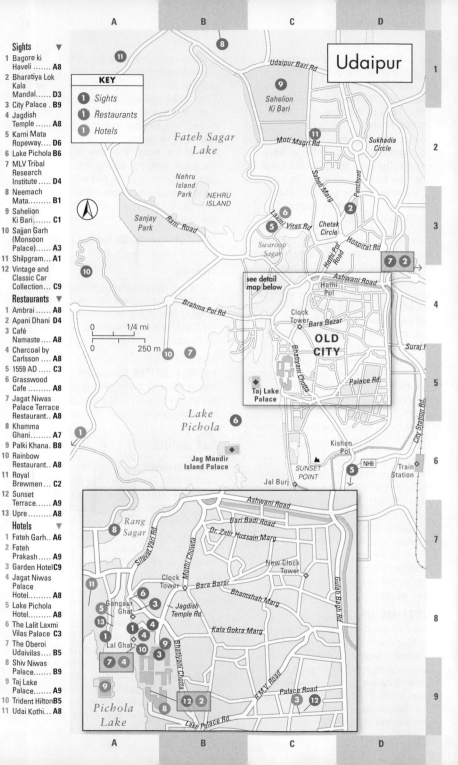

Batti, near Mohta Park ☎ *0294/252–9296* ✉ *From Rs. 45.*

City Palace

CASTLE/PALACE | The sprawling maharana's palace—the largest in Rajasthan—stands on a ridge overlooking the lake and the view of the city and Lake Palace from the top is one great reason to come here. Begun by Udai Singh and extended by subsequent maharanas, the sand-color City Palace rises five stories tall, with a series of balconies. Cupolas crown its octagonal towers, which are connected by a maze of narrow passageways—which make for perfect snapshot opportunities. The City Palace is part of a complex of palaces—two have been converted to hotels and one houses the current titular maharana, Arvind Singh of Mewar.

The main entry is through the **Badi Pol** (Great Gate), built in the 1600s. Next head through the **Tripolia Pol**, a triple arched gate built in 1725, which provides the northern entry. The road between this gate and the palace is lined with shops and kiosks of big brands and small boutiques. There's also a café.

The rooms and courtyards inside the City Palace Museum contain decorative art: beautiful paintings, colorful enamel, inlay glasswork, and antique furniture. Don't be surprised if you happen upon a fashion shoot in one of the colorful quarters. One of the more interesting features is the private bathroom of the maharaja on the third floor, which has a tree growing nearby and a grand padded toilet seat. It's useful to have the explanatory site publication, available in the book shop, or get an audio guide at the admission point. The hour-long sound-and-light show held at the palace's Manek Chowk chronicles the history of the House of Mewar—check ahead as timings can change without notice. ⌂ *City Palace Complex* ☎ *0294/252–8016* ✉ *From Rs. 300.*

Jagdish Temple

RELIGIOUS SITE | This 17-century imposing Hindu temple, the oldest in the city, was commissioned by Maharana Jagat Singh and is a major landmark in Udaipur's Old City for its architecture and height—the *shikhar* (or dome/spire) alone is 79 feet. It's usually abuzz with devotees and tourists, especially during the morning and evening aarti (prayer ceremony), when vendors set up makeshift flower stalls along the temple walls and sell offerings of marigolds. The temple is dedicated to Jagdish (an incarnation of Vishnu), and referred to as Jagdishji. Songs sung in his praise are often played through loudspeakers high on the temple's edifice. You're welcome to step inside, although the engravings on the temple's exterior walls are more interesting to look at. It's also one of the most central locations in the city, and an ideal location to use if you are meeting people. ⌂ *Jagdish Mandir, just north of City Palace.*

Karni Mata Ropeway

MOUNTAIN—SIGHT | Udaipur is one of the few places in India with cable cars, and these colorful gems will save you a 20-minute climb up to the scenic hilltop. You can take the ropeway (as it is called locally), to the top of Machchala Hill near Karni Mata temple and feast your eyes on the view of the city lakes and palaces. While it's a local destination, it's still relatively unknown among foreign tourists. ⌂ *Deen Dayal Park, Doodh Talai* ⊹ *At sunset hill* ⊕ *www.ropewayudaipur. com* ✉ *Rs. 100.*

★ Lake Pichola

HISTORIC SITE | You can't leave Udaipur without seeing the stunningly romantic **Lake Palace** (Jag Niwas, now a Taj hotel), which seems to float serenely on the waters of Lake Pichola. A vast, white-marble fantasy, the palace has been featured in many Indian and foreign films, including the James Bond film *Octopussy*. Unfortunately, the palace's apartments, courts, fountains, and gardens are off-limits unless you're a guest at the Taj Lake Palace Hotel. The equally isolated, three-story **Jag Mandir Island Palace** occupies Jag Mandir Island at the southern end of the lake, and is open to visitors from 10 to 6 (take a boat over). This palace has an elegant restaurant, the Darikhana (it serves Indian and continental cuisine, and is only open for dinner), as well as a more casual all-day café. Built and embellished over a 50-year period beginning in the 17th century, Jag Mandir is made of yellow sandstone, lined with marble, and crowned by a dome. The interior is decorated with arabesques of colored stones. Shah Jahan, son of the Mughal emperor Jahangir, took refuge in Jag Mandir after leading an unsuccessful revolt against his father. Legend has it that Shah Jahan's inspiration for the Taj Mahal came from this marble masterpiece. One-hour motorboat cruises (Rs. 400 morning rides, or Rs. 700 for a sunset cruise), start at the City Palace including a stop at Jag Mandir, leave from the jetty on the hour (daily 10–6) check for the exact spot at ticket counter; book a day ahead during the busy season. ⊠ *Udaipur* ☎ *294/252–8016.*

MLV Tribal Research Institute

MUSEUM | Stop in here if you're curious about Mewar's tribal communities. The institute has a compact museum of tribal culture and a good library on tribal life and issues. ⊠ *University Road, Ashok Nagar* ☎ *294/241–0958* ⊠ *Free.*

Neemach Mata

RELIGIOUS SITE | This hilltop temple in the new part of town is dedicated to the goddess of the mountain, also considered an avatar of Ambaji, and the climb to its summit (no vehicles are allowed) is rewarded by a beautiful view of the whole city and the Fateh Sagar lake. The shrine dates from the 17th century, although the building is newer. It's a steep, 20-minute climb on a paved, zigzag path, but you can pause often on the way up to take in the view (and catch your breath). Wear comfortable shoes

and be respectful as it's an active temple. ⊠ *North of Fateh Sagar Lake.*

Sahelion Ki Bari

GARDEN | FAMILY | Udaipur's famous Garden of the Maidens was founded in the 18th century by Maharana Sangam Singh for the 48 young ladies-in-waiting who were sent to the royal house as dowry. Back then, men were forbidden entrance when the queens and their ladies-in-waiting came to relax (though the king and his buddies still found their way in). The garden, on the banks of Fateh Sagar Lake, is lush with exotic flowers, carved fountains, a famous lotus pool, and monolithic marble elephants. The fountains don't have pumps. Designed to take advantage of gravity, they run on water pressure from the lakes. If the fountains are not working, ask one of the attendants to turn them on. ⊠ *Saheli Marg, north of the city, near Bharatiya Lok Kala Mandal* ⊠ *Rs. 50.*

Sajjan Garh (Monsoon Palace)

CASTLE/PALACE | High in the Aravali Hills just outside Udaipur, this fort–palace glows golden orange in the night sky, thanks to the lights that illuminate it. Once the maharana's Monsoon Palace and hunting lodge, it's now under government control and has lost some of its former glory. The panoramic view is spectacular from the fort's lofty tower, and locals claim you can see distant Chittaurgarh on a clear day. The winding road from the city to the top of Sajjan Garh, surrounded by green forests, is best navigated by car rather than rickshaw. On foot, it's a 45-minute uphill walk from the landing to the palace (or a taxi to the top will cost you Rs. 100 per person). ⊠ *Udaipur* ⊕ *www.tourism.rajasthan.gov. in* ⊠ *Rs. 150.*

Shilpgram

FESTIVAL | This rural arts-and-crafts village near Fateh Sagar lake 5 km (3 miles) west of Udaipur contains a complex with 34 re-creations of furnished village huts (authentic right down to their toilets)

Udaipur's City Palace

from various states across India, including Rajasthan, Gujarat, Maharashtra, and Odisha, with tribal relics on display. The town comes alive in late December with the nine-day **Shilpgram Utsav Festival,** when artists and craftspeople from around the country arrive to sell and display their works. Puppet shows, dances, folk music, and handicrafts sales take place year-round, however. There is a basic*dhaba* (eatery) inside the compound serving Indian food and tea. ✉ *Rani Rd., near Fateh Sagar Lake* ☎ *294/243–1304* 🎫 *Rs. 100.*

Vintage and Classic Car Collection
MUSEUM | The city's most elite wheels are found at the car museum, showcasing a small but gleaming selection of two dozen or so vintage (and still running) automobiles belonging to the local royal Mewar family. Look out for the 1939 Cadillacs, 1936 Vauxhall, and the 934 Rolls-Royce Phantom used in the Bond film *Octopussy,* which was largely filmed in and around the city. The museum is housed in the former Merwar State Motor Garage. ✉ *Lake Palace Rd.* 🎫 *Rs. 250.*

🍴 Restaurants

Ambrai
$$$ | **INDIAN** | Right on the shore of Lake Pichola opposite Lal Ghat, this lively outdoor restaurant with a pleasant bar has a hidden approach via narrow lanes and stunning views of the City Palace complex and the Lake Palace. It serves Rajasthani standards along with decent continental and Chinese dishes, though the views outshine the food. **Known for:** Lake Pichola views; sunset drinks; standard menu. [$] *Average main: Rs. 650* ✉ *Amet Haveli, opposite Lal Ghat* ☎ *294/243–1085* 🌐 *www.amethaveliudaipur.com.*

Apani Dhani
$$ | **INDIAN** | About half an hour's drive out of the center of town, and an upward climb on a hilltop, the restaurant offers traditional-style vegetarian Rajasthani thali. The local delicacies—dal baati (unleavened wheat bread eaten with lentils), *bajra* roti (millet rotis), garlic chutney, *sangri* (a desert vegetable)—are tasty. **Known for**: Rajasthan cuisine; folk theater;

Did You Know?

The main shrine at the Jagdish Temple, which is dedicated to Vishnu, is a four-armed image of the god, carved out of a single piece of black stone. You must climb a flight of 32 marble steps to reach the shrine.

tourist groups. $ *Average main: Rs. 425* ✉ *Pratap Nagar ByPass* ☎ *935/250–6351* ⊕ *www.apnidhani.com.*

Café Namaste

$ | CAFÉ | This little bakery and café in the Hotel Gangaur Palace, with courtyard or rooftop seating, sells fresh pastries and cakes, as well as delicious, real espresso. If you come for breakfast, try the baked beans on toast or the soft cinnamon rolls (not always available during summer months), apple crumble, or date-and-walnut pie. **Known for:** espresso; breakfast pastries; rooftop terrace with views of Lake Pichola. $ *Average main: Rs. 350* ✉ *339 Ashoka Haveli, Gangaur Ghat Marg* ☎ *294/242–2303.*

Charcoal by Carlsson

$$ | INTERNATIONAL | Looking for a spot to indulge your carnivorous cravings? With grilled meats and kebabs (cooked on a charcoal grill), Indian staples, and house-made corn tortillas for its famous tacos, this is an ideal restaurant for those needing a break from standard North Indian or vegetarian fare. **Known for:** grilled kebabs; tandoori; rooftop dining. $ *Average main: Rs. 450* ✉ *12 Lal Ghat* ✛ *Behind Jagdish temple* ☎ *294/256–0566.*

1559 AD

$$$$ | ECLECTIC | Named after the year when Udaipur was founded, 1559 occupies an elegant colonial bungalow, with indoor dining as well as alfresco dining in the large garden. Specialties include Rajasthani game birds (farmed, not hunted), prepared in traditional Indian and European styles, as well as salmon or rack of lamb; the menu also features pasta, pizza, and vegetarian specials such as *malai kofta* and paneer dishes. **Known for**: Rajasthani thali; landscaped patio seating; European cuisine. $ *Average main: Rs. 750* ✉ *P.P. Singhal Marg, near Fateh Sagar* ☎ *294/243–3559* ⊕ *www.1559ad.com.*

Grasswood Cafe

$ | CAFÉ | Authentic espresso drinks and fresh juice are the specialties at this café

on the corner of a busy intersection near Jagdish Temp. Free Wi-Fi and a/c make this postage-size but airy nook a hangout for tourists, but plenty of local merchants pop in for the high-quality coffee, too. **Known for:** fresh-squeezed juice; espresso drinks; small snacks. $ *Average main: Rs. 200* ✉ *26 Gadiya Devra* ✛ *Near foot bridge* ⊕ *www.grasswoodcafe.com* ▬ *No credit cards.*

Jagat Niwas Palace Terrace Restaurant

$$$ | NORTH INDIAN | In a converted haveli at the end of one of Lal Ghat's labyrinthine lanes, this restaurant has retained the mansion's lovely design and has spectacular views of the Lake Palace, especially at night, when the vistas capture the incredibly romantic essence of the city. There is a decently good range of continental, Chinese, and Indian food; wine, cocktails, and beer available—fish à la Jagat is a highlight during fishing season; otherwise try the laal maas (red meat curry) or *subz galouti kabab* (vegetarian kebabs). **Known for**: rooftop dining; lake views; international cuisine. $ *Average main: Rs. 600* ✉ *23–25 Lal Ghat* ☎ *294/242–2860, 294/242–0133* ⊕ *www.jagatcollection.com.*

★ Khamma Ghani

$$ | INDIAN | Overlooking the lake, this spacious restaurant with indoor and outdoor seating exudes ambience without being stuffy, and thus it's one of the best spots in Udaipur for stunning views and authentic food. Take a seat at a table or traditional floor seating alongside windows (*gokhra* seating) for a hearty meal of Indian or continental dishes. **Known for**: terrace seating; authentic tandoori; lively ambience. $ *Average main: Rs. 400* ✉ *63 Rang Sagar Lake* ✛ *Near Hotel Natural View.*

Palki Khana

$$$$ | EUROPEAN | Inside the City Palace complex, this casual café, is a perfect postmuseum stop—sit outside under Rajasthani umbrellas if you like to people-watch. The menu emphasizes

standard continental café fare, such as salads, sandwiches, pizza, and pasta. **Known for:** café eatery; drinks and cocktails; lunch spot. [$] *Average main: Rs. 750* ✉ *Shiv Niwas Palace, City Palace Complex* ☎ *294/241–9021* 🌐 *www.hrhhotels.com.*

Rainbow Restaurant

$$$ | **INDIAN** | Popular with tourists of all ages and backpackers, this family-run restaurant is a great place for Italian coffee and juices—the menu has an incredibly long list of fresh fruit juices and "mocktails." Tandoori food is the favorite here; try the butter chicken or a wide range of vegetarian dishes. It's the spot that local guides recommend for stunning views of Lake Pichola and the Lake Palace as the sun goes down. **Known for:** rooftop views; fresh juices; traditional Indian fare. [$] *Average main: Rs. 500* ✉ *27–28 Lal Ghat, Lake Pichola* ☎ *946/063–1484.*

Royal Brewmen

$$$ | **INTERNATIONAL** | Stop by this lively café and lounge, centrally located near a city garden and close to Fateh Sagar Lake, for some interesting blends of coffee, a quick bite, or to chill on the comfortable sofas. Sandwiches, burgers, and pizzas are on the menu, and Wi-Fi is free. **Known for:** coffee; variety of pizza; light snacks and lunch. [$] *Average main: Rs. 550* ✉ *Hitawala Complex, Saheliyo Ki Bari* ☎ *294/242–1571.*

Sunset Terrace

$$$ | **INTERNATIONAL** | Overlooking Lake Pichola, this café benefits from a constant breeze, and sitting on the terrace feels as if you've joined the aristocracy and have unlimited leisure—plus live instrumental music adds to the romance in the evenings. Order from a fixed-price menu or à la carte options; favorites include the butter chicken, kung pao chicken, prawns masala, paneer *lababdar* (soft white cheese in an onion and tomato gravy). **Known for**: sunset cocktails; date-night dinners with folk music; tourists relaxing with cold beers on hot afternoons. [$] *Average main: Rs. 700* ✉ *Fateh Prakash Palace, City Palace Complex* ☎ *294/252–8016* 🌐 *www.hrhhotels.com.*

Upre

$$$ | **INTERNATIONAL** | The name of the Lake Pichola Hotel's restaurant means "upstairs" in the local dialect, and that's exactly what it is—a rooftop spot beside the pool, with spectacular views of the City Palace complex and lake, especially charming and romantic when they are lighted up after dark (it can be hot at lunchtime). There's typical Rajasthani seating on high beds and against bolsters, too. **Known for:** big dinner crowds in high season (make reservations); drinks with on the rooftop with views; diverse menu. [$] *Average main: Rs. 550* ✉ *Lake Pichola Hotel, outside Chand Pol, Lake Pichola* ☎ *294/243–1197* 🌐 *www.1559ad.com.*

Hotels

Fateh Garh

$$$$ | **RESORT** | Environmentally friendly, community-minded, luxurious, and with an interesting backstory, this is one of Udaipur's notable boutique hotels, perched atop a hill adjacent to the Monsoon Palace. **Pros:** friendly, polite service; great food (though pricey); scenic location. **Cons:** a long drive away from the Old City; service does not match luxury feel or price level; expensive. [$] *Rooms from: Rs. 17000* ✉ *Sisarma 6 km (4 miles) from Udaipur* ☎ *869/694–5101* 🌐 *www.fatehgarh.in* 🛏 *50 rooms* 🍴 *Free Breakfast.*

Fateh Prakash

$$$$ | **HOTEL** | Part of the haughty City Palace complex, this 19th-century retreat on the eastern bank of Lake Pichola looks across the water at the Lake Palace, and oozes stateliness and history—royal portraits, antiques, chandeliers, ornate ceilings, and an abundance of crinkled-edged arches set the tone. **Pros:** well located and close to city sights; regal address;

spacious rooms. **Cons:** service, though warm, can be spotty; expensive; book in advance for high travel season. ⓢ *Rooms from: Rs. 45000* ✉ *City Palace Complex* ☎ *294/252–8016, 294/252–8017, 294/252–8018* ⊕ *www.hrhhotels.com* ⇲ *50 rooms* ◎l *Free Breakfast.*

Garden Hotel

$$$ | B&B/INN | The best reason to stay here is the hotel's proximity to city sights and access to a lovely garden barbecue restaurant out front. **Pros:** well located; clean bathrooms; spacious rooms. **Cons:** hotel lacks charm of others in Udaipur; bland breakfast buffet; most rooms lack views. ⓢ *Rooms from: Rs. 6500* ✉ *Sajjan Niwas Garden, Gulab Bagh Rd.* ☎ *294/241–8881* ⊕ *www.hrhhotels.com* ⇲ *29 rooms* ◎l *Free Breakfast.*

★ **Jagat Niwas Palace Hotel**

$$ | HOTEL | Overlooking Lake Pichola, this airy, whitewashed, 17th-century haveli hotel is one of the best medium-budget places to stay in Udaipur; you'd be hard-pressed to find better value (or better views). **Pros:** unsurpassed views of the lake and Aravali Hills; best value in town; short walk from shopping and restaurants. **Cons:** narrow approach only by auto-rickshaw; no pool or elevator; allot time between showers for hot water. ⓢ *Rooms from: Rs. 4600* ✉ *23–25 Lal Ghat* ☎ *294/242–2860, 294/242–0133* ⊕ *www.jagatniwaspalace.com* ⇲ *30 rooms* ◎l *Free Breakfast.*

Lake Pichola Hotel

$$ | HOTEL | Especially surprising given its price, this hotel has some great features, including a wonderful lakeside location, rooms with private terraces, suites with Jacuzzi or steam room, an Upre restaurant, and a rooftop pool. **Pros:** city and lake views; elevator; well priced and nearby the Old City with shops and cafés. **Cons:** difficult approach through narrow, crowded lanes; noisy at times; decor shows age. ⓢ *Rooms from: Rs. 5800* ✉ *Udaipur* ✛ *Outside Chandpol, on western side of Lake Pichola* ☎ *294/243–1197*

⊕ *www.lakepicholahotel.com* ⇲ *25 rooms* ◎l *No meals.*

The Lalit Laxmi Vilas Palace

$$$$ | HOTEL | Sumptuous lawns and views, grand terraces, palace pomp, and an interesting range of activities for guests—horse dancing, bagpiper recitals, puppet shows, snooker—are the highlights of Laxmi Vilas, a former palace constructed in 1911. **Pros:** tranquil; enviable location; breakfast buffet included. **Cons:** no pool; dining service can be slow; bathrooms are lackluster. ⓢ *Rooms from: Rs. 16000* ✉ *Opposite Fateh Sagar Lake* ☎ *294/301–7777* ⊕ *www.thelalit.com* ⇲ *55 rooms* ◎l *Free Breakfast.*

★ **The Oberoi Udaivilas**

$$$$ | HOTEL | On Lake Pichola, with sublime views of the Lake Palace, City Palace Complex, and ghats, this 30-acre property—a contemporary palace in its own right, reflecting the beauty of Mewar artistry—is one of India's most luxurious (and expensive) hotels. **Pros:** luxurious spa; great service and surroundings; expansive garden and sanctuary. **Cons:** extremely expensive; rather remote from the Old City (but a boat provides a shortcut); need to book far in advance for peak season. ⓢ *Rooms from: Rs. 61000* ✉ *Haridasji ki Magri* ☎ *294/433–300, 800/562–3764 reservations from U.S. and Canada* ⊕ *www.oberoihotels.com* ⇲ *90 rooms* ◎l *No meals.*

Shiv Niwas Palace

$$$$ | HOTEL | Once the royal guesthouse, where the maharaja of Udaipur had his guests stay, gracious Shiv Niwas on Lake Pichola is another part of the City Palace complex, and still features plenty of antiques and royal memorabilia in its decor. **Pros:** pretty pool and poolside restaurant with live music; spa; centrally located. **Cons:** some rooms lack views; a touch expensive for what you get; breakfast buffet okay but not spectacular. ⓢ *Rooms from: Rs. 17000* ✉ *City Palace Complex* ☎ *294/252–8016, 294/252–8016*

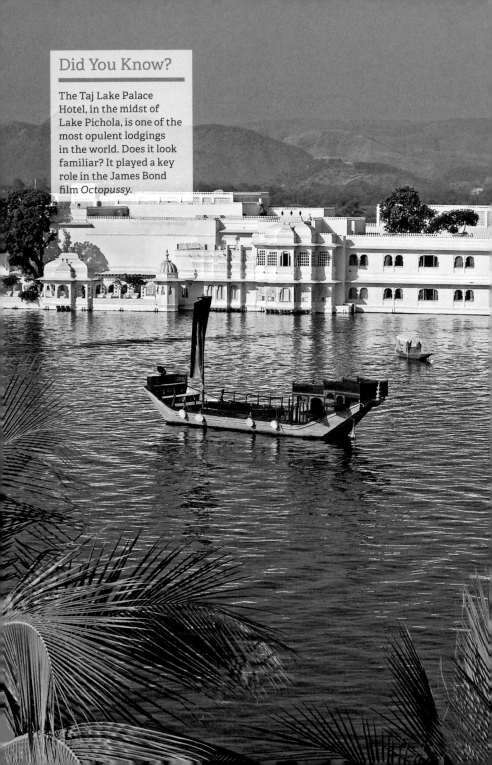

Did You Know?

The Taj Lake Palace Hotel, in the midst of Lake Pichola, is one of the most opulent lodgings in the world. Does it look familiar? It played a key role in the James Bond film *Octopussy*.

The private pools of the Oberoi Udaivilas hotel

⊕ *www.hrhhotels.com* ↬ *50 rooms* ⦿| *Free Breakfast.*

★ Taj Lake Palace

$$$$ | HOTEL | This ultraexclusive 250-year-old white-marble palace—location for the James Bond film *Octopussy*—floats like a vision in the middle of Lake Pichola, and you arrive, of course, by boat. **Pros:** exemplary service to match unique palatial setting; boat service to shore available all hours; spa on a boat. **Cons:** astoundingly expensive, and taxes can push up food and beverage costs by 25%; must book in advance for high season; some rooms have modest bathrooms. $ *Rooms from: Rs. 58000* ⊠ *Lake Pichola* ☎ *294/242–8800* ⊕ *www.tajhotels.com* ↬ *83 rooms* ⦿| *Free Breakfast.*

Trident Hilton

$$$$ | HOTEL | A more moderately priced option among Udaipur's luxury hotels, the Trident is removed from the downtown bustle, amid acres of beautiful gardens on Lake Pichola. **Pros:** heated pool is pleasant day or night; attentive service always comes with a smile; well priced for a luxury hotel. **Cons:** uninspiring rooms are on the small side; location is not central; must purchase Wi-Fi. $ *Rooms from: Rs. 13500* ⊠ *Haridasji Ki Magri, Mulla Tulai* ☎ *294/243–2200* ⊕ *www.tridenthotels.com* ↬ *145 rooms* ⦿| *No meals.*

Udai Kothi

$$$ | HOTEL | It's hard to pass up regal accommodations at moderate prices in luxury-driven Udaipur, particularly when the hotel's rooftop is one of the liveliest places in town. **Pros:** moderately priced for Udaipur; beautiful rooftop pool; elevator. **Cons:** only the suites have lake views; not central; must use tuk tuk, not car, to access small streets to hotel. $ *Rooms from: Rs. 8000* ⊠ *Hannuman Ghat, outside Chandpol* ☎ *294/243–2810* ⊕ *www.udaikothi.com* ↬ *50 rooms* ⦿| *Free Breakfast.*

Shopping

ART

B.G. Sharma Art Gallery

ART GALLERIES | Udaipur has many galleries that exhibit original work by burgeoning artists, which attracts serious art buyers. This gallery was started by B.G. Sharma, one of the preeminent miniature painters of India. Unlike most artists of miniature paintings, Sharma produced original ideas rather than copying traditional pictures, and made a huge contribution to advancing the Mughal, Kishangarh, and Kangra painting styles. Now his sons run the business but some of Sharma's legacy remains. As well as creating miniatures themselves in-house, they also sell the work of other painters. Check the authenticity of anything you want to buy. ☒ 3 Saheli Marg ☎ 294/241–4212 ⊕ www.bgsharmaart.com.

Gallery Pristine

ART GALLERIES | Specializing in both contemporary and folk art, this gallery has many small pieces by Shail Choyal, a guru of contemporary Indian painting. Other highlights include the stylized work of Shahid Parvez, a well-known local artist, as well as work from an expanding number of Udaipur's contemporary artists. ☒ 60 Bhatiyani Chohatta, Palace Rd. ☎ 294/242–3916.

Kamal Sharma Art Gallery

ART GALLERIES | You can often see the artist at work here. Kamal Sharma paints mainly birds and animals on paper, marble, silk, and canvas, in contemporary, experimental, and traditional styles. All the works are for sale. The gallery often holds workshops and rotating exhibits. ☒ 15–A New Colony, Kalaji-Goraji ☎ 294/242–3451 ⊕ www.kamalsharma. net.

HANDICRAFTS

Bhuwana

CRAFTS | A suburb of Udaipur on the road exiting the city towards Jaipur (15–20 minutes away from the city center), Bhuwana is the place to buy something carved in marble, be it an elephant almost as large as your car or a small knickknack like a soap tray or serving dish. There are rows and rows of shops here, where, with a little bargaining (never take the first price), you will get a good deal. Marble workshops are attached to many of the stores and you may be able to see artisans at work. Check with your hotel or local guide to arrange a car. ☒ Bhuwana.

Rajasthali

CRAFTS | If your time is limited, head straight to the area around the Jagdish Temple, where you'll find an array of shops stocking an almost overwhelming variety of leather-bound journals, deity statues, and knickknacks; if bargaining isn't your thing, though, head to an emporium instead. The government-run Rajasthali emporium (there's also a larger branch in Jaipur) sells high-quality Rajasthani arts and handicrafts, and is a good place to pick up a wool-stuffed washable quilt with a Rajasthani motif. The showroom at Jagdish temple is a bit run-down and looks dusty, but the prices here are fixed. ☒ Jagdish Chowk, near Jagdish Temple ☎ 294/242–9068.

Sadhna

CRAFTS | One of the oldest NGOs in India, working for the advancement of the village poor, Sadhna works with rural women in the Udaipur district and trains them to produce traditional appliqué work on cushion covers, bedspreads, silk stoles, bags, kurtas, light quilts, and jackets. Sadhna has gained popularity over the years, and the women also tour around the country to exhibitions in major cities during festivals. There's another branch near the Jagdish Temple in the Old City. ☒ Seva Mandir Rd., Fatehpura ☎ 294/245–4655 ⊕ www.sadhna.org.

University of Arts

CRAFTS | While you're in the Jagdish Temple area, make sure you check out the collection of more than 500 handmade wooden puppets in varying shapes and sizes at this small shop. Ask the folk artist proprietor, Rajesh Gurjargour, an excellent puppeteer, for a private demonstration. Miniature paintings, embroidered jackets, handcrafted soft toys, and knickknacks are also for sale. ⊠ *166 Jagdish Marg, off City Palace Rd.* ☎ *294/242–2591.*

JEWELRY
Ganta Ghar

JEWELRY/ACCESSORIES | From Jagdish Temple, stroll down to the Ganta Ghar (clock tower) and the area around it, a base for silver jewelry. Browse freely, but take care not to purchase items that are merely coated with silver-tone paint. Most of the silver shops here are run-of-the-mill and offer little variation in style and price. ⊠ *Udaipur.*

Ranakpur

96 km (60 miles) northwest of Udaipur.

This small, out-of-the-way village in the woodlands of the Aravali range is famous in all of Rajasthan for its astounding-looking Jain temples. It is said that site for the temples was gifted to the Jain merchant community by a Mewar king, Rana Kumbha in the 15th century, which how the place got its name. The temples are meticulously maintained by descendants of the original community and Ranakpur is an importance pilgrimage point for all Jains.

Sights

★ Ranakpur Jain Temple

RELIGIOUS SITE | A three-hour-plus uphill drive on winding roads from Udaipur, the 15th-century Jain Temple at Ranakpur is one of the most stunning examples of Jain temple architecture in the country. It is dedicated to Adinath, also called Rishabha, the first Jain tirthankar (a holy person who has attained enlightenment and takes rebirth to pass on the knowledge to others), and is a less crowded, more convenient, and perhaps more impressive alternative to Dilwara at Mount Abu. This white marble temple complex, rising out of the forest, is simply breathtaking. Not surprisingly, the temple took 65 years to build after (legend has it) it appeared in a dream to a minister of the Mewar kings. One of the five holiest places for India's Jains, the three-story temple is surrounded by a three-story wall and contains 27 halls supported by 1,444 elaborately carved pillars—no two carvings are alike. The relief work is some of the best in all of India. Below the temple are underground chambers where statues of Jain saints were hidden to protect them from the Mughals. As you enter, look to the left for the pillar where the minister and the architect provided themselves with front-row seats for worship. On one of the pillars is a carving of the creator of the temple. Another pillar is intentionally warped, to separate human works from divine ones—the builders believed only gods could be perfect, so they intentionally added imperfections to some of the columns to avoid causing insult. Outside are two smaller Jain temples and a shrine adorned with erotic sculptures and dedicated to the sun god. There are a few priests around who speak a little English and who act as guides; in return, you should make a small donation. Leather items—shoes, belts, wallets, and more—are not allowed inside the temple. They request that menstruating women not enter (though many modern Jain women ignore this), and there are strict instructions about dress code. You can use a camera, but they do not allow photographs of the deity. Leather is not allowed in the temple and can be deposited at the entry counter.

Although there are a couple of hotels in the vicinity, Ranakpur is best visited as a day trip from Udaipur, maybe stopping at Kumbalgarh Fort, 32 km (20 miles) away en route since Ranakpur opens to tourists late in the day. ✉ *Ranakpur* 🎫 *From Rs. 200.*

Hotels

Fateh Bagh
$$$ | **HOTEL** | The main reason to stay at this dramatic-looking royal retreat is to avoid taking on the twisting round-trip between Ranakpur and Udaipur in one day, because it's just a short drive from the Jain temple. **Pros:** serene setting; lovely pool; small spa. **Cons:** in the middle of nowhere; nearly two-hour drive to Udaipur; breakfast buffet is average. [$] *Rooms from: Rs. 6000* ✉ *Ranakpur Rd., Pali district* ☎ *293/428–6186* 🌐 *www.hrhindia.com* 🛏 *18 rooms* 🍴 *Free Breakfast.*

Kumbhalgarh

84 km (52 miles) north of Udaipur.

Perched high on a forested hilltop is the fort destination of Kumbhalgarh, 3,600 feet above sea level. The long Mewar dominance of this area of the country rested on the dynasty's skill of fortress building, and the fort is the main attraction here.

Sights

★ Kumbhalgarh Fort
MILITARY SITE | When you set eyes on this formidable, isolated fort, you'll understand its role in the history of these parts, and why it's venerated as a symbol of Rajput valor. This citadel, the largest wall in India, and the second longest wall in the world after the Great Wall of China, is situated some 3,600 feet above sea level. It was well equipped to withstand any kind of siege and was largely the reason the Rajasthani state of Mewar was able resist conquest by Mughal forces time and time again. Although there's less to see here than at Chittaurgarh, it's worth the 2½-hour drive from Udaipur and is a relatively smooth drive through lovely scenery. Kumbhalgarh Fort is also close enough to Ranakpur that you could visit both it and Ranakpur in one day. Ideally, you'll stop here on a car trip between Udaipur and Jodhpur.

Built in the 15th century by Maharana Kumbha, one of the mightiest rulers of Mewar, the fort's massive ramparts run 36 km (22 miles) and can be seen from a distance, and the outer wall encloses an area of 83 square km (32 square miles). You enter through colossal gates (Ram Pol) that might have scared off any enemy. The views of the countryside from Badal Mahal (Cloud Palace)—the fort is one of the highest points in the state—are far-reaching. At one time its ramparts nearly encircled an entire township, with nearly 400 temples (you can still see many of them today), self-contained to withstand a prolonged attack. The fort succumbed just once—to the army of Akbar when there was a shortage of water—and was the birthplace of the much-revered Maharana Pratap. There's a small, bland café that serves light snacks and drinks. Take a hat and bring some water with you, because Kumbhalgarh can be quite hot in the day and there's little shade. ✉ *Kumbhalgarh* 🎫 *From Rs. 200.*

Kumbalgarh Sanctuary
NATURE PRESERVE | Surrounding the fort, the modern-day Kumbalgarh Sanctuary makes for great treks. It is home to wolves, leopards, jackals, nilgai deer, sambar deer, and various species of birds. Inquire at your hotel if you're interested in going on a morning Jeep safari here. It's a pretty part of the country, though the wildlife is nothing too out of the ordinary. Tours start at about Rs. 1,500 per person. ✉ *Kumbhalgarh* 🕒 *Closed July–Sept.*

Mount Abu

185 km (115 miles) west of Udaipur.

Once the summer escape of Rajasthani royalty, who each had their oversized haveli here (which are still there), Mount Abu today is one of India's more popular—read crowded—hill stations. This is one of the few towns in Rajasthan where you can dine sumptuously on Gujarati food, given the proximity to the Gujarat border.

GETTING HERE AND AROUND

The road to Mount Abu is winding and rough in some areas, so make sure to leave early in the morning, skipping breakfast, if you're making a day trip from Udaipur or arriving here from Ahmedabad. Ideally, you should plan for an overnight stay.

Sights

High in the Aravali Hills, Mount Abu is situated on Nakki Lake and is Rajasthan's only hill station. It attracts hordes of tourists from the neighboring state of Gujarat, who come to enjoy the town's cool climate and pretty lakes. It's also a great place to stop if you like taking long walks or are simply looking to escape the heat during the unforgiving premonsoon months (April and May). The town's beautiful Dilwara Jain Temples bring plenty of pilgrims and admirers of art.

Mount Abu's ashram-cult hot spot, **Brahma Kumaris Spiritual University,** attracts thousands of followers from all over the world. Members of the sect don white robes or saris and study spiritual knowledge or Raja yoga meditation; you'll surely see them around town.

Dilwara Temples

RELIGIOUS SITE | The magnificent, awe-inspiring Dilwara Temples are a complex of five buildings made of marble between the 11th and 13th centuries, and have made Mount Abu a major pilgrimage center for Jains. Enter for free and admire (but do not photograph) the stunning intricacy of the carving that covers every inch of the temples, from doorway to dome. Each temple is dedicated to a different thirthankar (enlightened ascetic). The 13th-century Luna Vasahi and the 11th-century Vimal Vasahi temples are of special note. The highlight of the Luna Vasahi is its ceilings, covered with interconnected marble carvings; the Vinak Vasahi, with its beautiful white-marble columns and dome, is equally splendid. Non-Jains can visit between noon and 6 daily. *Cameras are not allowed in the temple; nor are leather items (bags, shoes, etc.).* ⊠ *Dilwara Rd.*

Guru Shikhar

VIEWPOINT | Past Peace Park, on Guru Shikhar Road, is Guru Shikhar, the highest point between South India's Nilgiri Hills and the Himalayas, in the north. From here you can enjoy excellent views of the countryside. It takes half an hour to reach here from the town of Mount Abu. From the parking lot, you must climb a few hundred stairs to reach the top, and in high season it can be quite crowded. **Don't venture this way after dark—the winding forest roads make for hazardous driving.** ⊠ *Mount Abu* ✣ *About 17 km (10 miles) from Mount Abu.*

Nakki Lake

LOCAL INTEREST | The sacred Nakki Lake, resting between green hills, is said to have been carved out by the gods' fingernails. Several types of boats ply the lake; rides cost approximately Rs. 300–Rs. 400 for half an hour. Around the shores of the lake are stalls selling local handicrafts. At Sunset Point, just southwest of the lake, you can take in a romantic Mount Abu sunset—but don't expect peace and quiet in the tourist high season. This is a major beauty spot, and you'll likely be joined by plenty of others. ⊠ *Nakki Lake.*

Did You Know?

Ranakpur Temple is supported by more than 1,444 marble pillars, no two carved alike; it's said that it's impossible to count them all.

Hotels

Cama Rajputana Club Resort

$$$ | **HOTEL** | Cradled in the Aravali hills, this late-19th-century club is where British officers and royalty from Gujarat and Rajputana came to escape the summer heat, and now it combines modern amenities with its country style. **Pros:** rooms belonging to the old club property are old-world; lovely lawns; clean pool. **Cons:** new blocks have modern rooms with nondescript furnishings; prices are much higher in winter; food is average. [$] *Rooms from: Rs. 9000* ✉ *Adhar Devi Rd.* ☎ *297/423–8205* 🌐 *www.cama-hotelsindia.com* 🛏 *42 rooms* 🍴 *Free Breakfast.*

Palace Hotel (Bikaner House)

$$$ | **HOTEL** | Set on 20 acres of grounds and featuring activities such as tennis and billiards, this family-run heritage hotel, built in 1893, is a sophisticated and hospitable getaway with something of the feel of a regal hunting lodge. **Pros:** service is excellent; spacious rooms; lovely grounds. **Cons:** no pool; conferences may have an impact on the experience; Internet is spotty. [$] *Rooms from: Rs. 8500* ✉ *Delwara Rd.* ☎ *297/423–8673* 🌐 *www.palacehotelbikanerhouse.com* 🛏 *33 rooms* 🍴 *Free Breakfast.*

Chittaurgarh

112 km (69 miles) northeast of Udaipur.

Chittaurgarh was for hundreds of years an important Rajput capital until it fell to Muslim conquerors from the north. Indian history books have made Chittaurgarh one of the most famous places in India, and the town attracts hordes of Indian tourists and students. The town of Chittaurgarh itself is an ugly, nondescript place, but the fort at Chittaurgarh is worth seeing.

Sights

Chittaurgarh

HISTORIC SITE | If any one of Rajasthan's many forts perched grandly on a hill were to be singled out for its glorious history and chivalric lore, it would be Chittaurgarh. It's also gargantuan in size, and there's plenty to explore on a day trip from Udaipur. This was the capital of the Mewar princely state from the 8th to the 16th centuries, before Maharana Udai Singh moved the capital to Udaipur, and the sprawling hilltop fort occupies roughly 700 acres on a hill about 300 feet high. It was besieged and sacked three times: after the first two conquests, the Rajputs recovered it, but the third attack clinched it for the Mughals for several decades. Chittaurgarh was also the home of the saint-poet Mirabai, a 16th-century Rajput princess and devotee of Lord Krishna who gave up her royal life to sing *bhajans* (hymns) in his praise.

The first attack of Chittaurgarh took place in 1303, when the Sultan of Delhi Allauddin Khilji became so enamored of the wife of then-king Rawal Ratan Singh, legendary beauty Rani Padmini, that he set out to attack the fort and win her in battle. Some 34,000 warriors lost their lives in this struggle, and the Sultan did not get Padmini: she and all the women in the fort committed *jauhar*—mass self-immolation—in anticipation of widowhood and assaults by invading armies. Frustrated, Khilji entered the city in a rage, looting and destroying much of what he saw.

The massive fort encompasses the palaces of the 15th-century ruler **Rana Kumbha,** where Udaipur's founder Udai Singh was born, as well as tiny picturesque palace of **Rani Padmini** surrounded by a small lake and some pleasant gardens. Legend has it that Khilji fell in love with Padmini by gazing at her reflection in the pond in front of her palace. The magic of this fort is to visit her palace and actually visually re-create that very famous scene of history. Also worth visiting in the fort are the victory towers—the ornate **Vijay Stambh** and **Kirti Stambh**—and a huge variety of temples, including **Kunbha Shyam, Kalika Mata,** and the **Meera temple** associated with the devotional poetess Mirabai. The **Fateh Prakash Mahal** displays some fine sculptures.

Plan to spend at least half a day in Chittaurgarh. Note that the sites are spread out and it can get quite sunny, so you may want to drive between some points and it is best to hire an auto-rickshaw to do the circuit (about Rs. 300–Rs. 500). ☎ *147/224–1089.*

Hotels

Hotel Amrit Manthan
$ | **HOTEL** | This fairly uninspiring business hotel serves its purpose as a rest stop for a day of exploring Chittaurgarh. **Pros:** hot water in shower; friendly staff; value hotel. **Cons:** basic lodging in bland hotel; need a tuk tuk to get to fort; rooms could use an update. [$] *Rooms from: Rs. 3400* ✉ *Nimbahera Rd.* ✣ *Behind Mundr Petrol Pump* ☎ *472/242–452* 🌐 *www.hotelamrit-manthan.com* 🛏 *50 rooms* 🍴 *No meals.*

Bundi

210 km (130 miles) south of Jaipur; 279 km (173 miles) from Udaipur.

Pretty Bundi in southeastern Rajasthan is famous for its *baoris* or stepwells, and art as well as its fort and palace. The town once had more than 50 stepwells, providing its only source of water. Many of the town's old buildings and havelis are today painted a striking indigo blue.

GETTING HERE AND AROUND

Although Bundi can easily be reached by train from Jaipur (via Kota), it's even more convenient to rent a taxi with a driver and get there by road (it's about a five-hour drive). Bundi can be done as a day trip, but it's more relaxing if you spend the night. The town is small enough to be navigated on foot, and most of the attractions are within a mile of each other. If you get tired of walking, auto-rickshaws are easy to find (negotiate a price suggested by your hotel before climbing in).

Sights

The magical little town of Bundi, with its winding lanes and unusual stepwells, appears to have been plucked straight from a fairy tale. It's a perfect getaway from the commotion of Jaipur.

The area now known as Bundi was populated by tribal people until the 13th century, when it was taken over by a clan of Rajputs, and after that was ruled by various dynasties like the Chauhans, who were Hada Rajputs, until the town was incorporated into the Republic of India after India's independence from the British. Rudyard Kipling is Bundi's most famous former resident, and it is popularly believed that it was during his stay in the little town that he decided to write *Kim*.

Most popular is the 14th-century **Taragarh** (Star Fort), tucked into a hillside above the town (but still within about 1½ km [1 mile] of the center). The run-down, poorly maintained fort, taken over by monkeys, was originally constructed to defend the principality of Bundi from invasion, although these days its biggest draw is its great views of the town and the surrounding countryside. Sunset is the best time to visit, but don't forget a flashlight for the way down. Don't carry food or you will attract monkeys, and carry an umbrella or a stick. **Bundi Palace** is another must-see, both for its impressive architecture and the amazingly well-preserved murals depicting the life of Lord Krishna that grace its interior walls. The palace also has its own*chitrashala* (art gallery), where beautiful old paintings are displayed. Bundi is also well-known for its dozens of baoris (stepwells), many of which have fallen in disrepair, which were used by local women to gather water in large vessels in the days before indoor plumbing and hand pumps. The most interesting of these is the steep **Raniji ki Baori** (Queen's Well), which is covered with carvings and stone latticework. The interiors of the nearby identical twin stepwells, **Nagar Sagar Kund,** feature banister-free flights of stairs that crisscross down into the well bellow—though you're not allowed to descend.

Hotels

Haveli Braj Bhushanjee
$$$ | **HOTEL** | Family owned and operated, this hotel in a 200-year-old sprawling haveli preserves many of its original features, including carved stonework, striking Bundi School of Painting murals, and other artwork, making a stay here like living in an art gallery. **Pros:** excellent location; warm staff; breakfast included. **Cons:** only vegetarian food served; no alcohol; no frills. [$] *Rooms from: Rs. 6500* ✉ *Bundi* ✣ *Below palace, opposite Ayurvedic Hospital* ☎ *747/244–2322* 🌐 *www.kiplingsbundi.com* 🛏 *18 rooms* 🍴 *Free Breakfast.*

Hotel Bundi Haveli
$ | **HOTEL** | This boutique heritage hotel, furnished with antiques, is in the heart of the town, with great views of the palace and fort. **Pros:** charming character; clean; value for money. **Cons:** a/c not always good; restaurant is expensive; food is bland. [$] *Rooms from: Rs. 3500* ✉ *107 Balchand Parra, near Naval Sagar Lake* ☎ *747/244–6716* 🌐 *www.hotelbundihaveli.com* 🛏 *12 rooms* 🍴 *No meals.*

Jodhpur

343 km (215 miles) west of Jaipur; 266 km (165 miles) northwest of Udaipur.

Jodhpur, Rajasthan's second-largest city, is known as the Blue City because of the pale-blue-painted narrow and tall houses of the jumbled and entrancing medieval Old City, which are especially impressive when viewed from the ramparts of Mehrangarh Fort. The city, at the base of a sandstone ridge, was the capital of the Marwar kingdom for five centuries, and it's encircled by a 9-km (6-mile) wall, which keeps out the desert sands. It was named after its 15th-century founder, Rao Jodha, chief of the Rathore clan of Marwar. The clan traces its lineage to Lord Rama, hero of the ancient Hindu epic the *Ramayana*.

There isn't that much to do in Jodhpur, aside from a few sites including the incredible Mehrangarh Fort, and some textile shopping, and many people use the city as a jumping-off point for Jaisalmer, or as a place to overnight on the way to Jaipur or Udaipur. It is also a great city to do a village tour, an opportunity you might not get in larger cities like Udaipur and Jaipur.

Check at the fort if any heritage tours are available. If you have time, Jodhpur is an especially good place from which to take a safari into the desert.

GETTING HERE AND AROUND

Getting around Jodhpur is relatively easy. The older part of the city that extends between the clock tower and the base of the Meherangarh Fort consists of narrow lanes, and it's faster and easier to hail an auto-rickshaw (they charge about Rs. 100 for a round-trip) to wander this part of town, since cars cannot enter. You can also walk the shorter distances in the quieter lanes or in the early morning, but at other times traffic moves rapidly and dangerously, and you will feel more comfortable in an auto-rickshaw even if it is a bumpy, careening ride. For attractions farther afield, auto-rickshaws can easily be hailed on the street.

TIMING

You could squeeze in all the main attractions in one full day, though this won't leave you much time to shop or really get a feel for the city, so try to spend two days here.

ESSENTIALS

TOURIST OFFICE Government of Rajasthan Tourist Office ✉ *RTDC Hotel Ghoomer Campus, High Court Rd.* ☎ *291/254–5083* ⊕ *www.rajasthantourism.gov.in.*

 Sights

Jaswant Thada

BUILDING | The royal marble crematorium was built in 1899 for Maharaja Jaswant Singh II. Capping the enormous white structure are marble canopies under which individual members of the royal family are buried. You may see people bowing before the image of the king, who is considered to have joined the ranks of the deities. It's a peaceful spot to stop, either on your way up to the fort or on your way down. *Remove shoes before entering.* ✉ *Jodhpur* ✛ *500 yds northeast of Mehrangarh Fort* ☎ *291/254–8790* 🎫 *From Rs. 50.*

Mahamandir

RELIGIOUS SITE | Built in 1812 just outside Jodhpur, this old, walled monastery complex—*mahamandir* means "great temple"—is not very well maintained but still contains a few hundred houses and a school. The photogenic monastery belongs to the Nath community, warrior-priests who worked closely with the royal family to arrange support in times of war. Mahamandir is best known for the 84 beautifully carved pillars that surround it. Prayers are offered morning and evening in the main temple. It's in the Mahamandir area of town near the railway tracks and a bit difficult to locate. Check locally for best times to visit or inquire with your hotel about stopping here as part of a city tour. It is also called Natho ka Mandir. ✉ *Mahamandir, on way to Mandore* ✛ *4 km (2½ miles) northeast of Jodhpur.*

Mandore Gardens

GARDEN | Within the old Marwar capital at Mandore (before the capital moved to Jodhpur), these gardens house the exquisitely sculpted red-sandstone, carefully looked-after *davals* (memorials or cenotaphs also called *chhatris*) to former rulers; the most impressive is the one dedicated to 18th-century maharaja Ajit Singh. The Hall of Heroes depicts 16 colorfully painted heroes and deities carved from a single piece of stone. The small **museum** on the grounds has sculptures from the 5th to the 9th centuries as well as ivory and lacquerwork. There are many monkeys here, and people seeking alms, and there is also a temple devoted to the 330 million Hindu gods. This is a tranquil place to visit except on weekends and holidays, when locals arrive for outings. It's worth a visit for the davals, but keep in mind that the gardens, while visually stunning, are not well maintained and are full of trash. ✉ *Mandore* ✛ *8 km (5 miles) north of Jodhpur* 🎫 *Gardens free; museum Rs. 50.*

★ Mehrangarh Fort

MILITARY SITE | This enormous hilltop fort was built by Rao Jodha in 1459, when he shifted his capital from Mandore to Jodhpur. Looking straight down a perpendicular cliff, the famously impregnable fort, about 500 feet above the city, is an imposing landmark, especially at night, when it's bathed in yellow light. Approach the fort by climbing a steep walkway, passing under no fewer than eight huge gates—if you're not up for the hike, you can take the elevator (Rs. 50) up two levels from the ticket office. The first gate, the **Victory Gate,** was built by Maharaja Ajit Singh to commemorate his military success against the Mughals at the beginning of the 18th century; the other seven commemorate victories over other Rajput states. The last gate, as in many Rajput forts, displays the haunting handprints of women who immolated themselves after their husbands were defeated in battle. Inside the fort, delicate latticed windows and pierced sandstone screens are the surprising motifs. The palaces—**Moti Mahal** (Pearl Palace), **Phool Mahal** (Flower Palace), **Sheesh Mahal** (Glass Palace)—and the other

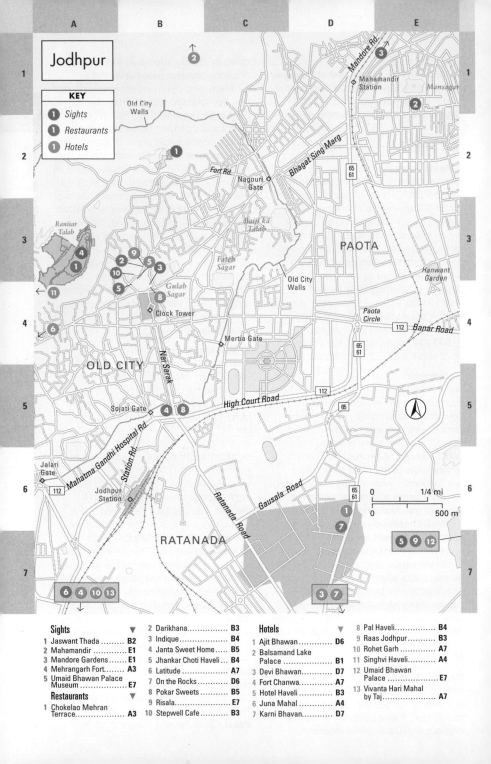

Jodhpur

KEY

- ① Sights
- ① Restaurants
- ① Hotels

Old City Walls

Ranisar Talab

Fort Rd.

Nagouri Gate

Baiji ka Talab

Bhagat Sing Marg

Mandore Rd.

Mahamandir Station

Mansagar

PAOTA

Fateh Sagar

Old City Walls

Hanwant Garden

Gulab Sagar

Clock Tower

Paota Circle

Banar Road

Mertia Gate

OLD CITY

Nai Sarak

High Court Road

Sojati Gate

Jalari Gate

Mahatma Gandhi Hospital Rd.

Station Rd.

Jodhpur Station

Ratanada Road

Gausala Road

RATANADA

0   1/4 mi
0   500 m

apartments are exquisitely decorated; their ceilings, walls, and floors are covered with murals, mirror work, and gilt and you should not miss viewing these chambers (though you can't go inside the rooms). The palace museum has exquisite rooms filled with lavish royal elephant carriages (*howdahs*), palanquins, thrones, paintings, and even a giant tent. It also has an interesting weapons gallery. From the ramparts there are great views of the city; the blue houses at sunset look magical. Another option is to take a zipline tour around the fort with **Flying Fox**; it's not for the fainthearted. The fort is possibly the best-maintained historic property in all Rajasthan, and offers an audio tour with headphones (included in the admission price for foreigners). There are two shops, open 9 to 5, run by the Mehrangarh Trust, that can be accessed without visiting the fort, that sell expensive but very attractive handicrafts. There's also a small craft bazaar in the outer courtyard that offers a variety of bargains. Apart from the fine-dining rooftop restaurant Mehran Terrace, there are also two cafés serving snacks and drinks where you can stop for a bite or a break. For an extra Rs. 30 you can visit 200-year-old Chokelao Bagh, a well-laid-out palace garden. ☒ *Fort Rd.* ☏ *291/254–8790, 291/254–8992* ⊕ *www. mehrangarh.org* ☒ *From Rs. 600.*

Umaid Bhawan Palace Museum

MUSEUM | Built between 1929 and 1942 at the behest of Maharaja Umaid Singh during a long famine, this public-works project employed 3,000 workers. Now part museum, part royal residence, and part heritage hotel, it has an art deco design that makes it unique in the state. Amazingly, no cement was used in construction; the palace is made of interlocking blocks of sandstone, something to admire when you stand under the imposing 183-foot-high central dome. The museum's collection includes a model of the palace, royal finery, collections of palace crockery and cut glass, menus,

Jodhpur's Sweetness

Jodhpur's famed tradition of hospitality, known as *mithi manuhar*, frequently takes the form of offers of food. Such items, especially *mithai* (sweets), are not to be missed. When you're offered a *mave ki kachori* (milk-based pastry), *besan ki barfi* (a fudgelike sweet made of chickpea flour), *mirchi bada* (fried, breaded green peppers), or *kofta* (deep-fried balls of potatoes or vegetables), don't resist: the offer will be repeated until you take some.

a sample of palace rooms (dining room and lounge), miniature paintings, stuffed big cats, and a large number of clocks. There's a photographic history of how the palace was designed as well as some grand old photographs of the palace, the royal family, and famous visitors. You may catch a glimpse of the titular Maharaja of Jodhpur, who still lives in one large wing, but you certainly won't miss the magnificent peacocks that strut around the palace's marble *chattris* (canopies) and lush lawns. ☒ *Umaid Bhawan Palace, Airport Rd.* ☏ *291/251–0101* ☒ *Rs. 100 (free to hotel guests).*

🍴 Restaurants

Chokelao Mehran Terrace

$$ | **NORTH INDIAN** | Sip a chilled beer or wine and enjoy spectacular views of Jodhpur city at this romantically lit restaurant high up within the royal Mehrangarh Fort. This touristy outdoor eatery is notable more for its ambience than the food, but if you're dining here, try the traditional Rajasthani food or standard tandoori favorites like mutton kebab and paneer tikka. **Known for:** city views; ambience; standard Indian fare. $ *Average main: Rs.*

400 ⊠ Mehrangarh Fort ☎ 291/255–5389, 254–8790 ⊟ No credit cards ◔ No lunch.

Darikhana

$$$$ | INTERNATIONAL | The mood in the evenings at this twinkling, partly open-air haveli restaurant, located in the shadow of the lit Mehrangarh Fort, is memorably romantic. Using as many locally sourced ingredients and spices as possible, Darikhana serves both Indian and international food, including pastas, Mediterranean, and Thai dishes; popular Indian dishes are the traditional Rajasthani laal maas (spiced, well-marinated mutton), chicken curry, *dahi* kebab, and the paneer dishes. **Known for**: cocktail menu; alfresco dining; high-end service. $ *Average main: Rs. 1200* ⊠ Raas, Tunwarji ka Jhalara, Makrana Mohalla ⊕ www.raasjodhpur.com.

Indique

$$$ | NORTH INDIAN | After a long day of sightseeing, stop at this recently renovated rooftop hangout at the Pal Haveli hotel in the Old City, where the ambience exceeds the quality of the food, which is slightly overpriced (though perfectly okay). Go for a sundown drink or dinner (kebabs and thalis are highlights) and take in stunning views of the nearby lake, the fort, the clock tower, and the Umaid Bhawan Palace. **Known for:** city views; sunset cocktails; Rajasthani staples. $ *Average main: Rs. 600* ⊠ Pal Haveli, Gulab Sagar ☎ 291/329–3328, 291/263–8344.

Janta Sweet Home

$ | INDIAN | Jodhpur's most famous sweet shop buzzes till 11 pm, so consider stopping here for dessert. It's a good place to sample regional delicacies; test your chilli tolerance level with the spicy *mirchi bada,* a huge pepper that's been breaded and deep-fried or, for something sweeter, try the local specialty: *mawa kachori* (a pastry filled with nut-based milk solid), *ghevar* (disc-shape sweet), *rabri laddu* (milk balls). **Known for**: freshly fried snacks; authentic Indian desserts; takeout. $ *Average main: Rs. 200* ⊠ 3

Nai Sarak ☎ 291/263–6666, 291/262–5559 ⊕ www.jantasweethome.com ⊟ No credit cards.

Jhankar Choti Haveli

$$ | VEGETARIAN | Join fellow travelers at this happening spot for a cup of masala chai or a meal in the garden courtyard oasis in the city. The restaurant, which also offers rooftop dining with fort views or indoor dining with a/c, is strictly vegetarian and alcohol-free, but even meat eaters will marvel at the Indian house specialties, which are well priced. **Known for:** vegetarian entrées; cashew curry; outdoor patio seating. $ *Average main: Rs. 400* ⊠ Jhankar Choti Haveli, Makarana Mohalla ☎ 291/261–2590.

Latitude

$$$$ | INTERNATIONAL | One of the better attempts at all-day, upscale cuisine in Jodhpur, the neo-Mughal-style restaurant serves continental and Indian food, with a few Rajasthani specialties, and there is a buffet (evenings) as well as à la carte options. Try Jodhpuri *gatte ki subz* curry (steamed chickpea flour dumplings in yogurt-base gravy) or the spicy Jodhpuri laal maas (lamb) curry, both typical of this region. **Known for**: all-day dining; Rajasthani thali; laal maas. $ *Average main: Rs. 900* ⊠ Vivanta by Taj–Hari Mahal Hotel, 5 Residency Rd. ☎ 291/222–3870 ⊕ www.vivantabytaj.com.

On the Rocks

$$$ | NORTH INDIAN | This jungle-theme and mostly outdoor restaurant in the new section of the city won't offer you the best meal you've ever had, but the food—rich and hearty—is good, the beer is cold, and it's an ideal rest stop for a quick drink or lunch. On weekends, its cavelike bar, Rocktails, is a hopping place. **Known for:** cocktail menu; outdoor seating; Rajasthani specials. $ *Average main: Rs. 600* ⊠ Circuit House Rd., next to Ajit Bhawan Hotel ☎ 291/510–2701 ⊕ ontherocksjodhpur.com.

Pokar Sweets

$ | **NORTH INDIAN** | Arrive at this extra-large food stall as early as 6 am (or as late as midnight) for an old North Indian favorite—piping hot puris and *alu* (deep-fried wheat bread served with potato curry)—or try traditional Jodhpuri sweets, snacks, dosas, and more. Don't expect ambience, but the food is made fresh and bakery items are in chilled cases. **Known for**: barfi (a fudgelike confection made of sweetened milk); potato alu; traditional sweets for holidays such as Diwali. [$] *Average main: Rs. 200* ✉ *Near Pokar Hotel, High Court Rd.* ☎ *982/902-3001* 💳 *No credit cards.*

Risala

$$$$ | **INTERNATIONAL** | If you're looking to feel like royalty and splurge on a wining-and-dining experience with impeccable service, head to this elegant, formal dining room adorned with portraits from the royal collection—or opt for the balcony overlooking verdant gardens. The contemporary European and unique Indian dishes are a welcome change from the usual Indian and Rajasthani fare, and the drinks menu is extensive, and includes internationally sourced wines. **Known for:** gourmet thali; impeccable service; afternoon high tea. [$] *Average main: Rs. 4500* ✉ *Umaid Bhawan Palace, Airport Rd.* ☎ *291/251-0101.*

Stepwell Cafe

$$ | **INDIAN** | A modern and cosmopolitan vibe greets you and the other patrons, who are mostly tourists, when you enter the small café next to the Toorji Stepwell and Raas. It's a perfect spot to sit in the a/c and have an afternoon break, and you can choose from cocktails, light meals, or an espresso made from an imported, Italian machine. **Known for:** coffee; classic cocktails; Indian and Italian comfort foods. [$] *Average main: Rs. 350* ✉ *Stepwell Sq.* ✥ *Next to Raas hotel* ☎ *291/263-6455* 🌐 *www.stepwell-cafe.com.*

Hotels

Ajit Bhawan

$$$$ | **RESORT** | This small, enchanting palace and village complex has several intriguing perks—like a pool with waterfalls and caves; a lobby stuffed with atmospheric royalty-related memorabilia, such as portraits of maharajas, spears, and heads of deer; and even a garage full of royal vintage cars available for rent. **Pros:** warm and inviting; cozy bar; near modern shops and restaurants. **Cons:** far from the Old City; tented rooms can be noisy; service can be slow during peak times. [$] *Rooms from: Rs. 15000* ✉ *Circuit House Rd.* ☎ *291/251-0674, 291/251-3333* 🌐 *www.ajitbhawan.com* 🛏 *100 rooms* 🍴 *Free Breakfast.*

Balsamand Lake Palace

$$$ | **RESORT** | Long a dreamy setting for royal getaways, this fine example of Rajput architecture offers a taste of country palace living at a reasonable price (unless you choose one of the suites, which are considerably more expensive than the rooms). **Pros:** quiet retreat on the outskirts of Jodhpur; ideal for nature lovers; suites have the best garden views. **Cons:** a bit out of the way; "deluxe" rooms are ordinary; pool hours may vary depending on season. [$] *Rooms from: Rs. 8500* ✉ *9 km (5½ miles) northeast of Jodhpur, Mandore Rd.* ☎ *291/257-1991, 291/257-1991* 🌐 *balsamandlakepalace.jodhanaheritage.com* 🛏 *35 rooms* 🍴 *Free Breakfast.*

Devi Bhawan

$ | **HOTEL** | One of the more moderately priced hotels in Jodhpur, this quiet hotel is in a spacious, pleasant garden, with plenty of spots to relax in the open air, and a nice pool. **Pros:** on a quiet street away from the city; pool and outdoor lounge; excellent value. **Cons:** not as many facilities as nearby hotels; Old City is far but the reception can call tuk tuk; no refrigerator in rooms. [$] *Rooms from: Rs. 3000* ✉ *1 Ratanada Circle, Defence Lab. Rd.* ☎ *291/251-1067* 🌐 *www.*

devibhawan.com 🛏 *25 rooms* 🍴 *No meals.*

Fort Chanwa

$$$ | **HOTEL** | This century-old, somber red fort in the dusty village of Luni is now a heritage hotel offering a real get-away-from-it-all experience. **Pros:** charming fort stay; good value; pool. **Cons:** remote location; few food options aside from hotel restaurant; some bathrooms small. [$] *Rooms from: Rs. 6500* ✉ *Luni* ✣ *58 km (36 miles) south of Jodhpur* ☎ *293/128–4216, 291/243–2460 reservations* 🌐 *www.fortchanwa.com* 🛏 *75 rooms* 🍴 *Free Breakfast.*

Hotel Haveli

$$$ | **B&B/INN** | An affordable option for those interested in staying in the heart of the Old City, this hotel, close enough for you to hear evening aarti (a Hindu prayer service) at the temples near the clock tower, is near the new retail area of Step-well Square, and has a rooftop restaurant with excellent views of the city. **Pros:** entrance on quiet street in the otherwise bustling Old City; impressive facade; well priced. **Cons:** rooms could be cleaner; multistory building with no elevator; can feel cramped. [$] *Rooms from: Rs. 10000* ✉ *Makrana Mohalla, behind clock tower, opposite Toorji Ka Jhalra (stepwell)* ☎ *291/261–4615, 291/264–7003* 🌐 *www.hotelhaveli.net* 🛏 *25 rooms* 🍴 *Free Breakfast.*

Juna Mahal

$ | **B&B/INN** | The quirky, charming, and nearly 500-year-old Juna Mahal, owned by a priestly family once attached to Jodhpur's royal temples, is tucked away from the congestion in one of the upper streets of the Old City (access is by auto-rickshaw) and resembles a carved dollhouse. **Pros:** cozy lodging; decent rooftop restaurant; great views. **Cons:** deep in the Old City; lots of steep steps; rooms and bathrooms are small. [$] *Rooms from: Rs. 3000* ✉ *Ada Bazaar, Daga St.* ☎ *291/244–5511* 🌐 *www.junamahal.com* 🛏 *5 rooms* 🍴 *Free Breakfast.*

Karni Bhavan

$$ | **HOTEL** | This homey, colonial-style bungalow offers unique-themed rooms (each is decorated in honor of local festivals and former principalities) with standard (don't expect to be wowed) amenities. **Pros:** 10-minute drive to airport; modestly priced; suites have small refrigerator. **Cons:** away from action in the Old City; no gym or spa; no kettle in the room. [$] *Rooms from: Rs. 4500* ✉ *Palace Rd., Ratanada* ☎ *291/251–2101, 291/251–2101* 🌐 *www.karnihotels.com* 🛏 *31 rooms* 🍴 *No meals.*

Pal Haveli

$$$ | **HOTEL** | Scoring high on location and heritage, this 300-year-old rambling haveli with an opulent feel is close to the clock tower in Old Jodhpur and has views of Mehrangarh Fort. **Pros:** centrally located; moderately priced; luxe decor and service staff. **Cons:** no pool; congested traffic can make getting in and out difficult and must be done by auto-rickshaw; larger rooms, even with a/c, remain warm in summer. [$] *Rooms from: Rs. 7000* ✉ *Gulab Sagar, near clock tower* ☎ *291/329–3328* 🌐 *www.palhaveli.com* 🛏 *20 rooms* 🍴 *Free Breakfast.*

Raas Jodhpur

$$$$ | **RESORT** | Located on the periphery of the older northeastern quarter, with marvelous views of Meherangarh, this pricey hotel is away from the thick of the commotion of Jodhpur, yet still offers a real flavor of the city—and the personal service is amazing. **Pros:** top-notch service; views; spa and pool with a view. **Cons:** you need to get here by auto-rickshaw (hotel can make arrangements); some rooms don't have fort views; expensive. [$] *Rooms from: Rs. 22000* ✉ *Tunwar ji ka Jhalara, Makrana Mohalla* ☎ *291/263–6455* 🌐 *www.raasjodhpur.com* 🛏 *38 rooms* 🍴 *Free Breakfast.*

Inside Jodhpur's Mehrangarh Fort

Rohet Garh

$$$$ | HOTEL | A great place to experience the lifestyle of Rajput nobility, this 17th-century desert fortress 40 km (25 miles) south of Jodhpur is both a heritage hotel and the home of its Rajput family, whose members are your hosts. **Pros:** rooms are spacious and suites are exceptionally large with tons of character; the bar area is like a semi-outdoors living room and has lovely views of the gardens; meals are included. **Cons:** small pool; not much to do at the hotel unless you venture out on an organized village safari; no refrigerator in rooms. $ *Rooms from: Rs. 11000* ⊠ *Pali district, Rohet House, Rohat* ☎ *844/828–5349* ⊕ *www.rohetgarh.com* ⇗ *38 rooms* ⎮⊚⎮ *Free Breakfast.*

Singhvi Haveli

$ | B&B/INN | More than 500 years old, this budget and mildly eccentric hotel is located at the highest point of the Old City, just below the fort, and has a great vibe—traditional, local, and chilled out. **Pros:** close to the fort; nice views; the hosts organize excellent village tours.

Cons: lots of steep stairs; bathrooms are average; few amenities. $ *Rooms from: Rs. 2500* ⊠ *Navchokiya, Ramdeo Ji ka chowk* ☎ *291/262–4293, 982/803–2515* ⊕ *www.singhvihaveli.com* ⇗ *11 rooms.*

★ Umaid Bhawan Palace

$$$$ | HOTEL | You can live like (and alongside) royalty at this magnificent palace, one of Rajasthan's grandest hotels, where the royal treatment begins the moment you arrive: bugles sound, drums play, petals are strewn at your feet, and an ornate canopy comes up to welcome you. **Pros:** impeccable, over-the-top service; the massive lawn is great for walks; excellent restaurants. **Cons:** extremely expensive; not close to the Old City; some rooms lack privacy. $ *Rooms from: Rs. 185000* ⊠ *Off S.H.61, north of Jodhpur Airbase* ☎ *291/251–0101* ⊕ *www.tajhotels.com* ⇗ *65 rooms* ⎮⊚⎮ *Free Breakfast.*

Vivanta Hari Mahal by Taj

$$$$ | HOTEL | Outside the Old City, this bustling hotel offers a respite from the hustle and bustle, and what it lacks in

excitement, it makes up for in hospitality and subdued charm—and children will enjoy the nightly puppet show. **Pros:** friendly service; large closets; pool. **Cons:** far from the Old City; busy hotel, not a real palace. [$] *Rooms from: Rs. 16000* ✉ *5 Residency Rd.* ☎ *291/243–9700* 🌐 *www.tajhotels.com* 🛏 *94 rooms* 🍴 *Free Breakfast.*

Nightlife

If you're looking for nightlife, you'll find Jodhpur rather sedate; your best bet is one of the hotel bars, which are usually open from 11 am to 2:30 pm and 6 pm to 11 pm, though some bars, like the Trophy Bar at the Umaid Bhawan Palace, are only open to hotel guests.

Mehrangarh Fort

FESTIVALS | Throughout the year, this fort hosts festivals and exhibits, such as Sufi music festivals and the Rajasthan International Folk festival in October. Inquire at your hotel or check the fort's website to see if anything is going on while you're here. ✉ *Fort Rd.* 🌐 *www.mehrangarh.org.*

Pulse the Bar

BARS/PUBS | The lobby bar within the Hotel Shri Ram Excellency is the closest thing in the city to an urban bar. Sit at the slick bar or a small table amid neon lights for cocktails and beer. A small food menu includes Chinese, continental, and Indian cuisines. ✉ *58 Residency Rd.* ✣ *Hotel Shri Ram Excellency* ☎ *291/261–4101* 🌐 *www.hotelshriramexcellency.com.*

Activities

Many hotels offer not-to-be missed excursions to outlying villages, and most can arrange desert safaris on request.

Flying Fox

TOUR—SPORTS | **FAMILY** | This expat-owned outfitter runs zipline tours of Mehrangarh Fort, an extraordinary way to get dramatic views of the city—if you can get over your fear of heights. By experiencing the thrills on six ziplines running across the fort and over lakes, you'll be rewarded with sights that few others see. Participants must be at least 10 years of age. *If you are visiting in summer, check ahead of time to confirm that this outfitter is open, as it often shuts down during June due to severe temperatures.* ✉ *Mehrangarh Fort* ☎ *91/98109–99390* 🌐 *www.flyingfox.asia.*

Jodhpur Village Safari

TOUR—SPORTS | If you want to get outside the city and see the dusty, rural villages around Jodhpur, a Jeep tour is your best bet. This operator offers full- and half-day tours that whisk you through small villages, some of which specialize in specific handicrafts like pottery and textiles, and a farming community, where you can get up close and personal with many goats. There must be at least two people for a tour. ✉ *81 Indra Colony Ratanada, Jaipur* 🌐 *www.jodhpurvillagesafari.com.*

Shopping

BAZAARS AND MARKETS

Sadar Bazaar

OUTDOOR/FLEA/GREEN MARKETS | Jodhpur's vibrant bazaars are among the city's key sights, particularly Sadar Bazaar and the Girdikot Bazaar, near the clock tower. Wandering among the tiny shops dotting these crowded, narrow lanes in the heart of town, you'll get a real feel for the life and color of Marwari jewelry, underwear, steel utensils, kitchenware, leather shoes, trinkets, wedding clothes—you can find just about everything here (including locksmiths and indigenous dentists sitting side by side on the street), and many of the local spice merchants here deal in saffron and other spices from all over India. Beware of tourist markups and young men guiding you to their "uncle's store." There are also plenty of stores to shop in if you don't like haggling in bazaars—most notably the government-run emporium. ✉ *Jodhpur.*

CLOTHING
Anokhi
CLOTHING | The local outlet of the popular brand Anokhi sells good-value Western clothes with an Indian flair, including cotton and hand-block prints that are sourced from national textile producers. ✉ *Shop No. 5, Rani Bagh, Ajit Bhawan, Circuit House Rd.* ☎ *291/251–7178, 291/251–7179* ⊕ *www.anokhi.com.*

Via Jodhpur
CLOTHING | Stepwell Square, adjacent to the Toorji Stepwell, is home to hip new boutiques and restaurants, and Via Jodhpur is one of them. The shop carries modern twists on Indian clothing for men, women, and children, as well as jewelry, scarves, and gift options. Expect Western prices. ✉ *Toorji Ka Jhalra (stepwell)* ⊹ *Near Raas Hotel* ☎ *982/919–0499* ⊕ *www.viajodhpur.in.*

HANDICRAFTS
Lalji Handicrafts Emporium
ANTIQUES/COLLECTIBLES | This place is a joy if you love antiques. Woodwork, antiques, leatherwork, and brass furniture comprise the collection here, which also includes unique painted boxes and *jharokhas* (carved doorways or windows) made of dark wood with brass decoration. ✉ *Umaid Bhawan Palace Rd., opposite Umaid Bhawan Palace* ☎ *982/902–5888* ⊕ *www.laljihandicrafts.com.*

Maharani Textiles and Handicrafts
HOUSEHOLD ITEMS/FURNITURE | Come here for a beautiful array of shawls, bedcovers, cushion covers, and wooden handicrafts. Bargain hard (they will pressure you, but stand your ground) and ignore tales about supplying to global designers. **If negotiating frustrates you, try considering the sales experience performance art.** ✉ *Tambaku Bazaat* ☎ *098/2902–6950.*

National Handloom Corp.
CRAFTS | For inexpensive textiles, including cotton dress fabric, plastic and glass bangles, and other handicrafts, check out this four-story emporium, where these items are hidden among the rows of discounted toasters and kitschy house decorations. It's fixed price (as opposed to haggling), caters to a local crowd, and is an easier experience than going from shop to shop where everyone is pressuring you to buy something. ✉ *66–67 Nai Sarak* ⊹ *Near Janta Sweets* ☎ *291/506–1103, 291/503–1198.*

Om Ganesh Export House
LOCAL SPECIALTIES | More like a warehouse, this store has several floors overflowing with textiles, rugs, and wooden items. Be prepared for some sly salesmanship. In particular, take the stories of supplying to global luxury brands with a grain of salt and be prepared to call their bluff when they tell you it's all fixed price; it's not. You will need to bargain. The experience will take some strength and stamina, but you may find it worth the effort, as there's an enormous and very handsome selection of goods here. ✉ *Gancha Bazar* ⊹ *In narrow street behind clock tower* ☎ *982/905–3950* ⊕ *www.omganeshexporthouse.com.*

Roopraj Durries
HOUSEHOLD ITEMS/FURNITURE | Buy your beautifully, painstakingly woven dhurrie from the man who made it at Salawas village (about 30 minutes outside Jodhpur). At this peaceful, pretty, and fairly remote hamlet of thatched homes there is a huge selection and you can see, step by step, how these colorful rugs are made. It is a memorable experience to witness this dying art—younger generations are not investing in the business. You can pay by credit card and then have it shipped by the store to your home. ✉ *Roopraj Durries Udhyog, Salawas* ☎ *998/240–0416* ⊕ *www.rooprajdurry.com.*

JEWELRY
Gems & Jewels Palace
JEWELRY/ACCESSORIES | This good local jewelry store specializes in traditional bridal jewelery styled according to Rajasthani royal tradition. ✉ *Rani Bagh, Ajit Bhawan, Circuit House Rd.* ☎ *982/805–3301.*

SPICES

M.V. Spices

FOOD/CANDY | Available here is a wide selection of spices, clearly marked and packed in plastic for travelers with a passion for cooking Indian food. The shop is small but clean and tidy, and clearly caters to a crowd concerned with quality and food safety. There's also a stand at the entrance to the Mehrangarh Fort, next to the café. ✉ *Shop 209B, Sadar Market* ✥ *Near clock tower* ☎ *291/510–9347* 🌐 *www.mvspices.com.*

Khimsar

90 km (56 miles) northeast of Jodhpur.

The 16th-century fort at Khimsar, a three-hour drive from Jodhpur, was once the province of one of Rao Jodha's sons. His descendants still live in the palace. Surrounded by a small village, green fields, and sand dunes, it's now a heritage hotel, and a delightful place to relax. The building is gorgeously floodlit at night.

🛏 Hotels

WelcomHotel Khimsar Fort

$$$ | **RESORT** | Relax and enjoy the fine service, as well as the peace and quiet, at this graceful palace and fort in the Thar Desert in rural Khimsar, a two-hour drive (90 km [56 miles]) from Jodhpur. **Pros:** retreat from city life; self-contained oasis; on-site restaurant. **Cons:** rooms could use an update; remote location; food average. [$] *Rooms from: Rs. 9000* ✉ *Khimsar, Nagaur district, Jodhpur-Nagaur Hwy., Khimsar* ☎ *1585/262–345 Jaipur, 141/222–9700 reservations* 🌐 *www.khimsar.com* 🛏 *85 rooms* 🍴 *No meals.*

Jaisalmer

663 km (412 miles) northwest of Udaipur; 285 km (177 miles) northwest of Jodhpur; 570 km (354 miles) west of Jaipur.

Jaisalmer seems like a mirage: its array of sandstone buildings are surrounded by the stark desert and illuminated in a gold hue by the sun. The ancient city is defined by its carved spires and palaces and the massive sandcastlelike fort that towers over the imposing wall that encircles the town. Jaisalmer is a remote and unusual city; it's out-of-the-way, but it's worth it if you want to see a different side of India, and if you want to take a safari.

Founded in 1156 by Rawal Jaisal, Jaisalmer is on the western edge of Rajasthan's Thar Desert, about 160 km (100 miles) east of the India–Pakistan border. The city started as a trade center: from the 12th through the 18th centuries, rulers here amassed their wealth from taxes levied on caravans passing through from Africa, Persia, Arabia, and Central Asia. Smugglers were also known to frequent Jaisalmer to work the profitable opium trade. The rise of Mumbai (known then as Bombay) as a major trading port in the 19th century, however, began to eclipse Jaisalmer. And when British India was partitioned into Pakistan and India at Independence, Jaisalmer's importance waned further when it lost its close access to the port town of Karachi (that went to Pakistan) and slowly became the sleepy place it is today.

Today Jaisalmer draws travelers attracted by the city's fairy-tale architecture and the mystery and harsh, remote charm of the desert. At night the golden fort is bathed in light, which illuminates its seemingly impregnable walls (most of the buildings inside are made out of yellow sandstone).

Jaisalmer is also known for its ornate 19th-century havelis—city mansions with facades so intricately carved that the stonework looks like lace. It's also worth wandering through the mazelike alleys and bazaars, in both the fort and off Gandhi Chowk, although the shopkeepers here can be at times annoyingly pushy, perhaps because they see fewer tourists than elsewhere in Rajasthan. You will find a very eclectic selection of handicrafts to choose with more items of leather and patchwork.

Safaris are a good way to see the desert. These are great fun, but choose your outfitter carefully—don't skimp and choose a cheap one, and choose a tour that offers a vehicle to take you to the desert. Take a light scarf to protect your face in case of a sandstorm, wear sunglasses, and use sunscreen.

Staying inside the fort area is the most atmospheric and memorable, but most of the hotels and guesthouses are outside its golden walls; if you do choose to stay in the fort, know that this part of town is easily and painlessly accessed by auto-rickshaw only (Rs. 50 from the fort gates to the central square in the fort).

GETTING HERE AND AROUND
Jaisalmer is not easy to reach. There is an airport that has recently been completed but not opened and, at this writing, there are no commercial flights. From Jodhpur, Jaisalmer is about five hours by car and more than six hours by train; from Jaipur the train ride is about 12 hours; from Delhi it's a grueling 17–18 hours by train. There are no direct trains to Jaisalmer from Udaipur.

With clean lanes, little traffic, and few crowds, Jaisalmer's fort and the surrounding areas are easily covered on foot (heat permitting), although you can also take an auto-rickshaw from the base of the fort to other parts of town. Rickshaws are not metered, so be sure to bargain and fix a price before setting off.

TAXI COMPANIES Hanuman Travels ✉ Hanuman Circle, Jaisalmer ☎ 299/225–0340 ⊕ www.hanumantravels.in. **Swagat Travels Bus Company** ☎ 941/476–1057, 2992/252–057 ⊕ www.swagatbus.in.

TIMING
Spend at least two nights in Jaisalmer. If you plan to go on a safari, set aside at least one extra night for this.

ESSENTIALS
TOURIST OFFICES Tourist Reception Centre ✉ Near Gadsisar Lake Circle, Jaisalmer ☎ 299/225–2406 ⊕ www.tourism.rajasthan.gov.in.

A GOOD TOUR
In Jaisalmer it's next to impossible to follow a straight path—the city is a maze of streets and passageways—so trust your instincts and don't be afraid to ask the locals for directions. You can't get too lost, because Jaisalmer is fairly small. The major landmark is the **Golden Fort**, which is every bit as labyrinthine as the rest of the city; allow several hours to explore the attractions within. After visiting there, walk north to the **Salim Singh-ki Haveli, Patwon-ki Haveli,** and **Nathmal-ki Haveli.** Finally, you can hail an auto-rickshaw and head southeast toward **Gadsisar Lake.** You can end your day with a puppet show at the Desert Culture Centre.

TIMING
You can do this tour in a day. If you spend a second day in town, visit the royal cenotaphs at **Bada Bagh** or the earlier capital of the Bhatti Rajputs at Lodarva and then head out of the city to **Sam Sand Dunes** for a sunset camel ride back.

Sights

Bada Bagh
MEMORIAL | Outside Jaisalmer proper, on the Ramgarh road, and on the shore of a small artificial lake, this site is home to a collection of picturesque yellow-stone cenotaphs (memorial temples) of Jaisalmer's Rajput rulers. There are royal cenotaphs in the overgrown and dusty gardens as well, with canopies under which members of the royal family are buried. Take your shoes off before climbing up to enter a cenotaph. Notice the beautifully carved ceilings and equestrian

statues of the former rulers. This is a half-hour excursion and only worth a look if you have time to spare. Make sure you, or the driver of the vehicle you take, knows the way; incorrect signage on this road can lead to unnecessary detours. ⊠ *6 km (4 miles) northwest of Jaisalmer, Jaisalmer* ☎ *2992/252–406* 🖂 *From Rs. 50.*

Desert Culture Centre and Museum

MUSEUM | Near Gadsisar Lake, this small museum has a collection of artifacts detailing the history of music, culture, and life in the desert, including camel decorations and an interesting opi-um-mixing box. They host nightly puppet shows during peak season. ⊠ *Gadsisar Circle, Jaisalmer* ☎ *2992/253–723* 🖂 *Rs. 100 (includes entry to puppet show).*

Gadsisar Lake (*Gadi Sagar Tank*)

NATIONAL/STATE PARK | Built in the 12th century, this freshwater lake surrounded by numerous golden-hue shrines is frequented by a spectacular and diverse avian community. Entry is through the impressive two-story Tilon ki Ol Gateway. Plan for a picnic and perhaps a short paddleboat excursion on a cool afternoon when the town is not overrun with local tourists including families and children, and bring some bread to feed the catfish. ⊠ *About 1 km (½ mile) southeast of Jaisalmer's fort, Jaisalmer* 🖂 *Free.*

★ Golden Fort (Sonar Qila)

MILITARY SITE | Jaisalmer's dazzling 12th-century fort, often likened to an oversized sandcastle, is unquestionably the most charming aspect of an already very charming city. Some 250 feet above the town, on Trikuta Hill, the fort has been inhabited for centuries and is a little town of its own; it's protected by a 30-foot-high wall and has 99 bastions, and several great pols (gateways) jut outward from the battlements. Built of sandstone and extremely brittle, the fort is rumored to be an architectural time bomb, destined to collapse in the face of a particularly aggressive

sandstorm—though it's withstood eight centuries. So lovely is this structure that the poet Rabindranath Tagore (1861–1941) was inspired to write the poem *Sonar Kila* after seeing it; this, in turn, inspired another creative Bengali—Satyajit Ray made a famous film by the same name.

Inside the web of tiny lanes are Jain and Hindu temples, palaces, restaurants, shops, and charming havelis. The fort is very clean and has a sleepy, time-has-stood-still vibe to it. The seven-story **Juna Mahal** (Old Palace), built around 1500, towers over the other buildings and is now home to the **Jaisalmer Fort Palace Museum and Heritage Centre**. A visit to the museum is worth the time: enter via the **Satiyon ka Pagthiya** (Steps of the Satis), where the royal ladies committed *sati,* self-immolation, when their husbands were slain.

Cars and larger vehicles are not allowed in the fort so you most hire an autorick-shaw (Rs. 50–Rs. 100) to take you. The walk up is also pleasant in cool weather. ⊠ *Jaisalmer* 🖂 *Free. Museum from Rs. 300.*

Gyan Bhandar

RELIGIOUS SITE | Within the fort, the Jain temple complex library contains more than 1,000 old manuscripts—some from the 12th century, written on palm leaf, with painted wooden covers—and a collection of Jain, pre-Mughal, and Rajput paintings. Typically open from 8 or 9 am to noon, but, especially in low season, it may be closed even during those hours. ⊠ *Jaisalmer.*

Jain temples

RELIGIOUS SITE | Make sure to visit the seven intricately decorated Jain temples within the fort. They were built from the 12th to 16th centuries, and house thousands of carved deities and dancing figures in mythological settings. The carvings of both the exteriors and the interiors are notable. There are a few rules to observe: photographing some

sculptures is not allowed; you'll have to leave any leather items at the gate; food, shoes, and cell phones are not allowed; and menstruating women are asked not to enter the temple. Open 8 am to noon. ⊠ *Inside fort, Jaisalmer* ⛄ *Rs. 200, including camera fee.*

Lodarva

RELIGIOUS SITE | Also called Luderwa, Lodarva was once the capital of the state in western Rajasthan ruled by the Bhatti Rajputs. The founder of "new" Jaisalmer, Rawal Jaisal, also of the Bhatti Rajput clan, lived here before shifting his capital to Jaisalmer fort on Trikuta Hill in the 12th century because Lodurva's location on a trade route through the Thar desert made it vulnerable to attack. Lodurva was attacked by both famous Afghan conquerors: Mahmud Ghazni, and later, Muhammad Ghori. The ruins of the former city are of interest to history buffs. The Jain temple complex is known for its *nag devta* (snake god), a live snake that appears on auspicious days and nights. The snake is worshipped because, as legend goes, it has been protecting this temple for thousands of years. The temples are famous for their graceful architecture and detailed carving. They, too, were ransacked by Ghori and were rebuilt in the 1970s. ⊠ *Jaisalmer* ✛ *16 km (10 miles) northwest of Jaisalmer* ⛄ *Rs. 100, including camera.*

Patwon-ki Haveli

HOUSE | Outside the fort, about 1½ km (1 mile) from the Gopa Chowk entrance, are the Patwon-ki Havelis—literally "five mansions"—a string of connected grand, ornately carved homes built by the Patwa brothers in the 1800s. The Patwas were highly influential Jain merchants who dealt in brocade (although it was rumored that they actually made their money on opium) back when Jaisalmer was an independent principality. The Patwa brothers forbade the repetition of any motifs or designs between their mansions, so each is distinctive. The first of these is arguably the most elaborate

and magnificent of all—in addition to exquisitely carved pillars and expansive corridors, one of the apartments in this five-story mansion is painted with beautiful murals. ⊠ *Near Mahavir Bhawan, Jaisalmer* ⛄ *From Rs. 150.*

Sam Sand Dunes

NATURE SITE | No trip to Jaisalmer is complete without a visit to this photographer's feast. Although the dunes have become somewhat touristy in recent years, with hawkers of all sorts dotting the sand, their wind-carved ripples still create fantastic mirages, and it's still a magical place to be. Many famous Hindi films were shot here. Expect some amount of heckling from persistent camel owners and girls offering to dance or sing for you, but don't let it put you off staying for the sunset, which is often spectacular.

A peculiar sort of peace descends on the dunes in the late evening, when the icy cold desert wind begins to blow, and this is the most enjoyable part of the dunes experience. Note there are no hotels here, but there are a few permanent camps, for which you need to book in advance; otherwise you must return to Jaisalmer at night. In summer or monsoon the going can be tough—heat, rain, sandstorms—but still try and take in the dunes. ⊠ *42 km (26 miles) west of Jaisalmer, Jaisalmer.*

Restaurants

Gaji's Restaurant

$$ | KOREAN | Korean food in India is not very typical, especially in dusty Jaisalmer, but Gaji's does a good representation of the cuisine with specialties including bibimbap and *omurice* (fried rice stuffed inside an omelet). It also offers a few Indian and Chinese dishes, and its rooftop dining room provides views of the city. **Known for**: Korean house specials; rooftop views; breakfast. [$] *Average main: Rs. 400* ⊠ *Rooftop of Gaji Hotel,*

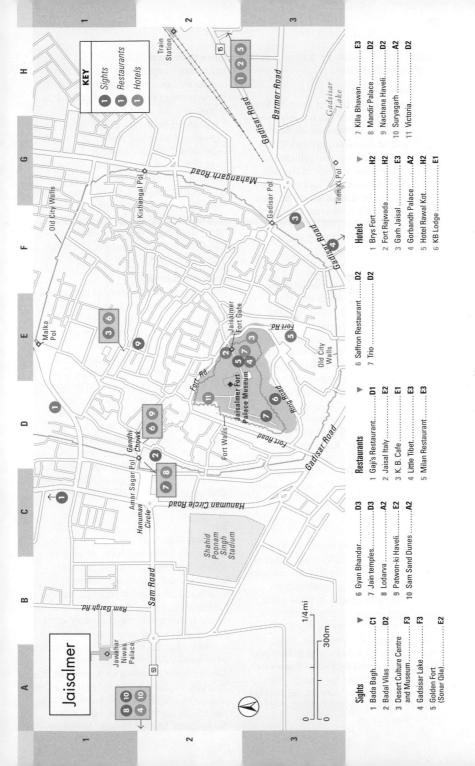

Jaisalmer

Kalakar Colony, Jaisalmer ✥ Near Sunset Point ☎ 982/903–0701.

Jaisal Italy

$$ | **ITALIAN** | At the base of the fort, this little Italian restaurant has a lovely vibe, an interior that is simple yet far from rustic, and an open rooftop area that is perfect for people-watching. It also has a huge advantage: it is one of the only restaurants in town with an indoor area with a/c comfort. **Known for:** Italian-style pasta; vegetarian dishes; a/c dining room. [$] *Average main: Rs. 350 ✉ By First Gate of fort, Jaisalmer ☎ 2992/253–504 ▭ No credit cards.*

K.B. Cafe

$$ | **NORTH INDIAN** | Rajasthani vegetarian food is the specialty at this small family-owned rooftop restaurant, but don't expect the palate-burning dishes that Rajasthan is known for—the spice levels here are significantly toned down to suit Westerners. If you haven't yet tried quintessentially Rajasthani dishes *dal bati churma* (lentils, rolls, and sweetened wheat and butter paste—sort of the Rajasthani equivalent of bread and butter) or *ker saangri* (desert vegetable), this is the place to do so. **Known for**: traditional thali; vegetarian dishes; rooftop dining. [$] *Average main: Rs. 450 ✉ K.B. Lodge Hotel, opposite Patwon-ki Haveli, Jaisalmer ☎ 299/225–3833 ▭ No credit cards.*

Little Tibet

$$ | **CAFÉ** | Most of the restaurants within the fort are vegetarian for historical reasons (mainly vegetarian Brahmin families lived in the fort), but a small section, where Rajput families live, have a few nonvegetarian restaurants—Little Tibet is one of them. It serves a mix of Tibetan (momos, vegetable and meat, great *thukpa* soups), Chinese, and Indian, with a few global items thrown in. **Known for**: meat dishes; Tibetan dumplings; rooftop seating. [$] *Average main: Rs. 350 ✉ Fort Kotri Para, Jaisalmer ☎ 779/195–7921 ▭ No credit cards.*

Milan Restaurant

$$ | **INDIAN** | Just behind the fort, this restaurant has an unassuming exterior that you might not even recognize as a restaurant, but what it lacks in decor, it makes up for in homemade cooking—especially meat dishes in the very vegetarian town of Jaisalmer. Milan's best dishes are the tandoori options: tandoori chicken and Jeera rice or vegetable curry is popular, as is the lal maas, a local favorite. **Known for:** traditional tandoori; chicken and mutton dishes; large portions. [$] *Average main: Rs. 350 ✉ Manak Chowk, Amar Sagar Pol, Jaisalmer ☎ 941/476–1614.*

Saffron Restaurant

$$ | **ECLECTIC** | The majority of the restaurants in Jaisalmer are vegetarian, prompting travelers in search of meat-based dishes to flock to this quiet, charming rooftop restaurant at the Nachana Haveli hotel complex. The menu includes a variety of Indian food, as well as Chinese and Italian options and a large array of all-day breakfast plates, but the emphasis is on traditional Rajasthani dishes, Indian, and tandoor (Indian clay-oven roasts), especially chicken delicacies. **Known for:** rooftop terrace; tandoori dishes; bar menu. [$] *Average main: Rs. 450 ✉ Nachna Haveli Hotel, Goverdhan Chowk ☎ 299/225–2110 🌐 www.nachanahaveli.com.*

Trio

$$$ | **NORTH INDIAN** | Serving rich North Indian and Rajasthani food, as well as some Chinese, quite a few continental dishes, and a choice of desserts which you don't find at other Jaisalmer restaurants, this rooftop restaurant is an old favorite with travelers even if the food is not outstanding. The tented roof top has a kitschy though charming look, with good views of the fort from the smaller open terrace area. **Known for:** rich Rajasthan cuisine; good for groups; meat and vegetarian dishes. [$] *Average main: Rs. 550 ✉ Gandhi Chowk, near Amar Sagar Gate, Mandir Palace, Jaisalmer*

☎ 2992/252–733 🌐 *www.royaldesert-camp.in* 💳 *No credit cards.*

Hotels

Brys Fort

$$$ | **HOTEL** | Created to look like a faux fort, Brys tends to verge more toward back-lot film-set fantasy than historical accuracy—for example, the lobby is graced with large marble elephants, peacock murals, and chandeliers—but it's a brave effort. **Pros:** one of the city's more modern hotels; attached restaurant; breakfast included. **Cons:** far from the center of the town (3½ km or 92 miles); rooms lack Rajasthani charm; some bathrooms could use an update. [$] *Rooms from: Rs. 7200* ✉ *Hotel Complex, Jodhpur Jaisalmer Rd., Jaisalmer* ✣ *Shortly beyond sprawling Indian Army base* ☎ *299/226–9100* 🌐 *brysfortjaisalmer.com* 🛏 *90 rooms* 🍴 *Free Breakfast.*

Fort Rajwada

$$$ | **HOTEL** | The hotel might not be particularly convenient, but its architecture and interior design are interesting, and the suites are quite luxurious. **Pros:** beautiful architecture and interiors; large pool. **Cons:** outside town; Wi-Fi spotty; service not up to luxury standards. [$] *Rooms from: Rs. 8200* ✉ *No. 1 Hotel Complex, Jodhpur-Barmer Link Rd., Jaisalmer* ☎ *299/225–4608* 🌐 *www.fortrajwada.com* 🛏 *100 rooms* 🍴 *Free Breakfast.*

Garh Jaisal

$$ | **B&B/INN** | This cozy haveli hotel, inside the 11th-century fort, is run like a homestay by the family who owns it, and makes for a special stay. **Pros:** quiet; clean surroundings; inside fort. **Cons:** no meals apart from breakfast; rooms have no TVs or phones; basic facilities. [$] *Rooms from: Rs. 5500* ✉ *Fort Kotari Para, Jaisalmer* ☎ *299/225–3836* 🌐 *www.hotelgarhjaisal.com* 🛏 *7 rooms* 🍴 *Free Breakfast.*

Gorbandh Palace

$$$ | **HOTEL** | Built of golden sandstone, this hotel away from the city center is spacious and elegant, and the rooms, with balconies, are arranged in haveli-style blocks around a series of small interior courtyards with skylights and fountains. **Pros:** spacious property; nice pool; music at night during high season. **Cons:** bland rooms; corridors could do with better lighting; hotel lacks intimacy. [$] *Rooms from: Rs. 7000* ✉ *1 Tourist Complex, Sam Rd., Jaisalmer* ☎ *299/225–3801* 🌐 *www.hrhhotels.com* 🛏 *85 rooms* 🍴 *Free Breakfast.*

Hotel Rawal Kot

$$$ | **HOTEL** | This comfortable, small, and well-maintained hotel is on the edge of town, with a great view of the fort from afar. **Pros:** friendly and helpful staff; quiet; large pool. **Cons:** a bit inconveniently located away from the main sights in Jaisalmer; isolated; busy in season. [$] *Rooms from: Rs. 7000* ✉ *3 Hotel Complex, Jodhpur-Jaisalmer Rd., Jaisalmer* ☎ *299/225–1874* 🌐 *www.hotelrawalkot.com* 🛏 *30 rooms* 🍴 *Free Breakfast.*

KB Lodge

$ | **B&B/INN** | Famous for its traditional Rajasthani thali, available in its rooftop eatery, comfy KB has accommodations that are equally authentic and striking and located smack in the center of town near the historic Patwon-ki Haveli. **Pros:** well located; good pricing; close to restaurants and sights. **Cons:** not particularly atmospheric; bathroom clean but basic; restaurant is vegetarian. [$] *Rooms from: Rs. 3500* ✉ *Patwon-ki Haveli, Jaisalmer* ☎ *2992/253–833* 🌐 *www.killabhawan.com* 🛏 *6 rooms* 🍴 *Free Breakfast.*

Killa Bhawan

$$$ | **HOTEL** | The location of this lovely, ancient, characterful hotel, built into the walls of the fort, could not be better—the views are great. **Pros:** views from the terrace; room rate includes breakfast; excellent service. **Cons:** steep stairs; no televisions and phones in the room;

some rooms have common bathrooms. $ *Rooms from: Rs. 9000 ⊠ Fort, 445 Kotri Para, Jaisalmer ☎ 02992/251–204 ⊕ www.killabhawan.com ⇌ 11 rooms ⏐⊙⏐ Free Breakfast.*

Mandir Palace

$$$ | HOTEL | Like something out of a fairy tale, this rambling 200-year-old palace-hotel at Gandhi Chowk with comfortable, neat, and clean (but not luxurious or memorable) rooms has a breathtakingly beautiful carved exterior that incorporates turrets, arched doorways, windows, and balconies. **Pros:** in the center of town near better restaurants; authentic ambience; nice pool. **Cons:** rooms do not reflect the character and heritage of the place; more expensive than other Jaisalmer hotels; inconsistent Wi-Fi. $ *Rooms from: Rs. 9000 ⊠ Gandhi Chowk, Jaisalmer ☎ 11/4603–5500, 2992/252–788, 299/225–2788 ⊕ www. mandirpalace.com ⇌ 28 rooms ⏐⊙⏐ Free Breakfast.*

Nachana Haveli

$ | HOTEL | A 10-minute walk from the Golden Fort, this 18th-century haveli exudes old-world charm and is owned and run by descendants of the Maharaja Kesri Singh, who ruled over Jaisalmer during the 1700s. **Pros:** central; reasonably priced; the rooftop Saffron (one of the better restaurants of the city). **Cons:** no pool; basic amenities; some windowless rooms. $ *Rooms from: Rs. 3800 ⊠ Gandhi Chowk, Jaisalmer ☎ 299/225–2110 ⊕ www.nachanahaveli.com ⇌ 12 rooms ⏐⊙⏐ No meals.*

Suryagarh

$$$$ | RESORT | Like a mirage in the desert, this contemporary, elegant fort turned enormous hotel rises out of the sand, luring you to its ramparts. **Pros:** scenic location; good service and food; indoor pool and spa. **Cons:** 13 km (8 miles) out of Jaisalmer in the middle of nowhere; need a driver to go into town; expensive, but worth the cost. $ *Rooms from: Rs. 25000 ⊠ Kahala Phata, Sam Rd., Jaisalmer ☎ 299/226–9269 ⊕ www.suryagarh. com ⇌ 90 rooms ⏐⊙⏐ Free Breakfast.*

Victoria

$$ | B&B/INN | There are very few comfortable lodgings located inside Jaisalmer fort, but this is one of them—but note that it is a climb to get to rooms on higher floors or the terrace. **Pros:** well located and well priced; some rooms have balconies; staff can book desert excursions. **Cons:** only breakfast is served; service is patchy; Wi-Fi not consistent. $ *Rooms from: Rs. 5500 ⊠ Kund Para, Jaisalmer ☎ 299/225–2150 ⊕ www.hotelvictoriajaisalmer.com ⇌ 11 rooms ⏐⊙⏐ Free Breakfast.*

🛍 Shopping

Jaisalmer is famous for its mirror work, embroidery, and woolen shawls. Local artisans also make attractive, good-quality wooden boxes, silver jewelry, leather items, patchwork bedcovers, mats and cushion covers, trendy cotton clothing, and curios. The main shopping areas are **Sadar Bazaar, Sonaron Ka Bas, Manak Chowk,** and **Pansari Bazaar,** all within the walled city, near the fort and temple areas. Sonaron Ka Bas, in particular, has exquisite silver jewelry. Avoid solicitors dispensing advice, take time to browse carefully, and bargain hard.

Khadi Gramudyog

CLOTHING | This shop has khadi (hand-spun cotton) shawls, Nehru jackets, scarves, and handmade rugs. ⊠ *Dhibba Para, near fort, in walled city, Jaisalmer.*

Chapter 7

MUMBAI

Updated by
Meher Mirza

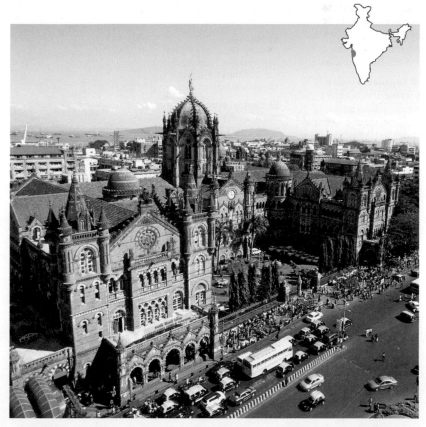

👁 **Sights**
★★★★☆

🍴 **Restaurants**
★★★★★

🛏 **Hotels**
★★★★★

👜 **Shopping**
★★★★★

🍸 **Nightlife**
★★★★★

WELCOME TO MUMBAI

TOP REASONS TO GO

★ **All of India in one city:** Mumbai is both modern and old-fashioned, rich and poor, beautiful and ugly—all of India concentrated in one metropolis.

★ **One big feast:** From down-home seafood joints to upscale temples of gastronomy, many of Mumbai's restaurants are the best in India.

★ **Experience India's bazaars:** The buzz of a typical Indian bazaar is fascinating, and Mumbai is packed with them; time to get shopping.

★ **Check out Chowpatty:** No visit to Mumbai would be complete without a nighttime stroll along this carnivalesque stretch of beach.

★ **The Ancient Caves of Ajanta and Ellora:** Take a side trip to see the awe-inspiring carvings and paintings here, using Aurangabad as a base.

Mubai is one of the largest cities in the world, with nearly 22 million people occupying just over 4,000 square km.

1 Colaba. The tip of Mumbai's peninsula is one of the oldest parts of the city.

2 Fort and Marine Drive. Visit this area for the best seafood in town.

3 Malabar Hill and Nearby. Mumbai's richest neighborhood also houses some of the city's most important holy sites.

4 Central Mumbai. The bustling city center has top dining and lodging options.

5 CST and Nearby. In the shadow of Mumbai's massive Victorian train station, you'll find some of the city's best street food and bazaars.

6 Elephanta Island. Just a short ferry ride from South Mumbai lie the ancient caves of Elephanta.

7 Juhu, Bandra, and the Western Suburbs. Northwestern Mumbai is famous for beaches and Bollywood studios.

8 Aurangabad and the Caves. Aurangabad is a base for exploring the cave temples of Ellora and Ajanta.

MALABAR POINT

Arabian Sea

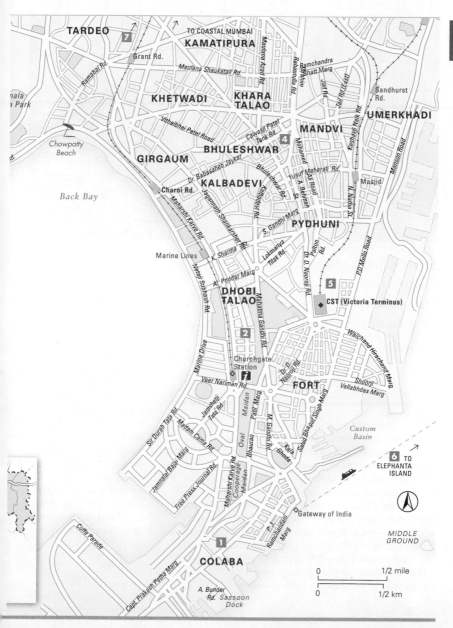

TARDEO

7

TO COASTAL MUMBAI

KAMATIPURA

Grant Rd.

Ramabai Rd.

Maulana Shaukatali Rd.

Mautana Azad Rd.

Rahimtulla Rd.

Ramchandra
Bhatt Marg

Jail Rd. East

Sandhurst
Rd.

KHETWADI

KHARA
TALAO

Rahimatullah
Rahim

Jail Rd.

Keshavji Naik Rd.

UMERKHADI

Vithalbhai Patel Road

Cawasji Patel
Tank Rd.

MANDVI

Manson Road

Chowpatty
Beach

BHULESHWAR

4

Mohamed
A. Rehman

Yusuf Meherali Rd.

Masjid

GIRGAUM

Dr. Babasaheb Jaykar

Bhuleshwar Rd.

A. Rehman

N. Naha St.

N. Natha St.

Charni Rd.

KALBADEVI

Pd. Makhatay

S. Gandhi Marg

Back Bay

Maharshi Karve Rd.

Jagannath Shankersheth Rd.

PYDHUNI

K. Sharma

Lokmanya
Tilak Rd.

Dr. D. Naoroji Rd.

Patton
Rd.

Pd. Mello Road

Marine Lines

Netaji Subhash Rd.

A. Poddar Marg

DHOBI
TALAO

Mahatma Gandhi Rd.

5

CST (Victoria Terminus)

Watchand Hirachand Marg

Marine Drive

2

Churchgate
Station

7

Dr. D.
Naoroji Rd.

Shoorji
Vallabhdas Marg

Veer Nariman Rd.

FORT

Oval
Maidan

Patel Marg

M. Gandhi Marg

Sahid Bhagat Singh Marg

Custom
Basin

Sir Durab Tata Rd.

Jamshetji
Tata Rd.

Madam Cama Rd.

Bhaurao

Kela
Ghoda

6

TO
ELEPHANTA
ISLAND

Jamnalal Bajaj Marg

Free Press Journal Rd.

Maharshi Karve Rd.

Cooperage
Maidan

Gateway of India

MIDDLE
GROUND

Cuffe Parade

1

COLABA

P.J.
Ramchandani
Marg

0   1/2 mile

0   1/2 km

Capt. Prakash Petha Marg

A. Bunder
Rd. Sassoon
Dock

EATING WELL IN MUMBAI

A plate of *bhel puri*

Mumbai has a robust tradition of eating out for cheap—you can dine out on a dime at working-class diners or stretch your dollar at bars and cafés—but it's also a modern metropolis with an exciting, extensive, and relatively affordable cosmopolitan dining scene.

With its origins as a fishing village, Mumbai is blessed with a strong coastal culinary tradition. And because it's also a historic port of commerce, Mumbai also has absorbed influences from foreign traders and settlers (among them, Portuguese, Iranians, and Brits) and Indian communities that came here for trade. The city's culinary traditions range widely, from Maharashtrian cooking to that of the Gujarati Hindus, Jains, and Parsis—the first two for their elaborate vegetarian contributions and the latter for its Persian- and British-influenced dishes. Regionally themed *thalis* (platters with lots of small dishes) are a popular way to sample an assortment of dishes from distinct cuisines.

DABBAWALAS

Dabbawalas, or tiffin carriers, are a symbol of Mumbai's industriousness. An institution since the late 1800s, they ensure that hundreds of thousands of professionals get fresh, home-cooked meals delivered daily to their offices. Wives and mothers fill containers, which are picked up and delivered by foot, bicycle, and train via a supply chain organized by an efficient system of coded marks.

BOMBAY SANDWICH

The Bombay sandwich is the hearty cousin of its delicate English ancestor. Bookended by buttered slices of white bread, its belly is filled with beetroot, cucumbers, potato, capsicum, tomatoes, onions, and a coat of chutney, all assembled in as many combinations as the customer may desire. This is then shoved into a greased toaster from which it emerges blistered and golden, then daubed with more butter and chutney, before serving.

Pav bhaji

EGGS KEJRIWAL

Years ago, Mr. Devi Prasad Kejriwal, member of Mumbai's tony Willingdon Club, tried to sidestep his Marwari community's strict vegetarianism by sneakily ordering eggs on toast that were concealed by a heavy blanket of cheese and chillies. Fortunately for us, not only did other members of the club quickly catch on to his secret, they took quite a shine to it. It soon became one of Mumbai's most well-known dishes.

BHEL PURI

Probably the most common street food you'll see in Mumbai is **bhel puri**; the crunchy, piquant, puffed-rice snack is sold on almost every street corner. Best savored during a stroll on Chowpatty Beach, *bhelwallas* blend the puffed rice with onion, coriander,

A bowl of lamb *dhansak*

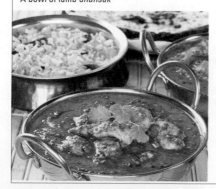

and a sprinkling of powdered spices like cumin, rock salt, and chilli powder; chutneys made of tamarind, dates, and jaggery (unrefined brown sugar), garlic, and coriander with green chillies. The addictive combination is tossed with fine shreds of fried gram (chickpea) flour and, sometimes, raw mango, then served in paper cones.

PAV BHAJI

Pav, the local word for leavened bread, comes from the Portuguese *pão;* "bhaji" is a curried vegetable dish. The combination, **pav bhaji,** is served late into the night on Mumbai's streets, but also in fast-food places and some hotel restaurants. A spicy mash of potato that's been fried and simmered into an orange paste is sopped up with soft white-bread rolls that have been lightly toasted with butter on a griddle. Slivers of raw onion, a squeeze of lemon, and a coriander garnish add a sharp kick.

DHANSAK

The flagship dish of the Parsi community, **dhansak** is a labor-intensive production that constitutes the big weekend meal. This stew always includes lentils and is only made with lamb or chicken and vegetables like gourds. It's a filling dish that is always eaten with caramelized white rice.

THE BAZAARS AND MARKETS OF MUMBAI

Produce at Crawford Market

Mumbai is not a city for sightseeing in the traditional sense—it's more a destination that you need to experience through your five senses, and there's no better way to do this than by going shopping in one of the city's teeming bazaars.

No one comes to Mumbai to shop at luxury boutiques—indeed, the locals don't, either, because high import taxes make it cheaper to buy name brands like Gucci abroad—they come to experience the racing pulse and frenzied pace of the markets. From handcarts tottering down crowded lanes, overloaded with antiques in Chor Bazaar, to succulent street food on the by-lanes of Bhendi Bazaar, to the overwhelming madness of the wholesale trade at Crawford Market, to the glittering gold of Zaveri Bazaar, Mumbai knows how to shop. If you consider yourself a bargainer, this is the place to test your skills—Mumbai merchants are some of the trickiest in the world, so be prepared to cut whatever price you're quoted in half, and then in half again.

THE ART OF THE BARGAIN

Unlike other parts of the world, where bargaining can sometimes take on a mean-spirited tone, in India the back-and-forth is part of the joy of shopping. Here bargaining is a game both you and the merchant are in on, so have fun with it: he's going to go extremely high, so you should go extremely low, then walk away when he won't come down. He'll likely call you back, with a smile on his face.

ANTIQUES, CHOR BAZAAR

Tourists—and locals—spend hours in crowded Chor Bazaar for the chance to dig out a hidden gem, lost beneath mountains of ancient antiques. Although the market's best finds are probably long gone, there is still the chance you might get lucky with vintage furniture or prints from decades gone by, but only if you bargain, and bargain hard. *Chor* is the Hindi word for thief, and if you're not firm—or don't have a local to help you with your purchasing—you're likely to get taken for a ride. ■ TIP→ **Do a round of the bazaar, taking notes on the items you like and which stall they're in; then, if you have a local friend, send him or her around the next day to buy the items for you, at a fraction of the quoted price.**

ANYTHING AND EVERYTHING (IN BULK), CRAWFORD MARKET

For an all-encompassing Mumbai market experience, look no farther than Crawford Market, where you can find everything from wholesale vegetables to knickknacks—it's definitely worth checking out, even if you're not planning to buy. To see Crawford in all its glory, go on a weekday, when the market, housed in a 140-year-old British Raj–era building, is packed with people bargaining over the price of Alfonso

Flower garlands for sale

A relics shop in Chor Bazaar

mangoes, tableware sets, and plastic bags. ■ TIP→ **Steer clear of the area that sells pets; the dogs, cats, and birds in this section of the market are not treated very well, and the scene is depressing and shouldn't be encouraged.**

CLOTH, MANGALDAS MARKET

More than 1,000 shops cram the far side of Crawford Market, in an area called Mangaldas, where the best fabrics in town are available at rock-bottom prices (sold by the bolt). If you're looking to get Indian clothing made, this is the place to pick up the fabric you need.

STREET FOOD AND JEWELRY, ZAVERI AND BHENDI BAZAARS

This pair of bazaars blend into one another, north of Crawford Market, and if you're looking for gold or, better yet, the best street food in Mumbai, this is the place to go. Shady is the name of the game here—from the money-laundering operations that most of the jeweler's in Zaveri engage in to the questionable hygiene of most of the street-food stalls; but if you want a great deal on jewelry, or have the stomach and the desire to taste the best of what Mumbai's carnivorous side has to offer, this is it.

MUMBAI'S HOLY SITES

The Knesseth Eliyahoo synagogue

Although it's not generally known for its religious heritage, Mumbai has a holy legacy going back hundreds of years, with sites dedicated to most of the world's major religions scattered throughout the city.

Not surprisingly, Hindu sites dominate any religious-oriented tour of Mumbai—from Siddhivinayak, central Mumbai's grand temple to Lord Ganesha, to Malabar Hill's peaceful, isolated Banganga water tank—but the city is also home to one of the world's most unusual mosques, Haji Ali Shrine, whose location in the Arabian Sea means it's only accessible during low tide; and colorful synagogues, like the sky-blue Knesseth Eliyahoo synagogue in Kala Ghoda. So if you need a break between booming bazaars and bumping bars—though, to be fair, some of these sites are likely to be just as busy as the hottest clubs in town—wander over to one of Mumbai's many temples, churches, mosques, or synagogues.

PAYING RESPECTS

How to be suitably respectful in a place of worship can be a little confusing—should you take off your footwear, cover your head, or remove your hat? Observe what others are doing and keep the following in mind: if you see a pile of shoes outside a temple, remove yours as well; if you see a collection box in front of an idol, drop in a coin or two; and if you're still not sure what to do, ask a local.

HAJI ALI SHRINE

This mosque lies in the middle of the Arabian Sea, just off one of Mumbai's busiest intersections. At high tide it looks like an isolated island in the middle of a bay, but during low tide the narrow 1-km (½-mile) pathway to the 500-year-old tomb is revealed. It's especially busy on Thursday and Friday, when upward of 40,000 pilgrims visit the site.

BANGANGA WATER TANK

According to the Hindu epic the *Ramayana*, the god Rama stopped at this spot while searching for his wife Sita, and asked his brother Lakshmana for some water. Lakshmana shot an arrow into the ground and water gushed out, creating what would become Banganga. The first tank, used for storing rainwater, is said to have been built here in the 11th century, and a more formal version was constructed in the 1700s. The current tank, built in the early 20th century, is a serene spot.

SIDDHIVINAYAK TEMPLE

Pilgrims travel from far and wide—often on foot—to visit the Siddhivinayak Temple, dedicated to Ganesh, the elephant-headed god. The shrine is renowned throughout the Hindu world for its purported wish-granting properties, and attracts worshippers of

Mount Mary church, in Bandra

At the Haji Ali shrine

every stripe—from Bollywood beauties to industrial titans to slum dwellers. Tuesday is Ganesh's day, and the road to the temple is especially busy then.

KNESSETH ELIYAHOO SYNAGOGUE

This pale, light-blue synagogue stands out among the gray and brown British Raj buildings of winding Kala Ghoda. It's worth a visit more for its exteriors than its interiors—the sparsely attended services are a sign of Mumbai's dwindling Jewish population.

JAIN TEMPLE

Officially known as Babu Amichand Panalal Adishwarji Jain Temple, but usually just referred to as the Jain temple, this small but very opulent (thanks to its diamond merchant benefactors) temple sits atop Malabar Hill, full of ornate sculptures and elegant frescoes, and topped with an arched dome extravagantly emblazoned with the 12 signs of the zodiac. The Jain temple is a testament to the wealth and status of a people who make up but a fraction of 1% of the Indian population.

Mumbai, sometimes called the Maximum City, after Suketu Mehta's 2004 nonfiction book of the same name, encapsulates the dynamism and chaos of modern India better than any other city. In this sprawling, muscular place by the sea you'll find everything from succulent street food to haute cuisine, bargain-basement bazaars to haute couture, humbling poverty to staggering wealth, sacred temples to hedonistic nightclubs.

Mumbai is in many ways the New York City of India, and many of the locals carry the same kind of chip on their shoulders—despite the madness, they wouldn't trade it for any other place on Earth. Mumbai is a city of extremes, where slum-dwelling strivers are making only a few dollars a day while working for billionaires and Bollywood stars. It's a 24-hour city stocked with some of the best late-night street food in the world, as well as fine-dining restaurants of renowned chefs. It's a cosmopolitan city of people from all over India that's nonetheless home to strident parochialism. It's a city of dreams for millions of Indians that, at the same time, affords so few any measure of comfort. And it's a beautiful city of silver towers when viewed by twilight from the Bandra-Worli Sea Link bridge over the Arabian Sea, but that sight quickly turns into a maze of winding, dirty streets and alleys when viewed up close.

Sensory overload is the name of the game on the island formerly known as Bombay (and yes, most locals still call it by its previous moniker; we use Bombay interchangeably with Mumbai in this chapter). The first thing that hits you when you arrive at the airport is the smell—spicy, fishy, and, to be honest, often not altogether pleasant. Next comes a crazed cab ride through the seemingly lawless streets (should your driver run a red light or, just as likely, drive on the wrong side of the road, try to remain calm). Then a traffic jam in the midst of a veritable symphony of honking, in which barefoot children, often holding infants, and tragically disfigured men and women knock at your window, begging for change. Persevere through, though; embrace and try to understand the natural hazards of the developing world, and you'll find yourself in the middle of a beautiful, often inspiring city.

There's plenty to see in Mumbai, but it doesn't have much in the way of the stationary monuments that London, Paris, Delhi, and other major cities possess. The art of experiencing Mumbai lies in eating, shopping, and wandering through the strikingly different neighborhoods and the various markets. Think of Mumbai as a 50-km-long (30-mile-long) open-air bazaar.

Colaba, headed by Gateway of India, is the tourist district and main drag for visitors, and from the Gateway of India to Colaba Market, along the main road, is a walkable stretch of hotels, pubs, restaurants, and interesting shops. Churchgate and Nariman Point are the business and hotel centers, and major bank and airline headquarters are clustered in skyscrapers on Nariman Point.

The district referred to as Fort—which includes Mumbai's hub, Flora Fountain—is filled with narrow, bustling streets lined with small shops and office buildings, as well as colleges and other educational facilities. Another upscale residential neighborhood, Malabar Hill, north of Churchgate on Marine Drive, is leafy and breezy, with fine, old stone mansions housing wealthy industrialists and government ministers.

Shopping and people-watching are most colorfully combined in Mumbai's chaotic bazaar areas, such as Chor Bazaar, Zaveri (jewelry) Bazaar, and Crawford Market (aka Mahatma Jyotiba Phule Market). Many of the city's newest and trendiest shops and restaurants are now out in the suburbs—where more and more people have been moving due to soaring real-estate prices and a lack of space—but South Mumbai still retains some of the very best.

Some travelers opt to stay in the suburbs, either in Bandra, at the end of the Bandra-Worli Sea Link; or in Juhu, a popular coastal suburb between Mumbai and the airports (about 20 km [12 miles] north of the city center). Juhu's beaches aren't clean enough for swimming, and

the place can be scruffy, but staying out here is a good way to observe everyday Indian life beyond the shadow of Mumbai's skyline. Sunday nights bring families down to the beach for an old-fashioned carnival, complete with small, hand-powered Ferris wheels, and lantern-lit snack stalls hawking sugarcane.

Planning

WHEN TO GO
HIGH SEASON: DECEMBER TO MARCH
Every year, Mumbaikars wait for the one-month period between mid-January and mid-February when the weather turns breezy and clear—a welcome respite from the sweltering heat (or pouring rain) that otherwise swamps the city. If you hit that sweet spot, you're golden—and you'll have also just missed NRI season, when the Non-Resident Indian relatives of locals visit from abroad during Christmas vacation (and prices explode). Because most tourists arrive in Mumbai in winter, it's important to make hotel and transportation arrangements ahead of time.

LOW SEASON: APRIL TO MID-SEPTEMBER
Mumbai's first summer starts at the tail end of March, increasing in heat and humidity until the monsoon breaks the cycle to cool things off, usually in mid-June; the rainy season lasts until mid-September, when another hot season comes around. None of these times are particularly pleasant—it's ungodly hot, then raining buckets, and then ungodly hot again. But those willing to test their mettle will find two joyous surprises: low hotel prices, and a monsoon that is not nearly as bad as you'd imagined (though hardly a walk in the park).

SHOULDER SEASON: MID-SEPTEMBER TO NOVEMBER

The Hindu festival season, when there seems to be (and often is) a religious holiday every other day, begins in August, but really starts rolling in September, attracting both domestic and international tourists. It will be hot and loud, but the Ganpati festival—during which Hindus transport massive, colorful idols of the elephant-headed god, Ganesh, to the sea—and other such festivities may just make it worth the sweat.

GETTING HERE AND AROUND
AIR TRAVEL

Mumbai's international airport, Chhatrapati Shivaji International Airport, is 30 km (19 miles) north of the city center. The domestic airport is at Santa Cruz, 4 km (2½ miles) away from the international airport. (Some domestic Air India flights leave, somewhat inexplicably, from the international airport. Many a domestic traveler has missed a flight by neglecting this crucial information, so always double-check your ticket before making your transportation arrangements.)

Arrive at the airport at least 75 minutes before takeoff for domestic flights, two to three hours before international flights (some airlines require three hours), and give yourself a cushion of time when leaving to avoid being stuck in the city's notoriously unpredictable highway traffic—it's better to wind up with some extra reading time at the gate than to endure the horror of watching your plane take off from the backseat cushion of a sweltering, motionless taxi. ■TIP➜ Mumbai airports are usually packed to their gills, and there are long lines for scanning luggage and checking in. However, in recent years a huge effort has been put into renovating both airports, and things are finally looking up. The recently renovated domestic airport is now one of India's finest, and is of international standard. Both airports have 24-hour business centers available to holders of major credit cards.

Most international flights arrive in the middle of the night. Be prepared: airports in Mumbai, like those in Delhi, Kolkata, or Chennai, are poorly run compared to those in other countries. Because airports typically run at or beyond capacity, many flights arrive at the same time. ■TIP➜ Make sure you secure a free baggage trolley first and send away the touts (and assorted individuals posing as porters, luggage loaders, personal trolley pushers, hotel/taxi providers, or customs clearance aids). Station yourself close enough to the right belt; check any stacks of luggage lined up against the wall in case your suitcases have come earlier.

If you have a lot of luggage, you can get a porter as soon as you disembark—right at the door of the airplane—they work for the airport and are identifiable by their uniforms. If you hire one, get his name, and he will meet you after you go through immigration, at the baggage belt. Do not negotiate rates beforehand—if he tries to do so, hire someone else. Pay him between Rs. 100 and Rs. 300 depending on how helpful he's been.

Immediately after you exit the customs hall there is a row of tourist counters for hotels, taxi hire, car hire, tourist information, cell-phone cards, and currency-exchange booths. If someone is meeting you at the airport, understand that he or she will have no idea when you will emerge from the airport, given the wait at immigration or at the baggage concourse, so don't panic.

AIRPORTS AND TRANSFERS

The trip from Chhatrapati Shivaji International Airport downtown to South Mumbai can take anywhere from 40 minutes if you arrive before 7:30 am or after 11 pm (many international flights arrive around midnight) to two hours, when traffic is at its worst. Some hotels provide airport transfers starting at Rs. 1,000 and going up to Rs. 3,000; some offer complimentary transfers if you're staying in a suite or on an exclusive floor or if the hotel is close to the airport.

To avoid hassles with taxis over prices, we strongly recommend heading to the prepaid-taxi counter outside the baggage-and-customs area to hire a regular cab, either air-conditioned or non-air-conditioned. Your rate is determined by your destination and amount of luggage, and is payable up front; Rs. 450 by day and Rs. 500 at night should get you to the center of town from the international airport, and from the domestic airport Rs. 50 less (tips aren't necessary and if your driver tries to charge you extra, show him the slip and firmly say "prepaid"). If you want an air-conditioned taxi and do not spot one, call Group Mobile Cool Cab Service or Gold Cabs, but remember, you'll have to wait even longer. Air-conditioned taxi fares are 25% higher than non-air-conditioned cabs. A trip to Colaba, for example, from the international airport will set you back Rs. 450 by day and Rs. 500 at night, and from the domestic airport Rs. 50 less. A word to the squeamish: most of the standard black-and-yellow cabs operating in Mumbai were built well over 20 years ago and seem to be held together by little more than duct tape and the driver's ingenuity. If you end up with an old Prestige (modeled on a Fiat), expect to see dirty, smelly upholstery (the drivers also sleep in the cars), a jerry-rigged trunk, and, quite possibly, a hole or two in the rusted metal floor. If you're on a budget, it's the way to go; but if you can afford it, spring for an overpriced Avis car, which includes a driver.

■ TIP→ **Even though metered taxis are available outside the domestic airport, and a police officer notes the taxi's license plates before dispatching you on your way, we advise against taking one.** The cabbies waiting at the domestic airport are often cheats with meters that run double-time.

A metered (not prepaid) taxi from the domestic airport to the downtown/south Mumbai area should cost Rs. 400, and from the international airport about Rs. 500 (more expensive at night). In any case, do not take a taxi that's outside the queue, or accept the offer of a taxi that's parked somewhere that requires you to walk out of the main airport area.

Finally, keep in mind that the route over Mumbai's Bandra-Worli Sea Link will cost you an extra Rs. 70, exclusive of what you've prepaid. The bridge, which cuts travel from the leafy Bandra to not-quite-midway-point Worli from 40 minutes to 7, offers stunning views of the ever-growing Mumbai skyline, and is definitely worth the extra money to save time.

AIRPORT INFORMATION Chhatrapati Shivaji International Airport ✉ *Airport* ⊕ *csia.in.* **Group Mobile Cool Cab Service** ✉ *Annie Besant Rd., 54/3, Worli* ☎ *22/2490–5152,22/2498–5353.*

BUS TRAVEL

Mumbai has a good bus system for traveling within the city, but navigating long routes and big crowds make it highly inadvisable for most short-term visitors.

CAR TRAVEL

Fairly good roads connect Mumbai to most major cities and tourist areas. Hiring a car and driver gives you a chance to watch the often-beautiful surroundings whiz by. Note that the driving can also be loud, hair-raising, and is definitely less than time-efficient for long distances.

Some distances from Mumbai: Aurangabad 388 km (241 miles); Panaji (Goa) 597 km (371 miles); Delhi 1,408 km (875 miles); Kochi (Kerala) 1,384 km (860 miles).

CARS AND DRIVERS

In certain areas, such as bazaars, you really have to walk for the full experience. Aside from these, having a car at your disposal is the most convenient way to travel around Mumbai, as you can

Some Mumbai History

Mumbai initially consisted of seven marshy Islands—Colaba, Old Woman's Island, Bombay, Mazgaon, Worli, Mahim, and Parel—that belonged to the Muslim kings of the Gujarat sultanate. The Muslims passed the parcel to the Portuguese (who occupied much of western India in the 16th and 17th centuries), who in turn gave it in 1661 to England's King Charles II as part of a dowry in his marriage to the Portuguese Princess Catherine de Braganza. The British established a fort and trading post that grew quickly in size and strength.

Soon enough, land reclamation joined the seven small islands into one, grafting a prototype for today's multifarious metropolis—today the islands, except for Old Woman's Island, are neighborhoods within Mumbai.

The pride of the British in Bombay, and in their power over western India, is memorialized in the city's most celebrated landmark—the Gateway of India, built to welcome King George V to India in 1911. It's now near a statue of the young 17th-century Maratha leader, Shivaji.

zip (or crawl, depending on the time of day) around town without the repeated hassle of hailing taxis. To arrange a hired car, inquire at your hotel's travel desk or contact a travel agency (you'll probably pay much more if you book through your hotel) or simply order an Uber or Ola (the local Uber equivalent) by using their apps. Both offer hourly bookings, share taxis, and intercity cabs, as well. You might get lower rates from private agents like Adarsh, Euro Cars, or Travel House: Rs. 1,800 to Rs. 2,000 for a full day (eight hours, or 80 km [50 miles]) in a car with air-conditioning and Rs. 1,700 or more for an air-conditioned sedan car like a Maruti Esteem. Meanwhile, an Ola mini will cost around Rs. 1,500 for the same amount of time/distance. Rates go up for Toyotas, Mercedes, and other luxury cars.

CONTACTS Euro Cars ✉ *105 Madhava, Bandra Kurla Complex, Bandra East* ☎ *22/4074–4074* ⊕ *www.eurocars-india. com.* **Travel House** ✉ *Crescent Business Park, 301/302, Andheri Kurla Rd., 3rd fl., near Saki Naka Telephone Exchange,*

Andheri East ☎ *22/4077–4071, 22/4077–4072* ⊕ *www.travelhouseindia.com.*

TAXI AND AUTO-RICKSHAW TRAVEL

Mumbai's sights are spread out, so getting around by taxi is a sensible—and cheap—option. You can flag down yellow-top black taxis anywhere in the city. All cabs are equipped with digital meters nowadays, so there is no question of any dreaded haggling. At this writing, the legal fare was Rs. 22 per km. Consult with your hotel's front desk to confirm the up-to-date rate before leaving to sightsee via local taxi.

Mumbai has plenty of on-call air-conditioned taxi services, but locals mostly use the convenient services of Uber and Ola (a local version of Uber)—the drivers are usually reliable and the estimated fare (usually correct to the rupee) is flashed on the app before the final booking is done. You can also use Meru Cab, but sometimes they miss your scheduled pickup time, so book the car for at least a half-hour earlier than you actually have to leave if you're headed to the airport, or do what the locals do and use Ola.

You can hire an air-conditioned taxi for a full day (eight hours or 80 km [50 miles], whichever comes first) for Rs. 1,000, and a half day (four hours) for Rs. 550. Ask your hotel what the going rates are in case they've gone up. Hiring a car and driver often presents a more comfortable ride at a better value than hiring a taxi for extended periods of time. Also, because there is no contract, you're not locked in, and if you don't like a particular driver, you can hire a different one the next day. Meru Cabs has an automated phone system, but if you stay on the line you'll eventually speak to an agent, and they'll send a confirmation by text message.

Auto-rickshaws are permitted only in Mumbai's suburbs, where you can flag them down on the street. Oftentimes, there will only be rickshaws available to you on the streets beyond Bandra, so it helps to get accustomed to using them. (Highway riding can sometimes feel a bit nerve-wracking when you're being driven without a door against a sea of trucks.) Rickshaws almost universally have digital meters now, and the fare, as of this writing, is Rs. 18 per km.

CONTACTS Meru Cabs ☎ *22/4422–4422* ⊕ *www.merucabs.com.*

TRAIN TRAVEL
Mumbai has two main train stations for travel outside of Mumbai (they also both act as stations for the local railroad). Chhatrapati Shivaji Terminus (CST), more commonly called Victoria Terminus, is the hub of Mumbai's Central Railway line. Churchgate and Mumbai Central Station are the hubs of India's Western Railway line. Make sure to go to the right train station.

To avoid the pandemonium at the stations, have a travel agent book your ticket; this costs a bit more but saves time and stress. Or book online: Indian Railways has a lumbering, heavily

trafficked website (⊕ *www.indianrail. gov.in*), so instead go to ⊕ *www.yatra. com* or ⊕ *www.makemytrip.com*—India's versions of Expedia and Priceline—where you can now book Indian Railway tickets in a much more user-friendly format. For information on confirming a ticket or on arrivals and departures, ask a local to make the phone call.

If you decide to book in person, head for the tourist counter established specially for foreign travelers. Eliciting information about trains on the telephone is usually impossible—local stations have no phone number, the national lines are usually busy, and the interactive voice-response numbers are in Hindi.

TRAIN INFORMATION Chhatrapati Shivaji Terminus (*CST, Victoria Terminus, or VT*) ⊠ *D. Naoroji Rd..* **Mumbai Central Station** ⊠ *Adjacent to Tardeo, Central Mumbai.*

EMERGENCIES
Pharmacies (chemists) in Mumbai are usually open daily until about 9 pm, and a wide variety of medications, including those that may require a prescription in the West, are available here over the counter. Hotels have house physicians and dentists on call. Your consulate can also give you the name of a reputable doctor or dentist and can assist you in locating the closest chemist. Otherwise, if you are in South Mumbai, try the emergency room at Breach Candy Hospital or nearby Jaslok Hospital— both are privately run and have highly regarded doctors. In north Mumbai, visit Lilavati Hospital in Bandra, or Kokilaben Dhirubhai Ambani Hospital further north in Andheri. Mumbai emergency services can't respond to an emergency as quickly as these services do in parts of the world with better roads and more manageable traffic.

MEDICAL CARE Breach Candy Hospital and Research Center ⊠ *60 Bhulabhai Desai Rd., Breach Candy* ☎ *22/2367–1888, 22/2367–2888.* **Jaslok Hospital** ⊠ *Dr. G.*

Deshmukh Marg, near Haji Ali, Pedder Road ☎ 22/6657–3333. **Kokilaben Hospital** ✉ Rao Saheb, Achutrao Patwardhan Marg, Four Bungalows, Andheri ☎ 22/3099–9999 ⊕ www.kokilabenhospital.com. **Lilavati Hospital** ✉ A–791, Bandra Reclamation, Bandra ☎ 22/2666–6666, 22/2656–8000, 22/2656–8063 for emergencies ⊕ www.lilavatihospital.com.

RESTAURANTS

Mumbai is India's melting pot, as well as its most cosmopolitan city, so it's no surprise that you can find nearly every regional Indian cuisine here, and some quality international food, too. You'll also find options ranging from casual to superchic.

Seafood from the Konkan coast—from Maharashtra south through Goa and all the way to Mangalore, in Karnataka—is a Mumbai specialty. The many seafood restaurants in Fort, from upscale Trishna to old-school Apoorva, have some of the best food in Mumbai. "Lunch home" is a typical Mumbai name for the slightly dingy seafood joints that bring in the crowds at lunchtime. North India is represented as well, with kebabs and tandoori. If you're looking for kebabs, head to restaurants specializing in Punjabi or Mughlai cuisine, or, if you have a fairly strong stomach, go to Khao Galli near Bhendi Bazaar; the late-night kebab snack option is Bade Miya behind the Taj Mahal Palace Hotel. Meat-heavy dishes from the North-West Frontier (the area of undivided India that's partly in modern-day Pakistan) are also popular, and closely related to Mughlai food: check out Neel, at the Mahalaxmi racetrack in Central Mumbai, for upscale versions. On the other end of the spectrum are Gujarati vegetarian thalis—combination platters of various veggies and lentils, though the ones in Mumbai tend to be a bit oilier than those from elsewhere in India. Soam, at the top of Marine Drive, is a great upscale place for thalis, and they're less oily here. You may also encounter some Jain food,

Ganesh Chaturthi

For two weeks every year, usually between August and September, Mumbai explodes with parades to celebrate Lord Ganesha, the elephant-headed god. During the Ganesh Chaturthi festival, idols of the god are worshipped throughout the city and then taken to the sea to be immersed—the two most popular beaches are Chowpatty and Juhu. Thousands of people walk, dance, and sing toward the beaches, where elaborately adorned idols as small as 6 inches and as large as three stories are dunked into the water.

which is also vegetarian but cooked without any root vegetables—and that includes onions and garlic. You'll find authentic South Indian vegetarian food— dosas (fried, crepelike pancakes), idlis (steamed rice cakes), wadas (also spelled vadas; savory fried, and often flavored, lentil-flour doughnuts), and simple, light thalis (combination platters)—all over the city.

There are many multicuisine restaurants around the city—usually fairly cheap, tacky joints that make good kebabs, decent Indo-Chinese food, and terrible continental food. (One rule of thumb for smaller or unknown places is that the further you depart from the Indian palate, the more likely you are to be burned with an unsavory dish.)

People eat late in India. Lunch is generally around 1-ish, and dinner is anytime between 8:30 pm and midnight—if you're meeting local friends, expect to eat around 9:30 or 10 pm. If you plan on eating at 7, reservations probably aren't necessary, and if you want to eat at 6,

Playing cricket in one of Mumbai's public parks

call ahead, because the restaurant may not even be open for dinner yet. Locals generally dress for dinner. They aren't formal, but they are usually well turned out. Shorts and anything sloppy or grungy are only acceptable at cafés and dives.

It's worth noting, too, that if you're staying in South Mumbai, there's no need to head out to the suburbs to eat. Nearby Lower Parel (roughly 25 minutes from Colaba Causeway by taxi), may lack tourist attractions, but it still manages to pack in some of the more popular new eating and drinking hubs in the city.

The restaurant scene in Mumbai is always evolving. To keep an eye on the latest openings, as well as nightclub events, parties and food or drink festivals, check local papers.

HOTELS

In Mumbai, unlike elsewhere in India, even midrange hotels can be shockingly overpriced, and a hotel shortage means that good deals are few. Many hotels in that middle range aren't quite up to Western standards of cleanliness, despite their high prices, but location means everything in Mumbai, and tourists may have to sacrifice a bit on substance to get proximity to the city's best attractions. Even hotels with the highest of prices can be full because of year-round demand, so you're well advised to make reservations a few months in advance.

Chains like the Taj, Oberoi, Hyatt, Marriott, InterContinental, Hilton, and Sheraton have huge hotels, most of them deluxe; these cater to leisure and business travelers, and movie stars with money to burn. Whether you reserve with a hotel directly or through a travel agent, always ask for a discount. Note that tariffs quoted in this book and at hotels do not include 12% tax. Room rates at the luxury hotels fluctuate depending on occupancy, and they offer the rate of the day; the earlier you book, the better the rate you'll get. If you're paying cash, convert your currency beforehand—most hotels give poor exchange rates.

Most of Mumbai's hotels are collected around three locations: in South Mumbai, primarily in Colaba; near Juhu Beach in the suburbs (note that the beach has been cleaned up, but it's not clean enough for swimming—even though you might see some local boys going in); and farther north, near the domestic and international airports. If you're going to be sightseeing, and you have the money, stay in South Mumbai rather than the suburbs. If you're here on business, the airport may be your ideal location, and there are several luxury hotels in the vicinity.

Mumbai's cheaper hotels, usually in South Mumbai, can be decent but are still probably overpriced for what you get. During the monsoon season (mid-June through late September), these hotels are overrun by large groups of vacationers from various Arab nations who come to Mumbai to enjoy the cooler weather and rain, during which time noise levels can be very high—solo women travelers should probably stay elsewhere during this time unless they really aren't going to be bothered by the stares.

Hotel reviews have been shortened. For full information, visit Fodors.com.

What It Costs

	$	$$	$$$	$$$$
RESTAURANTS				
	under Rs. 500	Rs. 500–Rs. 1,000	Rs. 1,001–Rs. 1,400	over Rs. 1,400
HOTELS				
	under Rs. 6,000	Rs. 6,000–Rs. 9,000	Rs. 9,001–Rs. 13,000	over Rs. 13,000

NIGHTLIFE

No other city in India knows how to have a good time quite like Mumbai. Here you'll find everything from dingy "permit rooms" (basically cafeteria-style rooms with a liquor license) so dirty they make an American dive bar look like the Rainbow Room, and clubs so fancy they make the Rainbow Room look like a permit room. Whatever destination you choose, they all hold their own special charms. If you're in the mood for a cheap tipple, and you appreciate the character of a down and dirty dive bar, head to Gokul, behind the Taj Mahal Palace; it's the most tourist-friendly of Mumbai's permit rooms.

If you're more inclined to clubbing, Mumbai has lots to choose from—though club owners seem to have decided that the only option that works in this city are lounges with blaring music and tiny dance floors: be forewarned, though, that prices are steep, and you'll often pay New York prices, or more, for your drinks. Note, too, that many clubs and bars have "couples" policies, wherein a "stag" (lone man) is not permitted to enter without a woman. This might be a circuitous attempt to prevent brawls, pickup scenes, and prostitution—or just a club owner figuring that in a country where many more guys are allowed to stay out late than girls, a club full of dudes isn't going to attract much business. To avoid an unpleasant encounter at the door, check with your hotel staff to find out whether your destination club or bar will allow you to enter if you're a man traveling alone or in a group of men. Dress nicely and you'll probably get in; an advance call from your hotel concierge might also make your entry smoother.

Revelry peaks from Thursday to Sunday night, with an early-twenties-to-mid-thirties crowd. Pubs open daily at around 6 or 7 (except a few, which open in the afternoon) and close by 1:15 am or a little later, depending, honestly, on how much they've paid the local cops. Some places collect a cover charge at the door. As in any metropolis, the reign of a nightspot can be ephemeral. ■TIP→ **Ask a young hotel employee to tell you where the best clubs or bars are, as trends change quickly in Mumbai.**

One area where the suburbs have it over the city is nightlife, and the after-dark scene in the wealthy enclaves of Juhu and Bandra thrive on suburbia's young nouveau riche as well as city folk willing to travel for a good night out.

PERFORMING ARTS

Nowadays, Mumbai's arts scene has gone as online as any other major city's, so your first stop should probably be the Internet. *You'll find the websites for all of the major playhouses below; check schedules accordingly.* For movies, go to ⊕ *www.bookmyshow.com* to book tickets at most Mumbai theaters. If you're old-school, you can check out the fortnightly culture calendar "Programme of Dance, Music and Drama," available free at the Government of India Tourist Office. The daily *Times of India* usually lists each day's films, concerts, and other events; on Friday the paper publishes a guide to city events called *What's Hot* that can be purchased at any newsstand. The afternoon paper *Midday* publishes highlights of the coming week's events in its pullout *What To Do? Where To Go?*, also available online (⊕ *www.mid-day.com*). Program information and details usually appear on the Maharashtra Tourism Development Corporation's (MTDC) city-guide programs, shown regularly on hotel in-house TV stations.

Performance tickets in Mumbai are usually quite inexpensive (from free to Rs. 500) and can be purchased from box offices or online.

Mumbai, aka "Bollywood," is the center of the Indian film industry—the largest film producer in the world. A typical epic Indian musical in the movie theater is three or so hours of song, tears, gun battles, and around-the-trees love dances; in other words, quite a spectacle. Most of these movies are in Hindi, but the plots are pretty basic, so you'll probably get the gist. Seeing a Bollywood movie in an Indian theater is an experience unlike what most Americans are used to: it's a very social scene, often with whole families or groups of friends talking and laughing and eating; indeed, the movie itself is often not the primary entertainment. It's definitely a unique experience, but not for everyone. And even if you go, don't feel obliged to stay to the end; the intermissions can be a convenient exit cue. The Inox is a convenient place to go, but there are other Bollywood theaters farther afield; check local entertainment listings.

Once, Mumbai was thick with elegant single-screen cinemas (popularly known as "talkies" from the time silent cinema gave way to talking films), some harking all the way back to the 19th century. Today though, the arc lights have dimmed on these decrepit structures, with younger audiences succumbing to the lure of fancier multiplex theaters. Still, it may be worth your while to catch a gander of some of the cinemas—charming art deco Liberty, with giant piano keys etched into its facade; glorious colonial-era Alfred Talkies, now a tired, seedy husk of its former self (best viewed from the outside); and plush Metro Adlabs, which has attempted to hold on to a whisper of its past, with glittering chandeliers and a sweeping wooden staircase.

For English-language movies, there are several options around Mumbai.

SHOPPING

Mumbai is a shopper's town: in the same day, you can sift through alleys full of antiques in Chor Bazaar, haggle for trinkets on the Colaba Causeway, and stop in at the Brioni showroom at the Taj

Mahal Palace Hotel for marked-up luxury goods (though we'd recommend you get your Chanel and Armani back home to avoid the huge import taxes).

The Causeway, Kemps Corner, and Breach Candy are all trendy shopping areas in South Mumbai; the latter two are chic and pricey. A walk down Colaba Causeway will probably take you past most of the things you want to buy in India—shoes, clothes, cheap knick-knacks, cheap cotton clothing, jewelry, and wraps—displayed at stalls lining the road; more expensive items are found in the air-conditioned shops and boutiques behind the stalls on this same road.

The arcades in top hotels offer a little bit of everything for a lot more money than anywhere else, but the merchandise is beautiful and the pace unhurried (and it's climate-controlled). If you're looking for the kind of stuff you can't get anywhere else in the world, and a more vibrant experience, throw yourself into the middle of one of Mumbai's famous bazaars. After all, odds are you didn't come to India to visit the Louis Vuitton boutique.

The city's department stores are good for one-stop shopping, and Fabindia and the Bombay Store both have a large number of branches in the city.

Throughout Mumbai many smaller shops are closed on Sunday (some of the suburbs are closed a different day: in Worli, up to Bandra, they're closed Monday; and in Bandra, up to the suburbs, they're closed Thursday, although many areas are also in the process of switching to Sunday). Malls, however, are open every day. They are especially crowded on the weekend (mall-gazing—that is, large-scale window-shopping—has become a new Mumbai leisure activity).

Once you've exhausted Mumbai proper, you can venture out to the suburbs, where prices tend to be lower and the malls more numerous. Linking Road in Bandra is a trendy place to shop, and Juhu's main strip, Juhu Tara Road, is lined with cutting-edge new boutiques, shops, art galleries, and restaurants.

Some good and cheap Mumbai buys: silver jewelry, handicrafts, hand-loomed cotton and silk clothing and household items, eyeglasses, DVDs, CDs, and books.

ACTIVITIES

Mumbai city, lashed by heavy monsoons and bleached by a scorching summer sun, isn't quite built for outdoor activities. However, very keen outdoor enthusiasts should head to the Sanjay Gandhi National Park (⊕ sgnp.maharashtra.gov.in) that fringes the edge of the city, in faraway Borivali. This 103-square-km (64-square-mile) forested area is thick with flora and fauna, including the rhesus macaque, barking deer, leopards, crocodiles, cobras, civets, and hyenas. It's usually a good idea to join a trekking group or hire a guide (preferably from the Bombay Natural History Society) before the walk. Closer to South Mumbai is Sewri jetty, where amidst a copse of mangroves, you may spot squadrons of elegant, pink flamingos, especially if you visit during November and May. Again, the Bombay Natural History Society is your best bet for tours; it has the most passionate, erudite guides. The seas surrounding the city are apt to be polluted at the best of times, but that shouldn't stop you from renting out speedboats, luxury yachts, or sailboats. Keep in mind though that the waters are extremely choppy and dangerous in the monsoons (June to September), and boats are not encouraged to sail out at all.

VISITOR INFORMATION

Don't count on hotels to stock general tourist information. The Government of India Tourist Office, near the Churchgate train station, has useful material; it's open weekdays 8:30–6, Saturday and holidays 8:30–2. There's information on trains, and the office

7

Mumbai PLANNING

The Great Bombay Name Change

In the mid-1990s, Shiv Sena, the Hindu nationalist party in power in Bombay, decided to change the city's name to Mumbai, a name often used in local languages that derives from Mumba Devi, the patron Hindu goddess of the island's original residents, the Koli fishermen. Many residents still call their city Bombay, however. The renaming of the city was simply the grandest example of an epidemic that has swept the former Bombay in the last 20 or so years—Crawford Market became Mahatma Jyotiba Phule Market, Victoria Terminus became Chhatrapati Shivaji Terminus, Marine Drive became Netaji Subhash Chandra Bose Marg. And those are just the big ones; indeed, nearly every road and lane in Mumbai has more than one name. Not only that, but each intersection often has its own name, too, and each individual corner might also have its own moniker (they're often named by local government officials or rich locals for members of their families).

The fact is, though, that as a tourist—and even as a local—you don't need to know any of the new names: no one calls Marine Drive anything but Marine Drive, and no one calls the Causeway anything but the Causeway. Although you will get the odd "CST" for Victoria Terminus, no one uses the new full name, so don't worry about pronouncing it: VT will do just fine.

oversees knowledgeable, multilingual tour guides, available directly from the office or through the MTDC (Maharashtra Tourism Development Corporation), or just about any travel agency. Rates are approximately Rs. 500 per half day for groups of one to four, Rs. 700 for a full eight-hour day (your guide will have lunch when you do, and you should pay for his lunch). Additional fees of Rs. 350 apply for trips beyond 100 km (62 miles), and for those involving overnight stays the rates could be still higher. Multilingual guides charge Rs. 300 extra, in addition to the regular fee.

The MTDC is open daily 9–6. Both MTDC and the Government of India Tourist Office have 24-hour counters at the airports. The MTDC also has counters at Chhatrapati Shivaji Terminus (Victoria Terminus) and the Gateway of India (it's a booth where the boats to Elephanta Island dock). MTDC phone numbers are not that useful, as they are always busy—visit in person or check the website.

TOURIST OFFICES Government of India Tourist Office ⊠ *123 Maharishi Karve Rd., Churchgate* ☎ *22/2207–4333, 22/2207–4334, 22/2203–3144, 22/2203–3145 recorded tourist background on Goa, Mumbai, Ahmedabad, and Aurangabad* ⊕ *www.incredibleindia.org.* **Maharashtra Tourism Development Corporation** (*MTDC*) ⊠ *Madame Cama Rd., opposite L.I.C. Bldg., Nariman Point* ☎ *22/2284–5678* ⊕ *www.maharashtratourism.gov.in.*

TOURS

Reality Tours and Travel

In recent years tours of one of Asia's largest slums, Dharavi, have become something of a cottage industry in Mumbai, especially after the popularity of the 2008 movie *Slumdog Millionaire,* which was set here. While the idea may seem like voyeurism, many of the companies who conduct the tours do so on a not-for-profit basis, and have explicit no-camera-allowed policies. On such a tour you'll normally meet up with a guide at Churchgate or

Mahim Station, and take the train with a group of no more than six other tourists to Dharavi, which is near the Mahim neighborhood. Here you'll see the variety of cottage industries—from jewelry making to recycling to leather working to blacksmithing—that make up an estimated $600 million annual economy. You'll see poverty, but Dharavi is not the kind of place you saw in those early scenes in *Slumdog*. Rather, it has a vibrant, functioning community, with its own post office, schools, temples, mosques, churches, and police force. It is, on balance, an incredibly safe place (and you'll be with a local guide) full of people striving for a better life in Mumbai, willing to live in cramped confines and not knowing where their next meal will come from—or even if there will be a next meal. The best of the tour operators, Reality Tours and Travel, explicitly takes no tips, and makes no profit: they use the fees (Rs. 400 per person) to fund a community center and a kindergarten in the area. ✉ *Mumbai* ☎ *98208–22253* ⊕ *www. realitytoursandtravel.com*.

PLANNING YOUR TIME

Spending two days in Mumbai is like sprinting a marathon. Even though the city may lack much in the way of monuments and historic sites, this is a place you have to experience to understand (and enjoy). Try cramming all of Mumbai into two days and you're likely to end up hating it, but give it a little longer and the abstract cacophony will start to make more sense and, ultimately, grow on you. Otherwise, the only impression you're likely to get is: hot, crowded, smelly, filthy. Give it a bit of time, and you'll begin to appreciate the madness, as opposed to being overwhelmed by it. We suggest spending a week in Maharashtra, with four–five days in Mumbai and a weekend trip to the Ellora and Ajanta caves, 370 km (229 miles) northeast of the city. You can take a round-trip overnight train to Aurangabad, the best place to base yourself for trips to the caves; alternatively, one-hour flights are readily available. If you have an extra day or two, head up to the gorgeously green Matheran (110 km [66 miles] away) or one of the other quaint hill stations nearby, where Maharashtra's landscape fuses stark, semiarid mountains and rock formations with lush, green countryside.

In Mumbai it's important to catch the flavor of the colonial city: this means walking around the Gateway of India, the Prince of Wales Museum, and Victoria Terminus. To take in a bazaar, head to Crawford Market or stroll down Colaba Causeway to do some bargain hunting. Lunching at a seafood restaurant in Fort and snacking at Chowpatty Beach off Marine Drive are both great experiences, as is people-watching with a beer at the Leopold Café in Colaba. A trip to the western suburbs—Bandra and Juhu, among others—will give you a good perspective on how Mumbai has grown, and where it's going next. A day trip to the ancient Elephanta Caves will show you where it came from.

In South Bombay—"Town" to the locals—indigenous heritage villages (*gaothans*), grand art deco buildings, and Victorian mansions, remnants of the British Raj, share space with towering high-rises, and long, rectangular parks, known as *maidans*. In the labyrinthine streets of Kala Ghoda, the sky-blue Knesseth Eliyahoo synagogue rubs shoulders with some of the city's hippest restaurants and cafés. Farther south from Kala Ghoda is Colaba, where the majestic Taj Mahal Palace Hotel holds court with the massive Gateway of India. On the western coast, the Queen's Necklace—as the lights along Marine Drive are affectionately known—stretch to tony Malabar Hill, where the Hanging Gardens provide some of the city's best non-skyscraper views. Farther north, the Haji Ali shrine, a popular pilgrimage spot for Muslims the world over, sits in the middle of the Arabian Sea like an ancient island tomb. Beyond that, the Bandra-Worli Sea Link, finally finished in 2009, connects the south to leafy Bandra, the king of the western suburbs. In between, and beyond, lie the very things that make Mumbai so confounding, and alluring, and so quintessentially Indian.

Colaba and Elephanta Island

Mumbai's main hot spot is full of bars, restaurants, and a long stretch of street stalls with everything from clothing to black-market DVDs to brassware and handicrafts set in front of name-brand stores from Nike, Puma, Lacoste, and many others. This part of South Mumbai is a bit of a one-stop shop for all of Mumbai. Beginning at Regal Circle, which is named for the 1930s art deco Regal Cinema, Colaba stretches southward, through winding lanes and bustling streets. You can stop by the Taj Mahal Palace Hotel for high tea and gaze out at the Gateway of India, standing sentinel over the sea, then wander up through cramped lanes filled with shops to the Colaba Causeway, South Mumbai's main drag. On the Causeway, you can haggle for knockoffs and bootlegs—start at one-third the asking price, at a maximum—or shop in the "official" stores if you're not in the bargaining mood, then stop in at Leopold Café or Café Mondegar for a beer, a snack, and some people-watching before heading deeper down into Colaba, where more stores, bargains, bars, and food await. Colaba is an easy place to end up spending an entire day just wandering, eating, drinking, and shopping with nothing particular in mind.

A 30-minute boat ride away from South Mumbai is Elephanta Island, where you can view caves dedicated to the Hindu destroyer deity, Lord Shiva. You can also be entertained by the resident monkeys.

⚠ It's not advisable to visit Elephanta during monsoon season.

 Sights

Elephanta Caves
ARCHAEOLOGICAL SITE | A quick 30-minute ferry ride from bustling South Mumbai, the UNESCO World Heritage site Elephanta Caves make an ideal half-day trip for anyone who wants a quick glimpse of India's ancient history. Once you arrive at the island, you climb a steep hill, on rough-hewn steps, past trinket sellers and beggars, to get to Shiva Cave; greenery abounds. The temple, carved out of the basalt hillside, is 130 square feet. Inside, each wall has elaborate, 16-foot-tall rock carvings of Lord Shiva, the destroyer, in his many forms, depicting famous events from the Hindu epics. The main sculptures are on the south wall, at the back.

The central recess has the most outstanding sculpture, the unusual Mahesamurti, the Great Lord Shiva—an 18-foot triple image. Its three faces represent three aspects of Shiva: the creator (on the right), the preserver (in the center), and the destroyer (on the left). Other sculptures near the doorways and on side panels show Shiva's usefulness. Shiva brought the Ganges River down to Earth, the story says, letting it trickle through his matted hair. He is also depicted as Yogisvara, lord of yogis, seated on a lotus, and as Nataraja, the many-armed cosmic dancer. The beauty of this stonework lies in the grace, balance, and sense of peace conveyed in spite of the subject's multiple actions. It's all very peaceful and serene. Then you step back outside and see the monkeys.

They are everywhere: climbing trees, hooting and hollering, looking for opportunities to get any human food you might be carrying—so we suggest you don't bring any with you (have lunch before you leave Mumbai, or wait until you get

The Elephanta Caves are filled with 1,500 year-old rock carvings depicting Shiva.

back). There are so many monkeys, and they are so comfortable around humans, that they almost distract you from the 1,500-year-old rock carvings. Almost.

It's unclear who did the carvings on Elephanta, but it is known that the island was originally called Gharapuri; the Portuguese renamed it after a large stone elephant was found near where their boat landed (the figure collapsed in 1814 and is now in mainland Mumbai's Victoria Gardens, also known as Jijamata Udyaan). Shortly before the temples were created, Mumbai experienced the golden age of the late Guptas, under whom artists had relatively free range. The Sanskrit language had been finely polished, and under the court's liberal patronage writers had helped incite a revival of Hindu beliefs. It was Shiva-ism—the worship of Shiva—that inspired the building of these temples.

The MTDC leads a tour, every day at 2 pm (book when you arrive), that is good but not essential, and runs a tiny restaurant on the island for refreshments and beer. In February a dance festival is held here.

Getting here: ferries for the one-hour trip (each way) depart daily every half hour from 9 to 2 from the Gateway of India and from noon to 5 from Elephanta Island every half hour, unless the sea is very choppy—don't visit Elephanta during monsoon season. You pay for your ferry and cave tickets separately. ⊠ *Ghara-puri, Elephanta Island* ⊕ *elephanta. co.in* ✉ *Ferry: up to Rs. 200 round-trip depending on boat/seat type; entrance fee: from Rs. 5 at start of climb; caves ticket: up to Rs. 350* ☉ *Closed Mon.*

Gateway of India

BUILDING | Mumbai's signature landmark, this elegant 85-foot stone archway was hastily erected as a symbol of welcome to Queen Mary and King George V of England when they paid a visit to India in 1911. In the years following, artisans added decorative carvings and lovely *jharoka*-work (window carvings), finishing in 1923. Less than 25 years later, the last British troops departed from India

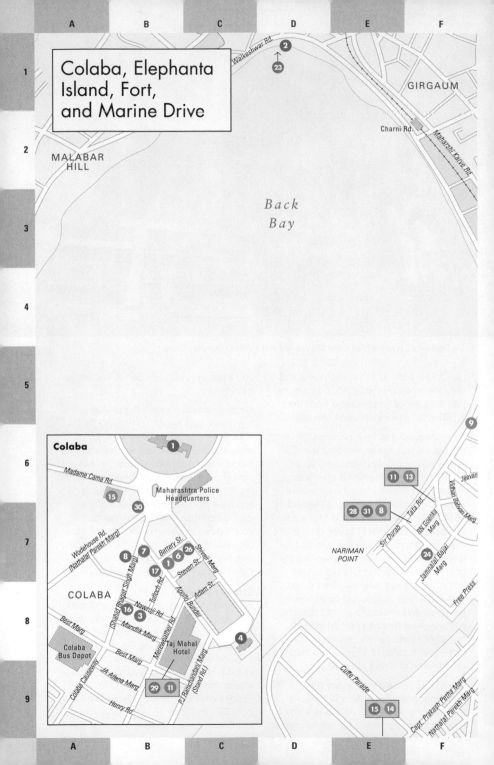

7

Sights ▼
1 Chhatrapati Shivaji Maharaj Vastu Sangrahalaya (formerly the Prince of Wales Museum)........ B6
2 Chowpatty Beach.................. D1
3 Elephanta Caves................... J7
4 Gateway of India................... C8
5 Jehangir Art Gallery............... H7
6 Knesseth Eliyahoo Synagogue......H4
7 Marine Drive G4
8 National Gallery of Modern Art....................... H6

Restaurants ▼
1 Ankur–The Coastal Bistro H6
2 Apoorva............................. I5
3 Bade Miya.......................... B8
4 Britannia & Co...................... J5
5 Burma Burma H6
6 Café Churchill H8
7 Café Mondegar B7
8 Delhi Darbar....................... B7
9 Gaylord............................. G5
10 Hotel Deluxe....................... I5
11 India Jones F6
12 K Rustom........................... G5
13 Kala Ghoda Café................... H6
14 Kebab Korner G5
15 Konkan Café E9
16 Leopold Café & Bar............... B8
17 Ling's Pavilion B7
18 Mahesh Lunch Home I5
19 Natural............................. G5
20 The Nutcracker H6
21 The Pantry......................... H6
22 Shree Thaker Bhojnalaya........ H2
23 Soam D1
24 Suzette Creperie & Cafe F7
25 Swati Snacks....................... G7
26 The Table B7
27 Trishna H6
28 Vetro............................... F7
29 Wasabi by Morimoto.............. B8
30 Woodside Inn B7
31 Ziya F7

Hotels ▼
1 Abode B7
2 Astoria G6
3 Bentley's........................... H8
4 Fariyas H9
5 Godwin............................. H8
6 Gordon House...................... B7
7 InterContinental Marine Drive ... G5
8 The Oberoi......................... F7
9 Sea Green F6
10 Sea Palace Hotel H8
11 Taj Mahal Palace B8
12 Taj Wellington Mews.............. G8
13 The Trident......................... F6
14 Vivanta by Taj–President E9
15 YWCA International Center....... B6

KEY
- Sights
- Restaurants
- Hotels
- Tourist information

through the same ceremonial arch. The monument serves as a launching point for boats going to Elephanta Island, and this is also where luxury liners like the *Queen Elizabeth 2* dock on their cruises. The majestic Taj Mahal Palace Hotel, built before the Gateway of India, in 1903, now stands just behind it. ⊠ *End of C. Shivaji Maharaj Marg, Colaba.*

🍴 Restaurants

Bade Miya

$ | **INDIAN** | Sitting behind the Taj Mahal Hotel for generations, Mumbai's most famous kebab joint is always packed, always greasy, and always tasty. Even though there's a strictly vegetarian section of the menu, you'll probably want to check out mutton *seekh* roll (succulent minced mutton kebab folded into a roti), the chicken *baida* roti (a sort of Indian quesadilla, with chicken and egg), or the more adventurous *bheja* fry (fried goat brains in a spicy gravy). **Known for:** quick, drive-through-style service; open till 1 am; always crowded so you know the food is fresh. $ *Average main: Rs. 200* ⊠ *Tullock Rd., behind Taj Mahal Hotel, Colaba* 🕾 *22/2202–1447* ▭ *No credit cards.*

Burma Burma

$$ | **BURMESE** | A trip to India can represent an opportunity for travelers to test the ropes at living vegetarian for a while (veg options constitute literally half of every menu here), but few major restaurants in the city have mastered all the possibilities of vegetarian like the charming Burma Burma. Ankit Gupta, the owner, is half Burmese, and demands authenticity, so short of a separate flight to Myanmar itself, you're not likely to find dishes as skillful as these in many other places; the restaurant also serves excellent teas (but no alcohol). **Known for:** nanji kaukswe (delicious noodles served in dry coconut powder); nanpeebya (Burmese bread served with creamy white peas);

shway aye, chilled coconut milk served in a glass with sweet bread. $ *Average main: Rs. 800* ⊠ *Kothari House, off M.G. Rd., Kala Ghoda* 🕾 *22/4003–6600.*

Café Churchill

$ | **BRITISH** | Dingy—but not dirty—Churchill specializes in British-style comfort food (e.g., starchy and simple roast beef and gravy with steamed veggies and mashed potatoes), and its red-and-white vinyl interior fits the food. The desserts are some of the best Mumbai has to offer—at any given time you'll find five kinds of chocolate cake (brownie, truffle, you name it), and five kinds of cheesecake in the dessert case. $ *Average main: Rs. 300* ⊠ *103–B Colaba Causeway, opposite Cusrow Baug, Colaba* 🕾 *22/2204–2604.*

Café Mondegar

$ | **CAFÉ** | Always packed, Mondy is a great place to grab an ice-cold Kingfisher draft and watch the crowds roll in—though unlike nearby Leo's, Mondy's doesn't have a full liquor license. Avoid the characterless air-conditioned room and instead post up at one of the cramped tables in the main space, where the jukebox plays at full blast and the walls are covered with cartoon murals of Mumbai life. **Known for:** greasy, spicy Chinese food that pairs excellently with icy beer; an iconic Mumbai restaurant; great location in the heart of touristy Colaba. $ *Average main: Rs. 300* ⊠ *Colaba Causeway, Colaba* 🕾 *22/2202–0591.*

Delhi Darbar

$ | **INDIAN** | **FAMILY** | Classic no-frills Mughlai food draws vacationing Arabs to this eatery; it has outlets throughout the United Arab Emirates, though this one's the flagship. It's loud and bustling—not the place for a romantic dinner—but the real reason to come is the top-quality nonvegetarian food, especially the meat, kebabs, and rice dishes. **Known for:** biryanis; butter chicken (or the paneer version for vegetarians); excellent

The Gateway of India, with the Taj Mahal Palace hotel in the background

location for Colaba shoppers. [$] *Average main: Rs. 300* ✉ *Colaba Causeway, near Regal Cinema, Colaba* ☎ *22/2202–5656* ⊕ *www.delhi-darbar.com.*

★ Kala Ghoda Café

$ | CAFÉ | Among the most beloved lunch spots for South Mumbai's workaday crowd, this quaint little café is the ideal spot to grab a soy latte and a quick bite while resting your feet. The fresh juices and salads are cheap but clean and safe for foreigners, the Wi-Fi is free, and the interior, while a bit cramped, is bright and pleasant—and best of all, the sandwiches, like the KGC Special (arugula, vegetarian mayo, and Padano cheese on grilled flat bread), are light but extremely tasty when snuggled up to a hot (or more preferably iced) cup of joe. **Known for:** great coffee; convivial atmosphere that encourages loitering (bring your laptop and get some work done); its location in trendy Kala Ghoda. [$] *Average main: Rs. 400* ✉ *10 Ropewalk La., Kala Ghoda, Fort* ⊕ *Turn into lane facing powder-blue synagogue* ☎ *22/2263–3866* ⊕ *www.kgcafe.in.*

Konkan Café

$$$ | SEAFOOD | Styled as an haute version of a typical Mangalorean home—all red clay and bright green—Konkan is in the Vivanta by Taj hotel (still "Taj President" to taxi drivers). It does all the chow your average home might serve, but it's more refined, with cleaner flavors and elegant presentation (food is served on copper thali plates lined with banana leaves), plus it has the added advantage of being one of the few coastal restaurants to offer a great, if expensive, bottle of wine. **Known for:** superb Taj-style service; prawn/fish gassi; mutton coconut fry. [$] *Average main: Rs. 1050* ✉ *Vivanta by Taj hotel, 90 Cuffe Parade, Colaba* ☎ *22/6665–0808* ⊕ *www.vivantabytaj.com/president-mumbai/dining/konkan-cafe-restaurant.html.*

Leopold Café & Bar

$ | CAFÉ | When it defiantly reopened just four days after the first shots of

The Great Irani Cafés 🍴

Mumbai has a special breed of teahouse that's fast disappearing. Called "Irani cafes" in local parlance, these corner shops were begun by the later waves of Zoroastrians, called the Iranis, who migrated to India in the 19th century from Persia to escape religious persecution. (Those who were part of much earlier waves are referred to as Parsis.) A community of about 75,000 remains in the country today, the majority in Mumbai.

Irani cafés probably arose out of the Iranis' need for a place to gather and exchange news. Simply furnished with solid bentwood chairs and cloaked in the appearance of yesteryear, they remain places where customers can tarry over endless cups of sweet tea for just a few rupees. Visiting these century-old cafés is a chance to glimpse a culture that has all but vanished. The clientele is usually very ordinary Mumbai *wallahs* (dwellers), more often than not old-timers who have been having chai and buns for the last 40 years in the same spot. Depending on which Irani cafe you visit, the menu will offer anything from *bun-maska* (a bun with butter), and typical Parsi cutlets, patties, mince and egg dishes, to fruitcakes and confectionery. Amid the ancient mirrors, upright chairs, marble tables, elaborate balconies, and portraits of the Prophet Zarathustra is sometimes a sign acquainting you with the dos and don'ts of the particular establishment. Beer is sometimes served. But credit cards? Goodness, no. Early or midmorning is a good time to visit. We recommend stopping by at Kyani's, the oldest surviving Irani cafe (1904); Ideal Corner (for its *dhansak*, a Parsi meat, lentil, and vegetable stew); Cafe Military for its spicy mince or brain masala, eaten with loaves of soft, white bread; Yazdani Bakery for its ginger biscuits and apple pie; and B Merwan & Co for its *mawa* cakes (small teacakes made with evaporated milk solids, and shot through with cardamom).

Traditional Irani cafés are dying out, almost overnight being converted to fast-food joints or else turning upscale and adding Chinese food or spaghetti to their menus. Several can be found in the Fort area, but some are as far afield as Mahim and Bandra.

November 2008 terrorist attacks were fired and 10 people were killed, the crowds were so big the police had to shut the place down all over again (the ownership has preserved bullet holes from the attack on its upstairs windows for people to see). Order a bottle of ice-cold Kingfisher beer to wash down the hearty, typical bar food—chicken tikka, french fries, that kind of thing, or go with the Chinese food that is actually the better bet. **Known for:** chilli chicken; chicken fried rice; exceedingly lively atmosphere. [$] *Average main: Rs. 450* ✉ *Colaba Causeway, Colaba* ☎ *22/2282–8185, 22/2202–0131* 🌐 *www.leopoldcafe.com.*

★ Ling's Pavilion

$$ | CANTONESE | Veering off from Colaba's arterial thoroughfare, Colaba Causeway, is Ling's Pavilion, a venerable Cantonese-style restaurant and Mumbai icon run by Baba Ling and Nini Ling, its third-generation owners. The decor is a sort of gracious 1970s time warp—pagoda-style roof and a likeness of a Chinese terra-cotta warrior at the entrance. **Known for:** soup dumplings, a riff on traditional xiao long baos; seafood chimney soup; its secret menu for Chinese diners (ask for it, as it is offered only when requested). $\boxed{\text{\$}}$ *Average main: Rs. 800* ✉ *Behind Regal Cinema, Mahakavi Bhushan Marg, 19/21, Colaba* ✛ *In lane that veers off from Cafe Mondegar* ☎ *22/2285–0023.*

The Nutcracker

\$\$\$\$ | **CAFÉ** | A short walk from the blue Kenesseth Eliyahoo synagogue is The Nutcracker, a tiny, pretty vegetarian restaurant with pink and white bougainvillea tumbling down its wooden windows, and mosaic tiled floors. Go for breakfast (or lunch, or dinner), and order any of the moreish egg concoctions. **Known for:** Emmenthal and truffle-oil scrambled eggs; salli eggs (deep-fried potato matchsticks blanketed by eggs; a quintessential Parsi dish); black-bean quesadilla. $\boxed{\text{\$}}$ *Average main: Rs. 5500* ✉ *Modern House, VB Gandhi Marg, Kala Ghoda* ☎ *22/2284–2430.*

★ **Swati Snacks**

\$ | **INDIAN** | A kilometer or two from Colaba Causeway lies Swati Snacks, a Mumbai stalwart and a great place to try the city's street food in clean, air-conditioned, somewhat canteen-style environs. Most popular are its *chaat* dishes (a smorgasbord of crunchy, creamy, spicy, sweet dishes), but you can venture further afield by ordering homely Gujarati fare from under the traditional specialities section of the menu. **Known for:** pao bhaji (spiced mashed vegetables with a dollop of butter, eaten with loaves of soft white bread); mung dal chilla (pulse-based pancakes); bhelpuri/sev puri/dahi batata puri (all delicious variations of chaat). $\boxed{\text{\$}}$ *Average main: Rs. 200* ✉ *Dalamal Tower, Free Press Journal Marg, Nariman Point* ☎ *22/6666–6880.*

★ **The Table**

\$\$ | **MODERN AMERICAN** | One of Mumbai's best restaurants, The Table was launched by a pair of Indian restaurateurs and a young American chef from San Francisco;

suitably enough, the food is American fare but is inflected with flavors from around the world. The lofted upper floor is perfect for romantic dinners; below is a more lively and sociable setting, with a large, eponymous, communal table extending from the bar. **Known for:** fresh, organic ingredients; boneless chicken wings; homemade breads. $\boxed{\text{\$}}$ *Average main: Rs. 750* ✉ *Kalapesi Trust Bldg., Chhatrapati Shivaji Maharaj Marg, Apollo Bunder, Colaba* ☎ *22/2282–5000* ⊕ *www. thetable.in.*

Wasabi by Morimoto

\$\$\$\$ | **JAPANESE** | On the second floor of the Taj Mahal Palace hotel and styled after an upscale but fairly authentic Japanese sushi joint, the wildly expensive Wasabi offers great service, a nice view toward the Gateway of India, and—we cannot emphasize this enough—great sushi. If you've got the cash, try one of the *omakase* menus (6 to 12 courses), which will take you through the best dishes, from whitefish carpaccio to rock-shrimp tempura to salmon nigiri, depending on what's freshest at the moment. $\boxed{\text{\$}}$ *Average main: Rs. 2000* ✉ *Taj Mahal Palace & Tower, Colaba* ☎ *22/6665–3366* ⊕ *www.tajhotels.com.*

★ **Woodside Inn**

\$\$ | **BRITISH** | The only real bar in town (in the American sense, at least) is modeled on an English pub, plays decent music (though sometimes too loud), has great snack food, and free Wi-Fi (that can sometimes be spotty), and some of the best-priced alcohol in town. Try the soy burgers, the pizzas—the four cheese is excellent—and the margarita's no slouch—or Franco's meatballs (a lamb and pork mix in a tangy tomato sauce). **Known for:** location, location, location—right at the head of Colaba Causeway; variety of local beers on tap; unusual burgers offered during Burger Festival. $\boxed{\text{\$}}$ *Average main: Rs. 550* ✉ *Indian Mercantile Mansion, Wodehouse Rd.,*

7

Mumbai COLABA AND ELEPHANTA ISLAND

Villages in Mumbai

Mumbai is a palimpsest of cultures: the city has been checkered with the footprints of the indigenous Koli fishing community, the British, the Portuguese, and a whole swath of communities in between. Some of these have found expression in quaint little heritage precincts that are scattered all over the city. Although most residents have succumbed to the pressure of avaricious builders, looking to grasp prime real estate, some spots remain: Khotachiwadi, a small, Portuguese-Goan-style hamlet in Girgaon; Mazgaon's idyllic Matharpacady, a handful of bungalows owned by Maharashtrians, East Indian Catholics, and Bohri Muslims; Worli Koliwada, an 800-year-old fishing village; and the Catholic hamlets of Ranwar and Chuim, in Bandra.

Regal Circle, Colaba ✥ Next to Sahakari Bhandar ☎ 22/2287–5752.

Hotels

★ Abode

$ | **B&B/INN** | Ensconced on the first floor of Colaba's Lansdowne House is a 100-year-old home made over into a hipster-chic boutique hotel with vintage furniture, chrome fans, and old-fashioned tiled flooring. **Pros:** an extra safety measure for women with women-run taxi service (a rarity); no-plastic policy; preloaded mobile phones for guests. **Cons:** small rooms with low ceilings; very small hotel (so book well in advance); no proper restaurant (although the food served is delicious). [$] *Rooms from: Rs. 5000* ✉ *Lansdowne House, MB Marg, Colaba* ✥ *Behind Regal Cinema* ☎ *80802–34066 mobile number* 🌐 *www.abodeboutiquehotels.com* 🛏 *20 rooms* 🍴 *Free Breakfast.*

Bentley's

$ | **HOTEL** | The best deal in Colaba—a clean, quaint, simple tourist joint in a prime South Mumbai location—is the kind of place young expats send visiting friends to stay at if they don't have room to host them themselves. **Pros:** cheap and clean; friendly, helpful owner; great location. **Cons:** can be a little musty; very basic rooms; no restaurant. [$] *Rooms from: Rs. 2000* ✉ *17 Oliver St., Colaba* ☎ *22/2284–1474* 🌐 *www.bentleyshotel.com* 🛏 *55 rooms* 🍴 *No meals.*

Fariyas

$$$ | **HOTEL** | Just a few minutes on foot from the Gateway of India, the Fariyas is a solid midrange hotel, well located in Colaba. **Pros:** well located; good views; in-house restaurants. **Cons:** smallish rooms; surprisingly expensive (though cheaper rates are often available online); decor is a bit fusty and tired. [$] *Rooms from: Rs. 10000* ✉ *25 Devshankar V, Vyas Marg, off Arthur Bunder Rd., Colaba* ☎ *22/6141–6141* 🌐 *www.fariyas.com* 🛏 *93 rooms* 🍴 *Free Breakfast.*

Godwin

$ | **HOTEL** | A great location at a decent price is the main selling point of this nine-story, low-frills hotel, but room standards (and views) vary, so opt for one of the 10 renovated deluxe rooms, with central air-conditioning and in-room amenities like coffeemakers. **Pros:** cheap (but not that cheap); well located; deluxe rooms have coffeemakers and a/c. **Cons:** shabby rooms; low-frills; room standards (and views) vary. [$] *Rooms from: Rs. 5500* ✉ *41 Garden Rd., off*

Colaba Causeway, near Electric House, Colaba ☎ *22/2287–2050, 22/2284–1226, 22/2287–1592* 🛏 *70 rooms* 🍴 *Free Breakfast.*

Gordon House

$$ | **HOTEL** | It's a unique stay at the well-located Gordon House, where the quirkily themed rooms, ranging from sunshine-yellow Mediterranean to minimalist Scandinavian, are a total departure from other, more somber, rooms offered by most hotels in the city. **Pros:** not your usual run-of-the-mill hotel; superb location; relatively pocket-friendly rates. **Cons:** the use of the gym is charged extra; rooms near the bar are extremely noisy; no pool or business facilities. [$] *Rooms from: Rs. 6500* ✉ *Battery St. 5, Colaba* ☎ *22/6124–5800* 🌐 *www.ghhotel.com* 🛏 *28 rooms.*

Sea Palace Hotel

$ | **HOTEL** | The location of this midrange hotel (with bargain prices given that it's Mumbai) is enough to make it a good choice—it's right on the waterfront near the Gateway of India (though the rooms themselves don't make great use of the view—they face the opposite direction, for the most part). **Pros:** attentive staff; cheap; great location. **Cons:** not well maintained; extremely basic breakfast; rooms are fairly small. [$] *Rooms from: Rs. 5200* ✉ *26 P.J. Ramachandani Marg, Colaba* ☎ *22/6112–8000* 🛏 *53 rooms* 🍴 *Free Breakfast.*

★ Taj Mahal Palace

$$$$ | **HOTEL** | Foreigners and wealthy Indians choose the Taj over other fancy hotels in town because it's a beautiful and regal landmark—worth visiting even if you don't stay here—with views past the Gateway of India to the Arabian Sea. The first hotel in what is now an international luxury chain, this Indo-Saracenic extravaganza was opened to the public in 1903. **Pros:** it's an icon; excellent location; city's best views. **Cons:** expensive; not particularly pet-friendly; the free room Wi-Fi is limited by usage and device. [$] *Rooms from: Rs. 17000* ✉ *Apollo Bunder Mumbai, Colaba* ☎ *22/6665–3366* 🌐 *www.tajhotels.com* 🛏 *610 rooms* 🍴 *Free Breakfast.*

Taj Wellington Mews

$$$$ | **HOTEL** | The well-placed Taj Wellington Mews's well-outfitted, elegant (but unremarkable) serviced apartments have all the amenities required for long-stay (and short-stay) guests. **Pros:** in-house deli and minimart; pet friendly; lots of business facilities. **Cons:** expensive; the deli is rather limited for long-stay guests; it doesn't have the opulence of its sister property, the Taj Mahal Palace & Towers. [$] *Rooms from: Rs. 16000* ✉ *Nathalal Parikh Marg, Apollo Bunder 33, Colaba* ☎ *22/6656–9494* 🌐 *www.tajhotels.com* 🛏 *80 rooms.*

Vivanta by Taj–President

$$ | **HOTEL** | Favored by business travelers, this hotel in the heart of charming Cuffe Parade also offers some great views, comfortable rooms, a choice of restaurants, and a hip bar. **Pros:** great in-house restaurants; its bar, Wink, is happening (though expensive); set in a quiet, nontouristy neighborhood. **Cons:** small rooms; a little far from the tourist heart of Colaba; free Wi-Fi is limited by device and usage. [$] *Rooms from: Rs. 9000* ✉ *90 Cuffe Parade, Colaba* ☎ *22/6665–0808* 🌐 *www.tajhotels.com* 🛏 *212 rooms* 🍴 *Free Breakfast.*

YWCA International Center

$ | **HOTEL** | The Y is about the cheapest you can go and still have decent, clean, and safe room. **Pros:** great for backpackers and those looking for very cheap accommodations; great location; good value for the price. **Cons:** institutional air; drab rooms; very basic amenities. [$] *Rooms from: Rs. 3250* ✉ *18 Madame Cama Rd., near Regal Cinema, Colaba* ☎ *22/2202–5053* 🌐 *www.ywcaic.info* 🛏 *31 rooms* 🍴 *Free Breakfast.*

Nightlife

Gokul

BARS/PUBS | The safest destination to test out one of Mumbai's infamous permit rooms offers a no-frills, dingy atmosphere—this is the kind of place you want to hit up for supercheap drinks (we're talking nearly retail prices per bottle, which you can order to your table) before you head to the club, or for a late-night drink postclubbing, if the owners have paid the cops enough to stay open past bar time that night. ⊠ *10 Tulloch Rd., behind Taj Mahal Palace hotel and next to Bade Miya, Colaba* ☎ *986/724–4668, 22/2284–8206.*

Koyla

BARS/PUBS | Koyla is a rooftop hangout with hookahs, Arabian music, a good breeze, and tasty barbecue bites. No alcohol is served. ⊠ *Gulf Hotel, Arthur Bunder Rd., near Radio Club, Colaba* ☎ *22/6636–9999.*

Social

GATHERING PLACES | This two-headed beast—a collaborative (although noisy) workspace by day that transforms into a buzzing gastropub by night—has pop and EDM streams from the speakers at full volume (so don't visit if you want a peaceful conversation). ⊠ *BK Boman Behram Marg, 24, ground fl., Apollo Bunder* ✛ *Behind Taj Mahal Hotel, opposite Starbucks* ☎ *22/2282–8484* ⊕ *www.socialoffline.in.*

Wink

BARS/PUBS | One of the more popular bars in South Mumbai, Wink is on the spendy side, as is common with bars in high-end hotels. The main draw is its chill house music. ⊠ *Vivanta by Taj–President Mumbai, 90 Cuffe Parade, Colaba* ☎ *22/6665–0975.*

 Performing Arts

Regal Cinema

FILM | One of the last in a dying breed of South Mumbai's gorgeous art deco theaters, Regal is a tourist treasure in its own right, and well worth the price of admission, regardless of the quality of the film itself. Here, flowing curtains still draw open at the start of a film and intermissions bubble over with gossip about the Hollywood and Bollywood stars on screen, harking back to a charming, almost forgotten time in India's pop culture landscape. ⊠ *Shaheed Bhagat Singh Rd., opposite Prince of Wales Museum, Colaba* ☎ *22/2202–1017.*

Sterling Cinema

FILM | Current English-language (and Bollywood) films are shown here. ⊠ *Tata Palace, Murzban Rd., off D. Naoroji Rd., near Victoria Terminus, Fort* ☎ *22/2207–5187, 22/6631–6677, 22/6622–0017* ⊕ *www.sterlingcineplex.in.*

🛍 Shopping

CLOTHING AND ACCESSORIES
Indian Textiles Company

CLOTHING | In the Taj Mahal hotel, this store sells quality silks, as does the Burlington store here. Both stores are convenient if you're staying here or nearby and need something quickly, but they are highly touristy and overpriced. Try something farther afield if you want to shop like a local. ⊠ *Taj Mahal Palace & Tower, Apollo Bunder, Colaba* ☎ *22/2202–8783.*

Khubsons Narisons

CLOTHING | Fine cotton and silk can be made into excellent shirts, trousers, or women's outfits in one day if need be. The store also sells ready-made women's clothing. There are two shops named Khubsons, back to back; make sure you have the right one (the one closer to Regal Cinema). ⊠ *49 Colaba Causeway,* opposite Colaba police station, Colaba ☎ 22/2202–0614.

★ Nappa Dori

SHOES/LUGGAGE/LEATHER GOODS | If you're scouring the city for tasteful, minimalist handmade leather bags and accessories, Nappa Dori is the place for you. The brand's origins were humble (it was birthed in a tiny space in Delhi's Hauz Khas village), but now its clientele includes Kiehl, Royce Chocolate, Qatar Airways (Nappa supplies pouches for its first- and business-class passengers), and celebrities such as Mira Nair, Eva Longoria, and Naomi Watts. ✉ *Sunny House, Mereweather Rd., 2, Colaba* ✛ *Behind Taj Mahal hotel* ☎ *22/2204–2162* ⊕ *www.nappadori.com.*

HANDICRAFTS AND HOME FURNISHINGS

Atmosphere

HOUSEHOLD ITEMS/FURNITURE | Exotic home furnishings and fabrics for the home are sold by the meter here. There's lots of expensive silk, and they'll organize tailoring for you. ✉ *Vaswani House, 7 Best Marg, Colaba* ☎ *22/2283–1877, 22/2283–1936* ⊕ *www.atmospheredirect.com.*

Central Cottage Industries Emporium

CRAFTS | The Mumbai branch of this government-owned chain is a decent place to buy souvenirs—though you won't be doing any bargaining, as all prices are fixed (and likely more than you'll pay elsewhere). It's therefore a good way to establish an upper bound for prices before you do any haggling in other places. It's packed with textiles, carvings, and myriad other traditional Indian handicrafts from all over the country, and there's a small but imaginative assortment of Indian costumes for kids, and traditional Indian toys. Mirror-work elephants, Indian dolls, wood and cane doll furniture, tiny brass tea sets, stuffed leather animals, and puppets can all be found on the second floor, as can kurtas and long skirt ensembles in cotton and silk. ✉ *Narang*

House, 34 Shivaji Marg, 1 block north of Taj Mahal hotel, Colaba ☎ *22/2202–6564, 22/2202–7537* ⊕ *www.thecottage.in.*

Good Earth

HOUSEHOLD ITEMS/FURNITURE | All sorts of housewares, including linens, pottery, and brass, are on offer here. There's one in Juhu, opposite the Marriott Hotel, and one in Lower Parel. ✉ *2 Reay House, adjacent to Taj Mahal Hotel, Colaba* ☎ *22/2495–1954* ⊕ *www.goodearth.in.*

India Circus

GIFTS/SOUVENIRS | Designer Krsnaa Mehta's quirky home decor and design brand is steeped in the bright, mischievous sensibilities of India. Think everything from wallpaper to cushions to glasses and spectacle cases. **There's also a branch at Phoenix Mills in central Mumbai.** ✉ *Dresswala House, Shahid Bhagat Singh Marg, 72, 1st fl., Kala Ghoda* ✛ *Near Lions Gate & Old Customs House* ☎ *908/284–8076 mobile* ⊕ *indiacircus. com.*

Kulture Shop

GIFTS/SOUVENIRS | Purveyors of art prints, stationery, T-shirts, bags, and other knick-knacks by the coolest new Indian graphic artists from around the world, this shop is changing the conversation on Indian art and identity. ■**TIP➜ You can visit its sister store (which is smaller but perhaps more convenient) in Kala Ghoda.** ✉ *Hill View 2, No. 201, 241 Hill Rd., above DCB Bank, 2nd fl., Bandra West* ✛ *Opposite Mehboob Studio* ☎ *22/2655–0982* ⊕ *www. kultureshop.in.*

JEWELRY

Mangal Palace Silver Shop

JEWELRY/ACCESSORIES | You'll find wonderful silver jewelry from all over India here, and there are some good bargains. ✉ *Colaba Market, Colaba* ☎ *22/2283–4333.*

PERFUME

Ajmal

PERFUME/COSMETICS | You'll find a wonderful selection of rare Indian and French perfumes stored in huge decanters here. It also stocks *agar* wood, a rare incense base, a kilo of which costs as much as a night at the Taj Mahal hotel. Sandalwood oil is another fragrance sold here. ⊠ *4/13 Kamal Mansion, Arthur Bunder Rd., Colaba* ☎ *098195–37886 mobile* ⊕ *www. ajmalindia.com.*

Fort and Marine Drive

Long, rectangular club grounds split Marine Drive starting at the Fort neighborhood, each one filled from end to end with countless overlapping cricket games. At one end there might be a gentle match between players in full white regalia, while the next comparable stretch of land is filled with 10 side-by-side matches, barefoot players whipping the ball and hurling their bodies through the air, laughing and talking trash. To the west, past Flora Fountain and the surrounding street-side secondhand booksellers, you'll find Churchgate Station and the Queen's Necklace (as Marine Drive's curved line of street lights is called). To the east, past the 130-year-old Gothic High Court building and Mumbai University's 260-foot Rajabhai Clocktower, in the labyrinthine streets of Kala Ghoda (a small area within the Fort neighborhood), some of the city's better-known seafood restaurants await, along with a completely incongruous, beautiful baby-blue synagogue. In Fort, the side streets are filled with vendors selling used books and bootleg software and DVDs, all at rock-bottom prices. Fort is a great place to see the kind of grandeur the British had in mind when they dreamed up "Bombay," and Marine Drive offers a wonderful walk along the Arabian Sea.

Sights

Chhatrapati Shivaji Maharaj Vastu Sangrahalaya (formerly the Prince of Wales Museum)

LOCAL INTEREST | FAMILY | Topped with Moorish domes, Mumbai's finest Victorian building and principal museum houses 30,000 artifacts, divided among art, archaeology, and natural history. While the building is stunning, the artifacts, most of which are extremely interesting, are unfortunately shown in a slightly dusty environment, with less-than-ideal lighting. The picture gallery contains scores of Mughal and Rajput miniature paintings, works by European and contemporary Indian artists, and copies of magnificent cave-temple paintings from Ajanta. ■ TIP→ The museum's new name is the Chhatrapati Shivaji Maharaj Vastu Sangrahalaya, but no one uses that name, so if you must ask for directions, call it the Prince of Wales Museum. ⊠ *M.G. Rd., near Regal Cinema, Fort* ☎ *22/2284–4519, 22/2284–4484* ⊕ *csmvs.in* ☞ *Rs. 500.*

★ Chowpatty Beach

BEACH—SIGHT | Chowpatty Beach and the rest of long, elegantly curved Marine Drive are the essence of the mammoth, cheeky, beautiful seaside beast that is Mumbai. Chowpatty gives a taste of the bazaar and *mela* (festival) rolled into one. By day—weekday, that is—it's a quiet, uncluttered stretch of sand, but by night it transforms into a carnival of food and hawkers and touts and amusements of every kind, all lit up like Christmas Eve. In a rapidly changing city, it retains some of the simple pleasures in which Mumbaikars indulged before the economy skyrocketed—and it remains an equalizer of sorts, with parents of every class and caste bringing their families here for an evening of fun. For the casual traveler, it offers a window into the many colors—and smells and tastes and sounds—of Mumbai.

Chhatrapati Shivaji Maharaj Vastu Sangrahalaya (formerly the Prince of Wales Museum) is one of the most beautiful buildings in Mumbai.

A hundred species of salesmen throng the beach in the evening, and especially on Sunday, selling everything from glow-in-the-dark yo-yos and animal-shaped balloons to rat poison. Men stand by with bathroom scales, offering complacent strollers a chance to check their heft. Hand-operated Ferris wheels and carousels are packed with children. A few stalls nearby distribute Mumbai's famously satisfying fast food—crunchy bhel puri (puffed-rice snacks), *ragda pattice* (potato cakes blanketed with spicy chickpea gravy), and pav bhaji (fried vegetable mash eaten with bread). From the beach, walk southeast down Marine Drive toward Nariman Point and you'll bump into flotillas of evening strollers, cooing couples wandering past the waves in a daze, and dogs and kids being walked by their respective minders. Just about the only thing the area lacks is water that's safe for swimming. ⊠ *Chowpatty.*

Jehangir Art Gallery

MUSEUM | Not a far stroll from Trishna and other famous restaurants, one of Mumbai's oldest contemporary-art galleries hosts changing exhibits of well-known Indian artists. Some of the work is lovely, and all of it is interesting for its cultural perspective. There's usually plenty of art outside as well—when it's not monsoon season the plaza in front of the building is full of artists selling their work. ⊠ *M.G. Rd., Kala Ghoda, Fort* ☎ *22/2284–3989* ⊕ *www.jehangirartgallery.com* ⊠ *Free.*

Knesseth Eliyahoo Synagogue

RELIGIOUS SITE | The attractive and ornate Knesseth Eliyahoo Synagogue is across from Jehangir Art Gallery, at the southern edge of Fort. Built in 1884 for Bombay's community of Baghdadi Jews, it's sky blue, with lovely stained-glass windows and intricately constructed second-floor balconies. You can visit daily between 10 and 6:30, and are welcome for Sabbath prayers on Friday evening. ⊠ *V.B. Gandhi*

Rd., Kala Ghoda, Fort ☎ *22/2283–1502* ☒ *Donation of Rs. 100 requested.*

Marine Drive

SCENIC DRIVE | Stretching for 3 km (2 miles) along the Arabian Sea, Marine Drive's promenade offers one of the best walks in Mumbai. After you've had your fill of the busy city, head out for a wander—if you're in the mood, you can stroll all the way from Nariman Point up to Malabar Hill. On the way, peer at the stately art deco buildings that flank the street, stop by **Dome,** on top of the Inter-Continental Hotel in Churchgate, for a sunset drink, or grab a snack at Chowpatty Beach, which is famous for Mumbai street food. If you're here at night, scope out the famed Queen's Necklace, as the streetlights along C-shape Marine Drive are affectionately known. ☒ *Mumbai.*

National Gallery of Modern Art

MUSEUM | A great place to see the works of legendary Indian artists M.F. Hussein and F.N. Souza, this imposing, classical-looking circular building has interiors that bring to mind a shrunk-down version of New York's Guggenheim Museum. Built in 1911 by Gateway of India architect George Wittet, it was once the Sir Cowasji Jehangir Public Hall, and the venue for the concerts of violinist Yehudi Menuhin and the rallies of Mahatma Gandhi—the hall still has the acoustics to match. Modern Indian art is displayed in an uncrowded, easy manner on four floors. It's not as spectacular as the Prince of Wales Museum across the street, but it's quiet, and worth a visit, especially if you're an art lover. ☒ *M.G. Rd., near Regal Cinema, Fort* ☎ *22/2288–1969* ⊕ *www.ngmaindia.gov. in* ☒ *Rs. 500.*

 Restaurants

Ankur–The Coastal Bistro

$ | **INDIAN** | Much of the Konkan cuisine of India's Western coast is inspired by its proximity to the sea—consequently, the menu here offers a rich haul of seafood, including many of Mumbai's signature fishes such as the pomfret, the rawas, and bony kane. All this marine abundance finds its expression in delicious dishes like *aajadina* (clams dry-fried in coconut), although you'll have to eat it all to a soundtrack of cheap synth-rock in a room that resembles a Swiss chalet, with sloping wooden roofs and pillars. **Known for:** paper-fine neer dosa (crepey flatbreads made from rice); fish or prawn gassi (piquant orange curry cooked in an earthen pot); sol kadi (a garlicky coconut milk drink stained pink with sour kokum fruit). $ *Average main: Rs. 350* ☒ *Meadows House, MP Shetty Marg, 77, Fort* ☎ *22/2265–4194.*

★ Apoorva

$$ | **INDIAN** | If you're searching for an authentic seafood "lunch home"—which implies unpretentious, tasty, and cheap—this old-school Kala Ghoda mainstay is spot on: slightly dingy, full of locals, with a too-cold a/c section that smells faintly of mothballs. Whichever main dish you choose, order an accompaniment of neer dosa—they are a little like rotis, but much lighter and fluffier, and made of rice; most Konkan restaurants have them, but none do them better than Apoorva. **Known for:** king prawn gassi (spicy gravied prawn dish); prawn or fish rawa fry, an Apoorva specialty; local kane fish smothered in Mangalorean spices and deep-fried to a crisp. $ *Average main: Rs. 550* ☒ *Vasta House (Noble Chambers), S.A. Brelvi Marg, near Horniman Circle, Fort* ☎ *22/2287–0335.*

★ Britannia & Co.

$ | **INDIAN** | At this old, dingy, and terribly atmospheric Irani restaurant, the nearly nonagarian and charming owner, Boman Kohinoor, has an obsession with the British royal family and thus pictures of royalty grace the restaurant's peeling walls. When he chants—and he will—"fresh lime soda sweet to beat the Mumbai heat!" you will order just that, but it's

Mumbai's Greatest Seafood Hits 🍴

Clams, squid, prawns, lobsters, crabs, and fish, rubbed with a spicy red masala or spiked with a green masala or simmered in a thick fragrant coconut gravy: this is what you'll find emanating from kitchens along the Konkan coast of India, stretching from Mumbai to Mangalore to Goa. If you love seafood, help make your Mumbai trip memorable by sampling the best of the local seafood cuisine.

Here's a list of what to look for on menus:

- ***Appam***: a Kerala-style steamed rice cake available in some Konkan joints
- ***Bombay duck bombil***: this Mumbai specialty has nothing to do with duck: Bombay duck is actually a type of fish that's either eaten fresh or dried out in the open—the dried version is extremely pungent and not for everybody. In this dish, it's batter-fried with semolina, and is light and flaky
- ***Kori roti***: a dry, crumbly rice roti
- ***Masala crab***: crab cooked in thick, almost dry, green or red masala
- ***Masala prawns***: prawns marinated in garlic and spices and then panfried
- ***Neer dosa***: a light crumpled soft-rice dosa meant especially for eating with seafood
- ***Prawn curry***: thinner than a ***gassi***, a red curry, with ***kokum*** (a sour berry)
- ***Prawn gassi***: small prawns simmered in a thick, tangy, spicy coconut gravy
- ***Surmai, pomfret, and rawas***: these three famous, fleshy fish of the region are either marinated and fried, baked in a tandoor, or cooked into a curry
- ***Teesri masala:*** tiny clams cooked in a dry coconut masala

the chicken or mutton berry *pulao,* with rice, chicken, gravy, and dried fruit, that will keep you coming back (and perhaps Boman telling you and your companion that you resemble Prince William and Princess Kate). **Known for:** chicken and mutton berry pulao—it's the only place you'll find it; local bombil fish fried the Parsi way; the old-fashioned interiors. [$] *Average main: Rs. 400* ✉ *Wakefield House, Strott Rd., opposite New Custom House, Ballard Estate, Andheri* ☎ *22/2261–5264* 💳 *No credit cards* 🕒 *No dinner.*

Gaylord

$$ | EUROPEAN | A genteel throwback to the continental dishes of the 1950s, '60s, and '70s, Gaylord opened in the 1950s and has consistently fed the city's sense of nostalgia by eschewing faddish culinary crazes and sticking to old-fashioned Indian and European dishes like lobster thermidore; it also has a bakery that sells bread, pastries, and other dainties. There is an air-conditioned section, but you want to sit outside on its pretty patio, fringed with a white latticed boundary. **Known for:** chicken à la Kiev; Swiss chicken (chicken breast with a belly of ham and cheese); roast chicken and bacon. [$] *Average main: Rs. 600* ✉ *Mayfair Bldg., Veer Nariman Rd., Churchgate* ☎ *22/2282–1259.*

Hotel Deluxe

$ | INDIAN | Inexpensive, shabby, and frankly a bit of a hole-in-the-wall, Hotel Deluxe (neither a hotel nor deluxe) has long been the default choice of eatery for homesick Keralites. The menu is vast, but tunnel your vision towards the special section; anything on there is bound to be excellent. **Known for:** flaky Malbari parottas; tiny karimeen fish, fried to a crisp; vegetarian thali (platter) served on a banana leaf. $ *Average main: Rs. 300* ✉ *Pitha St., 10A, Fort* ✤ *Opposite Citibank lane* ☎ *22/3395–6022* ▭ *No credit cards.*

India Jones

$$$ | **MODERN ASIAN** | Though the name implies something quite different, this restaurant actually serves Pan-Asian food and attracts a mix of couples and families out for a special occasion. A bubbling pond with wooden statues greets customers to an interior decked out with traditional Asian accoutrements—mini yellow catamaran sails over the lights, giant Japanese orchids, and various Asian scripts on the walls. **Known for:** Malaysian beef tenderloin satay; da long xai (ginger-flavored, wok-fried lobster with water chestnuts and asparagus); delicious all-you-can-eat dim sum lunch menu. $ *Average main: Rs. 1400* ✉ *Trident Hotel, Nariman Point* ☎ *22/6632–6330* ⊕ *www.tridenthotels.com.*

K Rustom

$ | **INDIAN** | In a somewhat dilapidated-looking store whose homemade ice creams hark all the way back to 1953, the pick of the menu is the ice-cream sandwich (slabs of ice cream slapped between two gossamer-thin wafer biscuits). A huge chunk of the menu is available year-round, but be sure to sample the seasonal flavors (such as mango) as well. **Known for:** walnut crunch; choco almond; rum 'n' raisin. $ *Average main: Rs. 100* ✉ *86, Veer Nariman Rd., Churchgate* ☎ *22/2282–1768.*

★ Kebab Korner

$$$ | **INDIAN** | Though they don't come cheap, the succulent kebabs at this hotel restaurant are perfect for those who don't want to risk Delhi belly (yes, even in Mumbai it's called that) at a hygienically challenged late-night spot.

Elegant and subdued, with excellent waitstaff, the restaurant's only drawback is the minimum 25-minute wait for your food—but good things take time, and the chicken seekh kebabs (ground chicken and spices), Chilean sea bass served in a green *hariyali* (spinach and mint) masala, and the chicken *pahadi* kebab (chunks of saffron-tinged chicken topped with egg whites) are worth the wait. **Known for:** tasty kebabs; Chilean sea bass; long wait. $ *Average main: Rs. 1400* ✉ *InterContinental Hotel, 135 Marine Dr., Churchgate* ☎ *22/3987–9999* ⊕ *www.ichotelsgroup.com* ☉ *No lunch.*

Mahesh Lunch Home

$$ | **SEAFOOD** | Somewhere between Apoorva and Trishna—geographically as well as atmospherically—Mahesh is a legendary Fort seafood restaurant (but can't compare with Ankur) that attracts the office-lunch crowd as well as packing them in during the evenings. Some of the character was stripped out of the place after it decided to go upscale, and the floor-to-ceiling marble might be a bit much, but the traditional Mangalorean seafood dishes are reliably good. **Known for:** clam and squid sukha (dry masala); fish gassi, made with local fish of your choice; neer dosa (paper-fine flatbreads). $ *Average main: Rs. 700* ✉ *8–B Cawasji Patel St., Fort* ☎ *22/6695–5559, 22/6695–5554* ⊕ *www.maheshlunchhome.com.*

Natural

$ | **CAFÉ** | Serving the best ice cream in town, Natural—which has the taste of Indian *malai* (sweets so creamy they're almost like cheese)—seems to be everywhere. All of the ice cream is made with fresh fruit or nuts, and contains no preservatives; highly recommended are the tender coconut, roasted almond, or seasonal Indian fruit flavors like cinnamon-tinged *chikoo* (a caramel-flavored fruit also known as sapodilla), custard apple, or mango. **Known for:** being open until midnight; fruit-flavored ice creams; chocolate chip ice cream. $ *Average* *main: Rs. 200* ✉ *Jyoti Sadan, 137 Marine Dr., next to InterContinental Hotel, Churchgate* ☎ *22/2202–7426, 22/6610–8000* 🌐 *www.naturalicecreams.in.*

The Pantry

$ | **MODERN AMERICAN** | Under the same ownership as Woodside Inn, this restaurant dispenses with the pubby atmosphere to focus on simple, rustic cuisine using local ingredients. The food is excellent and reasonably priced considering how refined it is, and although it'd be nice if it had a wine license—the white interiors, open kitchen, and general atmosphere all scream "wine bar"—the excellent baked goods and mains more than make up for the lack of booze. **Known for:** healthy breakfast options; delightful baked goods; fairly accommodating of gluten-free diners. [$] *Average main: Rs. 450* ✉ *Yeshwant Chambers, Military Sq. La., Kala Ghoda, Fort* ☎ *22/2270–0082* 🕒 *No dinner.*

Shree Thaker Bhojnalaya

$$ | **INDIAN** | The food at Shree Bhojnalaya makes an excellent primer for those venturing into vegetarian Gujarati thalis (a limitless set meal, served on banana leaves or on a metal plate called a thali). The restaurant is tiny, cheap, rather nondescript, and hidden away amidst the warren of Kalbadevi's lanes, but the extra peregrinating is well worth it—this is as close to homey Gujarati food as you will get in this city. **Known for:** aam ras (mango pulp, available in summer); undhiyu (a vegetable medley made of root veggies, available in winter); shreekhand (a sweet made from strained yogurt, available only on weekdays). [$] *Average main: Rs. 600* ✉ *Dadyseth Agiary La., 31, Fort* ☎ *87953–65431.*

★ Soam

$$ | **INDIAN** | This extremely popular restaurant is always likely to be packed with chattering families and friends, but the service is brisk and you'll soon get a seat amid the pale yellow walls, wooden benches, and loud aunties. Although most of the menu here is traditional Gujarati and Kathiawadi food, some dishes offer a modern take on the classics. **Known for:** panki (paper-thin pancakes folded into banana leaves and steamed); fada ni khichdi (broken wheat saturated with ghee); spinach and cheese samosas. [$] *Average main: Rs. 500* ✉ *Sadguru Sadan, ground fl., across from Babulnath Mandir, Chowpatty, Marine Drive* ☎ *22/2369–8080.*

Suzette Creperie & Cafe

$ | **FRENCH** | India's French influence might be strongest in sunny Pondicherry, on the east coast, but with two Frenchmen at the helm, this tiny crepe joint can provide a taste of it right here in Mumbai (branches have blossomed across Mumbai, including in Bandra and Powai). Try the Méditerranée, with grilled chicken, olive tapenade, mozzarella, and tomatoes, or the Italie, with arugula, a tomato coulis, mozzarella, and oregano, or build your own crepe from an extensive list of ingredients. **Known for:** Nutella crepes; cheerful atmosphere; buckwheat crepes from Britanny. [$] *Average main: Rs. 400* ✉ *Atlanta Bldg., Nariman Point* ☎ *22/2641–1431.*

Trishna

$$ | **SEAFOOD** | Although most of the items on Trishna's seafood menu are of respectable quality, you'd be remiss not to order the much-vaunted butter garlic crab—even if that was all this legendary Kala Ghoda restaurant served, it'd be full year-round. The succulent crab is available in myriad treatments—with Indian and Western spices, green *hariyali* masala, black (spicier) Hyderabadi masala—and Trishna maintains the quality that's made it a favorite with tourists for more than 30 years. **Known for:** the butter garlic crab and its brethren the squid and prawn; one of the few seafood restaurants that has an alcohol menu; prawns koliwada. [$] *Average main: Rs. 700* ✉ *7 Rope Walk La., next to Commerce House, Kala*

Marine Drive is also known as the Queen's Necklace due to its glittering lights.

Ghoda, Fort ☎ 22/2261–4991 ⊕ www.
trishna.co.in.

Vetro

$$$ | ITALIAN | Granted, Mumbai is not exactly known for its carbonara, so the bar isn't set too high, but Vetro could stack up against Italian food in any moderately sized American city. And if you're in the mood for a break from spicy food, this minimalist chic restaurant is perfect, with its wide variety of salads, pastas, and antipasti. Ⓢ *Average main: Rs. 1400* ✉ *Oberoi, Nariman Point* ☎ *22/6632–5757* ⊕ *www.oberoi-hotels.com.*

Ziya

$$$$ | INDIAN | Opened in 2010, Ziya quickly shot to the very forefront of Indian cuisine, and although other modern, more traditionally minded restaurants (like Neel) have taken its place at the top of the heap, it remains one of the most exciting restaurants to hit India in ages. Here, traditional Indian flavors receive nouvelle cuisine treatment from chef Vineet Bhatia, the first Indian chef to win Michelin stars. **Known for:** the tasting menu; dramatic view of the Queen's Necklace; the Ziya cocktails. Ⓢ *Average main: Rs. 2500* ✉ *Oberoi Hotel, Nariman Point, Nariman Point* ✛ *Just before NCPA complex* ☎ *22/3348–7783* ⊕ *www.oberoihotels.com.*

Hotels

Astoria

$$ | HOTEL | The Astoria, with its slightly severe 1930-ish art deco exterior, is a decent and reliable midrange hotel. **Pros:** good value; excellent location; very good deals for breakfast included in the package. **Cons:** functional but not-too-exciting rooms; roadwork for the upcoming metro lines may disturb guests; rather slow Wi-Fi. Ⓢ *Rooms from: Rs. 6500* ✉ *Churchgate Reclamation, Jamshedji Tata Rd., Churchgate* ☎ *22/6654–1234, 22/2287–1211* ⊕ *www.astoriaMumbai.com* ⏎ *68 rooms, 4 suites.*

InterContinental Marine Drive

$$$$ | **HOTEL** | Aside from the ideal Marine Drive location (near the commercial hubs of Nariman Point, Colaba, and Fort) and some of the city's biggest standard rooms, service is a big plus point at this hotel catering to a business clientele, with personal concierges and a complimentary in-room massage for every guest. **Pros:** 500-square-foot rooms are standard; sweeping views of the sea; there are often good online deals. **Cons:** rooms near the rooftop bar may be noisy; usual rates are quite high; business lounge may prove inadequate for business-focused travelers. [$] *Rooms from: Rs. 16000* ✉ *135 Marine Dr., Churchgate* ☎ *22/3987–9999* 🌐 *www.ihg.com/intercontinental/hotels/gb/en/mumbai/bomhb/hoteldetail* 🛏 *69 rooms* 🍴 *Free Breakfast.*

The Oberoi

$$$$ | **HOTEL** | Luxury and stellar service are the hallmarks here—every floor has a butler who will make reservations, collect your laundry, shine your shoes, supervise the room cleaning, and bring you chocolates. **Pros:** the world-famous restaurant Ziya; elegant rooms; great views of the Arabian sea. **Cons:** expensive; the contemporary design may be disappointing for those looking for a traditional "Indian" experience; Internet limited by device. [$] *Rooms from: Rs. 16000* ✉ *Nariman Point* ✥ *200 meters (656 feet) from NCPA* ☎ *22/6632–5757* 🌐 *www.oberoihotels.com* 🛏 *287 rooms* 🍴 *Free Breakfast.*

Sea Green

$ | **HOTEL** | For those looking to save money but still get a glimpse of the shimmering waters off Marine Drive, consider this classic hotel, whose main virtue is that it's a remarkable bargain relative to its location, halfway between heavyweights like the Oberoi and the InterContinental. **Pros:** good location; nice views; large, clean rooms. **Cons:** antiquated and rather worn; no business facilities or pool or gym; rather dismal breakfast. [$] *Rooms from: Rs. 4500* ✉ *145 Marine Dr., Churchgate* ☎ *22/6633–6525, 22/2282–2294* 🌐 *www.seagreenhotel.com* 🛏 *38 rooms* 🍴 *No meals.*

The Trident

$$$ | **HOTEL** | The Oberoi's posh and slightly less luxurious cousin continues the same tradition of excellent service, and because room rates vary according to occupancy, it can be a great value in the off-season. **Pros:** cheaper than the Oberoi, though not significantly lower in quality; a true high-rise with proper views; right at the heart of the business district. **Cons:** you're not staying at the Oberoi; the much-touted shopping center is rather blah; not a standout from the crowd of competing hotels. [$] *Rooms from: Rs. 13000* ✉ *Nariman Point, Nariman Point* ☎ *22/6632–4343* 🌐 *www.tridenthotels.com/mumbai-nariman-point/hotel.asp* 🛏 *550 rooms, 40 suites* 🍴 *No meals.*

🍸 Nightlife

Dome

BARS/PUBS | With some of the best views of the city, the open-air Dome attracts a young, good-looking crowd who sit, amid candlelight, on plush white sofas and chairs. It's one of the best sunset-drink spots in the city, and the fact that the menu includes a selection from the excellent Kebab Korner only sweetens the deal. Drinks are fairly expensive, but if you're on a budget, grab a Kingfisher for Rs. 450. That's hardly a steal, but you're paying for the view. ✉ *InterContinental Hotel, 135 Marine Dr., Churchgate* ☎ *22/3987–9999.*

Eau Bar

BARS/PUBS | Facing the Arabian Sea, this bar is elegant and more reserved than many of its peers, and attracts a rather high-class clientele for the live jazz band that plays each night. ✉ *The Oberoi hotel, Nariman Point* ☎ *22/6632–6220.*

Geoffrey's

BARS/PUBS | A relatively staid yuppie crowd likes to hang out in the clubby (in the British sense) setting here, but it's also one of the few bars with enough TVs to accommodate a big sporting event like Wimbledon or the World Cup. ☒ *Marine Plaza Hotel, 29 Marine Dr., Churchgate* ☎ *22/2285–1212.*

Inox

FILM | A good place to catch a Bollywood film, or the latest English one, is the upscale Inox. ☒ *CR2 shopping mall, opposite Bajaj Bhavan, Nariman Point* ☎ *808/021–1111.*

National Centre for the Performing Arts (*NCPA*)

ARTS CENTERS | This huge complex is home to the gracious **Jamshed Bhabha Hall,** a 1,000-seat auditorium that is Mumbai's ballet and opera theater, the Piramal Gallery, which hosts photography and art exhibitions, the **Godrej Dance Academy Theater,** a main venue for classical Indian dance performances as well as workshops and master classes, and several additional theaters, including the **Tata Theatre,** a grand 1,000-seat auditorium that regularly hosts plays, often in English, and classical concerts by major Indian and international musicians. The center also boasts a spacious and well-regarded Mediterranean restaurant, Amadeus, that occasionally holds wedding functions. Note that some NCPA performances are open to members only; a year's membership is Rs. 2,500. ☒ *Sir Dorab Tata Rd., Nariman Point* ☎ *22/2282–4567* ⊕ *www.ncpamumbai. com.*

★ Royal Opera House

MUSIC | Mumbai's grand opera house, which first opened to the public in 1911, has been painstakingly restored to its original baroque design and now hosts all manner of performances. Its pretty grounds encompass a café, Sunday markets, and a space for jazz performances called The Quarter. ☒ *Mama Padmanand Marg* ☎ *22/2369–0511* ⊕ *royaloperahouse.in.*

Shopping

ART AND ANTIQUES
★ Filter

ANTIQUES/COLLECTIBLES | This tiny jewel of a store sells edgy, kitschy collectibles like chocolate infused with South Indian coffee, cheeky shirts, and prints and posters by indie Indian brands. ☒ *VB Gandhi Marg, Kala Ghoda* ✛ *Straight down from blue synagogue* ☎ *22/2288–7070* ⊕ *www.filtershop.in.*

Gallery Chemould

ANTIQUES/COLLECTIBLES | This is an elegant gallery in the Fort district, full of works by modern masters like Atul Dodiya and rolling exhibitions. ☒ *Queens Mansion, G. Talwatkar Rd., 3rd fl., Fort* ☎ *22/2200–0211* ⊕ *www.gallerychemould.com.*

★ Phillips Antiques

ANTIQUES/COLLECTIBLES | Established in 1860, Phillips has the best choice of old prints, engravings, and maps in Mumbai. It also sells many possessions left behind by the British—Staffordshire and East India Company china, old jewelry, crystal, lacquerware, and sterling silver. ☒ *Waterloo Mans, Main Rd., Gpo, Fort* ☎ *22/2202–0564* ⊕ *www.phillipsantiques.com.*

BAZAARS AND MARKETS
Fashion Street

OUTDOOR/FLEA/GREEN MARKETS | This is a trove of cotton bargains in a long row of open-air stalls, with mounds of colorful, cheap, mainly Western clothing for all ages. The name is completely incongruous—there is nothing fashionable about this street, but the knock-offs are cheap (come prepared to bargain and bargain again). Come around 11 am, when the crowds are thinner and the sun has not yet peaked—and bargain. ☒ *M.G. Rd., opposite Bombay Gymkhana, Fort.*

Custom Tailors and Fine Fabrics

Mumbai's bazaars boom with some of the richest and widest varieties of cloth, and the Mangaldas Cloth Market has enough bales of material to carpet all of South Mumbai.

Buying clothes tailored to fit in Mumbai is not a difficult proposition: There are a number of tailors who can turn splendid fabric into custom-made clothing—Indian or Western—in a matter of hours, for ladies or men. The tailors are often armed with the latest catalogs and will faithfully copy a design from a picture. They're fast and competent, but be specific about what you want; their improvisations are not likely to go over well. If you have a shirt or trousers to give as a sample, they can generally make an exact copy. Make sure you preshrink cotton material and any lining before you give it in for stitching (rinse for a few minutes and drip dry; colored cottons need to be rinsed by themselves for just a few seconds to prevent too much bleeding). Fix a rate beforehand, and give an earlier deadline than necessary to allow for refittings if needed. If the material needs a lining, buy it yourself.

7

Mumbai FORT AND MARINE DRIVE

CLOTHING
★ Anokhi

CLOTHING | At this shop find lovely, colorful, and quality clothes with block-print designs from Rajasthan. ⊠ *Rasik Niwas, Metro Motors Lane, Dr. A.R. Rangekar Marg, off Hughes Rd., Marine Drive* ☎ *22/2368–5761, 22/2368–5308* ⊕ *www. anokhi.com* ⊠ *Govind Dham, 210 Waterfield Rd., Hughes Road* ☎ *22/2368–5761, 22/2640–8263* ⊕ *www.anokhi.com.*

The Bombay Shirt Company

CLOTHING | A one-of-a-kind tailoring store for Mumbai, The Bombay Shirt Company creates immaculate custom-made shirts for men and women from a selection of fabrics and styles that are showcased in the shop. You can also have them all made from scratch. ⊠ *Sassoon Bldg., The Fabindia La., No. 3, Kala Ghoda* ☎ *22/4004–3455* ⊕ *www.bombayshirts. com.*

Christina

CLOTHING | This is a tiny, classy boutique with exquisite silk blouses and shirts, scarves, ties, *dupattas* (long, thin scarves for draping), and silk-edge purses and wallets. ⊠ *The Oberoi hotel section of Oberoi Shopping Centre, Nariman Point* ☎ *22/2216–3269* ⊕ *www.christinaindia. com.*

★ Nicobar

CLOTHING | The hipster-ish brand Nicobar used to stock its merchandise at Good Earth until it decided to branch out with its own shop, a cheerful, eclectic emporium in Kala Ghoda. The clothes and accessories (for men and women) sport a breezy, contemporary, minimalist aesthetic; there's also a rather chic line of home decor items. It's a lovely shop. ⊠ *Nicobar Design Studio, 10, Ropewalk La., Kala Ghoda* ✛ *Next to Kala Ghoda Cafe* ☎ *22/2263–3888* ⊕ *www.nicobar. com.*

Roop Milan

CLOTHING | Primarily a sari shop, Roop Milan also sells a huge variety of fine silks upstairs. ⊠ *385 Laxmi Bldg., NC Kelkar Rd., Dadar West* ☎ *22/2431–6574.*

Sheetal

CLOTHING | This is probably the best suit shop in Mumbai, with an extensive collection of fabrics and impeccable tailoring. You can get a full suit made here in about five days if you ask for it to be expedited, with a trial fitting, for about Rs. 15,000. ✉ *Lal Bahadur Shastri Rd., Bail Bajar, Saki Naka* ☎ *22/2385–6565, 22/2387–6114* ⊕ *www.sheetalindia.com.*

DEPARTMENT STORES AND MALLS

★ **Bombay Store**

DEPARTMENT STORES | A must for souvenir shoppers, the friendly Bombay Store sells clothing and accessories for men, women, and children, silk by the meter, housewares, organic wellness products, and gifts. There are a number of branches in the city, but the Fort one is the most expansive. ✉ *Sir Pherozeshah Mehta Rd., Fort* ☎ *22/2288–5048, 22/2288–5049* ⊕ *www.thebombaystore.com.*

Fabindia

DEPARTMENT STORES | This store showcases the best of Indian fabrics—khadis (home-spun cotton), muslin, vegetable-dyed silks, and embroidered materials. You can find women's clothing (saris, kurtas, skirts, trousers, blouses, and *kurtis*) as well as men's shirts and kurtas, children's clothes, tablecloths, curtains, cushion covers—and napkins fashioned from these beautiful materials, some of which is also available by the meter. The Fort location is the address to head to—it's in a high-ceilinged, period building, with a wide selection—but there are a number of branches all over the city. ✉ *Jeroo Bldg., 137 M.G. Rd., Kala Ghoda, Fort* ☎ *22/2262–6539* ⊕ *www. fabindia.com.*

Le Mill

DEPARTMENT STORES | This pricey store stocks stylish clothes, perfumes, accessories, and bric-a-brac from Indian and international designers such as Isabel Marant and the Bombay Perfumery. This one's for the deep pocketed—and devoted dreamers. ✉ *Pheroze Bldg.,*

The Dhobi Ghats

Dhobi ghats are where washermen (dhobis) pound clothes clean day and night in enormous open-air laundries. Mumbai actually has several, but the Cuffe Parade ghat is the most conveniently located for tourists. If you're feeling more adventurous, a visit to Mumbai's main dhobi ghat, near Mahalak-shmi Station, a kilometer (half mile) beyond the racecourse, may make for better photo ops; here about 200 dhobis are at work in an area covering 7 acres—it's best viewed from the railroad bridge leading into Mahalakshmi Railway Station.

Chhatrapati Shivaji Maharishi Marg, 1st fl., Colaba ✛ *Above Indigo Deli* ☎ *22/2204–1925* ⊕ *www.lemillindia.com.*

EYEGLASSES

Ganko Optics

SPECIALTY STORES | This old and trustworthy family-run optician has good frame choices. ✉ *19 Tulsiani Chambers, ground fl., Nariman Point* ☎ *22/2283 2335.*

Lawrence and Mayo

SPECIALTY STORES | If you need some specs, a long-standing and reliable name in the eyewear business is Lawrence and Mayo. The main branch of this trusted brand is in Fort. ✉ *274 Dr Dadabhai Naoroji Rd., Kala Ghoda* ☎ *22/2631–3376* ⊕ *www.lawrenceandmayo.co.in.*

JEWELRY

Tanishq

JEWELRY/ACCESSORIES | Owned by the Tata Group, a venerable and enormous Indian conglomerate whose founder built the Taj Mahal hotel, Tanishq is a reliable place to buy gold jewelry. The prices, however, are a little higher than elsewhere. ✉ *Veer*

Nariman Rd., near Cricket Club of India (CCI), Churchgate ☎ *22/2282–1621* ⊕ *www.tanishq.co.in.*

MUSIC

Furtado's

MUSIC STORES | More than 150 years old, Mumbai's iconic music store sells all manner of Western musical instruments, music magazines, music books, and audio hardware. It now has an online store plus 20 branches around India; it even started a music school in 2011. ⊠ *Kalbadevi Rd., Dhobi Talao, Dhobitalao* ✛ *Near Metro cinema and Kyani's* ☎ *22/6622–5454* ⊕ *www.furtadosonline.com.*

Activities

Wankhede Stadium

CRICKET | Wankhede Stadium hosts Mumbai's major domestic and international cricket matches. In season—October through March—there are usually several matches a week. ⊠ *D Road, Churchgate.*

Malabar Hill and Nearby

This tony area is at the far end of Marine Drive, where some of the richest and most powerful people in Mumbai live. It's also probably the best place to see the sheer amount of money this city is made of—take, for instance, Antilia, the "quaint" house industrialist Mukesh Ambani recently completed on Altamount Road. Its $2 billion price tag, 560-foot height (27 floors), and 400,000 square feet of living space make it the most expensive, and largest, residential home on the planet. (That the 600-person-staffed behemoth is a mere 10 km [6 miles] from Dharavi, one of the largest slums in Asia, where 1 million people share less than 2½ square km [1 square mile] of land, highlights the extent of India's massive income gap.) Along the switchback roads of Malabar Hill you'll also find the ancient Babulnath Temple (a Shiva temple), the austere Jain Temple, the spring-fed Banganga water tank, and the verdant Hanging Gardens.

Sights

Babulnath Temple

RELIGIOUS SITE | To get the flavor of a large, traditional Indian temple that's nevertheless jammed in the heart of a busy city, a visit to the Babulnath Temple is a must. And climbing the few hundred steps to reach the temple, perched on a hillside, will also reward you with a panorama of South Mumbai. The first Babulnath Temple was apparently built by Raja Bhimdev in the 13th century and named after the *babul* trees (a type of acacia native to India) that forested this area. The architecture of this imposing shrine, one of Mumbai's most important, isn't especially remarkable, but it's interesting to watch the melée of worshippers coming, going, and milling about. Outside are rows of flower sellers hawking a temple-visit kit—coconut plus flowers plus rock sugar—and a cluster of vendors concocting sweets in *karhais* (large woks) in the open air. Temple authorities are sometimes prickly about allowing foreigners into the innermost areas, but it's worth a try; more often than not they don't object. For Rs. 2 you can avoid the climb and take the elevator. ⊠ *Babulnath Rd., Malabar Hill.*

★ Banganga Water Tank

RELIGIOUS SITE | This serene, criminally undervisited temple complex is considered one of the city's holiest sites. It's also the oldest surviving structure in Mumbai. The small, somewhat dilapidated temples are built around a holy pool of water and surrounded by the ever-encroaching houses of Mumbai's newer residents. Cows and people mingle freely here, as do bathers who come to obtain the purportedly healing powers of the water. Life around here harks back to earlier, more traditional times.

Touring the Malabar Hill area

■TIP➔ Do this tour by taxi; it's totally acceptable to have your taxi driver wait for you (do check with him before starting the ride); just ask him to keep the meter running.

After checking the tides to time your visit just right, take a taxi to the **Haji Ali Shrine** and have your taxi wait for you while you walk out on the jetty. Then drive to **Kamala Nehru Park,** take some air, enjoy the views,

and walk to the **Jain Temple.** From here you can either walk or take a taxi along Walkeshwar Road to the **Banganga water tank** area. Finally, have your taxi take you to **Babulnath Temple** and Gandhi's former home, **Mani Bhavan.**

Timing

This tour takes about three to four hours, depending on traffic.

✉ *Walkeshwar Rd., Malabar Hill* ✚ *Take lane just beyond Ghanshyamdas Sitaram Poddar Chowk* ▨ *Free.*

Haji Ali Shrine

RELIGIOUS SITE | Set far out on a thin, rocky jetty in the Arabian Sea, this striking, dilapidated white shrine was built in honor of the Muslim saint Haji Ali, who drowned here some 500 years ago on a pilgrimage to Mecca. When a coffin containing his mortal remains floated to rest on a rocky bed in the sea, devotees constructed the tomb and mosque to mark the spot. The shrine is reached by a long walkway just above the water. ■TIP➔ **At high tide the walkway is submerged, making the shrine unreachable. But walking there when the sea has completely receded is not too romantic, because the exposed rocks smell of garbage; choose a time in between.** The walkway is lined with destitute families and beggars ravaged by leprosy, some writhing, chanting, and (calling on the Muslim tradition of giving alms) beseeching you as you make your way down—this can be a deeply upsetting experience, but it's one that is unfortunately quintessentially Mumbai. Inside, the shrine is full of colored-mirror mosaics and crowded with worshippers praying over the casket, which is covered with wilted flower garlands. Men and

women must enter through separate doorways. On many evenings a busker plays *quawalis* (a style of Muslim music) after the sunset prayers. There's no admission charge, but you may consider giving between Rs. 20 and Rs. 50 to the mosque charity box. The shrine closes at 10 pm. ✉ *Off Lala Lajpatrai Marg, near Mahalaxmi Race Course, Central Mumbai.*

Jain Temple

RELIGIOUS SITE | What may be the most impressive temple in Mumbai belongs to the prosperous, strictly vegetarian Jains, the largely Gujarati followers of Lord Mahavira. The colorful interior of their main Mumbai temple is filled with marble, but at the same time it's understated and peaceful—check out the intricate work on the walls and ceilings. Jain worship here is rather different from the general chaos at Hindu temples; it's more introspective and humble in aspect, which reflects the Jain faith. At around 8 am daily, freshly bathed Jain devotees in swaths of unstitched off-white cloth walk here barefoot from their nearby—often quite ritzy—homes to pay homage to the splendid idol of Adinath, an important Jain prophet. (Jains show respect by arriving clean and without shoes—originally Jains used to wear only a silk cloth,

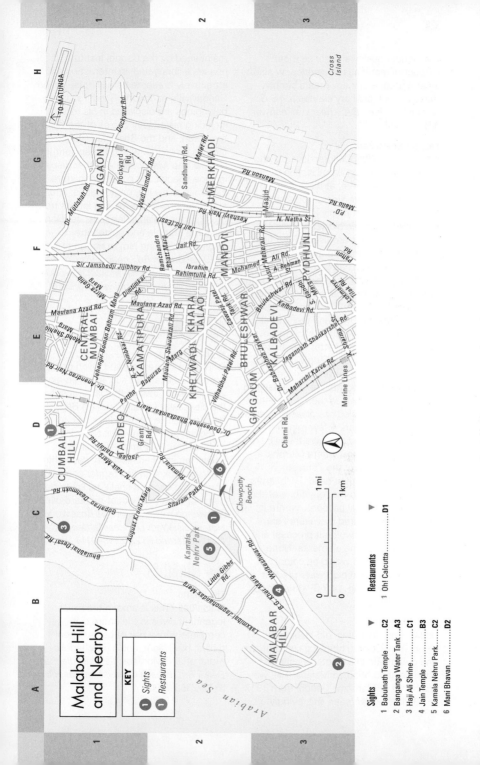

Malabar Hill and Nearby

KEY

① Sights

① Restaurants

Sights ▶

1 Babulnath Temple...............**C2**
2 Banganga Water Tank...**A3**
3 Haji Ali Shrine.................**C1**
4 Jain Temple.....................**B3**
5 Kamala Nehru Park......**C2**
6 Mani Bhavan.................**D2**

Restaurants ▶

1 Oh! Calcutta................**D1**

---

0 — 1km

0 — 1mi

the highest quality and hence most respectful material, but plenty now also wear cotton, and many others simply make do with ordinary clothes.) ✉ *B.G. Kher Marg, Teen Batti, near Walkeshwar, Malabar Hill.*

Kamala Nehru Park

CITY PARK | FAMILY | Children love playing on the "Old Woman Who Lived in a Shoe" structure here, at this small park on the eastern side of the top of Malabar Hill. It's primarily a children's playground—and an old-school one at that, so if your kids are used to the finer things, this park may seem impossibly quaint—but it also has gorgeous views of the city below that are worth checking out if you happen to be in the area. From the special viewpoint clearing you can see all of Marine Drive and the Mumbai skyline, from Chowpatty Beach to Colaba Point—try to come up after dark to see why Marine Drive, sparkling with lights, is known as the Queen's Necklace. Just across the road another park, the **Hanging Gardens** (also known as the Pherozeshah Mehta Gardens), also has pleasant views and a topiary garden. A few minutes north of here, heading down the hill, are the **Towers of Silence,** where Mumbai's Parsis—followers of the Zoroastrian faith—dispose of their dead. Pallbearers carry the corpse to the top of one of the towering cylindrical bastions, where it is left to be devoured by vultures and crows (a roughly two-hour process) and decomposed by the elements. None of this is visible to would-be onlookers, even relatives, and high walls prevent any furtive peeping. ✉ *B.G. Kher Marg, Malabar Hill.*

Mani Bhavan

HOUSE | This charming, old-fashioned three-story Gujarati house, painted brown and cream and in a quiet, tree-shaded Parsi neighborhood on Malabar Hill, was the home of Mahatma Gandhi from 1917 to 1934. Now overseen and lovingly maintained by the Gandhi Institute, it houses a library and an interesting and attractively presented small museum on Gandhi's life and work. Gandhi's simple belongings are displayed in his room, including his original copies of the Bible, the Koran, and the Bhagavad Gita (a famous discourse within the ancient Indian epic, the *Mahabharata*); other displays include spectacular colorful miniature dioramas of his life, photographs, and some important and moving letters from the fight for Indian independence. Don't miss the humble and polite letter to Adolf Hitler asking him to not go to war. ✉ *19 Laburnam Rd., near Nana Chowk, Gamdevi, Malabar Hill* ☎ *22/2380–5864* 🌐 *www.gandhi-manibhavan.org* 🎟 *Rs. 10.*

🍴 Restaurants

★ Oh! Calcutta

$$ | INDIAN | Rarely packed, even on Saturday night, because it's in an infrequently visited part of town, Oh! Calcutta serves the city's best (mustard-heavy) Bengali food in upscale surroundings of dark wood set off by simple black-and-white archival photos from the British Raj. **Known for:** smoked hilsa fish; daab chingri (prawns cooked in rich tender coconut served in a coconut shell); tel koi (whole perch cooked in a bath of mustard oil). [$] *Average main: Rs. 600* ✉ *Rosewood Hotel, Tulsi Wadi La., near Tardeo A/C Market, Tardeo* ☎ *22/2353–9114.*

🍸 Nightlife

The Ghetto

BARS/PUBS | This is among the most legendary dives in the entire city, complete with a pair of beat-up pool tables, black light, and a psychedelic mural of Jim Morrison. ✉ *30 Bhulabhai Desai Rd., Breach Candy, Malabar Hill* ☎ *22/2353–8418.*

Vasai Fort

Mumbai isn't known for its forts, and for good reason—most are rickety, ramshackle structures, encroached upon by shanties, and defaced with scribbled notes from visitors. Still, for those with a yen for peeling back the pages of the city's history, and several extra hours in hand, it might be worthwhile to travel to Vasai Fort. Originally built by the Portuguese in 1536, the fort was captured by the Marathas, and later the British. Unfortunately, its storied history hasn't quite prompted the ASI (Archaeological Survey of India) to work on preserving it; its moss-tumbled walls and somewhat decrepit condition are testament to this neglect. Nevertheless, it remains atmospheric as ever, with local couples using it a romantic backdrop for wedding shoots.

Pizza by the Bay

DANCE CLUBS | Rebranded from Not Just Jazz by the Bay, this had been one of Mumbai's few jazz venues, but with the name change went the music that had been the joint's hallmark. Still, while the music can sometimes be meh, the pizza is among the city's better pies, its location by the sea is beautiful, and it stays open until 1:30 am. ✉ *143 Marine Dr., Churchgate* ☎ *22/2282–0883, 22/2285–1876, 22/2282–0957.*

🎟 Performing Arts

G5A

ARTS-ENTERTAINMENT OVERVIEW | This venue, a remodeled warehouse, plays host to book readings, dance performances, music gigs, lectures, plays, and film screenings. It's a multifunctional space, with a study area, a vegetarian café, an open terrace area, and a main performance space. ✉ *Laxmi Mills Estate, Shakti Mills La., Mahalaxmi* ✣ *The same compound as Masque restaurant* ☎ *22/2490–9393* ⊕ *g5a.org.*

🛍 Shopping

Nalli

CLOTHING | The Mumbai branch of the famous Chennai store has a fair selection of classic silk saris. Have a look at the authentic gold-embroidered saris from Kanchipuram, in Tamil Nadu, as well as the Bangalore saris and the uncut silk sold by the meter. ✉ *Trimurti Apartments, Bhulabhai Desai Rd., Breach Candy, Malabar Hill* ☎ *22/2353–5577* ⊕ *www.nalli.com.*

Raymond

CLOTHING | This outlet for Raymond Mills, which makes some of India's finest men's suits, can tailor a first-rate suit for about Rs. 8,000 in about a week. During the wedding season (winter) it can get very busy. ✉ *J.K.House, Bhulabhai Desai Rd., Shop No. 15/16, Breach Candy* ✣ *Opposite Breach Candy Hospital* ☎ *22/2354–3371* ⊕ *www.raymondindia.com.*

🏃 Activities

Mahalaxmi Race Course

HORSE RACING/SHOW | Mumbai's Mahalaxmi Race Course, built in 1883, is one of the finest courses in Asia. A visit here in season is a social experience—for a few months each year, this green patch in Central Mumbai becomes an echo of London's Ascot racecourse in the 1950s, with posh accents, outfits that kill, and plenty of pomp and showiness. The season usually runs from November through April, with races on Thursday and Sunday. Upper-class admission in the Members' Area is about Rs. 300, depending on the race: this is definitely what you want, as opposed to the dirt-cheap general admission. Be sure to dress up, too—men should wear a tie for the Members' Area, though this requirement may not always be enforced. ⊠ *Near Nehru Planetarium, Mahalaxmi* ☎ *22/2307–1401* ⊕ *www. rwitc.com/comeracing/mumbairace-course.php.*

Central Mumbai

Unlike most other cities, the center of Mumbai has few historical sites, though it does include Mahalaxmi, home of the city's racetrack. Densely populated, it also encompasses areas like Lower Parel and Worli, but its cluster of gray tower blocks helps keep it from being the sort of place many tourists are going to want to visit. However, it is home to some of the best restaurants, bars, and nightlife in the city, and that alone may warrant a trip.

👁 Sights

★ Bhau Daji Lad Museum
LOCAL INTEREST | FAMILY | Best known for its excellently renovated Palladian and high-Victorian facade and interiors (it was awarded UNESCO's 2005 Award of Excellence in the field of cultural conservation), Mumbai's oldest museum houses a rather odd collection of artifacts that includes everything from clay models to lithographs and photographs. It also hosts talks, lecture series, and art and photography exhibitions in its Museum Plaza. A tiny museum shop offers a host of souvenirs for the folks back

home—fridge magnets of the Minton tiles adorning the museum floor, books on art, and the like. ⊠ *91A, Rani Baug, Babasaheb Ambedkar Rd., Byculla E* ✛ *In same compound as zoo* ☎ *22/2373–1234* ⊕ *www.bdlmuseum.org* ☑ *Rs. 100* ⊙ *Closed Wed.*

Magen Hassidim Synagogue
RELIGIOUS SITE | This Hasidic synagogue is probably Mumbai's most active synagogue, but being in Byculla, it's not really much of a tourist destination; it's also not always open to visitors. But if you're in the area—which is actually in the Muslim area of Madanpura—you can view this Bene Israel shrine from the outside and talk to locals. The congregation and caretakers at this well-attended shrine (with about 750 members) can lend insight into the future of this community. Although the communities of Baghdadi and Cochini Jews have dwindled to just a few thousand, the Bene Israel community continues to modestly prosper. Magen Hassidim is the face of India's modern Jews, the ones who generally don't plan to migrate to Israel and who are now part of the nation's mainstream. ⊠ *Maulana Azad Rd., near Fancy Market and Jula Maidan, Madanpura, Central Mumbai* ☎ *22/2301–2685.*

🍴 Restaurants

★ The Bombay Canteen
$$ | MODERN INDIAN | Indian food is often perceived to be a monolith of spicy curries and tandoori chicken, but for those looking to shatter these snap judgments, Bombay Canteen is the place to go. In a brilliant effort to champion the sort of ingredients that rarely make it into restaurant dishes, executive chef Thomas Zacharias and culinary director Floyd Cardoz (chef of New York restaurant Bombay Bread Bar) have wended their way around the country, subsuming ingredients like rat tail radish and colocasia roots into a playful menu with a global edge. **Known for:** regional cuisines in an

Bhau Daji Lad Museum, Mumbai's oldest museum, is known for its Victorian facade and interiors.

oft-changing seasonal menu; canteen cocktails infused with local ingredients; "small plates" that are fun riffs on snacks from across India. [$] *Average main: Rs. 800* ✉ *Process House, Kamala Mills, Lower Parel, Unit 1, Lower Parel* ✣ *Near Radio Mirchi* ☎ *22/4966–6666* 🌐 *www.thebombaycanteen.com* 🕒 *Closed Mon.*

Café Zoe

$$ | MODERN EUROPEAN | One of the city's most popular dining and drinking spots, the roomy, open, yet strangely utilitarian Café Zoe serves European and continental breakfasts, brunches, lunches, dinners, and drinks. Depending on what time you arrive at this converted industrial compound, the crowd may include young parents feeding their one-year-old daughter sweet bites of Belgian waffles, local journalists shoveling down hot minestrone soup while using the free Wi-Fi, dating couples sharing a romantic dinner of seafood and pasta, or young partygoers drinking cocktails in a dim but sensuous atmosphere after midnight. **Known for:** burgers and fries; crepes and waffles for brunch; happy hours, 5–9 pm. [$] *Average main: Rs. 600* ✉ *Todi Mills, Mathuradas Mills, Compound, Lower Parel* ☎ *22/2490–2065, 22/2490–2066* 🌐 *www.cafezoe.in.*

Ladu Samrat

$ | INDIAN | Once bustling Lalbaug was the beating heart of Mumbai's mill lands and center of its radical leftist political culture. The mills have since folded, but the area is still home to a clot of eateries serving excellent Maharashtrian cooking, and among the best is Ladu Samrat, an unfussy, eminently affordable, but rather threadbare restaurant serving homey vegetarian Maharashtrian snacks. **Known for:** sabudana vada (crisp-fried tapioca cakes); vada pao (fried potato cakes served with a slick of chutney, sandwiched within a soft white bread roll); pannha (a sweet-tangy drink made from green mango), excellent to mollify the spice of accompanying dishes. [$] *Average main: Rs. 200* ✉ *Habib Terrace, Lalbaug, Dr Ambedkar Rd., Parel, Shop*

Street-Food Favorites

Unlike most other Indian cities, Mumbai buzzes around the clock. Food carts appear every few yards serving *chaat* (Indian street snacks), and even the simplest food is transformed into something impressive. The choices are enormous—there are hot, spicy vegetable sandwiches, slices of green mango peppered with masala, sizzling kebabs, Chinese noodles with vegetables, fresh strawberry milk shakes, carrot juice, *kulfi* (cream-based Indian ice cream), fried fish, potato turnovers, masala peanuts, coconut water, green-chilli omelets in buns, and an almost endless array of exotic snacks associated with Mumbai, *such as those listed here.*

Much of this snack food is created right at the side of the road on open grills and stoves and then assembled in front of you. As you would imagine, the hygiene is often a little suspect, but don't dare avoid it, or you may miss out on some of the best available street food on our planet.

If you sample any of these street-side treats, follow some rules. Try food served hot on the spot. Avoid cold and room temperature sauces ("dry chutney" is often a helpful code for "no sauce" when ordering sandwiches like vada pav), and heavy dustings of herbs, such as coriander. If the plates don't look clean, or are dripping wet with unfiltered water, ask that food be either served or packed in a disposable container (a fresh plastic bag, a cup created from leaves, a paper plate, or newspaper) or bring your own container. Carry your own spoon and paper or plastic cup, if you want. And don't worry—the vendors

usually understand enough English to see the process through. Finally, those vendors who attract the biggest crowds and fame are likely to be safer than those who are ignored.

Mumbai's Street-Food Classics

■ *Andaa pav*: A spicy omelet made with chillies, onions, masala, and a bunch of spices, which is then fried and slapped into a pav.

■ *Bheja fry*: Spicy red masala and tomatoes fried with goat brains—it's really tasty!

■ *Boti roll*: Spicy pieces of grilled lamb kebab, chutney, and sliced onions rolled into a **roomali** roti (a thin, hand-tossed, and roasted white-flour pita).

■ *Dahi puri*: Tiny, flat, white-flour **puris** layered with boiled potatoes, three types of chutney made from tamarind, dates, and coriander leaves (cilantro), plus mung-bean sprouts and topped with curd, sev, and chopped cilantro leaves.

■ *Dahi wada*: Large flat dumplings of lentils, which are deep-fried to make **wadas,** and are then dipped in water to soak out the oil. The wadas are served spiced with a variety of masala powders, tamarind sauce, cilantro chutney, and yogurt.

■ *Frankie*: Spicy chicken and vegetables lashed with chutney, enveloped by an egg-smeared, panfried flatbread

■ *Vada (or wada) pav*: A cutlet made of mashed potatoes, spice, cilantro, and ginger that's coated in chickpea flour and deep-fried—which is then stuffed into a pav lined with hot garlic and red-chilli chutney.

No. 1–2, Parel ☎ 22/2471–0127 💳 No credit cards.

★ Masque

$$$$ | MODERN INDIAN | Owner Aditi Dugar and chef Prateek Sadhu, alumni of the Culinary Institute of America and a rapidly rising star in the Indian culinary landscape, comb the country for intriguing indigenous ingredients and make them the heroes in prix-fixe progressive menus that change every fortnight. Chef Sadhu's stints at Alinea, Noma, Le Bernardin, and French Laundry may have been the seed for his degustation menus, but the bedrock of all his dishes is staunchly Indian, albeit in a clean, pared-down way. **Known for:** contemporary wilderness-to-table cuisine; earthy, opulent design aesthetic; Sunday brunch. [$] *Average main: Rs. 3200 ✉ Laxmi Woollen Mills, Shakti Mills La., off E. Moses Rd., Unit G3, Lower Parel ✣ Same compound as Blue Tokai Coffee Roasters ☎ 22/2499–1010 🌐 www.masquerestaurant.com 🕒 Closed Mon.*

★ Neel- Tote on the Turf

$$ | NORTH INDIAN | Hands down the best upscale North Indian food in town for meat eaters, this restaurant in a beautifully designed building at the track makes the journey to the city center utterly worthwhile. Portions are big—as are the prices—and the food is heavy but sophisticated. **Known for:** seekh kebab (minced chicken or mutton kebabs); mutton shorba (bone marrow soup); z; raan (tenderised mutton leg roasted in a tandoor). [$] *Average main: Rs. 800 ✉ Mahalaxmi Racecourse, Gate 5 or 7, Mahalaxmi, Central Mumbai ☎ 22/6157–7777,22/4349–0000.*

The Tasting Room

$ | EUROPEAN | Popular with rich Mumbai housewives—who pack the place for lunch during the week—this Mediterranean restaurant serves gourmet food in a relaxed, tasteful setting. On the top-floor veranda of Good Earth (a designer furniture store), the Tasting Room shares its hosts' penchant for subtle Indian minimalism in warm earth tones. **Known for:** watermelon and feta salad; excellent location for those visiting the nearby shopping behemoth, Phoenix Mills; romantic dinner ambience. [$] *Average main: Rs. 300 ✉ Raghuvanshi Mansions, Raghuvanshi Mills, Tulsi Pipe Rd., Lower Parel, Central Mumbai ☎ 22/6528–5284, 22/2495–1954.*

Hotels

Four Seasons

$$$ | HOTEL | Extremely popular with businesspeople because of its central location between South Mumbai and the western suburbs, India's tallest hotel—33 stories—has a luxury rooftop bar that is one of the city's hottest (and most expensive) nightspots. **Pros:** central location between South Mumbai and the suburbs; business-friendly; small pets (under 16 pounds) are welcome. **Cons:** 20 minutes away from town; tragic view of nearby slums; some of the rooms don't effectively filter out noise from the main road. [$] *Rooms from: Rs. 11750 ✉ 114 Dr. E. Moses Rd., Parel, Central Mumbai ☎ 22/2481–8000 🌐 www.fourseasons.com/mumbai 🛏 202 rooms 🍴 No meals.*

ITC Grand Central

$$$$ | HOTEL | A bit out of the way, the imposing 30-story ITC Grand Central is not only trusted (ITC is a trusted chain of luxury hotels in India) it has a tremendous unique selling point—its excellent North Indian food at Kebabs and Curries. **Pros:** great Indian food; online booking through the company website will award you a wealth of extra perks; practices sustainability through rainwater harvesting, reduction of water consumption. **Cons:** poorly located; built in a rather chaotic, trafficked neighborhood; Wi-Fi not complimentary. [$] *Rooms from: 18000 ✉ 287, Babasaheb Ambedkar Rd., Parel ☎ 22/2410–1010 🌐 www.itchotels.*

Getaway to Matheran Hill Station

The most pleasant hill station to visit near Mumbai, Matheran, founded by British collector Hugh Malet, is cooler than Mumbai all year long due to the elevation, and it's particularly nice in the months leading up to and during the monsoon, when the hillsides burst into verdant bloom. One big attraction is the fact that Matheran is car-free, and the main forms of transportation are horses, hand-pulled rickshaws, and carts. The late Jimmy Lord, a crusty Parsi gentleman who established a Raj-style hotel (Lords Central) here, was responsible for the push to

hang on to Matheran's heritage: he was at the forefront of campaigns to keep the hill station free of vehicles. Over the years this hill station has grown from a tiny hamlet to a budget tourist resort. Horseback riding on the country paths beyond town is a pleasant and popular pastime. Matheran is famed for its handmade shoes, and stalls and stalls of footwear dot the town. Equally famous is the historic "toy" train by which you get here—it's not a toy but, rather, runs on a narrower-gauge track.

in/hotels/mumbai/itcgrandcentral.html ⭳ *242 rooms.*

St. Regis
$$$$ | **HOTEL** | At the luxurious St. Regis, the decor is opulent Indian—think ecstatically patterned stone inlay work, silver paneling, and gold-daubed rooms. **Pros:** great views; right in the new business/shopping district of Lower Parel; good spa facilities. **Cons:** an odd location for tourists; very expensive; some find the decor a little garish. $ *Rooms from: Rs. 17000* ✉ *Senapati Bapat Marg, Tulsi Pipe Rd., Gandhi Nagar, 462, Lower Parel* ⊹ *Right next to Phoeninx shopping mall* ☎ *22/6162–8000* ⊕ *www.stregismumbai. com* ⭳ *395 rooms.*

Nightlife

Aer
BARS/PUBS | The rooftop club at the Four Seasons is one of the most popular—and most expensive—bars in town, but it offers stunning views of the city in all directions, and is probably worth a drink. ✉ *Four Seasons Hotel, 114 E. Moses Rd., Worli, Central Mumbai* ☎ *22/2481–8444.*

The Barking Deer
BREWPUBS/BEER GARDENS | Stay long enough in Mumbai, and the words "cold beer on tap" start to sound like some distant faraway dream. This bar's founder, Greg Kroitzsh, a transplant from Vermont, decided to quit whining about India's headache-inducing bottles of Kingfisher Strong, and make the dream real. The Barking Deer brews its own pale ale, as well as Bombay Blonde, a tasty lager, and the Belgian Wit, a crisp wheat beer. Kroitzsh keeps on hand a nice sampling of imported bottled beers, and the pub fare, like the eggplant Parm sandwich, is well regarded. Weekend nights tend to become overcrowded with partyers, but afternoons present a quiet opportunity to relax and reflect on your trip. The best part? Happy hour (4–8) is two beers for the price of one. There's free Wi-Fi, too. ✉ *Mathuradas Mill Compound, Senapati Bapat Marg, Lower Parel* ☎ *22/6141–7400.*

Slink & Bardot
WINE BARS—NIGHTLIFE | This trendy spot draws the city's well-heeled set for its inventive cocktail concoctions, but also for chef Alexis Gielbaum's masterful French cooking (dinner only).

✉ *Thadani House, Worli Village, 329A, Worli* ✛ *Opposite Indian Coast Guard* ☎ *22/2430–1127.*

The White Owl

BARS/PUBS | This brewpub currently stands as a reminder of how tricky it is to get government permission to brew beer in Mumbai. Huge brass tankers have sat unattended behind the clean, inviting black-and-white checkered bar since its opening. Bottles of imported ales, stouts, and lagers are served instead; the atmosphere, pub food, and bar snacks, like hot, tangy sweet-potato-and-chives popcorn, make it well worth the visit. The brewing license is coming, we are told, but in the meantime, there are many reasons to keep coming back. ✉ *One Indiabulls Center, Tower 2 Lobby, Senapati Bapat Marg, Lower Parel* ☎ *22/2421–0231* ⊕ *www.whiteowl.in.*

Performing Arts

Canvas Laugh Club

THEATER | The popularity of stand-up comedy has been on the rise in Mumbai ever since India received its own version of Comedy Central on cable back in 2011. Located in a luxury mall, this theater is a great place to catch local comics tuning up their act. ✉ *Palladium Mall, 462 Senapati Bapat Marg, 4th fl., Lower Parel* ☎ *22/4348–5000, 22/4348–5010* ⊕ *canvaslaughclub.com.*

Nehru Centre Auditorium

MUSIC | One of Mumbai's major venues, this auditorium regularly showcases theater, music, and dance performances. ✉ *Dr. Annie Besant Rd., Worli, Central Mumbai* ☎ *22/2496–4676* ⊕ *www.nehru-centre.org.*

Prithvi Theatre

THEATER | FAMILY | Run by the famous Kapoor acting family (current Bollywood stars Kareena and Ranbir Kapoor are two of them), the theater stages plays each week, many in English, with reasonably priced tickets. It often hosts special programs for children, too. It's a 45-minute drive north from downtown Mumbai, or 20 minutes from the airport in nontraffic hours. An evening at Prithvi, which has an arty café and a carefully curated bookstore, can make for one of the more memorable cultural experiences in the city. ✉ *Janaki Kutir, Church Rd., Juhu* ☎ *22/2614–9546* ⊕ *www.prithvitheatre.org.*

🛍 Shopping

Ensemble

CLOTHING | This pricey store has exclusive men's and women's Indian and Western fashions, and lovely costume jewelry, all by high-profile Indian designers. Ask to see the rare Banarasi silk saris, in rich colors woven with real gold and silver thread. ✉ *Great Western Bldg., Lionsgate, Kala Ghoda, 130–132, Kala Ghoda* ☎ *22/2284–3227, 22/4056–4825* ⊕ *www.ensembleindia.com.*

Phoenix Mills

DEPARTMENT STORES | This ever-expanding shopping, entertainment, and dining area in an old mill is an island of prosperity and chic modernity amid slums and industry. The complex is divided into different segments. Phoenix Mills itself has department stores like **Big Bazaar,** outlet clothing shop **Pantaloons,** and Hamley's. Palladium is the luxury mall with stores like Burberry, Zara, Gucci, Diesel, and Royce, a company that sells high-end Japanese chocolates. Here, too, are a number of clubs (frequented by the teenage and college student set) and the Canvas Laugh Club, showcasing various comics of varying quality on a nightly basis. High Street Phoenix features major international chains. If you get hungry, outlets of Indigo Deli, Burger King, and McDonald's, among many others, await. ✉ *Phoenix Mills Compound, Senapati Bapat Marg, Lower Parel, Central Mumbai.*

CST and Nearby

Colaba may have the Causeway, but the commercial hub of Mumbai is centered on the bustling bazaars near Chhatrapati Shivaji Terminus. CST—also often referred to by its colonial acronym, VT, which stands for Victoria Terminus—is a sight in and of itself; in fact, it is a UNESCO World Heritage site. Nearby, you'll find three of Mumbai's most important bazaars and some excellent Muslim food. It's the perfect place to see a true slice of Bombay as it was before the high-rises, fancy hotels, and high-end restaurants moved in.

Sights

Chor Bazaar (*Thieves' Bazaar*)
MARKET | This narrow thoroughfare, in the center of classic Muslim Mumbai, is lined with dozens of stores crammed with antiques and general bric-a-brac: clocks, old phonographs, brassware, glassware, and statues; some of it quite cheap. Over the years the value and breadth of much of this stock has dwindled, but there's still a chance that you'll find an unusual, memorable piece. Haggle. In the same lane a number of shops are engaged in the profitable business of constructing new furniture that looks old; many will openly tell you as much. Some shops do stock genuine antique furniture from old Parsi homes. Around the corner, stolen cell phones and car stereos are being hawked. The Thieves' Bazaar got its name because it's always been the kind of place that sold goods that fell off the back of the truck—or back of the camel—and even today you can't be too sure of the provenance of your purchases. Getting to the Chor Bazaar will take you on a tour of an interesting and very staunchly Muslim neighborhood, where life has a completely different flavor from elsewhere in the city. ⊠ *Mutton St., off Sardar Vallabhbhai Patel Rd., off Mohammed Ali Rd., Mandvi, CST.*

CST (Chhatrapati Shivaji Terminus), aka Victoria Terminus
TRANSPORTATION SITE (AIRPORT/BUS/FERRY/ TRAIN) | Built by the British in 1888, this is one of India's—and probably the world's—busiest train stations, overflowing at rush hour with enormous, surging, scurrying crowds who use the suburban lines that also originate here (Mumbai's suburban trains carry 8 million people a day). Although it's been renamed Chhatrapati Shivaji Terminus, it's still commonly called Victoria Terminus or just VT, and it bears a hefty statue of Lady Progress on its imposing dome, the haughty structure combining Indian and Victorian Gothic architecture for an Eastern version of London's St. Pancras station. Why visit? To spend a few minutes admiring the enormous, incredible UNESCO World Heritage site, which is even more arresting lit up at night. It also houses a small museum within that opens every afternoon for a few hours. If you're brave, walk around the corner to the modern suburban extension of the station around rush hour—9 am or 5:30 pm—and experience Mumbai's maddening crowds. Even better, take a ride on a local train (but avoid the rush hour); many say you have not experienced Mumbai unless you have ridden one. ⊠ *D. Naoroji Rd., CST.*

Crawford Market
MARKET | Renamed Mahatma Jyotiba Phule market decades ago, but still known by its original name, this building was designed in the 1860s by John Lockwood Kipling (father of Rudyard, who was born in this very neighborhood). The market's stone flooring supposedly came from Caithness, Scotland. Check out the stone relief depicting workers on the outside of the building. Come here early in the morning for a colorful walk through Mumbai's fresh-produce emporium, and if it's late spring or early summer, treat yourself to a delicious

A Good Walk of Mumbai's Markets

This walk is not for the timid: it will be harried, the traffic is usually crazy, and the streets are dirty, but this is Mumbai, and the experience can't be beat.

Start off at grand, Victorian **CST**, then head north, just past the station, to **Crawford Market** (renamed Mahatma Jyotiba Phule, which no one ever uses). This is one of Mumbai's biggest wholesale fruit, poultry, and vegetable markets—though you can also buy retail—and it teems with traders and local buyers. To get around, it's best to just ask a local to point you in the direction of what you're looking for (or a good landmark), because street names mean almost nothing in Mumbai, and the roads here are winding and confusing. ■TIP→ **You're about to enter the belly of the bazaar beast, so keep an eye on your wallet, and it's a good idea not to carry anything of great value with you.** Head north and you'll end up on **Muhammad Ali Road,** the city's great Muslim ghetto, though its ragged appearance and generally filthy streets make it not for the faint of heart. Muhammad Ali Road begins to blend with **Bhendi Bazaar,** which, in turn, blends into **Zaveri Bazaar,** and these two bazaars contain all of Mumbai's best goldsmiths, as well as the city's not-so-secret money-laundering industry. Grab lunch in the air-conditioned confines of **Shalimar Restaurant** (*Bhindi Bazar Corner, Masjid Bunder Sind Harsh Rd. 022/2345–6630*) in Bhendi (order the *raan biryani,* a spicy rice dish made with goat leg), then hang a left to **Chor Bazaar,** where you'll dodge wooden carts piled high with goods and wind through the labyrinth of alleys, picking through thousands of shops and stalls for dirt-cheap antiques, vintage Bollywood posters, and furniture. ■TIP→ **If you can, bring a local with you and, after making a round together, have them go back and do the bargaining and purchasing for you, with you out of sight—they'll get much better deals without a foreigner around.** Next, head back toward Muhammad Ali Road and Bhendi Bazaar for some of the best Muslim street food Mumbai has to offer. If you're strong of stomach, go to Haji Tikha Wali (ask a local, he's well known) for *kheeri tikka,* marinated cow udders grilled right in front of you. Or, if it's late at night, to Walliji Paayawala, for cooked, spicy goat hooves with coarse Irani bread. During the day, you can get *chana bateta,* chickpeas cooked with spleen (yes, we know how terrible all of this sounds, but this is seriously tasty food); there's a whole row of stalls—just go for the one with the longest line. If you're adventurous, and relish food from regions far and wide, you won't be disappointed. And, on the honestly off chance you end up spending the night on the toilet or are otherwise chastened, at least you'll do so knowing you tried the best there is.

Timing: This walk will take a full day, and, again, it's not for the faint of heart—or those unwilling to experience India on its own chaotic, messy terms. Note that Crawford Market is closed Sunday, and Muhammad Ali Road, Bhendi Bazaar, and Chor Bazaar are essentially closed—that is, completely empty of the Muslims who make up their majority—on Friday, their holy day.

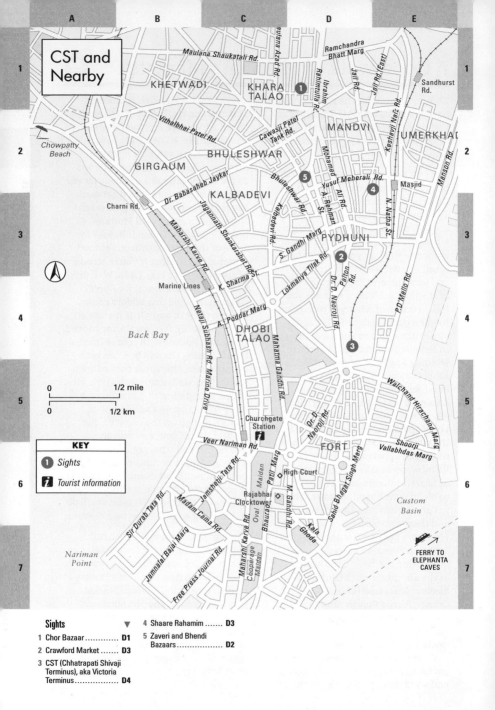

CST and Nearby

A **B** **C** **D** **E**

1

KHETWADI

Maulana Shaukatali Rd.

KHARA TALAO ❶

Maulana Azad Rd.

Ramchandra Bhatt Marg

Rahimtulla Rd.

Ibrahim Rd.

Jail Rd.

Jail Rd. (East)

Sandhurst Rd.

2

Chowpatty Beach

Vithalbhai Patel Rd.

BHULESHWAR

Cawasji Patel Tank Rd.

GIRGAUM

MANDVI

UMERKHAD

Keshavji Naik Rd.

Manson Rd.

3

Charni Rd.

Dr. Babasaheb Jaykar

KALBADEVI

Bhuleshwar Rd. ❺

Mohamed Ali Rd.

Yusuf Meherali Rd. ❹ Masjid

A. Rehman St.

N. Natha St.

S. Gandhi Marg

PYDHUNI

Maharshi Karve Rd.

Jagannath Shankarshet Rd.

Kalbadevi Rd.

Marine Lines

K. Sharma

Lokmanya Tilak Rd. ❷

Dr. D. Naoroji Rd.

Patton Rd.

P.D. Mello Rd.

4

Back Bay

Netaji Subhash Rd. / Marine Drive

A. Poddar Marg

DHOBI TALAO

Mahatma Gandhi Rd.

❸

5

0   1/2 mile
0   1/2 km

Churchgate Station

Veer Nariman Rd.

Dr. D. Naoroji Rd.

Walchand Hirachand Marg

FORT

Shoorji Vallabhdas Marg

KEY

❶ *Sights*

🛈 *Tourist information*

Jamshetji Tata Rd.

Maidan

Patil Marg

High Court

M. Gandhi Rd.

Sahid Bhagat Singh Marg

Custom Basin

6

Nariman Point

Sir Durab Tata Rd.

Madam Cama Rd.

Jamnalal Bajaj Marg

Free Press Journal Rd.

Maharshi Karve Rd.

Oval Maidan

Cooperage Maidan

Bhausar

Rajabhai Clocktower

Kala Ghoda

FERRY TO ELEPHANTA CAVES

7

Sights ▼

1 Chor Bazaar **D1**
2 Crawford Market **D3**
3 CST (Chhatrapati Shivaji Terminus), aka Victoria Terminus **D4**

4 Shaare Rahamim **D3**
5 Zaveri and Bhendi Bazaars **D2**

Alphonso mango—the experience has had many people rhapsodize that they've never truly had a mango until they ate one of these. Everything from cookies and party streamers to cane baskets is sold in other sections of the market—the meat section can be a bit hair-raising. In the middle lane (Sheikh Memon Street) of Crawford Market, is the chaotic **Mangaldas Market,** a covered, wholesale cloth market with a tremendous variety of fabrics at hundreds of indoor stalls. Across the street from the market's main entrance on the west, spread across a trio of lanes, is a smaller but popular bazaar area called **Lohar Chawl,** where the selection ranges from plastic flowers to refrigerators. ■TIP→ If you're headed to the market during the monsoon, wear rain boots or shoes you don't mind getting dirty. The floors can become quite mucky. ⊠ *D. Naoroji Rd., at L. Tilak Rd., CST.*

Shaare Rahamim (*Gate of Mercy*)
RELIGIOUS SITE | North of Crawford Market via P. D'Mello Road, past Carnac Bunder and right next to the Masjid train station, is the hard-to-find Shaare Rahamim, built in 1796. The mildly dilapidated synagogue is still in use, and you're welcome to peek inside. ⊠ *254 Samuel St., Mandvi, CST.*

Zaveri and Bhendi Bazaars
MARKET | Mumbai's crowded, century-old jewelry markets have shops filled with fabulous gold and silver in every conceivable design. The two bazaars are so intermingled at this point that it's impossible to tell where one ends and the other starts. If you notice people walking past with plastic bags full of cash, try not to stare—this is also a major hub for (certainly illegal, widely known, wholly tolerated) money laundering, completely out in the open, with no security measures in place. You'll find the bazaars a little beyond Fort in the neighborhood of Kalbadevi—a 10-minute walk northwest of Crawford Market. ■TIP→ One of the lanes leading off Zaveri Bazaar is called

Khao Galli (literally "Eat Lane") and its endless food stalls feed most of the bazaar workers daily; it's here that you'll find some of Mumbai's best—and most unusual— non–veg street food. ⊠ *Sheikh Memon St., Kalbadevi, Elephanta Island.*

Mumbadevi Temple
RELIGIOUS SITE | At the Bhuleshwar (the name of a neighborhood) end of Zaveri Bazaar is the six-century-old Mumbadevi Temple, a noisy, busy structure that houses the mouthless but powerful patron goddess who is the city's namesake. *Aarti,* evening prayers, take place at 6:30 pm. ⊠ *CST* ☎ *22/2242–4974.*

 # Shopping

BAZAARS AND MARKETS
Chor Bazaar
OUTDOOR/FLEA/GREEN MARKETS | In this bustling but tiny flea market you can find exactly what you don't need but have to have—old phonographs, broken nautical instruments, strange toys, dusty chandeliers, furniture, and brass objects ranging from junky knickknacks to valuable antiques and curios. Keep an eye on your purse or wallet and come relaxed—it can be chaotic. ⊠ *Mutton St., near Kutbi Masjid, off Mohammed Ali Rd., Mandvi, CST.*

Zaveri Bazaar
OUTDOOR/FLEA/GREEN MARKETS | A few blocks northwest of Crawford Market, this is the place to go for diamond, gold, and silver jewelry. The tumultuous streets are lined with tiny, decades-old family jewelry businesses. Duck into one and sip a customary cup of tea or coffee while a salesperson shows you the merchandise. Most shops are authentic, but beware of false silver and gold; it's difficult to spot the fakes, so it might be best to buy primarily for appearance and make intrinsic value a secondary consideration. ⊠ *Sheikh Memon St., Kalbadevi, CST.*

JEWELRY

Sheikh Memon Street

JEWELRY/ACCESSORIES | The most cost-effective place to buy jewelry is from a smaller outfit, such as **Narandas and Sons, Zaveri Naran Das,** or **Ram Kewalram Popley**—all on Sheikh Memon Street, which begins at Crawford Market and runs northwest through Zaveri Bazaar. Insist on knowing how many karats you're buying and whether or not the store will stand by the piece's purity. ✉ *Kalbadevi, CST.*

Tribhovandas Bhimji Zaveri

JEWELRY/ACCESSORIES | In business since 1865, this is said to be the largest jewelry showroom in India, with five floors of gorgeous 18-, 22-, and 24-karat gold, diamonds, and silver jewelry. ✉ *241–43 Zaveri Bazaar, Kalbadevi, CST* ☎ *22/2343–5656* 🌐 *www.tbztheoriginal.com.*

LEATHER GOODS

Daboo Street

SHOES/LUGGAGE/LEATHER GOODS | Brave bargain-hunters should take a trip to chaotic Daboo Street for all sorts of leather goods. ✉ *Off Mohammed Ali Rd., a 5-min walk south from Chor Bazaar, CST.*

Juhu, Bandra, and the Western Suburbs

The suburbs that make up the majority of Mumbai lie north of the island city, and spread out for miles on end, but visitors are likely only to visit the two main ones: Juhu and Bandra. Both house Mumbai's rich and famous, including most of its Bollywood stars (and studios). Being right in the middle of Mumbai, the main feature of **Juhu** is Juhu Beach, but it's not the kind of sandy oasis for swimming, or even sunbathing, even though it was recently cleaned up—you'll notice the locals, fully clothed, jumping around in the water, but theirs is a stronger constitution, so limit yourself to a sunset stroll. Instead, tourists are most likely to come here either for a hotel room or to sample one or two of its many bars and clubs. **Bandra,** the hub of hip Mumbai, is full of boutiques, trendy restaurants, and expats, and though it's low on sightseeing it's high on eating and drinking spots. If Bollywood's your thing, ask your cabbie or rickshaw driver to take you past the towering homes of superstars Shah Rukh Khan or Salman Khan, or past historic Mehboob Studios. If it isn't, stop in for a drink at one of the many watering holes on Waterfield Road. Other suburbs, such as Khar and Santa Cruz, are only worth a trip for the culinary offerings of certain restaurants.

🍴 Restaurants

The Blue

$$ | ASIAN | Tucked deep in the heart of one of Bandra's wriggling lanes, The Blue is a tiny, laid-back establishment with room for barely four tables, and a tiny open kitchen. It compensates for this lack of space with an unmatched selection of Japanese and Southeast Asian dishes pulled together in front of you by the wife-and-husband chef duo of Seefah Ketchaiyo and Karan Bane (previously Thai and Japanese chefs at the Four Seasons hotel's Asian restaurant San-Qi). **Known for:** sushi; yaki udon; som tam salad. [$] *Average main: Rs. 650* ✉ *Sai Pooja Bldg., on corner of 16th and 33rd Rds., Bandra West* ✣ *Near Mini Punjab* ☎ *22/3395–1655.*

Elco Restaurant

$ | INDIAN | For decades the food stalls in front of Elco Market have been serving some of the best—and cleanest—vegetarian street food Mumbai has to offer, and they were doing so well that the owners were able to open this two-floor restaurant inside the market, offering essentially the same food. One of Mumbai's most iconic experiences is standing by the pani puri vendor, as he stuffs boiled potato, sprouts, mint-fresh water,

The Deccan Odyssey

Following the success of Rajasthan's luxury Palace on Wheels train, India introduced a Maharashtra counterpart, the *Deccan Odyssey*. Traveling first class on Indian trains in the heyday of the British Raj could be a comfortable, lavish experience, with chefs and attendants taking care of the passengers' every need, in royal surroundings, as the train chugged through breathtaking countryside. The feeling is replicated aboard this train. The longest version of the trip takes you over seven nights and eight days down the Maharashtra coast to Goa before you swing upward to Pune, and to Ajanta, Ellora, and the vineyards of Nashik before returning to Mumbai. The train has several restaurants, lounges, and even a gym, but reservations are quite pricey, ranging from US$1,500 to US$11,500 depending on your choice of accommodations and the length of your journey. For more information, visit ⊕ *www.deccan-odyssey-india.com.*

and sweet chutney into an eggshell-thin sphere of fried flour and hands it to you in a plate woven together with leaves. **Known for:** the chaat, including the pani puri; all the fun of street food without any of the tummy upsets; ragda pattice (shallow-fried potato patties blanketed with a spicy curry of white peas). $ *Average main: Rs. 200* ⊠ *C–84 Elco Market, 46 Hill Rd., Bandra* ☎ *22/2645–7677* ⊟ *No credit cards.*

Gajalee
$ | SEAFOOD | Suburbanites love this quaint seafood joint near Juhu Beach, which compares favorably with the best coastal restaurants Fort has to offer. The Phoenix Mall branch is sleek and modern, while the original Vile Parle location is a bit tacky and dated but better regarded (as most originals are). **Known for:** the fried surmai fish (a type of mackerel); the big, fresh grilled tiger prawns; the "baby shark" masala (actually mori fish). $ *Average main: Rs. 400* ⊠ *Amrapali Shopping Centre, VL Mehta Marg, JVPD Scheme, Vile Parle, Juhu* ☎ *22/2610–7040* ⊕ *www.gajalee.com* $ *Average main: Rs. 500* ⊠ *Phoenix Mills, Block 3 ABC, Senapati Bapat Marg, Lower Parel, near Big Bazaar (department*

store), Central Mumbai ☎ *22/2495–0667, 22/2495–0668* ☉ *No dinner.*

Hakkasan
$$$$ | CHINESE | A Mumbai outpost of the Michelin-starred London original, this Bandra haunt is worth a visit for those who absolutely must have a fancy Chinese dinner. Even then, it's likely only worth dining here if you're in Bandra already. $ *Average main: Rs. 3500* ⊠ *Krystal Bldg., 206 Waterfield Rd., Bandra* ☎ *22/2644–4444* ⊕ *www.hakkasan.com/mumbai.*

Hemant Oberoi
$$$$ | MODERN INDIAN | After an illustrious career as the corporate chef helming the Taj hotel group's luxury division, Hemant Oberoi marked his retirement by opening his own fine-dining restaurant. The eponymous eatery serves Indian and Western food in a polished, modern avatar, but the true stars of the menu are Oberoi's signature dishes. **Known for:** the melt-in-the-mouth Brie and truffle souffle; Sunday brunch; the playful plating. $ *Average main: Rs. 1500* ⊠ *Jet Airways Godrej Bldg., G Block, Bandra Kurla Complex, 5, ground fl.* ☎ *22/2653–4757* ⊕ *www.hemantoberoi.com.*

Song and Dance, Bollywood Style

Bollywood, the famously spirited and wildly popular Indian film industry headquartered in Mumbai, is the largest movie production center in the world. Its devoted Hindi-speaking patrons number in the tens of millions.

For almost 40 years, the blueprint of Bollywood movies hasn't changed much: boy meets girl, boy and girl dance provocatively, but never kiss; something keeps them apart, usually some sort of injustice, or something having to do with religion or family; a poorly staged fight ensues in which one man takes on an entire village, and, finally, love conquers all and the pair live happily ever after. Often a dream sequence is used as an excuse for what basically amounts to a music video, often shot in the Swiss Alps, wherein famous actors otherwise unaffiliated with the movie's plot will appear, and lip synch. You may also notice pieces of your favorite American films popping up, uncredited (one popular Bollywood movie includes pieces of all the following films: *The Godfather, Pulp Fiction, Reservoir Dogs*, and *Goodfellas*; another took the plot of *I Am Sam* and turned it into a post-9/11 film, and managed to fit in a subplot featuring a Katrina-like situation in the American South).

Hindi films play a special role in the lives of the Indian people. Sure, it's a lot of musical gobbledygook, but for the poor and the illiterate, paying a few rupees for three solid hours of fantasy is a terrific bargain—and middle- and upper-class Indians are no less attached to their movies and the gods of Bollywood. An on-location film shoot, or the arrival of a Hindi star at a restaurant, will attract mobs; these actors and actresses are the demigods of India. (You'll also find them on TV and billboards, hawking everything from cell phones to cement.) The lion of the industry, Amitabh Bachchan, one of India's favorite superstars—think of him as a cross between Burt Reynolds and Ben Kingsley—has a temple dedicated to him in West Bengal.

Moviegoing tips: remember to stand up for the national anthem before the movie. You could try to brush up on your Hindi before you go, or have a local accompany you to provide a translation (you'll find that patrons talking in the movies is not uncommon; indeed, it's also not unusual for theatergoers to hold full-volume cell-phone conversations in the middle of the movie), but even though the movies are in a foreign language, the thin plotlines make it easy to follow along.

★ O' Pedro

$$ | **INDIAN** | **FAMILY** | Serving a whimsical, excellently executed menu of dishes inspired by the Catholic-dominated state of Goa, O'Pedro simultaneously pays homage to its Portuguese antecedents. Go at dinner time to avoid the clatter of the patrons who descend upon the restaurant for their lunch break from the nearby offices and to enjoy seeing the wood-fired oven lit up. **Known for:** excellent Goan breads such as poee eaten with choriz-studded butter; well-executed Hindu vegetarian Goan food in a state known for its love of pork and beef; decor that is bright with traditional and modern Goan elements. [$] *Average main: Rs. 800* ✉ *Plot number C–68, Jet*

Quick Bite 🍴

For a quick and essential bite, Mumbai has hundreds of fast-food, piping-hot-idli-crispy-dosa Udipi restaurants run by the Mangalorean Shetty community, known for proficiency in this delicious cuisine, which is an absolute must-try. The cooked food in these places is generally clean (raw foods and the restaurant floor may be less so). Many a traveler has become so addicted to eating dosas for snacks and for breakfast that they had to resist the temptation to consuming nothing else. If you're new to India and worried about getting sick from the food, dip your dosa, idli, or vada only in the hot sambar, and avoid the accompanying chutneys. Although the chutneys are quite delicious, cold and room-temperature dipping is better left for five-star hotels and fancier restaurants that cater to foreigners, where cleanliness is held to a slightly higher standard.

Airways, Godrej BKC, Unit 2, Bandra East ☎ *22/2653–4700* 🌐 *www.opedromumbai.com.*

★ Pali Bhavan

$$ | INDIAN | This Bandra West restaurant offers an intriguing tryst with regional pan-Indian flavors, the kind that rarely feature on restaurant menus in the city. Nurse a drink at the bar downstairs and then make your way upstairs to the romantic mezzanine floor; it sits choc-a-block with vintage photographs, wooden furniture, and candelabras on each table. **Known for:** bhindi kadhi (shatteringly crisp okra in a yogurt sauce); and a curry (Maharashtrian egg curry and rice); bagara baingan (peanut stuffed baby eggplant). [$] *Average main: Rs. 600* ✉ *10, Adarsh Nagar, Pali Naka, Bandra West* ✥ *Almost diagonally opposite Pali Village Cafe* ☎ *22/2651–9400.*

Pali Village Café

$$$ | EUROPEAN | Quality European bistro food—and the possibility of seeing a Bollywood star or two—draws suburbanites as well as townies on date night to this converted one-story restaurant in Bandra, but it's the romantic, old-school charm of its interior that keeps them coming back for more. While the rest of Mumbai runs headlong into the future, this place harks back to Bombay's bungalow roots with simple wooden tables, wrought-iron railings, and exposed brick. **Known for:** rustic-chic decor; wonderful wine selection; eclectic pizzas (apple, caramelized onions, and blue cheese is particularly playful). [$] *Average main: Rs. 1000* ✉ *Pali Naka, next to Janata Lunch Home, Bandra* ☎ *22/2605–0401.*

Salt Water Café

$$ | EUROPEAN | This unpretentious restaurant in Bandra Reclamation—a scenic, walkable section of Bandra—has a classic nouvelle cuisine menu and a simple rooftop terrace. It gets crowded on weekends, so be sure to make a reservation, preferably for the terrace, where the cover of giant palm trees somehow blocks out the cacophony from noisy Chapel Road below. **Known for:** great breakfasts; pretty sweet meaty dishes, especially the lamb shanks; great happy-hour deals. [$] *Average main: Rs. 700* ✉ *Rose Minar Annexe, 87 Chapel Rd., near Mount Carmel Church, Bandra* ☎ *22/2643–4441.*

Hotels

Citizen

$ | **HOTEL** | One of the cheapest decent hotels on the Juhu strip, and right on the beach, the Citizen is a deal in a city where you seemingly pay for every square inch. **Pros:** good value for money; on the beach; free Wi-Fi. **Cons:** far from South Mumbai and a bit of a drive from the airport; can be noisy; the food at the restaurant is adequate at best. [$] *Rooms from: Rs. 5000* ✉ *960 Juhu Tara Rd., Juhu* ☎ *22/6693–2525* 🌐 *www.citizen-hotelMumbai.com* 🛏 *48 rooms* 🍴 *Free Breakfast.*

Courtyard Marriott

$$$ | **HOTEL** | This Courtyard Marriott is plush, but guests hoping for local color will be disappointed; this is a sophisticated but generic luxury chain and its location (nearly fringing the airport) is rather uninspiring. **Pros:** airport shuttle; complimentary on-site parking; close to the new business center of BKC. **Cons:** far from tourist sites; not much of a view; the high-speed in-room Wi-Fi is expensive. [$] *Rooms from: Rs. 10000* ✉ *CTS 215 Carnival Cinema, Andheri Kurla Rd., Andheri* ☎ *22/6136–9999* 🌐 *courtyard.marriott.com* 🛏 *334 rooms.*

JW Marriott

$$$$ | **HOTEL** | **FAMILY** | At this grand, luxurious hotel you can retreat from the chaos of Mumbai but still step out and experience it, though the main sights are distant. **Pros:** massive Sunday brunch buffet; right on the beach; its Bombay Baking Company doles out great pastries and baked items. **Cons:** a bit far from city sights; not all rooms have great sea views; not very close to the airport. [$] *Rooms from: Rs. 13500* ✉ *Juhu Tara Rd., Juhu* ☎ *22/6693–3000* 🌐 *www.marriott.com* 🛏 *355 rooms* 🍴 *Free Breakfast.*

Novotel

$$$ | **HOTEL** | Built in the 1970s, this Western-style high-rise was completely renovated when Novotel took over in 2009, and the spacious lobby and large rooms now have a modern, sleek feel. **Pros:** beachside location; airport pickup included in price; close to suburban malls. **Cons:** far from downtown; somewhat shabby and run-down; city-facing rooms have rather dismal views. [$] *Rooms from: Rs. 10000* ✉ *Balraj Sahani Marg, Juhu* ☎ *22/6693–4444* 🌐 *www.novotel.com* 🛏 *215 rooms* 🍴 *No meals.*

Sofitel

$$$ | **HOTEL** | Step into a cavernous, airy, sunlit lobby with chandeliers and huge glass windows at this hotel that finds its inspiration in Indian and French art, effectively showcasing its East-meets-West credo. **Pros:** five in-house restaurants; close to a clutch of brand-new restaurants and offices in the BKC area; very courteous service and excellent attention to detail. **Cons:** oddly located for those wanting to spend time in the touristy south of Mumbai; not a great view at all; the rooms' curiouslyangled shapes may discomfit some. [$] *Rooms from: Rs. 11000* ✉ *C 57, Bandra Kurla Complex* ☎ *22/6117–5000* 🌐 *www.sofitel-mumbai-bkc.com* 🛏 *302 rooms.*

Taj Land's End

$$$ | **HOTEL** | Choose this opulent, ocean-facing hotel if you don't mind paying a decent buck for a luxurious stay far from the city's main sights but close to some of its best restaurants, bars, and clubs. **Pros:** amazing views; close to restaurants and nightlife; great business facilities. **Cons:** expensive; far from city's historic sites; the restaurants are not as celebrated as those at its sister restaurant, the Taj Mahal Palace & Towers. [$] *Rooms from: Rs. 11500* ✉ *Land's End, Bandstand area, Bandra* ☎ *22/6668–1234* 🌐 *www.tajhotels.com* 🛏 *526 rooms* 🍴 *Free Breakfast.*

Taj Santacruz
$$$ | **HOTEL** | The fifth Taj property in Mumbai, this hotel shares the high standards of all the others; each room offers all the regular mod-cons—free Wi-Fi, deep-soaking bathtubs, and DVD player. **Pros:** very close to the airport; very large rooms; large pool. **Cons:** a little difficult to find because of nearby construction activities; hard to find on GPS due to its proximity to the airport; pretty far from tourist areas in the south. [$] *Rooms from: Rs. 12500* ✉ *Off Western Express Hwy., Santacruz, Sahar* ✥ *Right next to Chhatrapati Shivaji International Airport* ☎ *22/6211–5211* 🌐 *www.tajhotels.com* 🛏 *279 rooms.*

Nightlife

antiSOCIAL
DANCE CLUBS | Housed in a defunct basement in Khar, antiSocial has rapidly become one of Mumbai's prime performance spaces and clubs. ✉ *Rohan Plaza, 5th Rd., Ram Krishna Nagar, Khar* ☎ *75063–94243.*

The Good Wife
BARS/PUBS | Run by siblings Ryan and Keenan Tham, The Good Wife supplies craft beer and European and East Asian fare to the accompaniment of pop and EDM. ✉ *The Capital, Bandra Kurla Complex, Block G, Bandra* ☎ *22/4003–9433.*

Monkey Bar
CAFES—NIGHTLIFE | This gastropub quickly gained a fan following for its food, but its cocktails are no laggard—order the Mangaa (vodka, mango, black salt) or the Don Draper (Ballantine's and bitters) and soak it all up with Rajasthani-style lamb tacos and the MoBar burger. ✉ *Summerville, Junction of 14th and 33rd Rds., Bandra* ☎ *2600–5215.*

Olive Bar and Restaurant
BARS/PUBS | This candlelit nightspot draws Mumbai's who's who for bites of top-notch antipasti, risotto, seafood salad, and sips of caipiroskas (caipirin is made with vodka instead of the rumlike cachaça). ✉ *14 Union Park, off Carter Rd., Bandra* ☎ *022/4340–8229* 🌐 *www.olivebarandkitchen.com.*

Shopping

Dhoop
CRAFTS | Here you'll find a superb, unusual collection of handicrafts that includes upside-down incense holders and palm-leaf lampshades. If you're staying in Bandra, you're only 15 or so minutes away. ✉ *Tridev Bldg., Plot No. 27A, 21st Rd., Dandpada, Anand Vihar Society, Khar* ☎ *22/2649–8646* 🌐 *www.dhoop.co.in.*

Linking Road
DEPARTMENT STORES | Starting from S.V. Road in Bandra all the way through a seemingly endless strip of stores, stalls, and tables of goods, you can bargain on belt buckles here one minute, and then pick up a designer dress on sale the next. It's also one of the more decent strips in the city to buy women's shoes. ✉ *Linking Rd., Bandra.*

OMO
CLOTHING | Short for On My Own, OMO is a small, out-of-the-way Bandra hotspot for women's cotton clothing, jewelry, and other accessories. ✉ *Serpis Villa, 53 Chimbai Rd., Bandra* ✥ *Behind St. Andrews Church* ☎ *22/2641–8140.*

Side Trips from Mumbai

Aurangabad and the Ajanta and Ellora Caves

Although they may never receive top billing on a brochure, an argument can certainly be made that the cave temples at Ajanta and Ellora, which rank among the wonders of the ancient world, make for as spectacular of a visit as one to Taj Mahal. The good thing about the reduced hype, of course, is that it translates to a less crowded and more intimate touring experience. And the best part for visitors of Mumbai? The sites are only a weekend trip away.

A less-than-an-hour flight and a reasonably short drive can put you inside a Buddhist cave filled with stunning paintings, or place you in front of a mighty temple carved from the hills, retelling the story of the Ramayana in intimate detail.

Dating back more than 2,000 years, the cave temples of Ajanta and Ellora represent the most elaborate and spectacular cave architecture in the entire country. Both have been listed as UNESCO World Heritage sites. Here, between the 2nd century BC and the 9th century AD, thousands of monks and artisan laborers carved cathedrals, monasteries, and entire cities of frescoed, sculptured halls into the solid rock. Working with simple chisels and hammers, and an ingenious system of reflecting mirrors to provide light into the dark interiors, they cut away hundreds of thousands of tons of rock to create the cave temples and other carvings. The work of these craftsmen inspires awe for the precision of their planning and knowledge of rock formations, their dedication to creating all this so far from the rest of India, and the delicacy and sheer quantity of the artwork. The cave temples span three great religions—Buddhism, Hinduism, and Jainism.

To best appreciate the caves, allow one full day for each site, and remember Ajanta is closed Monday, and Ellora is closed Tuesday.

Suggested itinerary: a weekend trip to Ajanta and Ellora, while making your base in Aurangabad, makes for a perfect trip from Mumbai. If you leave Mumbai on Friday morning, you can have dinner in Aurangabad—it's best to estimate more time, rather than less, when it comes to travel in India—and then head out early the next morning for the Ajanta caves, about a two- to three-hour drive away, for the day. Sunday morning you can head to the much closer (about 30 minutes), and more crowded, Ellora Caves, then head back to Mumbai that evening.

See the "Ajanta and Ellora Caves" feature in this chapter for more information.

GETTING HERE AND AROUND
To get to Ajanta and Ellora, you can take a train, bus, or plane to Aurangabad.

Aurangabad is about one hour from Mumbai by air (about US$50, one way), or 3½ hours from New Delhi (about US$80, one way); there are also flights (albeit with a stopover) between Aurangabad and Jaipur and Udaipur. Air India and Jet Airways fly to Aurangabad from Mumbai and Delhi. Schedules change every six months for these kinds of hop-and-a-skip flights, so check with the airlines for the most up-to-date information.

AIRLINE CONTACTS Air India ⊕ *www.airindia.com.* **Jet Airways** ⊕ *www.jetairways.com.*

There are only a few trains between Aurangabad and Mumbai, and the timing makes it difficult to see the caves in a timely manner. Indian Rail's *Tapovan Express* is the best option; it departs from Mumbai at 6:10 am and arrives a little after 1 pm.

The Government of India Tourist Office, across from the train station, provides a warm and informative welcome to Aurangabad and is open weekdays 8:30–6 and Saturday and holidays 8:30–2. The MTDC office in town (open Monday to Saturday 10–5:30; closed the second and fourth Saturday of the month) offers a variety of information about other destinations in Maharashtra, and it has a counter at the airport that's open when flights arrive.

TRAVEL AGENCY AND TOUR GUIDE CONTACTS Blossom Travel Services ⊠ *Hotel Ambassador Ajanta, Jalna Rd., Travel*

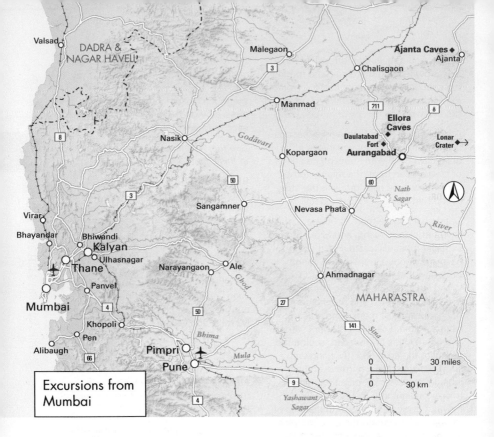

Excursions from Mumbai

Desk, Aurangabad ☎ 240/248–1955 ⊕ blossomtravels.com. **Saibaba Travels Aurangabad** ✉ Shop No. 88, Sindhi Colony, Jalna Rd., Aurangabad ☎ 240/235–1612 ⊕ www.saibabatravels.com.

VISITOR INFORMATION CONTACTS
Government of India Tourist Office ✉ MTDC Holiday Resort, Station Rd., 1st fl., Aurangabad ☎ 22/2204–4040 ⊕ www.maharashtratourism.net. **Maharashtra Tourism Development Corporation (MTDC)** ✉ MTDC Holiday Resort, Station Rd., Aurangabad ☎ 240/234–3169 ⊕ www.maharashtratourism.gov.in.

388 km (241 miles) east of Mumbai; 30 km (18 miles) southeast of Ellora; 100 km (62 miles) southwest of Ajanta.

With several excellent hotels, Aurangabad is a good base from which to explore the cave temples at Ajanta and Ellora,

but not a fantastic city for restaurants, and not likely a place where you would go without its accessibility to those jaw-dropping attractions.

India is still India, however, and Aurangabad does have a few intriguing sites if you have extra time before or after visiting the caves.

The city is known for its *himru* (cotton and silk brocade) shawls and saris, and its gorgeously and painstakingly decorated Paithani *zari*, which are fine gold-embroidered saris—zari is the name for the gold metallic thread; and Paithani is a village very close to Aurangabad. If you're interested, pop into the Aurangabad Standard Silk Showroom or Aurangabad Silk, both near the train station; Ajanta Handicrafts in Harsul, on the highway to Ajanta; or Himroo Saris, on the highway to Ellora. An even better option to view

Himru saris being woven is to venture over to the Himru Cooperative Society at Jaffer (also spelled Zaffar) Gate, an area in the western part of Aurangabad: there you can see the entire process in action in a traditional environment. The saris (which can be cut up and tailored into other items) are more reasonably priced here.

Bibi-ka-Maqbara

MEMORIAL | This 17th-century tomb is also known as the mini Taj Mahal; you can usually see it from the plane when you're flying into Aurangabad. A pale imitation of the original Taj Mahal, it is dedicated to the wife of the last of the six great Mughal emperors, Aurangzeb (founder of Aurangabad and son of the Taj Mahal's creator, Shah Jahan). It was supposed to be a shining, white-marble edifice, but money ran out, so only the bottom two feet of the monument were built with marble; the rest is stone with a facade of plaster. Somewhat awkwardly proportioned, the structure can be said to illustrate the decline of Mughal architecture. ✉ *550 yards north of Old Town, beyond Mecca Gate* 🎟 *Foreigners US$4 (Rs. 250).*

Daulatabad Fort

ARCHAEOLOGICAL SITE | The imposing fort, built in 1187 by a Hindu king, is surrounded by seven giant walls more than 5 km (3 miles) long. Daulatabad was once called Deogiri, or "hill of the gods," but was changed to "city of fortune" when the sultan of Delhi overtook it in 1308. Devote at least half a day to this fascinating fort, considered one of India's most impressive. There's a wonderful view of the plains from the acropolis (fortified city) on the top. As you enter the fort you go through a labyrinth—note the moats, spikes, cannons, and dark maze of tunnels designed to make the fort as impregnable as possible. Equally interesting is the Jami Masjid (large mosque) inside; it was made from horizontal lintels and pillars taken from Jain and Hindu temples. Local Hindus put a lot of store in a *puja* (worship) done at the top of the fort and then down below, at the exit. ✉ *13 km [8 miles] west of Old Town, on highway to Ellora Caves* 🎟 *Foreigners around US$2 (Rs. 100).*

Lonar Crater

NATURE SITE | About 160 km (100 miles) and 3½ to 4 hours east of Aurangabad, beyond Jalna, *not* on the highway to either Ajanta or Ellora, is the Lonar Crater. If you have a day free, or if you have an extra day because the caves are closed, visit this serene 50,000-year-old meteor crater. Off the beaten path and away from postcard sellers, bead hawkers, and soft-drink-stall owners, the 1,800-meter-long crater lake is one of India's more phenomenal sites. It's said to be Asia's largest and youngest crater. Lonar is a peaceful spot, full of wildlife and greenery. ✉ *Aurangabad.*

Most of the better choices for restaurants serve dishes representing multiple cuisine options—Indian (Mughlai and tandoori, or South Indian), Chinese, and the local variant of what passes for continental food. Stick with Indian cuisine outside the luxury hotels—Maharashtran and Hyderabadi fare is generally better prepared and tastier. Most restaurants here don't serve food outside typical meal hours.

Buddi Galli

$ | **INDIAN** | You'll have to drive a bit to reach the food street because Buddi Galli is on the fringes of the city, but once you reach it, your taste buds will thank you. Try the *naankhaliya,* Aurangabad's slow-cooked beef or mutton curry, fried *tikki* kebabs, and if you come during Ramzan, the *harees* (a hearty meat and lentil stew). **Known for:** meaty Muslim cooking; cantukky chicken (a take on KFC); Indian desserts like apricots with cream. [$] *Average main: Rs. 100* ✉ *Buddi Galli, Naralibag, Mumbai.*

Continued on page 360

AJANTA AND ELLORA CAVES

The centuries-old carved cave temples and cave paintings at Ajanta and Ellora are the product of awe-inspiring workmanship and span three great religions—Buddhism, Hinduism, and Jainism.

The caves at Ajanta and Ellora rank among the wonders of the ancient world. Here, between the 2nd century BC and the 5th century AD, great numbers (probably thousands) of monks and artisan laborers carved cathedrals, monasteries, and entire cities into the rock. Working with simple chisels and hammers, and an ingenious system of mirrors to send light into the interiors, the laborers cut away hundreds of thousands of tons of rock to create the cave temples and other carvings. The precision of the planning, the dedication of the laborers in such a remote location, and the delicacy and sheer quantity of the artwork make it obvious why both locations have been designated UNESCO world heritage sites.

CAVE PAINTINGS

Both Ajanta and Ellora have monumental facades and statues but Ajanta also has remarkable cave paintings that have survived the centuries. The paintings cover most of the cave surfaces, except the floor. They were created by spreading a plaster of clay, cow dung, chopped rice husks, and lime onto the rock walls, then painting pictures with local pigments: red ocher, copper oxide, lampblack, and dust from crushed green rocks. The paint brushes were made of twigs and camel hair. The caves are now like chapters of a splendid epic in visual form, recalling the life of the Buddha, and illustrating the life and civilization of the artisans.

(top) The magnificent Kailasa Temple, carved out of solid rock (left) The Ajanta cave painting of Padmapani, also known as "the one with the lotus in his hand"

THE AJANTA CAVES

Set in a wide, steep, horseshoe-shaped gorge above a wild mountain stream, the Ajanta caves reward travelers with a stunning glimpse into ancient India. Tucked in a setting that is lush and green after the monsoon, India's greatest collection of cave paintings dates back two millennia and is housed within massive carved stone caverns.

HISTORY

It's believed that a band of wandering Buddhist monks first came here in the 2nd century BC, searching for a place to meditate during the monsoons. Ajanta was ideal—peaceful and remote, with a spectacular setting. The monks began carving caves into the gray rock face of the gorge, and a new temple form was born.

Over the course of seven centuries, the cave temples of Ajanta evolved into works of incredible art. Structural engineers continue to be amazed by the sheer brilliance of the ancient builders, who, undaunted by the limitations of their implements, materials, and skills, created a marvel of artistic and architectural splendor. In all, 29 caves were carved, 15 of which were left unfinished; some of the caves were *viharas* (monasteries)—complete with stone pillars carved onto the monks' stone beds; others were *chaityas* (Buddhist cathedrals). All of the caves were profusely decorated with intricate sculptures and murals depicting the many incarnations of Buddha.

As the influence of Buddhism declined, the number of monk-artists became fewer, and the temples were swallowed up by the voracious jungle. It was not until about a thousand years

((top) An aerial view of the Ajanta caves (right) A carving of a reclining buddha in an Ajanta cave

later, in 1819, that an Englishman named John Smith, who was out tiger hunting on the bluff overlooking the Waghora River in the dry season, noticed the soaring arch of what is now known as Cave 10 peeking out from the thinned greenery in the ravine below. It was he who subsequently unveiled the caves to the modern world.

The paintings are dimly lit to protect the artwork, and a number are badly damaged, so deciphering the work takes some effort. The Archaeological Survey of India has, however, put a lot of effort into making the caves more viewable, including installing special ultraviolet lights to brighten certain panels. Shades and nets installed at the mouth of each cave keep out excess sun and bats.

PLANNING YOUR VISIT

A trip to the Ajanta caves needs to be well planned. You can see the caves at a fairly leisurely pace in two hours, but the drive to and from the site takes about two to three hours each way.

There's no longer direct access to the caves. All visitors are required to park their cars or disembark from their buses at a visitor center 3 km (2 mi) from the caves. From here, a Rs. 6 ticket buys you a place on frequently departing green Maharashtra Tourism

Development Corporation (MTDC) buses to the caves (it's Rs. 10 for an air-conditioned bus, but they travel less frequently). The visitor complex has stalls with people hawking souvenirs, film, sodas, water, and packaged and fresh hot snacks—plus unknown guides that need to be firmly dismissed.

WHAT TO BRING AND WEAR

Come prepared with water, lunch or snacks, comfortable walking shoes (that can be slipped on and off easily, because shoes are not allowed inside the caves), socks to pad about the cave in so you don't get your feet dirty, a small flashlight, a hat or umbrella for the heat, and patience. Aurangabad can be hot year-round, and touring 29 caves can be tiring.

PRACTICAL INFORMATION

✉ 100 km (62 miles) northeast of Aurangabad; about a 2–3 hour drive.

🎫 Admission Rs. 250 foreigners $5, light fee Rs. 5 (includes all caves), video camera fee Rs. 25, parking Rs. 50. Flash photography and video cameras are prohibited inside the caves (shooting outside is fine). There is a cloak room at the visitor center where you can check bags for Rs. 5.

🕙 Tues.–Sun. 9 am–5 pm (Closed Monday); arrive by 3:30

VISITING THE AJANTA CAVES

WHERE TO START

The caves are connected by a fair number of steps. It's best to start at the far end, at Cave 26, and work your way to Cave 1 to avoid a long trek back at the end. The initial ascent, before you reach the cave level, is also quite a climb, at 92 steps. Palanquins carried by helpers are available for the less hardy, for Rs. 400.

MOST IMPORTANT TO SEE

Opinions vary on which of the Ajanta caves is most exquisite: Caves 1, 2, 16, 17, and 19 are generally considered to have the best paintings; caves 1, 6, 10, 17, 19, and 26 the best sculptures. (The caves are numbered from west to east, not in chronological order.) Try to see all eight of these caves, at least.

Cave 1. Ajanta's most popular cave paintings are here; they depict the Bodhisattva Avalokitesvara and Bodhisattva Padmapani. Padmapani, or the "one with the lotus in his hand," is considered to be the alter ego of the Lord Buddha; Padmapani assumed the duties of the Buddha when he disappeared. Padmapani is often depicted with his voluptuous wife. When seen from different angles, the

magnificent Buddha statue in this cave seems to wear different facial expressions.

Cave 2. This cave is remarkable for the ceiling decorations and murals relating the birth of the Buddha. For its sheer exuberance, the painting of women on a swing is considered the finest. It's on the right wall as you enter, and when you face the wall it's on the left side.

Cave 6. This two-story cave has lovely detail. Climb the steep steps to the second floor, where there are pillars that emit musical sounds when rapped.

Cave 10. The oldest cave, this shrine dates from 200 BC, and is dominated by a large, squat *stupa* (a dome, or monument, to Buddha). The exquisite

brush-and-line work dates from AD 100: in breathtaking detail, the Shadanta Jataka, a legend about the Buddha, is depicted on the wall in a continuous panel. There are no idols of Buddha in this cave, indicating that idol worship was not in vogue at the time. (Cave 19, which dates from about the 5th century, does contain idols of Buddha, showing the progression of thought and the development of new methods of worship as the centuries wore on.) Guides and caretakers will enthusiastically point out the name of the Englishman, John Smith, who rediscovered the caves. His name, along with 1819 underneath, is carved on the 12th pillar on the right-hand side of this cave—though it's Cave 9, with its domed arch, that Smith first spotted.

Cave 16. The monk-artists seem to have reached their creative zenith here; the continuous narrative spreads both horizontally and vertically, evolving into a panoramic whole—at once logical and stunning. One painting is especially riveting: known as *The Dying Princess,* it's believed to represent Sundari, the wife of the Buddha's half-brother Nanda, who left her to become a monk. This cave has an excellent view of the river and may have been the entrance to the entire series of caves.

Cave 17. This cave has the greatest number of pictures undamaged by time. Heavenly damsels fly effortlessly overhead, a prince makes love to a princess, and the Buddha tames a raging elephant (resisting temptation is a theme). Other favorite paintings here

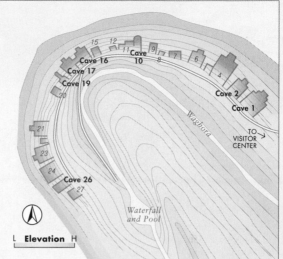

include the scene of a woman applying lipstick and one of a princess performing *sringar* (her toilette)—this last is on the right-hand wall as you enter, and as you face the wall on the farthest right pillar.

Cave 19. Dating from about the mid 5th century, when Buddhism was in full swing, the stone sculpture on the exterior of this magnificent cha-itya, or cathedral, is incredibly detailed. Inside, too, the faded paintings are overshadowed by the the sculptures. The standing Buddha is especially notable; compared with the stupas from earlier caves, this one is much more detailed and elongated.

Cave 26. This is the most interesting of the caves at the far end. An impressive sculpted panel of a reclining Buddha is on your left as you enter. It's believed to be a portrayal of a dying Buddha on the verge of attaining nir-

vana. His weeping followers are at his side, while celestial beings are waiting to transport him to the land of no tomorrows (no rebirths).

Unfinished caves. Several unfinished caves were abandoned nearby but are worth a visit if you're up for the steep, 100-step climb (alternatively, you can walk up the bridle path, a gentler ascent alongside the caves). From here you have a magnificent view of the ravine descending into the Wa-ghura River. An even easier way to reach this point is to stop your car as you return to Aurangabad, 20 km (12 mi) from the caves: take a right at Balapur and head 8 km (5 mi) toward Viewpoint, as it's called by the locals.

(top left) Religious figures carved out of the rock on the facade of an ancient Buddhist rock temple cave 26 (bottom left) Detail from Cave 2 (middle left) Buddha carving in Cave 6 (left) Inside Cave 26

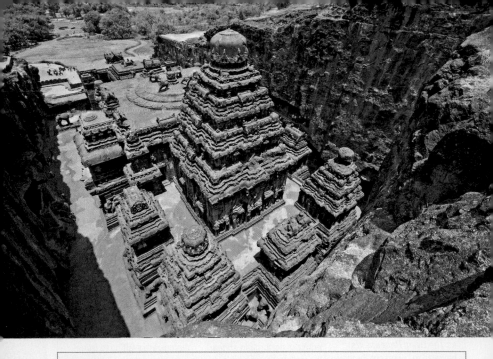

THE ELLORA CAVES

Unlike the cave temples at Ajanta, those of Ellora are not solely Buddhist. Rather, they follow the development of religious thought in India through the decline of Buddhism in the latter half of the 8th century, to the Hindu renaissance that followed the return of the Gupta dynasty, and to the Jain resurgence between the 9th and 11th centuries. Of the 34 caves here, the 12 to the south are Buddhist, the 17 in the center are Hindu, and the 5 to the north are Jain.

HISTORY

In the 7th century, religious activity shifted from Ajanta to a site 123 km (76 mi) to the southwest—known today as Ellora—although the reason for this move is not known. The focus at Ellora is sculpture, which covers the walls in ornate masses. The carvings in the Buddhist caves are serene, but in the Hindu caves they take on a certain exuberance and vitality—gods and demons do fearful battle, Lord Shiva angrily flails his eight arms, elephants rampage, eagles swoop, and lovers intertwine.

Unlike at Ajanta, where the temples were chopped out of a steep cliff, the caves at Ellora were dug into the slope of a hill along a north–south line, presumably so that they faced west and could receive the light of the setting sun.

WHEN TO GO?

Because Ellora is such a busy tourist destination, try to avoid coming here during school holidays from April to first week of June.

(top) Kailasa Temple (top right) Detail of a religious story carved into Kailasa (bottom right) One of the smaller rock-carved temples

The annual **Ellora Dance Festival**, held on one full moon night in December, draws top classical Indian dancers and musicians from around the country to perform outdoors against the magical backdrop of the Ellora Caves. For more information, ask at the tourist office or the Maharashtra Tourism Development Corporation.

PLANNING YOUR VISIT

Visiting the Ellora caves is in many ways easier than visiting Ajanta, though the rewards are different. Not only is Ellora closer to Aurangabad, when you get there, the line of caves is more accessible, all parallel to the road, and there are not many steps involved. Proximity to Aurangabad and the easy access makes seeing these caves a half-day's adventure; choose either

early morning or late afternoon. The winding drive to Ellora is very pleasant, through low-slung hills past old ruins as well as Daulatabad Fort (try to squeeze at least a half-hour stop there, too).

WHERE TO EAT?

You're best off packing a lunch from Aurangabad, but there are two decent options around caves: The **Ellora Restaurant** (☎ 24/372–4441), by the entrance, is a convenient place to stop for a cold drink and a hot samosa. The outdoor patio has fruit trees (home to many monkeys) and pink bougain-villea flowers. The restaurant closes before the caves do. Outside Kailasa Cave (number 16), past the many souvenir stall, is the Hotel Kailas with its attached restaurant, **Kailas**: it's a simple cafeteria-style restaurant serving basic vegetarian Indian food until 9:30 pm. The food isn't great, but it's a bit nicer than the Ellora Restaurant.

PRACTICAL INFORMATION

✉ 30 km (18 miles) northwest of Aurangabad; about a 1/2 hour drive

🎟 Rs. 250, video camera fee Rs. 25

🕐 Wed.–Mon. (closed Tuesday), 6 am–6 pm

VISTING THE ELLORA CAVES

WHERE TO START

Although the caves are spread out over a large area, they're parallel to the road. Arrange with your driver to pick you up at several points: start at Cave 1 and work your way to 16, where you should have your driver meet you and take you to Cave 21. Then head to Cave 29. Another short drive will take you to the Jain caves.

MOST IMPORTANT TO SEE

Cave 16, the Kailasa temple, is the star attraction here but make sure to see caves from each of the three representative religions so that you can compare and contrast.

The southernmost caves are Buddhist.

Cave 2. The facade of this impressive monastery is deceptively simple, but the interior is lavish: gouged into the block of rock is a central hall with ornate pillars and a gallery of Buddhas and Boddhisattvas seated under trees and parasols.

Cave 5. The largest of the Buddhist caves, this was probably used as a classroom for young monks. The roof appears to be supported by 24 pillars; working their way down, sculptors first "built" the roof before they "erected" the pillars.

Cave 6. A statue of Mahamayuri, the Buddhist goddess of learning—also identified as

Saraswati, the Hindu goddess of learning—is the focus here, surrounded by Buddhist figures. The boundaries between Hinduism and Buddhism are fuzzy and Hindus worship and recognize some Buddhist gods and goddesses as their own, and vice versa: Hindus, for instance, consider Buddha the avatar of Vishnu.

Cave 7. This austere hall with pillars is one of Ellora's two-story caves.

Cave 10. The carvings here are impressive: the stonecutters reproduced the timbered roofs of the period over a richly decorated facade that resembles masonry work. Inside this shrine—the only actual Buddhist chapel at Ellora—

the main work of art is a huge sculpture of Buddha. Check out the high ceiling with stone "rafters" and note the sharp echo. The cave has been dubbed the Sutar Jhopdi or Carpenter's Cave and called a tribute to Visvakarma, the Hindu god of tools and carpentry.

Caves 11 and 12. These two caves rise grandly three floors up and are richly decorated with sculptural panels.

Starting with Cave 13, the Hindu caves are the successors to the Buddhist ones, and a step inside will stop you in your tracks. It's another world—another universe—in which the calm contemplation of the seated Buddhas gives way to the dynamic cosmology of Hinduism. These caves were created around the 7th and 8th centuries.

Cave 16. Ellora is dominated by the mammoth Kailasa Temple (also known as Kailasanatha, or Kailash) complex, or Cave 16. Dedicated to Shiva, the complex is a replica of his legendary abode at Mount Kailasa in the Tibetan Himalayas. The largest monolithic structure in the world, Kailasa reveals the genius, daring, and raw skill of its artisans.

To create the Kailasa complex, an army of stonecutters started at the top of the cliff, where they removed 3 million cubic feet of rock to create a vast pit with a freestanding rock left in the center. Out of this single slab, 276 feet long and 154 feet wide, the workers created Shiva's abode, which includes the main temple, a series of smaller shrines, and galleries built into a wall that encloses the entire complex. Nearly every surface is exquisitely sculpted with epic themes.

Around the courtyard, numerous friezes illustrate the legends of Shiva and stories from the great Hindu epics, the Mahabharata and the Ramayana. One interesting panel on the eastern wall relates the origin of Shiva's main symbol, the lingam, or phallus. Another frieze, on the outer wall of the main sanctuary on the southern side of the courtyard, shows the demon Ravana shaking Mount Kailasa.

Cave 21. Of the Hindu caves north of Kailash, this cave, also called the Ramesvara, has some interesting sculptures, including the figurines of the river goddesses at the entrance. It's thought to be the oldest Hindu cave.

Cave 29. Past the seasonal waterfall, this cave, also called Dhumar Lena, is similar in layout to the caves at Elephanta, near Mumbai. Pairs of lion sculptures guard the staircases and inside are some interesting friezes.

The Jain caves are at the far end of Ellora, and definitely worth a visit, if just for the contrast. The Jain caves are more modest and subdued than the Hindu caves, but

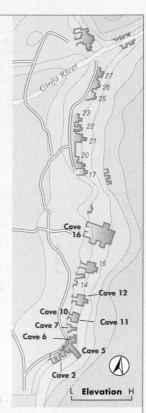

have some lovely artwork carvings. Climb through the many well-carved chambers and study the towering figures of Gomateshvara (a Jain mythological figure) and Mahavira (an important Jain sage).

Cave 32. The most notable of the Jain caves is a miniature Kailash Temple, on two levels. The bottom floor is rather plain, but elaborate carvings surround the upper story.

(top left) Seven carved buddhas, Cave 12 (middle left) seated buddha, Cave 10 (top right) Detail on Kailasa Temple (bottom right) Cave 29 detail

Planning Your Visit to the Caves

Getting to the caves

To see the caves from Mumbai takes several days: you'll base yourself in Aurangabad, which is about 400 miles east of Mumbai (an hour-long flight), and make separate day trips to Ajanta and Ellora. Allow one full day for each site, and remember Ajanta is closed Monday, and Ellora is closed Tuesday.

If you can make it only to either Ellora or Ajanta, choose Ajanta: it's farther, but the comparative lack of crowds and the pristine serenity of the forest are worth it.

Suggested itinerary from Mumbai:
A trip to Ajanta and Ellora, while making your base in Aurangabad, makes a perfect long weekend trip from Mumbai. If you leave Mumbai on Friday you can be in Aurangabad in the late afternoon, have dinner, and then head out early the next morning for the Ajanta caves, about a two- to three-hour drive away, for the day. Sunday morning, you can head to the much closer (about 30 minutes), and more crowded, Ellora Caves, then head back to Mumbai that evening.

Getting to Ajanta and Ellora from Aurangabad: From Aurangabad there are tour buses (check with the Government of India Tourist Office or the MTDC office), but this ends up being rather rushed. You're best off hiring a car and driver. An air-conditioned car for a full day will cost around Rs. 2,400 to Ajanta and Rs. 1,100 to Ellora. You can arrange a car for hire through your hotel, a travel agent, or the Government of India Tourist Office; fix a price in advance.

Hiring a guide

It's a good idea to hire a guide, who can explain the iconography and details about how the caves were built. The Government of India Tourist Office (*Krishna Vilas, Station Rd., Aurangabad 240/236–4999 or 240/233–1217 www.incredibleindia.org*) oversees about 45 expert, polite, multilingual tour guides. You can hire one through the tourist office; through the MTDC office (*MTDC Holiday Resort, Station Rd., Aurangabad 240/233–1513 www.maharashtratourism.gov.in*); or through a travel agent in Aurangabad.

For parties of one to four, the fees are about Rs. 1,000 for a full day to Ajanta, and about Rs. 750 for a full day to Ellora. Hiring a half-day guide (four hours) is about Rs. 450. An extra Rs. 400 or so is charged for trips of more than 100 km (60 miles). It's best to book ahead. There are also some guides available to hire at the ticket counters to the caves.

QUICK GUIDE TO THE CAVES

Ajanta	Ellora
Farther from Aurangabad (3-hour drive)	Closer to Aurangabad (½-hour drive)
Closed Monday	Closed Tuesday
29 caves were carved (15 are unfinished)	34 caves; Kailasa is the highlight
All Buddhist	Buddhist, Hindu, and Jain
Focus is on cave paintings	Focus is on sculpture
Caves chopped out of steep cliff	Caves dug into slope of a hill

Islami Hotel

$ | INDIAN | One of Aurangabad's most well-known restaurants, Islami Hotel is dingy, grotty, and ramshackle, with a very sparse menu—but don't be put off. It serves the most lush *paya*, a soup made with trotters that have been stewed overnight in a bath of spices and fat. **Known for:** cooking with offal (especially paya); tandoori roti; kheema (mince). $ *Average main: Rs. 100* ✉ *Delhi Gate* ☎ *98222–22549 mobile* ▬ *No credit cards.*

Madhuban

$$ | INDIAN | At one of Aurangabad's top restaurants, dark furniture, large paintings of Indian scenes, an abundance of green granite, crisp white tablecloths, and a chandelier composed of multiple *diyas* (traditional Indian lamps) set a regal tone, while a wall of windows opens onto a garden of lovely tropical trees and flowers. The menu might include butter chicken and dal *makhani*, a rich black lentil dish; tasty Indo-Chinese food— the chilli chicken, a spicy concoction, is recommended; and some Mexican and Italian food. **Known for:** buffet lunch; open-air dining under the stars; North Indian specialties. $ *Average main: Rs. 900* ✉ *Welcomgroup Rama International Hotel, R–3 Chikalthana* ☎ *240/265–3095.*

Tandoor

$$ | INDIAN | The hospitality manager Syed Liakhat Hussain is one good reason to visit this brightly lit, busy, and cheerful restaurant that stays open late; the other is the authentic and well-made tandoori food. Shoot for lunch instead of dinner if you're coming by auto-rickshaw, because in the evening it's difficult to find transportation (it's far from the main hotels). **Known for:** tandoori chicken; paneer tikka; biryani. $ *Average main: Rs. 500* ✉ *Shyam Chambers, Station Rd.* ☎ *98909–58466.*

The Tea House

$$$$ | CHINESE | This restaurant inside the local Taj is as good a place to sample the distinct flavor of Indo-Chinese—which blends powerful Indian spices and delicate Chinese preparation—as you're likely to find outside of Mumbai proper. The menu features an excellent array of teas (try the Darjeeling) and cocktails (the sweet but subtle mojito is especially nice), and unlike most of the rest of the pack in Aurangabad, the atmosphere here is quiet and refined. **Known for:** dim sum; golden honey shrimp; salt-and-pepper tofu. $ *Average main: Rs. 1600* ✉ *Vivanta by Taj–Aurangabad, 8–N 12 CIDCO, Rauza Bagh* ☎ *240/661–3737* ⊕ *www.tajhotels.com* ⊙ *No lunch.*

Most hotels in Aurangabad discount their rates if you ask. If you book directly, push for 15% off, or more—and make sure to ask whether the agreed-on rate includes breakfast and airport or train station pickup. Unless otherwise noted, all hotels listed are fully air-conditioned.

Lemon Tree Hotel

$$$ | HOTEL | This attractive contemporary hotel is a great choice, with the trappings of a luxury property, but offering reasonable prices. **Pros:** well-lit, cheerful hotel; comfortable rooms; excellent food. **Cons:** small bathrooms; free Wi-Fi access for one device only; the gym isn't perfectly equipped. $ *Rooms from: Rs. 6000* ✉ *R 7/2 Chikalthana, Airport Rd.* ☎ *240/6060–3030* ⊕ *www.lemontreehotels.com* ⇥ *106 rooms* ❑ *Free Breakfast.*

The Meadows

$ | HOTEL | Accommodations at this resort-style hotel, which has won architectural awards, are in simple cottages, each with a private patio, and though rooms are a bit spartan, it's wonderfully tranquil. **Pros:** service above average; good value; close to Ellora caves. **Cons:** far from the city; no pool; no fitness center. $ *Rooms from: Rs. 3000* ✉ *Aurangabad–Mumbai Hwy., Village Mitmita, Padegaon, 5 km (3 miles) from city center* ☎ *240/267–7412 to 16* ⊕ *www.themeadowsresort.com* ⇥ *52 rooms* ❑ *Free Breakfast.*

Vivanta by Taj–Aurangabad

$$ | HOTEL | Convenient for the caves, this gleaming Mughal palace, still called the Taj Residency by many, is all bright white marble and stone, inside and out—its windows and doors arch to regal Mughal points, and the grand dome over the lobby is hand-painted in traditional Jaipuri patterns. **Pros:** city's most elegant hotel; lovely ambience; wonderful in-house Chinese restaurant. **Cons:** rather expensive; service can be disorganized; rooms are a little tired. $ *Rooms from: Rs. 7500* ✉ *8-N 12 CIDCO* ☎ *240/661–3737* ⊕ *www.tajhotels.com* ⇌ *68 rooms* ⦿ *Free Breakfast.*

Welcom Hotel Rama International

$$ | HOTEL | A long driveway through the spacious grounds here leads to a place where efficient and friendly staffers create the kind of warm, intimate setting you'd normally associate with a smaller hotel. **Pros:** excellent value; attentive personal service; nice views. **Cons:** small pool; the restaurant food is average; slightly shabby rooms. $ *Rooms from: Rs. 7000* ✉ *R–3 Chikalthana* ☎ *240/663–4141* ⊕ *www.welcomhotelrama.com* ⇌ *137 rooms* ⦿ *Breakfast.*

Chapter 8

GOA

Updated by
Margot Bigg

👁 **Sights**
★★☆☆☆

🍴 **Restaurants**
★★★★☆

🛏 **Hotels**
★★★★☆

🛍 **Shopping**
★★★★☆

🍸 **Nightlife**
★★★★★

WELCOME TO GOA

TOP REASONS TO GO

★ **Sand and waves:** Goa's long, sandy, palm-fringed beaches are a key reason people come here. Some beaches offer relaxation under the sun, while the focus of others is partying, with scores of shacks serving cheap, cold beer and fresh seafood.

★ **Goan cuisine:** If you like your spicing heavy and your seafood caught fresh, you'll love the food in Goa.

★ **Backwaters:** Rivers flow across Goa to the Arabian Sea. Escape the crowds at a heritage home or country inn in a town like Loutolim, for a couple of days of quiet nature walks, home-style cooking, and warm hospitality.

★ **Parties:** Goa's party scene is no longer as hedonistic as in years past, but during peak season there's usually an afterparty (or three) to be found if you ask around a little.

★ **Portuguese architecture:** Goa was under Portuguese control until 1961, and its colonial past is stamped across its historic buildings, forts, churches, and charming Portuguese homes and mansions.

1 Arambol, Ashvem, Mandrem, and Morjim. Goa's less touristy side.

2 Vagator Beach. Vagator Beach has rugged shores.

3 Anjuna Beach. The original hippie destination.

4 Mapusa. Take a day trip to Mapusa for the market.

5 Calangute Beach, Candolin, and Around. This is the more developed part of Goa.

6 Sinquerim Beach. Large luxury resorts.

7 Panaji. This area has a European feel.

8 Bogmalo Beach. Known for watersports.

9 Cansaulim Beach. Cansaulim is home to a few sleepy villages.

10 Majorda and Utorda. This area is a convenient hub for exploring.

11 Colva. Discover Goa's party culture.

12 Loutolim. Off the beaten path.

13 Chandor. This village is home to ancient sites.

14 Benaulim. You'll find resorts and seclusion here.

15 Varca. Rural and unspoiled.

16 Cavelossim. Relax in this secluded area.

17 Palolem Beach. Numerous beachfront bars and restaurants.

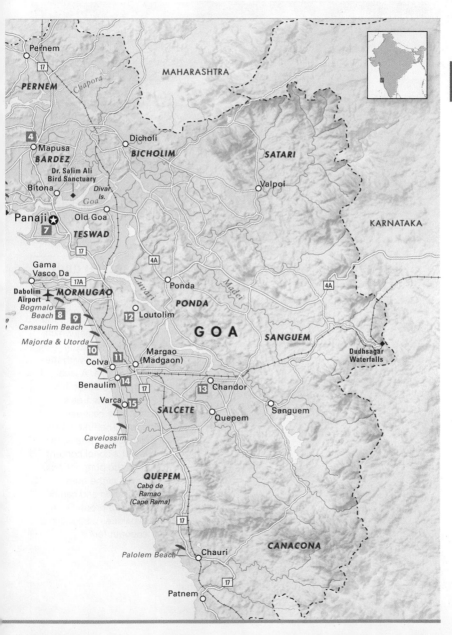

MAHARASHTRA

KARNATAKA

GOA

- Pernem
  - 17
- PERNEM
- Chapora
- Dicholi
- BICHOLIM
- SATARI
- Valpoi
- 4 Mapusa
- BARDEZ
- Dr. Salim Ali Bird Sanctuary
- Bitona
- Divar Is.
- Goa
- Panaji ★
- 7
- Old Goa
- TESWAD
- 17
- 4A
- Gama Vasco Da
- 17A
- Ponda
- Zuvari
- Mandvi
- 4A
- Dabolim Airport
- MORMUGAO
- Bogmalo Beach 8 9
- PONDA
- Cansaulim Beach
- 12 Loutolim
- GOA
- SANGUEM
- Dudhsagar Waterfalls
- Majorda & Utorda
- 10
- Colva 11
- Margao (Madgaon)
- 14
- Benaulim
- 17
- 13 Chandor
- Sanguem
- Varca 15
- SALCETE
- Quepem
- Cavelossim Beach
- QUEPEM
- Cabo de Ramao (Cape Rama)
- 17
- CANACONA
- Palolem Beach
- Chauri
- Patnem
- 17

EATING WELL IN GOA

Chicken vindaloo

Abundant seafood from the Arabian Sea, coupled with Goa's location on the spice route, ensures a wonderfully diverse cuisine.

Goan food is distinguished by the continued presence of Portuguese cooking techniques and ingredients. Chillies from the New World were incorporated into the local arsenal of spices relatively early, possibly with the arrival of Vasco da Gama in the late 15th century. The Portuguese also popularized eating pork, the use of vinegar, and certain desserts, and Goan Catholic eating habits continue to be influenced by these Portuguese methods, as well as those of the native Konkani-speaking inhabitants of the area.

The fact that Goa is a major tourist destination has also had an effect on the food you'll find here, and there are now plenty of international restaurants to be found, particularly in the north, where everything from Italian and Japanese to Greek and Mexican food can be found. There is also, of course, the gamut of Indian cuisines, from home-style Goan cafés to Punjabi restaurants that are comparable to anything in North India.

CASH(EW) CROP

An important cash crop in Goa, cashew trees grow all over the state. The tree, which is native to Brazil, came to Goa with the Portuguese. A local liquor is distilled from the cashew tree's fruit: the cashew apple. The first distillation, called *arrack*, has lower alcohol content than the pungent *feni*, which is the third distillation and can be up to 80 proof. Goan distilleries also make a coconut feni.

BEBINCA

A layered glutinous dessert, **bebinca** is traditionally eaten on special occasions, but due to its popularity with tourists, it is available in Goa all year round. The dish most likely evolved in Goa, probably with some Portuguese influence, but it has since migrated to Portugal as well. Making bebinca is a slow process: a batter of refined flour, coconut milk, egg yolks, and sugar is poured and baked, in layers, in a low-heat oven. The slight caramelizing between layers makes for an attractive tiger-stripe treat. You can buy bebinca in vacuum-sealed packages to take home.

The popular Goan sweet called *bebinca*

VINDALOO

A much-replicated Indian dish, vindaloo is the culinary pinnacle of the merging of Konkan and Portuguese cultures. A Portuguese meat dish cooked with red wine and garlic (*vinho* and *alhos*) was baptized in the fire of Goan spices and became vindaloo; the Goan version uses vinegar rather than wine for a slightly acidic-sweet taste. Vindaloo was originally a pork dish, but has since been adapted to chicken and lamb. It may include potatoes, too, and it generally incorporates red chilli for color and green chilli for spice.

SORPOTEL

A dish of Portuguese heritage that was adopted by Goan Christians, **sorpotel** (or *sarapatel*) is often somewhat toned down for tourists: it's an offal stew that is made using the liver, heart, and tongue of pork or other meats. By some accounts, the stew traditionally also includes the animal's blood, which some cooks still use as a thickener—but probably not in the version tourists encounter. This flavor is enhanced by the use of vinegar.

CHOURIÇO

If you happen to be in town on a market day, you might see strings of bulging Goan sausages gleaming dark red in the sun. Called **chouriço,** these are the local descendents of Portuguese chorizo, and are made with ground pork, vinegar, chilli, and other spices, and stuffed into casings. Chouriço can be very spicy or mild and varies in texture from dry to juicy. This type of sausage must be cooked, and is usually eaten with rice or *pao,* local Goan bread.

XACUTI

Chicken **xacuti** is one of Goa's most successful dishes outside of the state—and it can also be made with fish or lamb. It's a milder curry than some of the fiery red Goan curries.

A dish of roasted cashews

GOA BEACHES

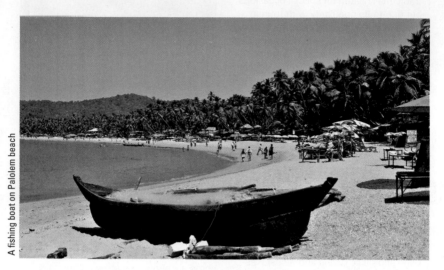

A fishing boat on Palolem beach

With its crescent-shape beaches of white sand and dramatic swaths of cliffs that hug the coastline, Goa continues to be a draw for both domestic and foreign travelers.

The northern beaches at Baga, Calangute, and beyond draw the biggest crowds and have plenty of beachside shacks, trendy bars and restaurants, booming nightlife, easy access to water sports, and an abundance of discount clothing and swimwear. There's a Wednesday flea market at the former hippie enclave around Anjuna, while arresting sunset views await visitors to the cliffs at Vagator. The northern-most beaches of Arambol, Ashvem, and Morjim are quieter and more scenic, though there's been a recent upswing in the number of cool little boutique hotels and the trendy bars around these beaches. Plush all-inclusive resorts dominate the southern coastline of Benaulim, Varca, and Cavelossim, where the beaches are quieter, cleaner, and with much fewer shacks in evidence. Palolem Beach, with its swaying palms and clean coastline, is becoming more popular, but quality accommodations and dining options still lag behind its northern counterparts.

MONSOON SEASON?

Most visitors go to Goa for the beach and the sun, though monsoon season (June to September), with its frequent downpours, is atmospheric and remarkably lush. It's also when the crowds are thinner and the prices lower—though most of the beach shacks and some of the larger properties are closed. And if your dream is to lie out on the beach or by the pool, this definitely isn't the time for you to visit.

WHAT SHOULD I WEAR?

The steady influx of foreign visitors over the years means that bikinis on the beach are commonplace. However, anything more risqué, like going topless or nude, is not acceptable, or legal. When you leave the beach, drape a sarong or throw on a cover-up to avoid untoward attention.

EATING AND DRINKING

Beach-shack dining is a signature experience in Goa—fresh seafood, a cold beverage, and a golden sunset. Along with catch of the day, a selection of North Indian mainstays, Goan curries, and simple Western dishes (think pastas and veggie burgers) are served.

RESTROOMS

Public restrooms can be dirty, so tuck some toilet paper in your beach bag, and bring some hand sanitizer. Facilities are cleaner at the nicer restaurants, but you'll probably be turned away if you're not a paying customer.

WATER SPORTS

The beaches at Calangute, Baga, and Colva in particular offer plenty of options for water sports, including parasailing, windsurfing, jet-skiing, and banana boating.

Arambol beach in northern Goa

BEACH CHAIRS

Beach chairs with umbrellas line the beaches in front of restaurants. If you're a customer, these are usually free to use; otherwise you can ask to rent one for a small, and negotiable, fee.

HAWKERS

You'll find plenty of vendors and stalls selling knickknacks, souvenirs, food, and drinks. Stick to the bottled beverages and be cautious of inflated prices. Vendors can be a nuisance, but a firm "No thank you," is all that's needed.

THE SUN

This is the tropics and the sun is strong. Wear good sunscreen and reapply often. Local brands with high SPF are available, but if you're particular about a specific brand, bring your own as prices here will be higher.

LIFEGUARDS

Major beaches have lifeguards during the day; smaller beaches do not. Undertows can be a danger in some areas, particularly in the monsoon season.

NEFARIOUS ELEMENTS

Goa's reputation for wild parties and easy drugs is not undeserved, but you can avoid any associated annoyances by sticking to recommended hotels, restaurants, and bars.

Sunset at the beach

Beguiling white sands, fresh and spicy seafood, and a cold drink under a glowing sun is Goa at its charming best. But there's plenty more: striking Renaissance cathedrals in Old Goa, ancestral homes surrounding the ragtag city of Margao, the ornate Hindu temples of Ponda, and Panaji's Portuguese historic district.

Those who know India well will tell you that Goa, the smallest state in the Indian federation, is an anomaly—a territory that is decidedly its own entity, shaped by a unique set of circumstances and influences.

Goa wasn't much of a tourist spot until the early 1960s, with the arrival of the first hippies from Europe, who were lured by the laid-back culture and picturesque beaches of Anjuna, Calangute, and Vagator. The lax law enforcement made it easy for the beaches to quickly become the site of wild parties, cheap alcohol, and plenty of drugs. The Anjuna flea market was established soon after, in the 1970s, as many of the foreign tourists started selling secondhand goods to fund an extended stay. It was around this time that the beach shacks appeared as well: temporary structures that multitasked as restaurants, bars, hotels, bookstalls, shops, or just places to hang out all day.

The era of electronic music in the 1980s changed Goa into a hot spot for raves, and all-night trance parties were all the rage for the subsequent two decades. This golden age of very loud and drug-flowing parties has subsided in recent years due to increased government action, though there are still underground events at a handful of beachfront venues, mostly located in Anjuna.

As Goa continued to attract more and more visitors, it caught the attention of well-heeled Indian tourists. Five-star hotels and resorts started popping up in the south, while package tours and charter flights from the United Kingdom and Russia became a common feature in the north. While Candolim and Calangute are popular with Indian tourists and retirement-age charter groups, younger budget travelers from abroad tend to congregate around the northern beaches around Morjim and Arambol, where it's not uncommon to see signs in Hebrew and Russian, but not English.

The Christmas/New Year's season is popular with travelers from all over the world, and hotels fill up fast during this period (and spike their rates accordingly). Domestic tourists are increasingly visiting Goa during January and February, though it's truly become a year-round destination for Indian travelers, who even brave the heavy monsoons to escape the pollution and hubub of urban life.

All this tourism has had an undeniable influence on Goa's way of life, economy, and identity, and in some areas today you can find a Greek restaurant, a

French-food shack, a German bakery, a pizza joint, and an Indian *dhaba* (bare-bones Indian food restaurant) all within a 5-mile radius. Much of Goa has evolved to cater to every breed of tourist—top-notch restaurants, boutique hotels, lovely heritage homes, luxury resorts, funky beach shacks, cheap and noisy hotels, and business hotels for the corporate retreats and conferences. You can still get away from it all, or you can just dive in and savor its still-wild reputation. But now, more than ever before, Goa offers so many more options that the hippies might be the only ones complaining.

MAJOR REGIONS

In **North Goa,** Calangute, Baga, and Anjuna were important stops on the hippie trails of the 1960s and 1970s, and continue to be at the beating heart of Goa's party scene. This coastal stretch is increasingly built up, but there are still some quiet areas around Mandrem beach (north of the Chapora River). Nearby, atop the hills, are a few beautiful old forts built of laterite, the local pitted red stone; they offer beautiful vistas of the curvaceous coastline. The villages that sit a few miles inland have charming bed-and-breakfasts and inns with rustic flavor.

You may also want to take an excursion to one of the popular markets. On Wednesday the bustling market in Anjuna, not far from the beach, is filled with inexpensive jewelry, cotton sarongs, colorful shoulder bags, handicrafts marketed by vendors from Goa, Karnataka, and other Indian states, and food stalls selling everything from bean burritos and brownies to Middle Eastern platters with hummus and falafel. There's also the Saturday night bazaar in nearby Arpora that is similar, and with even more food on offer, including whole roast chickens and Italian gelato. Goa's famed all-night beach parties are now history, but once the shacks close, follow the music (or the crowd) to the after-party, usually not publicized.

Goa's restaurant scene continues to refine and reinvent itself, with excellent restaurants serving both Goan and international cuisines. Stop by A Reverie in Calangute for its global fusion menu, Thalassa in Vagator for delicious Greek food, Ciao Bella in Assagao for a wonderful Italian meal, or Lila Café in Baga for a hearty morning-after recovery meal.

Panaji (also called Panjim) was once the capital of the former Portuguese colony and is now the state's capital. A scenic little city, it sits along the banks of the Mandovi River, about 29 km (18 miles) north of Goa's Dabolin airport. Apart from its own considerable charms—including the colonial architecture in the city's Fontainhas and Sao Tomé neighborhoods—the small city is a good base to explore Goa's Portuguese past, visible in the grand and ornate churches of Old Goa.

Margao, about 7 km (4 miles) inland from the coast, is the main town in **South Goa.** There's a bustling market, and it's worth exploring for its shopping areas, but only if you happen to be passing through; there's no reason to stay here. If you want to check out the sights, make Colva or Benaulim your base, and get the benefit of the beach and the nightlife after your day out. Excursions include the villages of Loutolim and Chandor, which have beautiful ancestral homes, some of which date from the early 1600s. The beaches of the south are more relaxing than those of the north; people here are less prone to partying, although there is more shack life in the south now than there used to be. Some of the state's most luxurious and expensive resorts are in this area.

8

Goa

Planning

WHEN TO GO
HIGH SEASON: OCTOBER THROUGH FEBRUARY

Goa's tourist season begins in October and peaks from the middle of December until after the New Year in January, when the skies are clear and parties are in overdrive. Anyone planning to visit over this time should prepare for sky-high lodging prices, and for beaches, hotels, and restaurants that are packed around the clock.

LOW SEASON: MAY TO SEPTEMBER

It's wise to avoid Goa in the months of May and September, when it is oppressively hot and humid, and very unpleasant even for the locals. During the monsoon months, from June through early September, most of Goa's hotels, beach-shack restaurants, and bars shut down due to the torrential rains and strong winds; violent surf makes water sports impossible, and visitors will struggle to find places to dine that are open. Farther inland the forests are lush, as are the rice plantations, which lie near Goa's many rivers, and most of the larger hotels stay open—it's always worth asking for "monsoon specials" if you are headed to Goa at this time of year.

SHOULDER SEASON: MARCH AND APRIL

Those who visit in the early spring can still enjoy gorgeous weather and Goa's beauty without feeling as if they're just part of a crowd.

GETTING HERE AND AROUND
AIR TRAVEL

Most travelers get to Goa by booking an international flight to Mumbai or Delhi, then hopping a domestic flight to Goa's Dabolim Airport, about 29 km (18 miles) south of Panaji, the state capital. Direct flights are available from many of India's major cities, and most can be booked online.

AIRPORT TRANSFERS

Buses are infrequent, so it's usually best to take a taxi from here to your destination. You can arrange for a prepaid taxi service at a counter inside the airport, or go straight outside and hire a private cab. Many resorts include airport transfers, or you can prearrange it for a fee. Alternatively, a government taxi desk outside the arrivals hall can organize a prepaid taxi. This is a better option than trying to negotiate fares with persistent drivers yourself. Either way, the fare to Panaji should not exceed Rs. 700.

AIRPORT INFORMATION Dabolim Airport
☎ *832/254–0806.*

BIKE OR MOTORBIKE TRAVEL

If you're in reasonable shape and confident riding on potholed, heavily traveled roads, consider renting a bicycle for a jaunt to save on taxi fares, especially if you simply want to get from your hotel to the beach and back. Don't expect more than one gear or anything resembling what you're used to; check the tires and brakes. You can rent motorbikes at bus stops, train stations, markets, and beach resorts and cars at the airport— your hotel will be able to arrange one as well. You'll need an international driver's license to drive anything larger than a 55-cc engine. However, Indian drivers and roads being what they are, think long and hard before renting any motorized vehicle you intend to drive yourself.

BUS TRAVEL

Several private bus companies connect Goa with Mumbai, Pune, Bengaluru, and Mangalore. They are more expensive than public transit but definitely faster and more comfortable. Try Paulo Travels (*832/663–7777* ⊕ *www.paulotravels. com*) for reliable service. Getting around Goa by bus is not advised unless you are traveling very light. Passengers are often packed in tight.

CAR TRAVEL
Goa can be easily explored from one end to the other by car. Everyplace is within a short drive of everyplace else.

TAXI AND AUTO-RICKSHAW TRAVEL
Goa has a unionized taxi system with fixed rates from point A to point B. They are expensive, but this is the best way to get around in Goa if money isn't a constraint. You don't really need to contact a tour operator, as there will usually be a taxi stand outside your hotel. If not, the hotel will call one for you from the nearest stand. Fares are not negotiable (in theory), and drivers charge a fixed rate displayed on a board at every taxi stand. If you are visiting a number of places and covering a lot of ground, it makes more sense to hire a taxi for a four- or eight-hour stretch (Rs. 1,500 for four hours), and pay an additional rate (Rs. 12) for every kilometer above 80 km (50 miles). Round-trip distances are calculated even for one-way journeys. Taxis levy a surcharge when they operate at night.

Most hotels can arrange taxis to take you around, either to the beach, restaurants, or shopping, and nothing is too far given the state's small size.

Auto-rickshaws, otherwise known as autos in India and "tuk tuks" elsewhere in Southeast Asia, are easy to find. They cost less than taxis, but there are no fixed rates, so before climbing in ask a local or a knowledgeable visitor what the fare should be to your destination. Autos are best for short distances in town rather than for jaunts across the state.

TRAIN TRAVEL
You can take a train or bus to Goa from Mumbai, but be warned: such trips can be long—at least 12 hours by train, 17 hours by bus—crowded, and uncomfortable. (Be sure to take a bus or train with reserved seating.) The Konkan Railway (⊕ *www.konkanrailway.com*) runs lines to Mumbai in the north and Mangalore in the south. The Madgaon station in

Festivals: Carnival

Carnival time remains the local's official season for nonstop revelry, directed by King Momo ("King of Misrule"), a Goan appointed by his peers as the life of the party. Festivities include fanciful pageants (with some 50 floats depicting elements of Goa's folk culture, or more contemporary messages like preservation of the environment), hordes of musicians strumming the guitar, and dancers breaking into the *mando*, a fusion of the Portuguese fado and the waltz.

8

Goa PLANNING

Margao is the main station, and there are smaller ones in Pernem, Thivim, Karmali, and Canacona. Book early online for train reservations: seats fill up quickly during the tourist season. Air-conditioned sleepers are best for overnight journeys.

For complete train schedules and fares, and to book tickets online, go to the Indian Railways website (⊕ *www.indianrail.gov.in*), where you can purchase and upgrade tickets, determine the kind of train you want, and review the rather extensive list of rules.

TRAIN INFORMATION Karmali station ☎ *832/228–5798.* **Margao station** ⊠ *2 km [1 mile] from main shopping area, Madgaon* ☎ *832/271–2790.*

ENGLISH-LANGUAGE MEDIA Golden Heart Bookshop ⊠ *Off Abade Faria Rd., Madgaon* ☎ *832/273–2450.* **Singbal's Book House** ⊠ *Opposite Mary Immaculate Conception Church, Panaji* ☎ *832/242–5747.*

TOURS AND VISITOR INFORMATION
There are dozens of private tour operators in Goa. The most reliable are run by the Goa Tourism Development

Corporation, which runs bus tours of both North and South Goa—departing from Panaji, Madgaon, and Colva Beach—as well as river cruises from the Santa Monica Pier in Panaji, and the Goa Department of Tourism. In Panaji, the Directorate of Tourism fields general inquiries. For assistance with reservations, including bus tours, contact the Goa Tourism Development Corporation (GTDC). There's also a 24-hour "Hello Information" number for Goa (*832/241–2121*), which is extremely useful for finding phone numbers.

CONTACTS Department of Tourism
✉ *Tourist Home, Patto Bridge, Panaji* ☎ *832/243–8750* ⊕ *www.goatourism. gov.in.* **Goa Tourism Development Corporation** ✉ *Paryatan Bhavan, 3rd fl., Patto, Panaji* ☎ *832/243–7132* ⊕ *www.goatourism.com.*

RESTAURANTS

If you like seafood and spicy food in general, you're in luck. You can spend all your time happily eating nothing but searingly hot (spicy) fish day in and day out, in the state's best restaurants as well as at the beachfront open-air shacks. But because Goa has such a huge tourist culture, food can be prepared to your liking—simply grilled or fried or with less spice, if you prefer. Goan food is typically big on flavor, whether it's chilli, tamarind, or coconut that dominates the dish. Make sure you order your meat (pork or beef) cooked through, and only order meat in the better-known larger restaurants, not at the beach shacks. Seafood is usually safe everywhere as long as it's fresh. If you're vegetarian, you'll get by fine, but vegetables are not as plentiful in the Goan diet as are fish, seafood, and meat.

HOTELS

Goa has every kind of lodging, from superexclusive posh resorts to beachside shacks appropriate only for beach bums and seen-it-all globe-trotters. Expect to get what you pay for, however, especially during peak season, from December to February, when the tourist hordes fill the hotels. Make sure you reserve a room far in advance of this time. During the monsoon season (June–October), prices drop by up to half and the resorts fill up with Indian visitors from the north. Unless noted otherwise, hotels have air-conditioning, TVs, and bathrooms with showers. *Hotel reviews have been shortened. For full information, visit Fodors.com.*

What It Costs			
$	$$	$$$	$$$$
RESTAURANTS			
under Rs. 300	Rs. 300– Rs. 499	Rs. 500– Rs. 700	over Rs. 700
HOTELS			
under Rs. 4,000	Rs. 4,000– Rs. 5,999	Rs. 6,000– Rs. 10,000	over Rs. 10,000

PLANNING YOUR TIME

It takes about a week to catch all of Goa's highlights—the beaches, Panaji, Old Goa, and the backwaters. If you're coming mainly for the beaches, a three- or four-day trip will suffice for swimming in the warm waters of the Arabian Sea, shopping at the colorful markets, and enjoying the flavors of Goan food. And there's a beach to suit every desire: those looking for seclusion and clear water can head north to Arambol, currently home to Goa's few remaining hippies, or Morjim, with its cool, quiet vibe. The resort-lined southern beaches offer swankier shacks and cold bottles of wine on quiet beaches, and for nonstop action, and for those who don't mind tourist hot spots, Baga in the north or Colva in the south are ideal. It's worth putting a day aside to see Panaji and to sample Goa's Portuguese ties firsthand, most apparent in the historic Fontainhas and Sao Tomé districts, as well as in the grand churches of Old Goa, built by the Portuguese in the 16th century.

A wonderful way to properly experience Goan life is to check in for two or three days at one of the state's heritage homes or properties. With antiques-filled guest rooms, attentive service, and delicious home cooking, the best of these places amount to a pleasurable window into Goa's past. Ultimately, much of Goa's charm lies in its ability to be so flexible: here you can choose between a tranquil retreat from modern life or party central, a resort spot for a perfect tan, or a destination from which to explore India's heritage.

Although it is the coastal areas that are the biggest draw for visitors to Goa, if you travel inland you'll find jungles, mountains, and agricultural areas. The north is known for its restaurants, bars and party-hearty beaches. In central Goa you'll find the mammoth ghost town that is Old Goa, as well as Panaji, the state capital. The less-traveled south is home to several high-end hotels and resorts, as well as small villages that allow a glimpse into Goa beyond the beach shacks and all-night parties.

Note that in addresses the terms *wadi, waddo,* and *vado* all mean "street."

Arambol, Ashvem, Mandrem, and Morjim

48 km (30 miles) northwest of Panaji.

The sands of Arambol are far less congested than those at Baga and Calangute, and as a result the area has become home to a new generation of hippies and free-spirited travelers. You'll catch this bohemian vibe in the European cafés and cheap hotels and shacks that cater to long-haul visitors. Arambol Beach, also known as Harmal, is rugged and lovely. The best stretch of it is tiny Paliem Beach, at the foot of Waghcolomb Hill. The scenery is spectacular: a freshwater pond stands at the base of

Monsoon Masala

Chances are you've never experienced anything like the monsoon in Goa. The downpours are heavy and sudden, and the raindrops so huge and close together it's as if someone is throwing buckets of water on you from a second-floor window. The rain may last for days or a mere 30 minutes, disappearing as quickly as it came. Even so, if you're in Goa during a rainy spell, don't let it slow you down. Wear your flip-flops, bring an umbrella, and carry on, as the locals do.

the hillside barely 200 yards from the sea. The sea is rougher here than at other beaches—it's still good for swimming, but a bit more fun for those who like a little surf. To avoid the crowds when it's high season, walk past the pond, and you'll find quieter tidal inlets and rock ledges.

A little farther south are the lovely, quiet beaches of Ashvem, Mandrem, and Morjim. Divided by little creeks, the beaches have spectacular windswept stretches of sand, a far cry from the overcrowded beaches south of the Chapora River. Mandrem offers the most accommodation and entertainment options, including a couple of well-tended luxury shacks. Morjim is popular because of the olive ridley turtles, which use its dark sands as a nesting ground during the winter. Hatchlings emerge at night after an eight-week incubation period. Conservation efforts have proved difficult, and it's unclear whether turtles will continue to return to nest here. Ashvem is quiet and relaxing in the daytime, but once the sun goes down the open-air beach parties in high season begin.

Goa's Past

Goa's coastal location has made it an influential trading post for many centuries. Hindu merchants flourished for centuries, trading spices, silk, pearls, horses, and ideas with Arab, East African, and Mediterranean cultures. Control of the region shifted between the Bahmani Sultanate of the Deccan Plateau and the Vijayanagar Empire in Hampi, to the east. Goa's fortunes were profoundly altered by the arrival in 1510 of Affonso de Albuquerque, a Portuguese explorer and naval officer who wrestled the tiny realm from the hands of the Sultan of Bijapur. For the next 450 years the Portuguese exerted major pressures as well as a strong influence on Goan culture, language, and religion—they converted many native Hindus and Buddhists to Catholicism by force. The Portuguese ruled with an iron first before, during, and after the rest of the Indian subcontinent was under the thumb of the British.

It was during this period, from the 16th to the 18th centuries, that the grandiose churches of Old Goa were built. The most illustrious structures here include Old Goa's Sé (cathedral) and the Basilica of Bom Jesus, where the remains of St. Francis Xavier lie in a silver casket entombed in a Florentine-style marble mausoleum. A string of cholera epidemics in this city built on swamps eventually saw its decline, and the Portuguese adopted Panaji as its new capital.

Although British-ruled India became a free country in 1947, the Portuguese retained their hold on Goa for 15 more years. They were finally driven out in 1961 through a land assault ordered by India's first prime minister, Jawaharlal Nehru. In comparison to some 30,000 Indian troops, the Portuguese force of 3,000 men was nominal.

In the decades since, Goa has retained its own identity, although tourism has changed it a great deal. In day-to-day life, Catholic traditions are evident in its whitewashed village churches, and European influence lives on in the Goans' love for pork, and even in local fashions. Goans, perhaps more than any other Indian state, are quite Western in their outlook, and it is that harmonious blend of East and West that sets it apart from most other parts of the country.

GETTING HERE AND AROUND

The best and fastest way of getting here is by taxi. A prepaid non-air-conditioned ride from the airport to Arambol should set you back about Rs. 1,200. From Panaji, it should take you about 40 minutes for a Rs. 600 taxi ride. Most hotels will arrange taxis, rent motorbikes, or loan bicycles.

Sights

Arambol Beach (*Harmal Beach*)
BEACH—SIGHT | Perfect for those keen on sampling a taste of the 1970s hippie trail, and still a favorite with Goa's free spirits, this lovely and rugged North Goan beach has long, wide swaths of clean sand and shallow water that's great for paddling. During the day it's quiet and relaxed, but come evening, the beachfront restaurants transform into informal nightlife venues, with some blasting music well into the night. **Amenities:** food and drink.

Best for: parties; sunrise; sunset; swimming. ✉ *Arambol Pernem.*

★ Ashvem Beach

BEACH—SIGHT | The white sands here are perfect for uninterrupted lazing. Sandwiched between Morjim and Mandrem beaches, Ashvem has a fair number of hippie beach shacks, but it still manages to hold onto its air of deserted idyll. Between September and February, this is a nesting spot for the olive ridley turtle, and you just might spot a few. No longer off the beaten track, the areas around the beach are now full of thatched beachside accommodations, like Yab Yum Resorts. And in season it's also home to some of Goa's best seasonal eating, notably at upscale La Plage. It's not as much of a destination for partyers as some of its neighboring beaches, and just a hop and a skip away from the beach are lush paddies and coconut groves. **Amenities:** food and drink. **Best for:** solitude; sunrise; sunset; swimming; walking. ✉ *Mandrem.*

Mandrem Beach

BEACH—SIGHT | This quiet hideaway in North Goa has the advantage of not being a popular destination on the tourist trail, which is why it's a top pick for honeymooners and for couples looking for a quiet getaway. There are a few beach shacks and the odd guesthouse in season, but you really have to make your own entertainment on this deserted stretch. **Amenities:** none. **Best for:** solitude; sunset. ✉ *Mandrem.*

Morjim Beach

BEACH—SIGHT | Best known as a home to olive ridley sea turtles, serene Morjim Beach is popular with those keen to see a nesting site of the species. Known to be quiet and peaceful, it is easy to see the attraction for these endangered marine creatures. In recent years, however, the village of Morjim has also become home to most of Goa's Russian expatriates, earning itself the title of "Little Russia," and this influx has brought with it a less peaceful atmosphere. Although the beach is still quiet during the day, it now has a thriving nightlife. **Amenities:** food and drink. **Best for:** swimming; walking; partyers. ✉ *Morjim.*

🍴 Restaurants

Fellini

$$ | **PIZZA** | Firmly established as the definitive destination for pizza (and giant calzones) in North Goa, Fellini is tucked away in the busy lanes of Arambol; it takes some finding, but it's worth the hunt. The interior is no-nonsense, with shack-style tables and seating. **Known for:** salami pizza; spinach and mushroom pizzas; good wine options. [$] *Average main: Rs. 500* ✉ *Socoillo Vaddo, Main Arambol Beach Rd., Arambol Pernem* ☎ *0091/98814–61224.*

La Plage

$$$$ | **INDIAN** | Don't let the casual air of the palm trees and simple white tables of this down-to-earth shack fool you. Conceived in 2003 by three old friends, the restaurant has become a must-visit destination for any food lover passing through Goa, serving excellent French food as well as comforting burgers and grills. **Known for:** fresh fruit cocktails; tiger prawn carpaccio; chocolate thali. [$] *Average main: Rs. 1500* ✉ *Ashwem Beach, Morjim* ☎ *98/2212–1712* 💳 *No credit cards* 🕒 *Closed May–Nov.*

🛏 Hotels

Elsewhere

$$$ | **HOTEL** | On a 500-yard-long spit of outstretched private land, surrounded on three sides by the waters of the Arabian Sea and Otter Creek, this beautiful, small property has attentive service and comprises four elegant beach houses and three tents that are separated from the mainland by the saltwater creek—access is via a private bamboo footbridge. **Pros:** semiprivate beach; lovely property; quiet. **Cons:** a 60-yard bamboo footbridge is the only access route; reservations have to

Sunset at Arambol beach.

be made via email; inflated prices during peak times. $ *Rooms from: Rs. 7400* ✉ *North Goa* ✛ *Mandrem* ⊕ *www.aseascape.com* ⊘ *Closed May–Sept.* ⇥ *7 rooms* ⊖ *No meals.*

Siolim House

$$$ | HOTEL | For the old-world charm of an aristocratic family home, stay at this elegant Portuguese villa on the south bank of the Chapora River, now converted into an all-suites boutique hotel. **Pros:** tranquil rural setting; free Wi-Fi; palatial rooms. **Cons:** no TV; no a/c in some rooms; the mattresses on some beds are old. $ *Rooms from: Rs. 9000* ✉ *Opposite Vaddy Chapel, Siolim, Bardez, Arambol Beach* ☎ *832/227–2138, 833/227–2941* ⊕ *www.siolimhouse.com* ⇥ *7 rooms* ⊖ *Free Breakfast.*

Yab Yum Resorts

$$$ | RESORT | Thatched and dome-shape roofs are tucked away in a shaded grove of palm trees at this fun and funky property just minutes from lovely Ashwem Beach. **Pros:** quiet beach; choice of domes or cottages; yoga classes offered.

Cons: no restaurant on premises; rooms lack soundproofing; expensive for what you get. $ *Rooms from: Rs. 7900* ✉ *Ashvem Beach, Mandrem* ☎ *832/224–7712, 832/651–0392* ⊕ *www.yabyumresorts.com* ⊘ *Closed late Apr.–mid-Oct.* ⇥ *17 rooms* ⊖ *Free Breakfast.*

Vagator Beach

25 km (16 miles) northwest of Panaji.

Jagged cliffs along sandy shores give a rugged wild atmosphere to the beaches at Vagator, which is split by a seaside headland that offers beautiful views on either side. On one side are the dark red walls of the old hill fort of Chapora, built in 1717, which was later taken twice from the Portuguese by the Marathas. (The Marathas ruled a principality that covers much of the modern-day state of Maharashtra, north of Goa.) The view from the ramparts is phenomenal, and farther up the shore are stretches of secluded sand. On the other side is beautiful

Water Sports in Goa

Goa offers a variety of water sports, from adrenaline-generating Jet Ski rides and parasailing to more light-hearted banana boat and catamaran rides.

Parasailing. This is the most exciting water-sport experience in Goa: you take off and feel the wind hitting you across the lovely palm-fringed coastline. There are two ways to do it: either you take off and land on a winchboat in the water, or you descend onto the beach. You will find plenty of operators during the tourist season, but some of them have questionable safety standards. Use licensed operators at the luxury resorts if you happen to be staying at one, or use one of those with a history of operating in Goa. Parasailing around Sinquerim-Candolim-Calangute offers a spectacular view of Fort Aguada. Other recommended areas are near the Arrosim-Cansaulim and Utorda stretches, and Mobor Beach, in the south. From Miramar you can catch views of the Mandovi River meeting the sea. Rides last for three to five minutes and cost between Rs. 400 and Rs. 1,000; boat-ride charges are extra. You need to be comfortable with both heights and water.

Jet-skiing and waterskiing. Watersports operators in Colva, Candolim, Calangute, Miramar, Arossim, Utorda, Benaulim, Mobor, and Rajbaga are also set up for jet-skiing. It's an exhilarating, energetic ride, which lasts from 2 to 15 minutes. Usually instructors accompany you on the rides, which cost upward of Rs. 1,500. If you want to go waterskiing, the cost is between Rs. 500 and Rs. 1,500 depending on the length of the ride and the time of year; operators are at Candolim, Calangute, Arossim, Utorda, Majorda, and Rajbaga.

Scuba diving and snorkeling. Goa is not a great location for these sports, but there are a couple of reputable places to try both. They can both also help you get PADI certified although the water in these areas isn't very clear.

8

Goa VAGATOR BEACH

Ozrant Beach, also called Mini-Vagator, near which you will find an impressive stone face of Shiva that was carved into a boulder by an unknown sculptor.

Little Vagator and Vagator come to life after dark. Beach shacks like Boom Shankar will have information on the ongoing beach parties. Nine Bar, above the beach, is for trance and house music lovers. This part of Goa has plenty of beach shack restaurants, but many disappear from one season to the next, or take on a different name. The best way to figure out where to eat is to ask fellow travelers for the name of the current favorite.

Sights

Vagator Beach

BEACH—SIGHT | The dark sands of Vagator Beach lead on from the red cliffs that line it. Vagator is popular with both local and foreign tourists; as a result, there are many vendors and stands catering to visitors, selling snacks, sliced local fruit, trinkets, and souvenirs. Plenty of bars and shacks are on hand to meet the needs of this mixed crowd, and in the high season most bars reverberate to the sounds of electronic music and reggae. Vagator's waters are choppier than some of North Goa's other beaches, which is why this beach isn't a top pick for swimmers. **Amenities:** food and drink; parking; toilets. **Best for:** sunset; partyers; walking. ✉ *Vagator Beach.*

🍴 Restaurants

★ Bean Me Up

$$$ | **VEGETARIAN** | An institution among expats and regular visitors, this health-conscious garden restaurant offers a huge menu of Indian and international dishes that eschew meat, eggs, and dairy without compromising on taste. While the food is the big draw for many, vegan or not, the ambience is equally enchanting, with a mix of shaded and uncovered seating in an enchanting plant-filled courtyard. **Known for:** lovely garden courtyard environment; healthy juices and smoothies; pizzas made with vegan cheese. [$] *Average main: Rs. 600* ✉ *1639/2 Deulvaddo* ✥ *On road that runs behind petrol pump* ☎ *77690–95356* 🌐 *www.beanmeup.in.*

Ciao Bella

$$$ | **ITALIAN** | At the helm of this delightful Italian restaurant—one of Goa's best (so get there early if it's a weekend)—are Mario and Simona, who are hands-on hosts who tend to customers as well as cook. Their personal touch is evident in every plate the kitchen sends out. **Known for:** black tagliatelle with salmon; spinach-and-ricotta ravioli; coffee granita. [$] *Average main: Rs. 800* ✉ *569 Assagao Baden Rd., Assagao* ☎ *97/6755–7673* ⏲ *No lunch. Closed Tues.*

★ Thalassa

$$$ | **GREEK** | Rugged Vagator Beach is the seductive backdrop for Mariketty Grana's popular whitewashed Greek restaurant, which is on top of a low cliff overlooking the rocky shores of Little Vagator. Thalassa's vibrant chef re-creates authentic food from her native Corfu, often served against a backdrop of live music and beautiful sunset views. **Known for:** kleftiko (slow-cooked lamb); hot feta cheese; moussaka. [$] *Average main: Rs. 800* ✉ *Little Vagator, Ozran Beach* ☎ *98/5003–3537* 🌐 *www.thalassaindia.com* ⏲ *No lunch; closed late May–Sept.*

Hotels

Casa Vagator

$$$ | **HOTEL** | Perched on a hillside high above the Arabian Sea, this smart and stylish contemporary hotel overlooks the wild beauty of Vagator Beach, which guests can reach by following a winding path that descends rather sharply. **Pros:** far from the hustle and bustle of Goa's beach scene; striking sunset views; delicious food. **Cons:** lots of stairs; small pool; the neighboring Nine Bar sometimes has thumping music at night. [$] *Rooms from: Rs. 9360* ✉ *H. No. 594/4 Vozran* ☎ *832/727–4931* 🌐 *casaboutiquehotels.com/hotel/casa-vagator* ⏲ *Closed roughly June–mid-Sept.* 🛏 *12 rooms* 🍴 *Free Breakfast.*

Sunbeam

$$$ | **HOTEL** | Set in a Portuguese family home in one of North Goa's most charming villages, Sunbeam is owned by Indian stylist Jivi Sethi, whose lively, unabashed approach to design is seen throughout the property. **Pros:** excellent food; beautiful family heirlooms and home-style touches; on-site massage room. **Cons:** power outages; lack of light in the Old House rooms; no online reservations (must be by phone or email). [$] *Rooms from: Rs. 7000* ✉ *E–13 Saunta Vaddo, Mapusa-Anjuna Rd., Assagao* ☎ *832/226–8525* 🌐 *www.justjivi.com* 🛏 *4 rooms* 🍴 *Free Breakfast.*

Anjuna Beach

20 km (12 miles) northwest of Panaji.

Discovered by the hippies in the late 1960s, Anjuna and its palm-lined beaches have had many seasons of glory. Although Anjuna can get very crowded and boisterous, its beach is still not as commercial as Calangute and doesn't have the large-scale luxury resorts you'll find at Sinquerim Beach and in the south. With coconut trees framing the sands against jagged laterite cliffs and boulders, the beach is as popular as ever. Drugs are all too easily available here, too, but they are also highly illegal—even if they seem to be part of the atmosphere. Anjuna is known for its Wednesday night **flea market**, where you can buy everything from jewelry and juice to art and antiques.

◉ Sights

Anjuna Beach
BEACH—SIGHT | This is Goa's original hippie haven. Those full-moon parties, now so synonymous with this beach state, first happened on the sands of Anjuna in the 1960s, and even today this northern beach is home to modern-day flower children, international travelers keen on sampling some of that hippie stardust, and everyone looking for a party. It's definitely not one of Goa's most beautiful beaches, but the steady influx of people means that it's got restaurants and bars galore. Anjuna's busiest on Wednesday, when the famed weekly Anjuna Flea Market takes place. The water is safe for swimming and you'll find lots of sunbathers and souvenir vendors year-round. **Amenities:** food and drink; water sports; parking. **Best for:** partyers; sunset; swimming; walking. ⌧ *Anjuna.*

🍴 Restaurants

Baba Au Rhum
$$ | BAKERY | This charming little French pizzeria and bakery, in a sleepy residential lane off the busy Anjuna road, is open all day and well into the evening, but it's best for breakfast. The ambience here is laid-back, the views are noteworthy, and there are regular live music performances. **Known for:** French breakfast pastries;

pizzas; tarts and cakes. $ *Average main: Rs. 300* ⌧ *Salim House, opposite Uttam Resorts, Arpora* ☎ *98220–78759* ☉ *Closed Tues.*

German Bakery
$$$ | INTERNATIONAL | Most Indian towns that are popular with overseas travelers have at least one "German bakery," which in local parlance indicates a casual (and usually not German-run) eatery with a solid selection of baked goods. Anjuna's German Bakery may very well be the best known such institution in the country, with its huge selection of cakes and pastries and delicious European-style dishes, with some Indian options. **Known for:** fresh pastries and chocolate cakes; live music performances; Western-style meat-based and vegetarian dishes. $ *Average main: Rs. 500* ⌧ *Flea Market Rd., Anjuna* ☎ *70579–01002* ⊕ *www.german-bakery.in.*

Lila Café
$$$ | CAFÉ | Cross the river, and you arrive at picturesquely situated Lila Café, by the banks of the Baga River. The daytime eatery is the perfect antidote to any late-night revelry and is popular among locals and tourists alike for its continental cuisine and freshly baked breads. **Known for:** fresh croissants; breezy open-air seating; delicious home-cooked breakfasts. $ *Average main: Rs. 500* ⌧ *Tito's White House, Calangute-Arpora-Siolim Rd., Anjuna* ☎ *832/227–9843* ⊕ *www.lilacafe-goa.com* ▤ *No credit cards* ☉ *Closed Tues. and June–Sept.*

🛏 Hotels

Casa Anjuna
$$$ | HOTEL | History, style, and attitude combine to make spending time in this 200-year-old Portuguese mansion turned boutique hotel a pleasure. **Pros:** beautiful setting; antiques-filled rooms; peace and quiet. **Cons:** 10-minute walk to the beach; rooms can be noisy; no room service. $ *Rooms from: Rs. 9360*

The Flea Market at Anjuna

Getting to the Wednesday flea market at Anjuna can be half the fun; you can take a bus or a motorcycle taxi, or a fisherman's boat from Baga, which takes 15 minutes or so. (Going by road takes half an hour.) There are still some old-school foreigners around manning the stands, but it really isn't their market anymore. Now the markets are dominated by Lamani, Kashmiris, and Tibetans, who sell all kinds of trinkets while dressed in striking clothing and jewelry, as well as craftspeople from elsewhere in India. The market is a splash of red and orange in a flat area above the rocky beach. Bead and white-metal bangles, necklaces and earrings, silver toe rings, embroidered shoulder bags, silk and cotton sarongs, and ethnic footwear are among the more common products on sale. If you look carefully, there are all sorts of other things here as well, from used motorbikes of uncertain age to do-it-yourself *mehendi* henna-tattoo kits. Buy a crochet bikini, tops and skirts embroidered with tiny mirrors, or a tie-dye bandanna, or just sit back at the market bar and down a ridiculously cheap beer while someone braids your hair deftly or offers to tattoo, pierce, or otherwise mutilate various parts of your anatomy. Be careful not to bargain unfairly, because you run the risk of a sarcastic "take it for free?" from one of the tribal women. When your day's bargains have been struck (and getting things for a third or less of the quoted price is not uncommon), join the rest of Anjuna down at the shore. The market only appears during the tourist season; during the monsoon there's a smaller market in Anjuna just above the main town beach.

✉ D'Mello Vaddo 66, Anjuna, Bardez ☎ 832/227–4123 🌐 casaboutiquehotels.com/hotel/casa-vagator 🛏 24 rooms 🍴 Free Breakfast.

Hotel Bougainvillea (Granpa's Inn)
$$ | HOTEL | This hotel occupies a 200-year-old restored Portuguese country house on an inland lane, and its small pool, lush garden, and simple, well-maintained rooms make it a well-priced place to stay in Anjuna. **Pros:** great value; funky atmosphere; rural setting. **Cons:** too far to walk to the beach; no a/c in some rooms; breakfast is simple. *[$] Rooms from: Rs. 4500 ✉ Anjuna-Mapusa Rd., Gaunwadi, Anjuna ☎ 832/227–3270, 832/227–3271 🌐 www.granpasinn.com 🛏 14 rooms 🍴 Free Breakfast.*

Laguna Anjuna
$$ | RESORT | A 10-minute walk from the beach, this quiet spot with elegant, minimalist cottages is in a tree-lined residential area. **Pros:** quiet, relaxed setting; excellent restaurant; beautiful garden with an expansive pool. **Cons:** not on the beach; complaints of room and pool maintenance issues; cleanliness level could be improved. *[$] Rooms from: Rs. 5824 ✉ Soranto Vado, Anjuna ☎ 832/227–4131 🌐 www.lagunaanjuna.com 🛏 25 rooms 🍴 Free Breakfast.*

Nilaya Hermitage
$$$$ | HOTEL | Roughly translated "a hidden dwelling," Nilaya is aptly named: this hip, hilltop retreat away from the beaches is etched out of laterite stone and enhanced with mosaic and ceramic tiles in a Goa-meets-Gaudi tableau. **Pros:** fabulous tiled pool; day cruises on the wooden sailing dhow; on-site ayurvedic spa. **Cons:** remote—taxi, car, or motorbike necessary; not on the beach; guests aren't allowed to bring outside food.

Secluded Sinquerim beach is home to luxury resorts and pristine beaches.

[$] *Rooms from: Rs. 20000* ✉ *Off Main Calangute Rd., Arpora* ☎ *832/226–9794* 🌐 *www.nilaya.com* 🛏 *13 rooms* 🍴 *No meals.*

Nightlife

Goa is known for its nightlife, and fans of electronic music (particularly house and psychedelic trance) will find lots of DJ nights at local beach shacks in Anjuna. For Bollywood and pop music, Baga is your best bet.

Curlie's Bar

BARS/PUBS | At the south end of Anjuna, Curlie's is something of an institution, with electronic music parties in season. With a great sea view and a basic menu, this is an essential pit stop for anyone who wants to sample the hard-partying side of Goa. ✉ *Anjuna* ✥ *On Anjuna Beach* ☎ *98/2216–8628.*

Nyex Beach Club

BARS/PUBS | Formerly known as Paradiso, this is one of Goa's most popular nightclubs. It's on a cliff near Anjuna Beach with fabulous views. ✉ *Anjuna* ✥ *Anjuna Cliff* ☎ *95455–50571.*

Primrose Music Club

BARS/PUBS | Situated between Anjuna and Vagator, this is a favorite spot to get the night started. It started off as a hot spot with the psychedelic trance crowd, and while those parties have moved indoors in keeping with new legislation, as is the case at most Goan nightspots, Primrose continues to be very popular in season (it's closed all monsoon). ✉ *Anjuna.*

Shore Bar

BARS/PUBS | The most popular place to down beer, watch the dramatic sunset over the Arabian Sea, and listen to loud music until the wee hours is the Shore Bar on the beach. The steps of this place are usually packed with people, especially on Wednesday after the flea market. Walk north from the market for about a kilometer to get here. ✉ *Anjuna* ☎ *0091/98223–83795.*

Mapusa

15 km (9 miles) north of Panaji.

Friday is the big market day in Mapusa (pronounced *map*-sa)—the main town in the Bardez district. People from adjoining villages and some transplanted hippies convene to sell everything from vegetables to blue jeans to handicrafts. It's an ideal place to buy souvenirs. Mapusa is not a place you'd want to stay for the night, and there's really nothing much to see here, but like Margao in the south, the town is good for brief forays to shop and take care of other necessities. Except for the lively Friday market, the town is a bit dreary.

Baga Beach

15 km (9 miles) northwest of Panaji; 2 km (1 mile) north of Calangute.

One of Goa's top party beaches, Baga is known for its hopping "shack life." If you're looking for a quiet spot to sunbathe, Baga probably isn't for you. But the many popular food and drink joints mean that it's a top spot for nighttime revelry, headlined by St. Anthony's for seafood (and karaoke) and the legendary Tito's Bar for club nights. The music at Baga nightclubs tends to be Bollywood and pop music. During the day, and in season, there are plenty of water sports on offer as well, including parasailing, windsurfing, and Jet Ski rides.

The beach drops steeply to the shoreline, where fishing canoes make use of the easy boat-launching conditions to provide rides, including trips to the Wednesday market at Anjuna Beach just around the bend (the ride to Anjuna takes 15 minutes by sea, but twice as long by road). A few hundred meters down the beach, to the south of the point where the steep slope meets the sand, you'll find relatively less-crowded areas where you can spread out your towel and sunbathe. The beach gets its name from the Baga River, which meets the sea at the beach's northern end.

👁 Sights

Baga Beach

BEACH—SIGHT | This long, narrow (at high tide) beach is one of Goa's most popular, and Baga is where you'll find nonstop action, cocktails around the clock, innumerable water-sports vendors, as well as some of North Goa's best-loved party spots like Tito's and Cavala (a short walk away from the beach). In the winter months this beach is filled with package tourists, so although you won't find peace at Baga, you will find everything else. **Amenities:** food and drink; water sports; lifeguards. **Best for:** partyers; sunset; windsurfing. ✉ *Baga.*

🍴 Restaurants

St. Anthony's

$$$ | **SEAFOOD** | This seasonal seaside restaurant, a bit above Baga's many beach shacks, serves an astonishing variety of dishes in a casual setting that draws big crowds due to its location at the mouth of the river. It hosts very popular karaoke nights; if you're keen to watch or participate, it's worth calling ahead to see when they're on. **Known for:** tuna steaks and pomfret; excellent riverfront location; karaoke nights. [$] *Average main: Rs. 600* ✉ *Near Baga River* ☎ *832/645–2396* 💳 *No credit cards.*

🛏 Hotels

Casa Baga

$$$ | **HOTEL** | This rambling, boutique hotel is one of the best places to stay in Baga—the lively beach scene is only a few minutes' walk away, and the friendly staff treat you like family, making up for any upkeep deficits. **Pros:** not on the noisy main road; exceptional staff; pretty grounds. **Cons:** sketchy plumbing; no fitness center; worn facilities. $ *Rooms from: Rs. 7600* ✉ *40/7 Saunta Vaddo, Baga* ☎ *832/227–6957, 832/228–2930, 832/228–2931* ⊕ *casaboutiquehotels. com/hotel/casa-baga* ↘ *14 rooms* ⦿ *Free Breakfast.*

Nightlife

Tito's

DANCE CLUBS | Probably the best known of all Goa's clubs, Tito's is always packed. Unlike the clubs and beach shacks further north in Anjuna and Vagator, which tend to attract a bohemian set, Tito's aims squarely at the mainstream, and is particularly popular with Indian and Russian tourists. Expect fashion shows, famous DJ mixers, theme nights, popular dance music, and expensive drinks. ✉ *Tito's La.* ☎ *832/227–5028,832/227–9895.*

Calangute Beach, Candolim, and Around

12 km (7 miles) northwest of Panaji.

Calangute is by far the most crowded of the northern beaches—it's an open stretch of white sand with an entrance area crammed with restaurants, stalls, and shops. The mood is especially festive during the high season in winter, when dozens of shacks serving inexpensive beer, mixed drinks, and seafood pop up on the beach.

The beach is accessible by concrete steps. ■**TIP**→ **Note the sign warning that swimming is dangerous—there's a fairly strong undertow here.**

Beyond the beach are some of the area's best restaurants and shopping. You'll also find hundreds of shops, including road-side trinket stalls, branches of the Oxford Bookstore and Café Coffee Day, ATMs, travel agencies, and Malini Ramani's boutique, filled with vibrant clothes. Most of these shops are on the stretch of road

running from St. Anthony's Chapel, past a market, to Baga. Candolim Church was first built in 1560 and dedicated to Our Lady of Hope; it was repaired in 1661 and received its current cake-icing look when the village Communidade remodeled it thanks to contributions from Candolim parishioners.

GETTING HERE AND AROUND
Calangute is at the center of the Bardez Coast, bordered by Candolim Beach to the south and Baga to the north. From the airport, a prepaid taxi costs around Rs. 600–Rs. 700.

Sights

Calangute Beach

BEACH—SIGHT | Crowded and sometimes dirty, particularly in the high season, Calangute Beach is the main destination for many package tourists in Goa. The rampant commercialization means that visitors can take their pick of activities, from water sports to shopping, but space and quiet are harder to find. The beach is accessible by concrete steps. There's a fairly strong undertow here, making swimming here dangerous. **Amenities:** food and drink; water sports; lifeguards. **Best for:** partyers; windsurfing. ✉ *Calangute.*

🍴 Restaurants

★ A Reverie

$$$$ | **INTERNATIONAL** | At this popular fine-dining restaurant, dishes are "re-visited, re-interpreted, and re-invented" with infused flavors, and all the food is beautifully plated. As the name suggests, A Reverie has a dreamlike, elegant ambience: the space is painted in warm earthy tones, but there are stylish overtones of bling; it's accented by dimmed lounge areas, crystal chandeliers, and wrought-iron decorative furniture. **Known for:** elegant seafood dishes; Goan pina coladas made with local cashew feni liquor; live jazz performances. $ *Average* *main: Rs. 2000* ✉ *Holiday St., next to Goan Heritage, Gaurovaddo, Calangute Beach* ☎ *98231–74927* 🌐 *www.areverie.com.*

Republic of Noodles

$$$$ | **ASIAN** | Slightly more expensive than is the norm in Goa, this Pan-Asian chain eatery inside the Lemon Tree Amarante Beach Resort features lovely interiors dominated by dark bamboo and sandstone with Indonesian accents. Diners can choose to sit at teppanyaki counters (with a built-in hot plate where the chef cooks and serves the food straight onto your plate) or at regular tables. **Known for:** fresh watermelon margaritas; seafood laksa (spicey noodle soup); Asian barbecue. [$] *Average main: Rs. 2000* ✉ *Lemon Tree Amarante Beach Resort, Vadi, Calangute* ☎ *832/398–8188.*

Souza Lobo

$$$ | **SEAFOOD** | Established in 1932, and now managed by the third generation of the Lobo family, this large, airy, no-frills restaurant on hectic Calangute Beach catches the exuberant sea breeze. The seafood is excellent, with a good selection of Goan and Western dishes, so it's no surprise that this place is almost always busy. **Known for:** kingfish steak peri-peri; Goan masala fried prawns; nightly live music. [$] *Average main: Rs. 500* ✉ *Calangute Beach* ☎ *832/227–6463, 832/228–1234* 🌐 *www.souzalobo.com.*

Hotels

Fortune Acron Regina

$$$$ | **HOTEL** | In a quiet location off the main road near Candolim, this resort from the Fortune Hotels group resembles a classy Portuguese mansion and is competent and professional in its service and facilities. **Pros:** tranquil location near a busy tourist area; lovely Goan-inspired exteriors and decor; excellent food and fresh juices. **Cons:** pricey for this type of hotel; not on the beach; lacks intimate feel of smaller properties. [$] *Rooms from: Rs. 10000* ✉ *376, off Fort Aguada Rd., Candolim* ☎ *832/398–8444* 🌐 *www.fortunehotels.in* 🛏 *102 rooms* 🍴 *Free Breakfast.*

Pousada Tauma

$$$$ | **HOTEL** | Less than a kilometer from the beach (a complimentary shuttle bus makes regular beach runs), this beautiful boutique hotel built of laterite (a local red pitted stone) is far enough from the noise but close enough to be part of the action when you want it. **Pros:** secluded setting; full ayurvedic treatments available; gorgeous grounds. **Cons:** pricey compared to similar hotels of its category; not on the beach; menu is limited. [$] *Rooms from: Rs. 19900* ✉ *Porba-Vaddo, Calangute* ☎ *832/227–9063* 🌐 *www.pousada-tauma.com* 🛏 *13 rooms* 🍴 *Free Breakfast.*

Activities

Odyssey Tours

TOUR—SPORTS | This company has a luxury yacht, *Solita,* with a license to carry 27 passengers on deck, plus four crew members, including a captain and engineer. It offers half-day dolphin-spotting cruises as well as bird-watching trips and sunset cruises. The yacht leaves from Britona, where it has its own jetty. In the afternoon it's available for private charter groups for Rs. 17,500 per hour, plus taxes. The yacht is operational October through May. ✉ *Calangute Beach* ☎ *88051–22221.*

Sinquerim Beach

10 km (6 miles) northwest of Panaji.

You can rent windsurfers and water skis at Sinquerim and Bogmalo, also in the Bardez district. Equipment rental is fairly cheap, but always check the condition of the equipment you use and make sure life jackets are provided. If possible, shop around at the other places on the beach for your best offer. Stretched out in front

Inner Peace

If there's anything that sums up the Goan attitude to life, it's *sussegado*, which means "take it easy." Even with the tourist influx exceeding the local population, the massive star resorts, and the party scene, there's a certain peace in Goa that is unlikely to ever be disturbed, because it comes from within. A part of this mood of daylong siesta can be attributed to a widespread love of excellent food and local alcohol—Goa brews its own *feni*, a potent and inexpensive concoction distilled from palm sap or cashew-fruit juice. If you're looking to imbibe the true spirit of Goa, try the coconut-palm feni—it smells less pungent than the cashew variety and goes down a little bit easier. You can buy the alcohol from just about anywhere in Goa (but make sure it's bottled properly) and down it with classic tender coconut water. A morning in the waves, tiger prawns at a seaside shack, and a couple of fenis, and you will come to discover why people come back to Goa year after year to rejuvenate, even as they complain about how crowded and dirty it's getting. Spend a week in the company of Goans, with their mellow attitude toward life and their legendary warmth—despite the heavy toll that tourism takes on their home state—and you may find yourself, for better or for worse, more than a little intoxicated by the Goan way.

of the luxury Taj hotel, this small, sandy beach can get crowded with tourists and vendors.

GETTING HERE AND AROUND

Sinquerim is the first beach you'll get to as you head northwest after crossing the Mandovi River from Panaji.

Sights

Fort Aguada

ARCHAEOLOGICAL SITE | Perched high on a hill, with wonderful views west across the Arabian Sea and east across Aquada Bay to Panaji, Fort Aguada was built in 1612 and named for the natural springs that supplied not only the fort but also passing ships. Surrounded by wild grass, the fort is in excellent condition. Inside, you can take a good look at the solid stone architecture and the old lighthouse. The fort's defenses actually enclosed a much larger area than the bastion at the top of the hill; a seaward bastion still juts into the Arabian Sea on Sinquerim Beach, near the Taj cluster of hotels. If you only have time for one of Goa's many forts,

hit Aguada—it's the best preserved and most magnificent. Hire a taxi if time is a constraint; it's not an easy walk, as it's 4 km (2½ miles) south of Sinquerim Beach and at least half the way is a fairly steep uphill. ⊠ *Sinquerim, Candolim.*

Sinquerim Beach

BEACH—SIGHT | Close to Panaji, Sinquerim is a quiet, well-kept beach and, with some of Goa's most expensive resorts in the area—including the Vivanta by Taj–Fort Aguada and the Taj Holiday Village—it tends to be a destination for well-heeled local tourists and older international travelers. Having said that, pockets of vendors and tourists can gather around some of the more populist beachfront hotels. Visitors can try their hand at water sports such as windsurfing and snorkeling, and while the water isn't crystal clear, it is clean and makes for a lovely afternoon of paddling about; consistent waves make for good bodysurfing. **Amenities:** lifeguards; water sports. **Good for:** snorkeling; sunrise; swimming. ⊠ *Bardez.*

Restaurants

Morisco

$$$$ | SEAFOOD | Situated within the Taj Fort Aguada Resort & Spa, Morisco offers elegantly presented seafood, Indian, and continental cuisine and great views of Fort Aguada. While the food is upscale, with prices to match, the ambience is casual. **Known for:** Fort Aguada views; tempura fried king prawns; local live music. $ *Average main: Rs. 1800* ⊠ *Taj Fort Aguada Resort & Spa* ☎ *832/664–5858* ⊕ *www.tajhotels.com.*

🛏 Hotels

Aashyana Lakhanpal

$$$$ | HOTEL | Right in the middle of acres of tropical foliage and within shout-ing distance of the sands of Candolim beach, this handsome and sprawling property provides an excellent base from which to explore North Goa. One large, five-bedroom villa, three two-bedroom cottages, and two Portuguese bungalows make up Aashyana Lakhanpal. **Pros:** airy bedrooms and lots of open space; won-derful swimming pool; great food and attentive service. **Cons:** the dense foliage attracts mosquitoes (be sure to carry repellent); the attentive service might feel overbearing to some; four- to seven-night minimum stays depending on the season. $ *Rooms from: Rs. 96900* ⊠ *Candolim Beach* ☎ *832/248–9225* ⊕ *www.aashyanalakhanpal.com* ⥲ *8 rooms* ⦿| *No meals.*

Marbella Guest House

$$ | B&B/INN | A restored Portuguese villa with clean rooms and antique furniture, this heritage guesthouse is a popular place among those who know Goa well, and it's only about half a kilometer from here down to Sinquerim Beach. **Pros:** quiet location; lots of local charm; open during monsoon season. **Cons:** no phones in room; breakfast not included; not on the beach. $ *Rooms from: Rs. 4800* ⊠ *Between Sinquerim and Candolim* beaches, Bardez district ☎ *832/247–9551* ⊕ *www.marbellagoa.com* ⥲ *6 rooms* ⦿| *No meals.*

★ Vivanta by Taj–Fort Aguada

$$$$ | RESORT | Constructed within the boundary and adjoining the ramparts of an old Portuguese fort built in 1612, this hotel has gorgeous views of the fort, sea, and beach. **Pros:** stunning location with direct fort access; beautifully furnished rooms; huge pool with beach views. **Cons:** not much within easy walking distance; expensive; may feel formal to some guests. $ *Rooms from: Rs. 11400* ⊠ *Sinquerim Beach* ☎ *832/664–5858* ⊕ *www.tajhotels.com* ⥲ *198 rooms* ⦿| *No meals.*

Vivanta by Taj–Holiday Village

$$$$ | RESORT | Housed in charming Goan village–style cottages and villas that face lush gardens or the broad expanse of Sinquerim Beach, all guest rooms at this Taj resort include private terraces, luxuri-ous bedding, marble bathrooms, and flat-screen TVs. **Pros:** spectacular setting; sophisticated yet friendly service; free use of facilities at adjacent Fort Aguada Beach Resort. **Cons:** lots of kids can mean lots of noise; Internet costs extra; big property requiring lots of walking. $ *Rooms from: Rs. 14000* ⊠ *Sinquerim, Bardez* ☎ *832/664–5858* ⊕ *www.tajho-tels.com* ⥲ *142 rooms* ⦿| *Free Breakfast.*

Activities

John's Boat Tours

TOUR—SPORTS | Dolphin-watching, snorkel-ing at Grand Island, crocodile-spotting in the river backwaters, and sea fishing are all available from John's. There are also jeep tours to nearby spice plantations, Dudhsagar Falls, and Hampi ruins in the neighboring state of Karnataka. ⊠ *Cando-lim Beach* ☎ *98/2218–2814, 70305–54400* ⊕ *www.johnboattours.com.*

Thunderwave Water Sports

WATER SPORTS | On Sinquerim Beach, Candolim, this operator has been offering winchboat parasailing for nearly 20 years. ⊠ *Near Taj Holiday Village, Arambol Beach* ☎ *832/249–9779, 98/2217–6985, 98/2217–6986.*

Panaji

600 km (372 miles) south of Mumbai.

Panaji has somewhat less of the poverty and hustle and bustle of India's other state capitals, and its palm-lined plazas, elegant Portuguese colonial architecture, and other sights are easy to explore. There are historic homes and churches, restaurants serving flavorful Goan cuisine, and many unique galleries and boutiques. The best way to see the older parts of the city is on foot—in fact, if you leave without having explored the backstreets at leisure, you haven't really seen the best it has to offer. For diehard sun-and-sand lovers, there's the city beach at Dona Paula, but Panaji isn't recommended for its beaches, as they tend to be dirty and crowded.

GETTING HERE AND AROUND
Expect to pay about Rs. 800 for the 40-minute taxi ride to reach Panaji from Dabolim airport. After that, it's an easy stroll to reach the city's main attractions, which are all in a central part of town. Banks and ATMs, tour operators, and airline offices are all generally found along the city's main arteries, in particular 18th June Road and 31st January Road.

ESSENTIALS
VISITOR INFORMATION Department of Tourism North Zone Office ⊠ *Paryatan Bhavan, Patto, 2nd fl.* ☎ *832/249–4200 or 243–8866* ⊕ *www.goa-tourism.com.*

 Sights

Church of Our Lady of Immaculate Conception
RELIGIOUS SITE | This grand shrine was a mere chapel before 1541. Soon after, in 1600, it became a parish, and its

structure was rebuilt entirely. Now the church almost entirely presides over one of Panaji's squares. The building's distinctive zigzag staircases are a 19th-century addition, and the church's large bell was originally in the Church of St. Augustine in Old Goa. An annual December festival here draws huge crowds. At the other times of the year the square is a peaceful place to linger. ⊠ *Near Municipal Gardens* ☞ *Free.*

Dr. Salim Ali Bird Sanctuary
NATURE PRESERVE | Just a short distance from Panaji, this delightful bird refuge is on the tip of Chorao, an island in the Mandovi. The ferry jetty for Chorao is on Ribander jetty on the southern bank of the Mandovi River, between Panaji and Old Goa, and boats travel regularly to the island and back. A taxi can bring you to the jetty for the 15-minute ride across the river. The Forest Department in Panaji organizes guided tours to Chorao. The tiny sanctuary, full of mangroves, is named after a dedicated Indian ornithologist. Although October through March is the best time to view migratory birds, the sanctuary is open year-round. ⊠ *3 km (2 miles) northeast* ☎ *832/222–4747.*

Fontainhas
NEIGHBORHOOD | The shady, narrow streets of this largely residential neighborhood do not seem Indian—they are clearly still Portuguese at heart. From tiny *balcaos* (colonnaded porches), inhabitants watch as their quiet, unchanging world goes by, and through the old windows you can hear people practicing the piano and violin. At the heart of Fontainhas is the little whitewashed Chapel of St. Sebastian, which dates only to the late 19th century—new by Goan standards. Its claim to fame is an old crucifix that was once housed in the infamous Palace of the Inquisition in Old Goa. ⊠ *Between Ourem Creek and Altinho.*

Sao Tomé
HISTORIC SITE | This crumbling old neighborhood contains the General Post

Office, a former tobacco trading house, and a maze of extremely narrow streets behind it. The tiny bars of this district are full of old-world character, and indeed you might need that drink to help banish the more grisly images of Goa's past—the area opposite the post office was once the site of Panaji's town executions. ✉ *Between M.G. and Emidio Gracia roads.*

🍴 Restaurants

AZ.U.R
$$$$ | **ECLECTIC** | The Goa Marriott's café and lounge, pronounced "As You Are," may be worth a visit for the bay views alone—fortunately, the quality of its limited yet choice menu won't disappoint, either. After dark, the coffee shop morphs into a relaxed evening lounge bar. **Known for:** calamari fritters; tea- and coffee-based beverages; Western-style sandwiches (think BLTs and croques monsieur). [$] *Average main: Rs. 1200* ✉ *Goa Marriott, Miramar Beach Rd.* ☎ *832/246–3333.*

★ Mum's Kitchen
$$$ | **INDIAN** | Smack-dab in the middle of Panjim, this Goan institution is indisputably the best place in town for home-style Goan food—and as most of the regulars are locals, the kitchen doesn't hold back on the spice. The menu is vast and enticing, so either visit as part of a large group, or when absolutely ravenous (but yet able to wait for a table; the service is brisk so the wait shouldn't be too long). **Known for:** semolina-fried Bombay duck; spicy prawn recheado; sausage curry, served with fresh poi (a Goan bread that's similar to a ciabatta). [$] *Average main: Rs. 700* ✉ *854 Martins Bldg., D.B. St., Panaji–Miramar Rd.* ☎ *98221–75559, 90110–95557* 🌐 *www.mumskitchengoa.com.*

Riorico
$$$ | **INDIAN** | Housed inside the Hotel Mandovi, this beautifully decorated restaurant offers formal tables with floral upholstered chairs and tablecloths and intricate ceilings embellished with curlicue designs plus a handful of terrace tables. The menu here is extensive and varied, and features an array of Portuguese-influenced seafood dishes along with Chinese and Western fare at lunch and dinner. **Known for:** caldeirada (poached fish layered with potatoes and tomatoes and cooked with white wine); semolina-fried fish and prawns; ornate interiors. [$] *Average main: Rs. 500* ✉ *The Mandovi Hotel, D.B. Marg* ☎ *832/222–4405 to 09* 🌐 *www.hotelmandovigoa.com.*

Ritz Classic
$$$ | **INDIAN** | If you can find it, you'll likely be the only foreigner at this family favorite serving traditional (and spicy) Goan specialties. Hidden away on the second floor of an anonymous block on the commercial 18th June Road, the restaurant is certainly worth looking for, attested to by the lines going out the door, especially at lunch. **Known for:** chicken xacuti (coconut and tamarind curry); grilled kingfish; spice-infused pomfret recheiado. [$] *Average main: Rs. 500* ✉ *Wagle Vision Bldg., 18th June Rd., 2nd fl.* ☎ *832/242–6417, 832/664–4796,832/222–1138.*

Sher-e-Punjab
$$$ | **NORTH INDIAN** | Popular with locals and foreigners alike, this casual spot serves butter-laden dishes inspired by the cuisine of North India's Punjab region. It's situated within the Hotel Aroma, and is a great place to take an air-conditioned break from the intense shopping of 18th June Road. **Known for:** mutton dry fry; Peshawari chicken; tandoori-baked meats. [$] *Average main: Rs. 500* ✉ *Hotel Aroma, 18th June Rd.* ☎ *832/222–7204* 🌐 *www.hotelaromagoa.com.*

Verandah Restaurant
$$$ | **ECLECTIC** | Located up a flight of stairs at the historic Panjim Inn, with indoor and outdoor seating, Verandah has an atmospheric location for those

seeking a casual spot to sample tasty, fairly priced Goan cuisine or continental food. Check the daily specials, particularly for seasonal seafood items. **Known for:** Goan prawn curry served with rice; pork sorpotel; Portuguese serradura (a whipped cream and biscuit dessert). [$] *Average main: Rs. 700* ✉ *E–212 31st January Rd., Fontainhas* ☎ *832/222–1122, 832/222–6523, 832/243–5628* 🌐 *www.panjiminn.com.*

Viva Panjim

$$ | **INDIAN** | A walk down a narrow alley in the Fontainhas district brings you to one of the city's best-value restaurants, where reliable Goan classics, conviviality, and bargain prices are the rule. Featuring the award-winning cuisine of chef Linda De Souza, this cheery hideaway is crowded with locals and tourists—indoor seating can get cramped, but tables are also available outside. **Known for:** chicken cafreal (marinated and cooked with fresh cilantro); prawn curry; kingfish vindaloo. [$] *Average main: Rs. 400* ✉ *H. No. 178 31st January Rd., behind Mary Immaculate High School, Fontainhas* ☎ *832/242-2405, 98/5047–1363* 🕐 *No lunch.*

Hotels

Goa Marriott Resort & Spa

$$$$ | **RESORT** | Walk into the lovely sea-facing lobby, where you can watch and listen to the crash of waves along the rocky shores, and you will find it hard to leave this upscale Western chain hotel with all the plush trimmings expected in a five-star establishment. **Pros:** courteous staff; beautiful location; extensive amenities. **Cons:** city beach isn't the best; a bit expensive; rooms run small. [$] *Rooms from: Rs. 14000* ✉ *Miramar Beach Rd.* ☎ *832/246–3333* 🌐 *www.marriott.com/hotels/travel/goimc-goa-marriott-resort-and-spa* 🛏 *180 rooms* 🍴 *Free Breakfast.*

Hotel Fidalgo

$ | **HOTEL** | At the corner of a crowded intersection on the bustling 18th June Road, this landmark business hotel offers all the amenities you'd expect at relatively reasonable prices, and with the convenience of being in the center of town. **Pros:** good value for money; convenient location; extensive on-site dining options. **Cons:** noisy commercial part of town; drab hallway carpets; pool faces a shabby building. [$] *Rooms from: Rs. 3800* ✉ *18th June Rd.* ☎ *832/222–6291 to 99* 🌐 *www.hotelfidalgo-goa.com* 🛏 *108 rooms* 🍴 *Free Breakfast.*

Panjim Inn

$$ | **B&B/INN** | Travelers who appreciate a sense of place love the warmth of the Panjim Inn, a unique hotel in the center of historic Fontainhas that was built in the late 1800s and incorporates the former family home of the owner, Ajit Sukhija. **Pros:** great location in the center of the historic district; friendly staff; relaxed atmosphere. **Cons:** traffic noise; no phones in rooms; some rooms are small. [$] *Rooms from: Rs. 5000* ✉ *E–212, 31st January Rd., Fontainhas* ☎ *832/222-6523, 832/222–1122, 832/243–5628* 🌐 *www.panjiminn.com* 🛏 *24 rooms* 🍴 *Free Breakfast.*

Panjim People's

$$$ | **HOTEL** | The four spacious and beautiful antiques-furnished rooms in this historic annex of the Panjim Inn, with their four-poster beds, carved rosewood dressers, and plenty of windows, are a reminder of the times when colonial homes stood along the banks of the river. **Pros:** spacious rooms; old-world charm; intimate ambience. **Cons:** some windows overlook a dumpster below; no elevator; rooms lack phones. [$] *Rooms from: Rs. 7500* ✉ *E–212, 31 January Rd., Fontainhas* ☎ *832/222–6523, 832/243–5628, 832/222–1122, 98/2357–2035* 🌐 *www.panjiminn.com/panjim-peoples.html* 🛏 *4 rooms* 🍴 *Free Breakfast.*

Pousada Panjim

$$ | **B&B/INN** | Several blocks from the street noise of Rua de Ourem, this vintage and stylish property built around

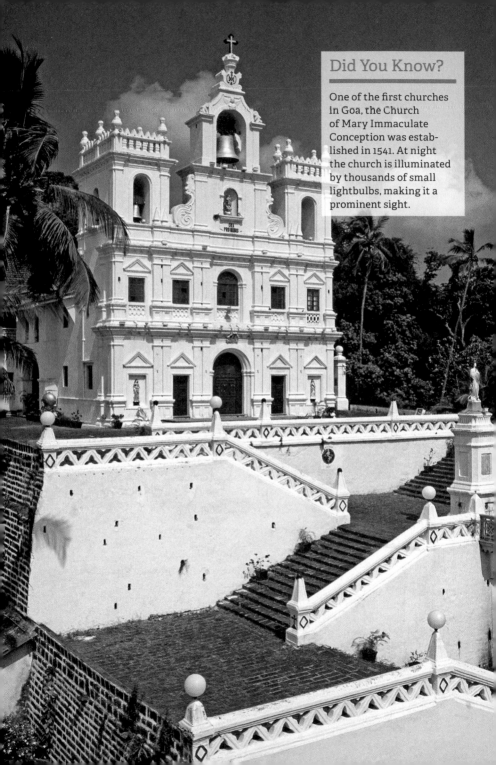

a central garden courtyard is noted for being one of the few Hindu homes in a predominantly Catholic neighborhood. **Pros:** quiet refuge in a noisy city; memorable, one-of-a-kind setting; exceptional value. **Cons:** no restaurant on premises; thin walls between rooms; expensive for what's offered. [$] *Rooms from: Rs. 5000* ✉ *E–212, 31 January Rd., Fontainhas* ☎ *832/222–6523, 832/243–5628, 832/222–1122, 98/2357–2035* 🌐 *www.panjiminn.com/panjim-pousada.html* 🛏 *9 rooms* 🍴 *Free Breakfast.*

Vivanta by Taj–Panaji
$$$ | **HOTEL** | This chain property is more business oriented than the average Panaji hotel, with the added oomph of high-tech features such as surround-sound home-theater systems, multimedia panels, and LCD screens in all rooms. **Pros:** 2,500-square-foot gym; lovely rooftop pool; spa with good menu of treatments. **Cons:** better suited to business travelers; no nearby beach access; rooms lack local charm. [$] *Rooms from: Rs. 7000* ✉ *D.B. Bandodkar Rd., St. Inez Junction* ☎ *832/663–3687* 🌐 *www.tajhotels.com* 🛏 *170 rooms* 🍴 *No meals.*

Activities

BOAT CRUISES

Casino Carnival
BOAT TOURS | Gambling, food, and drink can be enjoyed every night from 5 pm until 6 am aboard the *Casino Carnival,* a floating luxury casino that also has a TV–game room for those under 18, a toddlers' room with babysitters, and an open-air swimming pool. The dress code is smart-casual, which in India means no shorts, bikinis, or swimming trunks are allowed outside the pool area. ✉ *Casino Carnival Front Desk, Goa Marriott Resort and Spa, Panjim* ☎ *0091/8888–85314 to 47* 🌐 *www.casinocarnival.in.*

Department of Tourism
BOAT TOURS | In addition to several private operators, the Department of Tourism organizes river cruises, some with Goan cultural shows, music, and dinner. Most cruises depart from the Panaji jetty on the River Mandovi. ☎ *832/243–8750* 🌐 *www.goa-tourism.com/Cruise_menu.*

Shopping

Most stores are open 10 am to 7 pm, and 18th June Road (named after an anticolonial protest launched by a socialist leader in 1946) is the city's busiest shopping thoroughfare. It's nothing special, but it's worth a stroll if you are in the market for spices, nuts, or souvenirs.

Sosa's
CLOTHING | Come here for high-end Indian designers, including Goan favorite Savio Jon. Expect clothes in bright colors, with easy silhouettes, and made from cotton and silk, plus all manner of resort wear. ✉ *E–245 Rua de Ourem* ☎ *832/222–8063, 98/2338–1488.*

UK Dry Fruits
FOOD/CANDY | Goa is famous for its cashew crop, and this store has an excellent selection of cashew nuts. There are exotic varieties such as Pudina Lime, Hot Masala, and Szechuan—sample a couple before buying. You will also find a great selection of Goan curry pastes, powders, and spice mixtures. ✉ *18th June Rd.* ☎ *832/243–5455.*

Velha Goa Galleria
CERAMICS/GLASSWARE | This is the store for *azulejos,* a traditional Portuguese style of hand-painted tiles and ceramics. In addition to a selection of tiles, frames, and other ceramics, Velha Goa Galleria has the rights to sell the reproduced ceramic artwork of Goa's own celebrated cartoonist Mario Miranda. It's a fantastic spot for souvenirs and gifts. ✉ *4/191 Rua de Ourem* ☎ *832/242–6628* 🌐 *www.velhagoa.com.*

Old Goa

10 km (6 miles) east of Panaji.

Gorgeous Old Goa, with foliage creeping in around the ruins of old churches, served as the capital of the Portuguese colony until repeated outbreaks of cholera forced the government to move to Panaji in 1843. The shift out of Old Goa, however, had begun as early as 1695. It was a slow desertion—first the viceroy, then the nobility, then the customs. By the time the official declaration came, it was already a deserted, ruined city. There are several imposing and beautiful churches, convents, and monasteries that reveal its former glory. Most were begun at a time when European architectural styles were shifting toward the baroque. For anyone with an interest in religious architecture or Catholic history, Old Goa is a must-see destination, and merits a couple of hours of exploration.

GETTING HERE AND AROUND

Hop into a taxi or auto-rickshaw in Panaji to reach Old Goa. The 20-minute ride should cost around Rs. 400 by taxi or Rs. 250 by auto-rickshaw. It's a small area, and you can walk easily from one sight to another. It's worth hiring an English-speaking guide for a one-hour walking tour—they tend to find you around the entrance of the Basilica of Bom Jesus.

 Sights

Archaeological Museum

MUSEUM | A part of the Franciscan monastery behind the Church of St. Francis of Assisi, the Archaeological Museum has an intricately gilded and carved interior. The museum's collection is not entirely devoted to Catholic objets d'art; it also has bits and pieces from Goa's early Hindu history. It's worth a quick look around, if only to peruse the portrait gallery of Goa's viceroys. ⊠ *Across road from Basilica of Bom Jesus* ☎ *832/228–6133* ⊠ *Rs. 5.*

★ Basilica of Bom Jesus

RELIGIOUS SITE | Dedicated to the worship of the infant Jesus, the Basilica of Bom Jesus is also known throughout the Christian world as the tomb of St. Francis Xavier, patron saint of Goa, who was handed the task of spreading Christianity in the Portuguese colony. The saint's body has "survived" almost 500 years now without ever having been embalmed, and lies in a silver casket well out of reach of visitors. Built from local red stone around the turn of the 17th century, the tomb took the Florentine sculptor Giovanni Batista Foggini 10 years to complete. Once every 10 years the missionary's body is exposed to the public at close quarters, drawing thousands of pilgrims. ⊠ *Old Goa* ⊠ *Free.*

Museum of Christian Art

MUSEUM | Inside the Convent of St. Monica, the Museum of Christian Art has a number of objects of Christian interest, including paintings and religious silverware, some dating back to the 16th century. The convent was the first nunnery of its kind in the East, and functioned as one until the late 19th century. ⊠ *Holy Mount Hill* ⊕ *www.museumofchristianart.com* ⊠ *Rs. 30.*

Sé (St. Catherine's) Cathedral

RELIGIOUS SITE | The imposing white Sé (St. Catherine's) Cathedral—the largest church in Old Goa—was built between 1562 and 1652 by order of the king of Portugal. Fine carvings depict scenes from the life of Christ and the Blessed Virgin over the main altar, which commemorates St. Catherine of Alexandria. Several splendidly decorated chapels are dedicated to St. Joseph, St. George, St. Anthony, St. Bernard, and the Holy Cross. Only one of the cathedral's two original majestic towers remains; the other collapsed in 1776. ⊠ *Across road from Basilica of Bom Jesus* ⊠ *Free.*

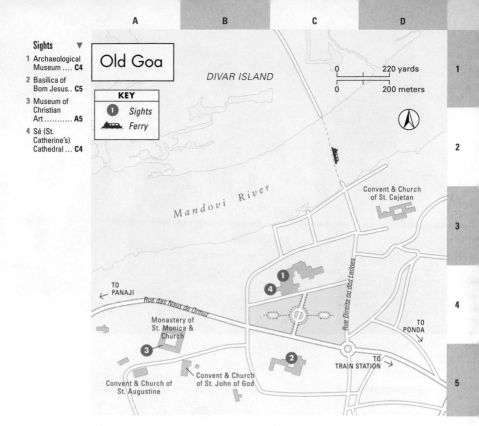

Sights ▼

1 Archaeological
Museum **C4**

2 Basilica of
Bom Jesus.. **C5**

3 Museum of
Christian
Art **A5**

4 Sé (St.
Catherine's)
Cathedral ... **C4**

Old Goa

DIVAR ISLAND

0   220 yards

0   200 meters

KEY

 Sights

Ferry

Mandovi River

Convent & Church
of St. Cajetan

TO
← PANAJI

Rue das Naus de Ormuz

Monastery of
St. Monica &
Church

Convent & Church of
St. Augustine

Convent & Church
of St. John of God

Rue Direita ou das Leilas

TO
PONDA →

TO →
TRAIN STATION

Dudhsagar Falls

50 km (31 miles) southeast of Panaji.

These imposing waterfalls make a good
day trip from Panaji or Calangute.

⊙ Sights

Dudhsagar Waterfalls

NATURE PRESERVE | With a name that
means "sea of milk," these waterfalls are
imposing, with water cascading almost
2,000 feet into a rock-ribbed valley. They
are at their most impressive when the
monsoons arrive, but this also makes the
approach road inaccessible, so the ideal
time for a trek here is between October
and the end of April. Pack refreshments
and beach towels, and plan to spend
a morning here; monkeys, birds, bees,
butterflies, and thick foliage complete

the wild experience. The Goa Tourism
Development Corporation runs tours
from Calangute (departing at 6:30 am,
Rs. 2,000) in air-conditioned buses or
jeeps, which include admission to the
falls, lunch, and bottled water.

Ponda

*29 km (18 miles) southeast of Panaji; 45
km (28 miles) from Dabolim Airport.*

Ponda itself is an uninteresting town, but
there are a number of temples in the hills
that surround it. The area came under
Portuguese control relatively late, in
1764, about 250 years after the Portuguese conquered Goa—which explains
why the temples were not destroyed.

Sé (St. Catherine's) Cathedral in Old Goa, the largest church in Asia

SIGHTS

Manguesh temple

RELIGIOUS SITE | One of the chief attractions of Ponda is this temple in Priol, 7 km (4 miles) before you reach Ponda. With its domes and other eccentric, un-Hindu architectural features, the temple has evidence of Islamic and Christian influences. Other temples in the vicinity include the always-crowded Shantadurga temple, with its distinctive tower, the Mahalsa temple, with its gargantuan (41-foot-high) oil lamp, and the Lakshmi Narasimha and Naguesh temples, with their lovely temple tanks (large pools with steps leading into them, so that the devout can bathe). ⊠ *Ponda.*

Bogmalo Beach

24 km (15 miles) north of Margao; 25 km (16 miles) south of Panaji.

Just a 4-km (2½-mile) ride away from Dabolim Airport, popular Bogmalo Beach has boating and water-sports facilities for diving and jet-skiing. Two tiny islands sit about 10 km (6 miles) out to sea.

 Sights

Bogmalo Beach

BEACH—SIGHT | This tiny crescent of fine sand is perfect for sunning and swimming (unless the water is rough). It's near a low, verdant hill topped by a few modern buildings on one side and the Bogmallo Beach Resort on the other. For the most privacy, walk down the beach to the far right—there are fewer fishing boats, shacks, and people. **Amenities:** food and drink; water sports; lifeguards. **Best for:** sunning; diving. ⊠ *Bogmalo Beach.*

 Hotels

Bogmallo Beach Resort

$$ | RESORT | This six-story high-rise beachfront hotel is a good choice for those needing easy access to the airport, but not much else. **Pros:** close to the airport; meal packages available; well-maintained rooms and facilities. **Cons:** not much character; Wi-Fi costs extra; on a mediocre beach. $ *Rooms from: Rs. 5750* ✉ *Bogmalo Beach* ☎ *832/253–8222 to 235* ⊕ *www.bogmalobeachresort.com* ⇨ *141 rooms* ⦿ *Free Breakfast.*

Coconut Creek

$$$ | **RESORT** | On a dense coconut plantation, just a two-minute walk (about 500 yards) from Bogmalo Beach and a 3-km (2-mile) drive from Dabolim Airport, this charming little resort with spotless, airy rooms, and a small swimming pool is run by friendly staff. **Pros:** private jungle setting; one of the nicest midrange resorts in South Goa; close to the airport. **Cons:** a/c problems in some rooms; noise from airplanes overhead; rooms are worn and need updating. $ *Rooms from: Rs. 8900* ✉ *Bogmalo Beach* ☎ *832/253–8100* ⊕ *www.coconutcreekgoa.com* ⇨ *20 rooms* ⦿ *Free Breakfast.*

Activities

Goa Diving

WATER SPORTS | Scotsman Willie Downey offers casual diving as well as PADI open-water courses. ✉ *Bogmalo Beach* ☎ *832/255–5117, 98/90221–00380* ⊕ *www.goadiving.com.*

Cansaulim Beach

16 km (10 miles) northwest of Margao.

This quiet, clean stretch of beach between Bogmallo and Colva has a fine location—it's conveniently close to both Dabolim Airport and Margao, and yet a good distance from the crowded north and the congested beaches around Colva. The only significant signs of life in these parts are the hotels and resorts in the vicinity, and a couple of sleepy villages.

It's a Stakeout

Goan taxi drivers stake out tourists by waiting outside hotels and restaurants. As soon as you walk out the door, three or four of them are at your side asking you if you want a cab, and where you are going. They find it hard to believe you'd want to walk when you can afford to pay for a ride.

⊙ Sights

Cansaulim Beach

BEACH—SIGHT | FAMILY | This remote stretch of beach between Bogmallo and Colva is quiet, making it ideal for relaxing. There are also some sporting activities and shopping available nearby. **Amenities:** none. **Best for:** solitude. ✉ *Cansaulim.*

🛏 Hotels

★ Park Hyatt Goa Resort and Spa

$$$$ | **RESORT** | In the very top bracket of the Goa resorts, the modern and sleek, 45-acre Hyatt has spacious rooms, great dining, an excellent spa, a library with 1,500 titles, a minitheater where you can watch movies, and the largest swimming pool in India (21,527 square feet). **Pros:** ultraluxurious; big rooms; top-notch spa and restaurants. **Cons:** very spread out; expensive; slow service. $ *Rooms from: Rs. 13500* ✉ *Arossim Beach, Cansaulim* ☎ *832/272–1234* ⊕ *www.hyatt.com* ⇨ *249 rooms* ⦿ *No meals.*

Majorda and Utorda

10 km (6 miles) from Margao.

Majorda and nearby Utorda, which both have a number of resorts, are rapidly sacrificing peace and quiet to larger volumes of tourists. Just north of Colva Beach, they are within cycling distance from

Take Home the Taste of Goa

If you haven't found your share of slippers, sarongs, bags, and bangles at Anjuna or the shack shops near the main beaches, pay a visit to a local grocery. Look carefully, and you'll find some great stuff to take home as a reminder of your stay in Goa or to give away as unusual epicurean gifts. There's high-quality *bebinca* (a rich, layered, dense 16-layer cake made of butter, sugar, egg yolk, and coconut) that has a long shelf life, making for easy packing; *feni* (Goan liquor) in fancy bottles (though it smells the same as the stuff in the downmarket bottles), which you'd be well advised to transport only in your carry-on baggage; *prawn balchao* (in a red chilli sauce) and *mackerel reicheado* (pickled prawns and mackerel soaked in red masala, which have to be fried once you get home); a variety of dried and wet *masalas* (spice mixes) from *cafreal* (green masala) and *vindaloo* (hot red masala) to *xacuti* (a masala with coconut and ground spices), and packets of *tendlim* (a pickled gourd). Chances are the store owner will wrap it for you with a grin to acknowledge that you know a bit about Goa after all.

Colva (5 km [3 miles]) and Betalbatim (3 km [2 miles]), both known for restaurants and shack life. If you stay here, you'll have yourself a good base from which to explore the sights around Margao.

Sights

Majorda Beach

BEACH—SIGHT | This wide stretch of golden sand is a good choice for travelers looking for peace and quiet. There are a couple of shacks set up here for those who want to order drinks or snacks, but for the most part the ambience is calm and uncrowded. **Amenities**: water sports; food and drink. **Best for:** swimming; solitude. ✉ *Majorda.*

Restaurants

Martin's Corner

$$$ | **INDIAN** | For more than two decades, this celebrated family-run restaurant has been serving meticulously prepared Goan specialties to residents and visitors in the Majorda area. What started as a humble diner with just a few tables and chairs is now among the most popular places to eat in town, featuring indoor and outdoor seating, regular live music, and great views of surrounding fields. **Known for:** pulao with spicy Goan chouriço sausages; masala fried king crab; good selection of drinks. [$] *Average main: Rs. 500* ✉ *Bin Waddo, Betalbatim, Salcette, Majorda* ☎ *832/288–0061* 🌐 *www.martinscornergoa.com.*

Hotels

★ Alila Diwa Goa

$$$$ | **RESORT** | Overlooking verdant rice plantations and the Arabian Sea, the Alila Goa is a cool open oasis of dark pitched roofs, breezy verandas, and serene courtyards. **Pros:** gorgeous property; delicious food; beautiful rooms. **Cons:** no direct beach access; expensive food and room rates; not much within walking distance. [$] *Rooms from: Rs. 19500* ✉ *48/10 Adao Vado Majorda, Salcette, Majorda* ☎ *832/274–6800* 🌐 *www.aliladiwagoa.com* 🛏 *171 rooms* 🍴 *Free Breakfast.*

The Kenilworth Beach Resort

$$$$ | RESORT | You may find your peace and quiet here: this large resort has an experienced and calm staff, thus lacking the frantic-to-please service typical of some other hotels in Goa; plus there's a marble lobby with lots of quiet corners for relaxing. **Pros:** all rooms have private balconies; beachfront location; scuba lessons with practice pool. **Cons:** sprawling and crowded at times; expensive room rates; can feel impersonal. $ *Rooms from: Rs. 11400 ⊠ Utorda, Salcete, Majorda ☎ 832/669–8888 ⊕ www. kenilworthhotels.com ⋑ 104 rooms ⊖ Free Breakfast.*

★ Vivenda Dos Palhacos

$$$ | B&B/INN | This 100-year-old restored Portuguese home—with a lovely front porch, elegant dining room, and cozy living room—has lots of pizzazz thanks to owners Simon and Charlotte Hayward, and yet maintains an intimate feel. **Pros:** personalized, friendly service; rooms with character; free Wi-Fi. **Cons:** no TV or phones in rooms; in an area with stray dogs; not on the beach. $ *Rooms from: Rs. 6000 ⊠ Costa Vaddo, Majorda, Salcette, Majorda ☎ 832/322–1119 ⊕ www. vivendagoa.com ⋑ 6 rooms ⊖ No meals.*

Colva

7 km (4 miles) west of Margao.

Colva Beach is a great place for family vacations. There are shacks selling snacks and souvenirs, and there are different beachfront activities. Vacationers here note that the beach tends to be clean and the water calm.

Sights

Colva Beach

BEACH—SIGHT | This is the most congested beach in South Goa. Its large parking and entrance areas are crowded with shacks selling snacks and souvenirs and young men offering mopeds for rent. The first 1,000 feet of the beach are hectic—stuffed with vendors, cows, and fishing boats—but the sand, backed by palm groves, stretches in both directions, and promises plenty of quieter spots. The water is good for swimming, and the restaurants and bar shacks are plentiful. **Amenities:** food and drink; toilets. **Best for:** swimming. ⊠ *Colva Beach.*

Hotels

Longuinhos Beach Resort

$$$$ | HOTEL | At this old Colva favorite, right on the beach, all rooms come with balconies and are comfortable and reasonably priced. **Pros:** easy beach access; one of the best midrange resorts in Colva; lovely grounds with sea views. **Cons:** a bit run-down; food is nothing special; property quality doesn't justify its high-season rates. $ *Rooms from: Rs. 66700 ⊠ Salcete, Colva Beach ☎ 832/278–8068 to 69 ⊕ www.longuinhosgoa.com ⋑ 53 rooms ⊖ Free Breakfast.*

Loutolim

10 km (6 miles) northeast of Margao.

Loutolim is among Goa's prettiest villages, with lush rice fields and tranquil village roads that lie under a canopy of forest trees. This is also a lovely area to view some fine examples of Goan-Portuguese architecture. There's not much by way of accommodations except for the charming Casa Susegad. If you are able to get a room, make Loutolim a stopover to experience nontouristy Goa and visit nearby spice plantations, the Brangaza house in Chandor, or the Miranda House—a well-preserved Goan country house. Lunch at one of Goa's most delightful restaurants, Fernando's Nostalgia, in the courtyard of the chef's house on the Ponda-Margao road, is a must if you venture this side.

🍴 Restaurants

★ Fernando's Nostalgia

$$$ | **INDIAN** | In the tranquil, slow-paced old village of Raia is one of the best restaurants in the state, set in the late chef Fernando's country house. Now run by his wife, the restaurant serves classic Goan and Portugese-Goan dishes, and there's live music Thursday through Sunday. **Known for:** fofos (shallow-fried fish and mashed potatoes, rolled in breadcrumbs and egg); Goan-style spinach soup; prawn almondegas (meatballs). [$] *Average main: Rs. 600* ✉ *608 Uzro, Raia* ☎ *832/277–7098, 832/277–7054, 98/98221–03467* 🌐 *fernandosnostalgia.wordpress.com.*

🛏 Hotels

Casa Susegad

$$$ | **B&B/INN** | Loutolim's laid-back charm is captured in Norman and Carol Steele's warm and inviting country inn, with its lovely rooms and great home-cooked food. **Pros:** relaxing ambience; lovely food; yoga lessons available in season. **Cons:** 30-minute ride to the beach; resident cats and dogs might disturb allergy sufferers; some rooms lack a/c. [$] *Rooms from: Rs. 7499* ✉ *Orgao Loutolim* ☎ *832/648–3368, 098/2210–6341* 🌐 *www.casasusegad.com* 🛏 *5 rooms* 🍴 *Free Breakfast.*

Chandor

15 km (9 miles) east of Margao.

This small, sleepy village occupies the site of Chandrapur, ancient capital of the region from AD 375 to 1053.

👁 Sights

Braganza House

HOUSE | The chief reason to visit Chandor is this 400-year-old house—a slice of living history. Two wings are occupied by two branches of the Braganza family, the Menezes Braganzas and the Braganza Pereiras. You can see the style in which the wealthy landed gentry must have lived until the land reformation that followed Independence in 1947; the great rooms are filled with treasures, including beautiful period furniture and Chinese porcelain. Although some parts of the house have been renovated and are in reasonably good shape, it takes a lot of effort to maintain the two wings, and contributions toward upkeep are expected. ✉ *Chandor* ☎ *832/278–4201, 832/278–4227* 🎫 *Donations welcome.*

Benaulim

9 km (6 miles) southwest of Margao.

Just 2 km (1 mile) south of Colva is the first of the beautiful, secluded beaches of South Goa—a far cry from the action-packed beaches of the north. Head to Benaulim and farther south only if you want to get away from it all. All this isolation comes at a price: the resorts are more expensive here.

GETTING HERE AND AROUND

Benaulim village has a small supermarket and is centered on a crossroads called Maria Hall. The beach is less than a kilometer from the village. There are some vendors, food shacks, and locals, but none of the crowds you'd find up north.

👁 Sights

Benaulim Beach

BEACH—SIGHT | Despite its proximity to crowded Colva, Benaulim beach is a world apart. Still relatively quiet, an increasingly rare commodity on Goa's beaches, this long swath of sand features only the odd souvenir hawker or stray dog, and is an excellent spot on which to park your beach towel. Of course, there are beach shacks, if you'd prefer a steady supply of beer and snacks as well as the comfort of a sun bed, and although it isn't as idyllic as Morjim or Mandrem farther north, with still water and soft sand, Benaulim is a great pick for a day in the sun. **Amenities:** food and drink; lifeguards; water sports. **Best for:** solitude; swimming; walking. ✉ *Benaulim Beach.*

🛏 Hotels

Taj Exotica

$$$$ | **RESORT** | Beside tranquil Benaulim Beach, well away from the mass-tourist clutter of Colva, is one of the most attractive places to stay in South Goa—and where the staff is kind and the rooms are spacious, too. **Pros:** excellent dining options; gorgeous setting; gorgeous rooms and villas, many with sea views. **Cons:** very spread out; very expensive; slow service at times. [$] *Rooms from: Rs. 23500* ✉ *Calwaddo, Salcette, Benaulim Beach* ☎ *832/668–3333* 🌐 *www.tajhotels.com* 🛏 *144 rooms* 🍴 *Free Breakfast.*

Varca

14 km (9 miles) southwest of Margao.

The scenery at Varca is rural: there are deep fields on either side of the road, and you may get the distinct feeling that you're heading nowhere in particular. This is an illusion. There are a number of resorts close to Varca village that take advantage of its perfect, unspoiled stretch of beach. Stay at Varca for the beach and for the opportunity to take long walks through the green Goan countryside.

👁 Sights

Varca Beach

BEACH—SIGHT | Another of the south's treasures, and only a short distance from Benaulim beach is Varca, a clean, quiet beach that manages the seemingly impossible feat of being nearly entirely hawker-free. Visitors from the area's resorts are treated to a quiet, palm-lined strip of beach that's perfect for unwinding with a good book. Beach shacks are thin on the ground in season, and nonexistent in the off-season, so plan to pack a picnic basket if you're headed there in the leaner months. **Amenities:** none. **Best for:** solitude; sunset; swimming; walking. ✉ *Varca.*

🍴 Restaurants

Carnaval

$$$$ | **ECLECTIC** | Low-hung black lamps light a woven bamboo ceiling, and quintessentially Goan Mario Miranda cartoons enliven the walls at this restaurant inside the Caravela Beach Resort. Here you'll find excellent fusion food and great desserts; unfortunately, it's only open for dinner. **Known for:** jerk potatoes peri-peri; crepes filled with Indian-style carrot halwa; tandoor-grilled tiger prawns with lemon-mustard sauce. [$] *Average main: Rs. 800* ✉ *Ramada Caravela* ☎ *832/669–5000.*

🛏 Hotels

Caravela Beach Resort

$$$$ | **RESORT** | A casino, a fusion Indian-Mediterranean restaurant, and a Polynesian eatery on the beach add to the mix of this cheery beachfront resort, which is spread out over 23 acres. **Pros:** lovely rooms with good views; attentive and eager-to-please staff; lots of good restaurants. **Cons:** public spaces could use a sprucing up; area lacks nightlife; expensive. [$] *Rooms from: Rs. 10500* ✉ *Varca Beach* ☎ *832/669–5000* 🌐 *www.caravelabeachresortgoa.com* 🛏 *199 rooms* 🍴 *Free Breakfast.*

Cavelossim

20 km (12 miles) southwest of Margao.

The last of the villages before the mouth of the Sal River, Cavelossim is also the end of the coastal road southward from Bogmalo. If you want to continue down the coast, you have to head back inland and take the national highway south, or take a country road up the river and use a ferry. Given that this is a rural area, Cavelossim is a surprisingly developed little place, with a shopping arcade; this is chiefly because of the presence of the Leela, arguably the most luxurious of the southern Goa resorts. The beach is clean and striking because it's at the mouth of the Sal River—serene and flanked by fields and coconut plantations.

This part of South Goa is an end in itself, and it's not a good base from which to explore the rest of the state (if you're keen on beach-hopping and other touristy activities, stay up north). It's the place to come when you want to relax, take up residence on the beach, and forget about everything, including trips to town.

GETTING HERE AND AROUND

From Dabolim Airport, it will take you about 45 minutes to reach Cavelossim.

Sights

Cavelossim Beach

BEACH—SIGHT | One of Goa's lesser-known stretches, Cavelossim Beach is starting to come into its own. With a few swanky hotels in the area, including the Leela Goa, Cavelossim is primarily popular with wealthy Indian visitors, due to the proliferation of upscale resorts in the area, and as a result is fairly clean, with soft white sand. If you're looking for swinging nightlife, this is not the beach for you, but it is worth a visit for those seeking relaxation, or perhaps some dolphin spotting—contact the area's boat operators who can organize sunset trips to spot the pods of dolphins that inhabit these waters. **Amenities:** food and drink; lifeguard; water sports. **Best for:** solitude; sunset; swimming. ✉ *Cavelossim Beach.*

Hotels

Holiday Inn

$$$ | **RESORT** | The chief advantage of this international chain is its uniform service and friendly vibe, and the private access to Mobor Beach is a blessing after the crowded beaches of North Goa. Spread over 25 acres, the hotel has a large pool that encourages long, all-day soaks, a poolside bar with excellent snacks, and comfortable, if generic, rooms. **Pros:** well priced for its lovely beach location; huge outdoor pool; expansive grounds. **Cons:** could use an update; rooms are generic; popular for weddings and can get loud. [$] *Rooms from: Rs. 7000* ✉ *Mobor Beach* ☎ *832/287–1303 to 312* 🌐 *www.holidayinngoa.com* 🛏 *203 rooms* 🍴 *Free Breakfast.*

★ **The Leela Goa**

$$$$ | **RESORT** | For flat-out, over-the-top luxury and sophistication, nothing in Goa can top this well-planned 75-acre resort that includes a secluded beach and a magnificent view of cliffs and coves. **Pros:** quiet; excellent in-house restaurants; super spa. **Cons:** Wi-Fi costs extra; not much to do in the areas surrounding the hotel; extremely expensive. [$] *Rooms from: Rs. 17601* ✉ *Mobor Beach* ☎ *832/662–1234* 🌐 *www.theleela.com* 🛏 *186 rooms* 🍴 *No meals.*

Palolem Beach

37 km (23 miles) southwest of Margao.

Until recently, Goa's southernmost sandy stretch—nicknamed Paradise Beach—really was like a dream. The visitors who made their way to Palolem, in the Canacona district, were nature lovers, privacy seekers, and the odd backpacker. It's no

longer quiet or under the radar, and every year the number of shacks, hotels, and restaurants goes up, although it continues to have a negligible club scene. Also increasingly popular with Indian tourists, Palolem is not the quiet haven of years past, but this mile-long, crescent-shape stretch of white sand remains one of the most beautiful beaches in India. Compared to Goa's other beach strips, accommodation options are thin on the ground, and tend more toward beach shack–style low-budget accommodations that pop up in season and pack up for the monsoon, but visitors will spot lots of construction works underway, and in another couple of seasons, Palolem will likely be rife with resorts and high-end properties.

For visitors not keen on lower-budget living, at present your best bet might be at the Lalit Goa, a few kilometers south, at Raj Baga.

GETTING HERE AND AROUND

From Dabolim Airport, a prepaid taxi will cost you about Rs. 1,200 to make the 67-km (42-mile) trip, which will take roughly 90 minutes.

Sights

Palolem Beach

BEACH—SIGHT | This once-deserted white-sand beach, backed by palm groves and low, green mountains, is still quieter than its northern counterparts, but Palolem is now a definite destination for sunseekers. It has a solid selection of cheap eateries and shacks, which have sprung up to cater to its bunch of hippie visitors. The farthest south of this coastline's developed beaches, it's no longer quite the idyll that first drew visitors this far south, but it is still very beautiful. **Amenities:** food and drink. **Best for:** solitude; swimming; walking. ✉ *Palolem Beach.*

Hotels

Ciaran's

$$ | B&B/INN | Suited to Palolem's long-term backpackers, Ciaran's has evolved over the years from beachfront, coco palm–thatched huts into proper cottages, all with an individual veranda and set around a small garden. **Pros:** good, hearty breakfasts; right on the seafront; free Wi-Fi. **Cons:** can be noisy in season; service slightly slow; rooms a bit gloomy in the daylight. [$] *Rooms from: Rs. 5250* ✉ *233/A Palolem Beach, behind Old Syndicate bank* 🌐 *www.ciarans.com* 🛏 *37 rooms* 🍴 *No meals.*

The Lalit Golf & Spa Resort Goa

$$$ | RESORT | They don't get much bigger than this sprawling 85-acre resort with spacious rooms and a 9-hole golf course lining the banks of the Talpona River on the south side. **Pros:** secluded; many on-site activities; incredibly luxurious facilities and accommodations. **Cons:** long walk between all the amenities; not close to the beach; extremely expensive. [$] *Rooms from: Rs. 7200* ✉ *Raj Baga, Cancona, 3 km (2 miles) from Palolem Beach* ☎ *832/266–771* 🌐 *www.thelalit.com* 🛏 *263 rooms* 🍴 *Free Breakfast.*

The Nest

$ | B&B/INN | A stone's throw from the sea, and reasonably priced, this rustic collection of beach huts is emblematic of accommodations in Palolem and a good place to get a no-frills beach hut experience. **Pros:** right on the beach; quiet; excellent views. **Cons:** basic bathrooms; some rooms lack a/c; rustic vibe overall. [$] *Rooms from: Rs. 2500* ✉ *Ourem Rd., Mohanbagh* 🌐 *www.thenestpalolem.com* 🛏 *15 rooms* 🍴 *No meals.*

Chapter 9

KERALA

Updated by
Christabel Lobo

👁 **Sights**
★★★★★

🍽 **Restaurants**
★★★★★

🛏 **Hotels**
★★★★★

🛍 **Shopping**
★★★★★

🍸 **Nightlife**
★★★★★

WELCOME TO KERALA

TOP REASONS TO GO

★ **Ease your stress:** There's no place better than Kerala to get an ayurvedic oil massage and a yoga session. Let your tension melt away and your body kick back into equilibrium.

★ **Sail along the scenic backwaters:** Luxury houseboats come with hotel comforts, but the real attraction is the traditional village life you see drifting by.

★ **Lounge by the sea:** Relax along an isolated stretch of sand in North Kerala, access backwaters minutes from the beach at Marari, or party on Kovalam's Lighthouse Beach.

★ **Indulge your taste buds:** Whether it's spicy, coconut-based curries, Portuguese- and Dutch-influenced dishes, or North Kerala biryani, traditionally cooked in a hollow piece of bamboo, Kerala's extensive menu is sure to win over your taste buds.

★ **Tap into the past:** Reflect on Kerala's colonial past in Kochi, as you watch the sun set over the Fort area.

The small state of Kerala is separated from the rest of the country by natural boundaries—the Arabian Sea to the west and the high Western Ghats to the east. The thickly forested and mountainous eastern edge can only be reached by road. Its hilly and fertile midlands are spotted with coconut farms and rice fields; its coastal lowlands are famous for the beaches and backwaters. Although most people never venture beyond the central backwater resorts and the well-developed beach towns in the south, the north's long beaches are also worth a visit.

1 Kochi. This colonial port city is packed with historical homes, churches, mosques, and a centuries-old synagogue where the city's small remaining population of Jews still worship.

2 Kumarakom. The rustic town of Kumarakom is where you'll find some of Kerala's nicest resorts.

3 Alleppey. Alleppey is the gateway to exploring Kerala's backwaters.

4 Thekaddy. This cool mountain town is tucked into the Cardamom Mountains.

5 Munnar. This is where you'll find Kerala's lush tea plantations.

6 Thiruvananthapuram (Trivandrum). Kerala's capital city is surprisingly calm.

7 Kovalam. Kovalom is home to laid-back beaches.

8 Varkala. This peaceful beach town is known for towering red sand cliffs.

9 Calicut. Calicut is the gateway to the lushly forested Wyanad district.

10 Kannur. This is the hearltand of Kerala's Muslim community.

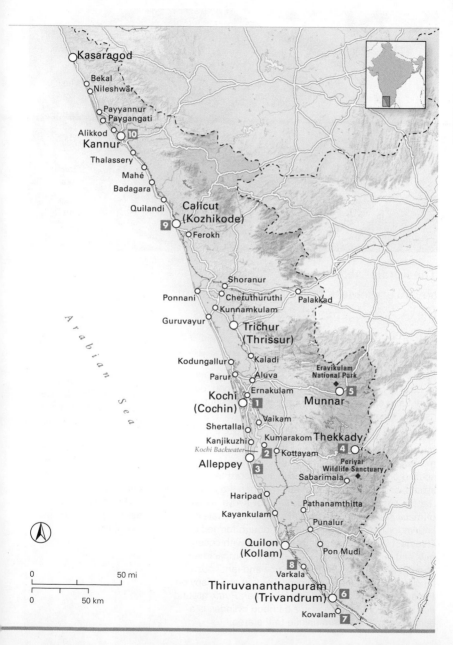

Kasaragod

Bekal
Nileshwar

Payyannur
Paygangati

Alikkod
Kannur **10**

Thalassery

Mahé
Badagara

Quilandi
Calicut
(Kozhikode)
9
Ferokh

Shoranur
Ponnani
Cheruthuruthi
Palakkad
Kunnamkulam
Guruvayur
Trichur
(Thrissur)

Kodungallur
Kaladi
Parur
Aluva
Eravikulam
National Park

Ernakulam
Kochi
(Cochin)
1
Munnar **5**

Vaikam
Shertallai
Kanjikuzhi
Kumarakom
Thekkady
Kochi Backwater
2
Kottayam
4
Alleppey
3
Periyar
Wildlife Sanctuary
Sabarimala

Haripad
Pathanamthitta
Kayankulam
Punalur

Quilon
(Kollam)
Pon Mudi
8
Varkala
Thiruvananthapuram
(Trivandrum) **6**
Kovalam **7**

A r a b i a n   S e a

0 ———— 50 mi
0 ———— 50 km

EATING WELL IN KERALA

Spicy fried chicken with curry leaves

The Kerala table is eclectic, savory, and adventuresome. Rice is the staple, coconut the essence, seafood the star, and spices the local zing.

Kerala means "land of coconuts" in Malayalam, and its cuisine certainly bears that out. Keralan food, both sweet and savory, uses every part of the coconut, and its milk, meat, and oil.

Expect distinctive meat and fish dishes—rich beef or mutton stewed in coconut milk, seafood, chicken and mutton (goat) fried up dry and spicy, *biryanis* (often spelled *biriyanis* locally) cooked in an assortment of spices, and fish curries. Vegetarian dishes are plentiful, like the sumptuous vegetarian *thalis* or *sadya,* a platter of many choices served on banana leaves. Kerala is known for *iddiappa,* thin strands of dough formed into little nests that are steamed and served with coconut milk and sugar for breakfast or as an accompaniment to curries. *Appam,* similar to the rice-and-lentil *dosa,* is an oil-free coconut-and-rice pancake, thin and crispy on the edges with a steamed, raised center. *Puttu,* ground rice and coconut steamed in a bamboo cylinder, is a common breakfast item unique to the area.

CHRISTIAN CUISINE

Kerala's Syrian Christian cuisine bears the stamp of all those who traversed its coasts. A typical day begins with *pallappam,* a rice pancake with Portuguese origins. Red meat is a major ingredient, with lamb *ishtew* (a stew with coconut milk), *urachi varutharachathu* (goat or beef cooked with ground coconut), and *ularthiyathu* (dry beef or goat with spices) all favorites.

MEEN POLLICHATHU

A central Kerala delicacy, **meen pollichathu** is a fragrant preparation of stuffed fish in a banana leaf. Any fish in season can be used, but the karimeen pearl spot is a freshwater local. The fish is marinated with various spices and a paste of diced tomatoes, onions, ginger, garlic, and coconut milk, then wrapped in a banana leaf sealed with a clove and cooked. This dish is available in almost every restaurant in Kerala.

MEEN PATHIRI

Malabar's stuffed fish pancakes, or **meen pathiri,** are found at almost every highway eatery in the northern part of the state. A *pathriri*—or *parota,* as it's often called—is a flat bread based on rice flour and coconut milk. This is filled with fish (usually kingfish, sardines, or pearl spot) that is shredded and cooked with spices, including chilli powder and turmeric. While some meen pathiri are so generously stuffed they look like a pie, in some parts of Malabar the pancake is flattened with a rolling pin after being stuffed. Chicken, egg, and mutton stuffings are also used.

IDIYAPPAM

String hoppers, or **idiyappam,** are made with rice flour and can be eaten with a curry, a stew, or at breakfast with *mutta* (egg) roast or simply with coconut

Idiyappam

milk. This Kerala staple can be sweet or savory and is a standard accompaniment to all meals, often garnished with grated coconut. Most often you will find it served with chicken stew.

PAZHAM PORI

An evening snack available from street vendors, cafeterias, and train stations across the state, **pazham pori** are plantain fritters—deep-fried delights that are best when served hot. A ripe Kerala-grown banana, which is very similar to a plantain, is chopped and coated in a flour-based batter before it's fried. A similar fritter is made using yams.

MEEN MULAKITTATHU

Using the fresh catch of the day, **meen mulakittathu,** or fish curry, is a staple at the dinner table. Traditionally cooked in a brass pot, the gravy is a combination of coconut milk and spices that are all grown in Kerala—and freshly crushed when the dish is cooked in traditional homes. Different kinds of fish can be used, although the most popular are pearl spot and kingfish.

PUTTU

Another specialty of the region, **puttu** is a puddinglike dish made from fresh-grated coconut and rice flour, molded into a cylindrical shape, and then steamed.

Fish curry

From pristine beaches and backwaters to extensive stretches of tea and spice plantations and rolling hills, Kerala, the narrow state running 560 km (350 miles) along India's western coast, is a land of diverse natural beauty. The scenery changes across the breadth of the state, and is dotted with waterfalls, fresh springs, and forests full of unique species of birds and wildlife. Kerala is also rich in history, with Hindu temples and Christian churches dating back hundreds or thousands of years and a culture that includes dance, martial arts, and age-old ayurvedic treatments.

From the more recent past, coastal cities preserve colonial mansions and 19th-century godowns (warehouses) used to store spices and teas and coffee from the plantations. Outside of the historic, spice-trading city of Kochi, attractions are rustic: quiet beaches spiked with palm trees line the west coast; the hilly eastern interior is heavily forested. Kochi is the anchor of low-lying central Kerala, a region dominated by lazy inland waterways, broad lakes, rice fields, and fishing boats; the backwater lifestyle is best experienced from the deck of a slow-moving houseboat. Farther inland, you'll find tranquil tea and spice plantations as well as two national parks and a sanctuary. At Periyar Wildlife Sanctuary,

near Thekkady, you can observe creatures in their native habitat from the comfort of a boat. Rajamala Wildlife Sanctuary, in the Eravikulam National Park near Munnar, is where you'll find the endangered Nilgiri tahr, a shy but sweet-tempered mountain goat. At Chinnar Wildlife Sanctuary you may have a better chance of seeing wild elephants or bison. The hills surrounding Thekkady and Munnar are lovely for trekking and rich in waterfalls and birdsong, especially in the rains. Southern Kerala is best known for the sparkling beaches near Kovalam, which lie south of the stately capital city, Thiruvananthapuram (Trivandrum), the home of the famous Padmanabhaswamy Temple. Undeveloped, conservative northern Kerala is the state's cultural heartland; you can witness some of the region's most spectacular festivals here. Kerala's Muslim community is concentrated in the north, and Christians are largely in the central and southern regions. Note that many of Kerala's low-slung, modest temples restrict entry to Hindus only.

MAJOR REGIONS

Kochi is the biggest city in Kerala and one of the largest port cities on the west coast.

In **Central Kerala**, between Kochi and Kollam (Quilon), to the south, is the immense labyrinth of waterways called *kayals,* through which much of the life of the Malayalee has historically flowed. From the vastness of Vembanad Lake to quiet streams just large enough for a canoe, the backwaters region, Kuttanad, has carried Kerala's largely coconut-based products from village to market for centuries, and continues to do so today. You can relax at some of Kerala's finest resorts, or briefly join the floating lifestyle by taking a boat cruise for a few hours or a few days. A houseboat cruise is one of the best ways to see the fascinating river village life of central Kerala and should not be missed. A day's worth is quite adequate, but a few days of cruising can be magical.

The terrain rises and the temperature drops as you move inland, up into the teak-forested hills of Thekkady and Munnar. Kerala's interior is elephant country—you'll find them roaming in Periyar Wildlife Sanctuary and even appearing in the mists of Munnar's tea plantations.

The beaches near Kovalam are **Southern Kerala's** main attraction—in fact, they're what brought Western tourists to the state in the first place, as the hippie scene from Goa moved down the coast. Parts of Kovalam are now overdeveloped and remain full of touts selling cheap tie-dyed clothes. There are, however, still some pleasant spots to relax within a few miles of the main beach.

Kovalam's hippie vibe sets it apart from other more solemn beach places in Kerala—the main drag on Lighthouse Beach is fairly lively, if a bit seedy. Just a half hour from Kovalam is Kerala's capital city of Thiruvananthapuram (Trivandrum), the former home of the rajas of Travancore and now home to Kerala's primary international airport. Varkala, slightly to the north of Trivandrum, has also gained tremendous popularity as a beach town. The place has a slow charm that grows on you. It's not as action-packed as Kovalam, but its numerous thatched food stalls, an ever-increasing number of low-budget hotels, and the pilgrims the town pulls in to see the Janardhana Swamy Temple all add to a festive feeling.

If Kerala is unspoiled India, then Malabar—as **Northern Kerala** was once known—is unspoiled Kerala. Arab traders landed here long before Vasco da Gama; many trading families converted to Islam and this part of the state retains strong Muslim influences. Various conquerors built forts along spectacular stretches of coastline, and some of Kerala's most unique and colorful religious festivals take place in this region. With the exception of the hill station of Wyanad, tourism has yet to make major inroads into the northern part of Kerala.

Planning

WHEN TO GO
HIGH SEASON: OCTOBER TO MARCH
Although Kerala used to have a second dip in visitor numbers during October's monsoon, this month now marks the beginning of the high season for all hotels and tour operators, with foreign tourists flocking in to take advantage of "monsoon tourism" deals. December and January are the peak tourist months, so be prepared to pay top rates around

Christmas and New Year's Eve. If you plan on visiting during that time be sure to book way ahead, as many hotels run on full occupancy. Because of Kerala's many Christians, this time of the year is quite festive and very enjoyable. The climate is ideal for the beach and backwaters, while the hills offer a cooler alternative.

LOW SEASON: MARCH TO JULY

By March the tourist season starts to wind down as temperatures soar to almost 40°C (105°F) and the air becomes humid. June brings in the monsoon season that has lasted up to mid-August the last few years. This rainy season deters tourists bound for the beaches and the backwaters, but it's supposed to be the best time for ayurvedic treatments. At the start of the monsoon it can rain continuously for many days at a time. Otherwise you get intermittent showers with lovely days of sunshine in between. The landscape is a really rich green, tourists are few, and hotel discounts are excellent. Thus, planning a visit after the middle of the rains or beyond may make sense for travelers who can handle a little rain. The hills, including Munnar and Kannur, are still pleasant during this time and often cater to domestic tourists escaping the heat in the plains.

SHOULDER SEASON: AUGUST AND SEPTEMBER

By mid-August the monsoons are over and the temperature is cooler. The Onam Festival is celebrated across Kerala around this time, and the Nehru Cup Snake Boat Race is held on the backwaters on the second Saturday in August. With the exception of dates around those two events, tourists can find some of the best deals during this period, and domestic vacationers often take advantage of this. The cooler temperature and good prices make this an ideal time to visit, although, because August is the tail end of the monsoon and the sea is on high tide, swimming in the ocean is restricted on several beaches. This is also bug season, so we advise packing insect repellent and lots of long pants to ward off the mosquitoes that can cramp evenings outside; we also suggest that, especially during this buggy season, you be wary of uncooked food or food cooked in less-than-trustworthy kitchens.

GETTING HERE AND AROUND

The most convenient way to get around Kerala is with a hired car and driver. The journey from Trivandrum to Kochi takes about five hours. Figure about Rs. 26 per km (½ mile) for a car and a halt charge of Rs. 200 per night. Shop around, and hire a car from a government-approved travel agency. There are prepaid taxi counters at both Trivandrum and Kochi airports. Figure on a minimum of about Rs. 2,700 per day for drives up to 150 km (93 miles) that take less than eight hours, in an air-conditioned medium-size car; taxes and overnight halt charges are extra. The charge for driving in the city in an air-conditioned medium-size car for up to 80 km (50 miles) and eight hours is about Rs. 1,800.

If you are doing a circular tour of Kerala it is best (and cheaper) to keep the same car and driver for the length of the trip. Drivers expect to be tipped at the end of each day. Additionally, when you stop somewhere to eat offer to pay for your driver's meal (though tourist-oriented restaurants often do feed drivers for free). Shop around, and hire a car from a government-approved travel agency or from your hotel (the latter will be more expensive).

In central Kerala, boat cruises offer a fascinating look at the backwaters where people still live. Most houseboats are based in the Alleppey district. When booking an overnight stay on one, make sure it comes equipped with solar panels and air-conditioning or a fan—otherwise you're in for a hot night. The going rate for a posh one-bedroom vessel with air-conditioning and meals for two is about Rs. 25,000 for two nights and three days, or Rs. 12,500 for one day on a one-bedroom boat and Rs. 15,000 for a two-bedroom boat.

AIR TRAVEL

Most international flights land in Trivandrum or Kochi, though Calicut airport also serves the Middle East and Sri Lanka. Air India, Jet Airways, Spice Jet, IndiGo, and Go Air cover domestic routes; most local carriers fly between Trivandrum, Kochi, and Calicut.

AIRPORT TRANSFERS

Calicut's Karipur Airport is 23 km (14 miles) south of town; a cab will cost roughly Rs. 900.

Kochi's international airport is about 40 km (25 miles) east of the city; abominable traffic can make it a two-hour trip. A taxi will cost about Rs. 1,200. The small airport in Trivandrum is 6 km (4 miles) west of the city center; taxis charge about Rs. 350 to get to the city and about Rs. 500 to reach Kovalam. Prepaid taxi booths operate in all three of these airports.

BOAT AND FERRY TRAVEL

A houseboat cruise is the quintessential way to experience Kerala. The District Tourism Promotion Council has houseboat information. Private companies, the K-Corporation (KTDC), and the Tourist Desk operate motorboat and houseboat tours from Alleppey; these only run when a minimum number of passengers has been reached. Prices range from Rs. 400 for one hour by motorboat to Rs. 8,500 for a 24-hour houseboat tour with meals. During the high season, Alleppey Tourism Development Cooperative (ATDC) has had daily ferry trips between Alleppey and Kollam (Rs. 400), but it takes eight hours and isn't recommended. There is also a public ferry from Alleppey to Kottayam (close to Kumarakom) for Rs. 40.

BOAT AND FERRY INFORMATION ATDC

✉ *Municipal Library, Thathampally P.O., 2nd fl., Alleppey* ☎ *477/226–4462,*

994/746–4171 transport dept. for houseboat and motorboat bookings ⊕ *www.atdcalleppey.com* **District Tourism Promotion Council (DTPC) Houseboat Information** ☎ *940/005–1796, 800/425–4747 tourist information* ⊕ *www.dtpcalappuzha.com.* **Houseboat Cruise** ☎ *471/231–6736 KTDC* ⊕ *www.ktdc.com.*

TAXIS AND AUTO-RICKSHAWS

Auto-rickshaws are a convenient and quick way to travel around town. In Trivandrum, figure Rs. 20 for the first 1½ km (1 mile) and Rs. 10 per additional kilometer—other cities will be slightly less. Don't be alarmed if your driver doesn't use the meter—it usually doesn't work (whether because it was intentionally broken or not is difficult to say). Make sure to agree on a fare before you get in, and don't trust a driver for unbiased shopping recommendations.

Auto-rickshaws (fix the price before you get in) are a good way to get around Fort Cochin; cabs are also a good option for longer distances around Kochi. Fares will run about Rs. 350 for an air-conditioned car for 25 km (15½ miles). Ask at any tourist office about the latest legal rates. Taxis hired at your hotel will have a slightly higher rate, but drivers are more likely to speak some English.

TAXI CONTACTS Kumarakom Taxi Service

✉ *Kumarakom P.O., Kottayam, Kumarakom* ☎ *944/739–0748* ⊕ *www.kumarakomtaxiservice.com.*

TRAIN TRAVEL

Rail journeys in Kerala can be scenic and more comfortable than traveling by car. The Himsagar Express—which travels from Kanyakumari, at India's southern tip, all the way up to Jammu and Kashmir—is a good train to take through Kerala, as is the Kerala Express and the Jan Shatabdi. December is a major pilgrimage season, so you'll need to book tickets in advance if you're traveling during this period. Check with KTDC for the latest schedules and fares, or try ⊕ *www.indianrail.*

gov.in, ⊕ indiarailinfo.com, or ⊕ www.
irctc.co.in and use a travel agent or your
hotel's travel desk to make bookings,
unless you don't mind standing in a
sometimes unruly line at the train station.

**TRAIN INFORMATION Ernakulam Junction
(South)** ✉ S. Railway Station Rd., Ernaku-
lam south, Ernakulam ☎ 484/237–6932.
Ernakulam Town Station (North) ✉ Xavier
Arakkal Rd., Ayyappankavu, Ernakulam
☎ 484/239–5198. **Thiruvananthapuram Cen-
tral Station** ✉ Chalai Bazaar, Thampanoor
Junction, Trivandrum ☎ 471/232–3066.

MONEY MATTERS
ATMS
ATMs are available in Kerala's major cities
of Kochi, Trivandrum, and Calicut, as well
as many smaller towns. Check for the
Cirrus or Plus sign, as some local banks
do not accept foreign cards. Make sure
your PIN is four digits.

CURRENCY EXCHANGE
Most of the major hotels have currency
exchange services, but it's wise to shop
around for the best deal. Thomas Cook
offers good rates. ANZ and any branch
of the Bank of India will change hard
currency.

TRAVEL AGENTS AND TOURS
The Kerala Tourism Development Corporation (KTDC) has several inexpensive
tours, including wildlife-spotting excursions to the Periyar Wildlife Sanctuary
and one- to two-week trips that follow
a pilgrim trail through Kerala's sacred
shrines. Kumarakom Taxi Service can
help with bookings and arrange a car and
driver for travel around Kerala. The Great
India Tour Company, one of Kerala's best
travel agencies, has offices throughout
South India. Trivandrum-based Tourindia
created the houseboat phenomenon and
offers unusual Kerala backwaters experiences, that is, much more authentic than
what you see elsewhere. One intriguing
two- to three-day trip—created by Tourindia and the forestry department—sends

you deep into the jungle with a local
guide, an armed escort, and a naturalist.

CONTACTS Destination Holidays ✉ Pallath
Bldg., Kurisupally Rd., 2nd fl., Kochi
☎ 484/235–0497, 404/235–7316 ⊕ www.
destinationskerala.com. **Great India Tour
Company** ✉ New Corporation Bldg.,
Palayam,, Trivandrum ☎ 471/301–1500.
Iris Holidays ✉ 32/1822 A, Edappally P.O.,
Ernakulam ☎ 999/500–4276 ⊕ www.
irisholidays.com. **Nakshathra Holidays**
✉ Princess St., Fort Kochi ☎ 974/685–
0074, 989/594–2933. **Tourindia** ✉ M.G.
Rd., near SMV High School, Trivandrum
☎ 471/233–1507 ⊕ www.tourindiakerala.
com.

VISITOR INFORMATION
Excellent brochures, maps, pamphlets,
and transportation information on all
of Kerala's districts are available at any
KTDC office. KTDC runs an around-the-
clock tourist information toll-free number
that can be dialed from within India.
In Kochi, the office is open daily 10–6.
Trivandrum's two KTDC offices—one in
town and one at the airport—are open
weekdays 10–5.

In Kochi, an alternative source of information is the Tourist Desk, a private,
nonprofit organization that conducts
moderately priced tours and provides
clear, straightforward information about
the state. In Kannur, the District Tourism
Promotion Council is quite active. Central
Kerala is well served by the ATDC. The
Government of India Tourist Office in
Ernakulam—open weekdays 9–5:30 and
Saturday 9–1—has its own vehicles,
boats, lodgings, and tours.

TOURIST OFFICES ATDC ✉ Municipal
Library, Thathampally P.O., 2nd fl., Alleppey ☎ 994/746–4171 ⊕ www.atdcallep-
pey.com. **Kannur District Tourism Promotion
Council** ✉ Edapally Panvel Hwy. (NH-17),
Caltex, Kannur ☎ 497/270–6336 ⊕ www.
dtpckannur.com.

RESTAURANTS

Until recently eating out was a relatively new concept in Kerala; the older generation viewed restaurants with a great deal of suspicion and the act of dining outside the home as some sort of tragedy. Most restaurants, as a result, catered to visitors and are often attached to hotels. (The word hotel, in fact, is often synonymous with restaurant.) But that has changed, and large cities and even roadside highway halts fairly bristle with places to eat.

In 2014, as part of a move to essentially ban alcohol consumption, the government of Kerala issued orders to close all bars that were not part of five-star hotels. Even though the state has since eased up on its regulations, most hotels still do not have liquor licenses and if they do, it's only to serve beer and wine.

HOTELS

Many Kerala resorts make use of traditional regional architecture, from tribal-style huts to elaborate wooden manors. Heritage properties transplant or reassamble traditional teakwood homes, or *tharavads,* while other hotels are newly built in the old style, helping to support traditional carpentry.

In cities, most hotels have air-conditioning, but many resorts in less populated and cooler areas do not. Beach properties often rely on fan and sea breezes, and in the hilly interior, air-conditioning is usually unnecessary and rooms may not even have fans. Some buildings have no window screens, so if a cool and/or bug-free sleep is part of your plan, ask about both and request a mosquito net/ curtains. Outside of cities, power supply is tenuous. Most hotels, even small ones, have their own generators, but they take a few seconds to kick in. Don't be surprised if you're left in the darkness for a moment—it's unavoidable. Most rooms are equipped with flashlights or an emergency light.

With the introduction in 2018 of the Goods & Services Tax in India, lodgings in Kerala now charge 12%–28% in taxes, depending on the daily room rate and facilities provided. You may be able to offset such fees with off-season discounts—around 50% during the monsoon season, from June to August. When booking during off seasons make sure you push hotels to give you the best possible rate; they discount quite a bit from the quoted rate or the rate on their websites. On the other hand, many hotels charge higher-than-usual rates in peak season, from mid-December to mid-January. *Hotel reviews have been shortened. For full information, visit Fodors.com.*

What It Costs			
$	$$	$$$	$$$$
RESTAURANTS			
under Rs. 300	Rs. 300– Rs. 499	Rs. 500– Rs. 700	over Rs. 700
HOTELS			
under Rs. 4,000	Rs. 4,000– Rs. 5,999	Rs. 6,000– Rs. 10,000	over Rs. 10,000

PLANNING YOUR TIME

The most convenient way to tackle Kerala is with a car and driver, allowing for the maximum amount of flexibility. Spend at least a day in Kochi, soaking in the beauty and the cultural offerings. A four-day itinerary can also include two days of ayurvedic massages and great local food in the resort town of Kumarakom and an overnight houseboat cruise through inland waterways. Drive inland to Thekkady or Munnar and spend two days viewing the wildlife in Periyar National Park (take the 4 pm boat cruise or a more adventurous jungle trek) and scenic Munnar, Kerala's Switzerland, with the added attractions of wild elephants and the Eravikulam National Park. The

Keralan Culture

A charming myth explains the creation of Kerala. Parashurama, an avatar of Vishnu, performed a series of penances to atone for a grievous sin, and the god of the sea rewarded his devotion by reclaiming Kerala from the deep. The reality is a little more prosaic: in 1956 the Malayalam-speaking states of Kochi and Travancore joined with the district of Malabar to form Kerala. The new Indian state became the first place in the world to adopt a communist government in a free election, an event that caused global speculation. Today this tropical enclave between the western mountains and the Arabian Sea is one of India's most progressive states, with a literacy rate of well over 95.5% and a life expectancy far higher than the Indian average. Even in the shabbiest backwater "toddy shop," where locals knock back glasses of potent coconut liquor, you'll find a copy of the day's newspaper in Malayalam, the local language. However, despite Kerala's very real accomplishments, unemployment remains endemic: it's close to 12.5%, and higher than the national average. Its citizens depend to a large degree on remittances (money sent from abroad). To be able to provide for their families back home, many Keralan men and women must leave to work in the Middle East.

The Malayalis make up India's most highly educated population; many are conversant in English, Hindi, and Tamil, as well as Malayalam. In the nearly three millennia before the 1795 establishment of British rule, Phoenicians, Arabs, Jews, Chinese, and Europeans came in droves, attracted by the region's valuable cash crops: tea, rubber, cashews, teak, and spices—notably black pepper (Kerala's "black gold") and cardamom.

Kerala's diversity is a testament to all those who passed by during the last few centuries. This state is unique in that its Hindu population (56%) is joined by relatively large numbers of Muslims (25%) and Christians (19%) (India's three largest religious communities).

Since Independence, people have begun using the place names that were used prior to British colonization. The strong British presence here makes name changes particularly germane; hence, Alleppey/Alappuzha, Calicut/Kozhikode, Cochin/Kochi, Quilon/Kollam, Trichur/Thrissur, and Trivandrum/Thiruvananthapuram. Official maps and tourist brochures reflect these changes, but both versions are still commonly used.

Kochi-Munnar-Thekkady circuit forms a trip with roughly equal distances between each point. Some travelers arrive in Kerala by car from Madurai, in Tamil Nadu; if that's your plan, visit Idukki on your way west toward the coast. Another option is to travel south from Thekkady to Trivandrum, Kerala's capital. Explore its sights and quiet lanes before heading for the mellow beaches, palm-fringed lagoons, and rocky coves near Kovalam and Varkala beach. If you want to get away from the crowds, head for the rarely visited north to see the extraordinary Theyyam festivals of Kannur and the pristine beaches along the northern coast.

Traditional Chinese fishing nets

Kochi

1,380 km (860 miles) south of Mumbai.

Kochi, formerly and still commonly known as Cochin, is one of the west coast's largest and oldest ports. The streets behind the docks of the historic Fort Cochin and Mattancherry districts are lined with old merchant houses, godowns (warehouses), and open courtyards heaped with betel nuts, ginger, peppercorns, and tea. Throughout the second millennium this ancient city exported spices, coffee, and coir (the fiber made from coconut husks), and imported culture and religion from Europe, China, and the Middle East. Today Kochi has a synagogue, several mosques, Portuguese Catholic and Syrian Christian (Saint Thomas Christian) churches, Hindu temples, and the United Church of South India (an amalgamation of several Protestant denominations).

The city is spread out over mainland, peninsula, and islands. Ernakulam, on the mainland 2 km (1 mile) from the harbor, is the commercial center and the onetime capital of the former state of Cochin. Willingdon Island, which was created by dredging the harbor, holds several luxury hotels as well as a navy base. The beautiful Bolghatty Island, north of Ernakulam, is a favorite picnic spot for locals. On it there's a government-run hotel in a colonial structure that was once used by the Dutch governor and later by the British Resident. Another local favorite is Cherai beach on Vypin Island, which is a 10-minute ferry ride from Fort Cochin but that takes about an hour total to reach. The Fort Cochin district, the area's historic center and the most important for area for sightseeing, is at the northern tip of the Mattancherry peninsula. Houses here often recall Tudor manors; some have been converted to hotels, others remain in the hands of the venerable tea and trading companies. South of Fort Cochin, in the Mattancherry district, is where you'll find the city's dwindling Jewish community (as of 2018, there are only five remaining Paradesi

Jews in Kochi). Their small neighborhood, called Jew Town, which is now dotted with cafés and shops selling curios and antiques, is centered on the synagogue. It's known for its antiques and curio shops.

GETTING HERE AND AROUND

Kochi is 212 km (132 miles) from Trivandrum and 193 km (120 miles) from Calicut. The efficient intercity express train Jan Shatabdi connects Ernakulam with Alleppey, Kollam, Trivandrum, and Calicut and is the quickest way to get to Kochi. There are slower trains connecting Kochi with Varkala and other smaller towns in Kerala. Express trains link Kochi with Mumbai, Bangalore, and Chennai. There are several flights a day from Delhi and Mumbai, Chennai, and Bangalore.

Cabs are a good option for getting around the city; public ferries and private boats go between Fort Cochin, Willingdon Island, and Ernakulam throughout the day. Ernakulam's main boat jetty is south of the Gateway Hotel Marine Drive hotel. Boats leave for Fort Cochin roughly every half hour, from 6 am to 9 pm. There are frequent ferries to Mattancherry, and limited service to Embarkation Jetty, on Willingdon Island's eastern tip. Ferry rides cost only a few rupees.

TIMING

Spend at least two days here to soak up the history and culture of the city, see all the sights, and enjoy some downtime relaxing by the harbor and dining on local delicacies.

ESSENTIALS

TOURIST OFFICES Government of India Tourist Office ⊠ *Malabar Rd., Willingdon Island* ☎ *484/266–9125, 800/425–4747 tourist information; toll-free in India* ⊕ *www.tourism.gov. in/tourism-offices.* **KTDC** ⊠ *Opposite Gateway Hotel Marine Dr., Ernakulam* ☎ *484/235–3234* ⊕ *www.ktdc. com* ⊠ *Vikas Bhavan P.O., Trivandrum* ☎ *471/231–6736* ⊕ *www.ktdc.com.*

Tourist Desk ⊠ *Main Boat Jetty, Ernakulam* ☎ *984/704–4688, 484/237–1761.*

TRAVEL AGENTS AND TOURS Great India Tour Company ⊠ *8th Cross, KC Joseph Rd., Panampilly Nagar* ☎ *471/301–1500, 484/286–4213* ⊕ *www.gitc.travel.* **Nakshathra Holidays** ⊠ *Princess St., Fort Kochi* ☎ *974/685–0074.*

Sita Travels
⊠ *KB Jacob Rd., Trivandrum, Fort Kochi* ☎ *124/470–3400* ⊕ *www.sita.in.*

Sights

Chinese Fishing Nets

LOCAL INTEREST | The precarious-looking bamboo and wood structures hovering like cranes over the waterfront are Kochi's famous Chinese fishing nets. Although they've become identified with the city, they're used throughout central Kerala. Thought to have been introduced by Chinese traders in the 14th century, the nets and their catch can be easily seen from Fort Kochi's Vasco da Gama Square. There's lots going on at the square—cooking, hawking, gaping (by tourists)—and don't miss the artistically decked-out tree in the center with tiger face, clowns, and fish painted on it. You can watch the fishermen haul up the nets around 6 am, 11 am, and 4 pm. They're particularly striking at sunset or at any time when viewed from the deck of a boat. ⊠ *Vasco da Gama Sq., Fort Kochi.*

Cochin Cultural Centre

DANCE | Kathakali performances in the air-conditioned room of the Cochin Cultural Centre start daily at 6 pm, though you should arrive an hour before the show to see makeup being applied. ⊠ *Behind No. 18 Hotel, K.B. Jacob Rd., near police station, Fort Kochi* ☎ *484/235–6366, 984/704–9542 cell phone* ⊕ *www.cochin-culturalcentre.com* 🎫 *Rs. 500.*

A Good Tour

The sleepy, tree-lined streets of Fort Cochin are perfect for a leisurely stroll. Start at the **St. Francis Church,** one of the earliest Indian churches to be built by Europeans. The Portuguese explorer Vasco da Gama was once buried here. Continue northeast along Church Street, passing colonial bungalows, to Vasco da Gama Square and the famed **Chinese fishing nets.** Follow River Road along the sea front past more colonial buildings. When you come to the end of the small Children's Park, take a right so that the edge of the park is on your right. At the park's far edge you'll hit tiny Princess Street—one of the first streets built in Fort Cochin, it's now crammed with shops, tour agencies, and modest European-style houses. The next major intersection is at Bastion Street. Take a left here and you'll soon see **Santa Cruz Cathedral Basilica** on your right. A six-minute walk south toward Bishop Kureethara Road will lead you to the grounds of the **Bishop's House,** which once served as the residence of the governor of Portugal

until the Dutch and British took over. The grounds here now contain the **Indo-Portuguese Museum,** originally built in 1910, featuring religious art and artifacts from the Santa Cruz Cathedral and 11 other Portuguese churches in Cochin. From here, hop in an auto-rickshaw to Mattancherry and visit the **Dutch Palace.** When you exit, take a right and follow the road as it turns a corner. Turn right again and you'll reach the **synagogue.** In the afternoon browse in the antiques and spice shops that line Jew Town Road, or head back north to the jetty and catch a ferry to Ernakulam for shopping on Mahatma Gandhi (M.G.) Road.

Timing

You can see Fort Cochin and Mattancherry in a day. Remember that all houses of worship close for a few hours around lunchtime. The Dutch Palace is closed on Friday, the synagogue is closed to visitors on Friday and Saturday, and many shops are closed on Sunday.

★ **Dutch Palace** (*Mattancherry Palace*)
CASTLE/PALACE | Built by the Portuguese in the mid-16th century as a gift for the Rajas of Cochin, this two-story structure reflects elements of traditional design while still looking colonial. It was extended by the Dutch when they took control of the area. The rajas, in turn, added some of India's best mythological murals—the entire story of the *Ramayana* is told on the walls in a series of bedchambers, which also have inviting window seats. In the ladies' ground-floor chamber, you can see a colorful, mildly erotic depiction of Lord Krishna with his female devotees. The coronation hall near the entrance holds a series of portraits

of monarchs (that interestingly show continuous familial resemblance) and some of the rajas' artifacts, including maps, swords, and a fantastic palanquin covered in red wool. The palace has rare, traditional Kerala flooring; it looks like polished black marble, but it is actually a mix of burned coconut shells, charcoal, lime, plant juices, and egg whites. ⊠ *Palace Rd., Mattancherry* ☎ *484/606–8716* 🖾 *Rs. 5* ⊙ *Closed Fri. and Sat.*

Galerie Wild Space

ART GALLERIES—ARTS | This intimate space features works of art by famed environmentalist and UNESCO-honored artist Paris Mohan Kumar. There's an organic clothing store next door (Aambal).

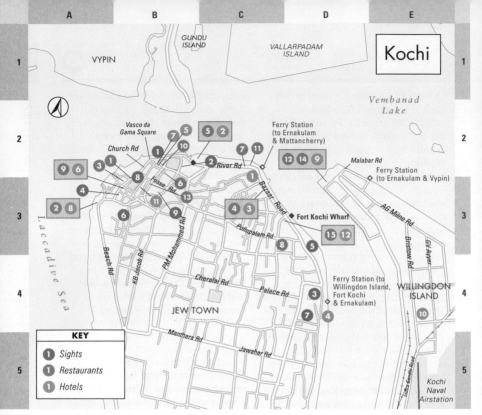

Kochi

KEY

- **1** Sights
- **1** Restaurants
- **1** Hotels

Sights ▼

1	Chinese Fishing Nets...	**B2**
2	Cochin Cultural Centre.	**B2**
3	Dutch Palace............	**D4**
4	Galerie Wild Space.....	**A3**
5	Gallery OED.............	**D3**
6	Indo-Portuguese Museum	**B3**
7	Pardesi Synagogue.....	**D4**
8	St. Francis Church......	**B2**
9	Santa Cruz Cathedral Basilica......	**B3**

Restaurants ▼

1	The Asian Kitchen by Tokyo Bay...............	**B3**
2	Bristow's Bistro.........	**A3**
3	David Hall...............	**B3**
4	East India Street Café...	**C3**
5	The History	**B2**
6	Kashi Art Café..........	**B2**
7	Fort House Restaurant..	**C2**
8	Kayees Rahmathullah...	**D3**
9	Malabar Junction.......	**B3**
10	Menorah.................	**B2**
11	Pepper House...........	**C2**
12	The Rice Boat..........	**D3**
13	Teapot Café.............	**B3**
14	Thai Pavilion............	**D3**
15	The Traders Deck.......	**C3**

Hotels ▼

1	Ayana Fort Kochi	**C2**
2	Brunton Boatyard.......	**B2**
3	Fragrant Nature Kochi	**C3**
4	Ginger House Museum Hotel.....................	**D4**
5	Koder House	**B2**
6	The Malabar House	**B3**
7	Old Harbour Hotel	**B2**
8	Old Lighthouse Bristow...................	**A3**
9	Taj Malabar Resort and Spa	**D3**
10	Trident....................	**E4**
11	Trinity....................	**B3**
12	The Waterfront Granary	**C3**

✉ *Napier St., Fort Kochi* ☎ *956/279–9777* 💲 *Free.*

Gallery OED

ART GALLERIES—ARTS | This large, modern space showcases works of contemporary art by Indian and foreign artists. ✉ *5/600, Bazaar Rd., Mattancherry* ☎ *944/710–8011* ⊕ *www.galleryoed.com* 💲 *Free* ⟳ *Closed Tues.*

Indo-Portuguese Museum

ARCHAEOLOGICAL SITE | Built on top of the remains of an old Portuguese fort—all that remains are a few stones located in the basement—the Indo-Portuguese museum was established in 1910 by Kochi bishop Dr. Joseph Kureethara in order to preserve the heritage of Portuguese Christian art and its influence in South India. The museum is divided into five main sections—Altar, Treasures, Procession, Civil Life, and Cathedral. There is a 16th-century pulpit made of teakwood that was originally located at St. Francis Church before being moved by the Dutch to Our Lady of Hope Church in Vypeen. Artifacts, which range from pure silver and gold statues and altarpieces to vestments worn by priests, have been collected from 11 churches in the Diocese of Cochin, including the Santa Cruz Cathedral Basilica. The museum is located on the lush grounds of the **Bishop's House** (which is not open to the public). If possible, ask for a guide to walk you through the museum. No photography is allowed. ✉ *Bishop's House, Bishop Kureethara Rd., Fort Kochi* ☎ *484/221–5400, 484/221–5401* ⊙ *Closed Mon.*

Kerala Lalita Kala Akademi Gallery

ART GALLERIES—ARTS | The former home of the Parishith Thampuran Museum now houses the Kerala Lalita Kala Akademi Gallery. There's not much here by way of explanation, but the traditional tile-roof building is cool and airy, and the interesting collection features contemporary works by Indian artists. ✉ *D.H. Rd., Ernakulam* ☎ *484/236–7748* 💲 *Free* ⟳ *Closed Mon.*

Head for Water

Traffic on land and the city's many bridges can be abominable. Private launches and small ferries zip through the waterways, making the journey as enjoyable as the destination.

Pardesi Synagogue

RELIGIOUS SITE | The first migration of Jews to Kerala is thought to have taken place in the 6th century BC, followed by a much larger wave in the 1st century AD, when Jews fleeing Roman persecution in Jerusalem settled at Cranganore (on the coast about 26 km [16 miles] north of Kochi). In the 4th century, the local king promised the Jews perpetual protection, and the colony flourished, serving as a haven for Jews from the Middle East and, in later centuries, Europe. When the Portuguese leader Afonso de Albuquerque discovered the Jews near Cochin in the 16th century, however, he destroyed their community, having received permission from his king to "exterminate them one by one." Muslim anti-Semitism flared up as well. The Jews rebuilt in Mattancherry but were able to live without fear only after the less-belligerent Dutch took control in 1663.

The rather small synagogue, built in 1568, houses four scrolls of the Torah kept in cases of silver and gold and is topped by an attractive clock tower that was added in 1760. Admire the collection of antique colonial Indian lights hanging from the center and the blue-and-white Chinese tiles on the floor (a gift from a Jewish businessman in the 18th century); no two tiles are alike. Also on view are the 4th-century copperplates that detail, in Malayalam, the king's decree that allowed the Jewish community to live in his kingdom. Before you enter the main synagogue there is a collection of paintings on the left highlighting the Jewish story in India. Photography and videography are not allowed in the synagogue. ⊠ *Synagogue La., Jew Town, Mattancherry* ☎ *800/425–4747* 🎫 *Rs. 5* ⊘ *Closed Fri., Sat., and Jewish holidays.*

Santa Cruz Cathedral Basilica
RELIGIOUS SITE | This Gothic-looking basilica, set in spacious grounds, has an interior that's colorfully painted with scenes and decorations that some find gaudy and others find gorgeous. The king of Cochin granted the Portuguese permission to build a fort and later a church in 1505 for their assistance in defeating the Zamorins of Calicut. For a while that structure was used as a Dutch armory. It was razed by the British in 1795, and in 1904 the current structure was completed, with a pillar of the original church within. Pope Paul IV elevated the church to a cathedral in 1558, and Pope John Paul II made it a basilica in 1984. ⊠ *Parade and K.B. Jacob Rd., Fort Kochi* ☎ *484/221–5799* ⊕ *www.santacruzcathedralbasilica.org.*

St. Francis Church
RELIGIOUS SITE | This stately church is the first European house of worship in India. The Portuguese flag first appeared in Fort Cochin in 1500, and Vasco da Gama arrived in 1502. The following year, Afonso de Albuquerque came with half a dozen ships full of settlers—he built the fort, and five friars in the crowd built this church in 1510. Da Gama returned in 1524 (his third trip) as Portuguese viceroy of the Indies, died that same year, and was buried in this church. You can still visit his gravestone inside the church, but his remains were shipped back 14 years later to Lisbon in 1538.

The church's history reflects the European struggle for colonial turf in India. It was a Catholic church until 1664, when it became a Dutch Reform church; it

Kochi Boat Tours

From Ernakulam's High Court or Sealord Jetty you can hire private boats, usually for about Rs. 500 an hour. The Kerala Tourism Development Corporation (KTDC) conducts two inexpensive boat tours of Kochi each day; the 3½-hour trips depart at 9 am and 2 pm from the Sealord Jetty, opposite the Sealord Hotel, between the Main and High Court jetties.

later became Anglican (1804–1947) and is now part of the Church of South India. Inside are beautifully engraved Dutch and Portuguese tombstones and the *doep boek,* a register of baptisms and marriages between 1751 and 1894; you can view a photographic reproduction—the original is too fragile. The first Portuguese was buried in 1562 and the first Dutch in 1664—their epitaphs are on view. ⊠ *Church St., between Parade Rd. and Bastion St., Fort Kochi* ☎ *484/221–7505* ⊕ *www.stfranciscsichurch.org.*

🍴 Restaurants

As Kerala's premier city, Kochi offers the most options for dining out. Many top hotels open outdoor seafood grills in season (November to February), where you can pick from the day's catch and have it prepared as you like. Try *karimeen,* also known as the pearl spot, a bony but delicious fish found only in central Kerala, prepared with spices wrapped in a banana leaf. Keep an eye out for unusual Portuguese-influenced dishes and do try the rare, eclectic Kochi Jewish cuisine. Lots of hotel restaurants feature live music, especially during peak season.

The Asian Kitchen by Tokyo Bay

$$$ | ASIAN | Located inside the historic Cochin Club, this casual open-air restaurant serves a diverse menu of Asian flavors, including Thai, Chinese, Malaysian, Indonesian, Singaporean, and Vietnamese cuisines. It's also the first restaurant in Kerala to serve sushi, sashimi, and teppanyaki, prepared with recipes from a chef from Japan. **Known for:** sushi (especially the tekka maki tuna roll); Thai red and green seafood curries; inexpensive dishes and large portions. $ *Average main: Rs. 500* ⊠ *Cochin Club, St. Francis Church Rd., Fort Kochi* ☎ *484/319–9366, 974/739–9333* ⊕ *www.tokyobay.in.*

Bristow's Bistro

$$$ | ECLECTIC | This tastefully decorated restaurant offers a flavor of Fort Kochi both with its food, and with its location overlooking the beach and sea. The buffet spread is varied and the à la carte options include choice dishes such as the stuffed red snapper, seafood platters, and desserts like the *chakkara choru* (a Malabari rice pudding) and Mattanchery sweet spice roll, made with grated coconut and jaggery (unrefined sugar). **Known for**: the seafood platter; Kerala desserts like chakkara choru (a Malabari rice pudding); seaside views. $ *Average main: Rs. 600* ⊠ *Old Lighthouse Bristow Hotel, Beach Rd., next to INS Dronacharya, Fort Kochi* ☎ *484/221–8711, 484/221–8611* ⊕ *www.oldlighthousehotel.com.*

David Hall

$$ | CONTEMPORARY | This rambling former Dutch home now serves as an art gallery—displaying the work of contemporary Indian artists and works from art camps held in villages across Kerala—and a spacious garden café extending out to a large back lawn. Best known for its delicious Italian pizza (made in a traditional stone oven in front of you) and panini, the restaurant changes its menu regularly, depending on what ingredients are in season, making for interesting choices and dependable freshness. **Known for:**

delicious Italian pizza made in a traditional stone oven; artsy vibe in a garden setting; displays from upcoming contemporary Indian artists. $ *Average main: Rs. 400* ⊠ *Opposite Parade Ground, Fort Kochi* ☎ *484/221–8298* ⊕ *www.davidhall. in* ☉ *Closed Mon.*

East India Street Café

$$ | CAFÉ | Located inside the luxe Fragrant Nature hotel, which formerly housed the East India Company's Kochi office, this quaint, colorful café, complete with its own red London telephone booth, is Kochi's first 24-hour eatery. The menu focuses mainly on classic British pub fare using produce grown at the hotel's own organic and pesticide-free farms. **Known for:** being open 24/7; the shrimp po'boy in a homemade hot dog roll; a/c indoors (a rarity in Kochi restaurants). $ *Average main: Rs. 300* ⊠ *Fragrant Nature Kochi, near SBI Calvathy, Calvathy Bazaar Rd., Fort Kochi* ☎ *484/221–3600* ⊕ *www.fragrantnature. com.*

Fort House Restaurant

$$ | SEAFOOD | Inside a budget hotel in a great location on the jetty, this simple, open-air restaurant doesn't skimp on quality or authenticity. The menu is almost entirely seafood—chicken and specialty items (like lobster) must be ordered in advance—and every dish is cooked to order and presented in a clay vessel. **Known for:** try the prawns Kerala and braised seerfish; waterfront dining; Kerala cuisine. $ *Average main: Rs. 300* ⊠ *Fort House Hotel, 2/6 A Calvathi Rd., Fort Kochi* ☎ *484/221–7103, 484/221–7173* ⊕ *www.hotelforthouse.com.*

★ The History

$$$$ | INDIAN | Alongside traditional Kerala fare you'll find unusual dishes bearing the stamp of the Middle East, Portugal, the local Jewish community, and the days of the British Raj with some age-old recipes having been passed on to the restaurant by local communities. The lofty, elegant dining room of this fine dining restaurant

is windowed on all sides, and capped with a gabled wooden ceiling (resembling an upturned ship) supported by massive wood beams. **Known for:** daily live sitar and tabla music performances; the railway mutton curry from the British Raj era; the vattalappam, a Syrian Christian version of caramel custard utilizing jaggery and coconut milk. $ *Average main: Rs. 800* ⊠ *Brunton Boatyard Hotel, 1/498, Calvetty Rd., Fort Kochi* ☎ *484/221–5461* ⊕ *www.cghearth.com/ brunton-boatyard/dining* ☾ *No lunch.*

★ Kashi Art Café

$$ | **INTERNATIONAL** | A favorite hangout for artists and young tourists, Fort Cochin's Kashi Art Café is about as funky as Kerala gets. The front room hosts rotating exhibitions, primarily of South Indian contemporary art, and light continental fare and Western-style coffee is served in the garden café at the rear. **Known for:** rotating art exhibit by Indian artists in front room; try a slice of the chocolate cake; airy garden vibe. $ *Average main: Rs. 300* ⊠ *Burgher St., Fort Kochi* ☎ *484/221–5769* ⊕ *www.kashiartgallery. com.*

Kayees Rahmathullah

$ | **INDIAN** | Known for its biryani, a rice dish cooked with meat and spices, this very modest restaurant is the original, and people say it's the best, with some of the most authentic and lip-smackingly good Kerala food you will find—but be ready for serious spice. There's usually a line for lunch on weekdays, and the menu may become more limited if you arrive late—they run out. **Known for:** the Malabar-style biryani; vegetarian dishes; Kayees' special jeera water (boiled with cumin seeds), an ayurvedically approved drink that aids digestion. $ *Average main: Rs. 200* ⊠ *New Rd., Mattancherry* ☎ *984/221–1234.*

★ Malabar Junction

$$$$ | **ECLECTIC** | The entire menu at this small restaurant, which is in a very elegant setting with an open side facing a garden and swimming pool, is comprised of a mix of regional specialties and Mediterranean cuisine contributed by both local and visiting chefs. The seafood is always fresh and perfectly cooked, and if you're craving Italian, the pastas, like the homemade cheese ravioli, are excellent. **Known for:** elegant setting with nightly traditional Kerala performances; large selection of Indian wines; chocolate samosas in mango sauce, the restaurant's signature dessert. $ *Average main: Rs. 900* ⊠ *The Malabar House, 1/268 Parade Rd., Fort Kochi* ☎ *484/270–4600* ⊕ *www.malabarescapes.com.*

Menorah

$$$ | **INDIAN** | A fine tribute to Cochin's rich Jewish history, Menorah is in the former mansion of one of the city's best-known Jewish families, and the fine table linens and stately surroundings recall the royalty, prime ministers, and dignitaries that once dined here. Traditional Cochin-Jewish cuisine is served—try the *chemeen ularth,* a prawn fry, or *plav,* a rice and chicken dish, and the mutta roast (eggs cooked with a variety of spices). **Known for**: unique Cochin-Jewish dishes like chemeen and squid ularth; excellent selection of pasta; quaint courtyard with a pool and outdoor seating. $ *Average main: Rs. 700* ⊠ *Koder House, Tower Rd., Fort Kochi* ☎ *484/221–8485* ⊕ *www.koderhouse.com.*

Pepper House

$$ | **CAFÉ** | This heritage building, which was once a former pepper warehouse, is now an art space and outdoor garden café with a menu that's constantly changing to showcase the best organic, local, and seasonal produce that Kochi has to offer. The art space hosts artists in rotation during the Kochi Muziris Biennale. **Known for:** homemade pastas; great coffee, especially the Americano; its design shop featuring local designers and art library. $ *Average main: Rs. 300* ⊠ *11/10 A and B, Kalvathy Rd., Fort Kochi*

☏ *484/221–5667* ⊕ *www.pepperhouse.in* ⊘ *Closed Tues. in May and June.*

The Rice Boat

$$$$ | **SEAFOOD** | This plush restaurant, which has windows on three sides, is long and shaped like a traditional wooden boat and is a favorite among Kochi's well-to-do crowd. The menu stresses seafood, as you might expect, with much of it often caught just a few hours before meal time in the Chinese fishing nets or in boats nearby. **Known for:** Kerala specialties like meen pollichathu, the local pearl spot cooked wrapped in banana leaf; an interactive kitchen where you can chat with the chef; great views of the harbor. $ *Average main: Rs. 1500* ✉ *Taj Malabar Resort & Spa, Willingdon Island* ☏ *484/664–3048* ⊕ *www.tajhotels.com.*

Teapot Café

$ | **ECLECTIC** | This quirky two-story café, off Princess Street and near the harbor, has teapots and kettles decorating every available space, including some dangling from the ceiling; some tables are made from wooden tea chests. There's a fair selection of both Indian and continental food—roast chicken and potatoes, prawn *moilee* (in a coconut curry), vegetable stew—but the café is best known for its sandwiches and freshly baked cakes and for being a terrific spot for sipping away on a cup of tea for an hour or more. **Known for**: its Indie rarebit sandwich; great selection of freshly baked cakes; open late until 9 pm (during the season). $ *Average main: Rs. 150* ✉ *Peter Celli St., Fort Kochi* ☏ *484/221–8035* ▭ *No credit cards.*

Thai Pavilion

$$$$ | **THAI** | This immensely popular place is Kerala's first Thai restaurant—so don't be surprised if the waiter explains each dish to you—and it has plentiful seafood as well as Vietnamese and Chinese dishes. The dining room is done up in warm woods, with silver and rich red accents on the ceiling and chairs, plus colorful murals and beveled glass windows that give you a glimpse of the Arabian Sea. **Known for:** pla rad prik, fish flavored with basil; Thai-style pork ribs; great views of the Arabian sea. $ *Average main: Rs. 950* ✉ *Taj Malabar Resort & Spa, Willingdon Island* ☏ *484/664–3000* ⊕ *www. tajhotels.com.*

The Traders Deck

$$ | **INDIAN** | The Kutchi Memom, who migrated to Kerala in the 1800s as traders from Gujarat, is one of Kochi's diverse resident groups, and you can get a taste of authentic Kutchi cuisine at this outdoor waterfront location. Located at Waterfront Granary hotel, this restaurant serves traditional Kutchi dishes, all passed down from the owner's family, like Kutchi Jo Machi, a traditional Kutchi fish curry, and Kutchi Ghau Jo Maani, prawns steamed in a banana leaf. **Known for:** Kutchi Ghau Jo Maani, steamed prawns in spices in a banana leaf; tables on the pier with great views of the harbor; the artifacts from the owner's personal collection. $ *Average main: Rs. 400* ✉ *The Waterfront Granary, 6/641, Bazaar Rd., Mattancherry* ☏ *484/221–1777, 484/221–1177.*

 ## Hotels

Ayana Fort Kochi

$$$$ | **HOTEL** | Set in a 200-year-old heritage building that once served as a Portuguese courthouse, Ayana Fort Kochi is an art deco lovers dream with its black-and-white tiled flooring, bright walls, and plush furnishings. **Pros:** thoughtful design and decor; in-room dining available; swimming pool offers rooftop views. **Cons:** no alcohol served in restaurant; rooms facing the street can get noisy; must book in advance especially during Biennale. $ *Rooms from: Rs. 15300* ✉ *Kalvathy Rd., opposite Coastal Police Station, Fort Kochi* ☏ *484/258–8919, 996/704–5098 cell phone* ⊕ *www.ayanahospitality.com* ⤳ *16 rooms* ⫯◎⫯ *Free Breakfast.*

★ Brunton Boatyard

$$$$ | **HOTEL** | Built in a combination of Dutch and Portuguese colonial styles, this elegant hotel is on the site of a former boatyard, facing the Chinese fishing nets and featuring antique fixtures and furnishings, right down to the light switches. **Pros:** all rooms and bathrooms are sea facing; plenty of amenities like a daily sunset cruise, cooking demonstration, and yoga; Wi-Fi in all rooms. **Cons:** pricey; doesn't offer nonsmoking rooms; beds so high you need a footstool to climb in. $ *Rooms from: Rs. 25700* ✉ *Calvetty Rd., Fort Kochi* ☎ *484/284–6500* ⊕ *www.cghearth.com* 🛏 *26 rooms* ❍❙ *Free Breakfast.*

★ Fragrant Nature Kochi

$$$$ | **HOTEL** | Conveniently situated between Fort Kochi and Jew Town, this luxury hotel with its landmark clock tower features an atrium-style lobby with marble flooring and a large trompe l'oeil paying homage to the building's original occupants—the East India Company. **Pros:** great ayurvedic spa; rooftop infinity pool offers sweeping views of Kochi harbor; three restaurants, including a 24/7 café, and a bar. **Cons:** luxurious but lacking Kochi's heritage charm; expensive; not all rooms offer sea views. $ *Rooms from: 16600* ✉ *Near SBI Calvathy, Calvathy Bazaar Rd., Fort Kochi* ☎ *484/221–3603, 484/221–3600* ⊕ *www. fragrantnature.com* 🛏 *41 rooms* ❍❙ *Free Breakfast.*

Ginger House Museum Hotel

$$$$ | **HOTEL** | Set in Kochi's bustling antiques bazaar, this luxurious boutique hotel has a unique policy: if you like *any* piece of furniture or artwork in the hotel—all collectible antiques—you can purchase it. **Pros:** every piece of furniture tells a story; picturesque views of the water away from the crowds; spacious rooms. **Cons:** expensive; must book in advance; no spa or gym. $ *Rooms from: Rs. 34000* ✉ *Ginger House Bldg., Jew Town, Mattancherry* ☎ *484/221–3400,*

954/444–5526 cell phone ⊕ *www.museumhotel.in* 🛏 *9 rooms* ❍❙ *Free Breakfast.*

Koder House

$$$ | **B&B/INN** | Unlike the sober Dutch mansions nearby, the three-story Koder House sticks out due to its brick exterior's fire-engine color and slightly unusual, Portuguese-inflected architecture. **Pros:** atmospheric; the restaurant, Menorah, serving unique Cochin-Jewish food is attached; prime location. **Cons:** staff can sometimes seem a little distracted; no elevator; ayurvedic spa is old. $ *Rooms from: Rs. 9000* ✉ *Tower Rd., Fort Kochi* ☎ *484/221–8485* ⊕ *www.koderhouse. com* 🛏 *6 rooms* ❍❙ *Free Breakfast.*

The Malabar House

$$$ | **HOTEL** | **Pros:** deluxe rooms open into private garden; restaurant, Malabar Junction, might be Kochi's best; hotel staff are friendly and helpful. **Cons:** book in advance during high season; no elevator; some rooms are noisy due to street traffic. $ *Rooms from: Rs. 9300* ✉ *1/268 Parade Rd., Fort Kochi* ☎ *484/270–4600* ⊕ *www.malabarhouse.com* 🛏 *17 rooms* ❍❙ *Free Breakfast.*

Old Harbour Hotel

$$$$ | **HOTEL** | Just opposite the Chinese fishing nets, this 1837 Dutch heritage building, a former brokerage house, features 13 tastefully decorated rooms with bright walls, antique fixtures, and contemporary Indian artwork. **Pros:** the airy and appealing restaurant serves very good Kerala delicacies; very good off-season discounts; prime Fort Kochi location. **Cons:** TVs only available on request; Wi-Fi signal is spotty; no room service. $ *Rooms from: Rs. 15986* ✉ *1/328 Tower Rd., Fort Kochi* ☎ *484/221–8006* ⊕ *www. oldharbourhotel.com* 🛏 *13 rooms* ❍❙ *Free Breakfast.*

Old Lighthouse Bristow

$$$ | **HOTEL** | This tastefully decorated hotel is the former home of the late Sir Robert Bristow, the architect of the modern port of Kochi, and it is one of the only

An antiques shop in Kochi

Kochi hotels that opens out onto a beach. **Pros:** spa offers a variety of ayurvedic massages; has an acclaimed seafood restaurant, Bristow's Bistro; Wi-Fi in all rooms. **Cons:** service is somewhat lacking; can be noisy because it's on the busy Fort Kochi beach; need to book in advance. $ *Rooms from: Rs. 9200 ✉ Beach Rd., next to INS Dronacharya, Fort Kochi* ☎ *484/221–8711, 484/221–8611* ⊕ *www.oldlighthousehotel.com* ⤳ *14 rooms* ⦿ *Free Breakfast.*

Taj Malabar Resort and Spa

$$$$ | RESORT | Isolated at the tip of Willingdon Island, this grand hotel offers a heritage sensibility and style with a stunning carved-wood ceiling in the lobby and a similarly styled bar with a harbor view. **Pros:** the spa offers good ayurvedic treatments; spacious rooms and great atmosphere in the public spaces; fantastic restaurants that are some of the best in Kerala. **Cons:** isolated on an island with little to do that's far from city landmarks; the heritage rooms—the ones to get and the reason for staying

here—aren't cheap; may be too large and impersonal for some. $ *Rooms from: Rs. 10880 ✉ Malabar Rd., Willingdon Island* ☎ *484/664–3000* ⊕ *www.tajhotels.com* ⤳ *95 rooms* ⦿ *Free Breakfast.*

Trident

$$$ | HOTEL | This tasteful and stylish hotel, across the harbor from Fort Kochi, is a low-rise, tile-roof building that wraps around a central courtyard and is outfitted rather plushly for both business and leisure travelers. **Pros:** well-priced rooms; gracious and helpful staff; quiet location. **Cons:** lacks atmosphere; nearly 25 minutes by ferry or road from the city's main attractions at Fort Kochi; older property in need of maintenance. $ *Rooms from: Rs. 9900 ✉ Bristow Rd., Willingdon Island* ☎ *484/308–1000* ⊕ *www.tridenthotels.com* ⤳ *77 rooms* ⦿ *Free Breakfast.*

Trinity

$$$ | HOTEL | Located in the former headquarters of the Dutch East India Company, this 150-year old heritage building is home to a small hotel with spacious

rooms. **Pros:** prime location; small property which is surprisingly quiet; friendly staff. **Cons:** no swimming pool; may be too intimate for some; restaurant is located a short walk away at sister property. $ *Rooms from: Rs. 7000* ⊠ *1/658 Ridsdale Rd., Parade Ground, Fort Kochi* ☎ *484/221–6669, 484/221–6666* ⊕ *www. trinityfortkochi.com* ⇨ *8 rooms* ⭕I *Free Breakfast.*

The Waterfront Granary

$$$ | HOTEL | Located on the bustling Bazaar Road, this quaint 1877 building originally functioned as a granary storing food grains before being renovated into a hotel showcasing the unique private collection of artifacts of the owners, who are part of Kochi's close-knit Kutchi Memom community. **Pros:** friendly and hospitable staff; The Traders Deck serves unique Kerala-Kutchi delights; complimentary boat ride to see Kochi by water. **Cons:** Wi-Fi is spotty in rooms; hotel entrance on busy narrow road; small swimming pool. $ *Rooms from: Rs. 7500* ⊠ *6/641 Bazaar Rd., Mattancherry* ☎ *484/221–1777, 484/221–1177* ⊕ *www. thewaterfrontgranary.com* ⇨ *16 rooms* ⭕I *Free Breakfast.*

 Nightlife

BARS

Armoury Bar

BARS/PUBS | Brunton Boatyard's bar and café is decorated, as its name suggests, with rifles and other such colonial-era weaponry, as well as chests and maritime artifacts. The rich wood rafters and views of the harbor make it an excellent place for a sundowner or a late-night drink. ⊠ *Brunton Boatyard, Calvetty Rd., Fort Kochi* ☎ *484/221–5461, 484/284–6500* ⊕ *www.cghearth.com/ brunton-boatyard.*

Divine Wine Lounge

WINE BARS—NIGHTLIFE | Located on the first floor of the upscale Malabar House hotel, this elegant wine bar showcases

---

---

red and white wines from all over India. They also serve an eclectic selection of tapas—the grilled prawns with lade-lemono and fresh prawns in crispy noodles are a must—which are all carefully chosen to accompany the wines on offer. ⊠ *The Malabar House, 1/268 Parade Rd., 1st fl., Fort Kochi* ☎ *484/270–4600* ⊕ *www.malabarhouse.com/divine-the-wine-lounge.html.*

Seagull

BARS/PUBS | Popular with both locals and tourists, Seagull is a great option for a chilled beer by the sea, especially if you opt to sit outside on the pier. There's also a restaurant offering a large selection of local seafood and other dishes. ⊠ *Hotel Seagull, Calvathy Rd., Fort Kochi* ☎ *803/007–7139* ⊕ *www.theseagull.in.*

★ Performing Arts

DANCE

Dating back to the 17th century, Kathakali is an art form in which elaborately made-up and costumed dancers tell epic stories using stylized hand gestures. For centuries, Kathakali performances were the only after-dark entertainment in Kerala; shows began at sundown and lasted all night. Today, for the benefit of tourists, performances are often shortened to one or two hours. Many centers also offer the chance to watch dancers being made up, which can be as entertaining as the show. Larger hotels all over the state organize impromptu and abridged performances of Kathakali and Mohiniyattam on their premises, either for free or for a small fee.

Greenix Village

DANCE | Kathakali performances are held daily at 6 pm in an air-conditioned room, with makeup being applied an hour earlier. The village also offers daily morning yoga and training classes and performances for Kerala's ancient martial arts. Additionally, it houses a cultural museum with impressive life-size Kathakali statues. ✉ *Kalvathy Rd., Fort Kochi* 🕿 *484/221–7000, 984/602–0091* ⊕ *www. greenix.in.*

Kerala Kathakali Centre

DANCE | This is a pleasant outdoor venue, where makeup starts at 5 pm and Kathakali shows follow at 6 pm daily. Indian classical dance classes are held on Saturday beginning at 8 pm. There are also martial arts shows, yoga, and meditation classes. ✉ *Near Santa Cruz Basilica, KB Jacob Rd., Fort Kochi* 🕿 *484/221–5827* ⊕ *www.kathakalicentre.com* 🎟 *Rs. 350.*

MARTIAL ARTS

Kerala's dramatic, high-flying martial art, Kalaripayattu, may be the oldest in Asia. Some think it started in the 12th century, others think it began earlier, and still others say later. Some scholars believe that Buddhist monks from India introduced Kalaripayattu to China along with Buddhism. Participants learn both armed- and unarmed-combat techniques. One of the more unusual skills involves defending yourself against a knife-wielding attacker using only a piece of cloth. In peak season, many hotels stage performances.

E.N.S. Kalari Centre

SPECTATOR SPORTS | If you call in advance, you can watch Kalarippayattu

practitioners here, before 5 pm daily. They only allow one or two people to come watch. ✉ *Nettoor, Ernakulam* 🕿 *484/270–0810, 944/707–0081 cell phone* ⊕ *www.enskalari.org.in.*

Shopping

The streets surrounding the synagogue in Mattancherry are crammed with stores that sell curios, and Fort Cochin's Princess Street, Prince Street, Rose Street, and Peter Celli Street have all sprouted small shops worth a browse. For more serious, exhaustive hunts for saris, gold jewelry, handicrafts, and souvenirs, head to M.G. Road in Ernakulam. Be suspicious of the word "antique" in all stores, and bargain hard.

ANTIQUES
Crafter's

CRAFTS | Local hotels often get their antiques here. The store is crammed with stone and wood carvings, pillars, and doors as well as such portable items as painted tiles, navigational equipment, and wooden boxes. Crafter's also has a café upstairs. ✉ *6/141 Jew Town Rd., Mattancherry* 🕿 *484/222–3346* ⊕ *www. crafters.in.*

Heritage Arts

ANTIQUES/COLLECTIBLES | Established in 1989 by antiques collector-turned-hotelier Manju, this is one of South India's largest antiques stores, with more than 100,000 square feet of warehouse space housing antiques from all over India. Don't miss the 108-foot-long iconic Kerala snake boat; it's more than 120 years old. ✉ *Jew Town Rd., Mattancherry* 🕿 *484/221–1145, 964/583–5129* ⊕ *www. heritageartscochin.com.*

BOOKS
Idiom Books

BOOKS/STATIONERY | Whether you're looking for a little information on Kerala or a little something to while away the hours, stop by Idiom Books, a small bookshop opposite the synagogue (there's also a

Kathakali dancers

branch in Fort Kochi, on Bastion Street). You can find an intriguing collection of recent Western and Indian fiction, as well as books on history, culture, cooking, and religion. ✉ *Jew Town Rd., Mattancherry* ☎ *484/222–5604, 484/221–7075* ✉ *1/348 Bastion St., near Princess St., Fort Kochi.*

CLOTHING
Anokhi

CLOTHING | This outlet of the popular and sophisticated Rajasthani handicrafts and clothing shop carries beautifully tailored women's clothing and linens for the home. ✉ *Ground fl., Bernard Bungalow, near Lilly St., Parade St., Fort Kochi* ☎ *484/221–6275* ⊕ *www.anokhi.com.*

Cinnamon

CLOTHING | This branch of the chic Bangalore boutique stocks stylish ethnic and modern housewares, silk scarves and purses, jewelry, and Indo-Western designer clothing. ✉ *1/658 Ridsdale Rd., Parade Ground, Fort Kochi* ☎ *484/221–7124, 484/221–8124.*

Fabindia

CLOTHING | Stop here for a range of colorful hand-printed cotton garments—skirts, pants, tops, kurtis, kurtas, men's shirts, and saris. The white tops are lovely. ✉ *1/281 Napier Rd., near Parade Ground, Fort Kochi* ☎ *484/221–7077* ⊕ *www. fabindia.com.*

Jayalakshmi

CLOTHING | A mind-blowing selection of saris (including the Keralan style), *lehangas* (long skirts with fitted blouses), and the like are on offer here, as well as Indian and Western clothes for men and children. ✉ *M.G. Rd., near Rajaji Rd., Ernakulam* ☎ *484/408–9899.*

HANDICRAFTS AND CURIOS
Fort Royal

CRAFTS | This is an expensive all-in-one shop with goods from all over India. You can find brocade work, marble inlay boxes, and Kashmiri carpets, plus local handicrafts and precious and semiprecious jewelry. ✉ *Dutch Cemetery St., behind Napier St., Fort Kochi* ☎ *484/221–7832.*

Indian Arts and Curios

GIFTS/SOUVENIRS | This is one of Kerala's oldest and most reliable curio shops. ⊠ *6/189 Jew Town Rd., Mattancherry* ☎ *484/222–8049.*

Indian Industries Arts and Crafts

CRAFTS | John Korula and his family have been running this shop since 1945. This shop's name is far more pedestrian than its contents—it's a virtual Aladdin's cave of curios and antiques—masks, statues, sculpture, Christian artifacts, and much more. And no one will follow you around the shop insisting you buy this or that, as does happen elsewhere. Note that it closes for a lunch break from about 1:30 to 3 pm. ⊠ *1/364 A, Princess St., Fort Kochi* ☎ *484/221–5393, 984/704–3566.*

Kairali

CRAFTS | A fixed-price government shop, Kairali has a good selection of local handicrafts and curios. ⊠ *M.G. Rd., near Jose Junction, Ernakulam* ☎ *484/235–4507* ⊘ *Closed Sun.*

Surabhi

CRAFTS | Run by the state's Handicrafts Cooperative Society, Surabhi has an impressive selection of local products. ⊠ *M.G. Rd., near Jose Junction, Ernakulam* ☎ *484/238–0144* ⊕ *www.surabhihandicrafts.com.*

Tribes India

CLOTHING | Indian tribal artisan work is sold through this cooperative store, which benefits the crafters directly. There's an unusual selection of crafts, including clothing and knickknacks. ⊠ *Ministry of Tribal Affairs, C/O Head P.O., Ridsdale Rd., Fort Kochi* ⊕ *www.tribesindia.com.*

Kumarakom

80 km (50 miles) south of Kochi.

Some of Kerala's finest resorts are hidden in this tiny, rapidly developing area on the shores of Vembanad Lake.

Kerala Crafts

Look for cups, vases, spoons, and teapots carved from coconut shells and baskets, floor and table mats, and carpets handwoven from coir (coconut fiber), and sleeping mats and handbags made of resilient, pliable kova grass. Other goods include brass lamps and other brassware, rosewood elephants, lacquered wooden boxes with brass fittings—traditionally used to store the family jewels—and metal polished assiduously to make mirrors from Aranmula, northeast of Trivandrum. Cinnamon, cloves, cardamom, and other spices are also sold throughout Kerala, as is coffee.

The quiet, rustic town of Kumarakom is a haven just outside the humming market town of Kottayam, deep in Central Kerala's wealthy and lush belt of rubber plantations, many of which have been owned for generations by Syrian Christians. The Christian population is quite noticeable here, with churches and Christian shrines popping up on the horizon every five minutes as you drive. Kerala Christians are particularly devout, and you will see more nuns and fathers here than in most of parts of the world—in fact, this area exports priests to the rest of the world. Christianity has been practiced in these parts longer than anywhere in the western world (historical records suggest that around 50 AD, two years before the Apostle Paul was spreading the gospel in Greece, in the port city of Thessaloniki, one of Jesus's original 12 disciples, Thomas, was preaching Christ in India, specifically in Tamilakam, which today is Kerala).

Novelist Arundhati Roy's birthplace, Ayemenem (featured in her 1997 novel *The God of Small Things*) is nearby; the Coconut Lagoon hotel is next to it. Birds abound in the backwaters, as well as in the sanctuary on the lake's eastern shore. Sailing the Vembanad Lake or exploring the canals is the most enjoyable exploring you could do while in Kumarakom, apart from visiting a selection of seafood restaurants. A small cruise of the lake and the shores nearest to your hotel may be enough to get the flavor of it. A larger part of your time should be devoted to roaming the backwater canals and peeking at a slice of Kuttanad life.

GETTING HERE AND AROUND

A prepaid cab from Kochi airport (Rs. 2,700 one way) is the safest and most hassle-free way of reaching Kumarakom.

There are few auto-rickshaws in the Kumarakom area, so your best bet for exploring is to either hire a car and driver from your hotel or a travel agency, or to take a speedboat, houseboat, or a small, traditional, motor-run ketch (about Rs. 1,000 an hour if hired through a hotel).

 # Hotels

Abad Whispering Palms

$$$ | **HOTEL** | Set on the banks of Vembanad Lake, this backwater hotel offers lake-facing cottages and garden rooms with private open-air bathrooms; three bamboo villas have their own private pool. **Pros:** friendly and helpful staff; nice views; ayurvedic rejuvenation center. **Cons:** rooms need an upgrade; lacks Kerala charm; open-air bathrooms. $ *Rooms from: Rs. 7500* ✉ *New Nazarath Rd., Konchumada* ☎ *481/252–3820, 481/252–3819* ⊕ *www.abadhotels.com* ⌇ *53 rooms* ⦿ *Free Breakfast.*

Coconut Lagoon

$$$$ | **RESORT** | This serene Kerala backwaters resort, bordered by the lake and the backwaters on three sides and crisscrossed with canals and footbridges, is dotted with white bungalows and two-story houses that are a mixture of rustic and modern but exceedingly comfortable. **Pros:** excellent ayurvedic center;

eco-friendly; staff naturalists lead tours of local bird sanctuary and the hotel's butterfly garden. **Cons:** pricey two-story mansions have bathroom and bedrooms on different floors (instead, opt for a bungalow); can only be reached by boat; older property in need of maintenance. $ *Rooms from: Rs. 31200* ✉ *Vembanad Lake* ☎ *481/252–8200, 481/252–8261* ⊕ *www.cghearth.com* ⌇ *49 rooms* ⦿ *All-inclusive.*

★ Kumarakom Lake Resort

$$$$ | **RESORT** | **FAMILY** | Set around a network of canals and pristine lawns, this lush 25-acre heritage resort is right on Lake Vembanad and is known for its palatial traditional villas, reassembled from 107 old houses, fitted with ornately carved teak wooden ceilings, colorful mythological murals, and open-air garden bathrooms with private pools. **Pros:** amazing meandering pool; gorgeous traditional setting; pottery and weaving classes. **Cons:** pricey; may be too large of a resort for some; open-air bathrooms attract insects at night. $ *Rooms from: Rs. 24000* ✉ *Kumarakom North P.O.* ☎ *481/252–4900, 481/252–4501* ⊕ *www.kumarakomlakeresort.in* ⌇ *59 rooms* ⦿ *All-inclusive.*

Taj Kumarakom Resort and Spa

$$$$ | **RESORT** | The brightly colored detached cottages at this tranquil resort set among rubber trees have broad verandas overlooking a small lagoon where guests can canoe or pedal boat. **Pros:** trees are populated by winged residents of the nearby bird sanctuary; excellent seafood restaurant; plenty of activities for children. **Cons:** not as carefully maintained as other Taj properties; pricey; very little lakefront or backwaters view. $ *Rooms from: Rs. 18000* ✉ *1/404 Kottayam* ☎ *481/252–5711, 481/252–5716* ⊕ *www.tajhotels.com* ⌇ *28 rooms* ⦿ *Free Breakfast.*

Zuri Kumarakom Resort and Spa

$$$$ | **RESORT** | Set along Lake Vembanad, this luxurious resort, known for its

impressive, giant four-headed statue of a Kathakali dancer in the gleaming lobby and boat-shape check-in desk, offers a variety of rooms from cottages with lagoon views to villas with private pools overlooking the lake. **Pros:** standard rooms are a good value; enormous modern spa with both ayurvedic and Western treatments; plenty of activities for kids. **Cons:** massage rates are rather high; lacks the elegance of its neighbors; rooms in need of minor renovation. [$] *Rooms from: Rs. 12500* ✉ *Karottukayal* ☎ *481/252-7272* 🌐 *www.thezurihotels.com* 🛏 *72 rooms* 🍴 *Free Breakfast.*

Alleppey

35 km (22 miles) southwest of Kumarakom.

This city was once known as the Venice of India, though most residents have abandoned their canoes for cars. Alleppey (Alappuzha) is an important gateway to the backwaters—tour operators abound, and several resorts 30 minutes out of the town are a good alternative to the pricier properties in Kumarakom.

Alleppey, from the tourist's point of view, is essentially an access point to the backwaters and does not offer much in the way of sights. It's a lively, noisy town of bazaars, with an unattractive beach, and the administrative headquarters of the surrounding district, so most visitors hurry through on their way to the lagoons. However, if you are looking to hire a houseboat for a day or more, Alleppey is the best place to do it.

GETTING HERE AND AROUND

Alleppey is a one-hour drive from Kochi. The safest and most hassle-free way of reaching your hotel outside Alleppey is using prepaid cabs booked and paid for at Kochi airport (Rs. 2,300 one way). The quickest way to get here is the Jan Shatabdi express train, which connects Alleppey with Ernakulam, Kollam, Trivandrum, and Calicut. There are slower trains connecting Alleppey with Varkala and other smaller towns of Kerala. Alleppey has plenty of auto-rickshaws, but the best way to get about Alleppey is by houseboat or another water vessel—the scenery is gorgeous, and the canals are practically right at your door in nearly any hotel you're likely to stay at here.

Sights

Kerala Kayaking

KAYAKING | A kayak tour of the Alleppey backwaters is a very peaceful way to see life along the backwaters and the lagoons up close. There are three tour options: a four-hour morning trip with breakfast (Rs. 1,500), a seven-hour day trip with lunch (Rs. 3,000), and a 10-hour full-day tour with breakfast and lunch (Rs. 4,500). All three come with a guide and a backup boat. ✉ *Near Vazhicherry Bridge, opposite Indian Oil Petrol Pump, Sanathanam Ward P.O.* ☎ *984/658-5674, 854/748-7701* 🌐 *www.keralakayaking.com/home.*

Nehru Trophy Boat Race

FESTIVAL | On the second Saturday in August throngs of supporters line the shore to watch the annual Nehru Trophy Boat Race, which starts with a water procession and concludes dramatically as the boats (propelled by as many as 100 rowers) vie for the trophy. The best way to see the race is from a houseboat that you have booked far in advance. Several other snake-boat races take place in the area from mid-July to mid-September. ✉ *Punnamada Lake* ☎ *477/225-1720, 477/224-3721* 🌐 *www.nehrutrophy.nic.in.*

St. Andrew's Basilica

RELIGIOUS SITE | At Arthunkal, 20 km (12 miles) north of Alleppey on the way from Kochi, stands the ancient St. Andrew's Basilica. The church makes for an interesting break. Made out of wood and coconut fronds, it was built in 1581 by Portuguese missionaries, in honor of

Jesus's disciple Andrew. A few years later the church was rebuilt in stone. When it was erected, St. Andrew's Basilica was considered holy by Hindus as well the missionaries; even the area's Hindu king visited the shrine. It's one of the oldest and more impressive churches in a state where you can spot a startling-looking church every few miles. ✉ *Arthunkal P.O., Alleppey district, Cherthala* 🌐 *www.arthunkalbasilica.com* ⏲ *Closed Sun.*

🍴 Restaurants

Most of the best food in the area is likely to be what's served in the hotel or resort you're staying at.

Chakara

$$ | **SOUTH INDIAN** | Raheem Residency, on Alleppey's main beach, is in an elegant old British-built bungalow dating from the 19th century, and its partially alfresco restaurant serves a variety of cuisines—Kerala, North Indian, and some Western dishes. Try the Alleppey fish curry, the Kerala prawns roast, or a chicken biryani (served only at lunch) and enjoy the beach view from the upper floor. **Known for:** Alleppey fish curry; scenic views in a colonial building; Kerala prawns roast. [$] *Average main: Rs. 350* ✉ *Beach Rd.* ☎ *477/223–9767, 477/223–0767* 🌐 *www.raheemresidency.com/restaurant.html.*

🛏 Hotels

Abad Turtle Beach

$$$ | **RESORT** | Although not as luxurious as some of its neighbors, this backwater resort with pretty white bungalows with terra-cotta roofs is set on a lovely 13-acre beachfront property that has ponds, lush coconut palm groves, and a small lagoon running through it. **Pros:** excellent location; bicycles for rent; ayurvedic center. **Cons:** busy in high season; no alcohol; no safes in rooms. [$] *Rooms from: Rs. 8500* ✉ *Varankavala, Pollathai P.O., Mararikulam* ☎ *478/286–0965, 989/589–0776* 🌐 *www.abadhotels.com/mararibeach* 🔑 *30 rooms* 🍽 *Free Breakfast.*

A Beach Symphony

$$$ | **HOTEL** | Set on Marari beach in a quiet neighborhood are four luxury cottages in a delightful garden hotel surrounded by palm trees. **Pros:** high levels of privacy; cottages have Wi-Fi; some offer private swimming pools. **Cons:** meal choices are limited; might be too quiet and intimate for some; spa needs soundproofing; beach is not very pristine. [$] *Rooms from: Rs. 9500* ✉ *Marari Beach Rd., Mararikulam* ☎ *974/429–7123* 🌐 *www.abeachsymphony.com* 🔑 *4 rooms* 🍽 *Free Breakfast.*

Lemon Tree Vembanad Lake Resort

$$$ | **RESORT** | The highlight of this relaxing resort with elegant rooms is the impressive infinity pool, which overlooks the mighty Vembanad lake. **Pros:** infinity pool overlooking the lake; well priced; lakeside hotel. **Cons:** modest, standalone resort and therefore isolated; lacks the Kerala charm; in need of minor renovation and maintenance. [$] *Rooms from: Rs. 7700* ✉ *About 13 km (8 miles) north of Alleppey, Janasakthi Rd., Kayippuram, Muhamma* ☎ *478/286–1970* 🌐 *www.lemontreehotels.com* 🔑 *27 rooms* 🍽 *No meals.*

Marari Beach Resort

$$$$ | **RESORT** | This 25-acre eco-friendly resort, built to resemble a traditional fishing village, offers a private and unspoiled palm-fringed beach, an excellent ayurvedic center, and easy access to the backwaters that Alleppey is most known for. **Pros:** luxury villas have their own pools; friendly and professional staff; on-site naturalist leads tours of the grounds and its butterfly garden. **Cons:** no TVs; beach is closed during monsoons; expensive during peak season. [$] *Rooms from: Rs. 27000* ✉ *17 km (10 miles) north of Alleppey, Pollathai P.O., Mararikulam* ☎ *478/286–3801* 🌐 *www.cghearth.com* 🔑 *62 rooms* 🍽 *Free Breakfast.*

Marari Villas

$$$$ | **RESORT** | Set on the secluded Marari beach—considered one of Kerala's finest—this select set of luxury villas each has its own butler and chef plus a fully equipped kitchenette. **Pros:** private setting on the beach; superattentive service; two villas have a private garden and pool. **Cons:** lacks the functionality of a hotel and might be too small for some; closed part of the year; part of the beach used by locals. $ *Rooms from: Rs. 14000* ⊠ *Vadkethayil House, Pollathai P.O.* ☎ *994/794–8707, 994/794–8868* ⊕ *www.mararivillas.com* ⊗ *Closed June and July* ⌨ *4 rooms* |◎| *Free Breakfast.*

★ Punnamada Resort

$$$$ | **RESORT** | Small design details, spacious grounds, and lake-view rooms with private patios just steps from the water make this large backwater resort sparkle. **Pros:** beautiful lake views and serene atmosphere; beer and wine available; good ayurvedic hospital and daily yoga classes. **Cons:** secluded location may be too quiet for some; open-air bathrooms at night attract insects; only one restaurant. $ *Rooms from: Rs. 14400* ⊠ *Punnamada, Kottankulangara, Punnamada* ☎ *477/223–3690, 477/223–3692* ⊕ *www.punnamada.com* ⌨ *36 rooms* |◎| *Free Breakfast.*

Thekkady

130 km (81 miles) east of Kumarakom; 195 km (121 miles) east of Kochi.

Due east of Kumarakom, Kottayam, and Kochi, this cool mountain town, thick with spice plantations, sits at 3,000 feet above sea level in the Cardamom Hills, midway between Kochi and the temple city of Madurai in Tamil Nadu. The hills are home to a range of wildlife, including (rarely spotted) tigers, as well as acres and acres of cardamom, cloves, allspice, vanilla, cocoa, and coffee. Most hotels and resorts are in Kumily town, about 4

km (2½ miles) from the Periyar Wildlife Sanctuary at Thekkady. Due to the high elevation, you don't need a room with air-conditioning here.

GETTING HERE AND AROUND

Thekkady is a six-hour drive from Kochi and five hours from Kumarakom. It can be an exhausting uphill drive, with many bends, and ideally it should be done in a good car, with a skilled driver and on an empty stomach. You can also reach Thekkady from Munnar (112 km or 70 miles; four hours). You will also need a hired car to get around the area, especially if you choose to stay outside Thekkady and Kumily town.

 Sights

Periyar Wildlife Sanctuary

NATURE PRESERVE | In the vicinity of Thekkady, the Periyar National Park is one of India's best animal parks for spotting elephants, bison, wild boar, oxen, deer, black-faced Nilgiri langurs, and lion-tailed macaques (two kinds of monkeys), as well as many species of birds. The best viewing period is March and April, when other watering holes have dried up and wildlife, including leopards and tigers, is forced to approach the lake to drink. Still, you have a good chance of seeing animals resident October through May.

Lake Periyar, its many fingers winding around low-lying hills, is the heart of the nearly 303-square-km (117-square-mile) sanctuary. Forget exhausting treks or long safaris. At this sanctuary, unlike any other in India, you lounge in a motor launch as it drifts around bends and comes upon animals drinking at the shores. ■**TIP➔ Be prepared: Indian children (and adults) love to scream and shout at wildlife sightings.** On a quiet trip, elephants hardly notice the intrusion, although younger pachyderms will peer at you out of curiosity and then run squealing back to their elders when your boat comes too close. If you're brave-hearted, you can spend a night doing a night trek (Rs. 2,000 per person), staying overnight in a jungle lodge. If you do go out in the forest, be prepared for leeches on the ground, especially during the monsoon. For information about treks in the park, contact the District Tourism Promotion Council (DTPC) in Idukki. ⊠ *Thekkady* ☎ *486/922–4571 forest department, 486/223–2248 District Tourism Promotion Council (DTPC)* ⊕ *www.dtpcidukki.com* ⊠ *From Rs. 300.*

 Restaurants

Ambadi

$ | NORTH INDIAN | Like the rest of the resort, the Ambadi's multicuisine restaurant has a rustic feel and is decorated with lots of wood. Head here for well-executed North Indian staples, such as kebabs and other tandoori dishes, butter chicken, and biryani, as well as Indo-Chinese options, Kerala specials, and Western dishes, including fish-and-chips and some pastas. **Known for:** North Indian kebabs and tandoori dishes; located inside a heritage hotel; walking distance to Periyar Wildlife Sanctuary. $ *Average main: Rs. 250* ⊠ *Ambadi Hotel, Ambadi Junction* ☎ *486/922–2194, 486/922–2195* ⊕ *www.hotelambadi.com.*

Tamarind Tree

$$$$ | SOUTH INDIAN | This all-day restaurant located in the Spice Village resort serves some of the best food in the area, including not-to-miss Kerala specialties. You can choose to eat inside the thatched main building, decorated with a colorful selection of cattle masks, on a veranda overlooking the pool, or in the garden. **Known for:** the panni kurumulaku roast, a peppery roast pork; the malli meen pudhina, a grilled fish with mint coconut sauce; all produce is locally sourced within a 50-mile radius. $ *Average main: Rs. 750* ⊠ *Spice Village, Kumily Rd., Kumily* ☎ *486/922–2315, 486/930–2555, 486/930–2500* ⊕ *www.cghearth.com.*

 Hotels

★ Hills and Hues

$$$$ | HOTEL | Built into the side of a steep hill, this tranquil hotel, located 6 km (3¾ miles) from the Periyar Wildlife Sanctuary, offers sweeping views of the verdant valley below and the Kerala-Tamil Nadu border. **Pros:** rooms have picture windows offering panoramic views; friendly staff; grows its own fruits and vegetables. **Cons:** steep slope to get to/from the restaurant; location might be too isolated for some; no alcohol served. $ *Rooms from: Rs. 13500* ⊠ *2nd mile, Amaravathy P.O., Kumily* ☎ *906/191–0000, 960/504–0033 cell phone* ⊕ *www.hillsandhues.com* ⊠ *6 rooms* ꙳ *Free Breakfast.*

Hotel Lake Palace

$$$$ | HOTEL | A ferry transports you to this former maharaja's hunting lodge, an enormous, red-tiled roof heritage bungalow, located on an island inside the Periyar Wildlife Sanctuary, where you can spot wildlife from your balcony. **Pros:** attentive service; the best lodge in Thekkady for watching wildlife; tranquil, especially at night. **Cons:** bathrooms need updating (not very luxurious, given the rates); you need to book in advance; entry into the resort possible only between 6 am and 6 pm. $ *Rooms from: Rs. 16000* ⊠ *Periyar Wildlife Sanctuary* ☎ *486/922–3887, 940/000–8589* ⊕ *www.lakepalacethekkady.com* ⊠ *6 rooms* ꙳ *All-inclusive.*

Niraamaya Retreats - Cardamom Club

$$$ | HOTEL | A fork in the road branches off to a mile-long, bumpy road that leads to a spice plantation holding this small resort that emerges like a little paradise from the undergrowth. **Pros:** great place to forget the rat race; good spa and excellent food; lovely outdoor pool overlooking the mountains. **Cons:** far away from any excitement; pricey; no alcohol. $ *Rooms from: Rs. 6000* ⊠ *256 V & V Estate, Spring Valley, 66th mile, Kumily* ☎ *471/226–7333, 804/510–4510* ⊕ *www.*

A houseboat on the backwaters

niraamaya.in 🛏 *13 rooms* 🍴 *Free Breakfast.*

Shalimar Spice Garden

$$$$ | **RESORT** | The emphasis is on serenity and relaxation at this rustic retreat inside a spice plantation that is 6 km (4¾ miles) off the main road to Kumily, reached by going down a rugged path and over a wooden bridge. **Pros:** gorgeous setting; rooms include complimentary slippers and heaters; pool. **Cons:** too isolated for some; built into a hill, so may be a steep walk for some; not a place to venture to during the monsoon. [$] *Rooms from: Rs. 17300* ✉ *Murikkady P.O., Kumily* ☎ *486/922–2132, 486/922–3232* 🌐 *www.shalimarspicegarden.com* 🛏 *20 rooms* 🍴 *Free Breakfast.*

Spice Village

$$$$ | **RESORT** | One of Thekkady's finest resorts, Spice Village has well-maintained thatch-roof cottages that are built into a hillside with lush plantings, including a spice garden that adds fragrance and privacy. **Pros:** great for spotting wildlife like a black-faced langur or a richly colored Malabar giant squirrel; restaurants use locally sourced, organic produce; fantastic collection of animal masks. **Cons:** easy to get lost in this large resort; cottages perhaps too close to each other in some parts; some guests have experienced slow service. [$] *Rooms from: Rs. 18700* ✉ *Thekkady-Kumily Rd., Kumily* ☎ *486/922–4514, 486/922–2315* 🌐 *www.cghearth.com* 🛏 *52 rooms* 🍴 *Free Breakfast.*

The Wildernest B&B

$$$ | **B&B/INN** | Less than a kilometer from the gates of the Periyar Wildlife Sanctuary stands a cute two-story cobblestone building with 10 cottage-style rooms. **Pros:** good value; intimate; prime location. **Cons:** no restaurant; not enough creature comforts for some; monkeys frequent the property. [$] *Rooms from: Rs. 6000* ✉ *Thekkady Road* ☎ *486/922-4030, 486/921–1471* 🌐 *www.wildernest-kerala.com* 🛏 *10 rooms* 🍴 *Free Breakfast.*

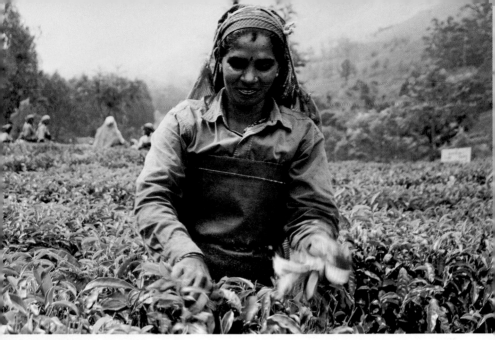

Picking tea leaves

Munnar

100 km (62 miles) north of Thekkady; 130 km (80 miles) east of Kochi.

On the drive from Thekkady to Munnar, a good road winds through lofty forests as well as spice and tea plantations. As you make the final climb to Munnar the hillside is richly carpeted with iridescent bushes and bushes of tea. Tea has been grown in Munnar for well over a hundred years, since about 1880. Like so many such areas in India, it reflects a long, virtually unchanged history—groups of workers heading out to pick the leaves, overstuffed sacks of the leaves heading to the factory, sleepy shacks clustered around a tea factory.

The town of Munnar itself is small and unattractive, though its Christ Church, less than a kilometer above the main town and built of British planters, is worth a quick visit for its atmosphere and the old memorial plaques inside.

Most of the land around Munnar is owned by the tea section of the huge Tata Group, resulting in a kind of unspoiled hill station, with acres of tea, coffee, and cardamom plantations amid hills, lakes, streams, and waterfalls. During your visit you can tour these plantations; arrange trekking, rock-climbing, paragliding, and river trips; or just sit on your hotel balcony with—what else?—a cup of tea, taking in the scenery. It's quite cool here, so you don't need to find a hotel with air-conditioning.

GETTING HERE AND AROUND

Munnar is easily accessed from Kochi or from Thekkady, both roughly four hours away using a car and driver—though note that it should be done in a good, powerful car, with a skilled driver. The initial climb is a treat as you wind through ravines, thick tropical jungle that includes sandalwood forests, and across many rivers.

You will also need a hired car to get around Munnar, especially if you should choose to stay outside the town.

⊙ Sights

Most lodgings can arrange a tea plantation tour, where you can walk through the steeply pitched, dense green hedges, and see how the leaf is processed.

You may like to also take a drive to see two of Munnar's lakes that have resulted in the area being compared to England's Lake District—the Sita Devi lake at Devikulum (7 km or 4 miles away) or Mattupetty Dam (13 km or 8 miles away). Cardamom plantations can be quite idyllic. The shade-loving spice needs plenty of forest cover, so a walk through a plantation feels like a stroll in the woods, complete with dappled sunlight, mountain streams, and birdsong.

Visit the Eravikulam National Park to catch a view of the rare Nilgiri tahr (mountain goat), and the Chinnar Wildlife Sanctuary (60 km or 37 miles) to see deer, bison, or elephants.

Chinnar Wildlife Sanctuary

NATURE PRESERVE | This wildlife sanctuary in the Annamalai Hills, which spreads 90 square km (35 square miles) across Tamil Nadu and Kerala, is considered a better place to spot elephants and wild oxen (gaur) than Periyar Wildlife Sanctuary. You also can look out for leopards, spotted deer, the Nilgiri tahr, yellow-throated bulbuls (songbirds), grizzled giant squirrels, crocodiles, sambar deer, langurs, and the bonnet macaque (both kinds of monkeys), and even an occasional tiger or a Manjampatti white (albino) bison. The entry fee is for the trekking program: paths lead along the Pambar and Chinnar rivers and past the mighty Thoovanam waterfalls, which are most impressive during the monsoons. Buses take you into the park, but you also can opt to stay in three-bed tree houses or four-bed log houses by booking in advance with the forest department. Bookings can be made at the wildlife warden's office in Munnar or online with an Indian credit card; it's about 90 minutes and 60 km (38 miles) from Munnar. ✉ *Munnar-Udumalpet Rd., Idukki District, Marayur* ☎ *486/523–1587 wildlife warden's office, 854/760–3222 Munnar Wildlife Department* ⊕ *www.munnarwildlife.com* ✇ *Rs. 100.*

Eravikulam National Park

NATURE PRESERVE | This well-maintained 97-square-km (24,000-acre) sanctuary, 15 km (9 miles) northwest of Munnar, is home to the endangered Nilgiri tahr (*Nilgiritragus hylocrius*), an ibex-like goat that inhabits the highest, wettest reaches of the Western Ghats in Tamil Nadu and Kerala. It has lost numbers to poaching and shrinking habitat, leaving a population of just 700–800 in the park, roughly half of the world's total number. Here you can get quite close to this endearingly tame creature, pushed to the brink of extinction in part because of its utter lack of suspicion of humans. There are often long lines in season to buy your ticket, so it's a good idea to book in advance, or head early. From the entrance a park bus takes you about 7 km (4½ miles) into the hill, from which you can walk nearly 1½ km (1 mile) farther, to a higher lookout point. No vehicles are allowed in the park, so be prepared to walk along the trails and footpaths. The craggy mountain views and gushing waterfalls in the monsoon add to the allure of this park. ■ **TIP→ The sanctuary is closed for about 90 days during the calving season, roughly from February to April (check ahead of time) and occasionally for a day or so during the monsoons if there have been heavy rains.** ✉ *Eravikulam National Park, Idukki* ☎ *486/523–1587, 830/102-4187, 854/760–3199 Forest Information Centre for enquiries and reservations* ⊕ *www. eravikulam.org* ✇ *Rs. 260.*

Tata Tea Museum

FACTORY | At one of the only museums of its kind in India, you can learn about the history of local tea growing and view the antique furnishings of an estate manager's bungalow. Another highlight is the 2nd-century BC urn found at one of the tea estates nearby. You also can sample this area's famous blends in the tasting room. ✉ *Kanan Devan Hills Plantations Company (P) Limited, Nullathanni Rd., Idukki* ☎ *994/640–5216 cell phone, 486/825-5272, 755/889–2441 cell phone* 🌐 *www.kdhptea.com* 🎟 *Rs. 80* 🕒 *Closed Mon.*

Top Station

VIEWPOINT | Take a drive to see the highest lookout points around Munnar, which offer great views of the tea estates below—one of the best is Top Station, 32 km (20 miles) and 40 minutes) from Munnar town and 1,700 feet above sea level, across the border in Tamil Nadu, in the Kanan Devan hills. It gets its name from once being the highest point of a ropeway from which tea from Munnar was sent down to the town of Kottagudi. ✉ *Idukki.*

🍴 Restaurants

The best restaurants in Munnar are within the resorts. It is best to call ahead to notify them of your visit, because you might go a long way to find them closed, or not much available.

Hill Spice

$$ | INTERNATIONAL | The airy, glass-roofed Hill Spice, at the Tall Trees resort, is a more elegant alternative to the restaurants in Munnar's main bazaar. The Kerala dishes are your best bet, though the restaurant offers thalis and buffet meals along with Indian, Indo-Chinese, and continental food. **Known for:** alfresco dining; great choice of Indo-Chinese dishes like hakka noodles and chilli chicken; located in a spice plantation. [$] *Average main: Rs. 350* ✉ *The Tall Trees resort, Bison Valley Rd.* ☎ *486/523–0593, 486/523–2716* 🌐 *www.ttr.in.*

🛏 Hotels

Blackberry Hills Retreat and Spa

$$$ | RESORT | A seriously steep walk downhill through green environs brings you to a clutter of whitewashed, terra-cotta-roofed cottages, clinging to the slope, where you get a bird's-eye view of tea plantations for miles around, including workers' settlements and a small blue-roofed church. **Pros:** its variety of organized treks, barbecues, and campfires; reasonably well priced; Wi-Fi available in rooms. **Cons:** no minibar in room; the low-key resort is in Pothamedu, 4 km (2½ miles) out of Munnar town; very steep climbs to the restaurant and reception. [$] *Rooms from: Rs. 8500* ✉ *Bison Valley Rd., Pothamedu Viewpoint* ☎ *486/523–2978, 486/523–2979, 944/770–6606* 🌐 *www.blackberryresorts.com* 🛏 *16 rooms* 🍽 *Free Breakfast.*

Fragrant Nature

$$$$ | HOTEL | Built into a steep cliff and in a style similar to the area's tea plantation bungalows, this luxury hotel offers sweeping views of Munnar Valley; that is, when it's not engulfed in a thick mist. **Pros:** one of the only hotels in Munnar to have a bar that serves alcohol; restaurants offer picturesque views of the valley below; plenty of daily activities like nature walks, tea plantation tours, and evening campfires. **Cons:** hotel is always busy no matter the season; pricey; thin-walled rooms. [$] *Rooms from: Rs. 12800* ✉ *V/1, Pothamedu, Bison Valley Rd., Idukki* ☎ *486/825–7800, 486/825–7888* 🌐 *www.fragrantnature.com* 🛏 *43 rooms* 🍽 *Free Breakfast.*

Kaivalyam Retreat

$$$ | B&B/INN | This simple, holistic yoga retreat on 11 scenic acres of vegetation and tea plantations is run by two yoga instructors and focuses on serenity and an organic lifestyle. **Pros:** nice views and peaceful; eco-friendly; the resort also offers spice plantation tours, bird-watching, and nature photography. **Cons:** can get noisy with families around; isolated (Munnar is 20 minutes away); reaching the property can be confusing (no signs). $ *Rooms from: Rs. 6000 ⊠ Pallivasal Estate, opposite Workers Recreation Center, Moolakadai ☎ 486/523–2628, 949/582–1617 ⊕ www.kaivalyamretreat. com ⌐ 16 rooms* ¦○¦ *Free Breakfast.*

Mountain Club

$$$$ | HOTEL | Fluttering eucalyptus trees frame an alluring resort of tile-roofed cobblestone cottages, some of them two stories, offering memorable views of Mattupetty Lake. **Pros:** ayurvedic treatments available; outdoor infinity pool; friendly staff. **Cons:** the restaurant is situated on a steep hill; no alcohol; popular, so expect crowds in high season. $ *Rooms from: Rs. 11500 ⊠ Chinnakanal Suryanelli Rd., Chinnakanal ☎ 486/824– 9978, 486/824–9979, 953/906–7830 ⊕ www.mountainclub.co.in ⌐ 50 rooms* ¦○¦ *Free Breakfast.*

Siena Village

$$ | HOTEL | Set in Chinnakanal, in lush green surroundings away from the commotion of Munnar, this fairly ordinary hotel offers rooms that capture the country-lodge feeling quite perfectly. **Pros:** outdoor buffet with musical performances and campfire during high season; play area and playroom for children; the semicircular restaurant also has panoramic vistas. **Cons:** rooms are basic; indifferent service; more than an hour's drive to any worthwhile sights in the area. $ *Rooms from: Rs. 5250 ⊠ 22 km (14 miles) east of Munnar, Chinnakanal ☎ 984/705–8996 reservations, 486/824–9261 ⊕ www. thesienavillage.com ⌐ 28 rooms* ¦○¦ *Free Breakfast.*

The Tall Trees

$$$$ | HOTEL | Getting around this hilly property is a workout—especially the hike to the skylight-topped restaurant— but the setting on 66-acre cardamom plantation is phenomenal. **Pros:** large rooms; hotel arranges lots of activities; peaceful location surrounded by lush

greenery. **Cons:** tiring walk uphill to the restaurant; rooms can smell damp during the monsoons; Munnar is 20 minutes away. $ *Rooms from: Rs. 11500 ⊠ Bison Valley Rd. ☎ 486/523–0593, 486/523–2716, 486/523–0593, 944/711– 1726 ⊕ www.ttr.in ⌐ 26 rooms* ¦○¦ *Free Breakfast.*

Windermere Estate

$$$$ | HOTEL | The hillside views on this working 55-acre cardamom, coffee, and vanilla plantation, are stunning, as are the grounds. **Pros:** service is warm and personalized; picturesque views; you are often eating the bounty of the plantation, including sweet carrots, cardamom-flower infused honey, tree-tomato juice, and fresh nutmeg pickle. **Cons:** basic amenities, no TVs or bar; electricity fluctuates in the rain, but there is a backup generator; Munnar is 5 km (about 3 miles) away. $ *Rooms from: Rs. 10450 ⊠ Bison Valley Rd., Pothamedu ☎ 484/242–5237 reservations, 486/523–0512 ⊕ www. windermeremunnar.com ⌐ 18 rooms* ¦○¦ *Free Breakfast.*

Thiruvananthapuram (Trivandrum)

222 km (138 miles) south of Kochi; 253 km (157 miles) southwest of Thekkady.

Built on seven low hills and cleansed by ocean breezes, Kerala's capital is surprisingly calm and pleasant, with wide avenues and some rather baronial buildings, a legacy of colonial times. Trivandrum's few sights and quiet lanes outside the town center make it an enjoyable place to spend part of a day or so, to have lunch, see a few landmarks, and shop a bit. Most leisure travelers decide to base themselves in any of the better-located hotels in Kovalam and then just make a visit to Trivandrum.

GETTING HERE AND AROUND

Trivandrum is 212 km (134 miles; about six hours or less) by road from Kochi. If you choose some of the coastal roads it is a lovely drive. The efficient intercity express train Jan Shatabdi connects Trivandrum with Kollam, Alleppey, Ernakulam, and Calicut in the north, and is the quickest way to get here. There are slower trains connecting Trivandrum with Varkala and other smaller towns in Kerala. Express trains also link Trivandrum with Mumbai, Bengaluru, and Chennai. Flights arrive many times a day from Chennai, Bengaluru, Delhi, and Mumbai, as well as a few international destinations.

It is easy to get around Trivandrum by auto-rickshaw, but be sure to fix the fare before you get in—no one goes by the meter rates, which are about Rs. 20 per kilometer. You can even take an auto-rickshaw from Kovalam into Trivandrum, but hiring a car from your hotel or a travel agent is the best option, both for getting here and then around the city.

 Sights

Kuthiramalika (Puthen Maliga) Palace Museum

CASTLE/PALACE | The 18th-century Kuthiramalika (Puthen Maliga) Palace Museum, or Horse Palace, built by the king of Travancore, has carved rosewood ceilings and treasures of the royal family, including an ivory throne, weapons, paintings, and gifts from foreign dignitaries. Life-size Kathakali figures stand in the dance room. Carved horses, for which the palace is named, line the eaves of an inner courtyard. Only one-third of the enormous compound is open to visitors; the entrance fee includes a knowledgeable guide. Also note that you must remove your shoes upon entering. ⊠ *Next to Padmanabhaswamy Temple, East Fort* ☎ *471/247–3952* 🎫 *Palace: Rs. 20* 🕙 *Closed Mon.*

Napier Museum

MUSEUM | FAMILY | In an 80-acre park at the north end of M.G. Road are the many attractions of the Museum and Art Gallery Complex. Each part of the complex requires a special ticket. At the Natural History Museum, a musty collection of animal skeletons, dioramas, and stuffed birds, head straight to the second floor to see an interesting model of a traditional *nalakettu* home (the traditional home of the Nairs, a warrior clan), complete with costumed figurines and a full explanation. The art museum's collection of local arts and crafts—including bronze and stone sculptures, ivory ornaments, and musical instruments—is as noteworthy as the building itself, with its almost Cubist pattern of gables, European-style minarets, and a decorative interior. Built in 1874, it was designed by Robert Chisholm, a specialist in Indo-Saracenic design, and was named after Lord Napier, the governor of Madras. Memorabilia donated by the royal family, including a golden chariot used by the Maharaja of Travancore, is displayed in the tiny Sree Chitra Enclave. On the opposite side of the park, the Sree Chitra Art Gallery has an eclectic collection of paintings, including works of the Rajput, Mogul, and Tanjore schools as well as those of India's most famous oil painter, Raja Ravi Varma; copies of the Ajanta and Sigirya frescoes; and works from China, Japan, Tibet, and Bali, along with canvases by modern Indian painters. ⊠ *Museum Rd.* ☎ *471/231–8294 director, 471/231–6275 administrative office* 🎫 *From Rs. 20* 🕙 *Closed Mon.*

Padmanabhaswamy Temple

RELIGIOUS SITE | The handsome Padmanabhaswamy Temple, dedicated to Vishnu, has a seven-story *gopuram* (entrance tower) that's as wide as it is tall to accommodate an unusual reclining statue of a very dark-skinned Vishnu (Padmanabha), lying in eternal slumber on a five-headed serpent. The date of its original construction has been placed at 3000 BC; legend has it that it was built

Trivandrum's Padmanabhaswamy Temple

by 4,000 masons, 6,000 laborers, and 100 elephants over the course of six months. In the main courtyard there's an intricate granite sculpture, supplemented by more stonework on the nearly 400 pillars supporting the temple corridors. Non-Hindus are not allowed inside the temple or inner sanctum but are welcome to view the impressive structure from the outside. The hours of opening reflect the eccentric uniqueness of this magnificent-looking and much revered house of worship: 3:30 am–4:45 am, 6:30 am–7 am, 8:30 am–10 am, 10:30 am–11:10 am, 11:45 am–noon, 5 pm–6:15 pm, 6:45 pm–7:20 pm, and a viewing of Vishnu can be booked online. You'll have to take off your shoes, photography is prohibited, and women should wear appropriate clothing (i.e., no shorts or sleeveless or revealing tops). Nearby there are little shops selling handicrafts. ✉ *Next to Kuthiramalika Palace Museum, Manjalikulam Rd., West Nada, East Fort* ☎ *471/245–0233 office, 471/246–6830 temple* 🌐 *www.sreepadmanabhaswamytemple.org.*

🍴 Restaurants

Azad

$ | INDIAN | Specialties at this chain restaurant (and this branch may be the best) include biryani, a flavorful rice cooked with chicken or mutton, and *kuthu paratha,* a Kerala Muslim delicacy of flatbread stuffed with minced fish and served from 4 pm onward. **Known for**: biryani; kuthu paratha; open late. [$] *Average main: Rs. 150* ✉ *Vazhuthacaud* ☎ *471/307–0603,471/233–6336.*

★ Chinapolis

$$$$ | CHINESE | This is Trivandrum's first fine-dining Chinese restaurant, and it serves authentic Cantonese, Hunan, Shanghai, Shandong, and Sichuan dishes; meals are accompanied by jasmine tea, which is a palate cleanser between courses. The decor, composed of intricate, black, wooden cutout panels, traditional Chinese lanterns, red damask table linens, and fine china, adds to the wonderful dining experience. **Known for:** the fried grouper in black bean chilli sauce with XO seafood and egg fried rice; authentic Chinese menu developed by head chef Wang Wen from Beijing; the date pancakes with ice cream are a must. [$] *Average main: Rs. 800* ✉ *Vivanta by Taj–Trivandrum, C V Raman Pillai Rd., Thycaud* ☎ *471/661–2345* 🌐 *www.vivantabytaj.com.*

Garden Grille and Bar

$$$$ | **INTERNATIONAL** | The food and buffet selection at the Hilton Garden Inn's all-day dining restaurant is varied and delicious, with everything from Kerala classics like *meen manga* curry to North Indian specialties, Italian pastas, and pizzas, and even a fresh salad counter. Beyond the food, a major draw is its staff; executive chef Shankar Chiranjeevi pays careful attention to diners likes and dislikes and makes sure to stop by every table to ask about their dining experience. **Known for**: wide variety of weekend brunch buffet selections; pizza made to order in a stone oven; serves alcohol. [$] *Average main: Rs. 850* ✉ *Hilton Garden Inn–Trivandrum, Punnen Rd.* ☎ *471/660–0000* 🌐 *www.trivandrum.hgi.com.*

★ **Villa Maya**

$$$$ | **INTERNATIONAL** | This former 18th-century Dutch mansion with its lush garden courtyard, classical architecture, and ancient art and relics dotting the grounds, once served as an *arumana ammaveedu* or home of the consorts of the king of Travancore. Regarded as Trivandrum's finest restaurant, this oasis in the heart of the city features an eclectic collection of dishes from Kerala, as well as Morocco and Italy, two countries that traded with Kerala. **Known for**: fine-dining heritage building containing 200-year-old antiques; wonderful outdoor garden seating area with ponds and fountains; its signature chocolate coffee fudge with hot caramel sauce and spiced blueberry and apple crumble for dessert. [$] *Average main: Rs. 750* ✉ *120 Airport Rd., Injakkal, West Fort* ☎ *471/257–8901, 471/257–8902* 🌐 *www.villamaya.in.*

Hotels

Fortune Hotel The South Park

$$$ | **HOTEL** | This large and well-located hotel, right in the middle of town, is primarily used by business travelers. **Pros:** good location and online rates; in-room Wi-Fi; there's a restaurant, bar, and coffee shop. **Cons:** large and impersonal; on a noisy street; the beds are fixed to the ground in the twin-bedded rooms. [$] *Rooms from: Rs. 7500* ✉ *Spencer Junction, M.G. Rd.* ☎ *471/233–3333, 984/703–0003* 🌐 *www.thesouthpark.com* 🛏 *76 rooms* 🍴 *Free Breakfast.*

Hilton Garden Inn

$$ | **HOTEL** | Set 2 km (1¼ miles) from two of Trivandrum's top sights —Padmanabhaswamy Temple and the Kuthiramalika Palace Museum—this seven-story business hotel offers wonderful views of the city and is known for its incredible staff and service. **Pros:** prime location; incredibly warm and helpful service; wonderful views of Trivandrum from some rooms. **Cons:** lacks traditional Kerala style; all rooms are carpeted; no spa. [$] *Rooms from: Rs. 5700* ✉ *Punnen Rd.* ☎ *471/660–0000* 🌐 *www.trivandrum.hgi.com* 🛏 *132 rooms* 🍴 *Free Breakfast.*

Varikatt Heritage

$$ | **B&B/INN** | This 150-year-old tiled-roof colonial bungalow, with its colorful history—as evidenced by the artifacts and photographs that embellish the home—is the location of this popular homestay run by an army colonel. **Pros:** charming, warm environment; well located; home-cooked daily breakfast. **Cons:** small; busy area, although the greenery helps shield the bustle; not for those seeking hotel amenities. [$] *Rooms from: Rs. 4500* ✉ *Punnen Rd.* ☎ *989/523–9055, 471/233–6057* 🌐 *www.varikattheritage.com* 💳 *No credit cards* 🛏 *4 rooms* 🍴 *Free Breakfast.*

Vivanta by Taj–Trivandrum

$$$ | **HOTEL** | This large and centrally located Taj property, with its hospitable staff, has a large outdoor swimming pool,

an ayurvedic spa, and a 24/7 gym, plus two restaurants, a bakery, and a bar. **Pros:** large outdoor swimming pool; excellent ayurvedic hospital; 24-hour in-room dining. **Cons:** primarily a business hotel; lacks the Kerala charm; bathrooms are small. $ *Rooms from: Rs. 8000* ✉ *C V Raman Pillai Rd., Thycaud* ☎ *471/661–2345* ⊕ *www.vivantabytaj.com* ⤳ *129 rooms* ❏*❖*l *Free Breakfast.*

🛍 Shopping

Most shops are closed Sunday, and smaller shops occasionally shut down for a few hours at lunchtime on weekdays.

ART AND ANTIQUES
Natesan's

ANTIQUES/COLLECTIBLES | This store is a respected and age-old art and antiques dealer. ✉ *M.G. Rd.* ✛ *Opposite Ayurveda College* ☎ *471/233–1594, 471/233–0689* ⊕ *www.natesansantiqarts.com.*

CLOTHING
Fabindia

CLOTHING | This popular chain is a great spot to pick up any kind of quality Indian cottons, both as clothing and for your home. ✉ *Anupama, 9/9/119 S. S. Kovil Rd., behind Tennis Club, Kowdiar* ☎ *471/231–7677* ⊕ *www.fabindia.com.*

Kalyan Silks

TEXTILES/SEWING | One of Kerala's largest stores for saris, Kalyan's also has cotton and gorgeous silk by the meter, and men's and women's traditional clothing. ✉ *M.G. Rd.* ✛ *Near Fine Arts College, Palayam* ☎ *471/233–8331, 471/233–7331.*

Pothys

DEPARTMENT STORES | This seven-story popular South Indian department store sells traditional Kerala saris, textiles, Western clothing, electronics, and more. There's also a grocery store in the basement. ✉ *Nikunjam Building, M.G. Rd., Vanchiyoor* ☎ *471/257–4133* ⊕ *www. pothys.com.*

HANDICRAFTS AND CURIOS
SMSM

CRAFTS | For Kerala handicrafts and souvenirs, check out this government emporium. ✉ *Statue Junction* ✛ *Behind Secretariat, Press Club Rd.* ☎ *471/233–1358, 471/233–0298.*

JEWELRY
Joyalukkas

JEWELRY/ACCESSORIES | The Trivandrum shop of global brand Joyalukkas is the best and largest store in town for gold and jewelry set with precious stones, including traditional Kerala-style ornaments. ✉ *East Fort Attakulangara Junction* ☎ *471/257–5035* ⊕ *www.joyalukkas. com.*

Kovalam

16 km (10 miles) south of Trivandrum.

Kovalam's numerous and delightfully clean and sandy beaches are lined with palm-fringed lagoons and rocky coves. Fishermen in *lungis* (colorful cloth wraps) drag in nets filled with the day's catch, then push their slender wooden boats out again with a Malayalam "Heave ho." Here you can spend the day lazing around on warm sand or rocky outcroppings, watch the sun set, then sit back as the dim lights of distant fishing boats come on. In peak season, outdoor shacks come to life right on the beach—just point to the fish of your choice and specify how you'd like it prepared. ■**TIP→ Be sure to find out how much it's going to cost—a little discreet bargaining might be in order.**

GETTING HERE AND AROUND
Kovalam is 235 km (146 miles; about six hours) by road from Kochi and 16 km (10 miles) from Trivandrum. It is easy to get around the town by auto-rickshaw. You can even take an auto-rickshaw from Kovalam into Trivandrum, but hiring a car from your hotel or a travel agent is the best option.

Sights

Overdevelopment had nearly ruined Kovalam, but it's experiencing something of a revival, with hotel expansion under control and a variety of lodging, some of it very luxurious, coming to the area and making it a place that attracts all kinds of tourists. The main beach, Lighthouse, has been cleaned up; the concrete promenade is lined with some interesting shops (selling mainly clothes), cheaper restaurants to catch a small bite, and budget hotels. It's well lit at night, allowing for a pleasant evening stroll as well as some semblance of nightlife and lots of people-watching. For peace and solitude, however, stick to the secluded beaches in villages to the north and south of Kovalam town.

Padmanabhapuram Fort and Palace

Believed to be the largest wooden palace in Asia, this magnificent, 17th-century, carved-teak palace, set on nearly 7 acres, and with fantastic murals and carved and painted ceilings, is across the border in neighboring Tamil Nadu, about a 1½-hour (73 km [45 miles]) drive south of Kovalam on National Highway 47 in a very serene location at the foot of the Velli Hills. Padmanabhapuram was once the capital of the Travancore rajas (Travancore was the southernmost state, which was combined with Cochin and Malabar to form Kerala). This palace, their home, gives a taste of the grandeur of those times. Don't miss the brass lanterns that apparently have been lit since the 1700s, or the palace tank (reservoir) that was used for bathing. This huge complex is one of the best-preserved examples of old wooden architecture in India and worth the excursion, especially if you are a royalty or history buff. ✉ *Thuckalay, Kanniyakumari* ☎ *465/125–0255* 🌐 *www.ktdc.com* 🕒 *Closed Mon.*

Restaurants

Bait

$$$$ | **INTERNATIONAL** | One of three restaurants at the Taj's sprawling 15-acre property, Bait is known for its fresh seafood cooked in local Keralan spices and international flavors; ask about the catch of the day, which comes straight from the local fishermen's haul. The open-air dining room with views of the Arabian Sea make for an unbeatable dining location, especially at sunset. **Known for:** beachside dining; the chef preparing on request a unique bait experience with the day's fresh catch; chemmeen manga curry (the local favorite). [$] *Average main: Rs. 970* ✉ *Taj Green Cove Resort & Spa, G.V. Raja Vattappara Rd.* ☎ *471/661–3000* 🌐 *www.tajhotels.com.*

Tides

$$$$ | **CONTEMPORARY** | This excellent beachside seafood restaurant located at the Leela serves up freshly caught fish supplied by the local Kovalam fishermen. You can have the day's fresh catch cooked in just about whatever style you like, including Indian, Chinese, Keralan, continental, Caribbean, and Middle Eastern; there are also vegetarian options available. **Known for:** Chinese wok-tossed lamb pepper and Singapore chilli crab; the ever-changing catch of the day; private beach access. [$] *Average main: Rs. 950* ✉ *The Leela Kovalam, Beach Rd.* ☎ *471/305–1234* 🌐 *www.theleela.com.*

Hotels

Beach & Lake

$$ | **RESORT** | The main draws of this basic resort sandwiched between the roar of the Arabian Sea and the ripple of a backwater lagoon are its ayurvedic treatments and serene surroundings. **Pros:** inexpensive; gorgeous views and fantastic location; friendly staff. **Cons:** basic accommodations; some rooms are non-a/c; few eating options near the hotel, and it's far from Kovalam. [$] *Rooms from: Rs. 4000*

✉ *Pozhikkara Beach, Pachalloor Village* ☎ *471/238–2086* 🌐 *www.beachandlakeresort.com* 🛏 *26 rooms* 🍴 *Free Breakfast.*

Ideal Ayurvedic Resort
$ | **RESORT** | This small, homey resort south of Kovalam near the beach (albeit a steep path to get there) has specialized in ayurvedic treatment since 1997. **Pros:** friendly staff; little to distract guests from their treatments; well priced. **Cons:** no alcohol served; a steep downhill walk to get to the beach; small hotel. [$] *Rooms from: Rs. 1800* ✉ *Just before Somatheeram, Chowara* ☎ *471/226–8632* 🌐 *www.ayuruniverse.com/services/ideal-ayurvedic-resort.html* 🛏 *28 rooms* 🍴 *Free Breakfast.*

The Leela Kovalam
$$$$ | **RESORT** | All rooms at this luxurious property are large and have balconies offering sea views; beachfront chalets also have private compounds. **Pros:** spectacular sunset views; private beach area; good ayurvedic center. **Cons:** pricey; large and slightly impersonal; getting to the bars and restaurants on Lighthouse Beach is a bit of a walk. [$] *Rooms from: Rs. 14200* ✉ *Beach Rd.* ☎ *471/305–1234* 🌐 *www.theleela.com* 🛏 *183 rooms* 🍴 *Free Breakfast.*

Manaltheeram Ayurveda Beach Village
$$$ | **HOTEL** | This strictly ayurvedic resort is quieter and even closer to the water than its neighboring sister property, Somatheeram Beach Resort. **Pros:** quiet, exclusive beachfront; some restaurant tables set up on the beach; lots of good handicraft, clothing, and knickknack shops nearby. **Cons:** the ayurveda on offer is below average; a little short on amenities; dishes with meat are limited, and need to be requested. [$] *Rooms from: Rs. 7400* ✉ *Manaltheeram Rd., Chowara* ☎ *471/226–6111 for reservations only, 471/226–6222* 🌐 *www.manaltheeram.com* 🛏 *61 rooms* 🍴 *Free Breakfast.*

Neelakanta
$$ | **HOTEL** | This beachfront budget hotel on Kovalam's main drag offers private sea-facing balconies in every room that let you see all the action—people strolling, sunbathing, swimming, and fishing—on the bustling Lighthouse Beach. **Pros:** beach views; swimming pool; friendly staff. **Cons:** not very well-lit stairwells; no elevators; rooms are basic. [$] *Rooms from: Rs. 4500* ✉ *Lighthouse Beach* ☎ *471/248–0321* 🛏 *30 rooms* 🍴 *Free Breakfast.*

Nikki's Nest
$$$$ | **ALL-INCLUSIVE** | Among bougainvillea, coconut palms, banana trees, orchids, and acacia stand thatch-roof, circular cottages and beautifully maintained traditional *nalukettu* (quadrangular buildings) wooden houses, most with commanding sea views, making this ayurvedic hotel a popular choice, though a minimum 14-night stay is required. **Pros:** great hilltop beach views; good value; good ayurvedic massages. **Cons:** uphill walk to the hotel from the beach; you must book in advance; minimum 14-night stay; Wi-Fi only available in common areas. [$] *Rooms from: Rs. 19000* ✉ *Azhimala Shiva Temple Rd., Chowara* ☎ *471/226–8822, 471/226–8821* 🌐 *www.nikkisnest.com* 🛏 *47 rooms* 🍴 *All-inclusive.*

★ Niraamaya - Surya Samudra
$$$$ | **RESORT** | Overlooking the sea, this rambling and simply beautiful resort, a top Kerala location that is built along a hillside, has an exquisite beach, lovely views, and a great deal of peace. **Pros:** a good place for yoga or the spa; some massive rooms; a don't-miss infinity swimming pool cut out of rock, and with underwater sculptures. **Cons:** can be a bit isolated; no activities for children; pricey. [$] *Rooms from: Rs. 20000* ✉ *10 km (6 miles) south of Kovalam, Pulinkudi* ☎ *804/510–4510* 🌐 *www.niraamaya.in* 🛏 *33 rooms* 🍴 *Free Breakfast.*

Somatheeram Ayurvedic Health Resort
$$$ | **RESORT** | This strictly ayurvedic resort, located 2 km (1 mile) south of Kovalam on 15 lush acres by the sea, offers lodging in traditional wooden houses and simple brick cottages. **Pros:** plenty of activities, including yoga and meditation; atmospheric; good ayurvedic spa. **Cons:** it's a big climb from the lower rooms to reception and the restaurant; nonvegetarian food is limited and alcohol is not permitted; resort rather large to get around. [$] *Rooms from: Rs. 7300* ✉ *Chowara P.O., south of Kovalam, Chowara* ☎ *471/226–6501, 471/226–6502* 🌐 *www.somatheeram.org* 🛏 *70 rooms* 🍴 *All-inclusive.*

★ **Taj Green Cove Resort & Spa**
$$$$ | **RESORT** | Set on 15 acres of manicured gardens, among hundreds of palm trees, this enormous Taj resort with a top-notch spa is easily one of the best places to stay in Kovalam. **Pros:** super location; three restaurants and a bar; handy to shops, local restaurants, and Lighthouse Beach. **Cons:** can be pricey in high season; Wi-Fi is slow; water too rough at beach to swim. [$] *Rooms from: Rs. 19800* ✉ *G.V. Raja Vattappara Rd., Samudra Beach* ☎ *471/661–3000* 🌐 *www.tajhotels.com* ⛳ *9-hole golf course* 🛏 *59 rooms* 🍴 *Free Breakfast.*

Varkala

51 km (32 miles) north of Trivandrum; 59 km (37 miles) north of Kovalam.

Varkala, a magically peaceful beach town, is on a small strip of coastline fringed by the sparkling Papanasam Beach, which stretches out below towering red cliffs.

Over the years, as Kovalam lost some its charm to overdevelopment and a flood of hippie tourists, quiet Varkala grew modestly. It's now considered one of Kerala's best beach destinations—one unmarred by the excessive bustle that haunts Kovalam at least some of the year. The relatively small number of hotels and the palm-thatched eateries that have sprung up along the beach and the Cliff (as it's known) haven't taken anything away from the rustic delightfulness of the place. There's a simple, laid-back air about Varkala—you can enjoy sun and sand and not be deprived of the liveliness of a seaside resort. Adding color and a festive feel are the many Hindu pilgrims who come to see Varkala town's ancient Janardhana Swamy temple. An amble to the Cliff makes an interesting sundown excursion, as much for the people-watching as for finding out what's cooking at the stalls that are set up there.

GETTING HERE AND AROUND

Varkala is 50 km (31 miles; less than 90 minutes) from Trivandrum airport. Book a prepaid taxi at Trivandrum airport for approximately Rs. 1,500 to reach here quickly and safely, without any hassles. Slower trains connect Varkala with Trivandrum and Kochi (check 🌐 *indiarailinfo.com*). There are not very large distances to negotiate in and around Varkala and most places are not that far on foot. But you can use auto-rickshaws (most fares, negotiated beforehand, would not come to more than Rs. 60), hire a motorbike or a bicycle, or else hire a car from the hotel or a local travel agency.

👁 Sights

Anchuthengu Beach and Anjengo Fort
HISTORIC SITE | The pristine Anchuthengu beach, 12 km (7½ miles) south of Varkala, is the location of a lighthouse and the ruins of the British Anjengo fort, built in 1695, which at various times was under Dutch and Portuguese attack. Anchuthengu ("Five Coconuts"), was the site of the first trade settlement of the East India Company, and therefore the beginning of British India. It was also the site of the first rebellion against the British, when locals, unhappy with the conduct of the British traders, banded together to oust them. All that remains

of the 1695 fort is its four walls and a few tombstones from the adjacent cemetery. Like so many other areas of southern and central Kerala, the sea pleasantly merges with the backwaters here—be sure to bring a camera. ⊠ *Anchuthengu.*

Janardhana Swamy Temple

RELIGIOUS SITE | Known as Dakshin Kashi, or the Varanasi of the south, Varkala is a major center for the worship of Vishnu. At the Janardhana Swamy temple, you can see what happens at a popular Hindu pilgrimage destination—the prayers; the morning and evening *aarti* (devotions), when the gods are feted with oil lamps; and the customs of the devotees. Non-Hindus are not allowed inside the inner sanctum, but you can certainly view the architecture and soak up the atmosphere of this pretty and very busy 2,000-year-old temple. *Photographs of the deity are not allowed, and there may be a charge for using a camera outside.* ⊠ *Temple Rd.* ☞ *Check with your hotel in case there is a change in temple times.*

Odayam and Thiruvambady Beaches

BEACH—SIGHT | Sparkling Odayam, the next beach north of Varkala, is considered part of the town but is about 2 km (1 mile) away. It's quieter and even prettier—well worth visiting for an afternoon of sun or to watch a spectacular sunset. Thiruvambady Beach, still more tranquil, is a black-sand beach a climb down from the Cliff. **Amenities:** food and drink. **Best for:** solitude; sunset; swimming; walking. ⊠ *Varkala.*

Varkala Beach

BEACH—SIGHT | A pristine strip of sand backed by a steep cliff, this is probably one of South India's prettiest yet most happening beaches. Unlike many Goan beaches, its beauty has not been marred by overdevelopment, such as hotels that are too close to the water. At what's also known as Papanasam beach, which means "to wash away your sins," a dip here may be a chance to dissolve your life's regrets in the Arabian Sea. You are bound to see plenty of pilgrims doing just that. Plenty of vendors will also come by, offering coconut water or slices of fresh pineapple. There are a few rip currents in these waters, so obey the signs. From the beach you can climb up to the Cliff for some souvenir hunting or to have a bite or a cool drink from the dozens of thatched shacks. **Amenities:** food and drink; parking (free). **Best for:** sunrise; sunset; swimming; surfing; walking. ⊠ *Varkala Beach.*

🍴 Restaurants

In high season, the Cliff above Varkala Beach has more than 100 thatched shacks serving a range of freshly cooked seafood. It's not fine dining, but there are great views, even at night, and lots of atmosphere. Caffé Italiano is known for its pasta, and Café Del Mar for spicy fried calamari, as well as for standard Italian and Indian dishes.

Coastal Kitchen

$$$$ | **INTERNATIONAL** | Open all day, and with an open-air patio on the cliff, Coastal Kitchen may just be Varkala's best restaurant, serving all regional and Kerala specialties as well as vegetarian options like eggplant curry. Don't miss the *karuvepilai* prawns, spicy and fried up with a lot of curry leaves, or the *meen polichathu,* fish fried in a wrapped banana leaf, or *nadan meen charu,* a local kind of fish curry; the desserts are good, too. **Known for**: karuvepilai prawns; beer and wine; cliffside dining. $ *Average main: Rs. 1000* ⊠ *The Gateway Hotel, Janard-hanapuram* ☎ *470/667–3300* ⊕ *www. gateway.tajhotels.com.*

🛏 Hotels

Hindustan Beach Retreat

$$$ | **HOTEL** | **FAMILY** | Comfortable, large but somewhat bland rooms are available in this modern block hotel a few yards from the sea. **Pros:** great location; well priced; daily yoga classes. **Cons:** ordinary hotel lacking Kerala charm; beach in front of hotel gets crowded; rooms in need of an upgrade. $ *Rooms from: Rs. 9000* ⊠ *Papanasam Beach, Janardhanapuram P.O.* ☎ *470/260–4254, 470/260–4255* ⊕ *www.hindustanbeachretreat.in* ⤵ *27 rooms* ⦿ *Free Breakfast.*

Maadathil Cottages

$$$ | B&B/INN | In these lovely, traditional, red-roofed Kerala bungalows, the only sounds you're likely to hear are the crashing of the waves from nearby Odayam and Edava beaches. **Pros:** splendid isolation, but still within good distance of Varkala; Odayam beach is a few steps away; wonderful hospitality from owner. **Cons:** might be too quiet for some; simple rooms; need to book in advance. $ *Rooms from: Rs. 6500* ⊠ *Odayam Beach, Manthara Temple Rd., Edava* ☎ *860/611–3495* ⊕ *www.maadathilcottages.com* ⤵ *12 rooms* ⦿ *Free Breakfast.*

The Sanctum Spring Beach Resort

$$ | HOTEL | Set in a lush garden, this cliff-side resort offers modest rooms, most featuring spectacular views of the Arabian Sea, and is within walking distance to Varkala Beach and the cliff above it, where a variety of seafood stalls pop up during high season. **Pros:** great location; decent value; higher rooms offer Arabian Sea views. **Cons:** can get noisy; older property in need of maintenance; Wi-Fi only in hotel lobby. $ *Rooms from: Rs. 4250* ⊠ *Helipad* ☎ *470/260–6993, 944/725–2058* ✎ *thesanctumspringvarkala@yahoo.co.in* ⊕ *www.sanctumspring.com* ⤵ *17 rooms* ⦿ *Free Breakfast.*

Nightlife

Many of the shacks along the Cliff, as well as a few of the restaurants facing the beach, stay open often beyond 11 pm offering drinks, beer, and small dishes as well as a taste of Varkala's modest nightlife.

Festival Time

January's Tiruvatira features folk dancing and singing by young Malayali women. In Trichur (Thrissur), the Pooram and Vela festivals (March and April) are among Kerala's best known. Pooram is an eight-day spectacle with parades of decked-out elephants, music, and fireworks. In the north, Kannur and Kasargode are known for the extraordinary Theyyam (November–May), a religious dance of tribal origin. The harvest festival, Onam (late August–early September), which lasts up to 10 days in some locations, is celebrated with floral displays and snake-boat racing.

Terrace at Clafouti Beach Resort

CAFES—NIGHTLIFE | This popular resort is known for its relaxed vibe and some of the freshest seafood around, including its butter-garlic crab. It serves wine, too, along with delightful seafood snacks in a terrace overlooking the roaring ocean. It is open throughout the year. Italian, Indian, and continental meals are also available. ⊠ *Clafouti Beach Resort, North Cliff* ☎ *470/260–1414, 470/302–1313* ⊕ *www.clafoutiresort.com.*

Varkala Cultural Centre

ARTS VENUE | Kathakali and Mohiniyattam performances take place here during the busy season, 5–7 pm. Come early to see the elaborate preperformance makeup being applied. ⊠ *North Cliff* ☎ *470/260–3612.*

Wait n Watch

BARS/PUBS | Year-round, Hindustan Beach Retreat's rooftop cocktail lounge, five floors up, is a good place to come for a drink and a view, 11 am until 10:30 pm. You can have snacks or dinner at the adjoining multicuisine restaurant. ⊠ *Hindustan Beach Retreat, Papanasam*

Beach, Janardhanapuram, P.O.
☎ *470/260–4254, 470/260–4255* ⊕ *www.*
hindustanbeachretreat.in.

Calicut

146 km (91 miles) northwest of Kochi.

This city doesn't hold much excitement
in itself, but Calicut (Kozhikode) has an
airport and is a good base for exploring
several interesting sights nearby, including the lushly forested Wyanad district
to the northeast. The city's historical ties
with the Middle East are clearly apparent
due to the strong Arab presence.

GETTING HERE AND AROUND

Calicut can be reached from Kochi by
car or by train. The efficient Jan Shatabdi
train connects Calicut with Ernakulam,
Alleppey, Kollam (Quilon), and Trivandrum
in the south; this is the quickest way to
get to Calicut. You can fly into Calicut
from Mumbai on Spice Jet, Jet Airways,
and Air India; from Chennai on Air India
and Spice Jet; and from Bengaluru on
Spice Jet. Several international flights
connect Calicut with the Middle East.
One can get around easily within town by
auto-rickshaw or by hiring a car.

◉ Sights

Tasara Centre for Creative Weaving

FACTORY | You can see weavers working
on giant hand looms here, and Tasara
also hosts programs for artists-in-res-
idence. Many different hand-loom
products are also for sale. Call ahead to
arrange a visit. ⊠ *7 km (4 miles) south of
Calicut, Beypore North* ☎ *495/241–4832,
944/646–8832* ⊕ *www.tasaraindia.com.*

🍴 Restaurants

Kingsbay

$ | SEAFOOD | Located inside a colonial
Portuguese bungalow, this restaurant is
popular with well-heeled locals and often

hosts a lively crowd. The friendly owner's
passion for food is much in evidence, and
the varied menu encompasses regional
and national cuisines, including South
and North Indian, Thai, and continental;
there aren't many vegetarian dishes on
the menu, and alcohol is not served.
Known for: squid and prawn masala
fry; seafood specialties from nearby
Mangalore; colonial Portuguese building. $ *Average main: Rs. 250* ⊠ *1414
Customs Rd., Vellayil* ☎ *495/405–4422,
755/987–7877* ⊕ *kingsbay.co.*

Mezban

$ | INDIAN | This modern and comfortable
restaurant, in a centrally located business
hotel, serves a range of local, Chinese,
North Indian, and continental dishes; popular choices include squid *tawa peralan* (a
dry curry prepared with numerous spices), prawn biryani, and chicken malabar
biriyani. The place gets busy for dinner,
especially on weekends, and as a result
the waiting time can vary and service can
be slow. **Known for**: squid tawa peralan;
variety of Malabar biryanis; friendly staff.
$ *Average main: Rs. 240* ⊠ *Hotel Asma
Tower, Mavoor Rd.* ☎ *495/408–8000,
495/404–1222* ⊕ *www.asmabusinessho-
tel.com/facilities#restaurant.*

Paragon

$$ | INDIAN | It's not much to look at,
and it can get noisy when crowded, but
this Calicut stalwart has been serving
tasty food since 1939. The chicken and
the prawn biryanis are both excellent
(come early for these), as is the prawn
thattukada, an unusual fried shrimp dish
that goes well with parathas (a flaky flat-
bread); other favorites include the prawn
pepper fry and tamarind fish curry. **Known
for**: open until midnight; tamarind fish
curry; prawn thattukada. $ *Average main:
Rs. 320* ⊠ *Kannur Rd.* ☎ *495/276–1020,
495/276–7020* ⊕ *www.paragonrestau-
rant.net.*

Zain's Hotel Restaurant

$ | SOUTH INDIAN | This brightly painted
former house near the beach, featuring

plastic chairs and tables laid out both indoors and outdoors for a no-fuss dining experience, is one of Calicut's most popular restaurants for authentic Moplah (Kerala Muslim) dishes. The owner-chef, Zainabi Noor Mohammed, not only prepares dishes using family recipes passed down through the generations, but he also creates innovative fusion dishes like mussel pie. **Known for:** biryani; unnakkaya (a sweet, banana- and coconut-based snack); different types of pathiri (North Kerala stuffed flatbreads). [$] *Average main: Rs. 150* ✉ *Convent crossroads, behind Beach Fire Station* ☎ *495/236–6311.*

Hotels

The Gateway Hotel, Calicut
$$$ | **HOTEL** | Calicut's premier hotel is frequented by airline crews and wealthy Omanis, who come for lengthy treatments at the well-regarded ayurvedic center. **Pros:** great pool; well-regarded ayurvedic spa; walking distance to Calicut beach. **Cons:** not much in the way of grounds; older property, in need of an upgrade; not as well maintained as other Taj properties. [$] *Rooms from: Rs. 7000* ✉ *P.T. Usha Rd.* ☎ *495/661–3000* 🌐 *gateway.tajhotels.com/en-in* 🛏 *74 rooms* 🍴 *Free Breakfast.*

The Raviz Resort and Spa, Kadavu
$$$ | **RESORT** | One of the first swank, world-class riverside and backwater resorts in the Calicut area (though a fair drive outside of town), Kadavu signaled Malabar's foray into tourism. **Pros:** stunning river views; good value; built in traditional Nallukettu architectural style. **Cons:** Calicut is 26 km (16 miles) away; hotel in need of maintenance; not all rooms offer views. [$] *Rooms from: Rs. 7000* ✉ *Kozhikode Bypass Rd., Azhinjilam P.O., Ferokh* ☎ *495/241–1111, 483/283–0027* 🌐 *www.theraviz.com* 🛏 *117 rooms* 🍴 *Free Breakfast.*

Westway Hotel
$$ | **HOTEL** | Attracting business clientele, this modern red-stone business hotel has a pleasant lobby with slim wooden pillars encircling it, and there's a beautiful terra-cotta-tile atrium with a traditional brass lamp. **Pros:** rooftop pool with nice city views; midsize rooms are comfortably furnished; great value and centrally located. **Cons:** a little noisy; no safes in rooms; an ordinary hotel with no local style. [$] *Rooms from: Rs. 5300* ✉ *Kannur Rd.* ☎ *495/276–8888* 🌐 *www.westwayhotel.com* 🛏 *63 rooms* 🍴 *Free Breakfast.*

Kannur

92 km (57 miles) northwest of Calicut.

The Kannur district is the heartland of the Moppilahs (Kerala's Muslim community). It's also a center for the hand-loom industry as well as the manufacture of *beedis,* potent hand-rolled cigarettes made from tobacco sweepings. The town itself was for many years at the center of the maritime spice trade. The ruling Kolathiri rajas profited from the spice trade as did the European colonists. Today Kannur is a good hub for visiting several coastal sights—to the north and the south—including forts and undeveloped beaches.

GETTING HERE AND AROUND

You can reach Kannur by road from Calicut in about two hours (93 km, 58 miles), either by bus or by a hired car. The Jan Statabdi and the Ernakulam–Kannur Intercity Express trains both go to Kannur, including from Kochi (a 5½-hour trip) or from Calicut (two hours or less). The sights around Kannur are all fairly far out of town, and your best option is to hire a car.

Theyyam

A haunting regional draw is a spectacular dance and tribal form of worship called Theyyam. It is thought to predate Hinduism in Kerala. Theyyams aren't usually held in traditional temples but rather in small shrines or family compounds. Dancers don elaborate costumes and terrifying makeup for the ritual dance, during which it's believed they become possessed by the spirit of the deity they represent, allowing them to perform such feats as dancing with a 30-foot headdress, a flaming costume, or falling into a pile of burning embers. The ritual can be accompanied by intense drumming, howling, and chanting. Theyyam season is from November to May.

■ TIP➔ You may want to avoid these if you're traveling with small children, especially the nighttime ones. You can ask around about the intensity of specific Theyyams.

Sights

The Kanhirode Weaver's Co-operative P&S Society Ltd.

FACTORY | The Kanhirode Weaving Cooperative is strewn with yarns of all colors, set out to dry after dyeing. You can watch the weavers at their giant, clackety-clacking looms, making bedsheets and upholstery for export as well as brightly colored saris. Cloth is available for purchase. ⊠ Off Kannur–Mysore Rd., 13 km (8 miles) east of Kannur ☎ 497/285–7865, 497/285–7259 ⊕ www.weaveco.com ⊠ Free ⊗ Closed Sun.

Sree Muthappan Temple

RELIGIOUS SITE | This unusual temple, one of the largest shrines of its type, sits on the bank of the Valapattanam River at Parassinikkadavu, 18 km (11 miles) from Kannur. It's devoted not to a Vedic god, but to Sree Muthappan, a folk deity of the Thiya community. One school of Hindu thought claims that he is a combined manifestation of both Shiva and Vishnu, another believes he is simply another avatar of Shiva in the form of a tribal hunter. Several colorful legends about him exist. Worship does not take the form of paying homage to an idol but to enactment of the lord's life: the temple hosts such Theyyam performances almost every day of the year. Though it's not as colorful as traditional outdoor festivals, you can at least get a taste of this mystical local form of dance. Because Sree Muthappan is usually pictured with a hunting dog, there is a statue in honor of dogs on the premises; friendly mutts roam the sanctuary, and offerings at the shrine take the form of bronze dog figurines. The temple is also unusual for the fact that toddy (fermented palm sap) and fish are both offered to Sree Muthappan. Non-Hindus are allowed to enter the temple but must dress modestly—shoulders and knees should be covered and no footwear is allowed inside. ⊠ Off NH–17, 18 km (11 miles) north of Kannur, Parassinikkadavu ☎ 0497/278–0722 ⊠ Free.

St. Angelo Fort (Kannur Fort)

MILITARY SITE | In 1505 the Portuguese built St. Angelo Fort, with the consent of the ruling Kolathiri Raja, in order to protect their interests in the area. After passing into Dutch and then British hands, it's now maintained by the Archaeological Survey of India. There are still a few British cannons intact, and lovely views of the fishing activity in Moppillah Bay. ✉ *Off NH–17,, 3 km (2 miles) north of Kannur* ☎ *497/273–2578* 🌐 *www.keralatourism.org/destination/st-angelo-fort-kannur/83* 🎟 *Free.*

Hotels

Ayisha Manzil

$$$$ | **B&B/INN** | A stay in this 1862 cliff-top spice-estate home may be the best way to experience what North Kerala is all about—people come for the gorgeous sea views and the food, whipped up by TV host and chef Faiza Moosa, who's famous for her traditional Mopla (Kerala Muslim) dishes. **Pros:** taxes, great meals, and nonalcoholic drinks are all included in rates; great views; palatial rooms with antique furnishings. **Cons:** expensive; need to book in advance; only beer available. [$] *Rooms from: Rs. 19250* ✉ *Court Rd., Thalassery* ☎ *490/234–1590, 984/700–2340* 🌐 *www.ayishamanzil.com* 🕒 *Closed Apr.–July* 🛏 *7 rooms* 🍴 *All-inclusive.*

Chapter 10

KOLKATA (CALCUTTA)

Updated by
Tania Bannerjee

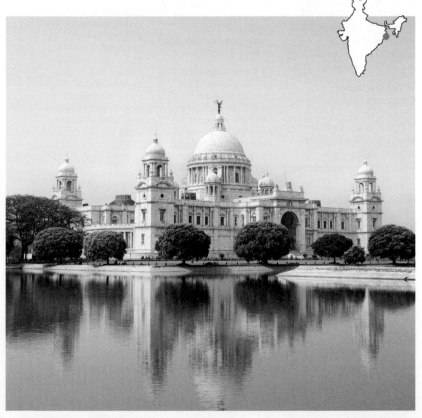

◉ Sights	🍴 Restaurants	🛏 Hotels	🛍 Shopping	🍸 Nightlife
★★★★☆	★★★★☆	★★★☆☆	★★★★☆	★★★☆☆

WELCOME TO KOLKATA (CALCUTTA)

TOP REASONS TO GO

★ **Eclectic Architecture:** The city is packed with gorgeous temples, mosques, universities, and colonial mansions and monuments.

★ **Walking City:** Kolkata is best seen on foot: stroll along the river promenade, walk across the Howrah Bridge, explore the bazaars, or wander around the sprawling Maidan park.

★ **Cultural Capital:** Catch an Indian classical music concert; watch a locally produced play; go gallery-hopping or head to the Indian Museum, considered one of the country's best.

★ **Foodie's Paradise:** Kolkatans are obsessive about their food. A visit to a traditional sweetshop is an absolute must, as is sampling the city's famous fish or Indo-Chinese dishes, created a century ago by Chinese immigrants.

★ **Book Bargains:** Kolkata's winter book fair is one of the biggest in the world, and year-round you can trust the stalls of College Street to surprise you with rare and cheap finds.

On the eastern bank of the Hooghly River, Kolkata is the commercial hub of northeastern India.

1 North Kolkata. The oldest part of the city is filled with the crumbling mansions of the former gentry, narrow streets and quiet alleys, grand university campuses, and heated social and political debates at street corners over cups of tea.

2 Central Kolkata. The bustling, congested downtown is anchored by B. B. D. Bagh, where business and government buildings are concentrated. Many of the city's finest shops and restaurants line Park Street.

3 The Maidan. This mammoth park is not only a good place to see sheep grazing and Kolkatans at play, it's also where you'll see some of India's finest colonial buildings, including the Victoria Memorial. Take a ride in an old tramcar, a service that has been in operation since 1902.

4 South Kolkata. This neighborhood has two distinct identities. On one hand, it has the noisiest streets, with vibrant shopping in crowded kiosks. But it's also a leafy world of elegant homes, restaurants, and exclusive clubs.

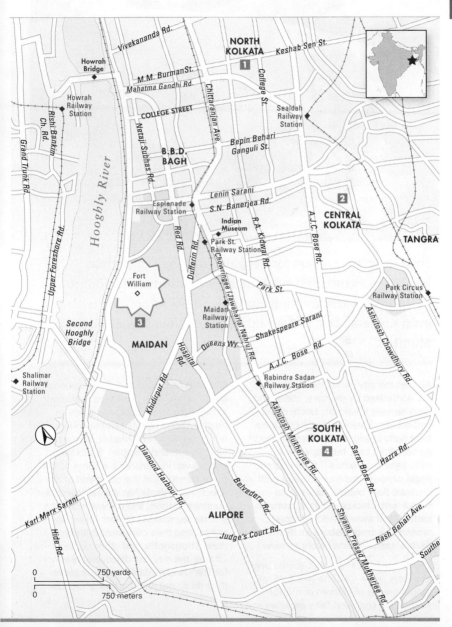

EATING WELL IN KOLKATA

A classic Calcutta (kati) roll

Food is a great passion for Bengalis, and they go to great lengths to ensure that every meal's a celebration. In addition to the great variety, eating out is also quite affordable, with even Kolkata's best restaurants cheaper than those in Delhi or Mumbai.

All over the city its narrow sidewalks are dominated by shanties, stalls, and carts serving breakfast, lunch, dinner, and snacks. Steaming-hot *luchi* (deep-fried puffy bread made of refined flour), curries, fried fish, fritters, samosas, rolls, kebabs, *momos* (Tibetan dumplings), chicken and mutton stew with unsliced flour bread, *chapatis* (flat bread) with chickpea curries, pastries, patties, and sweets—some streets resemble a smorgasbord for all the flavors, textures, and colors on view.

The street-food snack that scores over all others is the Calcutta (aka *kati*) roll, tender pieces of chicken or mutton wrapped in crisp and flaky *parathas* and served with onions and the occasional green chili. Calcutta rolls are available at most roadside stalls, and every neighborhood has its favorite source, but Nizam's in New Market; Kusum in Park Street; and Campari, Bedouwin, and Nawab in Gariahat are some of the more famous. On the other end of the spectrum, Kolkata has always loved its continental food, and colonial-era clubs and restaurants along Park Street are still putting their own spin on thermidors, Stroganoffs, and other classics. Of late, the city has discovered a yen for French-style cafés and patisseries— they do a neat job of artisanal breads, quiches, pies, *choux* pastries, cookies, and cupcakes.

BIRYANI

This flavorful dish of rice with meat and chicken in a rich gravy, with its roots in the Nawabi cuisine of Lucknow, takes many forms—one popular option is to get biryani with *chaap* or *champ*—marinated chicken or mutton slow cooked in large, thick pans. Specialty restaurants serving their own takes on the dish are in every neighborhood, but make sure you try it at a place that's popular, with lots of turnover. Shiraz, Rahmania, and Arsalan, with many branches throughout the city, are some of the more established options. Oudh 1590, in Deshpariya Park, near Gariahat, serves Nawabi cuisine in an upscale setting.

FISH

A much-loved and festive special is the *hilsa,* also called *ilish,* a delicate fish from the herring family that's found in fresh, salty, and brackish waters. Supplies have become limited, thanks in part to massive demand for its roe. Another favorite dish is the prawn *malai* curry, made with coconut milk, and its many variations, including one served in the shell of a tender (green) coconut. A common Bengali way of cooking fish is in mustard oil and in a mustard

Begali sweets

paste, making it quite pungent. Most sophisticated restaurants are mindful about toning down the flavors to appeal to foreign palates.

BEGALI SWEETS

The mind-boggling array of sweets sold at every corner shop attests to their importance in the Bengali diet. No trip to Kolkata can be complete without tasting the two things that the city could stake a copyright on. *Mishti doi,* or *mitha dahi,* is delicately sweetened yogurt; and *rashogolla* (*rasgulla*) are sugary, syrupy, spongy balls of soft curd cheese.

INDO-CHINESE FLAVORS

Kolkata is proud of its Chinese legacy and the community settled there is responsible for the hybrid cuisine served at most "Chinese" restaurants. The staples at are chili chicken, chow-mein-like *hakka* noodles, and mixed fried rice, all made with generous helpings of green chilies. The more authentic eateries in Tangra, Kolkata's Chinatown, serve chimney soup and pork dishes cooked in a unique style.

(top left) A classic Calcutta (kati) roll; (top right) a plate of Bengali sweets including rasgulla; (bottom right) samosas are favorite street-food snacks

Samosas are favorite street-food snacks

10

Kolkata (Calcutta) EATING WELL IN KOLKATA

Laid-back and vibrant, complacent and ambitious, politically charged but curiously indifferent, this is a city that contradicts itself at every turn of its famously winding alleys. A day in the life of Kolkata is India in all its colors, sound, chaos, and creativity—just one of the many reasons why a trip to the city is so essential.

Kolkata has been home to three Nobel laureates—the authors and intellectuals Rabindranath Tagore and Amartya Sen, and Mother Teresa—as well as the world-famous director Satyajit Ray, and many other notable authors, filmmakers, musicians, actors, scientists, reformers, freedom fighters, and famous athletes. In its three centuries of existence, it has been a jewel in the crown of the British Empire, a muse for many artists, the heart of India's freedom movement, and a symbol of everything that was wrong with colonialism and politics of divisiveness. It is a home of the homeless, who sleep on the pavements at night, and some of India's richest, living in restored heritage mansions and condos in skyscrapers. Although the name was officially changed from Calcutta to Kolkata in 2001, both names are used more or less interchangeably.

In 1690, Job Charnock, an agent for the British East India Company, leased the villages of Sutanati, Gobindpur, and Kalikutta and formed a trading post to supply his firm. Legend has it that Charnock had won the hearts of Bengalis when he married a local widow, thus saving her from *suttee* (the custom that called for a widow to throw herself on her husband's funeral pyre). (Recent research has suggested that the story of Charnock founding Calcutta is more lore than fact, and that the city existed in some form before the British East India Company agent arrived here in 1690.) Through Charnock's venture, the British gained a foothold in what had been the Sultanate of Delhi under the Moghuls, and the directors of the East India Company became Indian *zamindars* (landowners) for the first time. It was here, as traders and landowners, that British entrepreneurs and adventurers began what would amount to the conquest of India and the establishment of the British Raj. More than any other city in India, including New Delhi, Kolkata is tied to the evolution and the British presence. Having embraced 19th-century European humanism, such Bengalis as the poet Rabindranath Tagore and others revived their indigenous culture and made the first organized efforts to oust the British. Emotions here ran high early on, and agitation in Bengal broke away from what would later be called Gandhian politics to choose terrorism—one reason the British moved their capital from Calcutta to Delhi in 1911.

Amazing Festivals

The grandest Bengali festival of the year is the Durga Puja (Durga is an incarnation of Kali, Kolkata's patron goddess). The *pujas* (homage; literally, "worship") take place over several days in September or October. Thousands of devotees and revelers take to the streets, visiting different venues through the day and night. Food stalls, fairs, and live music stages come up in every corner. Colorful, sometimes handmade idols of Durga, sometimes more than 20 feet tall, are moved in large processions through the streets for several hours before reaching the river and being immersed there. The rites and processions blend tradition with innovation; themes at the puja venues are varied—war, tsunamis, film stars, and the White House and Obama have been faithfully re-created with local clay and other materials, lights, and sound effects.

Calcutta remained cosmopolitan and prosperous throughout the British period. But after Independence and Partition, in 1947, trouble began when the world's center of jute processing and distribution (Calcutta) was politically separated from its actual production center (the eastern Bengali hinterland). For Calcutta and the new East Pakistan, Partition was equivalent to separating the fingers of an industry from the thumb. Natural disasters—commonly cyclones and droughts, but also, as in 1937, earthquakes—had long sent millions from East Bengal (which later became East Pakistan) to Calcutta in search of shelter and sustenance; after Partition, a wave of 4 million political refugees from East Pakistan compounded and complicated the pressure. Conflict with China and Pakistan created millions more throughout the 1960s, and Pakistan's 1971 military crackdown alone sent 10 million temporary refugees into the city from what would soon become Bangladesh. By the mid-1970s, Calcutta was widely seen as the ultimate urban disaster. Riddled with disease and squalor, plagued by garbage and decay, the former heart of the British Raj, the "Paris of Asia," had quickly and dramatically collapsed.

However, the city kept on growing, and these days, greater Kolkata's entire metropolitan district covers more than 426 square km (264 square miles) and has more than 12 million people. It now has two municipal corporation areas (Kolkata and the near suburb of Howrah), 32 municipalities, 62 nonmunicipal urban centers, and more than 500 villages.

The tenure of the Marxist government in Bengal, which lasted for more than 30 years, from 1977 to 2011, pushed the state to the margins of contemporary India's power and economic structure. Many of its people had resigned themselves to being treated as second-class citizens, wistfully and passionately holding on to the city's glorious past. The government did try to infuse some life into the state's economy by inviting big-scale and IT industries to the state. But it also suffered serious backlashes in the form of violent clashes with the farmers, whose land the government had acquired for new industrial hubs. The change of regime to that of the All India Trinamool Congress, marked by the election of Mamata Banerjee to the position of chief minister of West Bengal in 2011, has brought a certain vigor and enthusiasm to the city. Buildings have received fresh coats of paint, and malls, IT hubs, restaurants, and small businesses seem invigorated. After a few unpardonable instances of violence against women, policing has been stepped up in certain areas, and the government is keen to put its best face forward.

Traffic policing may even be better than Mumbai and Delhi (motorists actually stop where they are supposed to at most signals) and police officers are able to fine errant motorists on the spot. Traffic signals in town play the music of Tagore, and some effort has been made to beautify the city, with varying results. In fact, some recent travelers have observed that in some ways Kolkata is cleaner, prettier, and less shabby than Mumbai, despite still being often used as the ultimate symbol of human strife. History may not always have been kind to the city, but Kolkata remains warm, rooted, thoughtful, and remarkably earnest.

Kolkata and Howrah (also written as Haora) straddle the Hooghly River, with Kolkata on the east side, and Howrah on the west. Across the Hooghly from Kolkata's old quarter, the Howrah district—which holds Kolkata's massive train station—is a constantly expanding suburb. On the eastern side of town is Salt Lake City, a planned, upscale residential community.

In Kolkata itself, the Howrah Bridge spills into Burra Bazaar, the vibrant wholesale-market area that anchors the city's commerce. North Kolkata includes Burra Bazaar and Kolkata University and extends to the distant neighborhood of Chitpur and the Jain Temple in Tala. The heart of Central Kolkata remains B. B. D. Bagh (Binoy Badal Dinesh Bagh, formerly Dalhousie Square), where commerce and government have been concentrated since British times. Central Kolkata also holds the expansive Maidan park, the crowded bazaar at New Market, and the upmarket shops and restaurants on Park Street. At the south end of the Maidan are the Victoria Memorial and Kolkata's racecourse. South Kolkata has the Kali

Temple and the late Mother Teresa's hospice in Kalighat and the National Library and zoo in Alipore, a posh residential community. To the east of the city is the Eastern Metropolitan Bypass (known simply as "the bypass"), which links south Kolkata to the north. The expanding city now stretches well beyond the bypass, which is now lined with five-star hotels, exclusive condominiums, malls, and parks that overlook vast stretches of agricultural lands and fisheries. The Chinese settlement in Tangra, famed for its Indo-Chinese cuisine, is a popular dining destination.

NIGHTLIFE

After a spell of gloom, the nightlife scene has been looking up, largely due to the city's deathless love for music, theater, and food. Venues in Park Street, Ballygunge, and even the satellite city of Salt Lake host local bands with a loyal following. They perform until midnight, which is late by the city's (and most of India's) standards.

During Durga Puja, the city remains up all night. Lounges, sheesha (hookah) bars, and discos all draw well-heeled young entrepreneurs, fashion designers, models, and professionals. Cabs run late into the night and are usually considered safe. Be cautious while traveling on your own, however, especially late at night.

Park Street boasts the most popular bars and lounges, most of them situated in hotels, except the local favorite Olympia, aka Oly Pub (unbelievably cheap drinks and service that follows a sort of secret code; waiters may refuse to serve you if you don't play by their rules). However, there are several new places all around town where you can have a drink too many, provided you have something to munch on as well.

Kolkata's clubs are technically open only to members and hotel guests, but you can get in for either a cover charge or a smile, depending on the doorman. All clubs retain good DJs for a mixture of Indian pop and Western dance music.

PERFORMING ARTS

Kolkata takes as much pride and interest in its vibrant, artistic present as it does its glorious past. Concerts, exhibitions, plays, book fairs, and literary and cultural festivals are held throughout the year. To find out what is happening, check ⊕ *bookmyshow.com*, ⊕ *timescity.com*, ⊕ *zomato.com*, ⊕ *10times.com*, ⊕ *exp-locity.com*, and similar websites.

The latest Bollywood, Hollywood, and Bengali films are shown at all the multiplexes in town, which are often inside malls. Check ⊕ *bookmyshow.com* for tickets and show times; local English-language newspapers all carry listings, too.

Many auditoriums host regular performances of music, dance, and theater—the most Bengali of the performing arts.

SHOPPING

Shopping in Kolkata bazaars is an adventure, and a test of your ability to shake off touts. In general, most shops are open six days a week and closed Sunday. Hours tend to be 10:30–8.

Kolkata has never been the place for trendy shopping, so you may want to concentrate on getting hand-loomed cloth, handicrafts, and artistic jute and metal gifts, most of which will cost you next to nothing. Things to look out for include long-necked terra-cotta Bankura horses, *dokra* metalwork, and Bengal saris, made in crisp cottons and luscious silks. And many galleries sell very affordable art.

ACTIVITIES

Kolkata still puts class first when it comes to sports, with the result that you need to be a member's guest to enter the golf and racing clubs. But if you'd like to just see a little cricket, head to the Maidan: on nice days it can sometimes seem like one big cricket pitch.

Planning

MAKING THE MOST OF YOUR TIME

You can see most of Kolkata's major sights comfortably in three days. Morning is a good time to hit the Maidan park and see Kolkatans playing sports and enjoying the outdoors before the afternoon sun forces them inside. The Victoria Memorial across from the park is a good place to escape the heat; its art exhibitions are fabulous. Take a tram ride around the Maidan to get a feel for how people once commonly traveled; some still do. It is slow, but delightful. Visit the Indian Museum and then hang around the art galleries and auditoriums in the vicinity, where plays and concerts are held throughout the year. Later, shop at New Market, and then join the locals for dinner, drinks, and dancing at the restaurants and hotel nightclubs on and around Park Street. Or take a leisurely boat ride down the Hooghly to catch the sunset and watch the two gorgeous bridges here light up.

The next day, visit College Street and walk around the university area and the secondhand bookstalls. From College Street, you can walk to Nakhoda Mosque, the Marble Palace, and the Rabindra Bharati University Museum, filled with Bengal-school paintings and Rabindranath Tagore memorabilia. For a dose of Jain culture, take a cab to the Pareshnath Temple. Continue on to Kumartuli to see artists create clay icons by the river. Another cab ride will take you to the Belur Math Shrine, then cross back to the Dakshineshwar Kali Temple.

If you have still have time in town, you can taxi down to Nirmal Hriday to visit the late Mother Teresa's first charitable home. And finally, hit South Kolkata's shopping hub, Gariahat, for handicrafts, saris, and art galleries (and lots of noise). End your time here at one of the many restaurants serving traditional and fusion Bengali cuisine.

Rickshaw Pullers

Kolkata is the last city on earth to use enormous Chinese-style rickshaws pulled by men on foot. The rickshaws were introduced in the 19th century by Chinese traders, and the British made it a legal form of transportation in 1919. Kolkata has about 6,000 licensed rickshaw operators, but at least as many operate without licenses. In 2005, the Communist government of West Bengal—concerned about its image as it positioned Kolkata as a technology hub—placed a ban on the human-powered vehicles. Government officials called the hand-pulled rickshaws "barbaric" and "inhuman"

and vowed not to renew operators' licenses. But the rickshaw-puller union continues to fight the ban, saying the hand-drawn rickshaws are a symbol of the old city. Though cycle-rickshaws have taken over in most areas, you may still find the hand-drawn ones operating in some parts of town. Recently Kolkata's mayor announced that the new government is keen to issue photo IDs to the licensed rickshaw pullers, most of whom are from the neighboring, impoverished states of Bihar and Jharkhand.

WHEN TO GO

Low Season: The hottest weather arrives in April and grows increasingly stifling through June, when the monsoon season begins. This runs through mid-September and cools Kolkata down, though the occasional downpour means you can expect a soaking or two.

Shoulder Season: After the monsoon, it's festival time. The biggest of all festivals is the Durga Puja, which takes place over two weeks in September or October. All of West Bengal virtually shuts down for four days; getting around may be difficult.

High Season: Around December the mild winter sets in and lasts until March. This is the best time to visit, but as a result making advance reservations for hotels, trains, and airplanes is essential. The annual book fair and several open-air, all-night music concerts featuring classical, jazz, and rock musicians enliven this time. If you visit around Christmas, you're likely to see such tangible signs of the season as Christmas lights and fruitcake-like desserts. The town of Shantiniketan

has its major festival, the Poush Mela, around the same time.

GETTING HERE AND AROUND
AIR TRAVEL

All international and domestic airlines use Netaji Subhash Chandra Bose International Airport, colloquially called Dum Dum Airport, 15 km (9 miles) north of the city. The terminal has prepaid taxi services; a ride downtown takes about 30 minutes and costs around Rs. 400. You can also book online with some of the fleet operators for an airport pickup or drop-off. Air-conditioned Volvo buses also service the airport from various parts of the city; these cost Rs. 40 or more. Bus service runs from 8:30 am to 9:30 pm.

AIRLINES AND CONTACTS Jet Airways ✉ *18/D Stephen Court Bldg., Park St., ground fl., Kolkata* ☎ *033/3989–3333* ⊕ *www.jetairways.com.*

AIRPORT Netaji Subhash Chandra Bose International Airport (*Dum Dum Airport; CCU*) ✉ *Jessore Rd., Dum Dum, Kolkata* ☎ *033/2511–8036* ⊕ *www.aai.aero/en/airports/kolkata* Ⓜ *Dumdum.*

BUS TRAVEL

Buses are slow, creaking, and unbearably crowded during rush hours. They will cost you next to nothing but will set you back in terms of time and comfort. The new air-conditioned buses are better. However, you should avoid them if you have a lot of luggage.

HAND-DRAWN AND CYCLE-RICKSHAW TRAVEL

Kolkata is the only city in the world to still have hand-pulled rickshaws: they're an efficient form of transportation for short distances. However, being carried around by a poor, barefooted man may be unsettling for some. Rickshaw fares fluctuate depending on the distance and the amount of traffic; negotiate ahead of time, using Rs. 20 per 10 minutes as a guide. Cycle-rickshaws, which are ubiquitous, offer a more comfortable ride for a similar price.

METRO TRAVEL

Kolkata's efficient metro system connects the airport with Garia, a South Kolkata locality that's the southernmost stop on the route. Tickets cost Rs. 5 for a 5-km (3-mile) ride and are available from machines and windows in every station. New routes have been added, with elevated lines joining the far-flung neighborhood of the expanding city to the airport and business district. Check ⊕ *www. kmrc.in* for the latest changes.

TAXI AND AUTO-RICKSHAW TRAVEL

The base fare for Kolkata taxis is Rs. 25, and then Rs. 12 for every kilometer. However, check with your hotel to confirm, because fares frequently change. If a driver refuses to turn the meter on, find another taxi. Traffic, unfortunately, plagues Kolkata, and it might bring your cab to a full stop amid humid air and diesel exhaust, so at rush hour you may just want to find a sweetshop and wait until it's over. Or better still, if your destination is along the metro's route, give the subway a try. A word of caution though—the office-hour crowd along the busy routes can be daunting even for those used to the rush-hour subway crush in places like New York.

Auto-rickshaws are cheaper (and sometimes dirtier) than taxis, but they're not as easy to find in the city center. Still, at rush hour they can be more efficient than taxis, which are more likely to get stuck in traffic.

The three-wheel auto-rickshaws used in Kolkata are often operated by unlicensed drivers and work much like buses, picking up passengers along fixed routes. Many taxi drivers are unfamiliar with the roads, so expect frequent stops for directions. Adding to the confusion is the haphazard way in which many streets have been renamed. Use your smartphone if possible to get around.

TRAIN TRAVEL

Howrah Junction, which sees tremendous amounts of train traffic every day, is divided into the neighboring Old and New Howrah stations. The main reservation office has a foreign-tourist section upstairs, open daily 9 am–1 pm and 1:30 pm–4 pm; you can buy tickets here with either foreign currency or a valid encashment certificate for rupees, so if you obtained your rupees from an ATM, go to the normal lines. There are also ticket offices on the first floor of Old Howrah Station, the second floor of New Howrah Station, and in Kalighat. Sealdah Station is used exclusively by trains to and from northern destinations such as Darjeeling. Tickets are sold on the platform level.

Getting to Central Kolkata by taxi from here takes 20 to 40 minutes, depending on traffic. Once you get downtown, it's usually best to hire a car and driver, which you can do from the travel agencies and rental agencies. Expect to pay Rs. 1,000 for eight hours and 70 km (50 miles), with an hourly and per-kilometer rate beyond that. Hailing a plain old taxi can be cheaper. Take a cab to or from the area you're visiting, then walk or find a sturdy cycle-rickshaw.

TRAIN INFORMATION Howrah Railway Junction ✉ *1 block south of west end of Howrah Bridge, Lower Foreshore Rd., Howrah* ☎ *033/2638–2581* ⊕ *www.irctc.co.in* ✉ *6 Fairlie Pl., North Kolkata* ☎ *033/2220–6811* ⊕ *www.irctc.co.in.* **Sealdah Station** ✉ *Bipin Behari Ganguly St., North Kolkata* ☎ *033/2350–3535* ⊕ *www.irctc.co.in.*

RESTAURANTS

Kolkata has experienced a growth in its vibrant restaurant culture since the mid-1990s. Restaurants here cater to a varied sensibility: Asian, Mexican, Italian, and, of course, Bengali and other Indian cuisines. The service is largely friendly, and many places are crowded enough, especially on weekends, to warrant reservations. Eating out in Kolkata is cheaper compared to cities like Delhi and Mumbai—and every bit as good in terms of quality. Restaurants are generally open daily 12:30 to 3 for lunch and 7:30 to 11 for dinner.

HOTELS

Kolkata has seen the launch of several top-end five-star hotels and establishments over the years, besides medium and budget options mainly for business travelers.

Unless otherwise noted, hotels have air-conditioning, room TVs, and do not include meals in the room price. Better hotels have currency exchange facilities, and most have rooms with bathrooms that have tubs. Some luxury hotels have exclusive floors with special privileges or facilities for the business traveler. *Hotel reviews have been shortened. For full information, visit Fodors.com.*

What It Costs

	$	$$	$$$	$$$$
RESTAURANTS				
	under Rs. 500	Rs. 500–Rs. 1,000	Rs. 1,001–Rs. 1,400	over Rs. 1,400
HOTELS				
	under Rs. 6,000	Rs. 6,000–Rs. 9,000	Rs. 9,001–Rs. 13,000	over Rs. 13,000

EMERGENCIES

GENERAL EMERGENCIES Fire ☎ *101* ⊕ *wb.gov.in/portal/web/guest/fire-and-emergency-services.* **Police** ☎ *100* ⊕ *www.kolkatapolice.gov.in.*

MEDICAL CARE Belle Vue Clinic ✉ *9 Dr. U.N. Brahmachari St., South Kolkata* ☎ *033/2287–2321* ⊕ *www.bellevueclinic.com.*

VISITOR INFORMATION

The West Bengal Tourist Office is open Monday through Saturday 10 to 5. The regional Government of India Tourist Office is well equipped to help baffled travelers; it's open Monday–Saturday 9–6. The Kolkata Information Centre is also helpful. The West Bengal Tourist Office is in the heart of Kolkata's business hub, but people here will only be able to give you information about destinations within the state. The Government of India Tourist Office, near the city center, gives more of an overall picture (including the state). The staff is friendly to boot.

CONSULATE U.S. Consulate ✉ *5/1 Ho Chi Minh Sarani, Central Kolkata* ☎ *033/3984–2400* ⊕ *in.usembassy.gov.*

TOURIST OFFICES Government of India Tourist Office ✉ *4 Shakespeare Sarani, Central Kolkata* ⊕ *Opposite AC Market* ☎ *033/2282–7731.* **Kolkata Information Centre** ✉ *1/1 A.J.C Bose Rd., South Kolkata* ⊕ *Near Maidan Police Station* ☎ *033/2223–2451* Ⓜ *Rabindra Sadan.*

West Bengal Tourist Office ✉ *3/2 B. B. D. Bagh, Central Kolkata* ☎ *033/2243–6440* ⊕ *www.wbtourism.gov.in.*

TOURS

These agencies can arrange a car and driver for local sightseeing or help make long-distance travel arrangements.

CONTACTS Ashok Travel and Tours (ITDC) ✉ *Everest Bldg., 46 C Jawaharlal Nehru Rd., Central Kolkata* ☎ *033/2288–0901* ⊕ *attindiatourism.com.* **Mercury Travels Ltd.** ✉ *Everest House, 46C Chowringhee Rd., Central Kolkata* ☎ *033/4057–8402* ⊕ *www.mercurytravels.co.in.* **Thomas Cook India Ltd.** ✉ *B. B. D. Bagh, Dalhousie, 2 Kiran Shankar Ray Rd., Shop No. 8, Central Kolkata* ☎ *033/2262–7756* ⊕ *www.thomascook.in.*

TELEPHONE NUMBERS

Phone numbers change with alarming frequency in Kolkata. Whenever you make a call and get a recorded message saying, "This telephone number does not exist," dial 1951 or 1952 or 197 to find out the new number. There are computerized as well as manual services.

North Kolkata

The streets in northern Kolkata are more crowded and narrower than those elsewhere in the city. This is where hand-pulled rickshaws still run along winding, skinny alleys, and old mansions seem to brood over the past. This—the old village of Sutanuti—is also where the Indians lived while the British spread their estates east and south of Fort William and Dalhousie Square (B. B. D. Bagh). The architecture reflects Italian and Dutch influences.

North Kolkata's attractions are somewhat scattered. You'll need to take taxis at least sporadically. The bazaar areas surrounding Mahatma Gandhi Road, universally known as M. G. Road, are at once intensely commercial and residential; tourists are only occasional, despite the fascinating sights and vibe. You may

attract some curious stares, but anyone you stop and speak to is bound to be friendly and welcoming.

⊙ Sights

Belur Math Shrine

RELIGIOUS SITE | This is the headquarters of the Ramakrishna Mission, a reform movement inspired by the mystic Ramakrishna Paramahansa, who died in 1886. Having forsaken his privileged Brahmin heritage, Ramakrishna preached the unity of religious faiths and an adherence to altruistic values for all people. His disciple, Swami Vivekananda, established the mission in 1898. The serene Belur Math Shrine, on the banks of the Hooghly, resembles a church, a temple, or a mosque, depending on where you're standing. Somber *aarti* (chants and hymns) are sung in the immense prayer hall every evening; visitors are more than welcome. Simple vegetarian meals, offered at the shrine, are then served to visitors who make a nominal donation. ✉ *Belur Rd., Howrah, Kolkata* ☎ *033/2654–1144* ⊕ *www.belurmath.org* 💲 *Free.*

College Street

NEIGHBORHOOD | FAMILY | This erudite destination smells of old books and history. This was the hotbed of the Bengal Renaissance movement, and it eventually became a symbol of revolutionary ideals and radical youth movements. Several walking tours are available around the elite Presidency College University, Kolkata University, Sanskrit College, Baptist Mission, Theosophical Society, and Hindu School. The pavements are dominated by bookstalls that are treasure troves for those with the inclination and time to discover a rare (and usually quite inexpensive) title. At Indian Coffee House, at 15 Bankim Chatterjee Street, you can grab a quick bite over a leisurely cup of coffee and get a whiff of the languid airs of the historic neighborhood. ✉ *North Kolkata* 💲 *Free* ⊙ *Closed Sun.*

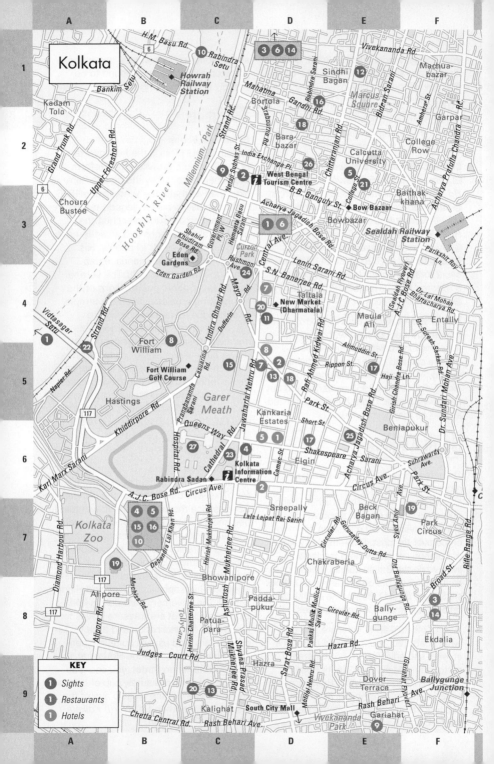

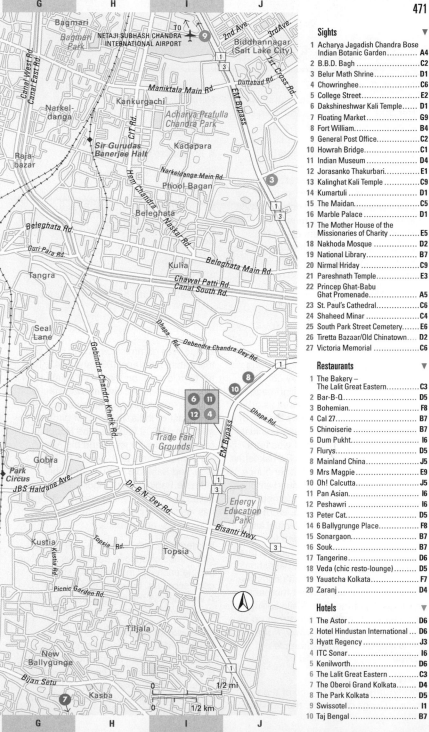

Sights ▼

1 Acharya Jagadish Chandra Bose
   Indian Botanic Garden............. A4
2 B.B.D. Bagh C2
3 Belur Math Shrine................. D1
4 Chowringhee....................... C6
5 College Street...................... E2
6 Dakshineshwar Kali Temple..... D1
7 Floating Market G9
8 Fort William........................ B4
9 General Post Office................. C2
10 Howrah Bridge..................... C1
11 Indian Museum D4
12 Jorasanko Thakurbari.............. E1
13 Kalinghat Kali Temple C9
14 Kumartuli D1
15 The Maidan......................... C5
16 Marble Palace D1
17 The Mother House of the
   Missionaries of Charity E5
18 Nakhoda Mosque D2
19 National Library.................... B7
20 Nirmal Hriday C9
21 Pareshnath Temple................ E3
22 Princep Ghat-Babu
   Ghat Promenade................... A5
23 St. Paul's Cathedral................ C6
24 Shaheed Minar C4
25 South Park Street Cemetery....... E6
26 Tiretta Bazaar/Old Chinatown.... D2
27 Victoria Memorial C6

Restaurants ▼

1 The Bakery –
   The Lalit Great Eastern............. C3
2 Bar-B-Q............................. D5
3 Bohemian........................... F8
4 Cal 27............................... B7
5 Chinoiserie B7
6 Dum Pukht.......................... I6
7 Flurys............................... D5
8 Mainland China.................... J5
9 Mrs Magpie E9
10 Oh! Calcutta....................... J5
11 Pan Asian........................... I6
12 Peshawri I6
13 Peter Cat........................... D5
14 6 Ballygrunge Place............... F8
15 Sonargaon.......................... B7
16 Souk................................ B7
17 Tangerine D6
18 Veda (chic resto-lounge)......... D5
19 Yauatcha Kolkata.................. F7
20 Zaranj D4

Hotels ▼

1 The Astor D6
2 Hotel Hindustan International ... D6
3 Hyatt Regency J3
4 ITC Sonar I6
5 Kenilworth.......................... D6
6 The Lalit Great Eastern C3
7 The Oberoi Grand Kolkata........ D4
8 The Park Kolkata D5
9 Swissotel I1
10 Taj Bengal B7

Calcutta to Kolkata

In 2001, Calcutta's name was officially changed to Kolkata. This transformation, like similar ones in India, was supposed to contribute to ridding the city of its colonial past. The two names are used interchangeably. Streets, too, have been renamed. Although some maps and street signs have only the new names, you're more likely to see just the old or both. Taxis and rickshaws use the names interchangeably, but old names are still favored, as most of the new names are ridiculously long and obscure. Here are a few of the most important name changes:

- Chowringhee Road/Jawaharlal Nehru (J. L. Nehru) Road

- Ballygunge Circular/Pramathesh Barua Sarani

- Bowbazar/B. B. Ganguly Street

- Harington Street/Ho Chi Minh Sarani

- Lansdowne Road/Sarat Bose Road

- Lower Circular Road/A. J. C. Bose Road

- Rippon Street/Muzaffar Ahmed Street

- Theatre Road/Shakespeare Sarani

Dakshineshwar Kali Temple

RELIGIOUS SITE | FAMILY | Far north along the Hooghly, this 19th-century complex with 13 temples is a major pilgrimage site for devotees of Kali, as well as other deities. The variety of temples makes this site a good introduction for the uninitiated to the Hindu pantheon. It was here that the 19th-century mystic Ramakrishna had the vision that led him to renounce his Brahmin caste and propound altruism and religious unity. His most famous disciple, Swami Vivekananda, went on to be a major force in the intellectual and spiritual growth of Kolkata, and founded the Ramakrishna Mission, headquartered in the Belur Math Shrine. Ramakrishna's room here is a museum. Don't miss the chance to spend some quiet moments on the banks of the river. Stalls selling local fast food line the busy street up to the temple. ⊠ *Dakshineshwar, Kolkata* ⊕ *www.dakshineswarkalitemple.org* ⊠ *Free.*

Howrah Bridge

BRIDGE/TUNNEL | FAMILY | One of the most enduring icons of the city, the Howrah Bridge was commissioned and built by the British between 1936 and 1943. The tall cantilevered bridge links Kolkata to Howrah and its bustling railway station, which serves as a gateway to the northeast of India. The web of girders stretches 1,500 feet over the Hooghly, crisscrossed with small and big fishing boats, ferries, and steamers. Now renamed Rabindra Setu, after Nobel laureate Rabindranath Tagore, who hailed from the city, the Howrah Bridge has fascinated poets, painters, writers, filmmakers, and tourists.

Bordered by thin walkways, the bridge's eight lanes of chaotic traffic bear 2 million people each day in buses, rickshaws, cars, scooters, bicycles, and pushcarts. A walk across the bridge provides terrific people-watching. ⊠ *Howrah* ⊠ *Free.*

★ Jorasanko Thakurbari

HOUSE | FAMILY | Rabindranath Tagore's sprawling and well-maintained mansion is a pilgrimage site for his fans and followers. A poet, philosopher, and Renaissance man, Tagore won the Nobel Prize for Literature in 1913. The nerve center of Calcutta's intellectual activity around the turn of the 20th century, Tagore's abode now holds memorabilia, including beautiful sepia photographs of the poet, his family, and his contemporaries. ✉ *Ganesh Talkies, 267, Rabindra Sarani, Jorasanko, North Kolkata* ☎ *033/2218–1744* ◷ *Closed Mon.*

★ **Kumartuli**

NEIGHBORHOOD | **FAMILY** | Home to hundreds of clay artists, this neighborhood is the most famous producer of idols of popular deities in the Hindu pantheon. The skilled craftsmen are especially in demand during the immense Durga Puja, which is usually held in the autumn. A walk around the maze of potters' settlements can be full of surprises. ✉ *North Kolkata* ☞ *Free.*

★ **Marble Palace**

CASTLE/PALACE | **FAMILY** | One of the strangest buildings in Kolkata was the inspiration of Raja Rajendra Mullick Bahadur, a member of Bengal's landed gentry. Mullick built the palace in 1855, making lavish use of Italian marble. It's behind a lawn cluttered with sculptures of lions, the Buddha, Christopher Columbus, Jesus, the Virgin Mary, and Hindu gods. Near a small granite bungalow (where Mullick's descendants still live), a large pool houses some exotic birds with large headdresses. The palace has an interior courtyard, complete with a throne room where a peacock often struts around the seat of honor. The upstairs rooms are downright baroque: enormous mirrors and paintings cover the walls (including works by Reynolds, Rubens, and Murillo), gigantic chandeliers hang from the ceilings, and hundreds of statues and Far Eastern urns populate the rooms. The floors bear multicolored marble inlay on a giant scale, with a calico effect. Even the lamps are detailed creations, especially those on the staircases, where metal women are entwined in trees with a light bulb on each branch. Movie producers use the palace for shooting films. Guides here expect tips and sometimes they can get adamant about it. ✉ *46 Muktaram Babu St., opposite Ram Mandir, Jorasanko, North Kolkata* ☎ *033/2269–3310* ☞ *Free; you must obtain a pass from the West Bengal Tourist Office 24 hrs in advance* ◷ *Closed Mon. and Thurs.*

Nakhoda Mosque

RELIGIOUS SITE | This massive red sandstone mosque, which can hold 10,000 worshippers, was built in 1926 by the Sunni Muslim community as a copy of Akbar's tomb in Agra. Each floor has a prayer hall. The top floor has views of the streets below, which are crowded with stalls selling everything from paperback Korans to kebabs. The tailors in the bazaar are known for their skillful embroidery and can craft traditional kurtas on short notice. ✉ *Bow Barracks, Rabindra Sarani, Chowringhee North, North Kolkata* ☞ *Free.*

Pareshnath Temple

HISTORIC SITE | **FAMILY** | Built in 1867 and dedicated to Pareshnathji, the 23rd of the 24 Jain *tirthankaras* ("perfect souls," meaning sages who have achieved Nirvana), this Jain temple is an uncharacteristically ostentatious one, with inlaid-mirror pillars, stained-glass windows, floral-pattern marble floors, fountains, a gilded dome, colorful fish in sparkling reservoirs, and chandeliers from 19th-century Paris and Brussels. The garden holds blocks of glass mosaics depicting European figures and statues covered with silver paint. ✉ *Badridas Temple St., Manicktala, Khanna, North Kolkata* ✛ *Near Raja Dinendra St.* ☞ *Free.*

Prinsep Ghat-Babu Ghat Promenade

PROMENADE | **FAMILY** | The promenade between the restored Prinsep Ghat (steps leading into the river), north to Outram Ghat and then Babu Ghat, has been spruced up to attract tourists and others seeking some spectacular photo ops. You'll find it under Vidyasagar Setu, the newer bridge that crosses the

The goddess Durga at a streetside temple in Kolkata.

Hooghly. The stretch has sweeping views of the riverbanks, old warehouses, the beautiful cable bridge, and steamers and smaller ships. There's a park at one end, with some food stalls favored by families; privacy-starved couples head to the quieter sections. The area is well policed and illuminated in the evenings, so if you feel adventurous, try a joyride in an oar-boat, as much an icon of the old city as the Howrah Bridge itself. Avoid late nights, though—stick to sunsets and sunrises. ✉ *Kolkata* ✥ *Near Fort Williams, Hastings* 🎫 *Free.*

Tiretta Bazaar/Old Chinatown

MARKET | FAMILY | Chinese settlers in Kolkata have given the city a few things to fall in love with, and the breakfast served at Tiretta Bazaar is one of them. Every morning, kiosks come up along the streets, catering to the dwindling Chinese population, as well as call-center employees, pub crawlers, and foodies. With the younger generation of Chinese migrants leaving the city, the market has shrunk considerably, as has the menu, though you can expect meatballs, fish soup, pork buns, and Chinese sausages. There are plans of reviving the neighborhood and turning it into a tourist hub. Until that happens, a quick trip here is a great way to sample authentic, even if a tad rustic, Chinese fare. Note that the vendors all disappear by 10 am. ✉ *Tiretta Bazar La., Tiretti, Central Kolkata* 🎫 *Free.*

🍴 Restaurants

Dum Pukht

$$$$ | INDIAN | FAMILY | Dum Pukht takes pride in the Awadhi cuisine it's known for. Curries cooked in handmade crockery, and grilled kebabs are the signature dishes. **Known for:** Dum Pukht biryani; slow-cooked food; master chef Zubair Qureshi. [$] *Average main: Rs. 4000* ✉ *ITC Sonar, 1 JBS Haldane Ave., Kolkata* ☎ *033/2345–4545* 🌐 *www.itchotels.in/hotels/kolkata/itcsonar/dining/dum-pukht.html.*

★ Pan Asian

$$$$ | ASIAN | FAMILY | This sleek, modern restaurant with massive ceilings is an

expat favorite in Kolkata. As the name suggests, the menu here covers a broad variety of dishes from Japan, Mongolia, Korea, Thailand, and China, all made with ingredients sourced from its very own kitchen garden. **Known for:** wine cellar; sushi and dim sum; teppanyaki-style cooking where chefs prepare food in front of the guests. [$] *Average main: Rs. 3000* ✉ *ITC Hotel The Sonar, 1 JBS Haldane Ave., Bypass and Beyond* ☎ *033/2345–4545* 🌐 *www.itchotels.in/hotels/kolkata/itcsonar/dining/pan-asian.html.*

★ Peshawri

$$$$ | NORTH INDIAN | FAMILY | Charming wooden elements and cushioned stools set this restaurant apart from its contemporary counterparts, transporting guests to simpler times. The delectable tandoor and kebab cooked in clay pots are the main crowd-pleasers. **Known for:** murgh malai kebab; silverware-free dining; offbeat decor. [$] *Average main: Rs. 2500* ✉ *ITC Sonar, 1 JBS Haldane Ave., Kolkata* ☎ *033/2345–4545* 🌐 *www.itchotels.in/hotels/kolkata/itcsonar/dining/peshawri.html.*

Hotels

Hyatt Regency

$$ | HOTEL | FAMILY | This sleek, tastefully designed business hotel has rooms with wooden floors and bathrooms with Italian-marble floors, glass sinks, and sunken rain showers. **Pros:** close to the airport and the Salt Lake City tech hub; great restaurants; good spa with reasonably priced massages. **Cons:** expensive taxi ride to the center of town; crowded during the wedding season (fall and early winter); some rooms need larger beds. [$] *Rooms from: Rs. 8500* ✉ *JA–1 Sector 3, Salt Lake City, Bypass and Beyond* ☎ *033/2335–1234* 🌐 *www.hyatt.com/en-US/hotel/india/hyatt-regency-kolkata/kolka* 🛏 *233 rooms, 13 suites* 🍴 *Free Breakfast.*

★ ITC Sonar

$$$$ | HOTEL | FAMILY | The Sonar resort has comfortable and modern rooms surrounding picturesque ponds and lush landscaped gardens. **Pros:** access to exclusive spa treatments like the Bengal Journey; Eva rooms exclusively made for female travelers; top-notch restaurants serving delectable cuisines. **Cons:** away from the heart of the city; the open spaces become inaccessible during rains; a high-rise construction nearby is threatening ITC Sonar's beauty. [$] *Rooms from: Rs. 15000* ✉ *1 Haldane Ave., Tangra, Bypass and Beyond* ☎ *033/2345–4545* 🌐 *www.itchotels.in* 🛏 *237 rooms, 7 suites* 🍴 *Free Breakfast; All-inclusive.*

Swissôtel

$ | HOTEL | A modern hotel catering to the white-collar professionals and other business travelers in the new satellite town of Rajarhat, this property is more about efficiency than style. **Pros:** nearest five-star hotel to Kolkata airport; next to a mall and multiplex; outdoor Jacuzzi. **Cons:** cut off from the heart of the city; too corporate; overcrowded and slow service. [$] *Rooms from: Rs. 5500* ✉ *City Centre New Town, Action Area 2 D, Plot–11/5 New Town Rajarhat, Central Kolkata* ☎ *033/6626–6626* 🌐 *www.swissotel.com/hotels/kolkata* 🛏 *147 rooms, 10 suites* 🍴 *No meals; Free Breakfast.*

Shopping

Bowbazar

JEWELRY/ACCESSORIES | FAMILY | Some of the country's most skilled goldsmiths and jewelry designers hail from Kolkata. And in Bowbazar, east of Chitpur Road, is where you will find them. The cheek-by-jowl shops that line the busy street sell good-quality traditional gold and silver jewelry, but there are also more trendy and chic designs in platinum, with diamonds and other precious and semi-precious stones. Prices are reasonable, because labor charges are less here than in other Indian cities. Each shop has an

Dakshineshwar Kali Temple is one of Kolkata's most colorful Hindu temples.

astrologer on hand to help you find the most auspicious stone based on your sign and birth date. ⊠ *B.B Ganguly St., North Kolkata.*

Rabindra Sarani

OUTDOOR/FLEA/GREEN MARKETS | Head up Rabindra Sarani from Lal Bazaar Road (near the West Bengal Tourist Office) and you'll soon enter an Islamic world. Women walk by in burqas (long, black, tent-shaped robes), their eyes barely visible behind veils. Men sit on elevated platforms selling Bengali kurtas (shirts) and pants, and colorful *lungis* and white dhotis (both are wraps) for men. Other vendors sell vials of perfume created from flowers. Rabindra Sarani is interesting all the way to Chitpur Road. ⊠ *North Kolkata.*

Salt Lake City Centre

SHOPPING CENTERS/MALLS | **FAMILY** | Designed by the award-winning Indian Charles Correa, this mall is favored by young couples and families for its abundant open spaces, restaurants, department stores, boutiques, and live shows.

⊠ *Sector 1, Block DC, Salt Lake, Bypass and Beyond* ☏ *033/2358–1011* ⊕ *www.citycentremalls.in.*

Central Kolkata and the Maidan

The British first built Fort William in the middle of a dense jungle. When disagreements led the local Bengali ruler, Siraj ud-Daula, to attack and destroy it, the British response was a quick and decisive battle led by Robert Clive. The Battle of Plassey (some 160 km [100 miles] north of town) transformed the British from traders into a ruling presence in 1757—after it, the forest was cut down in order to provide a clear line for cannon fire in case of attack. It's really from the year 1757 that modern Kolkata traces its history, and from the impenetrable Fort William (completed in 1773) that the city began its explosive growth.

Starting about 1 km north of the fort, Central Kolkata became the commercial

Calcutta's Anglo-Indians

Calcutta, once the capital of British Raj, is home to the country's largest population of Anglo-Indians, a fast-vanishing group of native English-speakers who are of mixed European and Indian ancestry. Anglos thrived under the British, who set aside important government jobs for them, especially ones having to do with the railways. Many others were successful teachers, secretaries, nurses, and singers. But after Independence many Anglo-Indians left for North America, England, and Australia, fearing hostility from other Indians, who identified them with the former rulers.

The exodus continues, but the dwindling community works hard to maintain its identity. Younger generations marry outside the community and are gaining familiarity with the Bengali language and culture. But at home, they eat chicken *jalfrezi* (with tomatoes and green chillies) and other Anglo-Indian dishes, attend the community's churches, and speak English with little trace of an Indian accent. At Christmas, Anglo-Indians from around the world come to dance, sing, and party on the narrow street that anchors Bow Barracks, a century-old neighborhood of Anglo-Indians behind Bowbazar Police Station in Central Calcutta. Among the most famous Anglo-Indians are singers Engelbert Humperdinck and Cliff Richard, who spent his early childhood in Calcutta. The moving documentary *A Calcutta Christmas* (1998) covers the lives of some elderly Anglo-Indians living in a home, in a city that's much different than the one they grew up in.

and political heart of the city. It was here that the British conducted business, and here that they built their stately homes. The immense area cleared for British cannons is now Kolkata's 3-square-km park, the Maidan, and Central Kolkata now goes beyond the Maidan to B. B. D. Bagh square and most of the commercial and residential areas to the east of the giant park.

Sights

B. B. D. Bagh

COMMERCIAL CENTER | FAMILY | With wide, buzzing streets lined with late-Victorian buildings and pavements taken over by vendors selling rice-based meals, snacks, fruits, clothes, accessories, books, magazines, and electronic devices, this square remains the heart of the city. Still referred to by its colonial name, Dalhousie Square, the regal buildings were built around a sprawling tank (water reservoir), Lal Dighi, for civil employees. Now they are home to international banks, and the state secretariat and other public offices. After office hours, the square falls silent; that's a good time to visit if you're interested in taking a closer look at its architectural and historic landmarks. ✉ *Central Kolkata ✛ East of Hooghly River, 2½ km (1½ mile) south of Howrah Bridge. Surrounding Lal Dighi* 🎫 *Free.*

Chowringhee

COMMERCIAL CENTER | FAMILY | North Kolkata may be the city's intellectual heart, but the slick commercial area east of the Maidan is the city's spinal cord. Now technically called Jawaharlal (or J. L.) Nehru Road, Chowringhee runs along the east side of the Maidan, with shops, hotels, and old Victorian buildings lining the other side of the wide pavement. In the evening, hawkers do their best with potential shoppers, and at night, the

Cricket matches are a favorite pastime in the central Maidan, the green lungs of Kolkata.

homeless bed down. ✉ *Central Kolkata* 💳 *Free.*

Fort William

MILITARY SITE | The irregular heptagon south of the Eden Gardens in the Maidan is surrounded by a moat almost 50 feet wide. Begun in 1757 after Robert Clive's victory at Plassey over Siraj ud-Daula, Fort William was designed to prevent any future attacks. The fort's walls, as well as its barracks, stables, and Church of St. Peter, have survived to this day chiefly because the fort has, in fact, never been attacked. The Indian government still uses the fort, but it's closed to the public. ✉ *Fort Williams, Hastings, Central Kolkata.*

General Post Office (*GPO*)

BUILDING | FAMILY | Built in 1864 and still in use as Kolkata's main post office, this building's massive white Corinthian columns rest on the site of the original Fort William, where the British were attacked in 1756 and many officers were imprisoned by Siraj ud-Daula in the infamous "Black Hole of Calcutta," a tiny space

that caused most of the group to suffocate. A postal museum, founded in 1884, has artifacts and stamps. The Philatelic Bureau is situated at the southwestern end of the building. ✉ *Netaji Subhash Rd., Fairlie Pl., Central Kolkata* ✛ *Near B. B. D. Bagh* ☎ *033/2242–1572* ⊕ *www. indiapost.gov.in* 💳 *Free* ⊘ *Closed Sun.*

Indian Museum

MUSEUM | FAMILY | India's oldest museum has one of the largest and most comprehensive collections in Asia, including one of the best natural-history collections in the world. The archaeology section has representative antiquities from prehistoric times to the Mughal period, including relics from Mohenjo Daro and Harappa, the oldest excavated Indus Valley cities. The southern wing includes the Bharhut and Gandhara rooms (Indian art from the 2nd century BC to the 5th century AD), the Gupta and medieval galleries, and the Mughal gallery.

The Indian Museum also houses the world's largest collection of Indian coins. Gems and jewelry are on display. The art section on the first floor has good collection of textiles, carpets, wood carving, papier-mâché figures, and terra-cotta pottery. A gallery on the third floor contains exquisite Persian and Indian miniature paintings, and banners from Tibetan monasteries. The anthropology section on the first floor is devoted to cultural anthropology. The museum plans to establish India's first comprehensive exhibit on physical anthropology. Some interesting specimens are an Egyptian mummy donated in 1880 by an English seaman, a fossilized 200-million-year-old tree trunk, the lower jaw of a 84-foot whale, and meteorites dating back 50,000 years. ⊠ *27 Jawaharlal Nehru Rd., Park St. Area, Central Kolkata* ☎ *033/2252–1790* ⊕ *indianmuseumkolkata.org* ⊠ *Rs. 500* ☉ *Closed Mon.* Ⓜ *Park Street.*

The Maidan

CITY PARK | FAMILY | Maidan, the green lungs of the city, and loved and prized by its people, stretches from the governor's house in the north to the National Library in the south, the Hooghly in the west, and the iconic Victoria Memorial in the east. The historic fields were created when the forests around the water bodies in the area were cleared out for the British army stationed at Fort William. The Maidan is now home to cricket fields, Eden Gardens, clubhouses of popular football (soccer) leagues, stadiums, monuments, statues of both British generals and Indian leaders, and a racecourse. Mornings see fitness enthusiasts and sports teams take to the grounds, while evenings are for families and couples enjoying the pony rides and fountains. ⊠ *Central Kolkata* ✥ *Around Victoria Memorial* ⊠ *Free.*

Shaheed Minar

MEMORIAL | FAMILY | On the north end of the Maidan stands a 148-foot pillar commemorating Sir David Ochterlony's military victories over the Nepalese in the border war of 1814–16. Built in 1828, the impressive monument has a curious design: the base is Egyptian, the column is Syrian, and the cupola is Turkish. Previously known as the Ochterlony Monument, now officially called the Shaheed Minar (Martyr's Tower), it has been the site of many political rallies and student demonstrations during Calcutta's turbulent post-Independence history. ⊠ *Dharmatala Bus Stop, Dufferin Rd., Central Kolkata.*

South Park Street Cemetery

CEMETERY | FAMILY | The graves and memorials here form a repository of British imperial history. People who lived within the Raj from 1767 on are buried here, and in the records of their lives you can see the trials and triumphs of the building of an empire. ⊠ *52 Park St., Central Kolkata* ✥ *Opposite Assembly of God Church* ☎ *033/2286–7104* ⊕ *www. christianburialboardkolkata.com* ⊠ *Free* Ⓜ *Park Street.*

St. Paul's Cathedral

BUILDING | FAMILY | Completed in 1847, the cathedral now has a steeple modeled after the one at Canterbury; previous steeples were destroyed by earthquakes in 1897 and 1934. Florentine frescoes, the stained-glass western window, and a gold communion plate presented by Queen Victoria are prize possessions. Birds congregate in the interior eaves. The lawns and the Parish Hall are a popular venue for marriages and other functions. ⊠ *Cathedral Rd, Central Kolkata* ✥ *East of Victoria Memorial and adjacent to Birla Planetorium* ☎ *033/2223–0127* ⊠ *Free* Ⓜ *Rabindra Sadan.*

★ Victoria Memorial

BUILDING | FAMILY | This massive, white marble monument was conceived in 1901 by Lord Curzon and built over a 20-year period. Designed in a mixture of Italian Renaissance and Saracenic styles, surrounded by extensive, carefully manicured gardens, and preceded by a typically sober statue of Victoria herself, it remains a major symbol of the British Raj as well as that of Kolkata itself. Inside the

10

Kolkata (Calcutta) CENTRAL KOLKATA AND THE MAIDAN

building is an excellent museum of the history of Kolkata (there's a lot to read, but it will really sharpen your sense of the British-Bengali relationship) and various Raj-related exhibits, including Queen Victoria's writing desk and piano, Indian miniature paintings, watercolors, and Persian books. Cameras and electronic equipment must be left at the entrance. In the evenings there's a sound-and-light show, with narration in English, about Kolkata's history. The lawns are used by locals, especially during winter, for family picnics and joyrides on horse-drawn carriages. ⊠ 1, Queen's Way, Central Kolkata ☎ 033/2223–1890 ⊕ www.victoriamemorial-cal.org ⊠ Rs. 500 ⊘ Closed Mon.

Restaurants

The Bakery - The Lalit Great Eastern
$$ | BAKERY | FAMILY | This renowned bakery is the hub of all cake shopping during Christmastime in Kolkata. The bakery is famous for its history, heritage, English breakfast spread, and high tea. **Known for:** egg patties called Dim Puffs; Belgian chocolate hazelnut crunch cake; elegant and rustic atmosphere. $ Average main: Rs. 600 ⊠ The Lalit Great Eastern, 1, 2, 3, Old Court House St., Dalhousie Sq.,Esplanade, Kolkata ☎ 033/4444–7777 ⊕ www.thelalit.com/the-lalit-kolkata/eat-and-drink/the-bakery/.

Bar-B-Q
$$ | CHINESE | FAMILY | This local favorite serves Cantonese, Szechuan, and Indian dishes in a setting that innovatively mixes Chinese and German-chalet style. Try the crisp fried chicken served with a mild sauce, the boneless chilli chicken, or the minced lamb cooked with cubes of tofu and hot garlic sauce. **Known for:** kung pao chicken; affordable prices; unique decor. $ Average main: Rs. 600 ⊠ 43–47–55, Park St. Area, Central Kolkata ☎ 033/4602–1224.

Flurys
$$$ | EUROPEAN | FAMILY | For breakfast or afternoon tea, Flurys serves nostalgia in a new, contemporary setting. Kolkata's first Swiss confectioner, Flurys serves omelets, croissants, and beans on toast for a classic English breakfast. **Known for:** cakes and desserts; upscale ambience; coffee and tea. $ Average main: Rs. 1350 ⊠ 18, Park St. Area, Kolkata ☎ 033/3099–0148 ⊕ www.flurys.com Ⓜ Park Street.

Peter Cat
$$ | ECLECTIC | FAMILY | This is one of the city's oldest restaurants, with an atmosphere that harkens back to its early days in the 1960s (some of the staff may actually date from those times, too). The Chelo kebab—a simple dish plated to resemble a cello with buttered saffron rice, a fried egg, two pieces of mutton (goat) kebabs, and one chicken kebab—is wildly popular. **Known for:** kebabs and chicken dishes; hard-to-get reservations; old-school ambience. $ Average main: Rs. 500 ⊠ 18 A, Stephen Court, Park St., Central Kolkata ✛ Opposite KFC Restaurant ☎ 033/2229–8841 Ⓜ Park Street.

Tangerine
$$ | ECLECTIC | Small and cozy, with minimalist furniture and plate-glass windows, this restaurant is run by a friendly, helpful staff. Don't-miss choices include prawn salad, fish-and-chips, lobster thermidor, and chilli crab. **Known for:** delicious seafood; cozy setting; affordable dining with an international menu. $ Average main: Rs. 1000 ⊠ 2/1, Outram St., Theatre Rd., Central Kolkata ☎ 033/2281–5450.

Zaranj
$$ | AFGHAN | FAMILY | With opulent furniture and ornate upholstery, Zaranj remains popular for its North-West Frontier cuisine and tandoori classics. The Zaranji raan, a favorite among guests, is a whole leg of goat marinated in Indian spices and slowly grilled—it takes a good 30 minutes to prepare, but it melts in your mouth. **Known for:** over-the-top decor; vegan and lactose-intolerant

options; old family recipes. $ *Average main: Rs. 1000* ✉ *26 Jawaharlal Nehru Rd., Central Kolkata* ☎ *90070–66664* ⊕ *www.zaranj.in/* Ⓜ *Park Street.*

 Hotels

The Astor

$$ | HOTEL | FAMILY | One of the least expensive and most comfortable hotels in the city, rooms here are somewhat small, but the lounge draws a hip crowd every evening. **Pros:** good value and location; a happening nightclub; a heritage feel. **Cons:** mostly catering to young people; no elevators; some rooms are noisy at night due to the nightclub. $ *Rooms from: Rs. 6500* ✉ *15 Shakespeare Sarani, Central Kolkata* ☎ *033/2282–9950* ⊕ *www.astorkolkata.com* ⇥ *34 rooms, 9 suites* ⦿ *Free Breakfast.*

Kenilworth

$$ | HOTEL | Popular with repeat visitors to Kolkata, this hotel has pretty gardens and two cheerfully furnished wings with comfortable and spacious guest rooms. **Pros:** located in the heart of the city; healthy food available; the Big Ben, a British-theme pub at Kenilworth, is very happening. **Cons:** ordinary furniture; a bit noisy; luxury tax is levied on every service. $ *Rooms from: Rs. 6800* ✉ *1–2 Little Russell St., Central Kolkata* ☎ *033/2282–3939* ⊕ *www.kenilworthhotels.com* ⇥ *98 rooms, 7 suites* ⦿ *Breakfast; No meals.*

The Lalit Great Eastern

$$ | HOTEL | FAMILY | In the heart of Kolkata's business district, this 19th-century heritage property was restored by Bharat Hotels Limited and turned into a classy business hotel with massive rooms in 2014; the property is well preserved with elements that highlight the building's history as a bakery. **Pros:** heritage walks with high tea are arranged within the hotel premises; rooms and facilities for specially abled people; the executive chef is a national award winner. **Cons:**

set in a chaotic, crowded location; there are no soothing city views around; small swimming pool. $ *Rooms from: Rs. 7500* ✉ *1,2,3 Old Court House St., Dalhousie Sq., Esplanade, Central Kolkata* ☎ *033/4444–7777* ⊕ *www.thelalit. com* ⇥ *190 rooms, 25 suites* ⦿ *Free Breakfast.*

The Oberoi Grand Kolkata

$$$ | HOTEL | FAMILY | One of the most elegant hotels in the country, this Victorian landmark in the center of town provides impeccable service. **Pros:** a heritage walk in the hotel is arranged by the concierge for guests; the central courtyard consisting of a garden and pool is breezy throughout the year; the heritage property is not remodeled and guests can feel the old-world charm. **Cons:** situated in a bustling, crowded part of the city; far away from airport; restaurants and food options are fewer compared to other luxury hotels. $ *Rooms from: Rs. 11000* ✉ *15 Jawaharlal Nehru Rd., Central Kolkata* ☎ *033/2249–2323* ⊕ *www.oberoihotels.com* ⇥ *209 rooms and suites* ⦿ *Free Breakfast.*

The Park Kolkata

$$$ | HOTEL | FAMILY | The location, good service, lively nightlife, and trippy interiors have made this into one of the busiest hotels in Kolkata. **Pros:** some of the hippest bars in town located nearby; rooms are spacious; easy connectivity to all places in the city. **Cons:** the area gets seedy at night; very noisy late at night due to the sound from the disco; poor housekeeping. $ *Rooms from: Rs. 12000* ✉ *17 Park St., Central Kolkata* ☎ *033/2249–9000* ⊕ *www.theparkhotels. com* ⇥ *132 rooms, 17 suites* ⦿ *Free Breakfast.*

 Nightlife

Big Ben

BARS/PUBS | Local professionals congregate in this pub, which has skilled bartenders. Coming from the speakers is a mix of rock, pop, and Bollywood music. Midweek theme nights and special offers on sangria pitchers help pack 'em in. ✉ *Kenilworth Hotel, 1–2 Little Russell St., Central Kolkata* ☎ *033/2282–3939* ⊕ *www.kenilworthhotels.com.*

Myx

DANCE CLUBS | Myx provides the perfect environment to dance the night away: good food, liquor, music, and a party atmosphere. ✉ *20G, Park St., Kolkata* ☎ *033/4007–8167.*

★ Phoenix

DANCE CLUBS | One of Kolkata's top nightlife hot spots, Phoenix boasts wonderful bartenders, a sci-fi ceiling illumination, and a crowd that loves to party. ✉ *15 Shakespeare Sarani, Kolkata* ☎ *98317–54003* ⊕ *www.astorkolkata.com.*

Someplace Else

BARS/PUBS | Kolkata's favorite pub is compact and always packed. Talented and popular local bands play rock, blues, alternative, and jazz, the venue hosts top international acts frequently. It's a great place to bond with musicians and music lovers—the city is teeming with both. ✉ *The Park Hotel, 17 Park St., Central Kolkata* ☎ *033/4004–9000* ⊕ *www.theparkhotels.com/kolkata/someplace-else.html.*

Tantra

DANCE CLUBS | Despite newer, younger venues around town, Tantra still draws the hottest crowd to its dance floor. Favored by those in their twenties, Tantra is where film stars and models let their hair down. ✉ *The Park Hotel, 17 Park St., Central Kolkata* ☎ *033/4004–9000* ⊕ *www.theparkhotels.com/kolkata.html.*

Shopping

AUCTIONS
Russell Exchange

AUCTIONS | On Sunday auctions take place along Russell Street. A trip to the oldest auction house, the Russell Exchange, run

by brothers Anwar and Arshad, or any of its neighbors, is invariably entertaining. Goods auctioned range from antiques and period furniture to crockery and cutlery. On Thursday, there's a sale of vintage clothes. ✉ *12C Russell St., Anandilal Poddar Sarani, Central Kolkata* ☎ *033/2229–8974.*

BAZAARS AND MARKETS
New Market

ANTIQUES/COLLECTIBLES | FAMILY | The century-old New Market, officially Sir Stuart Hogg Market, houses about 2,500 stores under one roof, selling cotton saris, Bankura clay horses, brassware, leather bags from Shantiniketan, silk from Murshidabad, khadi (handmade cotton) cloth, clothes for kids, wigs, poultry, cheeses, nuts, and other foods. The neighborhood is also home to several air-conditioned malls, department stores, restaurants, and stand-alone shops, while the sidewalks are taken over by street-food vendors and knickknack stalls. It's definitely the busiest shopping district in the region. ✉ *Central Kolkata* ⊕ *Off Jawahar Lal Nehru Rd.*

Salt Lake City Centre

SHOPPING CENTERS/MALLS | FAMILY | Designed by the award-winning Indian Charles Correa, this mall is favored by young couples and families for its abundant open spaces, restaurants, department stores, boutiques, and live shows. ✉ *Sector 1, Block DC, Salt Lake, Bypass and Beyond* ☎ *033/2358–1011* ⊕ *www.citycentremalls.in.*

BOOKS
Oxford Bookstore

BOOKS/STATIONERY | FAMILY | The café overlooking the chic street below serves teas and snacks at this store, one of the city's favorite spaces for books and book parties. There's a wide range of titles in English, as well as some in Indian languages and in French. Gifts and a DVD section round out the offerings. ✉ *17 Park St., Central Kolkata* ☎ *033/2229–7662* ⊕ *www.oxfordbookstore.com.*

HANDICRAFTS AND CURIOS

Central Cottage Industries Emporium

CRAFTS | FAMILY | For curios in a hurry and at fixed prices, head to Central Cottage Industries. It may seem a tad musty and salespeople may seem disinterested, but you may just find a good bargain. ✉ *7 Jawahar Lal Nehru Rd., New Market Area, Chowringhee, Esplanade, Central Kolkata* ☎ *033/2228–4139* ⊕ *www.cottageemporium.in.*

Konark Collectables

CRAFTS | FAMILY | Quaint little Konark Collectables carries handicrafts, curios, antiques, period furniture, and gift items. ✉ *Humayun Court, 20 Lindsay St., Central Kolkata* ☎ *033/2249–7657* ⊕ *www.konarkcollectables.com* Ⓜ *Esplanade.*

 Performing Arts

Academy of Fine Arts

ARTS CENTERS | FAMILY | This center of art and creative discourse was established in 1933 by Lady Ranu Mookerji, a close associate of Tagore who was known for her beauty and her patronage of the arts. In addition to the permanent collection of paintings and Tagore manuscripts, the Academy hosts live acts and theater festivals throughout the year. It's a popular meeting ground for the city's intellectuals, especially in winter. ✉ *2 Cathedral Rd., Maidan, Central Kolkata* ☎ *94330–63154* ⊕ *www.academyoffinearts.in* ▦ *Free.*

Galerie 88

ARTS CENTERS | FAMILY | Works by modern Indian artists are on view here. ✉ *28B Shakespeare Sarani, Park St. Area, Central Kolkata* ☎ *033/2290–2274* ⊕ *www.galerie88.in* ▦ *Free.*

Kalamandir Auditorium

THEATER | Theatrical and musical events are often staged here. ✉ *48 Shakespeare Sarani, Theatre Rd., Central Kolkata.*

Nandan

FILM | FAMILY | Popular with intellectuals and artsy young people, Nandan, the state-run theater in the Rabindra Sadan complex, shows art-house and independent films. ✉ *1/1 A.J.C. Bose Rd., Central Kolkata* ☎ *033/2223–1210.*

Rabindra Sadan

ARTS CENTERS | FAMILY | A popular venue for music, dance, and theater. ✉ *71, Acharya Jagadish Chandra Bose Rd., Central Kolkata* ☎ *033/2248–9917.*

Activities

Royal Calcutta Turf Club (*RCTC*)

HORSE RACING/SHOW | For horse-racing enthusiasts, the Royal Calcutta Turf Club retains an old-world air of sophistication. ✉ *11 Russell St., Central Kolkata* ☎ *033/2229–1104* ⊕ *www.rctconline.com.*

South Kolkata

Calcutta's rich and powerful moved consistently south as the city grew more and more crowded and unpleasant. Here you'll see an interesting mix of large colonial homes, modern hotels and businesses, open space, and crowded temple areas.

Sights

Acharya Jagadish Chandra Bose Indian Botanic Garden (*Indian Botanical Gardens*)

GARDEN | FAMILY | Across the Second Hooghly Bridge (Vivekananda Setu) in Howrah are these sprawling botanical gardens, first opened in 1786. Darjeeling and Assam teas were developed here. The gardens' banyan tree has one of the largest canopies in the world, covering a mind-boggling 1,300 square feet. On Sundays and holidays, locals turn out in droves to enjoy their day off. The winters are excellent for bird-watching. ✉ *Shibpur, Howrah* ✥ *Very near to Indian*

Institute of Engineering Science and Technology (IIEST) ☎ *033/2668–0554* 🗪 *Rs. 100* ⊗ *Closed Mon.*

Floating Market

LOCAL INTEREST | FAMILY | In the waterway, boats which double as shops can be found conducting daily business. Buyers can navigate the market by the wooden walkways. Be sure to bring mosquito repellent. ⊠ *Pond Block H, Block E, Baishnabghata Patuli Township, Kolkata* 🗪 *Free.*

Kalighat Kali Temple

RELIGIOUS SITE | Built in 1809, the Kali temple is one of the most significant pilgrimage sites in India, with shrines to Shiva, Krishna, and Kali, the patron goddess of Kolkata. Human sacrifices were reputed to be commonly practiced here on special days during the 19th century, but only goats are slaughtered now, then offered to the goddess with *bhang* (marijuana). The building rewards a close look: you'll see thin, multicolored layers of painted trim and swaths of tilework. Only Hindus are allowed in the inner sanctum, but the lanes and brilliant flower markets surrounding the temple are lovely in themselves. Beware of touts and aggressive priests. ⊠ *Anami Sangha, Kalighat Road, South Kolkata* ⊕ *kalighat-temple.com* 🗪 *Free* Ⓜ *Kalighat.*

The Mother House of the Missionaries of Charity

INFO CENTER | FAMILY | Awarded the Nobel peace prize in 1979 and beatified in 2003, Mother Teresa founded the Missionaries of Charity in Kolkata in 1950. Today the group works in 133 countries. The charity's work for those who have contracted HIV/AIDs, leprosy, and tuberculosis, including mobile dispensaries and shelters for orphans, draws volunteers and donors through the year. The headquarters has information on the missionaries' work and opportunities to volunteer with the various initiatives. It also houses the tomb of Mother Teresa. ⊠ *54A A.J.C Bose Rd., South Kolkata*

☎ *033/2249–7115* ⊕ *www.motherteresa. org* 🗪 *Free* ⊗ *Closed Thurs.*

National Library

COLLEGE | Once the house of the lieutenant governor of Calcutta, this hefty neo-Renaissance building has miles of books and pleasant reading rooms. The rare-book section holds some significant works, adding to the importance of this 2-million-volume facility. There are no displays, but you can take a short walk through the grounds. Day cards are issued to anyone interested in using the library's reading room. The staff are very helpful and will guide you through the process. ⊠ *Belvedere Rd., Block A, Alipore, South Kolkata* ⊕ *Near Taj Bengal* ☎ *033/2479–2968* ⊕ *www.nationallibrary. gov.in* 🗪 *Free.*

Nirmal Hriday (*Pure Heart*)

HOSPITAL—SIGHT | Mother Teresa's first home for the dying is now one of 300 affiliated organizations worldwide that care for people in the most dire need. Mother Teresa is buried in this building, which was her home for 44 years, until her death in 1997. ⊠ *251 Kalighat Rd., Kalighat, South Kolkata* ⊕ *Next to Kali Temple* ☎ *033/2464–4223* 🗪 *Free* ⊗ *Closed Thurs. and Sun.*

🍴 Restaurants

★ Bohemian

$$$ | MODERN INDIAN | FAMILY | In a residential neighborhood to the south, this restaurant takes the best and most unique ingredients and flavors of Bengali cuisine, and gives them a contemporary twist. Crab cakes come with mustard sauce and are baked with local greens in small clay saucers, river prawns are simmered in a coconut gravy with grapes, and desserts are delicately flavored with *gondhoraj*, a close cousin of the kaffir lime used in Thai dishes. **Known for:** gluten-free options available; busy atmosphere; bacon-wrapped chicken. 💲 *Average main: Rs. 1200* ⊠ *32/4 Old Ballygunge, 1st La.,*

The city's best street food can be discerned from the busiest stalls.

Ballygunge, South Kolkata ✛ Near Bondel Rd. ☎ 033/6606–4241 ◔ Closed Mon.

Cal 27

$$$$ | ECLECTIC | FAMILY | Cal 27 is an international restaurant offering a wide array of both vegetarian and nonvegetarian cuisine from ratatouille to Thai chicken curry. Overlooking the pool at the Taj Hotel, the restaurant has a laid-back and relaxing ambience. **Known for:** Indonesian nasi goreng; fine dining with a casual vibe; 24-hour service. Ⓢ *Average main: Rs. 3500* ✉ *Taj Bengal, 34B, Belvedere Rd., Alipore, Kolkata* ☎ *033/2223–3939* ⊕ *tajhotels.com/en-in/taj-bengal-kolkata/restaurants/cal-27-restaurant.*

Chinoiserie

$$$$ | CANTONESE | FAMILY | Popular with locals and tourists, the best Chinese fine-dining restaurant in the city has elegant interiors, with old mirrors, paintings, and glass pots that immediately catch the attention of the guests. Try the kung pao pork ribs, steamed scallop morsel, or the crispy lamb. **Known for:** attentive service; master chef Lian; upscale dining experience. Ⓢ *Average main: Rs. 4500* ✉ *Taj Bengal, 34B Belvedere Rd., Alipore, South Kolkata* ☎ *033/2223–3939* ⊕ *tajhotels.com/en-in/taj-bengal-kolkata/restaurants/chinoiserie-restaurant.*

Mainland China

$$$ | CHINESE | FAMILY | Kolkata's popular Chinese restaurant, now a national chain, is known for efficient service and spacious interiors with minimalist but comfortable furniture. Try their fish and prawn dishes or the elaborate and reasonably priced buffet. **Known for:** roast lamb in hot bean sauce; valet parking available; local favorite. Ⓢ *Average main: Rs. 1200* ✉ *Uniworth House, 3A Gurusaday Rd., Ballygunge, South Kolkata* ☎ *033/2283–7964.*

Mrs Magpie

$ | EUROPEAN | FAMILY | This pretty café is always buzzing with patrons lined up for pretty-as-a-picture cupcakes, tiered cakes, quiches, and pies, all served with excellent coffee and a flourish. There's also a hearty breakfast, and a high tea, which comes with scones, finger sandwiches, and fine Darjeeling tea. **Known for:** apple brandy; sweet and salty minicupcakes; cutesy decor. $ *Average main: Rs. 350 ⊠ 570, Lake Terrace Rd. Extension, Keyatala, Southern Ave., South Kolkata ☎ 033/4004–1114.*

Oh! Calcutta

$$ | **INDIAN** | **FAMILY** | Started in 2002, this is one of the most successful chains for traditional Bengali cuisine in upscale settings. All-time favorite dishes here include river prawns cooked in coconut milk and served in tender coconut shells. **Known for:** fish in mustard sauce; weekend lunch buffet; interesting and unusual menu during festivals. $ *Average main: Rs. 1000 ⊠ Forum Mall, 10/3 Elgin Rd., 4th fl., South Kolkata ☎ 033/3099–0461.*

★ 6 Ballygunge Place

$$ | **INDIAN** | **FAMILY** | This well-liked restaurant is known for its traditional and contemporary Bengali cuisine. Try the prawns or the hilsa (a local fish), wrapped in banana leaves and steamed in a mustard and coconut marinade. **Known for:** Malai prawn curry; colonial decor; local favorite. $ *Average main: Rs. 800 ⊠ 6 Ballygunge Pl., Ballygunge, South Kolkata ☎ 033/2460–3922.*

Sonargaon

$$$$ | **NORTH INDIAN** | **FAMILY** | This restaurant serving North Indian and Bengali dishes is a tasteful replica of a rural house, complete with a courtyard, a well, dark wood details, copper curios, and metal light fixtures. The traditional Bengali kebabs are wildly popular. **Known for:** vegetarian options; rustic countryside decor; impeccable service. $ *Average main: Rs. 4000 ⊠ Taj Bengal, 34B Belvedere Rd., Alipore, South Kolkata ☎ 033/2223–3939 ⊕ tajhotels. com/en-in/taj-bengal-kolkata/restaurants/ sonargaon-restaurant.*

★ Souk

$$$$ | **MIDDLE EASTERN** | **FAMILY** | This glitzy restaurant serves contemporary Middle Eastern and Mediterranean cuisine with flavors from Morocco, Greece, Turkey, and Egypt. The courteous staff delivers sound service. **Known for:** homemade hummus; Moroccan tagine; fine-dining atmosphere. $ *Average main: 3800 ⊠ Taj Bengal, 34B, Belvedere Rd., Alipore, Kolkata ☎ 033/2223–3939 ⊕ tajhotels. com/en-in/taj-bengal-kolkata/restaurants/ souk-restaurant ☉ Closed Mon.*

Yauatcha Kolkata

$$$$ | **ASIAN** | **FAMILY** | Set in the upscale Quest Mall, Yauatcha, a well-regarded dim sum house, is known for great dumplings, tea, and seafood—in short, everything Kolkata is obsessive about. The crispy duck, prawn, and chicken *shu mai* (dumplings) seem to be the overall favorites. **Known for:** turnip cake; chocolate hazelnut mousse; massive bar and liquor selection. $ *Average main: Rs. 2000 ⊠ Quest Mall, 5th fl., 33 Syed Amir Ali Ave., Park Circus, Beck Bagan, Ballygunge, South Kolkata ☎ 92222– 22800 ⊕ www.yauatcha.com/kolkata/ about-2.*

Hotels

Hotel Hindusthan International

$$ | **HOTEL** | You won't feel cramped inside this hotel where the crisp and modern standard rooms are 220 square feet. **Pros:** views of the city; seasonal fruit platter; a jewelry boutique in the hotel. **Cons:** small beds; cleanliness issues; noisy at night due to the nightclub. $ *Rooms from: Rs. 6575 ⊠ 235/1 A.J.C. Bose Rd., South Kolkata ☎ 033/4001–8000 ⊕ www. hhihotels.com ⤳ 176 rooms, 8 suites ⊚l Free Breakfast.*

★ Taj Bengal

$$$ | **HOTEL** | **FAMILY** | A fusion of traditional and contemporary Indian aesthetics, this hotel on the edge of the city center comes with spectacular views of the Maidan and the Victoria Memorial. **Pros:** the lobby allows lot of natural light; a wide array of in-house restaurants serving cuisine from all over the world;

Taj Khazana houses exclusive souvenirs from all over India. **Cons:** away from the corporate hub of the city; not a place for nightlife seekers; renovations take place after long intervals. $ *Rooms from: Rs. 10000* ✉ *34B Belvedere Rd., Alipore, South Kolkata* ☎ *033/6612–3939* ⊕ *www.tajhotels.com* ⇄ *229 rooms* ⦿ *Free Breakfast.*

Nightlife

★ Ozora
BARS/PUBS | The sky deck of Ozora has an unobstructed view of Kolkata, making this one of the best places to watch the sunset. ✉ *1858, Acropolis Mall, Rajdanga Main Rd., 20th fl., Kolkata* ☎ *033/3099–1287.*

 Performing Arts

Birla Academy of Art and Culture
ARTS CENTERS | **FAMILY** | The nondescript venue has some art on display, but the main draw is the auditorium, where some very talented musicians and dancers perform. Winters are especially favored for classical concerts. ✉ *108–109 Southern Ave., South Kolkata* ☎ *033/2466–6802* ⊕ *www.birlaart.com.*

Experimenter
ARTS CENTERS | **FAMILY** | This buzzy venue is where you will find works of award-winning contemporary artists from around the world. Bani Abidi, Nadia Kaabi-Linke, and Ayesha Sultana have all shown here. Experimental films and video art are also shown from time to time. ✉ *2/1 Hindusthan Rd., Gariahat, Dover Terrace, South Kolkata* ☎ *033/4001–2289* ⊕ *www.experimenter.in* ⬚ *Free.*

Shopping

BAZAARS AND SHOPPING MALLS
Forum Mall
DEPARTMENT STORES | **FAMILY** | Forum Mall has shops selling clothes, music, leather, toys, and lots more. ✉ *10/3*

Elgin Rd., Bhowanipore, South Kolkata ☎ *033/4023–5000* ⊕ *www.forumcourtyard.com* Ⓜ *Rabindra Sadan.*

Gariahat
SHOPPING NEIGHBORHOODS | South Kolkata's most popular and very congested shopping district is home to chic boutiques and bustling shops selling saris in all kinds of styles and prices. The pavements are taken over by hawkers selling clothes, toys, accessories, and handcrafted jewelry—it can be challenging to negotiate the crowd during peak hours. Intense bargaining is de rigueur on the street, but the air-conditioned shops offer respite from the heat as well as the haggling. The lanes away from Gariahat Road itself—Hindusthan Park Road, Dover Lane, Southern Avenue—are quieter and more upscale. Here, among the elegant homes of Kolkata's upper classes are where you will find art galleries, quirky and traditional Bengali restaurants, specialty shops, boutiques, and quaint cafés that are local favorites. Visit By Loom for hand-loomed saris, jewelry, and a cozy café. Bunkari sells saris, stoles, and scarves; Weaver's Studio has handloomed textiles. For a bite of Kolkata's famous kati rolls, try Bedouwin or Badshah, where crisp parathas are wrapped around succulent pieces of meat and finely chopped onions and served piping hot. For traditional Bengali meals, try 6 Ballygunge Place, Sholo Ana, Tero Parbon, or Bhojohori Manna. Le Petit De La Maison, The Bistro, Wise Owl, and French Loaf are some of the European-style eateries in the area. If the shopping and the crowds get to you, head to the Ramakrishna Mission, in Gol Park, for some quiet reflection. ✉ *Gariahat Rd., South Kolkata* ⊕ *Gariahat Crossing adjacent to flyover* Ⓜ *Kalighat.*

Quest Mall
CLOTHING | **FAMILY** | Kolkata's newfound love affair with malls is reflected in this massive and high-end example of the genre, home to Paul Smith, Emporio

Armani, Canali, Fendi, Gucci, Michael Kors—some 130 brands in all. Restaurants include SeraFina and Irish House. ⊠ *Beck Bagan Row, 33 Syed Amir Ali Avo., Park Circus, Dallygunge, South Kolkata* ☎ *033/2281–1111* ⊕ *www.questmall. in.*

South City Mall

CLOTHING | FAMILY | By some measures this is the largest mall in the region—there's parking for 1,800 vehicles. A huge number of major brands are available on its five floors, and there's also a sprawling food court and a multiplex. ⊠ *375 Prince Anwar Shah Rd., South Kolkata* ☎ *033/4007–2181* ⊕ *southcitymall.in.*

BOOKS

Seagull

BOOKS/STATIONERY | FAMILY | Specializing in art, social sciences, theater, and politics, this publishing imprint has a cozy store, which manages to devote space to art and literary discussions as well as an expansive and eclectic stock of books. ⊠ *31A S.P Mukherjee Rd., South Kolkata* ☎ *033/2476–5865* ⊕ *www.seagullindia. com.*

CLOTHING

Dakshinapan

CLOTHING | FAMILY | For those who want to browse through handicrafts and hand-loomed cloth and clothing from around the country, this no-fuss, no-frills mall is a good destination. Discovering gems in this sea of government shops may leave you parched, though. Head for Dolly's Tea Shop, on the ground floor, for refreshing hot and cool blends of the finest teas, handpicked by the owner, Dolly Roy, the world's first female tea auctioneer and India's first female tea taster. ⊠ *Near Dhakuria Bridge, 8/1B, Rohim Ostagar Rd., Jodhpur Park, South Kolkata.*

★ Sabyasachi

CLOTHING | FAMILY | Sabyasachi Mukherji, one of India's most well-known fashion designers, is from Kolkata; a trip to his flagship store is a crash course in Indian textiles and craftsmanship. Known for his saris and wedding clothes, Sabya (as he's popularly known) dresses many of India's top film stars and celebrities. ⊠ *P 545 Lake Rd., near Vivekananda Park, South Kolkata* ☎ *033/4064–8239* ⊕ *www. sabyasachi.com.*

Activities

Royal Calcutta Golf Club

GOLF | Established in 1829 by the British as the first golf course outside the United Kingdom, the Royal Calcutta Golf Club still caters to the city's elite. ⊠ *18 Golf Club Rd., Tollygunge, South Kolkata* ☎ *033/2473–1352* ⊕ *www.rcgc.in.*

Index

Photo Credits

Front Cover: SIME / eStock Photo [Description: The fort of Agra. Agra, India]. Back cover, from left to right: Aleksandar Todorovic/Shutterstock; infinity21/Shutterstock; Terraxplorer/iStockphoto. Spine: Kulpreet_Photography/iStockphoto. Interior, top from left to right: cmittman, Fodors.com member (1). mcgregorjn, Fodors.com member (2). mcgregorjn, Fodors.com member (5). **Chapter 1**: Experience India: Luca Tettoni / age fotostock (6–7). Sean Hsu/Shutterstock (8–9). Jan S./Shutterstock (9). Archna Singh/Shutterstock (9). Florinseitan | Dreamstime.com (10). Alexander Mazurkevich/ Shutterstock (10). CRS Photo/Shutterstock (10). Konstik | Dreamstime.com (10). Tetiana Photos/Shutterstock (11). Jpatokal / Wikimedia Commons (11). Yongyut Kumsri/Shutterstock (11). Mayank Makhija/Shutterstock (11). Dimaberkut | Dreamstime.com (12). Mik122 | Dreamstime.com (12). David Pearson / Alamy Stock Photo (12). Hypnocreative | Dreamstime.com (12). Pawe Borówka/Shutterstock (13). Richie0703 | Dreamstime.com (14). ZUMA Press, Inc. / Alamy Stock Photo (14). Flocutus | Dreamstime.com (14). Byelikova Oksana/Shutterstock (14). Byelikova | Dreamstime.com (15). photoff/Shutterstock (15). espies/Shutterstock (18). Manubahuguna | Dreamstime.com (18). arun sambhu mishra/ Shutterstock (18). Ppy2010ha | Dreamstime.com (18). Kumar7075 | Dreamstime.com (18). Kumar7075 | Dreamstime.com (19). Susansam90 | Dreamstime.com (19). Indian Food Images/Shutterstock (19). SMDSS/Shutterstock (19). Kaphoto | Dreamstime.com (19). Travellinglight | Dreamstime.com (20). Elena Veselova/Shutterstock (21). saiko3p/Shutterstock (22). Napoleonka/Shutterstock (22). suman14/Shutterstock (22). Ivanov Oleg/Shutterstock (22). Supamon R/Shutterstock (22). Mitrarudra | Dreamstime.com (23). Mashimara | Dreamstime.com (23). Don Mammoser/Shutterstock (23). Pikoso.kz/ Shutterstock (23). Murger | Dreamstime.com (23). F9photos | Dreamstime.com (24). saiko3p/Shutterstock (24). Saiko3p | Dreamstime.com (24). (c) Saiko3p | Dreamstime.com (25). Saiko3p | Dreamstime.com (25). Roop_Dey/Shutterstock (26). Saiko3p | Dreamstime.com (26). imagedb.com/Shutterstock (26). Traveleon73 | Dreamstime.com (26). Eldelik | Dreamstime.com (27). suronin/Shutterstock (27). Nstanev | Dreamstime.com (27). Leonid Andronov/Shutterstock (27). **Chapter 3**: Portrait of India: Photosindia com / age fotostock (49). James Burger / age fotostock (51). Marco Cristofori / age fotostock (52). Teresa Zau, Fodors.com member (53). Nikhil Gangavane/iStockphoto (53). Nick Hanna / Alamy (54). Vikram Raghuvanshi/iStockphoto (55). Ivan Vdovin / age fotostock (56). Alan Lagadu/iStockphoto (57). Rafal Cichawa/ Shutterstock (57). Jan S./Shutterstock (58). Walter Bibikow / age fotostock (59). Wikimedia Commons (60). paul prescott/ Shutterstock (61). AJP/Shutterstock (61). Lebedinski Vladislav/Shutterstock (62). paul prescott/Shutterstock (63). Christophe Boisvieux / age fotostock (64). JeremyRichards/Shutterstock (65). AJP/Shutterstock (65). Matthias Rosenkranz/Flickr, [CC BYND 2.0] (66). Vassil/Wikimedia Commons (67). jaimaa/Shutterstock (67). Dinodia / age fotostock (68). saiko3p/Shutterstock (69). Joe Gough/iStockphoto (70). Jehangir Hanafi/iStockphoto (71). Monkey Business Images/ Shutterstock (71). Joe Gough/iStockphoto (72). Colin & Linda McKie/iStockphoto (73). WITTY234/Shutterstock (74). Bartosz Hadyniak/iStockphoto (75). JTB Photo / age fotostock (76). Sid B. Viswakumar/Shutterstock (77). Rabouan JeanBaptiste / age fotostock (77). Ian Cumming / age fotostock (78). Wikimedia Commons (79). M Balan / age fotostock (80). testing/Shutterstock (81). NCPA Photo/ Harkiran Singh Bhasin (81). Eitan Simanor / age fotostock (82). **Chapter 4**: Delhi: szefei/Shutterstock (83). highviews/Shutterstock (86). sanskarshan/Wikimedia Commons (87). highviews/ Shutterstock (87). Varun Shiv Kapur/Flickr, [CC BYND 2.0] (88). Russ Bowling/Flickr, [CC BYND 2.0] (89). Kylelovesyou/ Wikimedia Commons (89). Amit kg/Shutterstock (99). Arco / TherinWeise / age fotostock (106). Dinodia / age fotostock (115). Sam DCruz/Shutterstock (118). McPhotos / age fotostock (121). Tibor Bognor / age fotostock (125). Oriental Touch / age fotostock (127). **Chapter 5**: Side Trips from Delhi: Rawpixelimages | Dreamstime.com (135). paul prescott/ Shutterstock (138). Bon Appetit / Alamy (139). Vibhisionksoni | Dreamstime.com (139). Mel Longhurst / age fotostock (148). Public Domain (152). J Hauke / age fotostock (153). Hashim/Wikimedia Commons (154). Gavin Hellier / age fotostock (154). Samir Luther/Wikimedia Commons (154). Samir Luther/Wikimedia Commons (154). Wikimedia Commons (154). Dinodia / age fotostock (155). John Henry Claude Wil / age fotostock (156). Rafal Cichawa/Shutterstock (157). William Donelson/Wikimedia Commons (157). Alexey Fateev/Shutterstock (157). Alexey Fateev/Shutterstock (157). JeremyRichards/Shutterstock (157). Tibor Bognar / age fotostock (161). Richard Ashworth / age fotostock (171). Jose Fuste Raga / age fotostock (172173). Aleksandar Todorovic/Shutterstock (180181). Christopher Soghoian/Flickr, [CC BYND 2.0] (182). Rumi Arpitadevi/Flickr/Flickr, [CC BYND 2.0] (183). Lebedinski Vladislav/Shutterstock (183). JeremyRichards/ Shutterstock (183). Aleksandar Todorovic/Shutterstock (183). Jon Larson/iStockphoto (184). Sequoy/Shutterstock (184). Sequoy/Shutterstock (184). Igor Plotnikov/Shutterstock (184). Bartosz Hadyniak/iStockphoto (184). Jeremy Edwards/

Photo Credits

Notes

Notes

Notes

Notes

Notes

Notes

Notes

Notes

Notes

Notes

Fodor's ESSENTIAL INDIA

Editorial: Douglas Stallings, *Editorial Director;* Margaret Kelly, Jacinta O'Halloran, *Senior Editors;* Kayla Becker, Alexis Kelly, Amanda Sadlowski, *Editors;* Teddy Minford, *Content Editor;* Rachael Roth, *Content Manager*

Design: Tina Malaney, *Design and Production Director;* Jessica Gonzalez, *Production Designer*

Photography: Jill Krueger, *Senior Photo Editor*

Maps: Rebecca Baer, *Senior Map Editor;* Mark Stroud (Moon Street Cartography), *Cartographers*

Production: Jennifer DePrima, *Editorial Production Manager;* Carrie Parker, *Senior Production Editor;* Elyse Rozelle, *Production Editor*

Business & Operations: Chuck Hoover, *Chief Marketing Officer;* Joy Lai, *Vice President and General Manager;* Stephen Horowitz, *Director of Business Development and Revenue Operations;* Tara McCrillis, *Director of Publishing Operations*

Public Relations and Marketing: Joe Ewaskiw, *Manager;* Esther Su, *Marketing Manager*

Writers: Kristin Amico, Tania Banerjee, Malavika Bhattacharya, Margot Bigg, Christabel Lobo, Meher Mirza

Editors: Teddy Minford

Production Editor: Jennifer DePrima

4th Edition

ISBN 978-1-64097-122-6

ISSN 2164–2222

Library of Congress Control Number 2018958610

SPECIAL SALES
This book is available at special discounts for bulk purchases for sales promotions or premiums. For more information, e-mail SpecialMarkets@fodors.com.

PRINTED IN THE UNITED STATES OF AMERICA

10 9 8 7 6 5 4 3 2 1

About Our Writers

Kristin Amico is a food and travel writer. In 2017 she quit her full-time job, sold most of her belongings, and bought a one-way ticket overseas. She has traveled across Europe and Asia. In addition to Fodor's, her work has appeared in *The Independent*, *USA Today*, *Hemispheres*, and *Roads & Kingdoms*. She updated the Rajasthan chapter.

Tania Banerjee is a freelance travel writer with roots in Kolkata, India. Tania chases destination stories with a human interest element in them. She gets a kick out of immersive travel and sinful desserts. Tania updated the Kolkata chapter.

Malavika Bhattacharya is an independent travel journalist whose work appears in publications such as *National Geographic Traveller*, *Travel + Leisure*, and *CNN.com*. Malavika writes about sustainable travel, the outdoors, India's remote wilderness, food, and culture. For this edition of Fodor's Essential India, Malavika updated the Delhi chapter.

Margot Bigg has lived and worked in India for many years and has written for a number of Indian publications, including local editions of *Rolling Stone*, *Condé Nast Traveller*, and *Time Out*. She's also the author of *Moon Living Abroad in India* and *Moon Taj Mahal, Delhi & Jaipur*. Margot contributed to the first edition of *Fodor's Essential India* and for this edition she updated the Experience, Portraits of India, and Travel Smart chapters. Find out more about her at ⊕ *www.margotbigg.com*.

Christabel Lobo is a freelance writer and certified Hatha Yoga teacher currently based in Mysore, India. Her writing has appeared in *Barclays Travel*, *ASEAN Tourism*, *BuzzFeed*, *Huffington Post*, two travel books—*The Trip That Changed My Life*, and *Taste the World*—and on her personal travel blog, Where's Bel. She also edits and manages social media for the kid-friendly food & family travel blog, Pint Size Gourmets. Christabel updated the Kerala chapter.

Meher Mirza is a food and travel writer based in Mumbai. Formerly the Copy and Features Editor at *BBC Good Food India*, she has also written for *Saveur*, *Serious Eats*, *Extra Crispy*, *Food 52*, *Roads & Kingdoms*, UK's *Evening Standard*, the *Times of India*, *Mint Lounge*, *The City Story*, and others. She updated the Mumbai chapter.